Flip to the
NFPA 70E

Work Involving Electrical Hazards

130.5(E)(2)

An arc fault incident can occur as a result of an open air event. However, arc fault events most often occur inside electrical equipment enclosures, and an enclosure can concentrate an arc flash event. Informative Annex D provides information on various methods of estimating the available incident energy and the arc flash boundary. The source documents listed in Table D.1 should be reviewed for the proper use and limitations of the techniques presented. NFPA 70E does not limit calculation methods to those listed, and other appropriate techniques may be available.

Public consensus is that, should an arc flash occur while an employee is performing a task on justified energized electrical equipment, the employee should be able to survive without permanent physical damage. Testing has concluded that 1.2 cal/cm^2 is the level at which exposed skin can suffer the onset of a second-degree burn. See the commentary following the term *arc flash hazard* in Article 100 regarding second-degree burns.

Properly rated PPE should limit the employee's injury to a second-degree burn if an arc flash were to occur while performing work within the arc flash boundary. There is no requirement to provide the employee with arc flash protection when the incident energy is below 1.2 cal/cm^2 since the expected injury from an incident will be survivable and nonpermanent.

Worker Alert

An incident energy of 1.2 cal/cm^2 is expected to limit your injury to one that is recoverable and nonpermanent. This does not necessarily mean that an injury sustained at this energy level will not result in your hospitalization.

△ (2) The arc flash boundary shall be permitted to be determined by Table 130.7(C)(15)(a) or Table 130.7(C)(15)(b) when the requirements of these tables apply.

There are two methods that can be used in an arc flash risk assessment to determine the arc flash boundary. One is the incident energy analysis method, which results in an arc flash boundary at a distance where the incident energy is 1.2 cal/cm^2. The second is the arc flash PPE category method, which results in an arc flash boundary selected directly from the tables in 130.7(C)(15). The 600-volt class motor control center (MCC) illustrated in Exhibit 130.4 shows the arc flash boundary distance when the risk assessment is conducted using the PPE category method. The shock protection boundaries are also shown for this specific equipment.

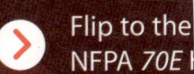

EXHIBIT 130.4

Three approach boundary distances for a 600-volt MCC.

Handbook for Electrical Safety in the Workplace   2018

"Worker Alert" features highlight crucial electrical safety information geared specifically for employees.

Enhanced exhibits help users to better visualize electrical safety concepts.

Summary of Technical Changes section provides an overview of major changes for the 2018 edition of the standard.

NFPA 70E Summary of Technical Changes: 2018

2018 Section	Comments	FR/SR Reference
Table 130.4(D)(b)	Revised title to include term "exposed". Revised to replace "100 Vdc" with "50 Vdc" to be in compliance with OSHA regulations. Adjusted restricted approach boundary distances for consistency throughout the tables.	SR 70
130.4(F)(2)	Deleted last sentence of former 130.4(D)(1) because bare-hand live line work is not within the scope of the standard.	SR 30
130.5	Reorganized into eight subsections to clarify arc flash risk assessment requirements.	FR 60, SR 31
130.5(A)	Revised parent text for clarity and usability. Added new list items to capture all of the prescriptive steps of an arc flash risk assessment.	SR 31
130.5(B)	Added requirement to consider multiple items when estimating the likelihood of occurrence and potential severity of injury.	SR 31
130.5(C)	Added requirement to implement the hierarchy of risk controls when additional protective measures are necessary. Added reference to Table 130.5(C) for determining need for protective measures.	FR 32, SR 29
Table 130.5(C)	Revised and relocated former Table 130.7(C)(15)(A)(a). Retitled last column as "likelihood of occurrence" to add clarity and to correlate with relocation into 130.5. Added new task for "opening a panelboard hinged door or cover to access deadfront overcurrent devices" to eliminate confusion with the task for "opening hinged doors." Revised Informational Notes No. 1 and 2 from "opening time" to "fault clearing time" for clarity. Revised Informational Note No. 3 to replace "short circuit current" with "available fault current." Modified Informational Note No. 5 for clarity. Relocated the former note for Equipment Condition into table to facilitate correlation to the "Normal" and "Abnormal" equipment conditions identified in Column 2. Revised table note to explain risk assessment and "likelihood of occurrence."	SR 31

Handbook for Electrical Safety in the Workplace

FIFTH EDITION

Edited by
Christopher D. Coache
Gil Moniz

With the complete text of the 2018 edition of NFPA *70E®, Standard for Electrical Safety in the Workplace®*

NATIONAL FIRE PROTECTION ASSOCIATION
The leading information and knowledge resource on fire, electrical and related hazards

Product Management: Debra Rose
Development and Production: Kenneth Ritchie
Copyediting: Kim Cervantes
Permissions: Josiane Domenici

Art Direction and Interior Design: Cheryl Langway
Cover Design: Twist Creative Group
Composition: Cenveo Publisher Services
Printing/Binding: Webcrafters, Inc.

Copyright © 2017
National Fire Protection Association®
One Batterymarch Park
Quincy, Massachusetts 02169-7471

All rights reserved.

Important Notices and Disclaimers: Publication of this handbook is for the purpose of circulating information and opinion among those concerned for fire and electrical safety and related subjects. While every effort has been made to achieve a work of high quality, neither the NFPA® nor the contributors to this handbook guarantee or warrantee the accuracy or completeness of or assume any liability in connection with the information and opinions contained in this handbook. The NFPA and the contributors shall in no event be liable for any personal injury, property, or other damages of any nature whatsoever, whether special, indirect, consequential, or compensatory, directly or indirectly resulting from the publication, use of, or reliance upon this handbook.

This handbook is published with the understanding that the NFPA and the contributors to this handbook are supplying information and opinion but are not attempting to render engineering or other professional services. If such services are required, the assistance of an appropriate professional should be sought.

NFPA *70E®, Standard for Electrical Safety in the Workplace®* ("NFPA *70E®*"), is, like all NFPA codes, standards, recommended practices, and guides ("NFPA Standards"), made available for use subject to Important Notices and Legal Disclaimers, which appear at the end of this handbook and can also be viewed at *www.nfpa.org/disclaimers*.

Notice Concerning Code Interpretations: This fifth edition of the *Handbook for Electrical Safety in the Workplace* is based on the 2018 edition of NFPA *70E*. All NFPA codes, standards, recommended practices, and guides ("NFPA Standards") are developed in accordance with the published procedures of the NFPA by technical committees comprised of volunteers drawn from a broad array of relevant interests. The handbook contains the complete text of NFPA 70E and any applicable Formal Interpretations issued by the NFPA at the time of publication. This NFPA Standard is accompanied by explanatory commentary and other supplementary materials.

The commentary and supplementary materials in this handbook are not a part of the NFPA Standard and do not constitute Formal Interpretations of the NFPA (which can be obtained only through requests processed by the responsible technical committees in accordance with the published procedures of the NFPA). The commentary and supplementary materials, therefore, solely reflect the personal opinions of the editor or other contributors and do not necessarily represent the official position of the NFPA or its technical committees.

REMINDER: UPDATING OF NFPA STANDARDS

NFPA *70E®, Standard for Electrical Safety in the Workplace®*, like all NFPA codes, standards, recommended practices, and guides ("NFPA Standards"), may be amended from time to time through the issuance of Tentative Interim Amendments or corrected by Errata. An official NFPA Standard at any point in time consists of the current edition of the document together with any Tentative Interim Amendment and any Errata then in effect. In order to determine whether an NFPA Standard has been amended through the issuance of Tentative Interim Amendments or corrected by Errata, visit the "Codes & Standards" section on NFPA's website. There, the document information pages located at the "List of NFPA Codes & Standards" provide up-to-date, document-specific information, including any issued Tentative Interim Amendments and Errata. To view the document information page for a specific NFPA Standard, go to http://www.nfpa.org/docinfo to choose from the list of NFPA Standards, or use the search feature to select the NFPA Standard number (e.g., NFPA *70E*). The document information page includes postings of all existing Tentative Interim Amendments and Errata. It also includes the option to register for an "Alert" feature to receive an automatic email notification when new updates and other information are posted regarding the document.

The following are registered trademarks of the National Fire Protection Association:

National Fire Protection Association®
NFPA®
National Electrical Code®, NFPA 70®, and NEC®
Standard for Electrical Safety in the Workplace® and NFPA 70E®

NFPA No.: 70EHB18
ISBN (book): 978-1-4559-1484-5
ISBN (PDF): 978-1-4559-1485-2
ISBN (e-book): 978-1-4559-1486-9
Library of Congress Control No.: 2017934720

Printed in the United States of America

17   18   19   20   21   5   4   3   2   1

Dedication

One-third of annual workplace fatalities are attributed to employees in construction and maintenance occupations. This edition of the *Handbook for Electrical Safety in the Workplace* is dedicated to construction and maintenance employees.

There are few occupations or work environments that do not use electrical energy in some form. Whenever an employee is interacting with electrical equipment, establishing an electrically safe work condition, or performing justified energized work, they may be put at risk of injury. Electrical injuries are not exclusive to electrical workers. Employees in many occupations have suffered injuries. Unsuspecting employees have suffered an electrical injury due to the action of another. Many more employees are protected by the requirements of NFPA *70E*® than those who are responsible for determining and providing them that protection.

First and foremost, NFPA *70E* is about protecting the employee. With human error being a major contributor in the cause of injuries, each employee has a direct impact on the safety culture and safety record of their employer. The actions of an employee often determine whether they will return home safely at the end of the day. Therefore, this edition is dedicated to construction and maintenance employees, with the expectation that each one takes an active role in their safety and the safety of those around them. This dedication also carries the hope that each one is protected from electrical injury every day.

PDF Navigation Tips

Find

To find a word or term in the PDF:

1. Select Find under the Edit menu or use the keyboard shortcut: CTRL + F for PC; COMMAND + F for Mac.
2. Type a word or term in the Find box. To specify Whole words only or Case-sensitive, use the drop-down arrow to the right of the Find box and toggle these criteria on or off.

The found term will be highlighted in the text. To go to other occurrences of the term, use the previous and next buttons that appear beside the Find box.

Advanced Search

Use the drop-down arrow to the right of the Find box and select Open Full Search. Additional search options are available by selecting Show More Options at the bottom of the pane. Options in the advanced search window include matching the exact word or phrase, matching only some of the words, and stemming (see below).

> **Stemming** finds words that contain part (the stem) of a specified search word. For example, a search for the word *opening* would find instances of *open, opened, opens*, and *openly*. Wildcard characters (* or ?) are not permitted in stemming searches. Stemming isn't available if either Whole words only or Case-sensitive is selected.

Links

Links to other sections of the document are colored red. When you click on a link and are directed to another page, use the following keyboard shortcut to return to the original page: ALT + <left arrow> for PC; COMMAND + <left arrow> for Mac.

Contents

Preface   vii

About the Editors   xi

NFPA *70E* Summary of Technical Changes: 2018   T1

PART 1

NFPA *70E*, Standard for Electrical Safety in the Workplace, with Commentary   1

ARTICLE 90

Introduction   7

CHAPTER 1

Safety-Related Work Practices   15

- **100** Definitions   16
- **105** Application of Safety-Related Work Practices and Procedures   45
- **110** General Requirements for Electrical Safety-Related Work Practices   49
- **120** Establishing an Electrically Safe Work Condition   82
- **130** Work Involving Electrical Hazards   107

CHAPTER 2

Safety-Related Maintenance Requirements   175

- **200** Introduction   176
- **205** General Maintenance Requirements   177
- **210** Substations, Switchgear Assemblies, Switchboards, Panelboards, Motor Control Centers, and Disconnect Switches   183
- **215** Premises Wiring   185
- **220** Controller Equipment   186
- **225** Fuses and Circuit Breakers   187
- **230** Rotating Equipment   189
- **235** Hazardous (Classified) Locations   190
- **240** Batteries and Battery Rooms   192
- **245** Portable Electric Tools and Equipment   193
- **250** Personal Safety and Protective Equipment   193

CHAPTER 3

Safety Requirements for Special Equipment   197

- **300** Introduction   197
- **310** Safety-Related Work Practices for Electrolytic Cells   198
- **320** Safety Requirements Related to Batteries and Battery Rooms   204
- **330** Safety-Related Work Practices: Lasers   212
- **340** Safety-Related Work Practices: Power Electronic Equipment   215
- **350** Safety-Related Work Requirements: Research and Development Laboratories   219

INFORMATIVE ANNEXES

- **A** Informative Publications   225
- **B** Reserved   231
- **C** Limits of Approach   233
- **D** Incident Energy and Arc Flash Boundary Calculation Methods   237
- **E** Electrical Safety Program   255
- **F** Risk Assessment and Risk Control   257
- **G** Sample Lockout/Tagout Program   271
- **H** Guidance on Selection of Protective Clothing and Other Personal Protective Equipment (PPE)   277
- **I** Job Briefing and Planning Checklist   283
- **J** Energized Electrical Work Permit   285
- **K** General Categories of Electrical Hazards   289
- **L** Typical Application of Safeguards in the Cell Line Working Zone   295
- **M** Layering of Protective Clothing and Total System Arc Rating   297
- **N** Example Industrial Procedures and Policies for Working Near Overhead Electrical Lines and Equipment   299
- **O** Safety-Related Design Requirements   305
- **P** Aligning Implementation of This Standard with Occupational Health and Safety Management Standards   309
- **Q** Human Performance and Workplace Electrical Safety   313

PART 2

Supplements   323

1. *National Electrical Code®* Requirements Associated with Safety-Related Work Practices   325
2. Electrical Preventive Maintenance Programs   331
3. Typical Safety Procedure (Procedure for Selection, Inspection, and Care of Rubber Insulating Gloves and Leather Protectors)   339

Index   351

Important Notices and Legal Disclaimers   359

Preface

The 2018 edition of the *Handbook for Electrical Safety in the Workplace* contains the latest information on electrical safety. More than 120 years have passed since March 18, 1896, when a group of 23 persons representing a wide range of organizations met at the headquarters of the American Society of Mechanical Engineers in New York City. Their purpose was to develop a national code of rules for electrical construction and operation. This was the first national effort to develop electrical installation rules for the United States. This successful effort resulted in the *National Electrical Code®* (*NEC®*), the installation code used throughout the United States and in many countries around the world.

The *NEC* addresses electrical installations and provides for safe operation of installed electrical equipment. NFPA *70E®* arose from the need to address the electrical safety of employees when they are interacting with electrical equipment in a manner other than under normal operation. Since its inception, NFPA *70E* has been tied to the Occupational Safety and Health Administration (OSHA). To have an understanding of how OSHA and NFPA *70E* are related and interact, it is important to understand the history of the Occupational Safety and Health Act (OSH Act). In 1970, Congress responded to the public's demand for safer workplaces and passed the OSH Act. Under this Act, employers are responsible for providing safe and healthful workplaces for their employees. In general, the OSH Act covers all employers and their employees in the 50 states, the District of Columbia, Puerto Rico, and other U.S. territories. The number of workplace injuries, illnesses, and deaths has fallen since OSHA began. However, there are still too many serious injuries and death, and there is still work to do.

29 CFR Section 1910.3(b)(1) addresses the historical relationship between the Act and the National Fire Protection Association (NFPA): "The relevant legislative history of the Act indicates congressional recognition of the American National Standards Institute and the National Fire Protection Association as the major sources of national consensus standards. National consensus standards adopted on May 29, 1971, pursuant to section 6(a) of the Act are from those two sources."

The OSH Act was signed into law by President Richard Nixon on December 29, 1970. The OSH Act created three independent branches. The first branch is OSHA, the administrative and prosecutorial branch under the U.S. Department of Labor. OSHA's role is to assure safe and healthful workplaces for America's working men and women by setting and enforcing standards, and providing training, education, and assistance. The second branch is the Occupational Safety and Health Review Commission (OSHRC), which is the independent federal agency created to decide contests of citations or penalties resulting from OSHA inspections of American workplaces. The third branch is the National Institute for Safety and Health (NIOSH), which helps ensure safe and healthful working conditions by providing research, information, education, and training in the field of occupational safety and health.

Originally OSHA adopted the *NEC* by reference as its electrical safety standard. Later, OSHA was confronted with several major issues when attempting to use the *NEC* in preparing updated electrical safety standards that would serve OSHA's needs. In addition to installation standards derived from the *NEC*, the need for requirements became apparent for electrical safety-related work practices and maintenance of electrical systems considered critical to safety. With the implementation of the OSH Act, a separate standard became necessary to provide requirements for safe work practices for people who might be exposed to electrical hazards.

On April 1, 1975, the National Electrical Manufacturers Association (NEMA) requested a meeting with the U.S. Department of Labor to discuss the possibility of a revised approach to the updating of the Electrical Occupational Safety and Health Standards (Subpart S of Part 1910). In May 1975, a meeting was held that led to the concept that a document be put together by a group representing all interests. The group would extract suitable portions from the *NEC* and from other documents applicable to electrical safety. With positive encouragement from OSHA, a proposal to prepare such a document was presented to the NFPA Electrical Section, which unanimously supported the development of a document to be used as a basis for evaluating electrical safety in the workplace.

On January 7, 1976, the Standards Council of the NFPA appointed the Committee on Electrical Safety Requirements for Employee Workplaces. To keep this document and the *NEC* well-coordinated, the new committee would report to the association through the *NEC* Technical Correlating Committee. The standard was visualized as consisting of four major parts: Part I, Installation Safety Requirements; Part II, Safety-Related Work Practices; Part III, Safety-Related Maintenance Requirements; and Part IV, Safety Requirements for Special Equipment. Each part was recognized as being an important aspect of electrical safety in the workplace, but the parts were sufficiently independent of each other to permit their separate publication.

The first edition of NFPA *70E®*, *Standard for Electrical Safety in the Workplace®* (1979), included only Part I, which dealt primarily with those electrical installation requirements from the *NEC* that were most directly tied to worker safety. In subsequent editions, the document expanded to include safety-related work practices, safety-related maintenance requirements, and safety requirements for special equipment. For the 2009 edition, installation requirements were removed because they were no longer necessary due to the wide adoption and use of the *NEC*. (This handbook includes a list of pertinent *NEC* sections in Supplement 3 to assist the user in understanding how the installation requirements of the *NEC* can make for a safer work environment.)

On January 16, 1981, OSHA revised its electrical installation standard for general industry as published in 46 FR 4034. This revision replaced the reference of the 1971 *NEC* with relevant requirements from Part I of the 1979 edition of NFPA *70E*. This simplified and clarified the electrical standard and updated its requirements to match the 1978 *NEC*. The OSHA standard was written to reduce the need for frequent revision and to avoid technological obsolescence. It was written mainly in performance-based language versus prescriptive-based language, as found in NFPA *70E*.

The electrical standards at the time in Subpart S of the General Industry Standards covered electrical equipment and installations rather than work practices. The electrical safety-related work practice standards that existed were distributed in other subparts of 29 CFR 1910. Although unsafe work practices appeared to be involved in most workplace electrocutions, OSHA had very few regulations addressing work practices necessary for electrical safety. Because of this, OSHA determined that standards were needed to minimize these hazards. OSHA's *Electrical Safety-Related Work Practices* became effective on December 4, 1990, and were based mainly on Part II of the 1983 edition of NFPA *70E*. Similar to the installation requirements, they were written mainly in performance-based language versus prescriptive-based language. The new standards addressed practices and procedures that were necessary to protect employees working on or near exposed energized and de-energized parts of electric equipment.

A violation of the General Duty Clause, Section 5(a)(1) of the OSH Act, exists if an employer has failed to furnish a workplace that is free from recognized hazards causing or likely to cause death or serious physical injury. The General Duty Clause is not used to enforce the provisions of consensus standards, although such standards are sometimes used as evidence of hazard recognition and the availability of feasible means of abatement. Since NFPA *70E* is substantially prescriptive based, OSHA looks to NFPA *70E* to fill out the performance-based requirements included in their standards, especially since NFPA *70E* is the American National Standard on the subject and sets the bar for safe work practices. This creates a symbiotic relationship between NFPA *70E* and the OSHA standards for electrical safety, which is of benefit to those interested in electrical safety.

To further increase the notice employers have of their obligations, some of OSHA's regulations/standards list in nonmandatory appendices national consensus standards that OSHA has determined are applicable. Employers are required to follow the OSHA regulations/standards and not the listed nonmandatory standards. However, once a standard is listed in the appendix, the presumption is the standard would be conclusive for enforcement purposes. Until and unless OSHA revokes a listing, employers will be assured that following the national consensus standard meets the employer's obligation under OSHA requirements.

Acknowledgments

Electricity can be a very dangerous occupational hazard. Almost all members of the workforce are exposed to electrical energy as they perform their duties every day. Since the creation of NFPA *70E*, employees have become more aware of the hazards of electricity and of how to protect themselves. This edition has been developed to not only address those that institute electrical safety programs but also the employee who must implement those programs to prevent their injury.

Handbooks are a team effort, and the editors of this book have been supported by an outstanding team of professionals. We wish to acknowledge with thanks the wonderful work of Debra Rose, Product Manager, and Ken Ritchie, Development and Production Editor, who supported us every step of the way. The editors also wish to acknowledge the contributions of former NFPA staff who served as staff liaisons to the committee and gratefully acknowledge the work of the editors who assembled previous editions of the handbook. The collective electrical safety expertise of former editors provided the solid foundation on which the 2018 edition of this handbook was built. This edition would not be possible without the tireless work of the dedicated professionals who serve on the Committee on Electrical Safety in the Workplace. Their work has saved and will save countless lives. The editors express a thank you to John Kjome, Technical Instructor, Minneapolis Electrical Joint Apprenticeship Training Committee (JATC), for his contribution to this edition regarding the safety and training of the employee.

Christopher wishes to thank his family, Heidi and Rebecca; and Gil wishes to thank his family for their patience, encouragement, and support they provided during the extended year it took to develop this edition.

About the Editors

Christopher D. Coache

Christopher is a senior electrical engineer at NFPA. Prior to joining NFPA, he was employed as an electrical engineer and as a compliance engineer in the information technology industry. He has participated in the International Electrotechnical Commission (IEC), Underwriters Laboratories (UL), and the Instrument Society of America (ISA) standards development. Chris serves as the staff liaison for NFPA 73, *Standard for Electrical Inspections for Existing Dwellings*; NFPA 110, *Standard for Emergency and Standby Power Systems*; NFPA 111, *Standard on Stored Electrical Energy Emergency and Standby Systems*; and NFPA *70E®, Standard for Electrical Safety in the Workplace®*. He is also an editor of the *National Electrical Code® Handbook* and the *National Fire Alarm and Signaling Code Handbook*. Chris is a member of International Association of Electrical Inspectors (IAEI) and IEEE.

Gil Moniz

Gil Moniz is a senior electrical specialist at NFPA and an NFPA-certified electrical safety compliance professional. Prior to joining NFPA, he served as a field representative for the National Electrical Manufacturers Association, an electrical inspector for the City of New Bedford, Massachusetts, a licensed master electrician in Massachusetts, and licensed journeyman in Massachusetts and Rhode Island. Gil served as chairman of Code Making Panel 1 for the 2011 and 2014 *NEC* and as a principal member of Code Making Panel 20 for the 2008 *NEC*. He served on the 2008 and 2012 New York State Residential Code Technical Subcommittees, Massachusetts Electrical Code Advisory Committee, New York City Electrical Advisory Board, New York City Electrical Code Revisions and Interpretations Committee, and as an advisor to the Rhode Island Electrical Code Subcommittee. Gil is also an editor of the *National Electrical Code® Handbook*.

NFPA 70E Summary of Technical Changes: 2018

This table provides an overview of major changes from the 2015 edition to the 2018 edition of NFPA 70E®, *Standard for Electrical Safety in the Workplace*®. Purely editorial and formatting changes are not included. For more information about the reason(s) for each change, visit www.nfpa.org/70E. The first revision (FR) and second revision (SR) numbers are given in the third column of this table for reference to the official documentation of the technical committee's actions.

2018 Section	Comments	FR/SR Reference
Article 90		
90.2(A)	Revised to include removal of equipment to the examples of activities covered by NFPA 70E, which correlates with a similar change to 90.2(A) of the 2017 NEC®. Revised language of informational note to clarify that energization is necessary for electrical hazards to be present.	SR 1
Figure 90.3	Revised figure to include "Introduction" and "Informative Annexes" and to correlate better with the requirements of this section.	FR 8
90.4	Deleted the list of informative annexes, which already appears in the table of contents.	FR 2
90.5(D)	Added new section to explain the informative annexes.	FR 3
Article 100		
Accessible, Readily (Readily Accessible)	Revised to correlate with the definition in the 2017 edition of the NEC. Revised the informational note to clarify the use of keys.	SR 3
Arc Flash Hazard	Revised to provide consistency with the definition of the term *shock hazard*. Revised Informational Note No. 1 and No. 2 to correlate with the risk assessment principles used throughout the standard.	FR 4, SR 2
Boundary, Arc Flash	Revised for clarity and to correlate with 130.5(E). Revised the informational note to provide additional information and improve clarity.	FR 9
Boundary, Restricted Approach	Revised for clarity by eliminating unessential language.	FR 5
Electrical Hazard	Replaced "blast" with "arc blast injury" for consistency with Informative Annex K.	FR 6
Electrical Safety	Revised language to correlate with the risk assessment principles of hazard identification and the hierarchy of risk controls used throughout the standard.	FR 10

NFPA 70E Summary of Technical Changes: 2018

2018 Section	Comments	FR/SR Reference
Electrical Safety Program	Added definition providing the pertinent components of an electrical safety program to enhance clarity and usability of the standard.	FR 13
Electrically Safe Work Condition	Added the adjective "temporary" to more accurately describe the term used in 120.5(8). Replaced "ensure" with "verify" to more accurately describe the result of the voltage test.	FR 11, SR 4
Enclosed	Revised language for consistency with other recognized occupational health and safety standards.	FR 80
Enclosure	Revised language for consistency with other recognized occupational health and safety standards.	FR 80
Fault Current	Added definition of a term used throughout the standard.	SR 8
Fault Current, Available	Added definition of a term used throughout the standard.	SR 8
Figure 100.0	Added figure to assist in understanding the arc-fault terms.	SR 8
Maintenance, Condition of	Added definition to clarify the term used in 110.1(C), 130.5(B), and 130.5(G).	FR 20, SR 5
Qualified Person	Revised to correlate with the risk assessment principles used throughout the standard.	FR 12
Risk Assessment	Revised to match language used in the definition of the term *risk*.	FR 7
Shock Hazard	Revised to clarify what NFPA *70E* considers a shock hazard.	FR 78, SR 6
Shock Hazard Informational Note	Added to clarify the parameters associated with the potential for injury due to shock.	SR 6
Working Distance	Added definition of a term used throughout the standard.	FR 15, SR 7
Article 105		
	Added "and procedures" to the title and in several other locations to correlate with the use of the phrase throughout the article.	SR 10
105.3	Separated employer and employee responsibilities into subsections for clarity and emphasis on each party's responsibilities.	FR 16
105.4	Added to emphasize hazard elimination as a priority in accordance with the hierarchy of risk control methods in 110.1(H)(3).	FR 17
Article 110		
110.1(B)	Added a documented inspection requirement for newly installed or modified electrical equipment to enhance worker safety.	FR 21, SR 11
110.1(C)	Added the phrase "condition of" to clarify the intent of this section. The term "maintenance" is used throughout the standard and has different meanings depending on the context.	FR 19
110.1(H)	Moved the hierarchy of risk control methods from an informational note to a requirement. Added requirement to take human error into consideration during a risk assessment and to correlate with requirements such as those in 130.6(A).	FR 24, SR 12
110.1(I)	Revised to require a job safety plan before work tasks begin.	FR 25
110.1(J)	Revised to require that an electrical safety program include investigation of electrical incidents.	FR 26

NFPA *70E* Summary of Technical Changes: 2018

2018 Section	Comments	FR/SR Reference
110.4, 110.5, 110.6, and 110.7	Revised former Section 110.4 to group similar requirements into separate sections.	FR 23
110.4(E)	Revised to clarify that the voltage source used to verify the operation of the test instrument is permitted to be different from that of the conductors or circuit parts.	SR 24
Article 120		
	Reorganized article to place requirements into logical order of developing and establishing an electrically safe work condition. Sections grouped by the terms "programs", "principles", "equipment", "procedures", and "process".	FR 30
120.2(E)	Relocated former 120.2(E)(5) because electrical circuit interlocks are more appropriately addressed under principles.	SR 25
120.2(F)	Relocated former 120.2(E)(6) because control devices are more appropriately addressed under principles.	SR 25
120.2(H)	Relocated and combined former 120.2(D)(3) with former 120.2(B)(9) to eliminate the redundancy of the two sections.	SR 25
120.4(A)(4)	Relocated former 120.2(D)(1) because the descriptive requirements for simple lockout/tagout are more appropriately addressed under procedures.	SR 25
120.4(A)(5)	Relocated former 120.2(D)(2) because the descriptive requirements for complex lockout/tagout are more appropriately addressed under procedures.	SR 25
120.5(6)	Replaced "policy" with "procedure" to describe action to be taken.	SR 25
120.5(7)	Replaced "a known voltage source" with "any known voltage source" to correlate with 110.4(E).	SR 25
120.5(7) Exception No. 1	Added exception recognizing a listed and labeled permanently mounted test device for the purpose of verifying the absence of voltage.	SR 25
Article 130		
	Renumbered applicable tables due to changes in 130.5 and 130.7(C)(15). Table 130.7(C)(15)(A)(a) was revised and relocated as Table 130.5(C). Section 130.7(C)(16) was incorporated into 130.7(C)(15).	FR 65
130.2	Added voltage level for clarity.	FR 47, SR 27
130.2(2)	Deleted exception because normal operation is already permitted in 130.2(A)(4).	SR 27
130.2(A)	Relocated informational notes for ease of reference. Revised titles of 130.2(A)(3) and 130.2(A)(4) for clarity.	FR 47
130.2(A)(4)(3)	Added list item to address proper interaction with electrical equipment.	FR 47
130.2(B)(1)	Added requirement to document the energized electrical work permit.	FR 47
130.2(B)(2)	Added requirement to describe the work to be done.	FR 47
130.2(B)(3)	Added ultrasound to the work permit exemptions.	FR 47
130.4	Revised section title to "Shock Risk Assessment" and revised parent text for clarity and usability. Reorganized subsections to capture all of the prescriptive steps of a shock risk assessment.	FR 32, SR 39
130.4(B)	Added requirement to apply risk controls to a shock risk assessment.	FR 32, SR 29
130.4(C)	Added requirement to document shock risk assessment.	FR 32, SR 2
Table 130.4(D)(a)	Revised title to include the term "exposed". Adjusted restricted approach boundary distances for consistency throughout the tables.	SR 70

NFPA 70E Summary of Technical Changes: 2018

2018 Section	Comments	FR/SR Reference
Table 130.4(D)(b)	Revised title to include term "exposed". Revised to replace "100 Vdc" with "50 Vdc" to be in compliance with OSHA regulations. Adjusted restricted approach boundary distances for consistency throughout the tables.	SR 70
130.4(F)(2)	Deleted last sentence of former 130.4(D)(1) because bare-hand live line work is not within the scope of the standard.	SR 30
130.5	Reorganized into eight subsections to clarify arc flash risk assessment requirements.	FR 60, SR 31
130.5(A)	Revised parent text for clarity and usability. Added new list items to capture all of the prescriptive steps of an arc flash risk assessment.	SR 31
130.5(B)	Added requirement to consider multiple items when estimating the likelihood of occurrence and potential severity of injury.	SR 31
130.5(C)	Added requirement to implement the hierarchy of risk controls if additional protective measures are necessary. Added reference to Table 130.5(C) for determining need for protective measures.	FR 32, SR 29
Table 130.5(C)	Revised and relocated former Table 130.7(C)(15)(A)(a). Retitled last column as "likelihood of occurrence" to add clarity and to correlate with 130.5. Added new task for "opening a panelboard hinged door or cover to access dead front overcurrent devices" to eliminate confusion with the task for "opening hinged doors." Revised Informational Notes No. 1 and 2 to change "opening time" to "fault clearing time" for clarity. Revised Informational Note No. 3 to replace "short circuit current" with "available fault current." Modified Informational Note No. 5 for clarity. Relocated the former table note for Equipment Condition into the table body to correlate with the "Normal" and "Abnormal" equipment conditions identified in Column 2. Revised table note to explain risk assessment and "likelihood of occurrence."	SR 31
130.5(D)	Relocated from 130.5(A).	FR 60, SR 31
130.5(E)	Relocated from 130.5(B).	FR 60, SR 31
130.5(F)	Relocated from 130.5(C).	FR 60, SR 31
130.5(G)	Relocated from 130.5(C)(1). Revised informational note to reference all of Informative Annex H to correlate with the relocation of Table H.3(b) into 130.5.	FR 60, SR 31
Table 130.5(G)	Revised and relocated Table H.3.(b) to be applicable as requirements rather than information.	FR 60, SR 31
130.5(H)	Relocated from 130.5(D).	FR 60, SR 31
130.7(A)	Revised language to correlate with text used elsewhere in the standard. Deleted former Informational Notes No. 2 and No. 3.	FR 36
130.7(B)	Revised to provide clarity on minimum requirements related to the condition of protective equipment, including following the manufacturer's instructions for maintaining protective equipment.	FR 37, SR 38
130.7(C)(7)	Replaced "energized electrical conductors or circuit parts" with "exposed energized electrical conductors or circuit parts" for consistent use of the term *exposed* with its definition and meaning. Added conditions (1), (2), and (3) to 130.7(C)(7)(a) to address use without leather protectors and to delete former exception. Revised table note on test intervals for clarity. Relocated standards and the first note from former Table 130.7(C)(7)(c) into an informational note to comply with the *NEC Style Manual*.	FR 38, SR 39

NFPA 70E Summary of Technical Changes: 2018

2018 Section	Comments	FR/SR Reference
130.7(C)(9)(c)	Deleted "underwear next to the skin" to have requirement apply to all under layers.	FR 39
130.7(C)(10)(b)(1)	Revised to clarify that either a hood or balaclava may be used to protect the head.	FR 77
130.7(C)(10)(e)	Revised to include dielectric footwear to correlate with 130.7(C)(8) where dielectric footwear is permitted as an alternative to leather.	FR 77
130.7(C)(11) and Exception	Relocated references to standards into an informational note to comply with the *NEC Style Manual*.	SR 42
130.7(C)(14)	Revised to require PPE to conform to applicable state, federal, or local codes and standards. Added two subsections regarding conformity assessment and marking requirements.	FR 84, SR 1
Table 130.7(C)(14)	Relocated former Table 130.7(C)(14) into Informational Note Table 130.7(C)(14) to comply with the *NEC Style Manual*. Added table entry for arc-rated gloves.	FR 84, SR 1
130.7(C)(15)	Revised title to better reflect content of section. Revised to clarify that the requirements contained within apply when the arc flash PPE category method is used for the selection of arc flash PPE. Revised reference to working distance in 130.7(C)(15)(A) and 130.7(C)(15)(B) by adding additional text similar to that found in 130.5(C)(1). Relocated former Table 130.7(C)(15)(A)(a) to Table 130.5(C).	FR 48
130.7(C)(15)(a)	Deleted former list item (1) because Table 130.7(C)(15)(a) is equipment based. Replaced "available short circuit current" with "fault current" for correlation in the standard for AC systems.	SR 35
Table 130.7(C)(15)(a)	Revised to clarify the working distance parameter as the "minimum" working distance. Replaced "short circuit current" with "available fault current" for consistent use of terminology and to correlate with the definition of *available fault current*. Replaced the reference to "Type 1 and Type 2" with voltage references because arc-resistant gear is only available as Type 1 or Type 2.	FR 48, SR 35
Table 130.7(C)(15)(a) Informational Note	Revised former table note for clarity and changed into an informational note to comply with the *NEC Style Manual*.	SR 35
130.7(C)(15)(b)	Deleted former list item (1) because Table 130.7(C)(15)(a) is equipment based. Replaced "available short circuit current" with "fault current" and "maximum fault clearing time" with "arc duration" for correlation in the standard for DC systems.	SR 35
Table 130.7(C)(15)(b)	Replaced "short circuit current" with "available fault current" for consistent use of terminology and to correlate with the definition of available fault current in Article 100. Deleted "or equal to" from the parameter "Greater than or equal to 250 V and less than or equal to 600 V" to correlate with the parameter "Greater than or equal to 100 V and less than or equal to 250 V." Changed both references to "Arc Flash PPE Category 1" to "Arc Flash PPE Category 2" for correlation with 130.7(C)(10)(b)(1) because the arc flash boundaries are at 36 inches.	SR 35
Table 130.7(C)(15)(c)	Relocated former Table 130.7(C)(16). Revised title of first column to "Arc Flash PPE Category" for clarity. Added Table Note "c" regarding other types of hearing protection that are permitted.	SR 35
130.7(D)(1)	Deleted all references to voltages to correlate with changes made elsewhere in the standard. Relocated references to standards into an informational note to comply with the *NEC Style Manual*.	FR 40

NFPA 70E Summary of Technical Changes: 2018

2018 Section	Comments	FR/SR Reference
130.7(D)(1)(e)	Revised to clarify circumstances under which portable ladders are required to have nonconductive side rails.	SR 3
130.7(D)(1)(f)	Replaced "accidentally contacted" with "unintentionally contacted" for consistency within this standard and with other well-recognized occupational health and safety standards.	FR 80
130.7(D)(1)(g)	Replaced "accidentally contacted" with "unintentionally contacted" for consistency within this standard and with other well-recognized occupational health and safety standards.	FR 80
130.7(E)(1)	Relocated references to standards into an informational note to comply with the *NEC Style Manual*. Removed the phrase "accident prevention."	FR 79, SR 4
130.7(E)(4) and Informational Note	Added subsection to address the need for an additional alerting technique. Added informational note to describe an additional alerting technique.	FR 41
130.7(F)	Relocated from 130.7(E)(4).	FR 42
Article 205		
205.3 Informational Note No. 2	Added to provide guidance and enhancement to safety-related maintenance practices.	FR 43, SR 46
205.7	Replaced "accidental contact" with "unintentional contact" for consistency within this standard and with other well-recognized occupational health and safety standards.	FR 44
Article 210		
210.2	Replaced "accidental contact" with "unintentional contact" for consistency within this standard and with other well-recognized occupational health and safety standards.	FR 80
215.2	Replaced "accidental contact" with "unintentional contact" for consistency within this standard and with other well-recognized occupational health and safety standards.	FR 80
Article 220		
220.2	Replaced "accidentally contacted" with "unintentional contact" and replaced "exposed" with "exposed energized" for consistency within this standard and with other well-recognized occupational health and safety standards.	FR 45
Article 230		
230.1	Replaced "accidentally contacted" with "unintentionally contacted" and replaced "exposed" with "energized" for consistency within this standard and with other well-recognized occupational health and safety standards.	FR 80, FR 46
Article 240		
240.1	Revised to clarify that some battery systems do not need additional ventilation. Added "and are present" to ensure that ventilation systems are provided when needed because of the battery chemistry.	SR 47
240.1 Informational Note	Added to clarify that the type of maintenance on "natural ventilation" systems would typically be limited to inspection and removal of any obstructions.	SR 47
Article 250		
250.2(A)	Revised to require that inspections conform to applicable state, federal, or local codes and standards.	SR 45

NFPA 70E Summary of Technical Changes: 2018

2018 Section	Comments	FR/SR Reference
Article 310		
310.4(A)(1)	Revised to provide clarity regarding the use of "exposed" with "energized" and for consistency with the rest of the standard.	FR 49
310.5(A) Informational Note No. 1	Revised to clarify the effects of shock and arc flash.	FR 50
310.5(C)	Replaced "hazard analysis" with "risk assessment" for consistency with the rest of the standard.	SR 49
310.5(D)(2)(a)	Deleted section references and table references to correlate with the move of references into informational notes and tables.	SR 64
310.5(D)(4)	Revised to provide clarity regarding the use of "exposed" with "energized" for consistency with the rest of the standard.	FR 51
310.5(D)(5)	Replaced "the placement of equipment or items" with "established by placing equipment or other items" to enhance clarity.	FR 52
310.5(D)(9)	Revised to require conformance to applicable codes and standards.	SR 62
310.5(D)(11) Informational Note	Changed "10 gauss" to "5 gauss" to align with IEEE 463 and the ACGIH.	FR 53
310.6(B)	Revised to require conformance to applicable codes and standards.	SR 63
Article 320		
320.1(12) Informational Note	Updated references to the current editions. Added reference to IEEE 1635 to address batteries that vent explosive gas.	FR 67
320.2 Prospective Short-Circuit Current Informational Note	Added to identify that some batteries rely on internal management systems to limit short-circuit current.	FR 58
320.3(A)(1)	Revised and added threshold voltages including dc voltages of 100 volts to align with Article 350.	SR 50
320.3(B)(1)(3)	Revised to enhance clarity and for consistency with industry practice.	FR 59
Article 330		
	Revised to focus on electrical hazards within the scope of the standard. Revised to delete nonelectrical hazards such as beam hazards.	FR 54, SR 51
330.4(B)	Revised to focus on electrical hazards within the scope of the standard.	FR 79
Article 340		
340.1 Informational Note	Relocated references to standards from 340.4 to an informational note to comply with the *NEC Style Manual*.	SR 65
340.5	Deleted former 340.5 because more accurate information can be found in other scientific works.	FR 55
340.5(B)	Revised to clarify that the employee is required to use the documents provided by the employer to identify the location of components that present an electrical hazard.	FR 56

NFPA 70E Summary of Technical Changes: 2018

2018 Section	Comments	FR/SR Reference
Article 350		
	Revised to address unique circumstances encountered in research and development laboratories.	FR 89, SR 52, SR 53
350.4	Added to permit an electrical safety authority (ESA) to act as AHJ in laboratory environments.	FR 89
350.5	Revised to address specific controls for personnel safety in laboratory environments.	FR 89
350.7	Added to define the specific requirements for documenting, labeling, and maintaining custom built equipment operating at less than 1000 volts.	SR 52
350.8	Added to define the specific requirements for documenting, labeling, and maintaining custom built equipment operating at more than 1000 volts.	FR 89
350.9	Added to define energy thresholds.	FR 89
350.10	Added requirement that energized electrical conductors and circuit parts be put into an electrically safe work condition.	SR 53
Informative Annex A		
	Relocated standards referenced from former Informative Annex B to the retitled Informative Annex A.	SR 67
Informative Annex B		
	Relocated standards referenced from Informative Annex B to the retitled Informative Annex A.	SR 67
Informative Annex C		
C.1	Replaced "accident" with "incident" for consistency with other well-recognized occupational health and safety standards.	FR 79
C.1.2.3(1)	Added "as applicable" to clarify that an energized electrical work permit is not always required when the restricted approach boundary is crossed.	FR 61
Informative Annex D		
D.4.1	Revised to include the date within the title of IEEE 1584-2002.	FR 62
D.5.1	Deleted the recommendation to use a multiplying factor for exposures where the arc is in a box or enclosure.	FR 66
Informative Annex E		
E.2(1)	Added the phrase "and procedures" to correlate with requirements in Article 120.	FR 63
E.2(6)	Replaced "on or near" with "within the limited approach boundary" for consistency.	FR 63
Informative Annex F		
	Rewritten to provide clarity for conducting a risk assessment and applying risk controls.	FR 64, FR 10, FR 8, FR 9, SR 54, SR 61

NFPA 70E Summary of Technical Changes: 2018

2018 Section	Comments	FR/SR Reference
Informative Annex G		
	Replaced "procedure" with "program" wherever the context indicated that the overall program was being referred to instead of a specific procedure.	FR 68
G.2	Added "employer's" to "lockout/tagout procedures" for clarity.	FR 68
G.5.7	Added the phrase "known source of voltage" to be consistent with other text regarding voltage testing.	FR 68
G.5.8	Added the phrase "known source of voltage" to be consistent with other text regarding voltage testing.	FR 68
G.10.1	Added the phrase "the requirements of" for clarity.	FR 68
Informative Annex H		
Table H.2	Revised Note b to replace "short circuit current" with "available fault current."	FR 82
Table H.3(b)	Relocated and revised as Table 130.5(G).	FR 69
H.4	Added to explain conformity assessment of PPE in 130.7(C)(14)(b).	FR 71, SR 55
Informative Annex I		
Figure I.1	Added three check boxes to correlate with Table 130.5(C): "Identify – Any evidence of impending failure?"; "Ask – Is the equipment properly installed and maintained?"; and "Prepare for an emergency – Is an AED available?" Added a reference to the energized electrical work permit and updated terms to correlate with the proper risk assessment terminology used throughout the standard.	FR 85, SR 56
Informative Annex J		
Figure J.2	Replaced mathematical symbols with text.	SR 57
Informative Annex K		
	Revised with updated information and data for electrical shock and arc flash injuries.	FR 72
K.2	Replaced "accident" with "incident" to correlate with other well-recognized occupational health and safety standards. Revised to provide the correct number of OSHA subpart V.	SR 58
K.3	Replaced "accidents" with "injuries" to correlate with other well-recognized occupational health and safety standards. Revised to provide the correct number of OSHA subpart V.	SR 58
K.5	Added to provide references to additional information on electrical hazards and injuries.	FR 72
Informative Annex M		
M.1.2	Revised to provide dual units of both calories and joules for consistency with terminology used for markings on equipment labels, arc-rated clothing, and PPE, which utilize calories/square centimeters as the primary units.	FR 81
M.3.1	Revised to provide dual units of both calories and joules for consistency with terminology used for markings on equipment labels, arc-rated clothing, and PPE, which utilize calories/square centimeters as the primary units.	FR 81

NFPA 70E Summary of Technical Changes: 2018

2018 Section	Comments	FR/SR Reference
Informative Annex N		
N.4.1	Replaced "accidental" with "unintentional" for consistency with other well-recognized occupational health and safety standards.	FR 80
N.4.3.2	Replaced "accidental" with "unintentional" for consistency with other well-recognized occupational health and safety standards.	FR 80
Informative Annex O		
O.2.3	Relocated former items from O.2.4 as being applicable to energy reduction methods.	FR 73
O.2.3(8)	Added shunt trip as an incident energy reduction method.	FR 73
O.2.4	Changed title from "Other Methods" to "Additional Safety-by-Design Methods." Added commonly used engineering controls that either reduce available current, restrict access to energized conductors and circuit parts, or reduce the likelihood of initiating an arc flash hazard. Relocated former items to O.2.3 as being applicable to energy reduction methods.	FR 73, SR 59
Informative Annex Q		
	Added to correlate with human performance concept added to Article 130 and to provide guidance on how this concept can be applied to workplace electrical safety.	FR 74, SR 69

PART 1

NFPA *70E*®, Standard for Electrical Safety in the Workplace®, with Commentary

Part 1 of this handbook includes the complete text and figures of the 2018 edition of NFPA *70E*®, *Standard for Electrical Safety in the Workplace*®. The text, tables, and figures from the standard are printed in black and are the official requirements of NFPA *70E*. Illustrations from the standard are labeled as "Figures." Additions, deletions, and changes to the code are indicated in the 2018 edition. See page 6 for information on the revision symbols used to identify changes from the previous edition.

In addition to standard text and informative annexes, Part 1 includes explanatory commentary that provides insight and other background information for specific sections in the standard. This commentary takes the reader behind the scenes into the reasons for the requirements or delves deeper into the subject of the requirements. The commentary provides a clear understanding of how those requirements are to be properly applied.

Commentary text, captions, and tables are printed in color to clarify identification of commentary material. So that the reader can easily distinguish between the illustrations of the standard and those of the commentary, line drawings, graphs, and photographs in the commentary are labeled as "Exhibits."

This edition of the handbook includes a list of Technical Changes, which precedes Part I. This provides the user with an overview of major code changes from the 2015 to the 2018 edition of NFPA *70E*. New to this edition is the "OSHA Connection" feature, which shows how the Occupational Safety and Health Administration's (OSHA's) electrical safety standards correspond with certain NFPA *70E* requirements. The "Worker Alert" feature, which is also new to the 2018 edition, highlights crucial electrical safety information specifically for the employee.

The focus of NFPA *70E* is more about protecting the employee who is put at risk of an injury from electrical hazards, rather than what the employer has done to meet their obligations. Although employers will use this standard to address safety issues brought forth when they put their employees at risk, the employees themselves must be knowledgeable of the requirements.

NFPA *70E* is so much more to the employee than the labeling of equipment and the use of PPE. Without fully understanding their roles, their options, and their personal impact on safety, employees may blindly accept undue risk of injury. Any task conducted in the vicinity of energized circuits puts an employee at risk, as Steve and Dela Lenz's situation illustrates.

Steve and Dela Lenz: One Family's Experience with an Arc-Flash Incident

Editor's Note: Although Steve was working on the exterior of an enclosure, the fact that he could not see what was behind the enclosure wall elevated the risk of exposure to an arc flash event. What happened to Steve emphasizes the importance of performing a thorough risk assessment. Although Steve was performing a seemingly innocuous task and could not have known that an arc flash would ensue, the level of incident energy that would result from a screw coming in contact with an energized conductor warranted performing this task with the equipment in an electrically safe work condition.

On a December morning in 2010, Dela Lenz was driving into town when her cell phone rang. It was 9 a.m. Steve Lenz, her husband of 20 years and father of their two children, was working a few towns over in an unoccupied building. "I've been burned bad," she recalls hearing. "I burnt my face off, and I'm on my way to the hospital."

The Job

Steve's job that morning was to install a monitoring box on the outside of a switchgear, a job he had done more than a dozen times. After reviewing the project with the engineer, it was determined that the best place to install the monitor was an entrance cabinet that carried parallel 500 kcmil 480-volt feeder wires with no live exposed parts. Although the wires were not secured in the cabinet, there should be more than 4 inches of clearance expected on the end of the gear he would be working on. Steve would use a self-tapping screw that would penetrate into the cabinet by less than half an inch. Steve considered the installation a "zero-risk job" — he would be on the outside of the switchgear, and the screws would fall at least 3½ inches from the live wires. He stayed behind alone at the job site to conduct the task.

The Incident

Steve drilled the top left, then the top right, the bottom right, and finally the bottom left. As the last screw came to a stop against the box flange, he heard a loud boom inside the cabinet and a buzzing sound, which were followed by a spray of metal and fire. Instinctively, he ducked. Backing up to avoid the flames, he hit a wall. Then, as he turned the corner, he realized he was on fire. After frantically ripping off his t-shirt and slapping out the flames, he looked down at his badly burned hands and felt an agonizing pain on his face. As he stood there, wondering what had just happened, a warm feeling on the left side of his neck crept upward. When he looked down at his torso, he realized he was still on fire. He started whipping at the flames and finally put them out.

The 29-year veteran electrician had just experienced an arc flash. The arc flash that Steve experienced occurred when he wasn't working in the cabinet; it had come through the side of the switchgear and the monitor box. The cabinet door was still closed.

The Aftermath

Badly burned, Steve looked around the smoke-filled room and realized there was nothing he could do. He grabbed his phone and called the engineer he had met with that morning. Steve explained that he had been in an electrical explosion and asked the engineer to secure the building. Then he went to his van, searched his GPS for the closest hospital, and called his wife.

Steve had told her he was driving himself to the hospital and that he would call her when he got there. Steve was surprised he could even speak. His lips felt like they were frozen. After urging Steve without success to wait for an ambulance, Dela headed in his direction. It would take her more than an hour to reach him. Feeling sheer panic, she somehow focused during the drive on what needed to be done. She remembered that Steve's mother was substitute teaching at the children's school so she called her mother-in-law. Dela told her that Steve had been in an accident and asked her to take the kids, then 12 and 15, out of class and explain to them what had happened to their dad.

Word traveled fast. Dela's phone didn't stop ringing. She couldn't answer all the calls. Steve was the provider of her family, the love of her life, and she had never imagined life without him. "I didn't know what to expect," says Dela. "Everything goes through your mind: Is he going to live? Is he going to be an electrician? Are we going to go bankrupt?"

Steve walked into the hospital with his keys dangling from the end of his finger. Doctors and nurses rushed Steve onto a gurney and covered him in yellow ice packs to stop the burning.

NFPA 70E®, Standard for Electrical Safety in the Workplace®

Part 1

As Dela and Steve would learn later, skin may keep burning for 72 hours after an arc flash incident. Covered in ice packs, Steve started shaking violently. A warm blanket was pulled up to his chin, and he blacked out. The next thing he felt was someone prying off his wedding ring. He awoke and offered to go to his van to get a tool to help, not realizing that more than 30 percent of his body was burned. He then blacked out again. His next vision was the spinning of blades in slow motion as three men hoisted him into a helicopter to transport him to a hospital with a specialized burn unit.

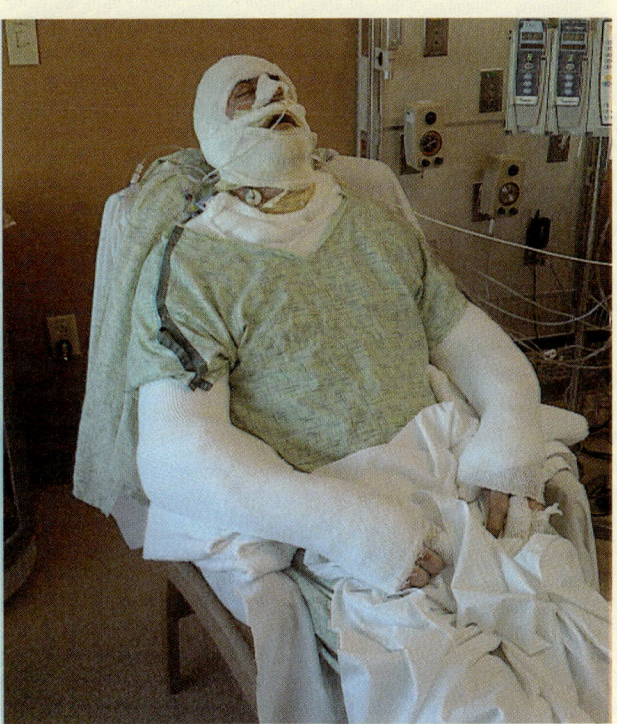

Steve 5 days after the accident. (Courtesy of the Lenz family)

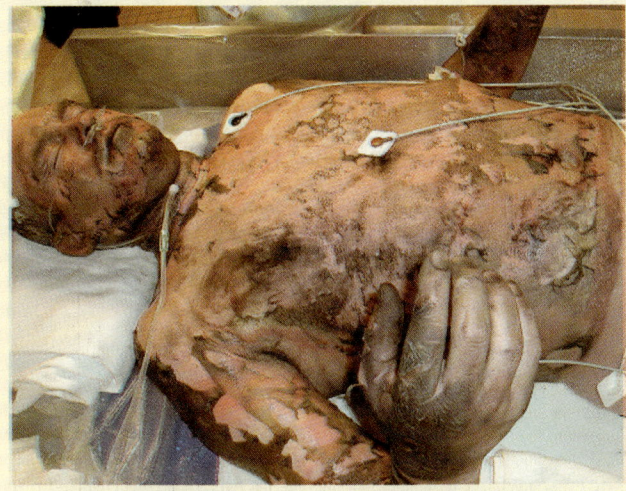

Steve on the day of the accident, immediately after admission to the hospital. (Courtesy of the Lenz family)

Dela headed straight to the second hospital after receiving a call from a nurse who was treating Steve. The next thing Steve remembered was waking up in a hospital bed wrapped in gauze.

Steve's mother brought the children to the hospital later that day. The man they had always viewed as invincible was unrecognizable. Gauze encircled his whole upper body. Only his swollen, blister-ridden eyes, burnt lips, and a small patch of neck were visible. His son touched one of his dad's wrapped hands, not knowing if Steve could acknowledge or even feel the touch. His strong-willed daughter shut down. Clad in gloves and gowns to prevent the spread of germs in the intensive care unit (ICU), they cried. "It's so painful to see your kids hurting," says Dela. "It was scary, and we didn't know what was going to happen."

Dela couldn't remember to eat that first week in the hospital. It came to mind only when she felt lightheaded. She eventually realized she had to take care of herself to stay strong for Steve. Steve was Dela's first priority, but everything else wouldn't just take care of itself. Her kids still needed their mother; her grandmother still needed help during the week, and everyone needed to be updated on Steve's condition. For the first time, Dela and Steve needed to ask for help instead of giving it.

Steve and Dela's children would spend the next month with their grandparents and aunt and uncle. Dela slept on a small sofa in the ICU. Out of 27 days, she spent only a few nights away from Steve's side — one night right after the accident to get the kids settled and another to stay in a nearby hotel room with them so they could be close to Steve over Christmas.

The kids visited often, but the distance between them and their father was more than just miles. In the required gown and gloves, their son would sit in the farthest chair and stare out the door and down the hallway. Their daughter had few words. "I was the guy who coaches baseball and basketball," says Steve. "Suddenly, I wasn't their indestructible dad; I was something different."

Dela remembers almost every moment in the hospital, while Steve has to piece together the bits he can recall — a result of many intense hallucinations brought on by the four narcotics, two nerve drugs, and amnesia medications it took to alleviate some of the pain. In his mind, it was always 9 a.m. in his small hospital room, which would meld into a farmhouse, then a hotel room, then a janitor's closet as he grasped for reality. During one episode, he thought that hospital staff was harvesting his organs. It was a fight for Steve to come back to reality, and Dela was his anchor. "When she was there I knew what I was seeing was real; when she wasn't I assumed I was hallucinating," says Steve.

Some memories were all too real. The trips to "the cleaning room" were the most painful. Nearly every day, burn techs would take Steve to a room and place him in a large metal trough. Then they would strip him down and scrub the dead skin off his arms and chest. Dela tried to stay a couple of times, but when Steve started vocalizing the pain she had to leave — she couldn't stand to see the pain in his face. After the agonizing 2-hour process, Steve would be wiped out for several hours. Soon, every time the burn techs walked into Steve's room, his heart monitor would go off as his blood pressure rose. "I remember it was like a game to me," Steve recalls. "It was like being tortured, and I wasn't going to make a sound."

As days passed, the hallucinations and detachment from reality were making Steve feel crazy, and the pain just got worse with each surgery.

Steve's first surgery occurred a few days after arriving at the hospital. The surgeons took all the dead skin off his chest and sides and covered the areas with cadaver skin to protect him until he was ready to have grafts from his own body. A silver spongy material was stapled directly to his skin. By the end of the third surgery, skin from his lower right leg and both his thighs covered his arms, chest, and collarbone. A large brace kept his arm from bending. Steve could hardly move following the surgery. The pain was nearly unbearable despite the massive amount of pain medication. The process of taking healthy "donor skin" from the body is said to be even more painful than the burns themselves.

Wearing an ICU gown and gloves 24 hours a day, Dela became Steve's personal nurse. She rarely left his side. She washed his burnt lips throughout the day, applied antibiotic ointment, fed him ice, helped him get up and around when possible, and called for help when he needed it. Steve maintains that his wife was the one who got punished through the whole ordeal.

Steve would go in and out of sleep during the day and then sleep at night. That's when Dela had time to contact family and friends and check on the kids to make sure what used to be her normal responsibilities were being covered. The nights got late, leaving Dela little sleep by the time the nurses started their rounds in the morning. "There was one day when I thought 'I have to get out of this room — I just have to get out of here; I'm going to go nuts,'" says Dela.

Steve and Dela were eager to get home, but Steve needed to eat on his own and gain strength before being released. His body was in hyperdrive, which means that his body was eating away at its own protein and muscle while trying to reverse the effects of the burn. His meals consisted of bags of what Steve referred to as "goo" squirted through a tube that had been placed in his nose. Steve lost 20 pounds over the course of a month, a significant amount for someone his size.

"I remember lying there one night, and I said to my wife, 'Why doesn't God just pull the plug — why doesn't he just finish?' because I realized I can't go back to who I was and I didn't see an end in sight," says Steve. "I felt like I was stuck in perpetual hell, and I couldn't get out."

Steve begged Dela not to sign the release for a fourth surgery. At that point, he was willing to risk serious infection to avoid the pain of taking more skin from his legs. But he needed the fourth surgery, and Dela signed the forms. This time they took large amounts of skin from the back of his left thigh and calf and grafted it to the sides of his upper body. "If you've never been burnt, you don't understand," says Steve. "It is so quick, it is so hard, and it lasts so long."

Going Home

Three days after the fourth surgery, Steve could go home. It was good news, but going home proved especially hard for Dela.

Steve went home with nine different prescriptions. Dela had not administered medication while Steve was in the hospital. Some were once a day, some twice a day, some three times a day; one was as needed. She learned the hard way that timing was essential for some of the meds. Then, on his first day back, Steve fell while Dela was changing his bandages. Steve wasn't hurt, but it was a sign of things to come.

Steve fell again on the second day. This time he blacked out in the shower and crashed through the shower door, landing in a pile of glass. The heat from the hot water, combined with his blood pressure medication and the fact that he had half the amount of blood in his body compared to a healthy person, had caused the blackout. Dela wrapped his new wounds then brought him to the hospital. After hours in the emergency room and numerous stitches, Steve was back home the next day.

"I was overwhelmed," admits Dela. Having him at home was harder than she had thought it would be. In addition to caring for Steve and finding out what worked and what didn't, Dela had the cooking, laundry, and all the other daily chores to manage again. She also had two kids who needed to continue their regular activities.

Steve's pain medication was changed a number of times as the doctors searched for the right combination. He finally ended up with a fentanyl transdermal patch, a narcotic used in chronic pain management. The patch, which had to be changed every 3 days, made the pain disappear. Steve began noticing that after 2½ days he would start to fidget and become cold, sweaty, and irritable. "I was miserable," says Steve. Although Dela and his doctor thought it was anxiety, Steve noticed that when he replaced the patch the symptoms vanished and he felt like himself again.

"I wish someone had told me that if you've been on narcotics for more than 3 weeks that you're addicted," says Steve, who never drank, did drugs, or let any substance control him. After his self-diagnosed dependency on narcotics was confirmed by his doctor, Steve ripped off the patch then gradually weaned himself off all medication. After 2 weeks, Steve was no longer dependent on pain medication, but he was in constant pain. Of the withdrawal, Steve says, "It was a crappy couple of weeks, but I guess compared to the month of December, it wasn't so bad."

Doctors estimated it would be 6 to 8 months before Steve was back to work, but by mid-March, just 10 weeks out of the hospital, Steve was working again. He was in pain, he was tired, and Dela had to go everywhere with him, but he was back.

Lessons Learned

Steve considers himself lucky. People die from arc flash accidents; many others are disfigured and live with chronic pain. Eight months and $300,000 worth of medical bills later, Steve had full mobility and faint scars, but his life was not the same. He is more cautious as an electrician. Although he still works alone, he takes precautions never considered before the incident. He covers everything with insulating rubber sheeting to protect himself from shock and burns when working in a cabinet or drilling into switchgear. He has an arc flash outfit, which includes a face shield, gloves, and an inexpensive shirt made of protective material. He also carries the knowledge that if he had been wearing the outfit, he might have returned home without a scratch that December day. "If I could change one thing, I would have worn the stupid $35 shirt," says Steve. "I would have put on the gloves; I would have put on the shield."

Steve comes from a family of electricians, received extensive training, and worked for a number of large companies before the incident. However, he had never had specific arc flash training. He learned the hard way and respects what some companies, like the one his brother works for, are doing to raise awareness and to prevent accidents through advanced arc flash training and arc flash risk assessments that provide employees guidance on specific jobs. "There is equipment, there are classes, there are warnings," says Steve. "It's just not in place in every application yet."

Steve and Dela's family members, who were always close, became even closer. Steve will never forget the looks on his kids' faces while he was in the hospital or the trauma his wife went through. "One tiny mistake, one oversight, a fraction of a second, a dropped tool, somebody else's mistake — it doesn't matter — it's going to catch you," says Steve. "We all think that we are indestructible, and I learned that I'm not indestructible: Hopefully I won't have to prove that to my kids again."

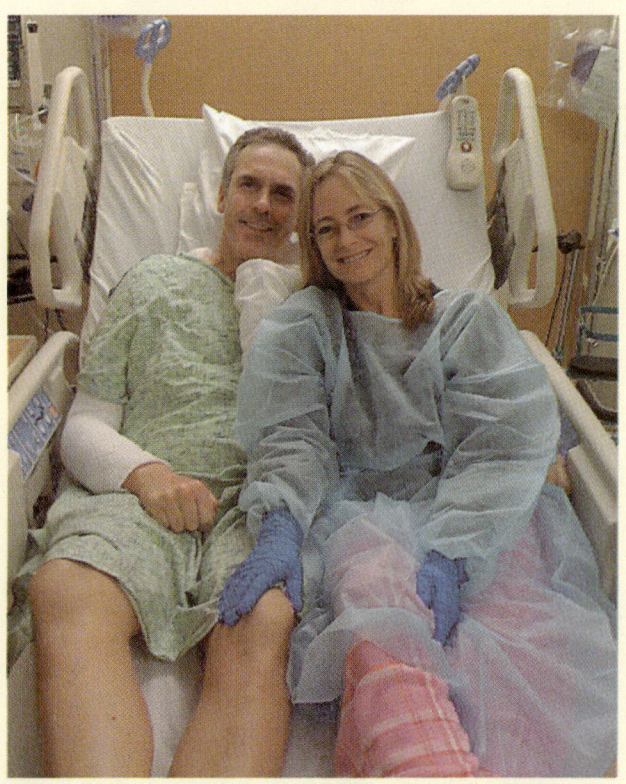

Twenty-one days after the accident, Steve and Dela watch a movie that Steve doesn't remember. (Courtesy of the Lenz family)

REVISION SYMBOLS IDENTIFYING CHANGES FROM THE PREVIOUS EDITION

Text revisions are shaded. A Δ before a section number indicates that words within that section were deleted and a Δ to the left of a table or figure number indicates a revision to an existing table or figure. When a chapter was heavily revised, the entire chapter is marked throughout with the Δ symbol. Where one or more sections were deleted, a • is placed between the remaining sections. Chapters, annexes, sections, figures, and tables that are new are indicated with an **N**.

Note that these indicators are a guide. Rearrangement of sections may not be captured in the markup, but users can view complete revision details in the First and Second Draft Reports located in the archived revision information section of each code at www.nfpa.org/docinfo. Any subsequent changes from the NFPA Technical Meeting, Tentative Interim Amendments, and Errata are also located there.

Shaded text = Revisions   Δ = Text deletions and figure/table revisions   • = Section deletions   **N** = New material

ARTICLE 90

Introduction

NFPA *70E®, Standard for Electrical Safety in the Workplace®*, provides enforceable responsibilities for employers and employees to protect against electrical hazards to which an employee might be exposed. It is an internationally accepted American National Standard that defines electrical safety–related work practices. The requirements at the heart of NFPA *70E* are suitable for adoption and implementation by agencies and employers charged with the responsibility of electrical safety plan development, implementation, and maintenance.

Following and fostering basic installation safety, maintenance, and prudent work procedure rules are essential to employee safety. This is accomplished by installing the electrical system in accordance with *NFPA 70®, National Electrical Code® (NEC®);* by maintaining the electrical system in accordance with NFPA 70B, *Recommended Practice for Electrical Equipment Maintenance* (in the absence of the specific manufacturer's instructions); and by following the safety policies, procedures, and process controls identified in NFPA *70E*. The technical committees for the *NEC,* NFPA *70E,* and NFPA 70B all report to the National Fire Protection Association (NFPA) through the NEC Correlating Committee. This promotes consistency between safety-related work procedures, installation requirements, and recommended maintenance procedures contained in the latest issued versions of these documents.

NFPA *70E* does not include design requirements, but system design considerations can have a significant impact on worker safety during installation, inspection, operation, maintenance, and demolition of electrical systems and components. When considered at the electrical system design stage, the use of elimination or substitution — as required by the hierarchy of risk control methods in 110.1(H) and explained in Informative Annex F — can often remove the hazard or lower the risk. The type and location of disconnect switches, for example, can play a role in the need for use of PPE when creating an electrically safe work condition. It is easier and less costly to implement safety features during the design phase than during (or after) the installation phase. Early discussions between engineers, designers, installers, maintainers, owners, and users of electrical systems can facilitate the implementation of safety features and enhance safe work practices.

The Occupational Safety and Health Administration (OSHA) looks to the prescriptive-based requirements of NFPA *70E* to fulfill the performance-based requirements included in its standards, especially since NFPA *70E* is the American National Standard on the subject and sets the bar for safe work practices. This symbiotic relationship between NFPA *70E* and OSHA electrical safety standards increases safety in the workplace.

Typically, NFPA *70E* is not adopted by legislation. It is most often used by employers voluntarily to help fulfill their obligations to OSHA. Compliance with the federal regulations is often not verified until an injury occurs. By default, this places both the employer and employee into the role of the authority having jurisdiction (AHJ) when it comes to proactively implementing and enforcing the requirements of NFPA *70E*.

Article 90, Introduction, should be the starting point for use of the standard, as it identifies the purpose, scope, and arrangement of the document. This information is essential for establishing a framework for applying the standard. The administrative topics of Purpose (Section 90.1) and Scope (Section 90.2) set the ground rules by which the standard is enforced. Users must first determine the standard's applicability to their situation, and Article 90 provides the information necessary to determine when the standard applies to a workplace and to determine proper compliance.

90.1 Purpose.

The purpose of this standard is to provide a practical safe working area for employees relative to the hazards arising from the use of electricity.

> The purpose of NFPA *70E* is to provide a practical, safe working area for employees, which is safe from unacceptable risk associated with the use of electricity in the workplace. By the use of an appropriate mix of risk controls from the hierarchy of risk control methods, as required by 110.1(H) and explained in Informative Annex F, the risks associated with the use of electricity can be reduced to an acceptable level.
>
> Work that is performed on exposed energized electrical conductors or circuit parts is dangerous. NFPA *70E*, like many safety standards, defines requirements that are based on the risk controls identified in the hierarchy of risk control methods, starting with the most effective risk control and ending with what is considered the least effective risk control. This standard utilizes or identifies all of the risk controls identified in this hierarchy, but the primary protective strategy when an electrical hazard is present must be to establish an electrically safe work condition. After this strategy is executed, all electrical energy has been removed from all conductors and circuit parts to which the employee could be exposed. Only under limited circumstances is energized electrical work allowed to be performed without creating an electrically safe work condition.
>
> NFPA *70E* establishes safety processes that use policies, procedures, and program controls to reduce the risk associated with the use of electricity to an acceptable level. The core objective here is practical, accomplishable electrical safety that results in the employee going home safe at the end of the day. The risk controls discussed in this standard are not impractical or unrealistic; they are sound, viable, workable applications of safety procedures and policies to be implemented by the employer and employee.
>
> When electrical equipment that has been properly installed and maintained is used in accordance with its listings and the manufacturer's instructions, the risk of injury from the use of electricity should be minimal, especially under normal operating conditions. Safety can only be what is reasonably actionable, and all risk associated with the use of electricity in the workplace may not be eliminated. The risk, however, must be reduced to an acceptable level. By reducing to an acceptable level the risks associated with the use of electricity, injuries — including fatalities — from the use of electricity in the workplace should be able to be managed to the extent that they are virtually eliminated.
>
> Prudent decision-making is necessary in order for employees to keep clear of situations where the risk of injury is unacceptable. Where the risk of injury is unacceptable, proper training and supervision will educate employees on how to avoid potentially dangerous situations.
>
> As is the very nature of a standard, each requirement contained within may not be the best practice that can be employed for a specific condition but is the minimum threshold of what must be done. A standard cannot contemplate all conditions that could exist for every piece of equipment, it cannot foresee every hazard present at every installation, and it cannot anticipate the actions of every employee at every company.

Introduction

90.2(A)(2)

Users should not limit themselves to meeting the minimum requirements — they should consider appropriate additional precautions beyond those provided in a standard to address their specific situation.

90.2 Scope.

The scope describes in general terms what this document covers and includes sufficient details to explain the range or limits of what is covered. It is important to understand that the *NEC* applies to electrical installations (premises wiring systems), and NFPA *70E* applies to employee workplaces that are located on premises that have premises wiring systems. A premises is a location that may consist of any combination of buildings, other structures, and grounds. When locations become employee workplaces, 90.2 clarifies which premises are intended to be covered by the work policies, procedures, and process controls found in this document.

(A) Covered. This standard addresses electrical safety-related work practices, safety-related maintenance requirements, and other administrative controls for employee workplaces that are necessary for the practical safeguarding of employees relative to the hazards associated with electrical energy during activities such as the installation, removal, inspection, operation, maintenance, and demolition of electric conductors, electric equipment, signaling and communications conductors and equipment, and raceways. This standard also includes safe work practices for employees performing other work activities that can expose them to electrical hazards as well as safe work practices for the following:

(1) Installation of conductors and equipment that connect to the supply of electricity
(2) Installations used by the electric utility, such as office buildings, warehouses, garages, machine shops, and recreational buildings that are not an integral part of a generating plant, substation, or control center

> Informational Note: This standard addresses safety of workers whose job responsibilities involve interaction with energized electrical equipment and systems with potential exposure to electrical hazards. Concepts in this standard are often adapted to other workers whose exposure to electrical hazards is unintentional or not recognized as part of their job responsibilities. The highest risk for injury from electrical hazards for other workers involve unintentional contact with overhead power lines and electric shock from machines, tools, and appliances.

Section 90.2(A) defines employee activities that require realistic safety-related work procedures. These activities include planned interaction with the electrical distribution system and connected equipment (such as installation, inspection, operation, maintenance, and demolition) and can also include unanticipated interaction (such as when employees are painting, tree trimming, or using lifts or ladders). This standard is also intended to cover employees when they are interacting with electrically powered machines, tools, and appliances.

Some complexes — such as college campuses and industrial, military, or multi-unit type facilities — frequently include utility-type generating facilities, utility-type substations, or utility-type electrical distribution systems. Often these installations are not electrically self-sufficient and are connected to utility power systems. The point of connection between the utility power system and the owner's electrical system is defined as the service point. The *NEC*, NFPA *70E*, and NFPA 70B are applicable to conductors and equipment on the load side of the service point, which is where the facility is responsible for the installation, operation, and maintenance during its full life cycle, from initial installation through operation and maintenance, up to and including its decommissioning and legal disposal.

OSHA Connection

The U.S. Department of Labor's Mine Safety and Health Administration (MSHA) by an agreement with OSHA endorsed the application of NFPA *70E* as "Arc Flash Accident Prevention Best Practices." This made it clear that NFPA *70E* applies to the mining industry workplace.

OSHA Connection

29 CFR 1910.269

The OSHA note to 29 CFR 1910.269(a)(1)(i)(A) considers equivalent generation, transmission, and distribution installations of industrial establishments that follow OSHA's rules regarding utility-type systems in 29 CFR 1910.269 effectively to be utility companies.

OSHA Connection

29 CFR 1910.269 Appendix A-2

OSHA provides a flowchart in 1910.269 Appendix A-2 for the application of 1910.269 (Electric Power Generation, Transmission, and Distribution) and Subpart S (Electrical) to the electrical safety–related work practices of qualified and unqualified utility workers.

Maintenance on the line side of the service point is the responsibility of the utility company. On the line side of the service point, utility-type safety rules are often followed, such as those included in ANSI C2, *National Electrical Safety Code*®. Although not required by NFPA *70E*, an employee on the line side of the service point that is not qualified to follow the utility-type safety rules is required by OSHA to follow the safety procedures identified in its general industry safety standards and as defined by NFPA *70E*.

The utility support facility (e.g., administration building, maintenance shop, vehicle garage) and the customer-owned substation are included within the scope of NFPA *70E*. Utilization-type distribution systems in a power plant — including building services such as lighting and heating, ventilation, and air conditioning (HVAC) — are included within the scope of NFPA *70E*. These systems are typically not wired as an integral part of the electric power generation installation. Various electrical equipment within the same area of a generating facility may or may not be covered by NFPA *70E*, as shown in Exhibit 90.1.

Dwelling units (residences) that become employee workplaces are included within the scope of this standard (and OSHA's electrical safety–related work procedure rules). Work performed by a contractor on a dwelling unit's backup generator, solar panels, or HVAC system are examples of such dwelling unit workplaces. Even though permanent existing wiring of a dwelling unit is not covered by the OSHA electrical safety standards, the OSHA safety-related work practices must be followed during a renovation in order to protect employees from recognized hazards presented by the electrical installation. In addition, equipment — such as portable tools and extension cord sets connected to the permanent wiring — is covered by the OSHA electrical safety standards.

EXHIBIT 90.1

Electric utility facility indicating some of the equipment covered and not covered within the scope of NFPA 70E. (Source: Thinkstock.com)

Introduction 90.2(B)(4)

(B) Not Covered. This standard does not cover safety-related work practices for the following:

(1) Installations in ships, watercraft other than floating buildings, railway rolling stock, aircraft, or automotive vehicles other than mobile homes and recreational vehicles

> All of the workplaces indicated in this exemption have the common feature of movement and transportation of people or material. Because such facilities may have special features and requirements, the electrical distribution systems in them do not have to be installed in accordance with the *NEC*, and they are not required to follow the safe work procedures included in this document. However, if the employer determines that the required level of safety can be achieved by following the rules in this document, the employer is not precluded from following them.

(2) Installations of railways for generation, transformation, transmission, or distribution of power used exclusively for operation of rolling stock or installations used exclusively for signaling and communications purposes

> Note that the exemption in 90.2(B)(2) applies only to utility-type systems used solely for rolling stock and is not for premises wiring systems. For example, general lighting for a railroad yard is covered by this standard. If the employer in a railroad yard determines that the desired level of safety can be achieved by following the rules in this document, the employer is not precluded from following them.

(3) Installations of communications equipment under the exclusive control of communications utilities located outdoors or in building spaces used exclusively for such installations

> Communication equipment installations under the control of private entities that are not utilities and premises wiring systems within building spaces used solely for communications equipment by a utility do not fall under the exemption in 90.2(B)(3). Interaction with this equipment is not exempt from the safe work practices of this standard.

(4) Installations under the exclusive control of an electric utility where such installations:

  a. Consist of service drops or service laterals, and associated metering, or
  b. Are located in legally established easements or rights-of-way designated by or recognized by public service commissions, utility commissions, or other regulatory agencies having jurisdiction for such installations, or
  c. Are on property owned or leased by the electric utility for the purpose of communications, metering, generation, control, transformation, transmission, or distribution of electric energy, or
  d. Are located by other written agreements either designated by or recognized by public service commissions, utility commissions, or other regulatory agencies having jurisdiction for such installations. These written agreements shall be limited to installations for the purpose of communications, metering, generation, control, transformation, transmission, or distribution of electric energy where legally established easements or rights-of-way cannot be obtained. These installations shall be limited to federal lands, Native American reservations through the U.S. Department of the Interior Bureau of Indian Affairs, military bases, lands controlled by port authorities and state agencies and departments, and lands owned by railroads.

> Wherever apparatus is owned by and under a utility company's sole control, the utility exemption in 90.2(B)(4) is in effect, and the utility company is not required to follow the safe work procedures in this standard for qualified persons. However, for persons who

> **OSHA Connection**
>
> **29 CFR 1910.269 Appendix A-2**
>
> OSHA provides a flowchart in 1910.269 Appendix A-2 for the application of 1910.269 (Electric Power Generation, Transmission, and Distribution) and Subpart S (Electrical) to the electrical safety-related work practices of qualified and unqualified utility workers.

are not qualified to work under the work procedures specifically applicable to a utility, OSHA's general industry safety-related work procedure rules apply, and therefore the safe work rules in this standard would apply.

90.3 Standard Arrangement.

This standard is divided into the introduction and three chapters, as shown in Figure 90.3. Chapter 1 applies generally, Chapter 2 addresses safety-related maintenance requirements, and Chapter 3 supplements or modifies Chapter 1 with safety requirements for special equipment.

Informative annexes are not part of the requirements of this standard but are included for informational purposes only.

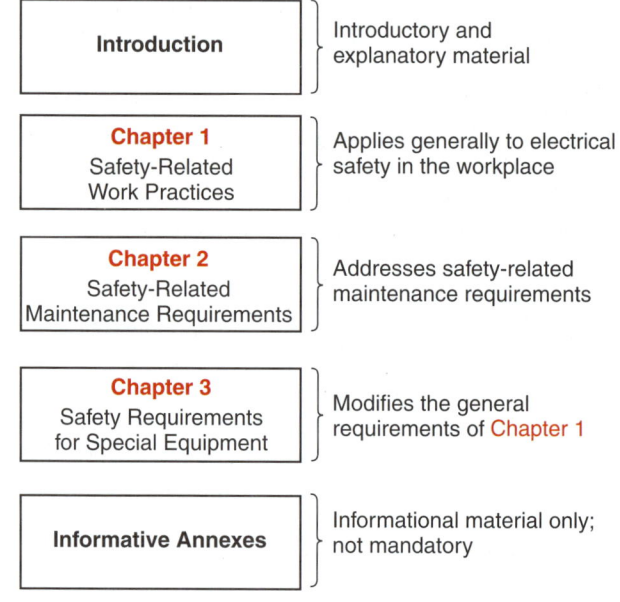

FIGURE 90.3 Standard Arrangement.

> The arrangement of this standard is such that the purpose and scope are given up front, followed by common rules with support material, and then the rules for more defined subject areas. At the end of the standard are the informative annexes — explanatory material covering specific subjects in detail.
>
> Chapter 1, Safety-Related Work Practices, is the heart of the standard. It provides general definitions, rules, and guidelines for electrically safe work practices. Chapter 2 deals with the maintenance necessary to ensure electrical safety from potential exposure to electrical hazards. The requirements contained in Chapter 1 and Chapter 2 generally apply to electrical safety in all workplaces.
>
> Chapter 3 covers unique and distinctive types of electrical equipment and systems in the workplace, as well as unique and distinctive workplace locations that call for specialized procedures. When the rules identified in Chapter 1 might result in unsafe conditions due to unique or unusual situations, Chapter 3 changes or modifies the work procedures in order to achieve the same goal — the establishment of safe work practices for employees while accommodating unique or unusual circumstances.

Introduction

90.4(C)

> The informative annexes provide additional, nonmandatory, explanatory material. Each informative annex covers a separate and distinctive subject area.

90.4 Mandatory Rules, Permissive Rules, and Explanatory Material.

(A) Mandatory Rules. Mandatory rules of this standard are those that identify actions that are specifically required or prohibited and are characterized by the use of the terms *shall* or *shall not*.

> Mandatory rules either compel or bar an action by the employee or by the employer. Mandatory rules in NFPA *70E* are necessary to keep employees safe in the work environment. They are particularly important when the risk of an incident from electrical hazards is determined to be unacceptable.

(B) Permissive Rules. Permissive rules of this standard are those that identify actions that are allowed but not required, are normally used to describe options or alternative methods, and are characterized by the use of the terms *shall be permitted* or *shall not be required*.

> Permissive rules are options or alternative methods of achieving equivalent safety — they are not requirements. Permissive rules use mandatory language and, as such, constitute rules by using terms such as "shall be permitted" or "shall not be required." A close reading of permissive terms is important because permissive rules are often misinterpreted. For example, the permissive term "shall be permitted" can be mistaken for a requirement. Substituting "[method A] is allowed" for "[method A] shall be permitted" generally clarifies the interpretation. When evaluating choices among options that are permitted, it is always advisable for the employer to make sure that the option selected does not increase the risk of injury from a potential electrical hazard above what is considered acceptable.

(C) Explanatory Material. Explanatory material, such as references to other standards, references to related sections of this standard, or information related to a rule in this standard, is included in this standard in the form of informational notes. Such notes are informational only and are not enforceable as requirements of this standard.

Brackets containing section references to another NFPA document are for informational purposes only and are provided as a guide to indicate the source of the extracted text. These bracketed references immediately follow the extracted text.

> Informational Note: The format and language used in this standard follow guidelines established by NFPA and published in the *National Electrical Code Style Manual*. Copies of this manual can be obtained from NFPA.

> Informational notes do not contain requirements, statements of intent, or recommendations. They present additional material that aids in the application of the requirement they follow. The information is intended to help the user understand the rule to which the informational note applies or to point to the location where other notable material can be found. Because informational notes are not requirements, they are not enforceable.
>
> A footnote is not an informational note — it is enforceable. When a footnote is included below a table in the body of the document, it is part of the requirements of this standard and is enforceable. Footnotes are as important as the requirements included in the table — in fact, the contents of the table are only applicable within the parameters included in the footnotes.
>
> Extracted material from the 2017 edition of the *NEC* appears in Article 100, Definitions. Each extracted definition is directly followed by a document number and

Handbook for Electrical Safety in the Workplace 2018

section reference, which identifies the source material extracted from another NFPA document. The extracted material included in the body of this document is part of the rules of this document and is enforceable.

N (D) Informative Annexes. Nonmandatory information relative to the use of this standard is provided in informative annexes. Informative annexes are not part of the requirements of this standard, but are included for information purposes only.

Additional explanatory material is located in the informative annexes. The term *informative* clarifies that these annexes contain additional information and do not contain recommendations or requirements. Each informative annex deals with a specific subject and includes information to help the user understand and implement the requirements contained in the body of the standard to improve electrical safety.

90.5 Formal Interpretations.

To promote uniformity of interpretation and application of the provisions of this standard, formal interpretation procedures have been established and are found in the NFPA Regulations Governing Committee Projects.

The procedures for formal interpretations of the requirements of NFPA *70E* are outlined in Section 6 of the *NFPA Regulations Governing the Development of NFPA Standards*. These regulations are included in the *NFPA Standards Directory*, which is published annually and can be downloaded from the NFPA website at www.nfpa.org.

Because most of the interpretations requested do not qualify for processing as a formal interpretation in accordance with the regulations named above, many interpretations are rendered as the personal opinion of NFPA electrical staff. Informal interpretation by NFPA technical staff is one of the benefits of association membership. Correspondence with NFPA staff is not a formal interpretation issued pursuant to NFPA regulations, and any opinion expressed is the personal opinion of the author and does not necessarily represent the official position of NFPA or the NFPA *70E* technical committee. The staff opinion is not provided as a professional consultation or service and is not to be relied upon as such. Also, NFPA technical staff do not issue opinions on the technical documents of other organizations even if the document is referenced in an NFPA document.

CHAPTER 1

Safety-Related Work Practices

Employees interacting with energized electrical conductors and circuit parts can be exposed to an unacceptable risk of injury from electrical hazards. This exposure can result in an electrical shock injury, electrocution, arc flash burn or thermal burn, injury from the molten metal, shrapnel or pressure blast, or a secondary injury as the result of a fall or from trying to avoid the exposure.

Where electricity is used in the workplace, NFPA *70E®, Standard for Electrical Safety in the Workplace®*, provides the safety-related work rules necessary to eliminate or reduce the risk associated with potential exposure to electrical hazards to an acceptable level. A hazard (source of possible injury) is separate from risk (a combination of the likelihood and severity of an injury). Not all hazards present a risk to the employee. Not all levels of risk are unacceptable. The hazard and risk terminology in NFPA *70E* is consistent with other national and international standards.

Electrical safety is like a three-legged stool. One leg depends on a safe installation. *NFPA 70®, National Electrical Code® (NEC®)*, stipulates the installation rules necessary to assure that an electrical installation is safe to operate. The *NEC* establishes safe installation rules for premises wiring systems for residential, commercial, institutional, industrial, and certain utility facilities.

For the second leg of the stool, these electrical installations are kept safe by following the preventive maintenance recommendations required by the manufacturer or those included in NFPA 70B, *Recommended Practice for Electrical Equipment Maintenance*. The preventive maintenance program for a facility must include an inspection and testing program that is performed by competent personnel. Electrical equipment must be maintained in order for it to be safely operated under normal conditions.

The third leg of the stool is NFPA *70E,* which addresses the protection of a worker when exposed to electrical hazards. NFPA *70E* provides the employer with the direction required to create an electrical safety program (ESP) for the facility. With the employer's ESP following the rules laid out in NFPA *70E*, the employees ought to be able to select and execute the safety-related work procedures required when the electrical equipment they are interacting with is in other than a normal operating condition.

Chapter 1 consists of five articles, which include the necessary information and essential safety-related work procedures required for employees to work safely where there is an unacceptable risk of injury from an exposure to electrical hazards in the workplace. The information and safety-related work procedures included in NFPA *70E* should form the basis of the employer's ESP. The following is a brief description of each article:

- Article 100 offers the terms and meanings necessary to understand this standard.
- Article 105 establishes the overall scope, purpose, and organization of Chapter 1 and distinguishes the responsibility of employers and employees.

- **Article 110** covers the overall requirements for formulating and implementing an electrical safety program, including policies, risk assessment, employee training, program and field auditing, documenting, and the relationships between the types of employers.
- **Article 120** provides the information necessary for creating an electrically safe work condition (ESWC). It provides the requirements for establishing a lockout/tagout program for a facility where electrical hazards are involved.
- **Article 130** defines the situations under which an ESWC must be established. It also describes the situations under which energized electrical work can be justified and the necessary requirements for working safely with energized electrical equipment.

Article 100 Definitions

Article 100 contains definitions of technical terms considered fundamental to the proper understanding of key requirements. Although these terms may be used or defined differently in another standard, these definitions are the ones that apply within the scope of NFPA *70E®*, *Standard for Electrical Safety in the Workplace®*. Understanding the vocabulary used in this standard is crucial to comprehending its requirements. When discussing a requirement, the parties involved must know the intended meaning of each term. This common understanding can increase electrical safety in the workplace. Many of the defined terms included in NFPA *70E* are taken directly from the *NFPA 70®*, *National Electrical Code® (NEC®)*. The definition of each term extracted from the *NEC* is identified by a bracketed reference of "[**70:**100]," which indicates it comes from Article 100 of that document.

Scope. This article contains only those definitions essential to the proper application of this standard. It is not intended to include commonly defined general terms or commonly defined technical terms from related codes and standards. In general, only those terms that are used in two or more articles are defined in Article 100. Other definitions are included in the article in which they are used but may be referenced in Article 100. The definitions in this article shall apply wherever the terms are used throughout this standard.

Official NFPA definitions are under the purview of the NFPA Standards Council, not the committee that is responsible for this document. Official definitions are the same in all NFPA documents. Many NFPA documents rely on or cross-reference each other, and having official definitions facilitates the consistency across documents. Commonly defined general terms are not defined in NFPA *70E* unless they are used in a unique or restricted manner. General terms are found in nontechnical dictionaries. Commonly defined technical terms, such as *volt* and *ampere*, are found in ANSI/IEEE 100, *IEEE Standard Dictionary of Electrical and Electronic Terms*.

Not all definitions are found in Article 100. Additional definitions can be found in Chapters 2 and 3, within the article in which they are used. For example, the definitions applicable to lasers can be found in 330.2, Definitions. An understanding of the definitions is paramount to understanding the rules in this standard.

Accessible (as applied to equipment). Admitting close approach; not guarded by locked doors, elevation, or other effective means. [**70:**100]

Definitions 100

> Access to equipment is necessary for operation, maintenance, and service, but this definition is also used to identify equipment that is accessible to unqualified persons. If a person has no impediment to reaching a piece of equipment, the equipment is considered accessible.

Accessible (as applied to wiring methods). Capable of being removed or exposed without damaging the building structure or finish or not permanently closed in by the structure or finish of the building. [**70:**100]

> Wiring methods located behind a panel designed to allow removal by tool or by hand are not considered permanently enclosed. These are also considered to be exposed wiring methods.

Accessible, Readily (Readily Accessible). Capable of being reached quickly for operation, renewal, or inspections without requiring those to whom ready access is requisite to take actions such as to use tools (other than keys), to climb over or under, to remove obstacles, or to resort to portable ladders, and so forth. [**70:**100]

> Informational Note: Use of keys is a common practice under controlled or supervised conditions and a common alternative to the ready access requirements under such supervised conditions as provided in *NFPA 70, National Electrical Code.*

> The definition of *readily accessible* does not preclude using locks on equipment doors or on doors of rooms, provided a key or lock combination is available to those for whom ready access is necessary. Locks are commonly used on electrical equipment and electrical equipment rooms to keep unauthorized persons away from electrical hazards and to prevent tampering. If a tool is necessary to gain access, the equipment is not readily accessible.

Approved. Acceptable to the authority having jurisdiction.

> This is an NFPA official definition. See the definition of the term *authority having jurisdiction (AHJ)* for a better understanding of the approval process. An understanding of terms such as *listed* and *labeled* can help the user to understand the approval process. Typically, approval of listed equipment is more readily given by an AHJ where the authority accepts a laboratory's listing mark. Other options may be available for the jurisdiction to approve equipment, including evaluation by the inspection authority or field evaluation by a qualified laboratory or individual. NFPA 790, *Standard for Competency of Third-Party Field Evaluation Bodies,* can be used to qualify evaluation services. NFPA 791, *Recommended Practice and Procedures for Unlabeled Electrical Equipment Evaluation,* can be used to evaluate unlabeled equipment in accordance with nationally recognized standards and any requirements of the AHJ.
>
> The importance of the role of the AHJ in the North American safety system cannot be overstated. The AHJ verifies that an installation complies with the standard, or, in the case of NFPA *70E,* that the established work procedure complies with the standard. The definition of the term *authority having jurisdiction* and its accompanying informational note are helpful to understand code enforcement and the inspection process.

△ **Arc Flash Hazard.** A source of possible injury or damage to health associated with the release of energy caused by an electric arc.

> Informational Note No. 1: The likelihood of occurrence of an arc flash incident increases when energized electrical conductors or circuit parts are exposed or when they are within equipment in a guarded or enclosed condition, provided a person is interacting with the equipment in such a manner that could cause an electric arc. An arc flash incident is not likely to occur under normal operating conditions when enclosed energized equipment has been properly installed and maintained.
>
> Informational Note No. 2: See Table 130.5(C) for examples of tasks that increase the likelihood of an arc flash incident occurring.

An arc flash hazard exists if a person is or might be exposed to a significant thermal hazard. A significant thermal hazard is one with an incident (thermal) energy of 1.2 calories per square centimeter (cal/cm^2) or more. Note that 1.2 cal/cm^2 is considered to be the energy level necessary for onset of a second-degree burn. The minimum requirements of this consensus standard use 1.2 cal/cm^2 because there is a probability that the employee will not suffer a permanent physical injury.

Merriam-Webster's Collegiate Dictionary defines a second-degree burn as "a burn marked by pain, blistering, and superficial destruction of dermis with edema and hyperemia of the tissues beneath the burn." This type of burn results in red, white, or splotchy skin, swelling, pain, and blisters. A second-degree burn penetrates the second layer of skin. When the first layer is destroyed, it separates from the second layer. The raw nerves in the second skin layer make this burn painful. If a second-degree burn is larger than 3 inches in diameter or is on the hands, feet, face, groin, buttocks, or a major joint, the Mayo Clinic suggests treating it as a major burn and getting immediate medical help. Exhibit 100.1 illustrates the damage to skin layers resulting from a second-degree burn to the hand from an arc flash.

EXHIBIT 100.1

Skin damage from a second-degree burn.

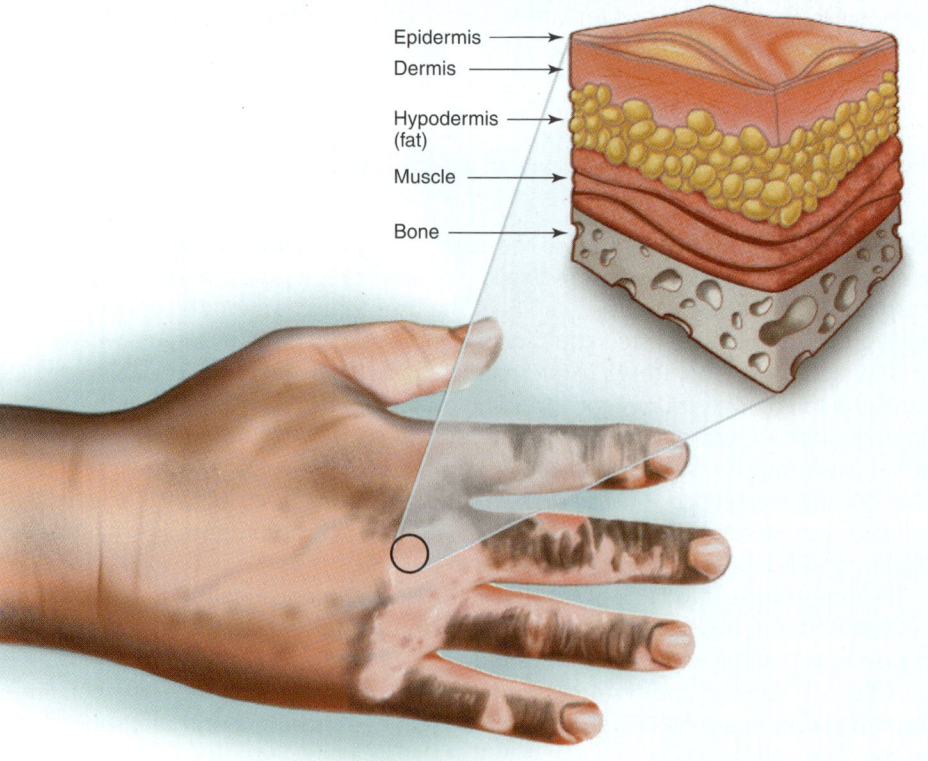

Definitions 100

Exhibit 100.2 shows an arc flash incident from the initial fault to the expiration of the arc. An arc flash incident can result in intense heat, shrapnel, molten metal, intense light, poisonous oxides, and pressure waves.

EXHIBIT 100.2

Photos of an arc flash. (Courtesy of Westex)

Arc Flash Suit. A complete arc-rated clothing and equipment system that covers the entire body, except for the hands and feet.

> Informational Note: An arc flash suit may include pants or overalls, a jacket or a coverall, and a beekeeper-type hood fitted with a face shield.

Historically, the term *arc flash suit* has not been used consistently throughout the industry. An arc flash suit is a complete system that has been evaluated. A suit is not a combination of individual components that have not been evaluated as a whole. Exhibit 100.3 shows an employee in a 40 cal/cm² arc flash suit with other necessary PPE for the assigned task. An arc flash suit does not provide protection for an employee's hands and feet, which must also be covered by adequate arc-fault protective equipment as shown in the exhibit.

EXHIBIT 100.3

A 40 cal/cm² arc flash suit. (Courtesy of Oberon Company)

Worker Alert

Arc-rated PPE does not necessarily prevent you from injury. Arc-rated PPE that conforms to the applicable standards and is properly rated for the anticipated incident energy should mitigate any burn injury you receive from an arc flash incident to one that is not permanent.

Arc Rating. The value attributed to materials that describes their performance to exposure to an electrical arc discharge. The arc rating is expressed in cal/cm² and is derived from the determined value of the arc thermal performance value (ATPV) or energy of breakopen threshold (E_{BT}) (should a material system exhibit a breakopen response below the ATPV value). Arc rating is reported as either ATPV or E_{BT}, whichever is the lower value.

Definitions

Informational Note No. 1: Arc-rated clothing or equipment indicates that it has been tested for exposure to an electric arc. Flame resistant clothing without an arc rating has not been tested for exposure to an electric arc. All arc-rated clothing is also flame-resistant.

Informational Note No. 2: *Breakopen* is a material response evidenced by the formation of one or more holes in the innermost layer of arc-rated material that would allow flame to pass through the material.

Informational Note No. 3: ATPV is defined in ASTM F1959/F1959M, *Standard Test Method for Determining the Arc Rating of Materials for Clothing*, as the incident energy (cal/cm^2) on a material or a multilayer system of materials that results in a 50 percent probability that sufficient heat transfer through the tested specimen is predicted to cause the onset of a second degree skin burn injury based on the Stoll curve.

Informational Note No. 4: E_{BT} is defined in ASTM F1959/F1959M, *Standard Test Method for Determining the Arc Rating of Materials for Clothing*, as the incident energy (cal/cm^2) on a material or a material system that results in a 50 percent probability of breakopen. Breakopen is defined as a hole with an area of 1.6 cm^2 (0.5 in^2) or an opening of 2.5 cm (1.0 in.) in any dimension.

> This definition correlates with the definitions in ASTM F1506, *Standard Performance Specification for Flame Resistant Textile Materials for Wearing Apparel for Use by Electrical Workers Exposed to Momentary Electric Arc and Related Thermal Hazards,* and ASTM F1891, *Standard Specification for Arc and Flame-Resistant Rainwear*. The term *arc rated* (AR) is consistent with the terminology used in these ASTM standards and provides consistency in the selection of protective apparel.
>
> Although all AR clothing is also flame resistant (FR), the inverse is not always true. FR clothing may not provide adequate protection from an arc flash. For electrical hazards, AR PPE is necessary rather than FR apparel because it has been specifically tested for protection against the thermal effects of an arc flash event. Manufacturers determine the arc and flame ratings for protective equipment. For clothing to be considered flame resistant, the material must withstand ignition or self-extinguish. Additional tests are required to achieve an arc rating. The material is exposed to arc flashes to determine how much energy the material repels before a wearer would be subjected to a second-degree burn. Workers must wear AR clothing when within the arc flash boundary to reduce the risk of serious injury or death caused by an arc flash.
>
> Labels on arc-rated clothing should include the rating, as shown in Exhibit 100.3. The arc rating should be visibly marked to ensure that correctly rated gear is used. An arc flash PPE category marking alone (such as 1 or 3) is not an arc rating and is only appropriate when the arc flash risk assessment is conducted using the arc flash PPE category method.
>
> Informational Notes No. 3 and No. 4 provide guidance on how arc thermal performance value (ATPV) and energy of breakopen threshold (E_{BT}) relate to the testing that is performed in accordance with ASTM F1959. The lower of these two values, as determined by testing, is the one used to label the PPE. Arc flash PPE testing determines the incident energy level at which the PPE has a 50 percent probability of successfully preventing a second-degree burn. Where arc-rated equipment is used at less than its rating, there can be a substantial increase in the probability of success. Properly rated PPE should limit the employee's injury to a second-degree burn when the PPE does not successfully withstand the incident energy presented.
>
> Many fabrics, including non-arc-rated cotton, polyester-cotton blends, nylon, silk, and wool fabrics, are flammable and can ignite and continue to burn, resulting in serious injuries. Furthermore, non-arc-rated synthetic materials, such as nylon, polyester,

polypropylene, and spandex, can melt into the skin from arc flash exposure, aggravating the burn injury.

Attachment Plug (Plug Cap) (Plug). A device that, by insertion in a receptacle, establishes a connection between the conductors of the attached flexible cord and the conductors connected permanently to the receptacle. [**70**:100]

The contact blades of general purpose attachment plugs have specific shapes, sizes, and configurations so that the plug cannot be inserted into a receptacle or cord connector of a different voltage or current rating. Locking and non-locking attachment plugs are available with options such as integral switches, fuses, or ground-fault circuit-interrupter protection.

> **Worker Alert**
>
> Regardless of your employer's safety plan, it is you who has the biggest impact on your personal safety. You are responsible for your own actions, and ultimately, you are the "AHJ" solely responsible for final assurance that a task can be and is performed safely.

Authority Having Jurisdiction (AHJ). An organization, office, or individual responsible for enforcing the requirements of a code or standard, or for approving equipment, materials, an installation, or a procedure.

Informational Note: The phrase "authority having jurisdiction," or its acronym AHJ, is used in NFPA documents in a broad manner, since jurisdictions and approval agencies vary, as do their responsibilities. Where public safety is primary, the authority having jurisdiction may be a federal, state, local, or other regional department or individual such as a fire chief; fire marshal; chief of a fire prevention bureau, labor department, or health department; building official; electrical inspector; or others having statutory authority. For insurance purposes, an insurance inspection department, rating bureau, or other insurance company representative may be the authority having jurisdiction. In many circumstances, the property owner or his or her designated agent assumes the role of the authority having jurisdiction; at government installations, the commanding officer or departmental official may be the authority having jurisdiction.

This is an NFPA official definition. The AHJ, where electrical safety of employees is involved, is the party (or parties) responsible for enforcing electrical safety requirements of NFPA *70E*. This could be the designee of a federal or state governmental agency, the commanding officer of a military base, a party designated by the owner or operator of a facility, a party designated by an employer, a party from an insurance company inspection department, the employer or employee themselves, or a combination of several of these.

Typically NFPA *70E* is not adopted by legislation. It is most often used voluntarily by an employer to help fulfill its obligations to OSHA. Compliance with the federal regulations is often not verified until an injury occurs. Throughout an organization there are many people responsible for various NFPA *70E* requirements. The employer must provide safety-related work practices and training for the employee. The employer must verify that the appropriate PPE is issued to the employee.

Notwithstanding, employees are required to implement the employer's training and practices. They are also responsible for their own actions. By default, this places both the employer *and* employee into the role of the AHJ when it comes to proactively implementing and enforcing the requirements of NFPA *70E*. Electrical safety is everyone's job. In some regard, everyone could be considered the AHJ at a facility, whether they are upper management, middle management, a supervisor, or an employee.

Definitions

Automatic. Performing a function without the necessity of human intervention.

> An automatic function or operation could be initiated by a mechanical operation. For instance, a high-pressure cutoff switch requires no human interaction to open the circuit upon detection of high pressure.

Balaclava (Sock Hood). An arc-rated hood that protects the neck and head except for the facial area of the eyes and nose.

> An arc-rated balaclava is shown in Exhibit 100.4. It fits tightly against the wearer's head and neck, and few air pockets exist between the balaclava and the wearer's skin. Only balaclavas having a tested arc rating in calories per square centimeter (cal/cm^2) can be used to meet the requirements of NFPA *70E*. Balaclavas intended only for warmth must not be worn as arc flash protection.

EXHIBIT 100.4

A balaclava sock hood made from two layers of rib knit material with an arc thermal performance value (ATPV) rating of 28 cal/cm^2. (Courtesy of Salisbury by Honeywell)

Barricade. A physical obstruction such as tapes, cones, or A-frame-type wood or metal structures intended to provide a warning and to limit access.

> The purpose of a barricade is to provide warning to approaching individuals that a hazardous condition exists. It is intended to limit approach to an unsafe condition (see the definition of *barrier*). A barricade might consist of warning tape and cones as shown in Exhibit 100.5.

Barrier. A physical obstruction that is intended to prevent contact with equipment or energized electrical conductors and circuit parts or to prevent unauthorized access to a work area.

EXHIBIT 100.5

Barricade used to keep unqualified persons from an area. (Courtesy of The T-CAP/www.TheTCap.com)

A barrier must be of sufficient integrity to eliminate the chance of unsafe contact. A barrier constructed from voltage-rated materials could be in physical contact with an energized conductor. Barriers constructed of other materials — such as wood, metal, or fiberglass — are installed to prevent contract with energized conductors or circuit parts.

Bonded (Bonding). Connected to establish electrical continuity and conductivity. [**70:**100]

Bonding is establishing an electrical connection between conductive elements of an electrical installation. Bonding does not necessarily rely on the presence of a ground connection.

Bonding Conductor or Jumper. A reliable conductor to ensure the required electrical conductivity between metal parts required to be electrically connected. [**70:**100]

Either of the terms *bonding conductor* or *jumper* may be used. A bonding jumper is an electrical conductor that is installed to join discontinuous or potentially discontinuous portions of conductive elements. The primary purpose of a bonding jumper is to ensure electrical conductivity between two conductive bodies, such as between a box and a metal raceway. The term *bonding jumper* is sometimes interpreted to mean a short conductor, although some bonding jumpers may be several feet in length.

Definitions

△ **Boundary, Arc Flash.** When an arc flash hazard exists, an approach limit from an arc source at which incident energy equals 1.2 cal/cm² (5 J/cm²).

> Informational Note: According to the Stoll skin burn injury model, the onset of a second degree burn on unprotected skin is likely to occur at an exposure of 1.2 cal/cm² (5 J/cm²) for one second.

The arc flash boundary is determined either through calculation or through the use of the PPE category method tables. The arc flash boundary separates an area in which a person is likely exposed to a second-degree burn injury from an area in which the potential for injury does not likely include a second-degree burn. Arc flash burns may still occur outside the arc flash boundary, but they should not be second-degree or worse. The arc flash boundary may be thought of as coming into existence when electrical equipment is in other than a normal operating state.

The minimum requirements of NFPA *70E* use 1.2 cal/cm² because there is a probability that the employee will not suffer a permanent physical injury. See the commentary associated with the term *arc flash hazard* for further information regarding the arc flash hazard and second-degree burns.

All body parts that cross into the arc flash boundary must be protected from the potential thermal effects of the hazard. The arc flash boundary is independent of the shock protection limited approach and restricted approach boundaries. See 130.2(4) and its associated informational note.

Exhibit 100.6 illustrates the three boundaries that must be determined through the risk assessments required by NFPA *70E*. The arc flash boundary may not always be the first boundary crossed by the employee assigned a task.

Boundary, Limited Approach. An approach limit at a distance from an exposed energized electrical conductor or circuit part within which a shock hazard exists.

The limited approach boundary is a shock protection boundary that is not related to arc flash or incident energy. The arc flash boundary may be greater than, less than, or equal to the limited approach boundary. This shock protection boundary is the approach limit for unqualified employees and is intended to eliminate the risk of contact with an exposed energized electrical conductor or circuit part. See Exhibit 100.6 for an illustration of the boundary.

△ **Boundary, Restricted Approach.** An approach limit at a distance from an exposed energized electrical conductor or circuit part within which there is an increased likelihood of electric shock, due to electrical arc-over combined with inadvertent movement.

The restricted approach boundary is a shock protection boundary that is not related to arc flash or incident energy. The arc flash boundary may be greater than, less than, or equal to the restricted approach boundary. This shock protection boundary is the approach limit for qualified employees. If a qualified employee crosses the restricted approach boundary they must be protected from unexpected contact with the conductors or circuit parts that are energized and exposed. See Exhibit 100.6 for an illustration of the boundary.

Branch Circuit. The circuit conductors between the final overcurrent device protecting the circuit and the outlet(s). [**70**:100]

EXHIBIT 100.6

An example of the three approach boundaries addressed by NFPA 70E.

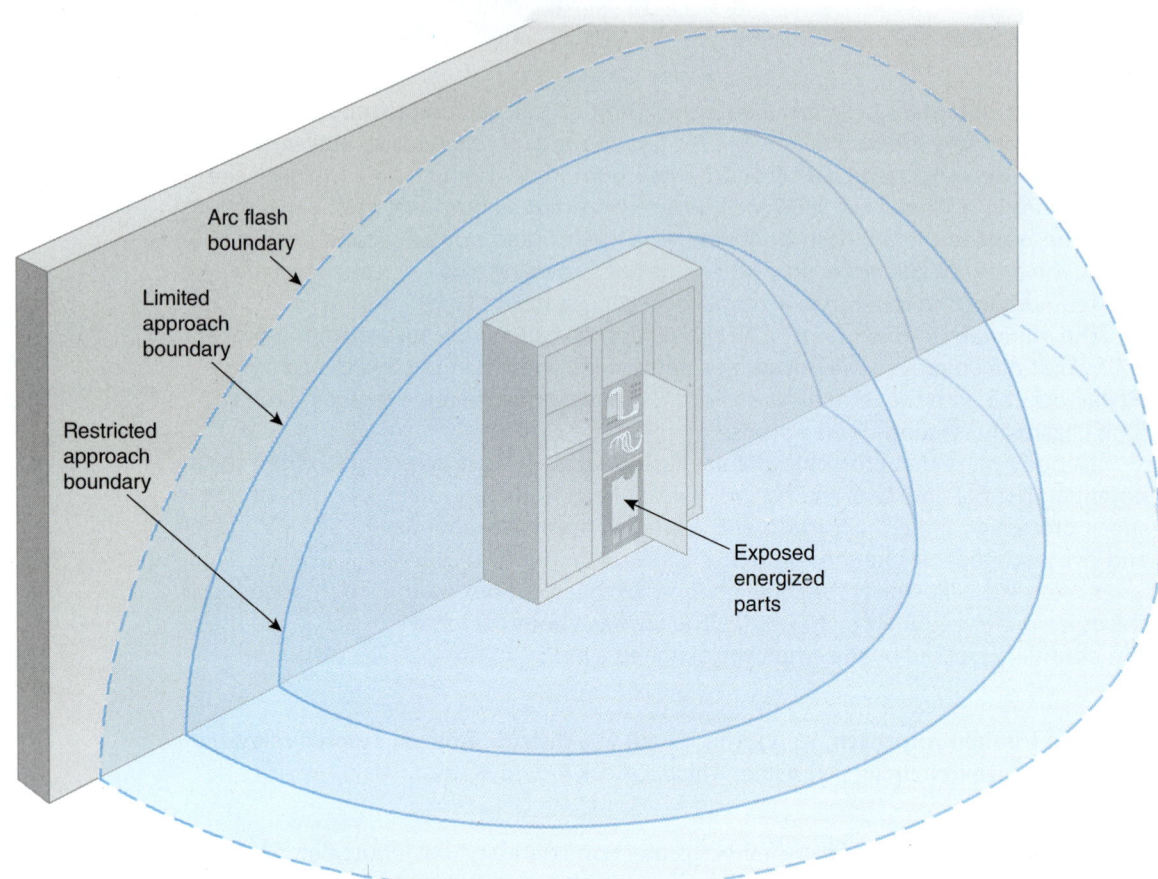

Conductors between the service equipment or other source of power supply and the final branch-circuit overcurrent protective device are feeders. The conductors between panelboards or between a generator and a panelboard are feeders. Conductors between an overcurrent device and outlets are branch circuits. The conductors that originate at overcurrent protective devices in a panelboard and supply receptacles, lighting, or other electrical equipment are branch-circuit conductors.

Building. A structure that stands alone or that is cut off from adjoining structures by fire walls with all openings therein protected by approved fire doors. [**70**:100]

A building is generally considered to be a roofed or walled structure that is intended for supporting or sheltering any use or occupancy. However, a separate structure, such as a billboard sign or radio tower, may also be considered to be a building. In general, a fire wall is a wall with a fire resistance rating and structural stability that separates buildings or subdivides a building to prevent the spread of fire.

Cabinet. An enclosure that is designed for either surface mounting or flush mounting and is provided with a frame, mat, or trim in which a swinging door or doors are or can be hung. [**70**:100]

Definitions 100

> Cabinets are enclosures in which an electrical assembly, such as a panelboard, is installed to enclose the energized electrical conductors and circuit parts under normal equipment operating conditions.

Circuit Breaker. A device designed to open and close a circuit by nonautomatic means and to open the circuit automatically on a predetermined overcurrent without damage to itself when properly applied within its rating. [**70:**100]

> Informational Note: The automatic opening means can be integral, direct acting with the circuit breaker, or remote from the circuit breaker.

Conductive. Suitable for carrying electric current.

> The term *conductive* refers to any material that is capable of conducting electrical current. If a material does not have an established voltage rating — such as voltage-rated rubber products — the material should be considered to be conductive.

Conductor, Bare. A conductor having no covering or electrical insulation whatsoever. [**70:**100]

Conductor, Covered. A conductor encased within material of composition or thickness that is not recognized by this *Code* as electrical insulation. [**70:**100]

> The uninsulated grounded system conductor within the overall exterior jacket of a Type SE cable is an example of a covered conductor. Covered conductors often resemble insulated conductors but should always be treated as bare conductors because the covering does not have an assigned insulation or voltage rating. Examples of where covered conductors may be used include busbars and overhead service conductors. See the definition and commentary for *conductor, insulated*.

Conductor, Insulated. A conductor encased within material of composition and thickness that is recognized by this *Code* as electrical insulation. [**70:**100]

> For the covering on a conductor to be considered insulation, it is generally required to pass minimum testing required by a product standard. One such product standard is UL 83, *Thermoplastic-Insulated Wires and Cables*. Only wires and cables that meet the minimum fire, electrical, and physical properties required by the applicable standards are permitted to be marked with the letter designations found in the *NEC*. Unless a voltage rating is marked on the insulation, a conductor generally should be considered as a covered conductor.

Controller. A device or group of devices that serves to govern, in some predetermined manner, the electric power delivered to the apparatus to which it is connected. [**70:**100]

> A controller can be a remote-controlled magnetic contactor, variable frequency drive, switch, circuit breaker, or other device that is normally used to start and stop motors and other apparatus. Stop-and-start stations and similar control circuit components that do not open the power conductors to the motor are not considered controllers.

Current-Limiting Overcurrent Protective Device. A device that, when interrupting currents in its current-limiting range, reduces the current flowing in the faulted circuit to a magnitude substantially less than that obtainable in the same circuit if the device were replaced with a solid conductor having comparable impedance.

> One important circuit characteristic that affects incident energy is the level of arcing current, which is dependent on the available fault current. Limiting the amount of current (energy) that is permitted through an overcurrent device during a faulted condition reduces the amount of available incident energy during an arcing fault. Installing a current-limiting overcurrent protective device is one method to reduce incident energy.
>
> The *NEC* recognizes two levels of overcurrent protection: branch-circuit overcurrent protection and supplementary overcurrent protection. Contrary to the name, branch-circuit overcurrent protective devices are used to protect service, feeder, and branch circuits. Supplementary devices are always used in addition to the branch-circuit overcurrent protective device.

Cutout. An assembly of a fuse support with either a fuseholder, fuse carrier, or disconnecting blade. The fuseholder or fuse carrier may include a conducting element (fuse link), or may act as the disconnecting blade by the inclusion of a nonfusible member.

> A cutout is usually associated with protection of a distribution conductor similar to those commonly used in utility distribution systems.

De-energized. Free from any electrical connection to a source of potential difference and from electrical charge; not having a potential different from that of the earth.

> The term *de-energized* describes a condition of electrical equipment and should not be used for other purposes. De-energized does not describe a safe condition.

Device. A unit of an electrical system, other than a conductor, that carries or controls electric energy as its principal function. [**70**:100]

> Switches, circuit breakers, fuseholders, receptacles, attachment plugs, and lampholders that distribute or control, but do not consume, electricity are considered to be devices. Devices that consume incidental amounts of energy, such as a ground-fault circuit interrupter (GFCI) receptacle with a pilot light, are also considered devices.

Disconnecting Means. A device, or group of devices, or other means by which the conductors of a circuit can be disconnected from their source of supply. [**70**:100]

> Disconnecting means can be one or more switches, circuit breakers, or other rated devices used to disconnect electrical conductors from their source of energy. Only a disconnecting means that is load rated should be used to disconnect an operating load.

Disconnecting (or Isolating) Switch (Disconnector, Isolator). A mechanical switching device used for isolating a circuit or equipment from a source of power.

Definitions 100

These devices are intended to be operated after interrupting and removing the load current.

Dwelling Unit. A single unit providing complete and independent living facilities for one or more persons, including permanent provisions for living, sleeping, cooking, and sanitation. [**70:**100]

Electrical Hazard. A dangerous condition such that contact or equipment failure can result in electric shock, arc flash burn, thermal burn, or arc blast injury.

> Informational Note: Class 2 power supplies, listed low voltage lighting systems, and similar sources are examples of circuits or systems that are not considered an electrical hazard.

> **Worker Alert**
>
> The requirements of this standard protect you from two of the recognized electrical hazards — electric shock and arc flash burn. There are other hazards associated with electrical energy, some of which are not fully understood. There is no public consensus on the methods for determining these other hazards or on the methods of protecting you from these hazards.

Although this definition includes four separate hazards, NFPA *70E* currently addresses only two directly — electric shock and arc flash burn. As part of the risk assessment, it is necessary to determine the need for and an appropriate method of protecting the employee from the other hazards. Other known arcing fault hazards include flying parts, molten metal, intense light, poisonous oxides, and generated pressure waves (blasts). Additional electrical hazards might be associated with an arcing fault.

Power limited circuits are not normally considered to be an electrical hazard, and electrical equipment energized at less than 50 volts is not normally considered to be an arc flash hazard. However, the effects of an arcing fault are related to available incident energy. In some instances, such as for a 48-volt battery bank, the arcing fault hazard might be significant at this lower voltage.

Electrical Safety. Identifying hazards associated with the use of electrical energy and taking precautions to reduce the risk associated with those hazards.

Electrical safety is a condition that can be achieved by doing the following:
- Identifying all of the electrical hazards
- Generating a comprehensive plan to mitigate exposure to the hazards
- Providing protective schemes, including training for both qualified and unqualified persons

N **Electrical Safety Program.** A documented system consisting of electrical safety principles, policies, procedures, and processes that directs activities appropriate for the risk associated with electrical hazards.

Electrically Safe Work Condition. A state in which an electrical conductor or circuit part has been disconnected from energized parts, locked/tagged in accordance with established standards, tested to verify the absence of voltage, and, if necessary, temporarily grounded for personnel protection.

Establishing an electrically safe work condition (ESWC) is the only work procedure that ensures that an electrical injury cannot occur. However, verifying absence of voltage is an activity where the risk of injury from electrical hazards is unacceptable. Until the ESWC is established, an unacceptable risk of injury exists and employees must be protected from the hazards present.

Δ **Enclosed.** Surrounded by a case, housing, fence, or wall(s) that prevents persons from unintentionally contacting energized parts.

Handbook for Electrical Safety in the Workplace 2018   29

Enclosure. The case or housing of apparatus — or the fence or walls surrounding an installation to prevent personnel from unintentionally contacting energized electrical conductors or circuit parts or to protect the equipment from physical damage.

> Enclosures are required to be marked with a number that identifies the environmental condition for which they may be used. *NEC* Table 110.28 summarizes the intended uses of the various standard types of enclosures rated 1000 volts nominal or less for nonhazardous locations. Enclosures that comply with the requirements for more than one type may be marked with multiple designations.

Energized. Electrically connected to, or is, a source of voltage. [**70**:100]

> The term *energized* is associated with all voltage levels, not just those levels that present a shock hazard. Energized equipment or devices are also not limited to those that are connected to a source of electricity. Batteries, capacitors, circuits with induced voltages, or photovoltaic systems must also be considered energized. Electrolytic processes are also considered energized.

Equipment. A general term, including fittings, devices, appliances, luminaires, apparatus, machinery, and the like, used as a part of, or in connection with, an electrical installation. [**70**:100]

Exposed (as applied to energized electrical conductors or circuit parts). Capable of being inadvertently touched or approached nearer than a safe distance by a person. It is applied to electrical conductors or circuit parts that are not suitably guarded, isolated, or insulated.

> Some electrical equipment contains conductors that are uncovered and guarded only by the enclosure. Wires and tools inserted through equipment ventilation openings could contact energized conductors; therefore, the level of exposure is determined based on the equipment, task to be performed, and associated tools.
> Some panelboards are equipped with an internal cover. Once the outer cover is removed, the wiring gutter is accessible. However, inadvertent contact is not prevented by the internal cover, and the conductors and circuit parts are considered exposed.

Exposed (as applied to wiring methods). On or attached to the surface or behind panels designed to allow access. [**70**:100]

> Wiring methods located above lift-out ceiling panels are considered to be exposed.

N **Fault Current.** The amount of current delivered at a point on the system during a short-circuit condition.

> A fault current is a current that leaves the intended circuit path to return to the source of supply. The term, as used in this standard, refers to an abnormal current beyond the usual range within the circuit. In the electrical industry, fault current is often referred to as short-circuit current.

N **Fault Current, Available.** The largest amount of current capable of being delivered at a point on the system during a short-circuit condition.

Definitions

Informational Note No. 1: A short circuit can occur during abnormal conditions such as a fault between circuit conductors or a ground fault. See Figure 100.0.

Informational Note No. 2: If the dc supply is a battery system, the term *available fault current* refers to the prospective short-circuit current.

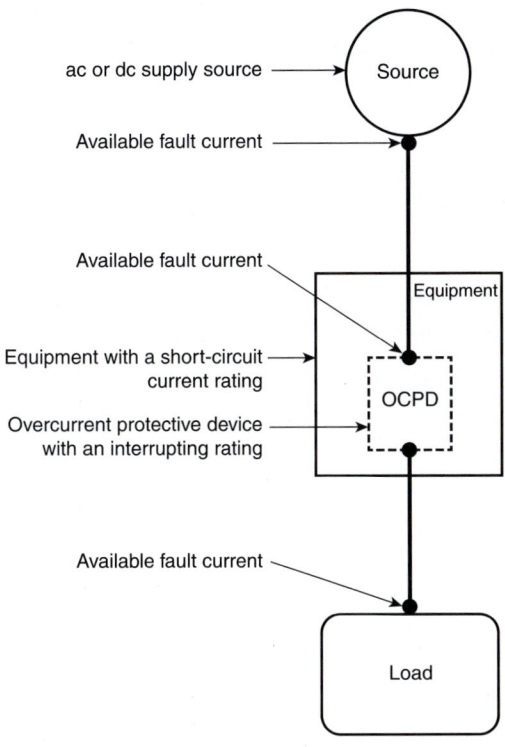

△ FIGURE 100.0 Available Fault Current.

Fitting. An accessory such as a locknut, bushing, or other part of a wiring system that is intended primarily to perform a mechanical rather than an electrical function. [**70**:100]

> Examples of fittings include condulets, conduit couplings, electrical metallic tubing (EMT) couplings, and threadless connectors.

Fuse. An overcurrent protective device with a circuit-opening fusible part that is heated and severed by the passage of overcurrent through it.

Informational Note: A fuse comprises all the parts that form a unit capable of performing the prescribed functions. It may or may not be the complete device necessary to connect it into an electrical circuit.

Ground. The earth. [**70**:100]

> The term *ground* is commonly used in North America. For installations within the scope of the *NEC*, ground literally refers to the earth, which is used as a reference point to establish system potential and to limit line surges. In some electronic circuits, the term is used to describe a reference point, which may not be ground (earth).

Ground Fault. An unintentional, electrically conducting connection between an ungrounded conductor of an electrical circuit and the normally non–current-carrying conductors, metallic enclosures, metallic raceways, metallic equipment, or earth.

> Any fault is unintentional and normally unexpected. A fault results in an electrical current being imposed in an unintended circuit, which could include a person. One of the primary purposes for grounding an electrical system is to provide a path for fault current that excludes a person.
>
> Two types of faults can occur in an electrical circuit — a bolted fault and an arcing fault — and each type results in different hazardous conditions. An example of a bolted fault is a de-energized circuit with safety grounds installed for maintenance purposes, which is then re-energized with the safety grounds still in place. The most common type of fault is an arcing fault, which might result from a conductive object falling into the circuit or from a component failure.
>
> Bolted faults and arcing faults exhibit different characteristics and present different hazards. The primary hazard associated with a bolted fault is shock or electrocution. If a bolted fault exists too long, the mechanical force or pressure produced by the current can cause conductors to move significantly, resulting in an arcing fault. An arcing fault normally is associated with a thermal and physical hazard. Arcing faults also can present a shock or electrocution hazard.

Grounded (Grounding). Connected (connecting) to ground or to a conductive body that extends the ground connection. [**70:**100]

Grounded, Solidly. Connected to ground without inserting any resistor or impedance device. [**70:**100]

Grounded Conductor. A system or circuit conductor that is intentionally grounded. [**70:**100]

> In most instances, one conductor of an electrical circuit is intentionally connected to earth. That conductor is the grounded conductor. A grounded system results in the overcurrent protective device functioning in response to the first occurrence of a ground fault in the circuit. An equipment grounding conductor is not a grounded conductor.

Ground-Fault Circuit Interrupter (GFCI). A device intended for the protection of personnel that functions to de-energize a circuit or portion thereof within an established period of time when a current to ground exceeds the values established for a Class A device. [**70:**100]

> Informational Note: Class A ground-fault circuit interrupters trip when the current to ground is 6 mA or higher and do not trip when the current to ground is less than 4 mA. For further information, see ANSI/UL 943, *Standard for Ground-Fault Circuit Interrupters*.

> GFCI devices do not prevent a shock that could startle or cause a reflex action of a person. GFCI devices operate quickly in the 4 mA to 6 mA range to minimize the chance of electrocution or serious shock injury.
> Exhibits 100.7 through 100.9 show examples of devices that provide GFCI protection.

▲ **Grounding Conductor, Equipment (EGC).** The conductive path(s) that provides a ground-fault current path and connects normally non–current-carrying metal parts of equipment together and to the system grounded conductor or to the grounding electrode conductor, or both. [**70:**100]

Definitions

EXHIBIT 100.7

A portable GFCI with open neutral protection that is designed for use on the line end of a flexible cord. (Courtesy of Legrand®)

EXHIBIT 100.8

A temporary power outlet unit commonly used on construction sites with a variety of configurations, including GFCI protection. (Courtesy of Hubbell Wiring Device–Kellems)

EXHIBIT 100.9

A 15-ampere duplex receptacle with integral GFCI that also protects downstream loads. (Courtesy of Legrand®)

Informational Note No. 1: It is recognized that the equipment grounding conductor also performs bonding.

Informational Note No. 2: See 250.118 of NFPA 70, National Electrical Code, for a list of acceptable equipment grounding conductors.

> Under normal conditions a person typically must be exposed to a potential difference of 50 volts or more for a shock hazard to exist. One of the primary purposes for an EGC is to reduce the potential difference (voltage) between surfaces that an employee is likely to touch, thereby minimizing the chance of shock injury or electrocution.
>
> In a solidly grounded electrical system, the EGC also provides an effective ground-fault current path that facilitates the operation of circuit overcurrent protective devices when a ground fault occurs. This function of the EGC is extremely important in minimizing the duration of a ground fault in a circuit.

Grounding Electrode. A conducting object through which a direct connection to earth is established. [**70:**100]

Grounding Electrode Conductor. A conductor used to connect the system grounded conductor or the equipment to a grounding electrode or to a point on the grounding electrode system. [**70:**100]

Guarded. Covered, shielded, fenced, enclosed, or otherwise protected by means of suitable covers, casings, barriers, rails, screens, mats, or platforms to remove the likelihood of approach or contact by persons or objects to a point of danger. [**70:**100]

It is unlikely that people or objects will contact equipment, circuits, or conductors that are guarded. Although guarding provides protection from exposure to shock or electrocution, it is still possible for persons to be exposed to arc flash hazards. The fenced-in substation shown in Exhibit 100.10 effectively removes the likelihood of approach or contact by persons.

EXHIBIT 100.10

An equipment enclosure. This equipment is said to be guarded.

Hazard. A source of possible injury or damage to health.

Hazards can refer to all aspects of technology, environmental factors, and activities that create risk. In addition, ANSI/AIHA Z10, *American National Standard for Occupational Health and Safety Management Systems*, defines a hazard as a condition, set of circumstances, or inherent property that can cause injury, illness, or death.

Hazardous. Involving exposure to at least one hazard.

Incident Energy. The amount of thermal energy impressed on a surface, a certain distance from the source, generated during an electrical arc event. Incident energy is typically expressed in calories per square centimeter (cal/cm^2).

NFPA *70E* does not dictate the use of a particular method of determining incident energy. Incident energy calculations are based on thermal energy only. ASTM standards require PPE ratings to be in calories per square centimeter (cal/cm^2) rather than joules per square centimeter, joules per meter squared, or calories per square inch. Regardless of the unit of measurement, selection of proper PPE dictates that the incident energy and PPE thermal rating be expressed using the same term.

Definitions

> Predicting the amount of available incident energy is crucial in selecting appropriate PPE. Properly rated PPE prevents injury from melting or burning clothing or from direct skin exposure due to the increased temperature during an arcing fault. Using PPE rated above the calculated incident energy value can raise the probability of the employee being protected.

Incident Energy Analysis. A component of an arc flash risk assessment used to predict the incident energy of an arc flash for a specified set of conditions.

> The calculated incident energy from the installation-specific assessment is the predicted energy that an employee will be exposed to if an arc flash incident occurs. See the commentary to 130.5(G).

Insulated. Separated from other conducting surfaces by a dielectric (including air space) offering a high resistance to the passage of current.

> Informational Note: When an object is said to be insulated, it is understood to be insulated for the conditions to which it is normally subject. Otherwise, it is, within the purpose of these rules, uninsulated.

Interrupter Switch. A switch capable of making, carrying, and interrupting specified currents.

> Interrupter switches are a disconnecting means rated to interrupt load current. The manufacturer's product label typically provides the interrupting rating of the switch.

Interrupting Rating. The highest current at rated voltage that a device is identified to interrupt under standard test conditions. [**70**:100]

> Informational Note: Equipment intended to interrupt current at other than fault levels may have its interrupting rating implied in other ratings, such as horsepower or locked rotor current.

> The interrupting rating is generally expressed in root-mean-square (rms) symmetrical amperes and is specified by a fault current magnitude only. Where instantaneous phase trip elements are used, the interrupting capacity is the maximum rating of the device with no intentional delay. Where instantaneous phase trip elements are not used, the interrupting capacity is the maximum rating of the device for the rated time interval. Circuit breakers also have a short-time current rating, which is the ability of the breaker to remain closed for a time interval under high fault current conditions. The short-time rating is used to determine the ability of the circuit breaker to protect itself and other devices and to coordinate with other circuit breakers so the system will trip selectively.

Isolated (as applied to location). Not readily accessible to persons unless special means for access are used. [**70**:100]

> Isolated conductors, devices, or equipment are protected from accidental contact by an unqualified person because a special means, such as a tool or key, is required to gain access. Standard tools such as Phillips head screwdrivers are not considered to be a special means.

Labeled. Equipment or materials to which has been attached a label, symbol, or other identifying mark of an organization that is acceptable to the authority having jurisdiction and concerned with product evaluation, that maintains periodic inspection of production of labeled equipment or materials, and by whose labeling the manufacturer indicates compliance with appropriate standards or performance in a specified manner.

> This is an NFPA official definition. Labeled equipment, devices, or conductors have an identifying mark to indicate that they meet the requirements defined by the appropriate standards. These marks are most often a third-party symbol used to indicate not only that an evaluated sample has complied with the standard but also that production units continue to comply. The mark must be of an organization acceptable to the AHJ. Labeled equipment must be approved and used in accordance with instructions supplied as part of the labeling or listing. Exhibit 100.11 shows a motor control center label indicating a third-party evaluation to both United States and Canadian product standards.

EXHIBIT 100.11

A motor control center label showing a third-party identifying mark.

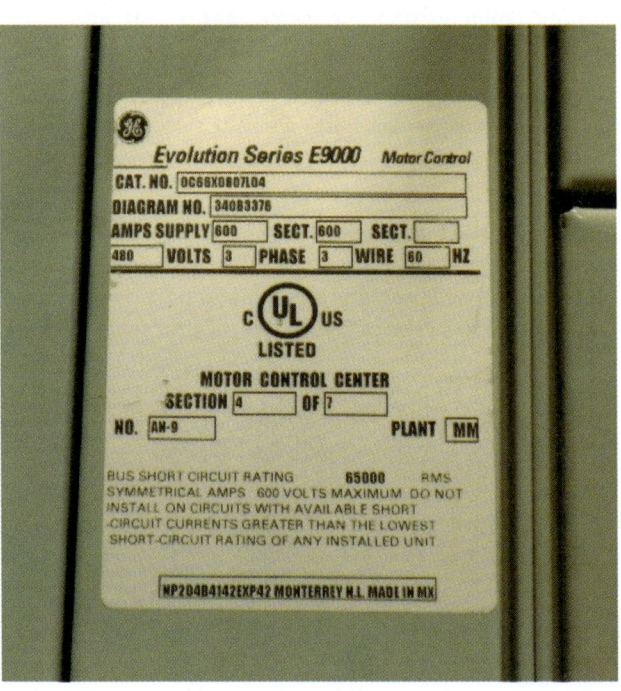

OSHA Connection

29 CFR 1910.7(b)

The term *nationally recognized testing laboratory (NRTL)* means an organization that is recognized by OSHA to test for safety and to list, label, or accept equipment or materials.

Listed. Equipment, materials, or services included in a list published by an organization that is acceptable to the authority having jurisdiction and concerned with evaluation of products or services, that maintains periodic inspection of production of listed equipment or materials or periodic evaluation of services, and whose listing states that either the equipment, material, or service meets appropriate designated standards or has been tested and found suitable for a specified purpose.

> Informational Note: The means for identifying listed equipment may vary for each organization concerned with product evaluation; some organizations do not recognize equipment as listed unless it is also labeled. The authority having jurisdiction should utilize the system employed by the listing organization to identify a listed product.

> This is an NFPA official definition. Listing is the most common method of third-party evaluation of the safety of a product. These organizations evaluate equipment in

Definitions 100

> accordance with appropriate product standards and maintain lists of products that comply. NFPA codes and standards do not use the OSHA term *nationally recognized testing laboratory (NRTL)* because the acceptance of the listing organization is the responsibility of the AHJ. Even when not required by this standard, listed equipment is often employed to facilitate approval.

Luminaire. A complete lighting unit consisting of a light source, such as a lamp or lamps, together with the parts designed to position the light source and connect it to the power supply. It may also include parts to protect the light source or the ballast or to distribute the light. A lampholder itself is not a luminaire. [**70:**100]

N **Maintenance, Condition of.** The state of the electrical equipment considering the manufacturers' instructions, manufacturers' recommendations, and applicable industry codes, standards, and recommended practices.

> The condition of maintenance for a piece of equipment plays a major role in the safety of not only the maintenance employee but also the person operating the equipment. Improperly maintained or damaged equipment cannot be assumed to function normally or to provide the protection for the operator that would be afforded by proper installation and maintenance.

Motor Control Center. An assembly of one or more enclosed sections having a common power bus and principally containing motor control units. [**70:**100]

> A motor control center typically contains combination motor starters, fusible safety-disconnect switches, circuit breakers, power panels, solid-state drives, and similar components. A motor control center is not to be confused with switchgear or a switchboard. It is important to understand the difference when using Table 130.7(C)(15)(a) and Table 130.7(C)(15)(b), because the arc flash hazard PPE categories are based on the type of equipment and voltage level.

Outlet. A point on the wiring system at which current is taken to supply utilization equipment. [**70:**100]

> The term *outlet* is frequently misused to refer to receptacles. Although a receptacle is an outlet, not all outlets are receptacles. Other types of outlets include lighting outlets, smoke alarm outlets, and motor outlets.

Overcurrent. Any current in excess of the rated current of equipment or the ampacity of a conductor. It may result from overload, short circuit, or ground fault. [**70:**100]

> Informational Note: A current in excess of rating may be accommodated by certain equipment and conductors for a given set of conditions. Therefore, the rules for overcurrent protection are specific for particular situations.

Overload. Operation of equipment in excess of normal, full-load rating, or of a conductor in excess of rated ampacity that, when it persists for a sufficient length of time, would cause damage or dangerous overheating. A fault, such as a short circuit or ground fault, is not an overload. [**70:**100]

Panelboard. A single panel or group of panel units designed for assembly in the form of a single panel, including buses and automatic overcurrent devices, and equipped with or without switches for the control of light, heat, or power circuits; designed to be placed in a cabinet or cutout box placed in or against a wall, partition, or other support; and accessible only from the front. [**70**:100]

Premises Wiring (System). Interior and exterior wiring, including power, lighting, control, and signal circuit wiring together with all their associated hardware, fittings, and wiring devices, both permanently and temporarily installed. This includes: (a) wiring from the service point or power source to the outlets; or (b) wiring from and including the power source to the outlets where there is no service point.

Such wiring does not include wiring internal to appliances, luminaires, motors, controllers, motor control centers, and similar equipment. [**70**:100]

> Informational Note: Power sources include, but are not limited to, interconnected or stand-alone batteries, solar photovoltaic systems, other distributed generation systems, or generators.

Premises wiring includes all wiring downstream of the service point to the outlets. However, a premises wiring system does not have to be supplied by an electric utility. For example, a generator or photovoltaic system can supply a stand-alone premises wiring system. The premises wiring for these systems includes the power source as well as the wiring to the outlets.

Qualified Person. One who has demonstrated skills and knowledge related to the construction and operation of electrical equipment and installations and has received safety training to identify the hazards and reduce the associated risk.

In a broad context, any person doing any task should have the training to do that task, to know something about the equipment they are interacting with, and to know how to avoid injury. Anyone interacting with electrical equipment that is not under normal operating conditions [see 130.2(A)(4) and associated commentary] is at risk of an injury from the use of electricity and should be qualified to perform the assigned task under the requirements of NFPA *70E*.

A qualified employee must understand the construction and operation of the equipment or circuit associated with the planned work task. An employee could be qualified to perform one work task and not be qualified to perform a different task on that same piece of equipment. An employee could also be qualified to work on one piece of equipment but not another similar piece of equipment.

Many state and local government licensing programs have training requirements that must be met for a person to be considered qualified. The applicant must be examined initially and then periodically after procuring a license. The license in and of itself does not make a person qualified under the requirements of NFPA *70E* for all tasks or equipment that may be encountered. For example, often the licensing of electricians qualifies them for installing electrical equipment in accordance with the *NEC* but may not qualify them to maintain that same equipment. Electrical work requires continuing education and demonstration of the necessary skills in order to maintain the requisite skill level to work safely. It may be helpful to understand the following definitions:

- **Licensure.** The granting of licenses, especially to practice a profession or trade.
  Note: Licensure normally requires the passing of an examination and that certain qualifications be met. Where licensure is in effect, certain tasks or trades may only be performed by licensed individuals.
- **Certification.** The act of making something official.

Worker Alert

It is crucial to acknowledge the fact that you may not be qualified for the task that you are assigned. As a qualified employee, you should recognize that new equipment, a different set of procedures, or the ability to perform a similar task may make you *unqualified* to perform the scheduled task on the specific equipment.

> *Note:* Certification generally requires the passing of an examination and that certain qualifications be met. However, certifications are issued by private organizations, not by government entities, such as NFPA's Certified Electrical Safety Compliance Professional certification. The value given to certification may depend upon the reputation of the organization issuing the certification.
>
> - **Registration.** The act or process of entering names on an official list entitling the party to practice a profession, such as a Registered Professional Electrical Engineer. *Note:* Registration is similar to licensure in that it requires the passing of an examination and that certain qualifications be met.
>
> Part of being a qualified person is recognizing that energized electrical work is permitted only under the conditions specified in 130.2(A). A qualified person must understand electrical hazards associated with the scheduled work task and must be able to react appropriately to all hazards associated with the task. They must be trained to understand and apply the details of the electrical safety program and procedures provided by the employer. A qualified person should be able to understand the risk assessments and the proper application and the limitations of PPE. They must understand the limitations of test equipment such as voltage testers, how to select appropriate equipment, and how to apply that equipment to the planned work task.
>
> The phrase "has demonstrated skills" requires that the person must actually demonstrate the ability to perform the task. It may be necessary to demonstrate the ability to perform the task while using appropriate PPE to ensure that the restricted lighting and field of view of the arc flash suit hood or the dexterity limitations of voltage-rated gloves with leather protectors do not hinder the employee.

Raceway. An enclosed channel of metal or nonmetallic materials designed expressly for holding wires, cables, or busbars, with additional functions as permitted in this standard. [**70**:100]

Receptacle. A receptacle is a contact device installed at the outlet for the connection of an attachment plug. A single receptacle is a single contact device with no other contact device on the same yoke. A multiple receptacle is two or more contact devices on the same yoke. [**70**:100]

> The term *receptacle* is frequently misused. A receptacle is a device installed at an outlet. However, not all outlets are receptacle outlets. See the definition of *outlet*.

Risk. A combination of the likelihood of occurrence of injury or damage to health and the severity of injury or damage to health that results from a hazard.

> Risk is not only the likelihood that an incident could occur, but it also includes the severity (seriousness) of the resulting injury or damage that may result from the hazard. A risk could have a high probability of an incident occurring, but the result could be a minor injury. Conversely, it may have a low likelihood of occurring but present the potential for severe injury. See the commentary on Informative Annex F for more information.

Risk Assessment. An overall process that identifies hazards, estimates the likelihood of occurrence of injury or damage to health, estimates the potential severity of injury or damage to health, and determines if protective measures are required.

> Informational Note: As used in this standard, *arc flash risk assessment* and *shock risk assessment* are types of risk assessments.

Risk assessment includes hazard identification. Risk assessment is about risk mitigation. Implementing risk control involves application of the safety controls from the hierarchy of safety controls in accordance with the process required by 110.1(H)(3) and identified in Informative Annex F.

Service Drop. The overhead conductors between the utility electric supply system and the service point. [**70**:100]

The *NEC* contains requirements covering the interface (service point) between the utility conductors (service-drop or service lateral) and the premises conductors (overhead service conductors or overhead service-entrance conductors).

Service Lateral. The underground conductors between the utility electric supply system and the service point. [**70**:100]

Service Point. The point of connection between the facilities of the serving utility and the premises wiring. [**70**:100]

> Informational Note 1: The service point can be described as the point of demarcation between where the serving utility ends and the premises wiring begins. The serving utility generally specifies the location of the service point based on the conditions of service.

The service point is the point of demarcation on the wiring system where the serving utility ends and the premises wiring begins. It is the transition point where the rules of NFPA *70E* and the *NEC* apply. Only conductors physically located on the premises wiring side (load side) of the service point are covered by the *NEC*. The utility typically specifies the location of the service point. Exact locations of the service point may vary from utility to utility as well as from occupancy to occupancy. The service point might be at the transformer or substation for an industrial installation, or at the weatherhead and drip loop for a small commercial occupancy. Exhibit 100.12 shows two examples of service point locations.

EXHIBIT 100.12

Service point.

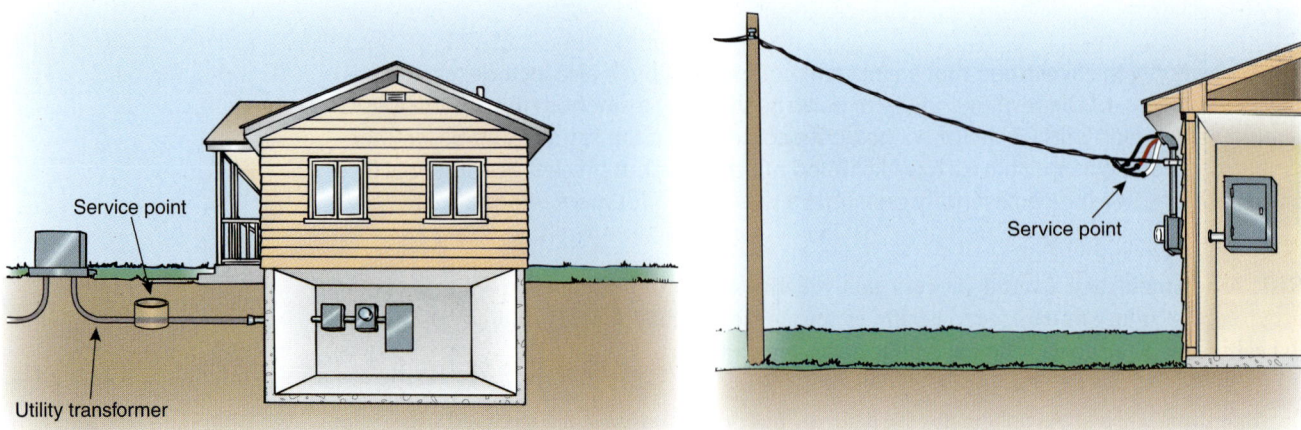

Definitions

Shock Hazard. A source of possible injury or damage to health associated with current through the body caused by contact or approach to energized electrical conductors or circuit parts.

> Informational Note: Injury and damage to health resulting from shock is dependent on the magnitude of the electrical current, the power source frequency (e.g., 60 Hz, 50 Hz, dc), and the path and time duration of current through the body. The physiological reaction ranges from perception, muscular contractions, inability to let go, ventricular fibrillation, tissue burns, and death.

A person's tolerance to an electrical current through the body varies depending on the path of the current through the body and on the applied voltage. The tolerated level also varies from person to person. The perception of a 60 Hz alternating electrical current occurring near 1 mA and 5 mA is a level typically considered to cause an involuntary reaction. Pain may be felt at a slightly higher current, and involuntary muscle contractions may occur around 20 mA. Direct current and higher frequencies have an effect on tolerance levels. Although exposure to any energized component may present a shock hazard, a shock hazard is generally considered to exist at a voltage of 50 volts or greater. See also commentary to 340.4, which focuses on the effects of electricity on the human body.

Short-Circuit Current Rating. The prospective symmetrical fault current at a nominal voltage to which an apparatus or system is able to be connected without sustaining damage exceeding defined acceptance criteria. [**70**:100]

The short-circuit current rating (SCCR) is marked on equipment, as shown in the bottom section of the label in Exhibit 100.11. The available input current must not exceed this rating. Wire, bus structures, switching, protection and disconnect devices, and distribution equipment will be damaged or destroyed if their short-circuit ratings are exceeded. SCCR was formerly known as "withstand rating," and some other standards may still use that terminology.

Overcurrent protective devices should be selected to ensure that the SCCR of the components are not exceeded should a short circuit or high-level ground fault occur. The overcurrent protective device must limit the let-through energy to within the SCCR of the electrical components. The SCCR is the actual symmetrical root-mean-square (rms) fault current that can be withstood for a period of time. It could be 3 cycles, 15 cycles, 30 cycles or some other time period depending upon the standard to which the equipment or component was tested.

Utility companies usually determine and provide information on available short-circuit current levels at the service equipment. Literature on how to calculate short-circuit currents at each point in any electrical distribution system can be obtained by contacting the manufacturers of overcurrent protective devices.

Single-Line Diagram. A diagram that shows, by means of single lines and graphic symbols, the course of an electric circuit or system of circuits and the component devices or parts used in the circuit or system.

A single-line diagram illustrates a complete system or a portion of a system using graphic symbols. Recorded copies of this drawing should be marked by red-lining or other method to illustrate all changes made to the system. The availability of an up-to-date and accurate single-line diagram that identifies sources of energy and locations of disconnecting means is key to implementing procedures for establishing an electrically safe work condition. Exhibit 205.1 and Figure D.2.2 both show an example of a single-line diagram.

Special Permission. The written consent of the authority having jurisdiction. [**70**:100]

Step Potential. A ground potential gradient difference that can cause current flow from foot to foot through the body.

> Any current path through the body other than from foot to foot is touch potential. Exhibit 100.13 illustrates the difference between step and touch potential and possible injuries resulting from electric current passing through the human body. Although the insulating quality of voltage-rated gloves or footwear may be one component of a system to mitigate step and touch potential hazards, these cannot be used as the primary means of employee protection. See 130.7(C)(8) for more information on foot protection.

EXHIBIT 100.13

Step and touch potential.

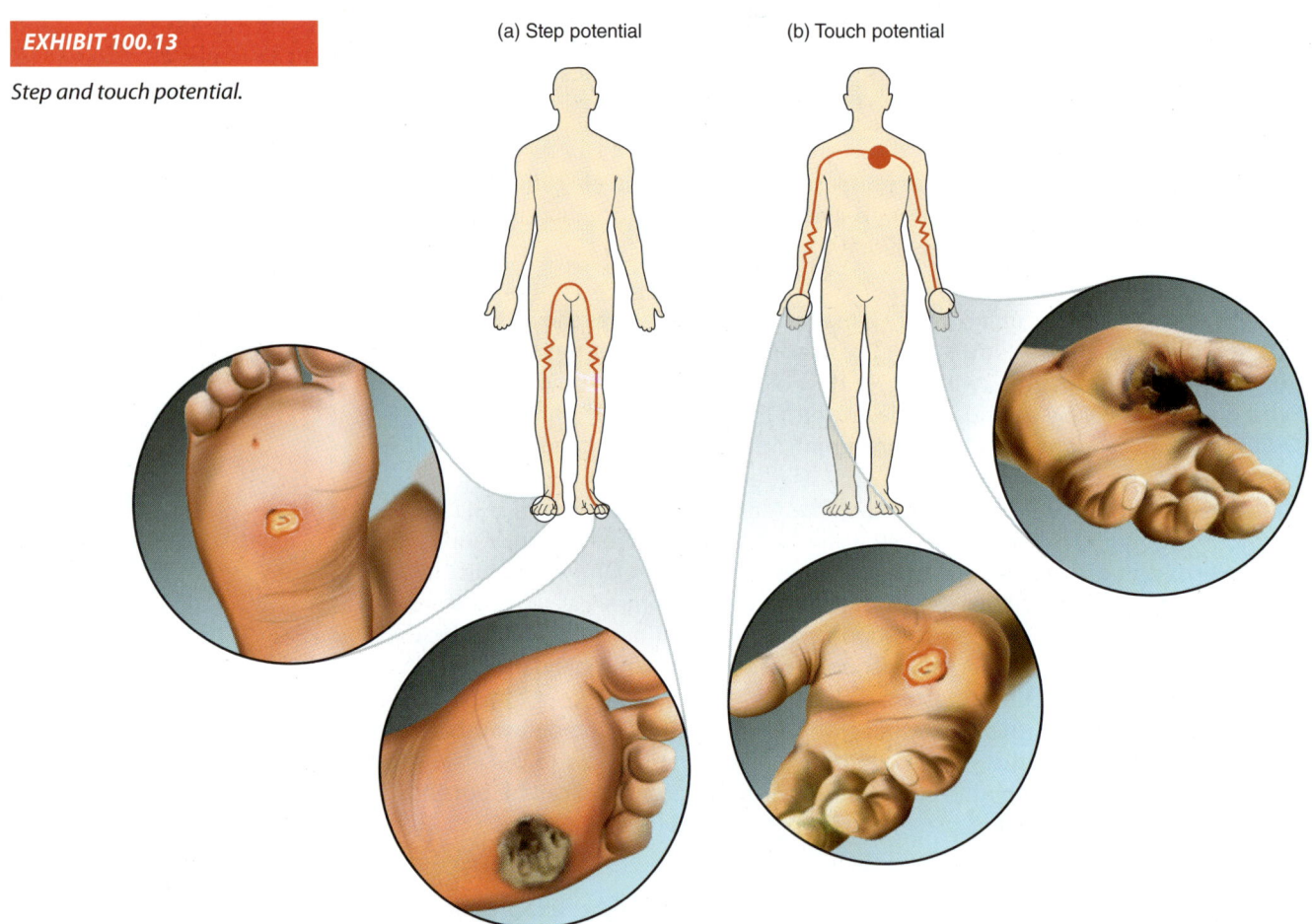

Structure. That which is built or constructed. [**70**:100]

Switch, Isolating. A switch intended for isolating an electric circuit from the source of power. It has no interrupting rating, and it is intended to be operated only after the circuit has been opened by some other means. [**70**:100]

> Isolating switches, while not intended nor rated to open a circuit under load, can provide a means to install lockout devices after the load current has been removed.

Definitions

Switchboard. A large single panel, frame, or assembly of panels on which are mounted on the face, back, or both, switches, overcurrent and other protective devices, buses, and usually instruments. These assemblies are generally accessible from the rear as well as from the front and are not intended to be installed in cabinets. [**70**:100]

> Switchgear or motor control centers do not meet this definition. However, many electrical employees apply the term *switchgear* to switchboards and motor control centers. It is important to understand the difference when using Table 130.7(C)(15)(a) and Table 130.7(C)(15)(b) because the arc flash hazard PPE categories are based on the type of equipment being serviced and voltage level.
>
> Modern switchboards are totally enclosed to minimize the probability of spreading fire to adjacent combustible materials and to guard live parts. Service busbars are isolated by barriers from the remainder of the switchboard to avoid inadvertent contact by personnel or tools during maintenance.

Switchgear, Arc-Resistant. Equipment designed to withstand the effects of an internal arcing fault and that directs the internally released energy away from the employee.

> Only switchgear specifically identified as being arc resistant provides protection from an internal arcing fault when the equipment is closed and operating normally. If doors and covers (including fasteners) are not completely closed, employees are exposed to the hazards associated with an arcing fault just as if no arc-resistant rating existed. Exhibit 110.14 shows an examples of arc-resistant switchgear and metal-clad switchgear.

EXHIBIT 100.14

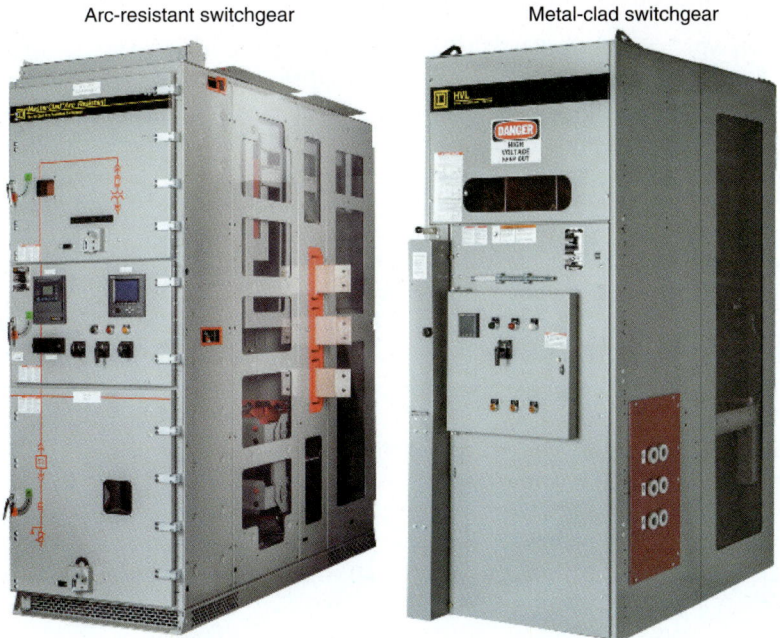

An exterior comparison of arc-resistant switchgear (left) and metal-clad switchgear (right). (Courtesy of Schneider Electric)

Switchgear, Metal-Clad. A switchgear assembly completely enclosed on all sides and top with sheet metal, having drawout switching and interrupting devices, and all live parts enclosed within grounded metal compartments.

Switchgear, Metal-Enclosed. A switchgear assembly completely enclosed on all sides and top with sheet metal (except for ventilating openings and inspection windows), containing primary power circuit switching, interrupting devices, or both, with buses and connections. This assembly may include control and auxiliary devices. Access to the interior of the enclosure is provided by doors, removable covers, or both. Metal-enclosed switchgear is available in non-arc-resistant or arc-resistant constructions.

Switching Device. A device designed to close, open, or both, one or more electric circuits.

> A switching device can be any device that is rated for this use. Splicing devices located in mid-conductor sometimes are rated for use as disconnecting devices and therefore are acceptable as switching devices.

Touch Potential. A ground potential gradient difference that can cause current flow from hand to hand, hand to foot, or another path, other than foot to foot, through the body.

> Any current path between two points on a body, other than from foot to foot, is called touch potential. (See Exhibit 100.13 and the commentary following the definition of the term *step potential*.)

Ungrounded. Not connected to ground or to a conductive body that extends the ground connection. [**70**:100]

Unqualified Person. A person who is not a qualified person.

> Any person who has not received the specific training to perform a task or to recognize that an electrical hazard exists and how to avoid that hazard or who has not shown demonstrated ability is an unqualified person. An employee qualified to perform a specific task may be unqualified to perform other tasks. The characteristics of being qualified and unqualified are task-dependent.

Utilization Equipment. Equipment that utilizes electric energy for electronic, electromechanical, chemical, heating, lighting, or similar purposes. [**70**:100]

Voltage (of a Circuit). The greatest root-mean-square (rms) (effective) difference of potential between any two conductors of the circuit concerned. [**70**:100]

> Informational Note: Some systems, such as three-phase 4-wire, single-phase 3-wire, and 3-wire direct-current, may have various circuits of various voltages.

Voltage, Nominal. A nominal value assigned to a circuit or system for the purpose of conveniently designating its voltage class (e.g., 120/240 volts, 480Y/277 volts, 600 volts). [**70**:100]

> Informational Note 1: The actual voltage at which a circuit operates can vary from the nominal within a range that permits satisfactory operation of equipment.

Worker Alert

Often the most appropriate person to determine your qualification level for a given task is *you*. It is ultimately your responsibility to recognize if you do not have the skills necessary to perform a task safely.

Application of Safety-Related Work Practices and Procedures

Informational Note 2: See ANSI C84.1, *Electric Power Systems and Equipment — Voltage Ratings (60 Hz).*

N Working Distance. The distance between a person's face and chest area and a prospective arc source.

Informational Note: Incident energy increases as the distance from the arc source decreases. See 130.5(C)(1) for further information.

> Required arc flash PPE is based on the incident energy at the working distance. Often arms and hands are placed closer to the hazard than the chest. Additional arc flash protection may be necessary for any body part that is closer than the specified working distance.

Working On (energized electrical conductors or circuit parts). Intentionally coming in contact with energized electrical conductors or circuit parts with the hands, feet, or other body parts, with tools, probes, or with test equipment, regardless of the personal protective equipment (PPE) a person is wearing. There are two categories of "working on": *Diagnostic (testing)* is taking readings or measurements of electrical equipment with approved test equipment that does not require making any physical change to the equipment; *repair* is any physical alteration of electrical equipment (such as making or tightening connections, removing or replacing components, etc.).

> A person required to perform a task involving intentional contact with an energized electrical conductor or circuit part is considered to be working on the energized part. The person is subject to all associated requirements, including the selection of the appropriate level of PPE. Regardless of the use of PPE, measuring voltage with probes is an example of a diagnostic task involving working on energized parts that exposes an employee to an electrical hazard.
>
> Two distinctly different types of tasks are included within this definition: diagnostic testing and repair. The two categories suggest that different procedural approaches may be necessary depending on the complexity of the task and the employee's exposure to electrical hazards.

Worker Alert

The protection afforded by this standard is based on this working distance. It is important to understand that your hands and arms are typically closer to the energized circuit than this distance. Leaning toward the equipment to gain a better viewpoint exposes your head and face to greater energy levels. These closer distances require additional protection of these body parts that often exceeds the labeled protection level.

Application of Safety-Related Work Practices and Procedures

Article 105

Article 105 establishes the overall scope, purpose, and organization of Chapter 1. It differentiates between the responsibilities of the employer and those of the employee. The employer has the responsibilities of providing safety-related work procedures, training employees in the practices, supervising the employees, auditing, and documenting. The employees are responsible for applying the work procedures in accordance with their training and demonstrated ability.

> OSHA's electrical safety standards are derived from NFPA *70E*. Since NFPA *70E* is the American National Standard for electrical safety in the workplace, it sets the minimum consensus requirements for safe electrical work procedures. NFPA *70E* establishes the minimum standard of care. OSHA's electrical safety standards are mainly performance based, whereas NFPA *70E* is mainly prescription based. NFPA *70E* fleshes out how the performance-based requirements in the OSHA standards should be met by providing and defining the minimum standard industry practices necessary for electrical safety. OSHA is the law, but NFPA *70E* outlines how to comply with OSHA's electrical safety requirements.

105.1 Scope. Chapter 1 covers electrical safety-related work practices and procedures for employees who are exposed to an electrical hazard in workplaces covered in the scope of this standard.

> Chapter 1 outlines the electrical safety procedures necessary to protect employees from the dangers inherent with the use of electricity. The chapter also defines the responsibilities for creating an electrical safety program (ESP) and implementing the procedures included in the program. An electrical safety procedure should include all employees who interact with systems, equipment, components, or parts that use electricity.
>
> Injuries associated with the use of electricity are not limited to unique employees, specific industries, or a particular segment of specific industry. The applicability of this standard does not depend on the employee's craft; on whether the facility is classified as residential, commercial, institutional, or industrial; on whether the employee is qualified or not; on the business of the employer; or on the employees' level of training. For work locations covered by NFPA *70E*, no industry segment or work discipline is omitted. The fundamentals identified in this standard are intended to protect all types of employees in workplaces identified. However, the fundamentals may be used protect employees in workplaces excluded under 90.2(B), if the employer chooses to adopt the work procedures.

Worker Alert

First and foremost, NFPA *70E* is about protecting you from injury when you are interacting with electrical equipment. It covers you when operating equipment under normal conditions as well as when performing other tasks on the electrical equipment.

105.2 Purpose. These practices and procedures are intended to provide for employee safety relative to electrical hazards in the workplace.

Informational Note: For general categories of electrical hazards, see Informative Annex K.

> Employees may be exposed to unacceptable risk of injury while interacting with energized electrical conductors and circuit parts that are not under normal operating conditions. When electrical equipment is not properly installed or maintained, even the risk associated with normal operation of electrical equipment may be unacceptable.
>
> The requirements of NFPA *70E* are suitable for use in situations where the potential harm from the use of electricity poses unacceptable risk. This standard specifies the electrical safety–related work procedures required to protect all types, categories, and classes of employees and others — whether or not they are qualified or unqualified to interact with energized electrical equipment — under normal or other than normal operating conditions. Normal operating conditions are defined in 130.2(A)(4).

Application of Safety-Related Work Practices and Procedures

105.3(B)

105.3 Responsibility.

N **(A) Employer Responsibility.** The employer shall have the following responsibilities:
(1) Establish, document, and implement the safety-related work practices and procedures required by this standard.
(2) Provide employees with training in the employer's safety-related work practices and procedures.

> Electrical safety is a shared responsibility between employers and employees. Employee electrical safety requires a collaborative effort between workers and management. Compliance with safety regulations is not just an employer responsibility. The Occupational Safety and Health Act of 1970 specifically requires that employees comply with the applicable OSHA regulations. The responsibilities are divided between employer and employee.
>
> Employers are required to have an electrical safety program (ESP) for employees that includes the requirements identified in 110.2 and 110.3. The employees are required to put into practice policies and procedures of the ESP, which includes the training to perform the task at hand safely and the use of required tools and safety equipment. The best results are achieved by collaboration and cooperation between labor and management, including the use of cross-functional teams and outside experts as determined necessary.
>
> It is the employer's responsibility to create an ESP that includes policies, procedures, and process controls to document that program and to implement the program through training, auditing, and enforcement that is appropriate to the risk associated with the potential electrical hazards. The employer's ESP needs to address all situations that can lead to the potential exposure of an employee to an electrical hazard. Where the employer has an overall occupational health and safety management system in place, the ESP is a component of such a program and needs to be integrated in the system.
>
> Development and implementation of ESPs and their work procedures requires the knowledge, expertise, and commitment of both management and labor. Management must provide the assets needed as well as coordinate planning, scheduling, and best methods of meeting deadlines. The required tasks are normally performed by employees who tend to have familiarity and expertise in the use of the actual systems and equipment. Sometimes the required expertise is lacking, and it has to be developed. It is in the organization's interest and the interest of the individuals involved that each and every employee goes home safe and sound. Commitment of both parties is necessary and required.
>
> Managers and supervisors must demonstrate the safety behaviors they expect their employees to follow. A comprehensive safety program can easily be rendered ineffective if management does not support the safety principles or does not encourage a safety culture. Management must allow the time necessary for the employee to follow the documented safety procedures and must convey that safety takes precedence over speed. Employees who perceive the opposite will take shortcuts and expose themselves to an increased risk of injury.

N **(B) Employee Responsibility.** The employee shall comply with the safety-related work practices and procedures provided by the employer.

> NFPA *70E* is not just about the actions an employer took before the incident investigation. NFPA *70E* is about preventing the worker from being injured. Regardless of the

---

OSHA Connection

Public Law 91-596, "Occupational Safety and Health Act of 1970" SEC. 5.(a) Duties

Each employer must furnish to each of his employees employment and a place of employment which are free from recognized hazards that are causing or are likely to cause death or serious physical harm to his employees.

Worker Alert

In order for there to be an effective safety culture, you must incorporate the provided training, practices, and procedures. Taking short cuts, skipping steps of a procedure, or failing to don protective gear are risky decisions that lie with you, not your employer. You should work to improve safety by providing effective feedback on the training, practices, and procedures.

Handbook for Electrical Safety in the Workplace 2018

> **OSHA Connection**
>
> Public Law 91-596, "Occupational Safety and Health Act of 1970" SEC. 5.(b) Duties
>
> Each employee must comply with occupational safety and health standards and all rules, regulations, and orders issued pursuant to this Act which are applicable to his own actions and conduct.

employer's electrical safety plan, it is the employee who has the biggest impact on his or her own electrical safety.

Employers are required to provide safety-related work practices and training to their employees as part of their job. The employer must teach the employee to be self-aware of the hazards and actions taken and should also instill in the employee a sense of self-discipline. An employer must also train the employee to perform the tasks, recognize the hazards, and understand the potential injury from those hazards, as well as how to protect themselves from those hazards.

Employees are responsible for implementing each of these into their work. An employer may train, audit, and retrain employees. Regardless of training, it is the employee who will make decisions and take actions that may or may not result in injury. Employees have a responsibility to know their limitations — only they can determine if they are truly qualified to safely perform a task on a piece of equipment.

N 105.4 Priority. Hazard elimination shall be the first priority in the implementation of safety-related work practices.

> Informational Note: Elimination is the risk control method listed first in the hierarchy of risk control identified in 110.1(H).

> Once a hazard has been identified, it should be determined if the hazard can be eliminated. If there is no hazard, there is no risk of injury from a hazard. During the electrical system design stage, methods should be employed to eliminate the hazard in its entirety. In this first context, elimination is removal of the hazard entirely so that it never exists. This often is not an option for installed equipment. Elimination can be also be achieved by applying other controls, such as through the establishment of an electrically safe work condition, but the initial attempt should be full elimination of the hazard.

105.5 Organization. Chapter 1 of this standard is divided into five articles. Article 100 provides definitions for terms used in one or more of the chapters of this document. Article 105 provides for application of safety-related work practices and procedures. Article 110 provides general requirements for electrical safety-related work practices and procedures. Article 120 provides requirements for establishing an electrically safe work condition. Article 130 provides requirements for work involving electrical hazards.

> Article 105 sets the tone for Chapter 1 by defining the scope, purpose, and responsibilities of the parties involved. The practices and procedures contained in Article 110 must be established before work is performed on any electrical equipment and circuit parts. The requirements in Article 120 eliminate the hazards associated with the use of electricity by creating an electrically safe work condition, through de-energizing, lockout/tagout, and verification that there is no voltage, as well as temporarily grounding equipment as necessary. The practices and procedures in Article 130 generally cover interaction with energized electrical equipment and circuit parts.

General Requirements for Electrical Safety-Related Work Practices

Article 110

Work practices set the policy and direct employee activity in broad terms. They may be incorporated as part of an employer's overall occupational health and safety management system. The work practice should address planning all tasks and protecting employees from hazards. The work practice will also incorporate the electrical safety work program, which fills in the details of how to put the practice to use. For example, work procedures will direct an employee on how to maintain electrical equipment or use a specific test instrument. Principles of work practices should include the following:

- Establish an electrically safe work condition
- Plan all tasks
- Anticipate unexpected events
- Identify the hazard and minimize the risk
- Protect the employee
- Use correct tools
- Ensure employee qualifications and abilities
- Inspect and maintain electrical equipment

110.1 Electrical Safety Program.

Section 110.1, Electrical Safety Program, is presented first in order to promote the importance to employees and employers of having a documented electrical safety program (ESP). The employer's electrical safety program needs to address all situations that can lead to the potential exposure of an employee to an electrical hazard. Where electrical safety is involved, high ethical standards should exist and be enforced. As illustrated in Exhibit 110.1, an ESP includes many different components.

(A) General. The employer shall implement and document an overall electrical safety program that directs activity appropriate to the risk associated with electrical hazards. The electrical safety program shall be implemented as part of the employer's overall occupational health and safety management system, when one exists.

> Informational Note No. 1: Safety-related work practices such as verification of proper maintenance and installation, alerting techniques, auditing requirements, and training requirements provided in this standard are administrative controls and part of an overall electrical safety program.
>
> Informational Note No. 2: ANSI/AIHA Z10, *American National Standard for Occupational Health and Safety Management Systems*, provides a framework for establishing a comprehensive electrical safety program as a component of an employer's occupational safety and health program.
>
> Informational Note No. 3: IEEE 3007.1, *Recommended Practice for the Operation and Management of Industrial and Commercial Power Systems*, provides additional guidance for the implementation of the electrical safety program.
>
> Informational Note No. 4: IEEE 3007.3, *Recommended Practice for Electrical Safety in Industrial and Commercial Power Systems*, provides additional guidance for electrical safety in the workplace.

EXHIBIT 110.1

Components of an electrical safety program.

Occupational Health & Safety Management System

- Management Commitment Policy
- Planning
- Implementation & Operation
- Evaluation & Corrective Action
- Management Review

Electrical Safety Program Procedures
- Job briefing
- Establishing an electrically safe working condition
- Test before touch
- Working while exposed to electrical hazards (justification; energized electrical work permit)
- Auditing (program and field work)
- Program controls (metrics)

Health & Safety Risk Management Program
- Risk Assessments
- Training
- Hierarchy of Risk Controls

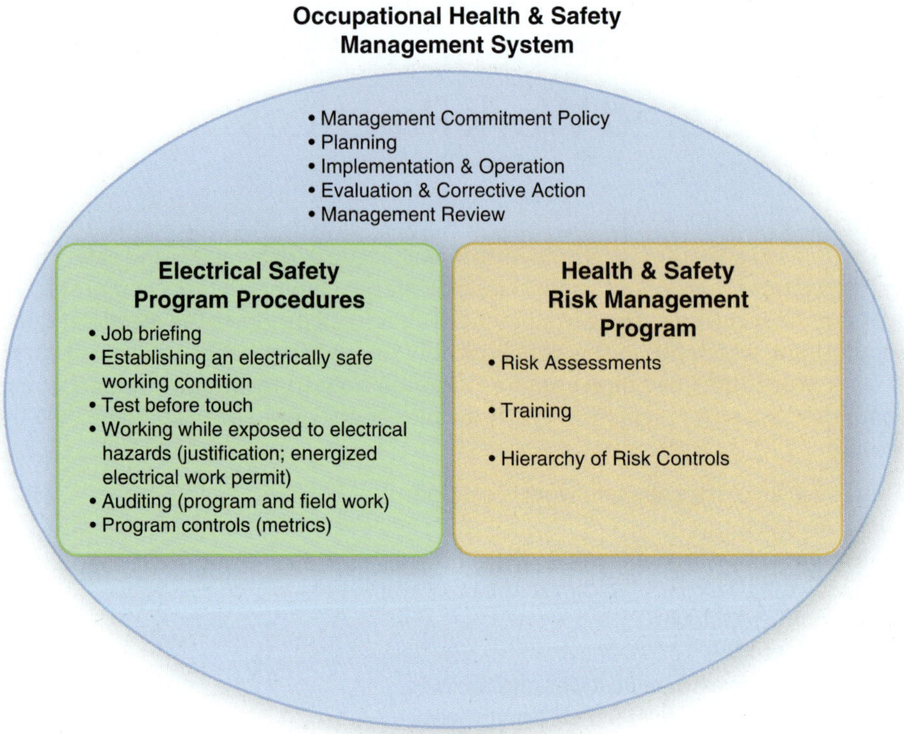

It is the employer's responsibility to create and document an electrical safety program that includes policies, procedures, and process controls. The employer must implement the program through training, auditing, and enforcement that is appropriate to the risk associated with the potential electrical hazards. Where the employer has an overall occupational health and safety management system in place, the electrical safety program must be a component of such a program that is integrated in the system.

The employer may have developed an occupational health and safety management system in accordance with ANSI/AIHA Z10, *American National Standard for Occupational Health and Safety Management Systems*. In the same way that NFPA *70E* provides information on electrical safety-related work procedures, ANSI/AIHA Z10 provides guidance on developing and implementing an overall occupational safety management system. The ANSI/AIHA Z10 document provides a framework into which the electrical safety program can fit.

N **(B) Inspection.** The electrical safety program shall include elements to verify that newly installed or modified electrical equipment or systems have been inspected to comply with applicable installation codes and standards prior to being placed into service.

Often building systems are inspected by an authority outside of the employer/owner. Much of the equipment that falls under the purview of NFPA *70E* does not have a governmental electrical inspector verifying that the installation complies with applicable codes, standards, and instructions. Equipment is often installed by an employee or outside contractor, with no governmental oversight. Without proper installation, the equipment cannot be depended on to operate correctly or to perform its required safety functions. The employer/owner must determine how to enforce and determine compliance with *NFPA 70®*, *National Electrical Code® (NEC)*, for equipment installed under these circumstances.

Case Study

110.1

Scenario

Joe, a journeyman electrician with 28 years of experience, and Al, an electrical apprentice, were removing a set of circuit conductors from a circuit breaker installed in a 480Y/277-volt, 3-phase, 4-wire, 800-amp main breaker service panelboard. The panelboard supplied power to the entire building. Due to the cost associated with having the utility company disconnect the power to the building, their employer decided to have them proceed with this task by simply placing the main circuit breaker into the off position to de-energize the panelboard busbars. The service conductors into the line side terminals of the main circuit breaker were still energized and exposed.

Joe began removing the conductors from a branch circuit breaker in the upper left-hand side of the enclosure. Al was standing on a ladder 4 or 5 feet away and was manually supporting the conduit that contained the circuit conductors. The bare equipment grounding conductor being removed was still connected to the equipment grounding terminal in the enclosure. As the conductors were being removed, the equipment ground conductor accidently contacted an energized terminal on the main circuit breaker, and an arc flash event ensued.

Result

Al saw a large flash and heard a loud noise, followed rapidly by two more explosive noises. Then, Al noticed that Joe's synthetic clothing was in flames. Al patted out the flames on his partner with his hands and burned himself in the process. He then led Joe out of the smoke-filled room and called 911 for assistance.

Joe sustained second- and third-degree burns over nearly 50 percent of his body. He required surgery for removal of destroyed skin and restorative skin grafts. He needed physical therapy for a year and after another year returned to work full time. Al was treated for second-degree burns and released.

Analysis

Unless the establishing of an electrically safe work condition (ESWC) introduced a greater hazard or increased risk or was infeasible (neither of which was indicated), the employer should not have authorized the work. The facts suggest that the company placed a higher priority on the cost of the utility establishing an ESWC than the personal safety of Al and Joe. If an ESWC had been properly established prior to the removal of the circuit conductors, this incident would not have occurred.

An assumption was made that simply opening the main circuit breaker was adequate enough protection for the assigned task, rather than establishing an ESWC. Within the enclosure there were exposed energized circuit parts that were not addressed. Proper risk assessments and work procedures would have identified that an electrical hazard existed within the enclosure — even with the load side of the circuit breaker de-energized. The work should have been considered as energized work due to the presence of exposed electrical hazards within the enclosure. If the task were properly justified, a written permit would have been necessary. The permit would have been approved by the owner, responsible management, or safety officer. The energized work permit would have specified the written procedures necessary to conduct the task safely and any necessary protective equipment, and would have used the hierarchy of risk controls to address the exposed energized circuit parts. The exposed parts of the service conductors and main circuit breaker could have been shielded by an appropriate insulating barrier. The exposed parts of the circuit conductors, including the equipment grounding conductor, could have been insulated. Appropriate PPE could have been used or worn.

Relevant NFPA *70E* Requirements

This was not simply a case of the need for Joe and Al to don proper PPE. If the company had followed the requirements of NFPA *70E*, Al and Joe might not have been injured. The employer ignored the following primary safety principles:

- Create an electrical safety program [110.1].
- Establish an electrically safe work condition [130.2].
- Properly justify energized work [130.2(A)].

Joe and Al also hold some responsibility for the incident. As employees they should have been aware of their responsibilities under NFPA *70E*. In addition to the requirements listed above, they should have been aware of the following:

- Their ability to meet the definition of a qualified person [100]
- Their need for awareness and self-discipline [110.1(D)]
- The training they should have received from their employer [110.2]

(C) Condition of Maintenance. The electrical safety program shall include elements that consider condition of maintenance of electrical equipment and systems.

> An electrical safety program must consider the condition of maintenance of the equipment and its component parts. Without proper maintenance, the equipment cannot be depended on to perform its required safety functions, such as interrupting fault currents within its characteristic time–current curves. Proper maintenance can be achieved by following the manufacturer's instructions or the recommendations included in NFPA 70B, *Recommended Practice for Electrical Equipment Maintenance*.
>
> Proper maintenance applies not only to the equipment where the task is being performed but also to any remote disconnect and the circuit's overcurrent device, for example.

> **Worker Alert**
>
> When interacting with electrical equipment, you should be aware if the equipment has not been maintained. Maintenance personnel know if the company's priority is to maintain its high-value or production equipment, rather than *all* electrical equipment. Without a comprehensive maintenance program, you are put at risk when operating or interacting with equipment.

(D) Awareness and Self-Discipline. The electrical safety program shall be designed to provide an awareness of the potential electrical hazards to employees who work in an environment with the presence of electrical hazards. The program shall be developed to provide the required self-discipline for all employees who must perform work that may involve electrical hazards. The program shall instill safety principles and controls.

> Human factors are generally recognized as one of the leading causes of injuries. When employees are conducting work, they are typically solely responsible for their actions. After employees have gone through training, received supervision, and been provided procedures to follow, it is their own actions (or lack thereof) that will impact their safety. In the hierarchy of risk controls, awareness generally means being able to recognize warning signs. In this section, awareness refers to attentiveness to self, others, and the situation. According to this section, awareness can apply to any of the following:
>
> - Recognizing when the risk of a potential electrical hazard is unacceptable
> - Understanding a possible sequence of events that could lead up to exposure to an electrical hazard
> - Being alert to other personnel who could enter the work area
> - Realizing that work conditions could change
> - Understanding that personal circumstances — such as weariness, exhaustion, boredom, or distraction — can affect performance and result in unsafe conditions
>
> By instilling awareness and self-discipline, employees begin to accept that their own actions often are a primary cause of injuries. Short cuts, such as failing to don appropriate PPE or conducting unjustified energized work, begin to be questioned. Employees begin to realize that the rush to complete a task before the end of a shift or the fatigue from extended hours may put them at risk. Aware and self-disciplined employees understand the potential harm a certain action could subject them to and realize that it is not worth the risk. Employees may also start to correct or point out unsafe actions of other employees.
>
> Having an electrical safety program is not enough, in itself; employees must follow the policies and effectively implement the procedures. The employer provides the personal and other protective equipment required. The equipment owner ensures that the warning labels required by 130.5(H) are installed. However, the employee has to be able to select, wear, and use the equipment appropriate for the specific hazards involved.

> **Worker Alert**
>
> Regardless of your employer's policies and training programs, it is your own action — or inaction — that often can prevent you from returning home uninjured at the end of the day. Your awareness and self-discipline on the job cannot be understated.

General Requirements for Electrical Safety-Related Work Practices

Case Study

Scenario

Ellen was an electrician at a chemical manufacturing facility. Carl, the senior electrician, was qualifying Ellen to perform energized tasks on production line equipment. The company had an established electric safety work program with documented procedures for each task to be performed. Routine maintenance was conducted on the production line equipment to minimize lost production time. Risk assessments were conducted, and labels with the results were applied to the equipment. In order for Ellen to better understand the unique production line equipment, the first task scheduled was simple diagnostic testing. Even though the task was exempted by NFPA *70E*, company policy required that an energized work permit be completed prior to performing the task. A job briefing was held to make sure that Ellen fully understood the task and work procedures. Carl demonstrated how to visually inspect all the equipment necessary for the task.

The enclosure where the task was to be performed was labeled with an incident energy of 6.4 cal/cm^2 at a working distance of 18 inches. The label stated that a minimum PPE arc-rating of 8 cal/cm^2 was required to work on the equipment. Both Carl and Ellen dressed in PPE since they would be within the 7-foot arc flash boundary. Although Ellen would be conducting the task, company policy required Carl to also wear shock PPE for safety even though he would not be within the restricted approach boundary.

After opening the access panel, Ellen proceeded to perform the diagnostic evaluation by connecting an analyzer to check power quality. After the testing had begun, Ellen bumped into the side of the enclosure, which then released a nut that had been spot-welded to the inside of the enclosure to bolt the access panel in place. When Ellen reached deeper into the equipment to retrieve the nut, an arc flash occurred.

Result

Ellen suffered severe second-degree burns over the left side of her body from the face to the waist. She was released from the hospital after three days and returned to work after another three weeks. Carl was not injured during the incident.

Likely Cause of Incident

The incident primarily occurred as a result of human error. Ellen's impulse reaction to retrieve the nut through blindly reaching into the enclosure was the root cause. Although she was not yet qualified to perform the task on her own, Ellen should have had training that provided her with a better understanding of the risks and hazards associated within the energized equipment, not just for the assigned task.

Subsequent investigation into the incident revealed the primary cause for the severity of injury. Although Ellen's employer placed a priority on the maintenance of the production line equipment to maximize revenue, the electrical distribution equipment had not been maintained since its initial installation 16 years prior. Testing of the circuit breaker, which was relied upon to limit the incident energy, was found to have a fault clearing time nearly double that used for the incident energy calculation. Examination of the device revealed that the environment within the chemical facility had degraded the trip mechanism. Although the PPE worn by Ellen was rated for 10 cal/cm^2, it was subjected to an estimated incident energy level of 21.4 cal/cm^2.

Analysis

Although Ellen holds some responsibility for the incident since her blind reaching directly initiated the arc flash, her employer missed its responsibility to protect her from the energized electrical hazards that they subjected her to. Maintenance of equipment as required by NFPA *70E* is not limited to only the equipment being worked on — it is applicable to all the overcurrent devices upstream from that equipment. This is true whether the policy is to establish an electrically safe work condition or for justified energized work to be authorized. Proper maintenance is necessary whether the arc flash analysis is conducted under the incident energy method or the PPE category method. Whenever an arc flash hazard exists, it is the proper function of protective devices that will limit the severity of injury to a worker during an incident. Ellen was fortunate that the PPE she was wearing performed beyond its rating, thereby preventing a permanent injury or her death.

(E) Electrical Safety Program Principles. The electrical safety program shall identify the principles upon which it is based.

> Informational Note: For examples of typical electrical safety program principles, see Informative Annex E.

A company's primary safety and business objectives will guide the development of the safety program. Electrical safety program principles are the company's safety policies. As such, they are safety guidelines for the employees. These principles direct employee activity.

An employee may not interact with electrical equipment safely if the employer favors keeping the production line running or getting power back on as quickly as possible. Unless the company's core safety principles and expectations of performing energized work safely are upheld, the employee will justify taking shortcuts and engaging in substandard work practices to meet those goals.

An employer's policies might include the following:

- Electrical hazards are to be identified and minimized.
- Every job is to be planned.
- First-time procedures are to be documented.
- Unexpected events are to be anticipated.

Examples of such polices are found in the sample electrical safety program outline found in E.1 of Informative Annex E.

(F) Electrical Safety Program Controls. An electrical safety program shall identify the controls by which it is measured and monitored.

Informational Note: For examples of typical electrical safety program controls, see Informative Annex E.

Electrical safety program controls are the company's electrical safety metrics for determining if the electrical safety program is effective and efficient. Metrics are measurable points to determine performance. They also can be used to determine if improvements to the safety program are required and, if so, what needs to be changed. Some program controls are found in the sample electrical safety program outline found in E.2 of Informative Annex E.

There are two common metrics used to determine the effectiveness of something: lagging metrics and leading metrics. Lagging metrics provide a reactive view of a safety program. Lagging metrics for a safety program could include the total time lost to injuries, the costs spent on worker compensation, or the amount of training that an employee has received. Leading metrics are used to identify and correct contributing factors before an incident occurs. Leading metrics for a safety program could include the number of hazards identified and eliminated, the reduction in number of energized work permits authorized, or the amount of work procedures altered for de-energized work rather than energized. A combination of these metrics can enhance a safe work program.

(G) Electrical Safety Program Procedures. An electrical safety program shall identify the procedures to be utilized before work is started by employees exposed to an electrical hazard.

Informational Note: For an example of a typical electrical safety program procedure, see Informative Annex E.

The electrical safety program must be documented. It must include the policies, procedures, and process controls necessary for the employees to work safely.

A procedure should be specific for the task to be performed. It should contain a defined scope, the required qualifications and number of employees involved, the hazards associated with the task, the limits of approach, the safe work practices to be followed, and the required PPE. It should also include the required tools and necessary precautionary techniques. Electrical diagrams, equipment preventative maintenance requirements, visual job aids, and manufacturer's data sheets should also be provided where they are warranted. The procedure should be discussed and reviewed during

> **Worker Alert**
>
> Your employer must provide you with documented procedures before you begin the task. You must review and understand them prior to starting. Improvising in the field is dangerous.

General Requirements for Electrical Safety-Related Work Practices

the job briefing so that it can be agreed that it sufficiently addresses the scheduled task before work has begun.

Electrical safety should be a continual improvement process, and all procedures should be periodically reviewed. A procedure is the best practice at the current time; some companies use the term *standard operating procedure* (SOP). Over time, situations can change and new methods developed. When situations change and the risk of injury exists, the employee must be able to identify and implement the necessary procedures for safe work where the potential for electrical hazards exists.

△ **(H) Risk Assessment Procedure.** The electrical safety program shall include a risk assessment procedure and shall comply with 110.1(H)(1) through 110.1(H)(3).

The flowchart in Exhibit 110.2 illustrates the process of conducting risk assessments. The chart references the main subsections pertinent to each type of assessment and those applicable to each leg of the chart. This exhibit is not intended to absolve users of their responsibility to read and understand the applicable NFPA *70E* requirements.

(1) Elements of a Risk Assessment Procedure. The risk assessment procedure shall address employee exposure to electrical hazards and shall identify the process to be used by the employee before work is started to carry out the following:

(1) Identify hazards
(2) Assess risks
(3) Implement risk control according to the hierarchy of risk control methods

Hazards must be first recognized in order to reduce the risk of injury. A program should be implemented to identify hazards proactively and to identify, analyze, and minimize risks. NFPA *70E* currently addresses only two hazards directly: electric shock and arc flash burn. As part of the risk assessment, it is necessary to determine the need for and an appropriate method of protecting the worker from all electrical hazards. The definition of *electrical hazard* in Article 100 includes any of the following: electric shock, arc flash burn, thermal burn, or arc blast. Other known hazards include flying parts, molten metal, intense light, poisonous oxides, and generated pressure waves (blasts).

As defined in Article 100, a *risk assessment* is "an overall process that identifies hazards, estimates the potential severity of injury or damage to health, estimates the likelihood of occurrence of injury or damage to health, and determines if protective measures are required." Risk assessment is about risk mitigation. Risk assessment involves a determination of whether protective measures are necessary. If they are deemed necessary, these protective measures come from the safety control categories in the hierarchy of risk controls. See also 110.1(H)(3) and F.3 for more on the hierarchy of risk controls.

A risk assessment procedure is a fundamental guideline for employees to follow to work safely. This risk assessment procedure must be documented and available to employees. For this procedure to be effective, it should point out the steps that employees must take where the risk of injury from a potential electrical hazard is unacceptable, and the employees must be trained to perform this procedure correctly each time risk is assessed. Where electrical hazards are involved, there are at least two components to a risk assessment procedure — a shock risk assessment per 130.4 and an arc flash risk assessment per 130.5. Furthermore, justification in accordance with 130.2(A) might also be considered part of the risk assessment procedure.

> **Worker Alert**
>
> Energized work exposes you to more electrical hazards than current standards are able to protect against. Being aware of other hazards will help you to determine the actions to take to prevent injury.

EXHIBIT 110.2

Risk assessment flow chart.

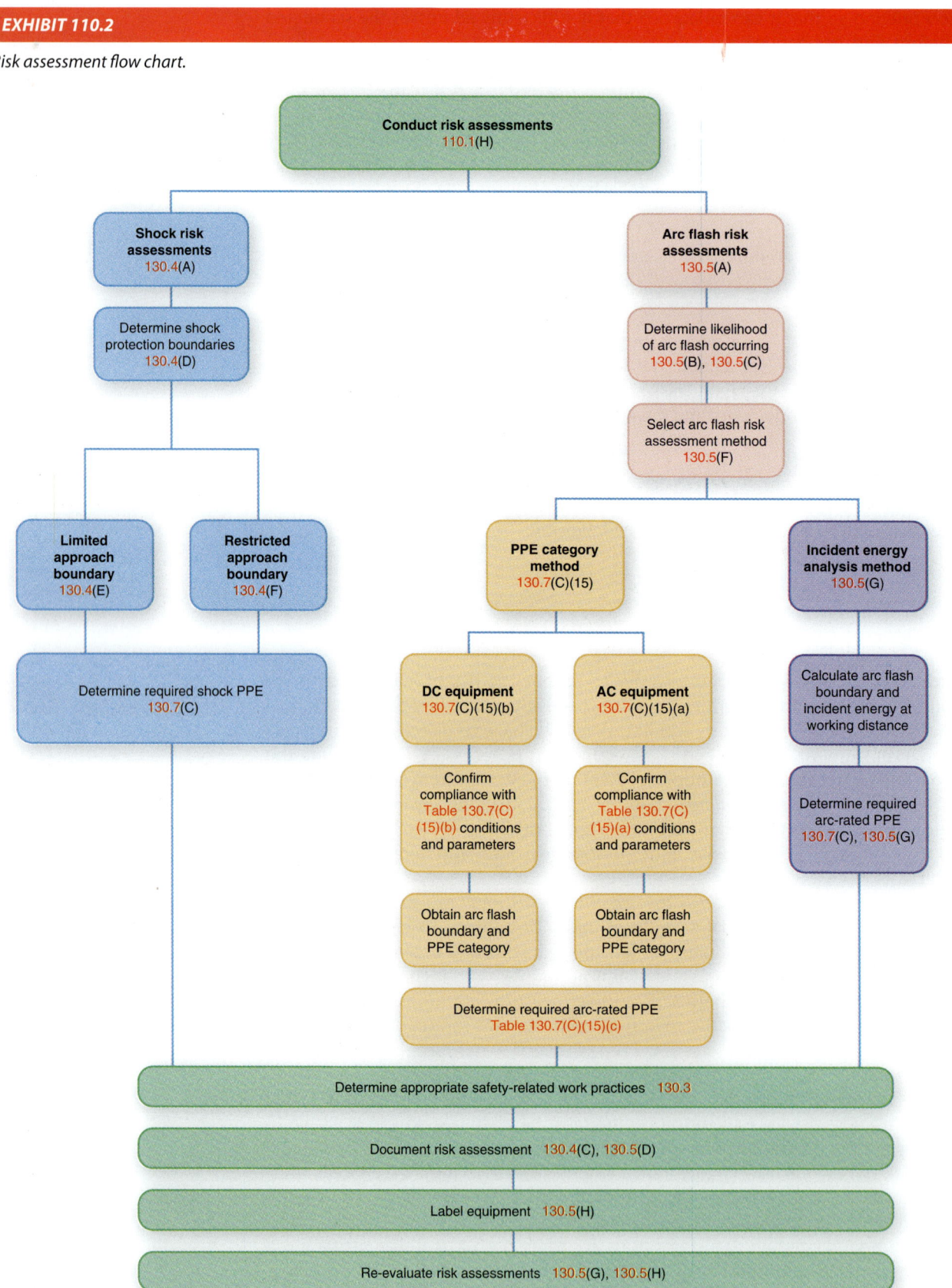

General Requirements for Electrical Safety-Related Work Practices

N (2) Human Error. The risk assessment procedure shall address the potential for human error and its negative consequences on people, processes, the work environment, and equipment.

> Informational Note: The potential for human error varies with factors such as tasks and the work environment. See Informative Annex Q.

> Equipment meeting the normal operating conditions seldom exhibits an injury-causing failure on its own. Electrical incidents are often the result of human error. Employees do not intentionally initiate an electrical incident that results in a "near miss" or an injury. Human error can be either a conscious or inadvertent act. Employees may slip or may take their eyes off the task at hand. They may decide not to follow the standard procedure or not to don the appropriate PPE. Training is a key factor in limiting these human errors.
>
> If taking shortcuts, skipping procedures, or routinely breaking rules is not addressed, employees begin to consider their actions as being condoned by the employer. If the employer is aware of these issues and does not promote safety, employees will assume they are permitted to continue the unsafe work practice.
>
> Safe work practices help establish human behaviors, which in turn aid in preventing an error from occurring. A behavior-based safety approach is an important method of addressing electrical safety in the workplace. This safety approach will assist employees to recognize that such errors are a leading cause of injury and that they need to take responsibility for their own safety. As the process permeates throughout a facility, employees begin to correct actions taken by peers. Eventually, voluntary compliance with the safe work practices increases as employees realize that their decisions influence safety.

Worker Alert

Equipment typically does not cause an injury without some error by you or your employer. Improper maintenance, failure to don PPE, and a slip of the hand are all forms of human error that can defeat even the best conceived safety program.

N (3) Hierarchy of Risk Control Methods. The risk assessment procedure shall require that preventive and protective risk control methods be implemented in accordance with the following hierarchy:

(1) Elimination
(2) Substitution
(3) Engineering controls
(4) Awareness
(5) Administrative controls
(6) PPE

> Informational Note No. 1: Elimination, substitution, and engineering controls are the most effective methods to reduce risk as they are usually applied at the source of possible injury or damage to health and they are less likely to be affected by human error. Awareness, administrative controls, and PPE are the least effective methods to reduce risk as they are not applied at the source and they are more likely to be affected by human error.
>
> Informational Note No. 2: See ANSI/AIHA Z10, *American National Standard for Occupational Health and Safety Management Systems*, for more information regarding the hierarchy of risk control methods.
>
> Informational Note No. 3: The risk assessment procedure could include identifying when a second person could be required and the training and equipment that person should have.
>
> Informational Note No. 4: For an example of a risk assessment procedure, see Informative Annex F.

Worker Alert

If a risk assessment defaults to the category tables for PPE or does not include elements of control prior to PPE, you may be put at a higher risk of severe injury than necessary for a properly justified energized task. You should be aware of the other means or methods that could be used prevent or mitigate possible injuries.

> A risk assessment will not only determine the hazard, but as the name suggests, it will also determine the risk associated with conducting the task. Risk assessments must be

conducted whether equipment will be placed into an electrically safe work condition or justified energized electrical work will be authorized. The PPE category method does not remove the need to implement the hierarchy of risk controls. The assessments apply whether it is intended to use the PPE category method or the incident energy analysis method.

The hierarchy is listed in order of the most effective to the least effective and must be applied in this descending order for each risk assessment. Once a hazard has been identified, it first must be determined if the hazard can be eliminated. During the electrical system design stage, methods should be employed to eliminate the hazard in its entirety. In the electrical system design and equipment selection phase, it is easier to utilize the most effective controls of elimination and substitution to limit the risk associated with anticipated justified energized work. In this first context, elimination is the removal of a hazard so that it does not exist. This removes the potential for human error when interacting with the equipment.

Full elimination of the hazard is often not an option for installed equipment. Although elimination also can be achieved by applying other controls such as through establishing an electrically safe work condition, these other controls introduce a potential for human error. Therefore, the initial attempt should be full elimination of the hazard. Informative Annex F describes what is involved in conducting a risk assessment and the benefits that each control provides. It also explains the potential effect of the controls on the hazard and the risk.

Another aspect of elimination that is often overlooked is the removal of the employee from the area containing the hazard. NFPA *70E* addresses safe work practices for the employee conducting a task where there is a hazard. The risk of injury is substantially reduced when the employee is not in proximity to a hazard. For example, if the racking of an energized breaker is a justified task, then the use of a remote racking system would not place the employee at risk of injury if an incident were to occur.

The result of each risk assessment should be evaluated to determine if the hierarchy of controls could be further employed to lower the risk or reduce the hazard. Only after all other risk controls have been exhausted should PPE be selected. PPE is considered the least effective and lowest level of safety control for employee protection and should not be the first or only control element used.

The primary method of worker protection required by NFPA *70E* and OSHA is for equipment to be placed into an electrically safe work condition when a hazard or risk of injury exists. When the result of a risk assessment determines that a hazard or risk of injury exists, it is unacceptable to justify energized work simply with the ability to require PPE. Properly rated arc flash PPE limits the severity of injury but does not necessarily prevent an injury if an incident occurs.

(I) Job Safety Planning and Job Briefing. Before starting each job that involves exposure to electrical hazards, the employee in charge shall complete a job safety plan and conduct a job briefing with the employees involved.

N **(1) Job Safety Planning.** The job safety plan shall be in accordance with the following:

(1) Be completed by a qualified person
(2) Be documented
(3) Include the following information:
   a. A description of the job and the individual tasks
   b. Identification of the electrical hazards associated with each task
   c. A shock risk assessment in accordance with 130.4 for tasks involving a shock hazard

General Requirements for Electrical Safety-Related Work Practices

d. An arc flash risk assessment in accordance with 130.5 for tasks involving an arc flash hazard

e. Work procedures involved, special precautions, and energy source controls

> A task must be planned in detail in order for there to be an effective job briefing. If the task is being conducted for the first time, work procedures must be developed before work begins. If the planning reveals shortcomings in the safe work program or procedure, these should be addressed before the task is performed. It should be verified that necessary equipment will be available to perform the task.
>
> NFPA *70E* currently addresses only two hazards directly — electric shock and arc flash burn. As part of the risk assessment, it is necessary to determine the need for and an appropriate method of protecting the employee from all electrical hazards. The definition of *electrical hazard* in Article 100 includes any of the following: electric shock, arc flash burn, thermal burn, or arc blast. Other known hazards include flying parts, molten metal, intense light, poisonous oxides, and generated pressure waves (blasts).

N **(2) Job Briefing.** The job briefing shall cover the job safety plan and the information on the energized electrical work permit, if a permit is required.

> Where exposure to potential electrical hazards is involved, the employee in charge should be qualified for the tasks to be performed (i.e., for working at the applicable voltage). The job briefing and planning checklist located in Informative Annex I can be referenced as needed. The employee in charge must be able to communicate what is required to the employees involved. (In some instances, this could require knowledge of a second language.) If the tasks involved require the skills of a licensed electrician, then it might be wise for a licensed electrician to perform the job briefing.
>
> The job briefing needs to be performed before the work tasks are started. However, it should not be performed so far ahead that the employees involved might forget what was covered. The job briefing should include a discussion of the work procedure so that all parties fully understand the procedure before beginning the task. The job briefing also gives employees the opportunity to express any concerns they have about the task, the procedure, and their safety.

Worker Alert

The job briefing must cover all aspects of the assigned task. Equipment, procedures, PPE, hazards, risk control methods, and so forth must all be addressed in a manner that you fully understand and are in agreement with. The job briefing is your opportunity to have any safety concerns addressed prior to starting the task.

N **(3) Change in Scope.** Additional job safety planning and job briefings shall be held if changes occur during the course of the work that might affect the safety of employees.

Informational Note: For an example of a job briefing form and planning checklist, see Informative Annex I, Figure I.1.

> A deviation from the work plan may put a worker at risk. Tightening a lug instead of establishing an electrically safe work condition or holding a flashlight while performing a task that required temporary lighting can dramatically affect the work procedure or risk assessment. A wisp of smoke drifting from a ventilation opening or gaining equipment access from another direction can dramatically alter the hazard or risk the employee is exposed to. Any change in scope, procedure, task, safety, and so forth must not be done without consideration for the effect of that change on the risk assessment, work permit, and worker safety.

Worker Alert

You may find a reason to change the scope of the task after work has begun, or someone else may request that you do additional work. Neither should occur without modifying the work plan. Additional hazards not anticipated with those tasks could expose you to injury. Your protection from the additional hazard or risk may not be addressed by the original work permit.

Handbook for Electrical Safety in the Workplace   2018

Worker Alert

It is important for you to report near misses. Every electrical shock is a potential electrocution. A thermal burn means that all hazards were not properly addressed. A minor injury that resulted from a missing step in the work procedure may be the step that saves your life next time the procedure is performed.

N **(J) Incident Investigations.** The electrical safety program shall include elements to investigate electrical incidents.

> Informational Note: Electrical incidents include events or occurrences that result in, or could have resulted in, a fatality, an injury, or damage to health. Incidents that do not result in fatality, injury, or damage to health are commonly referred to as a "close call" or "near miss."

Incident investigations should not be limited to those where an employee is injured to the point where medical attention is required. Employees should be encouraged to report any potential injury situation. Near misses are often injuries that did not occur by chance. An electric shock has the potential to become an electrocution under the right conditions.

The investigations required by NFPA *70E* are not for the purpose of assigning blame. They are intended to improve worker safety. Employers and employees must accept their responsibilities and work together to find the causes of incidents and near misses. The electrical safety program, work procedures, protective equipment, test instruments, and so forth may require revision to prevent another near miss occurrence or a future injury or death.

(K) Auditing.

(1) Electrical Safety Program Audit. The electrical safety program shall be audited to verify that the principles and procedures of the electrical safety program are in compliance with this standard. Audits shall be performed at intervals not to exceed 3 years.

Auditing and enforcement is a critical part of any electrical safety program. It is vital that the electrical safety program — as well as the auditing and enforcement actions — be documented for the benefit of the employees and of the company.

The process control points and actions (i.e., the items capable of being measured) need to be determined for there to be effective auditing. The safety principles and procedures should be compared with the requirements in this standard. This comparison not only verifies compliance with the standard, but it is also one way to ensure that an electrical safety program is updated to be in accordance with the latest adopted edition of NFPA *70E*, which is on a 3-year revision cycle. An audit is necessary for enforcement and to ensure that employees are following program principles and procedures.

(2) Field Work Audit. Field work shall be audited to verify that the requirements contained in the procedures of the electrical safety program are being followed. When the auditing determines that the principles and procedures of the electrical safety program are not being followed, the appropriate revisions to the training program or revisions to the procedures shall be made. Audits shall be performed at intervals not to exceed 1 year.

Auditing field work involves going into the field — wherever employees are performing their required tasks and there is the potential of exposure to electrical hazards — to gather information. At intervals not exceeding 1 year, it is important for an employer to confirm employee compliance with its own electrical safety regulations by watching employees perform their electrical safety related tasks and ensuring that they are using PPE appropriate for the task to be performed. The procedures being verified become the metrics used to verify the required performance.

When it has been confirmed that the electrical safety program principles or procedures are not being followed, corrective action must be taken. This corrective action should consist of either applicable modification of the training program or a revision to the procedures, such as increasing the frequency of training or adding

General Requirements for Electrical Safety-Related Work Practices

follow-up verification of compliance. Employee involvement in creating a safer work environment should be fostered. Training employees to report near misses or incidents brought about by human error or insufficient procedures should be encouraged. However, it is important that an enforcement program be established for willful violations of the employer's safety regulations.

An audit should also be used to confirm that all electrical hazards are addressed, to measure program effectiveness, for developing program improvement, and to evaluate any program and physical conditions that have changed. An audit should also evaluate incidents to determine any necessary change to the electrical safety program.

N **(3) Lockout/Tagout Program and Procedure Audit.** The lockout/tagout program and procedures required by Article 120 shall be audited by a qualified person at intervals not to exceed 1 year. The audit shall cover at least one lockout/tagout in progress. The audit shall be designed to identify and correct deficiencies in the following:

(1) The lockout/tagout program and procedures
(2) The lockout/tagout training
(3) Worker execution of the lockout/tagout procedure

The objective of the audit is to make sure that all requirements of the lockout/tagout procedure were properly executed and that employees are familiar with their responsibilities. The audit must determine whether the requirements contained in the published procedure are sufficient to ensure that the electrical energy is satisfactorily controlled. The audit should also identify and correct any deficiencies in the procedure, employee training, or enforcement of the requirements.

(4) Documentation. The audits required by 110.1(K) shall be documented.

110.2 Training Requirements.

Training can be defined as the process by which someone is taught the skills that are needed for the job. Training can be seen as teaching (presenting the required information) and learning (absorbing the information and being able to perform the required skill) together. Until the skill is learned, the employee has not been trained. To be considered qualified, the person has to demonstrate an understanding of the required knowledge and the ability to perform the task safely. To be competent, it might be said that the person being trained should be able to show proficiency in performing the task, so as to be able to do the task safely and efficiently. However, the prime goal here is safety, not efficiency.

Δ **(A) Electrical Safety Training.** The training requirements contained in 110.2(A) shall apply to employees exposed to an electrical hazard when the risk associated with that hazard is not reduced to a safe level by the applicable electrical installation requirements. Such employees shall be trained to understand the specific hazards associated with electrical energy. They shall be trained in safety-related work practices and procedural requirements, as necessary, to provide protection from the electrical hazards associated with their respective job or task assignments. Employees shall be trained to identify and understand the relationship between electrical hazards and possible injury.

> Informational Note: For further information concerning installation requirements, see *NFPA 70, National Electrical Code.*

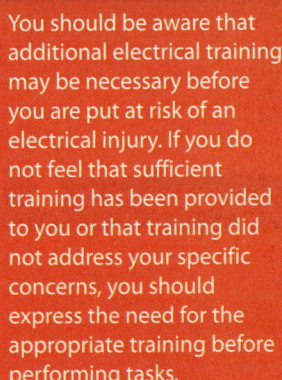

Worker Alert

You should be aware that additional electrical training may be necessary before you are put at risk of an electrical injury. If you do not feel that sufficient training has been provided to you or that training did not address your specific concerns, you should express the need for the appropriate training before performing tasks.

These training requirements are necessary at some level for all employees. The requirements are necessary when the risk of an injury from a potential electrical hazard is not reduced to an acceptable level by the pertinent installation requirements. For example, an employee using portable electrical equipment in contradiction of the manufacturer's instructions or published safety warnings must recognize the hazards. Employees interacting with electrical equipment should understand that safe operation requires proper installation and maintenance.

All employees should be trained to refrain from operating equipment where evidence of impending failure is present, such as arcing, overheating, loose equipment parts, visible damage, unusual noises or odor, or deterioration of condition. When any of these indications exist, the risk from electrical hazards may be unacceptable.

Employees who may be exposed to unacceptable risk of injury from the use of electricity in the work environment need to be trained to identify the following:

- Situations that may involve unacceptable risk, including recognizing evidence of impending failure
- The actual or potential hazards involved with the situation
- The degree or level of the actual or potential hazard
- How the degree or level of the hazard can determine the seriousness of any potential injury
- The means of avoiding or mitigating actual or potential exposure to electrical hazards

The training required depends upon various factors, such as the tasks to be performed, whether the employee is a manager, supervisor, or worker, whether the employee is an unqualified person, or whether the employee is or needs to be a qualified person (see commentary following the definition of *qualified person* in Article 100).

Depending upon their job functions and the tasks assigned to them, different groups or levels of employees could be trained in a variety of subjects, including the following:

- Utilizing safe work practices
- Creating an electrically safe work condition (ESWC)
- Selecting, caring for, and using insulating or insulated tools and equipment, including test instruments
- Interpreting arc flash hazard equipment labels
- Determining if energized electrical work is justified
- Determining if an energized electrical work permit is required
- Selecting, caring for, and using PPE, including the types of arc ratings
- Selecting and using alerting techniques, such as safety signs and tags, barricades, and attendants

The degree of training should be appropriate and based on the tasks that the employee will be performing. Where the risk of receiving an electrical injury from energized electrical equipment is minimal (acceptable) — such as when operating equipment that is properly installed, maintained, and enclosed — the electrical safety training required may be minimal.

Even though 110.2(A) stipulates the essential types of training required, the key concepts in training are (1) the employee understanding the relevant factors, and (2) the employee demonstrating the ability to work safely. The key to working safely is to always remain vigilant and not let one's guard down, even for a second.

Worker Alert

A license, diploma, or certificate does not necessarily make you a qualified person under the requirements of NFPA *70E*.

(1) Qualified Person. A qualified person shall be trained and knowledgeable in the construction and operation of equipment or a specific work method and be trained to identify and avoid the electrical hazards that might be present with respect to that equipment or work method.

General Requirements for Electrical Safety-Related Work Practices

110.2(A)(1)

A *qualified person* is defined in Article 100, and by default this person must be competent. The general definition of competent is having sufficient skill, knowledge, or experience for a specific purpose. A worker could be competent to install a light fixture but not qualified under NFPA *70E* to troubleshoot that fixture while it is energized.

The only place in NFPA *70E* in which the term *competent person* is used is Article 350. That definition, which uses *qualified person* as its basis, includes responsibility for all work activities or safety procedures related to custom or special equipment and is only applicable to Article 350.

In order to be considered qualified for a particular task or work assignment, an employee should have internalized the requisite knowledge regarding the electrical system involved and the required procedures. The employee must have received the safety training identified in 110.2. Exhibit 110.3 is provided to assist the employer and employees in understanding some of the traits necessary to be considered a minimally qualified person under NFPA *70E* requirements, depending on the requirements of the specific tasks (e.g., responding to medical emergencies).

EXHIBIT 110.3

Traits of a qualified person.

Trained and knowledgeable in …
- Construction of equipment
- Operation of systems and equipment
- Specific work procedures for assigned tasks
- Identification of electrical hazards
- Avoidance of electrical hazards
- Selection of test equipment
- Safety-related work practices
- Normal operating conditions of specific electrical equipment
- Self-awareness and self-discipline

Able to identify and understand the …
- Specific hazards associated with electrical energy and equipment
- Relationship between electrical hazards and possible injury
- Electrical hazards regarding procedures to be used
- Approach boundary distances
- Indication of impeding equipment failure

Familiar with proper use of …
- Required special precautionary techniques
- Personal protective equipment
- Insulating and shielding materials
- Insulated tools
- Test equipment

Has skills and techniques to …
- Distinguish exposed energized electrical parts from other parts of electrical equipment
- Determine nominal system voltage of exposed energized electrical parts
- Inspect and test personal protective equipment
- Inspect test equipment

Has necessary decision-making process to be able to …
- Perform job safety planning
- Assess associated risk with electrical hazards
- Select appropriate risk control methods

Demonstrated ability and capability to …
- Perform procedures necessary to safely conduct the assigned task
- Establish an electrically safe work condition

Retraining is necessary when …
- Inspection indicates employee not properly complying with safety related work practices
- New equipment, including PPE, or new technology introduced into work environment
- New or revised procedures are to be used
- Scheduled for task not associated with regular job duties
- Retraining has not occurred within 3 years
- Requested by employee

Handbook for Electrical Safety in the Workplace 2018

> A person may be qualified to perform a specific task on specific equipment while being unqualified to perform another task on the same piece of equipment. Qualification does not necessarily carry over to a similar piece of equipment nor to the identical task on a different piece of equipment. Work practices, procedures, and hazards can vary by the task and the equipment. Qualification is not necessarily based on title, licensure, and so forth. For example, a licensed HVAC technician may not be qualified for working in high-voltage switchgear. In order to be qualified, the person must have knowledge and demonstrated skills regarding specific hazards, work practices, and procedural requirements.

(a) Such persons shall also be familiar with the proper use of the special precautionary techniques, applicable electrical policies and procedures, PPE, insulating and shielding materials, and insulated tools and test equipment.

(b) A person can be considered qualified with respect to certain equipment and tasks but still be unqualified for others.

(c) Such persons permitted to work within the limited approach boundary shall, at a minimum, be additionally trained in all of the following:

(1) Skills and techniques necessary to distinguish exposed energized electrical conductors and circuit parts from other parts of electrical equipment

(2) Skills and techniques necessary to determine the nominal voltage of exposed energized electrical conductors and circuit parts

(3) Approach distances specified in Table 130.4(D)(a) and Table 130.4(D)(b) and the corresponding voltages to which the qualified person will be exposed

(4) Decision-making process necessary to be able to do the following:
   a. Perform the job safety planning
   b. Identify electrical hazards
   c. Assess the associated risk
   d. Select the appropriate risk control methods from the hierarchy of controls identified in 110.1(G), including personal protective equipment

> This section deals with the limited approach boundary, which implies shock risk. The employee performing the task should be able to identify exposed energized electrical conductors and circuit parts from those that are considered to be effectively guarded, insulated, or isolated. The employee also should be able to determine the nominal system voltage of the exposed energized components and circuit parts concerned. Normally, the nominal system voltage is identified on the equipment nameplate and on the arc flash hazard equipment label of 130.5(H). Where the nominal voltage cannot be readily determined in this way, checking the one-line diagram for the facility, or checking the nameplates of upstream or downstream equipment, may be helpful.
>
> Once the nominal system voltage level is determined, the employee must be aware of the distances specified in the shock approach boundary tables in 130.4 and follow the rules applicable at each boundary point — the limited approach boundary and the restricted approach boundary.
>
> As stated in 110.1(H), risk assessment includes identifying the hazards — electrical or otherwise — for the task at hand, assessing the associated risk, and then selecting the appropriate safety control from the categories identified in the hierarchy of risk controls. NFPA *70E* currently addresses only two hazards directly: electric shock and arc flash burn. It is necessary to determine the need for and an appropriate method of protecting the worker from all electrical hazards. The definition of *electrical hazard* in

General Requirements for Electrical Safety-Related Work Practices

Article 100 includes any of the following: electric shock, arc flash burn, thermal burn, or arc blast. Other known hazards include flying parts, molten metal, intense light, poisonous oxides, and generated pressure waves (blasts).

Although this standard is concerned with electrical hazards, employees need to be concerned with all potential hazards for the work tasks they are assigned.

(d) An employee who is undergoing on-the-job training for the purpose of obtaining the skills and knowledge necessary to be considered a qualified person, and who in the course of such training demonstrates an ability to perform specific duties safely at his or her level of training, and who is under the direct supervision of a qualified person shall be considered to be a qualified person for the performance of those specific duties.

Part of this training is about learning how to select and use the personal and other protective equipment required to perform the task safely. Training may be completed in incremental steps. Once the instructor is sure that the employee is ready, the employee would be allowed to perform the procedure with the instructor close by to help out as necessary. Until the employee shows a level of confidence at the task — the ability to perform the task safely with the minimum ability required in the instructor's opinion — the employee should not be allowed to perform the procedure without the instructor watching close by. However, once this level of knowledge and ability is reached, the employee may then be considered a qualified person to perform that particular task.

(e) Employees shall be trained to select an appropriate test instrument and shall demonstrate how to use a device to verify the absence of voltage, including interpreting indications provided by the device. The training shall include information that enables the employee to understand all limitations of each test instrument that might be used.

The employee must know how to safely use the test instrument to perform the required measurement task. This use requires an understanding and a capability of interpreting all readings and indications given by the test instrument. It also includes knowing the different settings, limitations, and operating modes of the device, as well as the proper terminal into which leads are to be installed. If the device has a duty rating or category rating, the employee needs to know how to comply with the rating. The employee must also be able to select test instruments suitable for the parameters of the system and the location where they will be applied on the electrical distribution system. The employee must be familiar with and understand all of the required information contained in the operating and maintenance instructions provided with the test instrument.

Exhibit 110.4 shows an example of a test instrument used for measuring voltage. Note the different voltage ratings for Category III and Category IV. Understanding these ratings is critical to the safe use of the meter. See also the commentary following 110.4(B) regarding meter category ratings.

(f) The employer shall determine through regular supervision or through inspections conducted on at least an annual basis that each employee is complying with the safety-related work practices required by this standard.

In order to ensure safety, compliance with the requirements of this standard and with the employer's electrical safety program is an ongoing and continuous activity. Where there is potential exposure to electrical hazards, each employee should receive occasional observation by a mentor (such as a supervisor or senior person), or with checkups

EXHIBIT 110.4

Meter for measuring voltage. (Courtesy of Fluke Corporation)

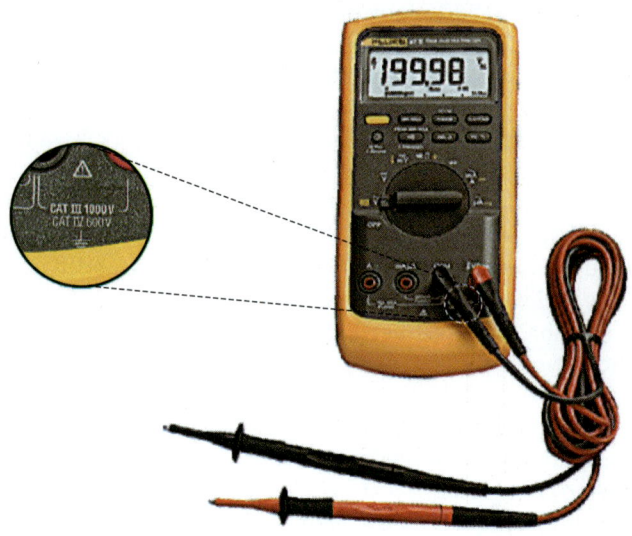

conducted on at least an annual basis. This may be part of the required field work audit required per 110.1(K)(2).

(2) Unqualified Persons. Unqualified persons shall be trained in, and be familiar with, any electrical safety-related practices necessary for their safety.

Employees not considered qualified persons must have the knowledge and skills necessary for their safety when interacting with electrical equipment, which includes normal operation of the equipment. The following is a list of some of the situations that unqualified persons may encounter and need to be aware of:

- *General potential hazards* — Understand and recognize potential hazards, including the relationship between exposure to potential electrical hazards and possible bodily injury.
- *Attachment plugs* — Understand how to properly remove an attachment plug from a receptacle.
- *Damaged equipment* — Do not use damaged electrical equipment (fixed or portable); damaged cables, cords, or connectors; or damaged receptacles.
- *Impending failure of equipment* — Be aware of what the signs of impeding failure of electrical equipment may be and do not remain around electrical equipment where there is evidence of impending failure.
- *Receptacle plugs/caps* — Do not remove attachment plugs (caps) from receptacles where the combination is not load-break-rated.
- *Tripped circuit breakers* — Do not reset a circuit breaker after an automatic trip. Always notify a qualified person to determine the cause.
- *Flammable materials* — Do not use flammable materials near electrical equipment that can create a spark.
- *Overhead power lines* — Be aware of the proper approach distance from overhead power lines.
- *Alerting techniques* — Be aware of alerting techniques such as safety signs and tags, barricades, and warning attendants. Know to remain outside the shock protection or arc flash protection boundaries when energized work is being performed.

> **Worker Alert**
>
> Examples of an unqualified person interacting with electrical equipment can include a janitor responsible for turning on lights in the facility at the start of the day or a machine operator starting a machine at the beginning of the shift. Both must be trained in safety practices related to these tasks.

General Requirements for Electrical Safety-Related Work Practices

- *Limited approach shock boundary* — Do not cross the limited approach shock boundary unless advised and continuously escorted by a qualified person.
- *Restricted approach boundary* — Never cross the restricted approach boundary.

All employees should be given some basic, commonsense rules for avoiding electrical accidents and injuries. These rules include the following:

- Do not overload circuits, such as by running multiple appliances from a single outlet.
- Never plug in equipment with a damaged electrical cord or use an extension cord that has damaged insulation.
- Never use electrical equipment, such as a power tool or appliance, if it is sparking, smoking, or otherwise seems to be malfunctioning.
- Keep metal objects, large and small, away from electrical equipment.

(3) Retraining. Retraining in safety-related work practices and applicable changes in this standard shall be performed at intervals not to exceed 3 years. An employee shall receive additional training (or retraining) if any of the following conditions exists:

(1) The supervision or annual inspections indicate the employee is not complying with the safety-related work practices.
(2) New technology, new types of equipment, or changes in procedures necessitate the use of safety-related work practices different from those that the employee would normally use.
(3) The employee needs to review tasks that are performed less often than once per year.
(4) The employee needs to review safety-related work practices not normally used by the employee during regular job duties.
(5) The employee's job duties change.

> Electrical safety in the workplace is not a static subject. Generally, retraining is required when there are changes in situations, policies, procedures, or equipment. Since improvements in electrical safety often dictate changes to this standard, retraining of employees may be necessary when a new edition is published. The employer should keep track of the tasks employees are qualified to perform and schedule retraining to make certain their qualifications do not lapse.

△ **(4) Type of Training.** The training required by 110.2(A) shall be classroom, on-the-job, or a combination of the two. The type and extent of the training provided shall be determined by the risk to the employee.

> When developing and implementing an electrical safety training program, the employer may determine that certain parties could be helpful in developing the training material and the training methods and in presenting the material in a clear fashion. Some, all, or a combination of the following parties could be included: consultants, engineers, manufacturer's representative or agents, safety professionals, teachers (including those with experience in curriculum development), trade persons, contract employees, independent contractors, employees (workers), managers, and supervisors.
>
> NFPA *70E* does not specify who is qualified to provide training. The employer is to determine the qualifications of the instructor. The employer must be familiar enough with the requirements in both NFPA *70E* and the applicable federal regulations to determine the suitability of the instructor. Reputation, experience, credentials, or education may be determining factors used by the employer. The instructor should have knowledge of the procedures regardless of the title or position held. An engineer, supervisor,

Worker Alert

You are the only one who truly knows when your skills are not current or not sharp enough to safely perform a task. Updating and refining your skills can help prevent injury.

or experienced worker could each have the appropriate knowledge. The instructor needs to be competent in teaching methods and trade practices and knowledgeable on the subjects presented. Employees will trust that a qualified person has been selected to conduct the employer's training.

Training can be of the classroom or on-the-job type, or a combination of the two. The connotation of these types of training is that they are instructor-led programs, whether in person or in nontraditional classrooms. NFPA *70E* does not specify the type of classroom training permitted. The employer must determine whether the method employed conveys the necessary level of training and if it imparts the knowledge necessary for employees to perform their duties safely. If an employer needs to communicate work instructions or other workplace information to employees at a certain vocabulary level or in a language other than English, electrical safety training also needs to be provided to those employees in the same manner.

It is incumbent on the employer to verify that the employees have acquired the knowledge and skills necessary to perform their job tasks safely. Retraining needs to be provided when practices indicate that the employee has not retained or acquired the requisite understanding or skill. Employees should be tested to demonstrate ability in performing the required tasks safely and in a timely manner. If the employer has not conveyed the training to employees in a manner or type they were capable of understanding, then the instruction or training has failed to meet the employer's training obligations and needs to be revised.

Although training required by NFPA *70E* and OSHA regulations is expected to be instructor-led, other forms of training may be used to augment classroom instruction. In actuality, an appropriate training mix will include some of the following methods, as well as others not mentioned:

- *E-book or tablet-based.* Training that uses an e-book or tablet-type computer for training.
- *Self-paced.* Training for which the pace of learning is determined by the student.
- *Web-based or on-line.* Training performed on the internet, through a website, or utilizing web-based applications.

OSHA considers classroom and on-the-job training to be the most effective training types. These forms of training facilitate interaction between employees and the trainer. For computer-based training to be as effective as classroom training, it must be interactive and participatory.

N (5) Electrical Safety Training Documentation. The employer shall document that each employee has received the training required by 110.2(A). This documentation shall be in accordance with the following:

(1) Be made when the employee demonstrates proficiency in the work practices involved
(2) Be retained for the duration of the employee's employment
(3) Contain the content of the training, each employee's name, and dates of training

Informational Note No. 1: Content of the training could include one or more of the following: course syllabus, course curriculum, outline, table of contents, or training objectives.

Informational Note No. 2: Employment records that indicate that an employee has received the required training are an acceptable means of meeting this requirement.

Governmental rules may require the safety training documentation to be retained for a longer period of time, which could exceed 7 years after the employee leaves. Where

General Requirements for Electrical Safety-Related Work Practices

outside training is used, information about the training organization or instructor may also prove useful.

N **(B) Lockout/Tagout Procedure Training.**

N **(1) Initial Training.** Employees involved in or affected by the lockout/tagout procedures required by 120.2 shall be trained in the following:

(1) The lockout/tagout procedures
(2) Their responsibility in the execution of the procedures

Employers, including independent contractors, must provide training for all employees who might be involved in the process of establishing an electrically safe work condition (ESWC). Employees must be trained and be able to understand the process prior to attempting to establish an ESWC in the field. Training in the method to be employed for the task can help minimize the possibility of errors in implementing an unfamiliar process. Each employee associated with performing the job must be trained to understand his or her role in the lockout/tagout process and accept individual responsibility for the integrity of the lockout/tagout process. All employees must receive additional training whenever the established procedure is changed.

Contract employer procedures may be different from host employer procedures. Contractors and facility owners must exchange information about creating an ESWC — along with any information about characteristics specific to the facility — and ensure that their respective employees understand all issues that are important to the other employer. Employees who have been reassigned (either permanently or temporarily) must be trained to understand their new role in the lockout/tagout procedure.

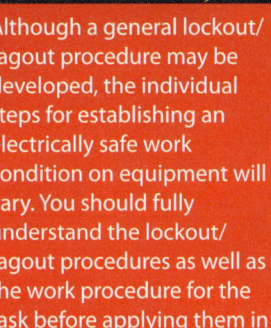

Worker Alert

Although a general lockout/tagout procedure may be developed, the individual steps for establishing an electrically safe work condition on equipment will vary. You should fully understand the lockout/tagout procedures as well as the work procedure for the task before applying them in the field.

N **(2) Retraining.** Retraining in the lockout/tagout procedures shall be performed as follows:

(1) When the procedures are revised
(2) At intervals not to exceed 3 years
(3) When supervision or annual inspections indicate that the employee is not complying with the lockout/tagout procedures

(3) Lockout/Tagout Training Documentation.

(a) The employer shall document that each employee has received the training required by 110.2(B).

(b) The documentation shall be made when the employee demonstrates proficiency in the work practices involved.

(c) The documentation shall contain the content of the training, each employee's name, and the dates of the training.

Informational Note: Content of the training could include one or more of the following: course syllabus, course curriculum, outline, table of contents, or training objectives.

Training documentation can be either hard copy or electronic. Whatever format is used, the record must be retained for the duration of the employee's employment in accordance with 110.2(A)(5).

(C) Emergency Response Training.

> **Worker Alert**
>
> You may instinctively react to your friend's predicament without considering the consequences. Proper training and your personal awareness of the situation will not only allow you to help your friend but will keep you safe. Remember that many electrocutions occur to the person responding to the initial victim.

Δ **(1) Contact Release.** Employees exposed to shock hazards and those responsible for the safe release of victims from contact with energized electrical conductors or circuit parts shall be trained in methods of safe release. Refresher training shall occur annually.

A victim of an electrical accident may be incapable of releasing the energized electrical conductor or circuit part because muscles contract when electrical current is running through the body. Extreme caution is a primary consideration when responding to an electrical accident. Anyone attempting to rescue a victim who is in contact with an energized electrical conductor or circuit part is exposed to the same hazard and must identify and avoid the hazard and take the appropriate action. The victim's survival depends on a safe and rapid response. Before first aid can be provided, the victim has to be safely moved from the energized electrical conductors and circuit parts.

A quick response is essential during an electrical shock incident — seconds gained or lost can decide the life or death of a victim. Often shutting off the equipment is the most efficient way to safely release an employee. However, a shock rescue kit equipped with all necessary personal and other required protective equipment can save rescue personnel vital time. The shock rescue kit could include items such as an insulated rescue stick or hook, a voltage detector, a cable cutter with insulated handles, an insulating platform or pad, insulated rubber gloves, insulated dielectric overshoes (boots), safety and first aid instructions, a roll of adhesive warning tape, and a can of talcum powder. The composition of the kit should be dependent on the situation in which it would be used.

> **Worker Alert**
>
> Training requirements include cardiopulmonary resuscitation (CPR) and artificial external defibrillator (AED) use, since contact with an energized conductor or circuit part can result in sudden cardiac arrest. If you are responsible for responding to medical emergencies, you must be aware of the location of the first aid supplies and AED.

Δ **(2) First Aid, Emergency Response, and Resuscitation.**

(a) Employees responsible for responding to medical emergencies shall be trained in first aid and emergency procedures.

(b) Employees responsible for responding to medical emergencies shall be trained in cardiopulmonary resuscitation (CPR).

(c) Employees responsible for responding to medical emergencies shall be trained in the use of an automated external defibrillator (AED) if an employer's emergency response plan includes the use of this device.

(d) Training shall occur at a frequency that satisfies the requirements of the certifying body.

Informational Note: Employees responsible for responding to medical emergencies might not be first responders or medical professionals. Such employees could be a second person, a safety watch, or a craftsperson.

> **OSHA Connection**
>
> 29 CFR 1910.151(b)
>
> Employers must ensure that — in the absence of medical services near the workplace — an adequately trained person is available to render first aid to an injured employee. Adequate first aid supplies must also to be readily available.

No matter how well prepared the facility may be, where human beings are involved, accidents will occur. Employers need to have policies, procedures, and trained personnel available to deal with an injury or illness on the job.

The employer must determine who will be responsible for responding to an emergency for electrical incidents within the facility. NFPA *70E* does not dictate that a second worker or supervisor be responsible for responding to emergencies, and it does not prohibit the use of off-site response. Whomever is responsible for first aid, the person(s) must be trained for providing that response. Different levels of response may dictate different training requirements. For example, an employee may be a first responder for cardiopulmonary resuscitation (CPR) purposes, but the subsequent

General Requirements for Electrical Safety-Related Work Practices

arrival of the facility heath care professional may bring more advanced and detailed training to the scene.

For information regarding the contents of a generic first aid kit, refer to ANSI Z308.1, *Minimum Requirements for Workplace First Aid Kits and Supplies*. Although the listed contents should be adequate for small worksites, employers at larger or unique facilities should determine the need for additional types of first aid supplies as well as additional quantities. Employers should assess the specific needs of their worksite periodically and augment the first aid kit appropriately.

△ **(3) Training Verification.** Employers shall verify at least annually that employee training required by 110.2(C) is current.

> **OSHA Connection**
>
> OSHA Publication 3317-06N (2006), *Best Practices Guide: Fundamentals of a Workplace First-Aid Program*, identifies four essential elements for first aid programs to be effective and successful. It also includes best practices for planning and conducting safe and effective first aid training.

First-aid training courses should include instruction in both general and workplace hazard–specific knowledge and skills. First aid responders may experience long intervals between learning cardiopulmonary resuscitation (CPR) and automated external defibrillator (AED) skills and putting them to practice. It may be beneficial to refresh first aid skills periodically to maintain and update knowledge and skills even if a certification for CPR or AED is valid. Instructor-led retraining for life-threatening emergencies might occur annually to keep necessary skills sharp. Retraining for non-life-threatening response might occur periodically to help retain the knowledge.

First aid training is offered by nationally recognized and private educational organizations, including the American Heart Association, the American Red Cross, and the National Safety Council. NFPA *70E* does not advocate any specific first aid course. First aid courses should be customized for the specific work environment. Unique conditions at a specific worksite may warrant additional elements to a standardized first aid training program.

The training organization sets the minimum level required for its first aid training program. Assessment of successful completion of the first aid training program should include instructor observation of acquired skills and written performance assessments. NFPA *70E* requires that the employer verify at least annually that training for employees who are first aid responders is current.

> **OSHA Connection**
>
> 29 CFR 1910.269(a)(2)(v)(C) and 1926.950(b)(4)(iii)
> Retraining does not mean that the employee be formally recertified in first aid. The retraining requirements may be met when the employee has an opportunity to refresh himself or herself on, and demonstrate proficiency in, appropriate first aid skills each year.

△ **(4) Documentation.** The employer shall document that the training required by 110.2(C) has occurred.

Documentation reinforces the importance of training and training verification for the employer's first aid responders.

- **110.3 Host and Contract Employers' Responsibilities**

Generally, the host employer may be seen as the party contracting for the premises where the work is to be performed. There are circumstances where one division of a company could be the host employer to another division's employees and the other division's employees seen as the contract employer. The host employer may not always be the owner of the facility. There are also situations where the host employer is the on-site employer (not the owner of the facility), and a contract employer is the one that is obligated to perform the work. A service contractor, such as a vending machine operator sending employees to a site, would be considered a contract employer.

The concept of host employer and contract employer has some flexibility, since the terms are not defined within NFPA *70E*. It may be possible to pass from the role of contract employer to host employer and from host employer to contract employer,

Handbook for Electrical Safety in the Workplace 2018

depending on the particular work agreement involved. The AHJ that is enforcing this standard makes the final decision regarding the terms.

(A) Host Employer Responsibilities.

(1) The host employer shall inform contract employers of the following:

(1) Known hazards that are covered by this standard, that are related to the contract employer's work, and that might not be recognized by the contract employer or its employees
(2) Information about the employer's installation that the contract employer needs to make the assessments required by Chapter 1

Any employer should be aware of energized electrical work being conducted within its facility, whether the task is performed by an internal employee or a contract employee. The information to be passed back and forth during the documented meeting required by 110.3(C) should be determined ahead of time. Each party should clearly communicate the information they require and the information they expect to provide, including the exchange of electrical safety programs. Where there is ambiguity, there is the potential for problems because the various parties may have different expectations.

When justification of energized work is being proposed, the host employer should include the information needed to complete and submit an energized electrical work permit for the signature of the host employer's management. See 130.2(A) for requirements specific to energized work. The host employer should also provide the contractor employer with the host's electrical safety-related rules that will be required to be followed while onsite.

(2) The host employer shall report observed contract employer–related violations of this standard to the contract employer.

Informational Note: Examples of a host employer can include owner or their designee, construction manager, general contractor, or employer.

Using a contract employee does not absolve the host employer of enforcing its own safe work practices. The host employer may be responsible for limiting access to energized electrical equipment regardless of who is conducting the work. The host employer may also be responsible for emergency response if an incident does occur.

(B) Contract Employer Responsibilities.

(1) The contract employer shall ensure that each of his or her employees is instructed in the hazards communicated to the contract employer by the host employer. This instruction shall be in addition to the basic training required by this standard.

The contract employer is often referred to as the independent contractor. The host employer is generally expected to have greater knowledge of the special conditions, unique situations or features of equipment, and specific hazards other than electrical hazards present in its facility. The host employer must convey this information to the contract employer, and the contract employer in turn must provide this information to the employee performing the work at the host facility.

Worker Alert

Although the contract employer is responsible to pass this information onto his or her employees, you are ultimately responsible for your own actions. As a contract employee working at an unfamiliar site, you must be aware of all hazards associated with the job, including work procedures involved, special precautions, energy source controls, and PPE requirements. If you do not receive the information required by this section, ask your employer.

(2) The contract employer shall ensure that each of his or her employees follows the work practices required by this standard and safety-related work rules required by the host employer.

> Contract employers need not follow only their own electrical safety-related practices but may be required to follow the host employer's electrical safety-related practices. The contract employer should provide employees the necessary training on correct work procedures and the necessary personal and other protective equipment to perform the job safely. For example, the contract employer is responsible for ensuring that employees implement the host employer's lockout/tagout procedures if they are more stringent than their own. If the contract employer's lockout/tagout will be utilized, the host employer should be made aware of the steps involved with that procedure.
>
> To ensure that the host's required practices do not violate the requirements of NFPA 70E, it is important to know the rules included in Article 120, Article 130, and, where special equipment, systems, or facilities are involved, Chapter 3. Likewise, NFPA 70E is not an allowance to utilize practices that are less stringent than an employer's safety-related practices.

△ **(3)** The contract employer shall advise the host employer of the following:

(1) Any unique hazards presented by the contract employer's work
(2) Hazards identified during the course of work by the contract employer that were not communicated by the host employer
(3) The measures the contractor took to correct any violations reported by the host employer under 110.3(A)(2) and to prevent such violation from recurring in the future

> Where conditions and situations regarding equipment or procedures need to change as a result of the work being performed by the contract employer, the contract employer must make the host employer aware of the new conditions. For example, in situations in which an additional task is necessary or the utility company has increased the size of the transformer serving the facility, the contract employer must notify the host employer. The contract employer has an obligation to inform the host employer of the resulting increase in hazard level. Either situation may require a re-evaluation or modification of the work permit.
>
> When the utility has increased the size or efficiency of the transformer, a new risk assessment may need to be performed for the facility. When the contract employer notices that such a change might cause the newly installed equipment to be used above its ratings, the contract employer should inform the host employer of the situation. The contract employer may prefer not to perform work when the equipment, task, risk assessment, work practices, or work scope changes do not adequately protect their employees.

(C) Documentation. Where the host employer has knowledge of hazards covered by this standard that are related to the contract employer's work, there shall be a documented meeting between the host employer and the contract employer.

> A documented meeting may be prudent regardless of prior knowledge of hazards by the contract employer. The host employer should be aware of all energized electrical work being conducted within their facility by a contractor. Documentation should include whether energized work by the contractor is or is not permitted. If energized diagnostic tests are necessary, the contractor must inform the host of that need. Hazards observed by the contractor and the steps taken to mitigate an injury should be

documented. The training provided to associated employees and the decision of which employer's lockout/tagout procedure to follow should be documented.

110.4 Test Instruments and Equipment.

Test instruments within an organization should be standardized to facilitate their use. The organization should determine the manufacturer, type, and model for the test instruments to be used, as well the types of systems and the locations where they can be used. The organization should also determine if it will be providing the test instruments or if it will allow employees to use their own test instruments, which may create some unique problems and situations. Each test instrument may require its own set of policies and procedures. Procedures and policies need to be developed and refined before any test instrument is used.

(A) Testing. Only qualified persons shall perform tasks such as testing, troubleshooting, and voltage measuring on electrical equipment operating at voltages equal to or greater than 50 volts.

Careful consideration should be given to circuits operating under 50 volts where conditions such as a wet environment or high available fault current are encountered. If it is determined that an electrical hazard does exist, only those persons considered as qualified are permitted to perform tasks such as testing, troubleshooting, voltage measuring, or similar diagnostic work.

(B) Rating. Test instruments, equipment, and their accessories shall be as follows:

(1) Rated for circuits and equipment where they are utilized
(2) Approved for the purpose
(3) Used in accordance with any instructions provided by the manufacturer

> Informational Note: See UL 61010-1, *Safety Requirements for Electrical Equipment for Measurement, Control, and Laboratory Use – Part 1: General Requirements*, for rating and design requirements for voltage measurement and test instruments intended for use on electrical systems 1000 volts and below and UL 61010-2-033, *Safety Requirements for Electrical Equipment for Measurement, Control, and Laboratory Use — Part 2-033: Particular Requirements for Hand-Held Multimeters and Other Meters, for Domestic and Professional use, Capable of Measuring Mains Voltage*.

The point on the electrical distribution system where a specific voltage test meter may be used is often indicated by a category designation. The transient overvoltage protection, fusing, and probes for these meters vary for the location in which they can be used. For example, Category III test instruments may be rated CAT III–600 V or CAT III–1000 V. The 600 V instrument is rated for transients up to 6000 volts, whereas the 1000 V instrument is rated for transients up to 8000 volts. However, a CAT II–1000 V instrument is rated only for transients up to 6000 volts.

Using an inappropriate meter for the measurement location could initiate an electrocution or arc flash incident. The four categories that are typically employed for indicating the location of use for test equipment are as follows:

Category IV: Three-phase utility connections and outside
Category III: Inside distribution (feeders and branch circuits)

Worker Alert

A qualified person in this context has knowledge related to the operation of the test instruments and the electrical equipment being tested. To be a qualified person, you must have received safety training needed to identify and avoid the hazards involved with the use of the test instrument on the specific piece of equipment. The use of the instrument on other equipment may require further qualification.

General Requirements for Electrical Safety-Related Work Practices

110.4(D)

> Category II: Single-phase receptacle level (30 feet from CAT III locations, 60 feet from CAT IV locations)
> Category I: Electronic equipment
>
> Exhibit 110.5 illustrates the locations where various categories apply within an electrical system.

EXHIBIT 110.5

Examples of equipment and locations suitable for Category II, Category III, and Category IV rated test instruments.

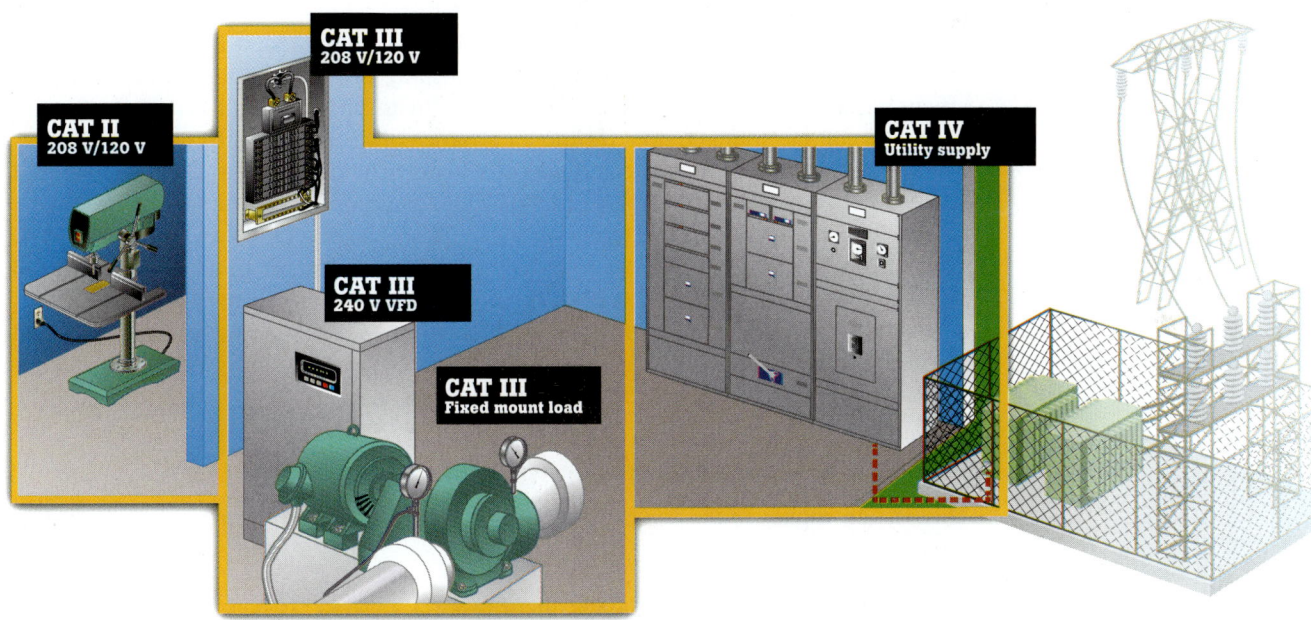

(C) Design. Test instruments, equipment, and their accessories shall be designed for the environment to which they will be exposed and for the manner in which they will be utilized.

> Test instrument accessories, such as probes and leads, are part of the equipment design and should be treated with the same care as the instrument. Making or modifying accessories must be avoided. There are a variety of special accessories for test instruments available from the test equipment manufacturer.
>
> Test instruments must be selected for the conditions of use. Contacting an exposed energized electrical conductor or circuit part with a test instrument to measure voltage normally results in a small arc, immediately before contact is made or when contact is broken. Therefore, such test instruments must not be used where concentrations of flammable gases, vapors, or dusts occur.

(D) Visual Inspection and Repair. Test instruments and equipment and all associated test leads, cables, power cords, probes, and connectors shall be visually inspected for external defects and damage before each use. If there is a defect or evidence of damage that might expose an employee to injury, the defective or damaged item shall be removed from service. No employee shall use it until a person(s) qualified to perform the repairs and tests that are necessary to render the equipment safe has done so.

Worker Alert

You must look for damaged insulation, cracks to the instrument or probes, exposed metal, or missing covers. You must also verify that the instrument is properly rated for the system you will be testing. You must only use probes identified for use with the test equipment.

Handbook for Electrical Safety in the Workplace   2018

If a defect is found during the visual inspection, a tag or label should be attached to the instrument indicating that the instrument is defective and not to be used. The instrument should be removed from service until repairs have been made by a qualified person. A defective lead or probe should not be repaired; it should be destroyed and replaced with a new one.

(E) Operation Verification. When test instruments are used for testing the absence of voltage on conductors or circuit parts operating at voltages equal to or greater than 50 volts, the operation of the test instrument shall be verified on any known voltage source before and after an absence of voltage test is performed.

When a test instrument is used to test for absence of voltage, a zero reading might mean that no voltage is present during the testing, or it could mean that the instrument has failed. Therefore, proper operation of the test instrument must be verified on a known voltage source before testing for absence of voltage. After the voltage test has been conducted, the proper operation of the test instrument must again be verified on a known voltage source to ensure that a failure did not occur during the testing for absence of voltage.

Although this verification applies to conductors or circuit parts operating at 50 volts or more, under certain conditions (such as wet contact or immersion) even circuits operating under 50 volts can pose a shock hazard. The 50-volt limit does not rely on the frequency of the circuit — it applies to all frequencies. See Exhibit 120.4 for an illustration of the procedure to test for absence of voltage.

- **110.5 Portable Cord- and-Plug-Connected Electric Equipment.**

This section applies to the use of cord- and plug-connected equipment, including cord sets (extension cords).

Portable electrical equipment is electrical equipment that is cord- and plug-connected and is capable of being readily moved from one location to another location with relative ease. Requirements under this section do not include portable cordless equipment powered by battery power packs. However, the cord- and plug-connected battery charger used to recharge the battery power pack for the cordless equipment is included.

(A) Handling and Storage. Portable equipment shall be handled and stored in a manner that will not cause damage. Flexible electric cords connected to equipment shall not be used for raising or lowering the equipment. Flexible cords shall not be fastened with staples or hung in such a fashion as could damage the outer jacket or insulation.

Raising, lowering, or moving portable equipment by the flexible electric cord can damage the cord and equipment, exposing conductors that could leave an employee vulnerable to injury. Such practices should be prohibited as part of the electrical safety plan.

NEC Section 400.9 requires flexible cord to be used only in continuous lengths without splice or tap where initially installed. *NEC* Article 590 applies to temporary electric power and lighting installations and requires flexible cords and cables to be protected from damage when being used or handled. In accordance with *NEC* 590.4, flexible cords and cables (extension cords) should be of the hard- or extra-hard-usage type, as identified in *NEC* Table 400.4. In accordance with *NEC* 590.4(J), flexible cords and cables

General Requirements for Electrical Safety-Related Work Practices

110.5(C)

should be supported in place at intervals that ensure that they will be protected from physical damage.

Extension cords are permitted to be laid on the floor or ground and to run through doorways, windows, or similar openings, provided they are protected from damage. One method of protection could be preventing the doors from closing by means of fasteners or blocking.

Proper storage of portable equipment and the flexible electric cords connected to the equipment is just as important as proper handling. The cord listing defines indoor storage as protection from sunlight or weather, or both. Cords improperly stored (such as those exposed on work trucks) without this necessary protection will potentially suffer UV and weather damage.

(B) Grounding-Type Equipment.

(a) A flexible cord used with grounding-type utilization equipment shall contain an equipment grounding conductor.

An equipment grounding conductor is an integral part of the safety system built into equipment by manufacturers that provides significant protection from shock or electrocution. The flexible cord must have a grounding-type attachment plug, and the receptacle supplying the equipment must be a grounding-type receptacle.

Equipment grounding conductors are not required on tools that are double insulated. Double-insulated tools have two completely separate sets of insulation and must not be connected to the equipment grounding conductor of the supply circuit.

(b) Attachment plugs and receptacles shall not be connected or altered in a manner that would interrupt continuity of the equipment grounding conductor.

Additionally, these devices shall not be altered in order to allow use in a manner that was not intended by the manufacturer.

All components of the circuit must provide the same integrity as the equipment grounding conductor. Attachment plugs and receptacles are constructed, tested, and listed for specific use. Altering these devices in a manner not intended by the manufacturer compromises the integrity of the equipment grounding conductor continuity. Removal of the grounding pin, or twisting the blades or pins of a plug to enable the plug to mate with a receptacle of a different configuration, is prohibited by this requirement.

(c) Adapters that interrupt the continuity of the equipment grounding conductor shall not be used.

Field-fabricated adapters that use a plug of one configuration on one end and a cord cap of a different configuration on the other end that interrupts the continuity of the equipment grounding conductor is prohibited.

(C) Visual Inspection and Repair of Portable Cord- and Plug-Connected Equipment and Flexible Cord Sets.

(a) *Frequency of Inspection*. Before each use, portable cord- and plug-connected equipment shall be visually inspected for external defects (such as loose parts or deformed and missing pins) and for evidence of possible internal damage (such as a pinched or crushed outer jacket).

> **OSHA Connection**
>
> 29 CFR 1910.304(b)(3)(ii)(C)(3)
>
> Each cord set, attachment cap, plug, and receptacle of cord sets, and any equipment connected by cord and plug must be visually inspected before each day's use for external defects. Additional subparts of this section require documented tests before first use, before equipment is returned to service following any repairs, before equipment is used after any incident that can be reasonably suspected to have caused damage, and at intervals not to exceed 3 months.

Handbook for Electrical Safety in the Workplace 2018

> **OSHA Connection**
>
> 25 CFR 1910.334(a)(2)(i)
> Portable cord- and plug-connected equipment and flexible cord sets must be visually inspected before use on any shift for external defects. Inspection before each shift is not necessary if the equipment and cord sets remain connected once they are put in place and are not exposed to damage.

Exception: Stationary cord- and plug-connected equipment and flexible cord sets (extension cords) that remain connected once they are put in place and are installed such that the cord and plug are not subject to physical damage during normal use shall not be required to be visually inspected until they are relocated or repaired.

Damaged portable cord- and plug-connected equipment and flexible cord sets might expose the employee to shock or electrocution. Visual inspections might not identify all possible problems, but a thorough visual inspection does provide significant assurance that the equipment and cord sets will be safe to use. The inspection should include a careful examination of each end of the cord or cord set and ensure that all pins and blades are in place and unmodified. During this inspection, it is a good practice for the employee to run a hand along the complete surface of the cord. The surface should be smooth with no indentations, cuts, or abrasions. Any anomaly should be inspected further to ensure the integrity of the cord insulation and the conductivity of the equipment grounding conductor.

Although no additional inspection is required until the equipment is moved to another location, periodic inspection of the equipment grounding conductor is recommended. The repair of hard-service cord and junior hard-service cord 14 AWG and larger is permitted if the conductors are spliced in accordance with *NEC* 110.14(B) and the completed splice retains the insulation, outer sheath properties, and usage characteristics of the cord being spliced. The in-line repair is not permitted if the cord is reused or reinstalled.

The repair of the receptacle or plug end of an extension cord is covered by product listing requirements. Receptacle and plug ends are available as listed components for use with listed extensions cords. Repairs must be performed in accordance with the listing requirements. Exhibit 110.6 shows a listed extension cord repaired with a recognized component (receptacle) thereby maintaining the listing of the cord set.

EXHIBIT 110.6

An extension cord repaired with a new receptacle. (Courtesy of Noel Williams)

(b) *Defective Equipment.* If there is a defect or evidence of damage that might expose an employee to injury, the defective or damaged item shall be removed from service. No employee shall use it until a person(s) qualified to perform the repairs and tests necessary to render the equipment safe has done so.

Defective or damaged portable cord- and plug-connected equipment and flexible cord sets that have been removed from service should be identified as defective by a

General Requirements for Electrical Safety-Related Work Practices

tag or other method warning personnel that the item should not be used. The warning should remain with the item until repairs have been completed by a person qualified to perform the repairs and tests necessary to render the equipment safe have been completed.

(c) *Proper Mating.* When an attachment plug is to be connected to a receptacle, the relationship of the plug and receptacle contacts shall first be checked to ensure that they are of mating configurations.

Attachment plugs and receptacles are available in many configurations to ensure proper polarity of connections and prevent the interconnection of different electrical systems, thereby avoiding potentially dangerous conditions. It is also important to check the attachment plug to ensure pins have not been damaged or removed.

(D) Conductive Work Locations. Portable electric equipment used in highly conductive work locations (such as those inundated with water or other conductive liquids) shall be approved for those locations. In job locations where employees are likely to contact or be drenched with water or conductive liquids, ground-fault circuit-interrupter protection for personnel shall also be used.

Informational Note: The risk assessment procedure can also include identifying when the use of portable tools and equipment powered by sources other than 120 volts ac, such as batteries, air, and hydraulics, should be used to minimize the potential for injury from electrical hazards for tasks performed in conductive or wet locations.

Portable cord- and plug-connected equipment that is used in the rain can expose workers to a shock or electrocution hazard. Portable electric equipment used in a wet or damp location must be suitable for that location. In such locations it is recommended that equipment powered by sources other than 120 volts ac — such as batteries, air, and hydraulics — be used to minimize the potential for injury from electrical hazards. GFCI protection is required where employees work with portable tools in a wet or damp location.

(E) Connecting Attachment Plugs.

(a) Employees' hands shall not be wet when plugging and unplugging flexible cords and cord- and plug-connected equipment if energized equipment is involved.

(b) Energized plug and receptacle connections shall be handled only with insulating protective equipment if the condition of the connection could provide a conductive path to the employee's hand (e.g, if a cord connector is wet from being immersed in water).

(c) Locking-type connectors shall be secured after connection.

Locking-type attachment plugs and receptacles and some other portable cord-connecting devices are designed to provide a connection that is secure from accidental withdrawal. For example, the locking type attachment plug system shown in Exhibit 110.7 must be inserted into the mating receptacle and turned to the secure position.

(F) Manufacturer's Instructions. Portable equipment shall be used in accordance with the manufacturer's instructions and safety warnings.

EXHIBIT 110.7

A locking type attachment plug and receptacle. (Courtesy of Hubbell Inc.)

> Any instructions included with the equipment must be followed for its safe operation. Listed equipment has been evaluated for safe use only within the context of these instructions.

110.6 Ground-Fault Circuit-Interrupter (GFCI) Protection.

(A) General. Employees shall be provided with ground-fault circuit-interrupter (GFCI) protection where required by applicable state, federal, or local codes and standards. Listed cord sets or devices incorporating listed GFCI protection for personnel identified for portable use shall be permitted.

> Listed GFCI protection identified for portable use incorporates open neutral protection. Open neutral protection de-energizes the load if there is a loss in continuity in the neutral conductor leading to the device. A typical Class A GFCI receptacle installed in a box with a flexible cord will not provide this additional protection.
>
> GFCI protection is required by *NEC* Article 590 for all temporary installations involving construction, remodeling, maintenance, and repair or demolition of buildings, structures, or equipment. However, using a GFCI device wherever employees use cord-and-plug-connected equipment is a best practice. Exhibits 100.9 through 100.11 show examples of ways to implement the GFCI requirements specified in *NEC* 590.6(A) for temporary installations.

(B) Maintenance and Construction. GFCI protection shall be provided where an employee is operating or using cord sets (extension cords) or cord- and plug-connected tools related to maintenance and construction activity supplied by 125-volt, 15-, 20-, or 30-ampere circuits. Where employees operate or use equipment supplied by greater than 125-volt, 15-, 20-, or 30-ampere circuits, GFCI protection or an assured equipment grounding conductor program shall be implemented.

> Informational Note: Where an assured equipment grounding conductor program is used, a special purpose ground-fault circuit interrupter may provide additional protection. See Informative Annex O.

(C) Outdoors. GFCI protection shall be provided when an employee is outdoors and operating or using cord sets (extension cords) or cord- and plug-connected equipment supplied by 125-volt, 15-, 20-, or 30-ampere circuits. Where employees working

General Requirements for Electrical Safety-Related Work Practices

outdoors operate or use equipment supplied by greater than 125-volt, 15-, 20-, or 30-ampere circuits, GFCI protection or an assured equipment grounding conductor program shall be implemented.

> Informational Note: Where an assured equipment grounding conductor program is used, a special purpose ground-fault circuit interrupter may provide additional protection. See Informative Annex O.

> The required GFCI protection can be achieved using a listed portable GFCI device or a device installed as part of the premises wiring system. Where the cord- and plug-connected equipment is supplied by a circuit rated greater than 125 volts, GFCI protection or an assured equipment grounding conductor program must be implemented.
>
> Section 590.6(B)(3) of the 2017 *NEC* describes the requirement for an assured equipment grounding conductor program as follows:
>
> > A written assured equipment grounding conductor program continuously enforced at the site by one or more designated persons to ensure that equipment grounding conductors for all cord sets, receptacles that are not a part of the permanent wiring of the building or structure, and equipment connected by cord and plug are installed and maintained in accordance with the applicable requirements of 250.114, 250.138, 406.4(C), and 590.4(D) [of the *NEC*].
> >
> > (a) The following tests shall be performed on all cord sets, receptacles that are not part of the permanent wiring of the building or structure, and cord-and-plug-connected equipment required to be connected to an equipment grounding conductor:
> >
> > (1) All equipment grounding conductors shall be tested for continuity and shall be electrically continuous.
> > (2) Each receptacle and attachment plug shall be tested for correct attachment of the equipment grounding conductor. The equipment grounding conductor shall be connected to its proper terminal.
> > (3) All required tests shall be performed as follows:
> >
> >   a. Before first use on site
> >   b. When there is evidence of damage
> >   c. Before equipment is returned to service following any repairs
> >   d. At intervals not exceeding 3 months
> >
> > (b) The tests required in item (3)(a) shall be recorded and made available to the authority having jurisdiction.

OSHA Connection

29 CFR 1926.404(b)1)(iii)

The assured equipment grounding conductor program requirements for construction sites are very similar to the *NEC* requirements for an assured grounding program.

(D) Testing Ground-Fault Circuit-Interrupter Protection Devices. GFCI protection devices shall be tested in accordance with the manufacturer's instructions.

> Installation and testing instructions are provided with all listed GFCI devices. Many devices are required to be tested on a monthly basis.

110.7 Overcurrent Protection Modification. Overcurrent protection of circuits and conductors shall not be modified, even on a temporary basis, beyond what is permitted by applicable portions of electrical codes and standards dealing with overcurrent protection.

> Informational Note: For further information concerning electrical codes and standards dealing with overcurrent protection, refer to Article 240 of *NFPA 70, National Electrical Code*.

> All overcurrent devices must comply with the requirements of the *NEC*. The protection provided may be of the overload, short-circuit, or ground-fault type, or a combination of these types, depending on the application.
>
> Overcurrent devices are important components of a safety system to prevent conductors and equipment from exceeding their rating and ability to safely conduct current. Exceeding the conductor or equipment rating can result in overheating, which can lead to ignition of the insulation or nearby flammable material or result in device and component failure.

Article 120 Establishing an Electrically Safe Work Condition

> The main premise of providing an electrically safe work environment for the employee is that equipment be placed into an electrically safe work condition (ESWC) unless used under normal operation. Both OSHA and NFPA *70E* require this to be the default condition. Article 120 provides the steps for establishing and the method of controlling the ESWC. All of the requirements in Article 120 must be applied before an ESWC is achieved. The act of creating an ESWC requires that appropriate PPE be worn and work procedures be followed. Until verification of the ESWC, it cannot be assumed that equipment is disconnected from energy sources and that it is safe to work on as de-energized.

N **120.1 Lockout/Tagout Program.**

N **(A) General.** Each employer shall establish, document, and implement a lockout/tagout program. The lockout/tagout program shall specify lockout/tagout procedures to safeguard workers from exposure to electrical hazards. The lockout/tagout program and procedures shall also incorporate the following:

(1) Be applicable to the experience and training of the workers and conditions in the workplace
(2) Meet the requirements of Article 120
(3) Apply to fixed, permanently installed equipment, temporarily installed equipment, and portable equipment

> It is the employer's responsibility to establish lockout/tagout procedures that are part of creating an electrically safe work condition (ESWC) that will protect employees from hazardous energy sources during service and maintenance. A single lockout/tagout procedure may not be possible for all installed equipment. Procedures should indicate which pieces of equipment they apply to. They should detail the specific steps necessary to achieve an ESWC for those pieces of equipment. In order to be effective the procedure must be written in a manner that can be understood by the qualified person tasked with establishing an ESWC.

N **(B) Employer Responsibilities.** The employer shall be responsible for the following:

(1) Providing the equipment necessary to execute lockout/tagout procedures
(2) Providing lockout/tagout training to workers in accordance with 110.2
(3) Auditing the lockout/tagout program in accordance with 110.1

Establishing an Electrically Safe Work Condition

120.2(B)

(4) Auditing execution of the lockout/tagout procedures in accordance with 110.1

Informational Note: For an example of a lockout/tagout program, see Informative Annex G.

> Not only is the employer responsible for developing, implementing, and enforcing lockout/tagout procedures, the employer must also provide training and initiate audits. The training must ensure that each employee understands the necessity of an installed lockout or tagout device as part of the program. The audit must ensure that the lockout/tagout procedure is effective and is being properly implemented. The employer is also required to provide the equipment necessary to execute the procedure — locks, multi-lock tree, tags, PPE, and any other tools needed to complete the lockout/tagout procedure.

120.2 Lockout/Tagout Principles.

N **(A) General.** Electrical conductors and circuit parts shall not be considered to be in an electrically safe work condition until all of the requirements of Article 120 have been met.

Safe work practices applicable to the circuit voltage and energy level shall be used in accordance with Article 130 until such time that electrical conductors and circuit parts are in an electrically safe work condition.

Informational Note: See 120.5 for the steps to establish and verify an electrically safe work condition.

> De-energized equipment is not equipment placed into an electrically safe work condition (ESWC). Installing locks and tags does not ensure that electrical hazards have been removed. Until an ESWC has been established, employees must use work practices that are identical to working on or near exposed live parts. These work practices (including use of PPE) should be appropriate for the voltage and energy level of the circuit as if it were known to be energized.
>
> With a proper risk assessment and when performed under the conditions that permit normal operation, the act of establishing an ESWC should remove hazards before the equipment is opened. Although establishing an ESWC must be considered energized work, ideally it should not be exposing the employee to any energized circuits. The ESWC voltage measurement should always be zero. The procedure, including the use of PPE, is necessary to protect the worker when something goes wrong.
>
> Where an ESWC exists, there is no electrical energy in proximity of the work task(s). The danger of injury from electrical hazards has been removed, and neither protective equipment nor special safety training is required.

(B) Employee Involvement. Each person who could be exposed directly or indirectly to a source of electrical energy shall be involved in the lockout/tagout process.

Informational Note: An example of direct exposure is the qualified electrician who works on the motor starter control, the power circuits, or the motor. An example of indirect exposure is the person who works on the coupling between the motor and compressor.

> Any employee who could be exposed to unacceptable risk of an electrical hazard when executing a work task (even if the assigned task is not electrical) must be involved in the lockout/tagout process. Temporary and contract employees also must understand how the lockout/tagout procedure that is part of creating an electrically safe work condition influences their exposure to electrical hazards, and they must participate in the process. When multiple employers are involved in the work process, such as when

Worker Alert

You must notify other affected employees that you will be implementing a lockout/tagout system and provide them with the reason for its implementation.

an independent contractor is involved, Section 110.3 requires each employer to share information about hazards and procedures.

(C) Lockout/Tagout Procedure. A lockout/tagout procedure shall be developed on the basis of the existing electrical equipment and system and shall use suitable documentation including up-to-date drawings and diagrams.

> A procedure must be developed for each lockout/tagout that is part of creating an electrically safe work condition (ESWC). Up-to-date, accurate single-line diagrams provide essential information that is needed when creating an ESWC. The purpose of the information is to clearly indicate all sources of electrical energy that are or might be available at any point in the electrical circuit. If the diagram is inaccurate, employees could be injured as a result of one or more sources of energy that are not removed. See Annex G for a sample lockout/tagout procedure.

(D) Control of Energy. All sources of electrical energy shall be controlled in such a way as to minimize employee exposure to electrical hazards.

> All sources of energy — including stored energy and mechanical energy — must be removed by operating all applicable disconnecting means. After the disconnecting means is opened, all employees who might be exposed to the electrical hazard should be involved with the lockout procedure.

(E) Electrical Circuit Interlocks. Documentation, including up-to-date drawings and diagrams, shall be reviewed to ensure that no electrical circuit interlock operation can result in re-energizing the circuit being worked on.

> A diagrammatic drawing is commonly used to determine the possibility for a circuit to be re-energized from backfeeds or through the operation of a remote interlock. It is crucial that the drawing be up to date and that it accurately depict the installation. As an installed circuit or system changes, the single-line diagrams, schematic diagrams, or similar drawings that are on record should be marked to document the change in the system.

(F) Control Devices. Locks/tags shall be installed only on circuit disconnecting means. Control devices, such as push-buttons or selector switches, shall not be used as the primary isolating device.

> Some control devices are fitted with a mechanism designed to accept a lock. However, these control devices are not to be used as the primary means for de-energizing circuits or equipment. Control devices do not render a circuit inoperative; therefore, installing a tag or a lock on a control device does not meet the objective of a primary isolating device. If the device being locked or tagged does not create a break in the conductors providing energy to the equipment or circuit, the device must not be used as a lockout or tagout point. Although the installation of a lock on these control devices is not prohibited, the use of an identified lockout/tagout device for that purpose is not permitted.

Establishing an Electrically Safe Work Condition

(G) Identification. The lockout/tagout device shall be unique and readily identifiable as a lockout/tagout device.

> Uniquely and readily identifiable lockout/tagout devices must be durable, substantial, and standardized. Standardization can be achieved by color, shape, or size. The print and format on tagout devices should also be standardized. Employees must be able to recognize a lockout/tagout device, and there cannot be any possibility of confusing lockout/tagout devices with locks or tags used for other purposes, such as information tags and process control locks. See 120.3(C) and 120.3(D) for lockout and tagout device requirements.

(H) Coordination. The following items are necessary for coordinating the lockout/tagout procedure:

(1) The electrical lockout/tagout procedure shall be coordinated with all other employer's procedures for control of exposure to electrical energy sources such that all employer's procedural requirements are adequately addressed on a site basis.

> A project could involve contractors and employers other than the facility owner. Since each employer is required to implement a lockout/tagout procedure, different requirements can exist. The lockout/tagout procedures must be coordinated with outside employers — independent contractors who service and/or maintain equipment that require lockout/tagout. To make sure that the requirements of each procedure are understood and observed, each employer might need to amend one or more procedures. Contractors and facility owners must exchange information about creating an electrically safe work condition and ensure that their respective employees understand all issues that are important to the other employer.
>
> When the lockout/tagout procedure for different employers must be implemented on the same work site, the procedures must be coordinated with each other and employees of each employer must be instructed about any unique aspect. Training in the method to be employed for the task can help minimize the possibility of errors in implementing the unfamiliar process. The basic concerns of each employer must be addressed in the written lockout/tagout plan. Employees must understand the change and the necessity for the change.

(2) The procedure for control of exposure to electrical hazards shall be coordinated with other procedures for control of other hazardous energy based on similar or identical concepts.

> All lockout/tagout procedures must clearly and specifically outline the scope, purpose, authorization, rules, and techniques to be utilized for the control of hazardous energy.
>
> Other standards may require an employer to implement a procedure for control of exposure to other hazardous energy sources. For instance, the general control of hazardous energy procedure and the electrical lockout/tagout procedure that is part of creating an electrically safe work condition could have similar or identical requirements for locks and tags. The electrical lockout/tagout procedure could be integrated into an overall control of hazardous energy procedure; however, that procedure needs to address all the issues identified in this standard.

(3) Electrical lockout/tagout devices shall be permitted to be similar to lockout/tagout devices for control of other hazardous energy sources, such as pneumatic, hydraulic, thermal, and mechanical, if such devices are used only for control of hazardous energy and for no other purpose.

Worker Alert

You should exercise caution when working on a group of machines that work together in a coordinated manner. This type of machinery typically has a number of electrical supplies and can have multiple sources of energy. You need to have knowledge of each machine's purpose and functionality in order to identify all possible sources of hazardous energy.

OSHA Connection

29 CFR 1910.147

Energy sources are defined as "any source of electrical, mechanical, hydraulic, pneumatic, chemical, thermal, or other energy."

Devices used for control of hazardous energy must be easily recognizable and be the only devices the employer uses in conjunction with the control of hazardous energy. Electrical lockout/tagout devices should have the same physical characteristics as devices used for control of other forms of energy so that employees can easily recognize lockout devices used to control energy sources.

(I) Forms of Control of Hazardous Electrical Energy. Two forms of hazardous electrical energy control shall be permitted: simple lockout/tagout and complex lockout/tagout [see 120.4]. For the simple lockout/tagout, the qualified person shall be in charge. For the complex lockout/tagout, the person in charge shall have overall responsibility.

The objective in controlling exposure to electrical energy is to ensure that all possible sources of electrical energy are disconnected and cannot be re-energized unexpectedly. The two types of control are the simple lockout/tagout and the complex lockout/tagout, which are administrative controls (procedures) from the hierarchy of safety controls. See Informative Annex G for a sample lockout/tagout procedure.

In a simple lockout/tagout, the qualified person(s) de-energizes one source of electrical energy and is responsible for their own lockout/tagout. A written lockout/tagout plan is not required. A simple lockout/tagout does not place the limit at a single person conducting work on the equipment and may require that multiple locks be applied.

A complex lockout/tagout typically involves more than one energy source and more than one disconnecting means. It requires a single person with overall responsibility and a written plan prepared in advance for each lockout/tagout application.

120.3 Lockout/Tagout Equipment.

(A) Lock Application. Energy isolation devices for machinery or equipment installed after January 2, 1990, shall be capable of accepting a lockout device.

OSHA Connection
29 CFR 1910.147(c)(2)(iii)
Whenever replacement or major repair, renovation, or modification of a machine or equipment is performed, and whenever new machines or equipment are installed, energy isolating devices must be designed to accept a lockout device.

Many *NFPA 70®*, *National Electrical Code®* (*NEC®*) requirements for disconnecting means require that the equipment have a method built in that allows it to be locked in the open position. Any disconnecting means that cannot be locked in the open position must not be used as an energy isolation device.

(B) Lockout/Tagout Device. Each employer shall supply, and employees shall use, lockout/tagout devices and equipment necessary to execute the requirements of 120.3. Locks and tags used for control of exposure to electrical hazards shall be unique, shall be readily identifiable as lockout/tagout devices, and shall be used for no other purpose.

Each employer must provide the necessary equipment — such as locks, tags, chains, wedges, key blocks, adaptor pins, and self-locking fasteners — for employees to control exposure to electrical hazards.

Lockout/tagout devices for control of exposure to electrical energy can be identical to lockout/tagout devices used for the control of hazardous energy from other energy sources, but these devices must not be used for any other purpose. See the commentary following 120.2(G) for identification of lockout/tagout devices.

Δ **(C) Lockout Device.** The lockout device shall meet the following requirements:

Establishing an Electrically Safe Work Condition

120.3(D)(5)

(1) A lockout device shall include a lock — either keyed or combination.
(2) The lockout device shall include a method of identifying the individual who installed the lockout device.
(3) A lockout device shall be permitted to be only a lock, if the lock is readily identifiable as a lockout device, in addition to having a means of identifying the person who installed the lock.

> Even though a uniquely identified lock used as a lockout device may be used in conjunction with other components, the fundamental lockout device must be a lock. The lockout device must include information that identifies the person who installed the lock and must be installed in a manner that prevents operation of the energy isolation device.

(4) Lockout devices shall be attached to prevent operation of the disconnecting means without resorting to undue force or the use of tools.

> The lockout device must be capable of withstanding the environment to which it is exposed for the maximum period of time that exposure is expected. It must also be substantial enough to prevent removal without the use of excessive force or unusual techniques, such as the use of bolt cutters or other metal cutting tools.

(5) Where a tag is used in conjunction with a lockout device, the tag shall contain a statement prohibiting unauthorized operation of the disconnecting means or unauthorized removal of the device.
(6) Lockout devices shall be suitable for the environment and for the duration of the lockout.
(7) Whether keyed or combination locks are used, the key or combination shall remain in the possession of the individual installing the lock or the person in charge, when provided by the established procedure.

> The method of locking (by key or combination) must prevent unauthorized removal of the lock, and the person who might be exposed to an electrical hazard must be in control of the electrical energy. To accomplish that purpose, the key to the lock must remain in the possession of the person who installed it.

(D) Tagout Device. The tagout device shall meet the following requirements:

(1) A tagout device shall include a tag together with an attachment means.
(2) The tagout device shall be readily identifiable as a tagout device and suitable for the environment and duration of the tagout.
(3) A tagout device attachment means shall be capable of withstanding at least 224.4 N (50 lb) of force exerted at a right angle to the disconnecting means surface. The tag attachment means shall be nonreusable, attachable by hand, self-locking, nonreleasable, and equal to an all-environmental tolerant nylon cable tie.
(4) Tags shall contain a statement prohibiting unauthorized operation of the disconnecting means or removal of the tag.

> The device must be easily recognizable as a tagout device and must be securely attached to the energy isolation device to alert employees that equipment is not to be operated until the tag is removed.

(5) A hold card tagging tool on an overhead conductor in conjunction with a hotline tool to install the tagout device safely on a disconnect that is isolated from the work(s) shall be

Handbook for Electrical Safety in the Workplace   2018

permitted. Where a hold card is used, the tagout procedure shall include the method of accounting for personnel who are working under the protection of the hold card.

> The work environment for utility employees often leads to the disconnecting means being located several miles away from the work site. Utility systems have successfully relied on a hold card to provide warning that operating a disconnecting means would place employees in danger. Utility workers are trained to respect the system associated with the hold card, which results in a positive and effective system of energy control.
> When tagout is employed, at least one additional safety measure, such as removing the cutout, must be used in addition to the use of the hold card. Employees of utility systems must be covered by a written policy that describes how the hold card system functions. Where contract employees perform utility maintenance or construction, the contract employer must provide a program that is at least as effective as the program of the utility authorizing the contractor's work.

OSHA Connection

29 CFR 1910.333(b)(2)

The employer must maintain a written copy of the procedures and make it available for inspection by employees.

120.4 Lockout/Tagout Procedures.

The employer shall maintain a copy of the procedures required by this section and shall make the procedures available to all employees.

> Although an employer is responsible for providing the lockout/tagout procedure, employees should be involved in gathering the information to generate the procedure. The procedure must be implemented as a step in the process of establishing an electrically safe work condition. The lockout/tagout procedure can be included in an overall lockout/tagout procedure for an employer or site, or it can be a stand-alone procedure. In either instance, all the requirements of Article 120 must be addressed.

Δ **(A) Planning.** The procedure shall require planning, including the requirements of 120.4(A)(1) through 120.4(B)(14).

> The planner might be the person in charge, the supervisor, a person competent in establishing an electrically safe work condition, or the qualified employee performing the task themselves. Regardless of who develops the plan, the qualified persons performing the task should be involved in the development of any plan that affects their safety. The plan must identify the location, both physically and electrically, that requires a lockout or tagout device.
> The lockout/tagout procedure must include a detailed method of achieving the objectives of 120.2(A) and (B). A complete procedure must indicate whether the plan must be in writing and whether any authorization is necessary.

(1) Locating Sources. Up-to-date single-line drawings shall be considered a primary reference source for such information. When up-to-date drawings are not available, the employer shall be responsible for ensuring that an equally effective means of locating all sources of energy is employed.

> A crucial requirement in the lockout/tagout procedure is to determine all possible sources of electrical supply to the specific equipment. Although applicable up-to-date drawings must be the initial source of information, when they are not available other sources can include manuals, panel schedules, and information tags. The system should be visually inspected so that all hazards are properly identified. Where a single-line

Establishing an Electrically Safe Work Condition

120.4(A)(4)

drawing is not available, it may be appropriate to generate one as part of gathering information from other sources.

(2) Exposed Persons. The plan shall identify persons who might be exposed to an electrical hazard and the PPE required during the execution of the job or task.

The plan must identify those who might be exposed to an unacceptable risk from an electrical hazard, either directly or indirectly. The act of establishing an electrically safe work condition is considered to be performing work on an energized circuit until all steps in 120.5 have been completed. The plan must also identify what PPE employees must use during the implementation of the lockout or tagout and during the execution of the job or task.

(3) Person in Charge. The plan shall identify the person in charge and his or her responsibility in the lockout/tagout.

The person in charge may be the individual implementing a simple lockout procedure or the individual responsible for overseeing a complex lockout procedure. Responsibilities of the person in charge might include implementing the energy control procedures, communicating the purpose of the operation to the servicing and maintenance employees, coordinating the operation, and ensuring that all procedural steps have been properly completed.

(4) Simple Lockout/Tagout Procedure. All lockout/tagout procedures that involve only a qualified person(s) de-energizing one set of conductors or circuit part source for the sole purpose of safeguarding employees from exposure to electrical hazards shall be considered to be a simple lockout/tagout. Simple lockout/tagout procedures shall not be required to be written for each application. Each worker shall be responsible for his or her own lockout/tagout.

Exception: Lockout/tagout is not required for work on cord- and plug-connected equipment for which exposure to the hazards of unexpected energization of the equipment is controlled by the unplugging of the equipment from the energy source, provided that the plug is under the exclusive control of the employee performing the servicing and maintenance for the duration of the work.

Lockout/tagout procedures that involve a qualified person(s) de-energizing one set of conductors or one circuit part source for the sole purpose of safeguarding employees from exposure to electrical hazards are considered to be a simple lockout/tagout. A simple lockout/tagout is not limited to a single employee or limited to the application of a single lock. Employees are responsible for their own individual lockout/tagout.

Consider this example of a simple lockout/tagout procedure, where a single disconnect switch provides energy for equipment, such as a motor, and where an employee intending to service the motor opens the disconnecting means, de-energizing the motor circuit. The only way to guarantee that the disconnecting means remains open and the motor stays de-energized is to lock the disconnecting means in the open position and affix the appropriate tag. Although no written lockout/tagout plan is needed, a simple lockout/tagout must be a planned activity. A simple lockout/tagout may involve more than a single person and may require that multiple locks be applied.

Worker Alert

You must notify other affected employees that you will be implementing a lockout/tagout system and provide them with the reason for its implementation.

120.4(A)(5) — Article 120

Worker Alert

If you are the person in charge, you must develop a written plan of execution and communicate that plan to all persons engaged in the job or task. You will be held accountable for safe execution of the complex lockout/tagout plan. You must ensure that each person understands the electrical hazards to which they are exposed and the safety-related work practices they are to use.

(5) Complex Lockout/Tagout.

(a) A complex lockout/tagout procedure shall be permitted where one or more of the following exists:

(1) Multiple energy source
(2) Multiple crews
(3) Multiple crafts
(4) Multiple locations
(5) Multiple employers
(6) Multiple disconnecting means
(7) Particular sequences
(8) Job or task that continues for more than one work period

> The conditions listed in 120.4(A)(5)(a) increase the complexity and difficulty of a lockout/tagout. Multiple energy sources as referenced in Item (1) are not limited to electric power; they could be compressed air, hydraulic, mechanical, pneumatic, natural gas, steam, thermal, or water. A process or machinery with multiple operations are examples of Item (7).

(b) All complex lockout/tagout procedures shall require a written plan of execution that identifies the person in charge.

> If one or more of the conditions listed in 120.4(A)(5)(a) exist, the lockout/tagout is defined as complex, and a person in charge must be assigned. The primary responsibility of the person in charge is to directly implement a complex lockout/tagout procedure.

(c) The complex lockout/tagout procedure shall vest primary responsibility in an authorized employee for employees working under the protection of a group lockout or tagout device, such as an operation lock or lockbox. The person in charge shall be held accountable for safe execution of the complex lockout/tagout.

> The person in charge must be both a qualified person and an authorized employee. This person coordinates personnel and ensures continuity of lockout/tagout protection for all employees working under the protection of a group lockout/tagout device. The person in charge is accountable for developing, implementing, and monitoring the plan.

(d) Each authorized employee shall affix a personal lockout or tagout device to the group lockout device, group lockbox, or comparable mechanism when he or she begins work and shall remove those devices when he or she stops working on the machine or equipment being serviced or maintained.

> To adhere to the basic principle that each employee be in control of the hazardous energy, all persons involved in the work task must affix their own personal lockout device to the group lockout device or to each individual lockout point. The person in charge is responsible for ensuring adherence to this principle. Exhibits 120.1 and 120.2 show examples of complex lockout/tagout devices.

Establishing an Electrically Safe Work Condition

120.4(B)(2)

EXHIBIT 120.1

Lockbox.

EXHIBIT 120.2

Disconnect switch with locks from more than one individual.

(e) All complex lockout/tagout plans shall identify the method to account for all persons who might be exposed to electrical hazards in the course of the lockout/tagout.

> The person in charge is responsible for ensuring that all employees are protected by the complex lockout/tagout. This person is also responsible for administering the removal of the devices and the release for return to service. Each employee must understand the process by which the person in charge will implement this responsibility.

(B) Elements of Control. The procedure shall identify elements of control.

(1) De-energizing Equipment (Shutdown). The procedure shall establish the person who performs the switching and where and how to de-energize the load.

(2) Stored Energy. The procedure shall include requirements for releasing stored electric or mechanical energy that might endanger personnel. All capacitors shall be discharged, and high-capacitance elements shall also be short-circuited and grounded before the associated equipment is touched or worked on. Springs shall be released or physical restraint shall be applied when necessary to immobilize mechanical equipment and pneumatic and hydraulic pressure reservoirs. Other sources of stored energy shall be blocked or otherwise relieved.

Worker Alert

Typical examples of stored energy sources are capacitors used for power factor correction and motor starting. There are many other sources, such as cable capacitance, where you could encounter stored energy.

Electrical energy can be generated electrical power, stored energy (such as in a capacitor), or static electricity. Generated electrical power can be turned off or on, whereas stored or static electricity can only be dissipated or controlled. Although the most common energy source is electrical energy, the procedure should consider all forms of energy that might be present, such as hydraulic energy (liquid under pressure), pneumatic energy (gas/air under pressure), or mechanical motion (kinetic energy, energy of motion). The procedure must indicate the appropriate steps to control these sources of energy, such as the blocking of springs.

(3) Disconnecting Means. The procedure shall identify how to verify that the circuit is de-energized (open).

Creating an electrically safe work condition always includes the verification of lack of voltage. Additional visual verification that the disconnecting means is physically open can involve looking through an observation port or opening a door and observing the position of the contacts in the disconnecting means. In other cases, such as where arc chutes are involved, the contacts are not readily visible and observation of the contacts is not possible. Employees must be instructed how to determine that all conductors are disconnected from the source of energy.

(4) Responsibility. The procedure shall identify the person who is responsible for verifying that the lockout/tagout procedure is implemented and who is responsible for ensuring that the task is completed prior to removing locks/tags. A mechanism to accomplish lockout/tagout for multiple (complex) jobs/tasks where required, including the person responsible for coordination, shall be included.

(5) Verification. The procedure shall verify that equipment cannot be restarted. The equipment operating controls, such as push-buttons, selector switches, and electrical interlocks, shall be operated or otherwise it shall be verified that the equipment cannot be restarted.

The operation of control devices, such as pushbuttons, may not be the only means to verify that equipment cannot be restarted when creating an electrically safe work condition. Additional measures may be necessary for the specific equipment.

(6) Testing. The procedure shall establish the following:

(1) Test instrument to be used, the required PPE, and the person who will use it to verify proper operation of the test instrument on a known voltage source before and after use
(2) Requirement to define the boundary of the electrically safe work condition
(3) Requirement to test before touching every exposed conductor or circuit part(s) within the defined boundary of the work area
(4) Requirement to retest for absence of voltage when circuit conditions change or when the job location has been left unattended
(5) Planning considerations that include methods of verification where there is no accessible exposed point to take voltage measurements

The lockout/tagout procedure must include the requirements necessary to ensure that all employees know whether they are exposed to an electrical hazard. The procedure must identify acceptable test instruments and contain a requirement to ensure that

Worker Alert

There have been many incidents where a worker was injured by assuming that the equipment was still in an electrically safe work condition after returning from lunch. Visually inspecting the lockout/tagout device is not enough to ensure the equipment is still in a de-energized state or cannot be restarted. You must retest for absence of voltage when the job location has been left unattended.

Establishing an Electrically Safe Work Condition

120.4(B)(7)

the test instrument is functioning properly before and after each use. Employee training must ensure that each qualified employee is familiar with the requirements for testing voltage. See Exhibit 110.4, which shows a test instrument used for measuring voltage.

Employees who use test instruments must understand the limitations of the instrument, how to use the device, how to protect themselves from any associated hazard, and how to interpret all possible indications provided by the test instrument. The integrity of the test instrument must be verified before and after the voltage test. Exhibit 120.13 illustrates of the correct procedure to test for absence of voltage.

If the work task has no exposed point for measuring voltage, the procedure or plan must identify the method for verifying that all conductors and circuit parts have been de-energized.

OSHA Connection

29 CFR 1910.334(c)(2)
Testing instruments and equipment must be visually inspected for external defects or damage before being used to determine de-energization.

(7) Grounding. Grounding requirements for the circuit shall be established, including whether the temporary protective grounding equipment shall be installed for the duration of the task or is temporarily established by the procedure. Grounding needs or requirements shall be permitted to be covered in other work rules and might not be part of the lockout/tagout procedure.

Applying temporary protective grounding devices is an important part of establishing an electrically safe work condition, but it may not be required in all cases. Where it is possible for de-energized conductors or circuit parts to contact other exposed energized conductors or circuit parts, temporary protective ground devices rated for the available fault duty should be applied. The procedure must define any requirement for placement of temporary protective grounding equipment. If other work rules consider and address temporary protective grounding, the lockout/tagout procedure is not required to address the same issue. However, employees must be aware that the lockout/tagout procedure is augmented by other work rules that cover the use of temporary protective grounding equipment. Establishing general rules assists an employee who is attempting to determine if use of temporary protective grounding equipment is necessary.

Some grounding and testing devices are designed to be inserted (racked) into a compartment from which a circuit breaker or disconnect has been removed. These devices can be inserted only into specific spaces. See Exhibit 120.3.

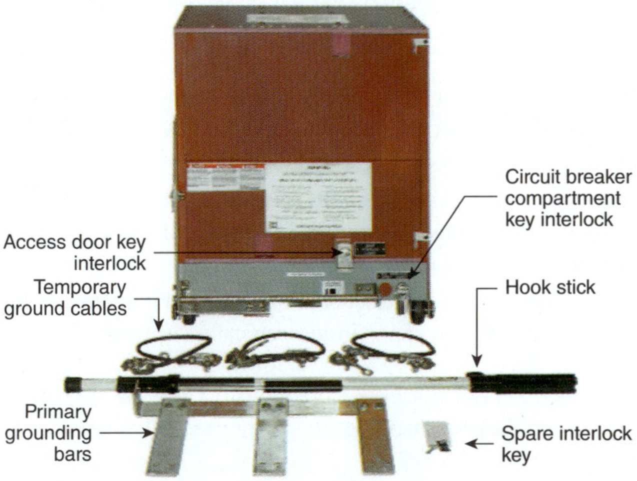

EXHIBIT 120.3

A ground and test device for rack systems. (Courtesy of Schneider Electric)

Handbook for Electrical Safety in the Workplace 2018

> **Worker Alert**
>
> The transfer of responsibility for lockout/tagout is much more than just exchanging locks and tags. Be sure that you review the procedure and coordinate with the person in charge. Be aware of all aspects of the task, including all possible sources of energy, placement of temporary grounding equipment, and other employees involved in the project.

(8) Shift Change. A method shall be identified in the procedure to transfer responsibility for lockout/tagout to another person or to the person in charge when the job or task extends beyond one shift.

> When work extends beyond one shift and there are personnel changes, the procedure must provide for the orderly transfer of responsibilities between off-going and incoming employees to ensure the integrity of the electrically safe work condition and the continuity of lockout or tagout protection. The process of transferring of responsibility from the off-going shift's person in charge to the incoming shift's person in charge must be clearly defined in the procedure. Off-going employees who had installed locks and tags during their shift should remove their locks and tags, and the incoming employees must install their individual locks and tags.

(9) Coordination. The procedure shall establish how coordination is accomplished with other jobs or tasks in progress, including related jobs or tasks at remote locations as well as the person responsible for coordination.

> When more than one task or job is in progress, the actions of one employee might have an impact on the actions of others. One person must be assigned responsibility for ensuring that work tasks by others — such as different tradesmen or contractors — are coordinated, to minimize the possibility of one person's actions adversely impacting another's.

(10) Accountability for Personnel. A method shall be identified in the procedure to account for all persons who could be exposed to hazardous energy during the lockout/tagout.

> Typically, the person in charge [see 120.4(A)(3)] is assigned to account for everyone involved in the work task, including contract employees.

(11) Lockout/Tagout Application. The procedure shall clearly identify when and where lockout applies, in addition to when and where tagout applies, and shall address the following:

> Tagout is permitted in lieu of lockout only in cases where equipment design precludes the installation of a lock. If tagout is permitted, the procedure must define individual responsibility and accountability clearly for each person that would be potentially exposed to an electrical hazard. In addition, all employees must receive training regarding the limitations of tags.

(1) Lockout shall be defined as installing a lockout device on all sources of hazardous energy such that operation of the disconnecting means is prohibited, and forcible removal of the lock is required to operate the disconnecting means.
(2) Tagout shall be defined as installing a tagout device on all sources of hazardous energy, such that operation of the disconnecting means is prohibited. The tagout device shall be installed in the same position available for the lockout device.
(3) Where it is not possible to attach a lock to existing disconnecting means, the disconnecting means shall not be used as the only means to put the circuit in an electrically safe work condition.

> A disconnecting means that does not accept a lockout device must not be the only means of controlling the energy source. Tagout must be supplemented by at least one additional safety measure.

Establishing an Electrically Safe Work Condition

(4) The use of tagout procedures without a lock shall be permitted only in cases where equipment design precludes the installation of a lock on an energy isolation device(s). When tagout is employed, at least one additional safety measure shall be employed. In such cases, the procedure shall clearly establish responsibilities and accountability for each person who might be exposed to electrical hazards.

Informational Note: Examples of additional safety measures include the removal of an isolating circuit element such as fuses, blocking of the controlling switch, or opening an extra disconnecting device to reduce the likelihood of inadvertent energization.

> If the equipment cannot be locked, tagout is permitted when an additional safety measure is employed and the employer's procedure clearly identifies the acceptable methods to be used as the additional safety measure. The informational note provides examples of additional safety measures.

(12) Removal of Lockout/Tagout Devices. The procedure shall identify the details for removing locks or tags when the installing individual is unavailable. When locks or tags are removed by someone other than the installer, the employer shall attempt to locate that person prior to removing the lock or tag. When the lock or tag is removed because the installer is unavailable, the installer shall be informed prior to returning to work.

> The procedure for removal of a lockout/tagout under these circumstances should include measures to ensure that the lockout/tagout can be safely removed and that the employee who removes the lockout/tagout device documents its removal. The person who originally installed the device must be informed that the lockout/tagout device was removed before the person returns to work and should be briefed on the current status of the equipment.

(13) Release for Return to Service. The procedure shall identify steps to be taken when the job or task requiring lockout/tagout is completed. Before electric circuits or equipment are re-energized, tests and visual inspections shall be conducted to verify that all tools, mechanical restraints and electrical jumpers, short circuits, and temporary protective grounding equipment have been removed, so that the circuits and equipment are in a condition to be safely energized. When applicable, the employees responsible for operating the machines or process shall be notified when circuits and equipment are ready to be energized, and such employees shall provide assistance as necessary to safely energize the circuits and equipment. The procedure shall contain a statement requiring the area to be inspected to ensure that nonessential items have been removed. One such step shall ensure that all personnel are clear of exposure to dangerous conditions resulting from re-energizing the service and that blocked mechanical equipment or grounded equipment is cleared and prepared for return to service.

> Inspection of the work area should also ensure that all guards and covers are installed properly and that everyone in the area is notified that the lockout/tagout devices will be removed and the equipment could start. The person in charge must make sure that all employees are safely positioned or removed from the area before removing the lockout devices. The equipment should be verified as being placed back into a normal operating condition before being re-energized. See 130.2(A)(4).

(14) Temporary Release for Testing/Positioning. The procedure shall clearly identify the steps and qualified persons' responsibilities when the job or task requiring lockout/tagout is to be interrupted temporarily for testing or positioning of equipment; then the steps shall be identical to the steps for return to service.

> Informational Note: See 110.4 for requirements when using test instruments and equipment.

If the equipment is not going to be returned to service after testing or repositioning, all lockout/tagout devices should be reinstalled immediately. Temporarily restoring electrical energy to reposition equipment or to facilitate testing is very hazardous and should be avoided.

Worker Alert

The process for establishing and verifying an electrically safe work condition (ESWC) may be one that you complete many times, but it should not be treated as a routine task. Every time you establish an ESWC, you must carefully consider each step of the process. In most facilities, establishing an ESWC should occur more often than performing energized electrical work.

OSHA Connection

29 CFR 1910.333(b)(2)

The steps to de-energize equipment are met by the application of 120.5.

120.5 Process for Establishing and Verifying an Electrically Safe Work Condition.

De-energization itself does not create an electrically safe work condition (ESWC). The process of establishing an ESWC includes turning off the power, verifying lack of voltage, and ensuring that the equipment cannot be re-energized while work is being performed. An ESWC does not exist until all of the Article 120 requirements have been completed. The act of establishing an ESWC requires that task be considered as energized work.

When an ESWC is achieved and verified, no electrical energy is in the immediate vicinity of the work task(s). Danger of injury from an electrical hazard has been reduced to an acceptable level, PPE is not needed, and unqualified persons can perform non-electrical work such as cleaning and painting near electrical equipment. When the equipment is re-energized, the employees must be capable of executing the task(s) in a manner that will not create unacceptable risk from electrical hazards.

Establishing and verifying an electrically safe work condition shall include all of the following steps, which shall be performed in the order presented, if feasible:

(1) Determine all possible sources of electrical supply to the specific equipment. Check applicable up-to-date drawings, diagrams, and identification tags.

It is crucial that all possible sources of information be used to identify and locate all sources of energy. These sources include single-line diagrams, panelboard schedules, elementary or schematic diagrams, electrical plans, identification signs and tags on electrical equipment, and consultation with workers who routinely service the equipment. Although most electrical equipment is supplied by a single source, occasionally there are multiple sources such as emergency or standby generators, photovoltaic or fuel cell systems, or a separate control power source. The single-line diagram in Exhibit 120.4 depicts an electrical system fed by two separate sources. Section 408.4(B) of the *NEC* requires marking, shown in Exhibit 120.5, when a panelboard, switchboard, or switchgear is fed by two sources.

Usually equipment is labeled. However, a sneak circuit (hidden path) could exist that can only be identified by reviewing diagrammatic-type drawings, which identify additional sources. Diagrammatic-type drawings must be maintained and kept up to date, just as is required for single-line diagrams to provide accurate information.

Circuits containing transformers must be checked to verify that all links or disconnects are opened to prevent any potential backfeeds. This is especially important when connecting temporary power in situations when equipment is taken out of service for repair or maintenance.

Establishing an Electrically Safe Work Condition

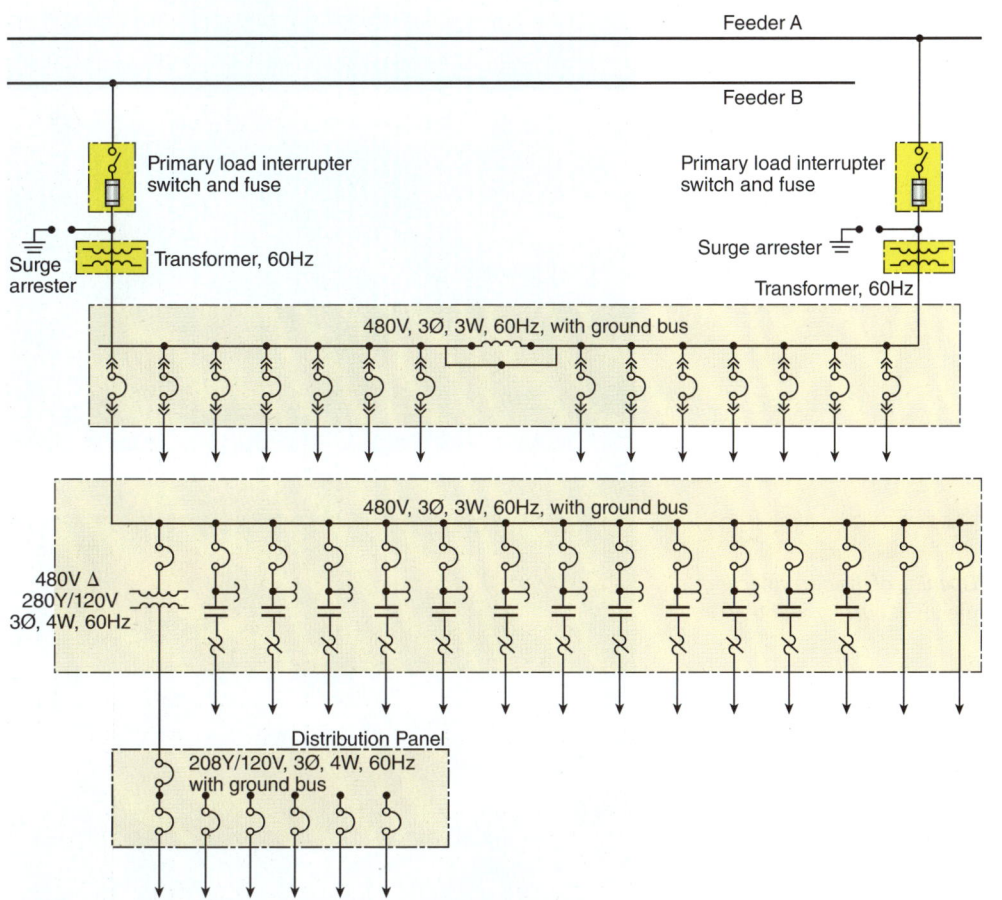

EXHIBIT 120.4

Single-line diagram.

EXHIBIT 120.5

Marking indicating equipment is fed by two sources. (Courtesy of Bobby Gray)

(2) After properly interrupting the load current, open the disconnecting device(s) for each source.

Before operating any disconnecting device, it should be verified whether or not the device is capable of opening the load current. When the rating of a disconnect device is not sufficient to interrupt the load current, the load must be interrupted by another action prior to opening the device. Otherwise, the disconnecting device might be destroyed, initiating a significant failure that could escalate to an arcing fault within the equipment.

Even when the equipment is load-rated, interrupting large full-load currents can reduce the life of the disconnecting device. Motor-driven equipment should be stopped and other electrical equipment de-energized to reduce the amount of current in the circuit before the disconnecting device is operated. Exhibit 120.6 shows the interrupting of the load by stopping the equipment prior to opening the disconnecting means. Exhibit 120.7 shows the opening of the disconnect device. The equipment label in Exhibit 120.8 indicates the need to disconnect additional power sources.

EXHIBIT 120.6

Interrupting the load. (Courtesy of Bobby Gray)

EXHIBIT 120.7

Opening of the disconnecting means. (Courtesy of Bobby Gray)

EXHIBIT 120.8

Marking of a disconnect that does not remove all power sources.

Establishing an Electrically Safe Work Condition

(3) Wherever possible, visually verify that all blades of the disconnecting devices are fully open or that drawout-type circuit breakers are withdrawn to the fully disconnected position.

Disconnecting devices occasionally malfunction and fail to open all phase conductors when the handle is operated. If the disconnecting mechanism does not operate freely, it should not be forced open. The circuit should be de-energized by means of an upstream device. Where possible after operating the handle of the disconnecting device, the employee should observe the physical opening in each blade of the device, such as through a viewing window. Notice that the blades in Exhibit 120.9 have been fully separated from the retention jaws. Opening a door or removing a cover to verify open contacts could expose an employee to electrical hazards. Therefore, the employee must continue to be protected from those hazards by PPE until all steps for the verification of the electrically safe work condition have been completed.

EXHIBIT 120.9

Verifying the opening of contacts.

(4) Release stored electrical energy.

Electrical energy may be stored in batteries, capacitors, inductors, or other discrete electrical components. These components may be internal or external to the equipment being worked on. Stored electrical energy may also be present in electrical cables. Depending on the equipment or system design, it may take a considerable amount of time before the dissipation of storage energy has occurred. The equipment in Exhibit 120.10 requires at least 15 minutes of discharge time and carries a reminder to verify the lack of voltage. Time itself must not be relied upon for depletion of stored energy.

(5) Release or block stored mechanical energy.

The procedure includes requirements for releasing mechanical energy that might endanger personnel. Springs must be released or physical restraint must be applied when necessary to immobilize mechanical equipment. Other sources of stored energy must be blocked or otherwise relieved. The mechanical energy in the press shown in Exhibit 120.11 has been blocked.

EXHIBIT 120.10

Equipment requiring dissipation of stored energy. (Courtesy of Schneider Electric)

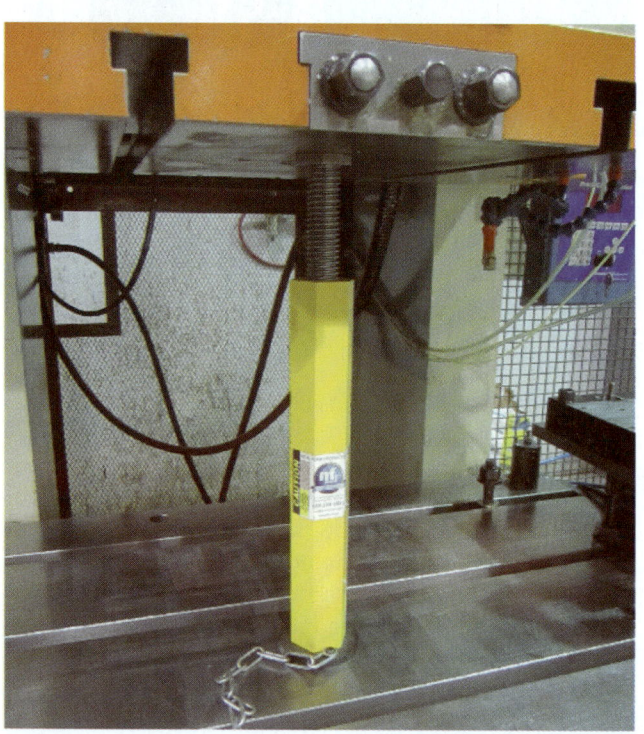

EXHIBIT 120.11

Blocked stored mechanical energy. (Courtesy of Metal form Products Co. Ltd)

(6) Apply lockout/tagout devices in accordance with a documented and established procedure.

Only qualified persons should apply lockout/tagout devices in accordance with the employer's documented and established policy. The lockout device is typically a specifically identified padlock to keep the disconnecting means open and to isolate the equipment from all potentially hazardous energy sources. Tags identify the persons responsible for applying and removing the locks. Exhibit 120.12 shows an employee attaching a lock and tag to the open switch.

Establishing an Electrically Safe Work Condition

120.5(7)

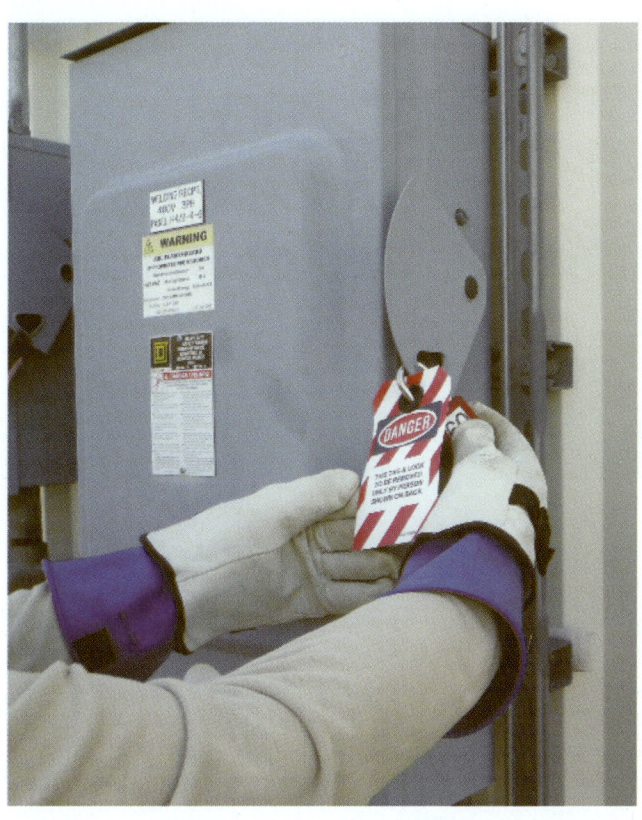

EXHIBIT 120.12

Applying a lock and tag to a switch. (Courtesy of Bobby Gray)

(7) Use an adequately rated portable test instrument to test each phase conductor or circuit part to verify it is de-energized. Test each phase conductor or circuit part both phase-to-phase and phase-to-ground. Before and after each test, determine that the test instrument is operating satisfactorily through verification on any known voltage source.

> In each instance, the qualified person must determine the absence of voltage on each conductor to which the person could be exposed. That determination must be made by measuring the voltage to ground and the voltage between all other conductors using a voltage detector rated for the maximum voltage available from any potential source of energy. In an abnormal situation where there is no connection to earth, the test instrument might indicate an absence of voltage to ground and thereby indicate that the equipment ground path needs to be re-established.
>
> The test instrument should be selected on the basis of the service and duty. The rating of the device must be at least as great as the expected voltage and for the transient voltage expected at the test point. Categories also define where on the electrical system distribution system the test instrument may be used. See the commentary following Item (3) to 110.4(B) for test instrument ratings.
>
> The three-step testing procedure is shown in Exhibit 120.13. First, the test instrument is used to test a known source to verify that the tester is operating properly, as shown in part (a). Then the test instrument is used to confirm that the equipment to be de-energized has zero voltage, as shown in part (b). The tester is used again in part (c) to test a known source to confirm that the test instrument has not failed during the testing process.

Worker Alert

A person in charge may be assigned certain responsibilities in establishing an electrically safe work condition. If you are an exposed worker, you must be involved in the lockout/tagout process. You may want to double-check for a de-energized state when working on equipment.

EXHIBIT 120.13

Lack of voltage verification procedure.

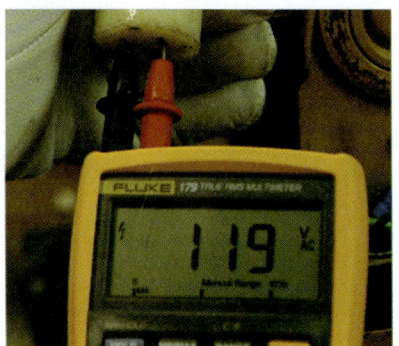

(a)

(b)

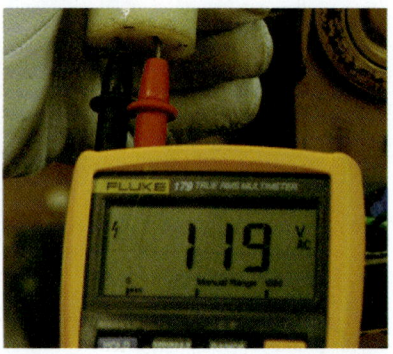

(c)

Exception No. 1: An adequately rated permanently mounted test device shall be permitted to be used to verify the absence of voltage of the conductors or circuit parts at the work location, provided it meets the all following requirements: (1) It is permanently mounted and installed in accordance with the manufacturer's instructions and tests the conductors and circuit parts at the point of work; (2) It is listed and labeled for the purpose of verifying the absence of voltage; (3) It tests each phase conductor or circuit part both phase-to-phase and phase-to-ground; (4) The test device is verified as operating satisfactorily on any known voltage source before and after verifying the absence of voltage.

Typically measurement devices indicate when voltage is present, but lack of indicating a voltage does not guarantee the equipment has been de-energized. For this reason, these mounted devices are designed to run internal diagnostics, verify operation on a known voltage source, confirm contact with the circuit, and verify the lack of voltage. These measurement devices do not use equipment voltage to verify the operation of the device. A secondary test source is available to perform this function. The device will then actively indicate the lack of voltage. See Exhibit 120.14 for an installed absence of voltage tester indicating that equipment is de-energized. Absence of voltage testing equipment for fixed installations is listed to UL 1436, *Standard for Outlet Circuit Testers and Similar Indicating Devices*.

Exception No. 2: On electrical systems over 1000 volts, noncontact test instruments shall be permitted to be used to test each phase conductor.

Informational Note No. 1: See UL 61010-1, *Safety Requirements for Electrical Equipment for Measurement, Control, and Laboratory Use, Part 1: General Requirements*, for rating, overvoltage category, and design requirements for voltage measurement and test instruments intended for use on electrical systems 1000 volts and below.

Informational Note No. 2: For additional information on rating and design requirements for voltage detectors, refer to IEC 61243-1, *Live Working — Voltage Detectors — Part 1: Capacitive type to be used for voltages exceeding 1kV a.c.*, or IEC 61243-2, *Live Working — Voltage Detectors — Part 2: Resistive type to be used for voltages of 1kV to 36 kV a.c.*, or IEC 61243-3, *Live Working — Voltage Detectors — Part 3: Two-pole low voltage type*.

Establishing an Electrically Safe Work Condition

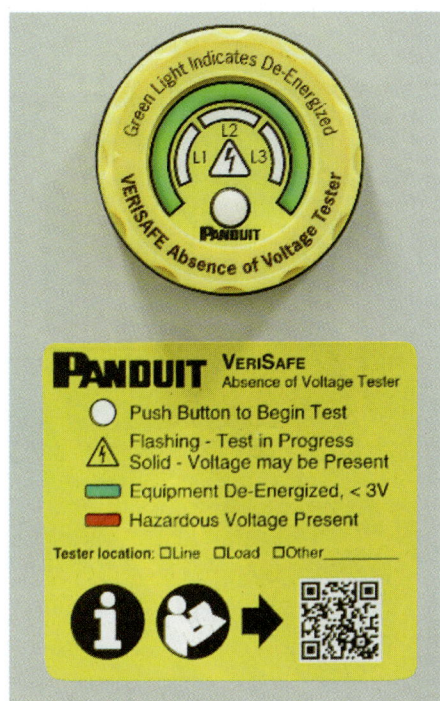

EXHIBIT 120.14

*Absence of voltage tester.
(Courtesy of Panduit Corp.)*

(8) Where the possibility of induced voltages or stored electrical energy exists, ground the phase conductors or circuit parts before touching them. Where it could be reasonably anticipated that the conductors or circuit parts being de-energized could contact other exposed energized conductors or circuit parts, apply temporary protective grounding equipment in accordance with the following:

> The purpose of temporary grounding is to provide protection against electrical shock to personnel while working on de-energized circuits. Temporary protective grounds are critical safety devices used to create a circuit path so that the circuit overcurrent protective device can operate upon accidental energizing of the circuit. De-energized circuits could be accidentally energized from many energy sources, including human error (such as switching errors), equipment failure, mechanical failure, stored charges from capacitors, static buildup, or induced voltage feedback from adjacent circuits. Exhibit 120.15 shows a 3-phase system with temporary grounding installed.
>
> Energized conductors and equipment in high-voltage installations can induce hazardous voltages in adjacent conductors and equipment that are de-energized. Failure of a conductor support system or conductor can result in the inadvertent re-energizing of a de-energized conductor. For instance, more than one outside overhead line might be installed on a single pole and when the conductor supported at a higher elevation is damaged, it could fall onto a lower installed conductor and re-energize the lower conductor.
>
> Protective grounding equipment is necessary to protect employees from a potentially hazardous voltage, such as that caused by the following accidental instances:
>
> - A long conductor installed in proximity to the de-energized conductor could induce a hazardous voltage onto the otherwise de-energized conductor (magnetic coupling).
> - An employee inadvertently connecting a conductor that is not locked out can add a source of energy and re-energize the circuit under repair.
> - Other situations that could reintroduce voltage to a conductor under repair could be identified by the risk assessment procedure.

Worker Alert

Applying temporary protective grounding equipment is the last step in establishing an electrically safe work condition (ESWC). You are required to use PPE for all steps of establishing the ESWC. Temporary grounding is not necessary for all ESWC.

EXHIBIT 120.15

Installed temporary grounding system. (Courtesy of Eaton)

> **Worker Alert**
>
> Temporary protective grounding equipment must be capable of conducting the maximum available fault current and to facilitate the operation of the protective device. You must make sure that personal protective ground equipment components, such as cables that are not properly sized or connectors that are not designed for the connection, are not used.

a. *Placement.* Temporary protective grounding equipment shall be placed at such locations and arranged in such a manner as to prevent each employee from being exposed to a shock hazard (i.e., hazardous differences in electrical potential). The location, sizing, and application of temporary protective grounding equipment shall be identified as part of the employer's job planning.

> Employees must fully understand the system and the equipment to be worked on to select the appropriate temporary protective grounding device(s) and to determine their placement. The protective grounding device must be installed on the conductor at a point between the person and the source of energy. Care must be taken to properly locate the conductors so that the movement of the conductors from mechanical forces does not cause harm to the employee. Equipment grounding conductors or equipment grounding terminals are a likely point of attachment for temporary protective grounding equipment. If the unexpected source of electricity could be from both directions in the electrical circuit, temporary protective grounding equipment must be installed on both sides of the employee.
>
> Employees who work within the area of the dc bus for a battery system must be trained to understand the unique hazards associated with ungrounded dc voltage. Normally the dc voltage is ungrounded. Although in normal settings an equipment grounding conductor decreases exposure to an electrical hazard, in cell areas any conductor that is grounded increases exposure to an electrical hazard. See the informational note for 320.3(C)(1), which describes four grounding schemes employed in battery systems.

b. *Capacity.* Temporary protective grounding equipment shall be capable of conducting the maximum fault current that could flow at the point of grounding for the time necessary to clear the fault.

Establishing an Electrically Safe Work Condition

120.5(2)(3)

Grounding devices are available in many forms; the clamp and cable types are most commonly used. Some equipment manufacturers provide grounding devices for switchgear, which are built on a frame for inserting into a space or cubicle that normally holds a circuit breaker or fusible switch. Exhibit 120.16 shows a typical set of safety grounds.

EXHIBIT 120.16

A safety-grounding assembly. (Courtesy of Salisbury by Honeywell)

Temporary safety grounding equipment must also be capable of withstanding the high mechanical stress imposed when conducting fault current. The equipment must have a rating established by the manufacturer, and it must be applied within that rating. Selecting the appropriate temporary grounding device with an established fault-duty rating for the circuit is paramount. Inadequately rated protective grounding equipment can introduce a hazard that otherwise would not exist.

Informational Note: ASTM F855, *Standard Specification for Temporary Protective Grounds to be Used on De-energized Electric Power Lines and Equipment*, is an example of a standard that contains information on capacity of temporary protective grounding equipment.

The employer is responsible for providing equipment capable of protecting the employee who is put at risk of an injury during energized work. The employer must verify that issued temporary protective grounding equipment meets the appropriate consensus standard. See 130.7(C)(14)(b) and associated commentary regarding equipment compliance. An employer may not be competent in determining that purchased equipment complies with the standard. Often, in order to facilitate acceptance of the equipment, listed equipment is employed even when a standard, such as NFPA *70E,* does not require listing.

   c. *Impedance.* Temporary protective grounding equipment and connections shall have an impedance low enough to cause immediate operation of protective devices in case of unintentional energizing of the electric conductors or circuit parts.

The objective of temporary protective grounding is to create a circuit path so that the overcurrent protective device can operate upon accidental energizing of the conductor that has been temporarily grounded.

The impedance of the ground-fault current return path through earth should be verified on a frequency determined through use. If the impedance of the ground-fault return path is high, the overcurrent device is likely to not operate or might not operate rapidly enough to protect the employee and limit damage to the equipment. Therefore, creating a path for ground-fault return current other than through the earth is necessary to achieve the immediate overcurrent device operation upon accidental energizing of conductors or of equipment that is being worked on by personnel.

Cable size, cable length, and proper attachment of temporary protective grounding equipment are all important factors to be considered in creating a low impedance path. Cables must be of adequate length for the task but should not interfere with the worker within the defined boundary of the work area. Excessive cable length could increase cable impedance and employee exposure when conducting fault current and should be avoided to reduce possible injury due to cable whipping action from high fault currents.

Case Study 120.5

Scenario

Nathan was employed by an electrical contractor (contract employer) and had been working at a wastewater treatment plant for 6 weeks, installing and testing high-voltage equipment. One seemingly routine task was to install new relays on the door of a 13,800-volt switchgear cubicle. As he prepared to install the relays on a door of the new equipment, Nathan assembled his tools and opened (disconnected) the main high-voltage switch. The procedure called for him to perform a visual inspection of the switch blades to ensure they had opened properly, but he was interrupted by Dave, the general contractor. Dave was upset that the relays hadn't already been mounted, and he instructed Nathan to finish this job as soon as possible.

Had Nathan remembered to inspect the switch, he would have discovered that one blade of the three-phase switch had failed to open. Nathan didn't have a functioning tester suitable for this level of voltage. Without it, he had no way to determine if the load side of the switch was de-energized. To mount the relays, Nathan had to drill several holes in the cabinet door. As Nathan stretched into the cabinet to plug in the drill, his right leg got close enough to the 13,800-volt bus for the electricity to jump the air gap and enter his leg. This developed into an arc flash. The extreme temperatures at the arc terminals vaporized the bus material and propagated into a huge fireball and arc blast.

Result

This arc flash event lasted only 4 milliseconds, yet it ignited Nathan's clothes, resulting in third-degree burns over 40 percent of his body. Nathan was wearing a polyester shirt which fused into his skin. He was also wearing a large metal belt buckle, a plastic watch, and his wedding ring. During the incident, the belt buckle burned a hole in his stomach, the watch melted into his wrist, and the wedding ring nearly severed his finger. He was transported to a burn unit, where he began his battle for survival. At the burn center, he underwent several months of excruciatingly painful treatments and skin grafts necessary to recover from his severe burn injuries. Nathan did not return to work as an electrician.

Analysis

Nathan's injuries could have been prevented if an electrically safe work condition (ESWC) had been established. Additionally, if barricades had been set up and the general contractor (unqualified person) was kept out of the work area, Nathan would not have been distracted from verifying that the disconnecting device was fully opened and all phases had been disconnected.

There was no indication whether Nathan had worn appropriate shock and arc-rated PPE for establishing the ESWC. Although Nathan assumed that the equipment he was working on was de-energized, the fact that he was wearing conductive objects exacerbated his injuries. In accordance with 130.6(D), wearing of jewelry and other conductive articles is prohibited where there is a potential for electrical contact with exposed energized conductors or circuit parts.

Likely cause of incident

There are two possible situations that could have occurred during this incident. The first is the assumption that Nathan was qualified for the task of establishing an ESWC for the specific equipment. However, if he were qualified he would have verified the ESWC before removing the necessary PPE, if he had indeed been wearing it prior to the incident. He would have had the proper test equipment for verification of the lack of voltage. He would have had the awareness and self-discipline required by 110.1(D) to not be distracted by the general contractor.

The second and more likely situation is that Nathan was unqualified for the task and that he considered the task routine and not worth the time to follow all necessary procedures. A worker with this mindset often will consider the use of PPE to be a burden at the cost of suffering injuries just as Nathan had. In either situation, Nathan decided not to don the PPE that provided the last chance to prevent the injury he suffered.

Work Involving Electrical Hazards

Article 130

While Article 120 describes the process of creating an electrically safe work condition (ESWC), Article 130 defines the situations under which an ESWC must be established. Work that is performed on exposed energized electrical conductors or circuit parts is dangerous. NFPA *70E* and the OSHA regulations require that, first and foremost, employees must work with equipment de-energized and in an ESWC unless operated under a normal condition. Therefore, the primary protective strategy must be to establish an ESWC. After this strategy is executed, all electrical energy has been removed from all conductors and circuit parts to which the employee could be exposed. Section 130.2(A) explains the limited situations under which energized electrical work may be justified.

△ **130.1 General.** Article 130 covers the following:

(1) When an electrically safe work condition must be established
(2) Requirements for work involving electrical hazards such as the electrical safety-related work practices, assessments, precautions, and procedures when an electrically safe work condition cannot be established

All requirements of this article shall apply whether an incident energy analysis is completed or if Table 130.7(C)(15)(a), Table 130.7(C)(15)(b), and Table 130.7(C)(15)(c) are used in lieu of an incident energy analysis.

Energized electrical conductors and circuit parts must be put into an electrically safe work condition (ESWC) before an employee performs work within the limited approach boundary or interacts with equipment where an increased likelihood of injury from an exposure to an arc flash hazard exists. An ESWC is established when the electrical conductors or circuit parts have been disconnected from energized parts, locked out/tagged out in accordance with established standards, tested to ensure the absence of voltage, and grounded if determined necessary. An ESWC does not exist until all eight steps of 120.5 have been completed.

Under both NFPA *70E* and OSHA, work is required to be performed in a verified de-energized state (ESWC) unless energized work can be justified. There are only three conditions given in 130.2(A) under which energized work is permitted. Normal operation of most equipment does not meet the definition of the term *working on* as defined in Article 100. Normal operation [see 130.2(A)(4)] of equipment is not expected to place an employee at an inherent risk of injury.

There are two methods for conducting an arc flash risk assessment when energized electrical equipment is involved. The arc flash PPE categories method uses the tables within NFPA *70E*. The incident energy level method consists of a variety of possible calculation approaches. Regardless of the method selected, the requirements of Article 130 apply, including the requirement that an ESWC be the primary method of establishing a safe work environment for employees.

130.2 Electrically Safe Work Conditions. Energized electrical conductors and circuit parts operating at voltages equal to or greater than 50 volts shall be put into an electrically safe work condition before an employee performs work if any of the following conditions exist:

(1) The employee is within the limited approach boundary.
(2) The employee interacts with equipment where conductors or circuit parts are not exposed but an increased likelihood of injury from an exposure to an arc flash hazard exists.

Worker Alert

When there is potential for you to be injured by electricity, the primary work practice must be to shut the equipment off. Under certain conditions (such as a damp environment or lacerated skin on your hands), shock or electrocution can occur at values below 50 volts.

Case Study

Scenario

Mark, an electrician, and John, a helper with no formal electrical training, were installing a new three-phase circuit between an existing, energized 480-volt panelboard and a new piece of machinery. Mark used protective insulating gloves with leather protectors but did not use any other PPE. During the process, Mark attempted to install a missing bolt from a circuit breaker mount onto an energized busbar. He lost control of the bolt while attempting to screw it into place. Either the bolt or the mount then contacted another busbar phase, resulting in an arc flash. John was standing some distance away when the incident happened and was uninjured. John was able to find the facility owner and demonstrate what had happened with the arc flash incident involving Mark. During that time, a second electrical arc flash occurred at the panelboard, the cause of which is unknown. The facility owner was standing some distance away and was not hurt.

Result

Mark temporarily lost his sight and received first- and second-degree burns to his head, face, and forearm. John was also not wearing any PPE at the time of his incident. He received second-degree burns to his head, face, neck, arm, and hand. The nylon jacket he was wearing caught fire and melted to his skin causing third-degree burns. John required surgery for removal of destroyed skin and restorative skin grafts. John did not return to work.

Analysis

Accidents typically occur due to a chain of events or mistakes that lead up to the actual event. If one of the links in the chain of events is eliminated, the accident most likely would not have happened.

There are no facts presented to suggest either that it was infeasible or that a greater hazard or increased risk would have been created if the power to the panelboard had been turned off to establish an electrically safe work condition (ESWC). The facts suggest that Mark and John were unqualified for the task they were assigned. If an ESWC had been established prior to the attempted replacement of the missing bolt from the circuit breaker, this incident would not have occurred.

Justified energized work does not prevent an incident from occurring or prevent equipment damage. Even if the task were properly justified, an incident such as this might still have occurred, albeit with a less severe injury to Mark who would have had appropriate protection from all electrical hazards.

Relevant NFPA *70E* Requirements

If the company that Mark and John worked for had followed the requirements of NFPA *70E*, they might not have been injured. The employer ignored the following primary safety principles:

- Create an electrical safety program [110.1].
- Establish an electrically safe work condition [130.2].
- Properly justify energized work [130.2(A)].

If it could have been demonstrated that working within the energized equipment was justified, the employer should have done the following:

- Considered the possibility of human error [110.1(H)(2)]
- Conducted a shock risk assessment [130.4]
- Conducted an arc flash risk assessment [130.5]
- Created an energized electrical work permit [130.2(B)]

Mark and John also hold some responsibility for the incident. As employees they should have been aware of their responsibilities under NFPA *70E*. In addition to the requirements listed above, they should have been aware of the following:

- Their ability to meet the definition of a qualified person [100]
- Their need for awareness and self-discipline [110.1(D)]
- The training they should have received [110.2]

Under both NFPA *70E* and OSHA, work is required to be performed in an electrically safe work condition (ESWC) unless energized work can be justified. If an employee is within the limited approach boundary or interacts with energized electrical equipment, conductors, or circuit parts in such a manner that there is a likelihood of injury from exposure to a potential arc flash event, the primary method of protection must be that energized conductors and circuit parts are put into an ESWC. The requirements for creating an ESWC are found in Article 120. The act of creating an ESWC uses the risk controls of administration and elimination from the hierarchy of risk controls. Elimination is considered the most effective form of risk control available.

The boundary for establishing an ESWC is the limited approach boundary. However, the point at which an energized electrical work permit is required is the restricted approach boundary or when there is a potential exposure to an arc flash. Note that the ESWC is required to be established based on a shock protection boundary. This is not dependent upon the potential for arc flash to occur. Unless energized work is justified,

Work Involving Electrical Hazards 130.2(A)(2)

it is not permitted to expose an employee to a shock hazard regardless of the ability to use PPE.

The phrase "interacting with the equipment" could involve opening or closing a disconnecting means or pushing a reset button. However, if equipment is installed in accordance with the requirements of NFPA 70®, National Electrical Code® (NEC®), and the manufacturer's instructions, and it is properly maintained and operated normally, the chance of one of these actions initiating an arcing fault is remote. Normal operation of equipment involves interacting with the equipment, but for most equipment this does not meet the definition of working on as defined in Article 100. Normal operation [see 130.2(A)(4)] of equipment is not expected to place an employee at an inherent risk of injury. An arc flash hazard is more likely to exist where a circuit breaker is racked in or out of switchgear, or where the equipment does not meet the normal operating conditions stated in 130.2(A)(4).

Properly protecting employees from electrical hazards requires more than using the various tables within NFPA 70E. Many factors must be considered and many requirements applied before an employee is put at risk of an injury. The flow chart in Exhibit 130.1 illustrates a sample of the necessary thought process. Exhibit 130.1 does not absolve users of their responsibility to read, understand, and properly apply the requirements.

(A) Energized Work.

(1) Additional Hazards or Increased Risk. Energized work shall be permitted where the employer can demonstrate that de-energizing introduces additional hazards or increased risk.

> Informational Note: Examples of additional hazards or increased risk include, but are not limited to, interruption of life-support equipment, deactivation of emergency alarm systems, and shutdown of hazardous location ventilation equipment.

The additional hazards do not have to be electrical hazards, and the increased risk does not have to be from electrical hazards. Hazards can include chemical, mechanical, or environmental hazards — such as those associated with chemical plants, refineries, or ethanol production facilities.

The requirements in Article 130 intend to protect employees when energized electrical work is justified. Protecting an employee does not prevent an incident from occurring, nor does it prevent damage to the equipment if an incident does occur. Before authorizing energized work with the justification of a greater hazard, consideration should be given to the result of an incident that may occur. Not only would equipment failure present the greater hazard, but the equipment could be inoperable for a considerably longer time than during a scheduled outage. If the greater hazard would not be presented immediately upon equipment failure, the work may be able to be conducted in an electrically safe work condition before the greater hazard presents itself.

For example, the proposed justification may be that life support equipment must be worked on while energized. There must be an alternate plan if an incident does occur during repair and the equipment is rendered inoperative. How will life support be maintained when such an event occurs? Another example is a hazardous area ventilation system that may depend on the continuity of electrical power. However, temporary ventilation may be available. Often, the alternate plan provides the reasoning and ability to conduct the work de-energized.

(2) Infeasibility. Energized work shall be permitted where the employer can demonstrate that the task to be performed is infeasible in a de-energized state due to equipment design or operational limitations.

> **OSHA Connection**
>
> **29 CFR 1910.333(a)(1)**
>
> Live parts must be de-energized before the employee works on or near them. Energized work requires the employer to demonstrate that de-energizing introduces additional or increased hazards or is infeasible due to equipment design or operational limitations. Live parts that operate at less than 50 volts to ground must be evaluated to determine if there is an increased exposure to electrical burns or to explosion due to electric arcs.

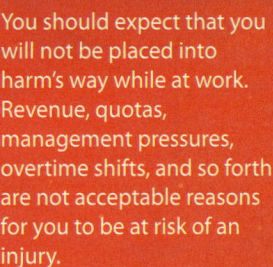

> **Worker Alert**
>
> You should expect that you will not be placed into harm's way while at work. Revenue, quotas, management pressures, overtime shifts, and so forth are not acceptable reasons for you to be at risk of an injury.

EXHIBIT 130.1

A sample thought process flow chart for conducting electrical work.

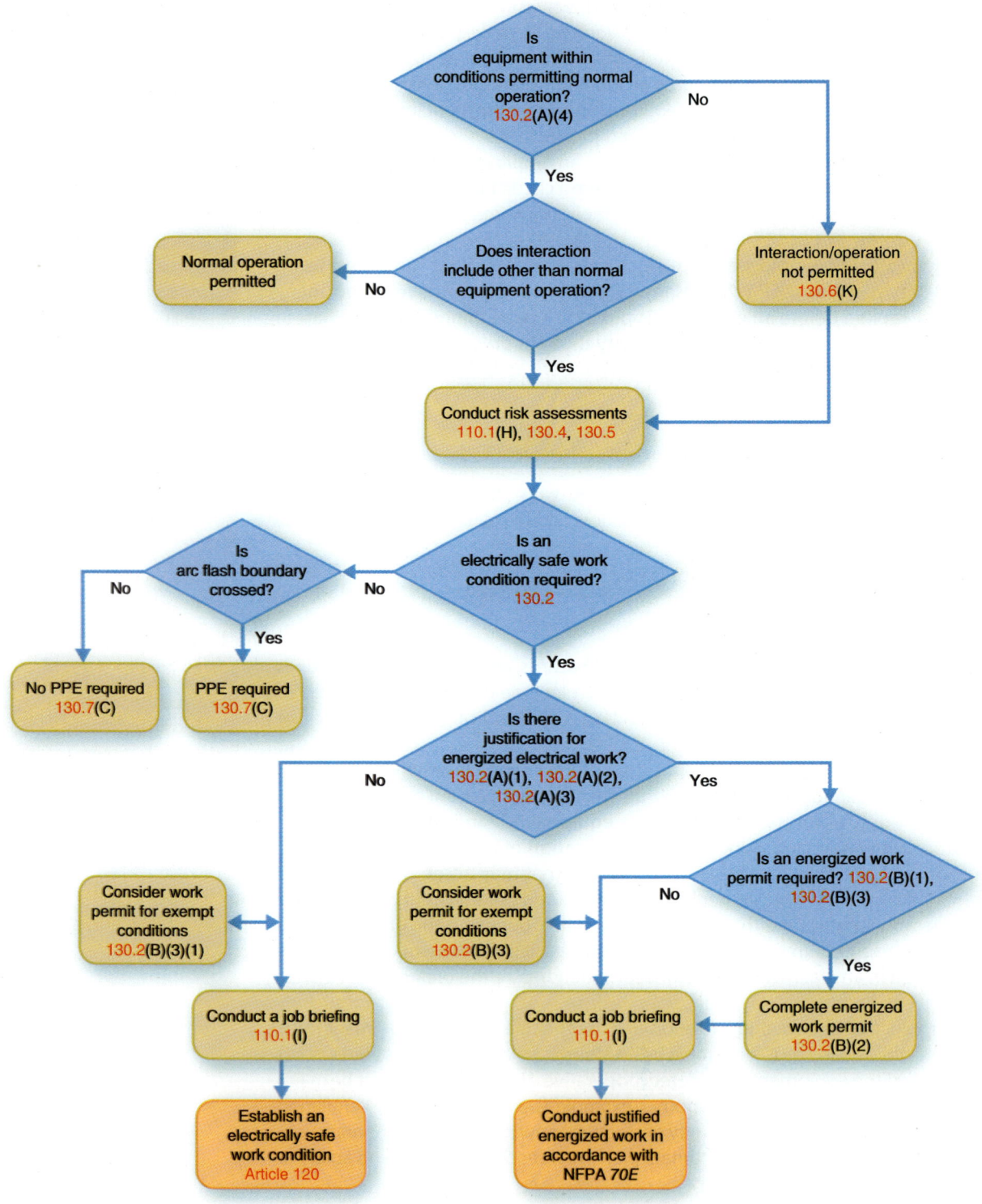

Work Involving Electrical Hazards

130.2(A)(3)

Informational Note: Examples of work that might be performed within the limited approach boundary of exposed energized electrical conductors or circuit parts because of infeasibility due to equipment design or operational limitations include performing diagnostics and testing (for example, start-up or troubleshooting) of electric circuits that can only be performed with the circuit energized and work on circuits that form an integral part of a continuous process that would otherwise need to be completely shut down in order to permit work on one circuit or piece of equipment.

Infeasible does not mean impractical. That it is infeasible to establish an electrically safe work condition is most often determined by the task to be performed, not the equipment being worked on. In many situations, due to equipment design limitations, diagnostic work such as voltage or temperature measurement, troubleshooting, and testing of electrical equipment is infeasible to perform without the employee being exposed to energized conductors and circuit parts. With the advent of remote programming and monitoring ports, however, what was considered to be infeasible may have changed. If it is feasible to install a remote programming port to program a motor control center bucket electronic overload relay, opening the door and exposing an employee to energized electrical conductors and circuit parts may no longer be justified.

What is considered infeasible for older designed equipment may not be infeasible for newly designed equipment. With the advent of remote racking systems, it may no longer be feasible for the employee to be in front of or even within the room where justified energized work involves replacing a circuit breaker in switchgear.

(3) Equipment Operating at Less Than 50 Volts. Energized electrical conductors and circuit parts that operate at less than 50 volts shall not be required to be de-energized where the capacity of the source and any overcurrent protection between the energy source and the worker are considered and it is determined that there will be no increased exposure to electrical burns or to explosion due to electric arcs.

This justification for energized work essentially addresses only shock to the employee. Under normal conditions, electrical conductors energized at a voltage less than 50 volts do not present an electrical shock hazard. This allowance does not apply to any system operating at 50 volts or less without first considering if there is a risk of exposure to electrical burns or to explosions from electrical arcs. If there is a potential for arc flash or thermal burn to occur, working on the energized low voltage circuit is not permitted unless justified through the allowance of 130.2(A)(1) or (A)(2).

A thermal hazard can exist in circuits that have a significant capacity to deliver energy, even when the voltage level is less than 50 volts. For instance, battery installations can be connected so that an arc resulting from a short circuit could present a significant thermal hazard. Burn injuries from the use of electricity can be one of the three types that follow:

- An electrical burn that occurs when sufficient electrical current flows through the body
- A thermal burn that results from the skin touching a hot surface or contacting clothing that has caught fire
- An arc flash burn from the radiation from an arc flash event

An arc flash event could occur provided there is a large enough battery (even if less than 50 volts) or as a result of discharge from a capacitor. If an uninsulated wrench is left across the terminals of a 12-volt battery for an extended period of time, it can become red hot and can easily burn skin if touched without appropriate protection.

Many control circuits operate at a voltage level less than 50 volts. Creating an open circuit or short circuit in one of these control circuits could result in a different type of hazard. An interruption or other unintended action within an industrial process can result in exposure to a chemical hazard or creation of an unacceptable environmental condition.

> **OSHA Connection**
>
> 29 CFR 1910.303(b)(1)
>
> Electric equipment must be free from recognized hazards that are likely to cause death or serious physical harm to employees. OSHA noted that industry consensus standards may "recognize" a hazard and indicate that there is a feasible means of correcting such a hazard.

Δ **(4) Normal Operating Condition.** Normal operation of electric equipment shall be permitted where a normal operating condition exists. A normal operating condition exists when all of the following conditions are satisfied:

Normal operation of equipment involves interacting with the equipment, but for most equipment this does not meet the definition of *working on* as defined in Article 100. If equipment meets all of these criteria, there is no reason to assume that it is inherently unsafe. When equipment is considered to be operating normally or the employee is operating that equipment, the risk associated with normal operation is generally considered to be acceptable. Normal operation of equipment is typically conducted by someone other than a qualified person under NFPA *70E*.

These normal operating conditions apply to the normal operation of the equipment for its intended function. For example, normal operation does not include the installation or removal of a circuit breaker. Neither of these is considered the normal operation of that circuit breaker for its intended purpose of overcurrent protection. Closed door racking of a breaker may not adequately protect the employee. PPE for the maximum possible hazard must be used during the operation. Remote racking is a protective technique that can be used to keep the employee outside the arc flash boundary.

(1) The equipment is properly installed.

Much of the equipment that falls under the purview of NFPA *70E* does not have a governmental electrical inspector verifying that the installation complies with applicable codes, standards, and instructions. Equipment is often installed by an employee or an outside contractor with no governmental oversight. Without proper installation, the equipment cannot be depended on to operate correctly or to perform its required safety functions.

The employer/owner must determine how to enforce and determine compliance with the *NEC* for equipment installed under these circumstances. The employer/owner must make sure that all equipment is properly installed. If not, the employee is being put at risk of an injury when normal operation of that equipment is attempted.

(2) The equipment is properly maintained.

At the time it was properly installed, equipment was in a new condition and everything was expected to be in order. Since that point in time, the equipment will slowly begin to show signs of wear and tear. Motors, circuit breakers, and even transformers are not pieces of equipment that should be ignored. They require maintenance. Most manufacturers will provide recommendations on what is minimally required to maintain their equipment. Some industries provide guidance on maintenance. NFPA 70B, *Recommended Practice for Electrical Equipment Maintenance*, contains a wealth of information on the subject.

Work Involving Electrical Hazards

130.2(A)(4)

> Proper maintenance is not just the act of fixing, adjusting, or filling fluids. There is a time aspect that is just as important. A piece of equipment may only need proper maintenance every year or two in one installation. That same piece of equipment in another installation may require monthly maintenance to be considered properly maintained. The employer/owner must make sure that any equipment is properly maintained. If not, the employee is being put at risk of an injury when normal operation of that equipment is attempted.

(3) The equipment is used in accordance with instructions included in the listing and labeling and in accordance with manufacturer's instructions.

> For employees to safely interact with equipment, they must understand the conditions, methods, functions, and sequences for safely operating the equipment. Equipment is supplied with its manufacturer's operating instructions. If the equipment is listed, these instructions typically include the specifics necessary to operate the equipment within the parameters of that listing. Operating equipment contrary to these instructions puts the employee at risk of an injury when operation of that equipment is attempted.

(4) The equipment doors are closed and secured.

> This requirement demands some judgment by the employee at the time of equipment operation. A panelboard hinged door is meant to be opened for someone to gain access for the normal operation of an HID circuit breaker. This is different from an access door that is intended to be closed and secured during operation of a transformer. This differentiation requires proper training of the employee interacting with the equipment. If the inappropriate door is open, the employee is at risk of an injury when normal operation of that equipment is attempted.

(5) All equipment covers are in place and secured.

> This requirement demands some judgment by the employee at the time of equipment operation. The bolted cover, to which the hinged access door for a panelboard is attached, is intended to stay in place when operating the breaker. This requires proper training of the employee interacting with the equipment. If the covers are absent or unsecured, the employee is at risk of an injury when normal operation of that equipment is attempted.

(6) There is no evidence of impending failure.

> Informational Note: The phrase *properly installed* means that the equipment is installed in accordance with applicable industry codes and standards and the manufacturer's recommendations. The phrase *properly maintained* means that the equipment has been maintained in accordance with the manufacturer's recommendations and applicable industry codes and standards. The phrase *evidence of impending failure* means that there is evidence such as arcing, overheating, loose or bound equipment parts, visible damage, or deterioration.

> Typically the employer/owner is not aware of the daily condition of equipment in the facility. The burden of determining the condition of the equipment is often the responsibility of the employee interacting with the equipment, since conditions can change on a daily basis. This involves training that employee to understand the potential failure

modes and to identify signs of the impending failure of the equipment. These signs vary greatly by the type of electrical equipment. The smell of ozone, presence of smoke, sound of arcing, visible damage, or warning lights are all possible indications of potential equipment failure. There also may be some unusual cases that are undetectable, such as rodents or snakes getting into equipment through unsealed openings. If any of these signs are present, the employee is potentially at risk of an injury when normal operation of that equipment is attempted.

(B) Energized Electrical Work Permit.

Employers are required to provide procedures that prevent injury to employees. Work that does not take place within an electrically safe work condition always exposes employees to potential injury.

No matter how simple the task, there is no such thing as routine work where electrical safety is involved. NFPA *70E* does not specifically prohibit issuing an energized electrical work permit for simple or repetitive tasks. However, before issuing this type of open permit, due consideration must be given to the fact that no energized work should be considered as "routine" work. A simple task may not be routine if performed on different equipment. Conducting a task repeatedly may not be routine after an extended work shift. Repetitive work may not be routine work, even if the employee is trained to understand the risk associated with exposure to the potential electrical hazards that can be involved and is wearing appropriate PPE, as situations can easily change.

△ **(1) When Required.** When work is performed as permitted in accordance with 130.2(A), an energized electrical work permit shall be required and documented under the any of following conditions:

(1) When work is performed within the restricted approach boundary
(2) When the employee interacts with the equipment when conductors or circuit parts are not exposed but an increased likelihood of injury from an exposure to an arc flash hazard exists

The phrase "interacting with the equipment" could involve opening or closing a disconnecting means or pushing a reset button. However, if equipment is installed in accordance with the requirements of the *NEC* and the manufacturer's instructions, and it is properly maintained and operated normally, the chance of one of these actions initiating an arcing fault is remote. An arc flash hazard is more likely to exist when equipment is operated when not under normal operating conditions or when not operated normally, such as when a circuit breaker is racked in or out of switchgear.

Once energized electrical work is properly justified, the hierarchy of risk controls has been employed, and the justified work can safely be conducted, the basic purpose of the energized electrical work permit (EEWP) is to ensure that people in responsible positions are involved in the decision whether or not to accept the increased risk associated with working on energized electrical conductors or circuit parts. An additional benefit of the EEWP is that its review might initiate a decision to perform the work de-energized.

It is good practice to consider the use of an EEWP even when one is not required. This demonstrates that proper consideration was given to all aspects required to protect an employee when diagnostic work is being done.

Work Involving Electrical Hazards 130.2(B)(3)

△ **(2) Elements of Work Permit.** The work permit shall include, but not be limited to, the following items:

(1) Description of the circuit and equipment to be worked on and their location
(2) Description of the work to be performed
(3) Justification for why the work must be performed in an energized condition [see 130.2(A)]
(4) Description of the safe work practices to be employed (see 130.3)
(5) Results of the shock risk assessment [see 130.4(A)]
   a. Voltage to which personnel will be exposed
   b. Limited approach boundary [see 130.4(E), Table 130.4(D)(a), and Table 130.4(D)(b)]
   c. Restricted approach boundary [see 130.4(F), Table 130.4(D)(a), and Table 130.4(D)(b)]
   d. Personal and other protective equipment required by this standard to safely perform the assigned task and to protect against the shock hazard [see 130.4(E), 130.7(C)(1) through (C)(16), and 130.7(D)]
(6) Results of the arc flash risk assessment [see 130.5]
   a. Available incident energy at the working distance or arc flash PPE category (see 130.5)
   b. Personal and other protective equipment required by this standard to protect against the arc flash hazard [see 130.5(F), 130.7(C)(1) through (C)(16), Table 130.7(C)(15)(c), and 130.7(D)]
   c. Arc flash boundary [see 130.5(E)]
(7) Means employed to restrict the access of unqualified persons from the work area [see 130.3]
(8) Evidence of completion of a job briefing, including a discussion of any job-specific hazards [see 110.1(I)]
(9) Energized work approval (authorizing or responsible management, safety officer, or owner, etc.) signature(s)

Informational Note: For an example of an acceptable energized work permit, see Figure J.1.

△ **(3) Exemptions to Work Permit.** Electrical work shall be permitted without an energized electrical work permit if a qualified person is provided with and uses appropriate safe work practices and PPE in accordance with Chapter 1 under any of the following conditions:

(1) Testing, troubleshooting, or voltage measuring
(2) Thermography, ultrasound, or visual inspections if the restricted approach boundary is not crossed
(3) Access to and egress from an area with energized electrical equipment if no electrical work is performed and the restricted approach boundary is not crossed
(4) General housekeeping and miscellaneous non-electrical tasks if the restricted approach boundary is not crossed

> The energized electrical work permit (EEWP) exemptions require that safe work practices be followed and that appropriate PPE be worn, which includes both shock protection PPE and arc flash protection PPE as necessary. It is good practice to use an EEWP even when it is not required. The EEWP will document the task, PPE, and work procedures that are necessary. An employee conducting voltage measurement without an EEWP may notice a loose conductor in a terminal and consider that it may need to be tightened. The use of an EEWP here will remind the employee that the only authorized task is a voltage measurement. Tightening the terminal is a separate task outside the scope of the original EEWP and could put the employee at risk of an injury for a condition that was not considered.

Worker Alert

You should be aware of what is required on an energized electrical work permit. Each item plays a role in protecting you when energized work is justified. You should make sure all items are adequately covered and all gaps filled in prior to beginning any task.

Worker Alert

Although an energized electrical work permit is not required for the conditions listed here, you are still permitted to generate one. You may want a work permit to document what is expected of you and how you will be protected when conducting justified, energized work when testing or troubleshooting or for voltage measurement.

> **OSHA Connection**
>
> **29 CFR 1910.333(c)(9)**
>
> Employees must not perform housekeeping duties at such close distances to live parts that there is a possibility of contact. Adequate safeguards (such as insulating equipment or barriers) must be provided.

Note that 130.2(B)(3)(1) limits the work to be conducted to diagnostic tasks. A work function is diagnostic when it is used to identify the condition of equipment or its parts to assure the condition of the equipment or to identify and eliminate potential problems. This would include the verification of an electrically safe work condition. Should a planned diagnostic task change to a repair task, the work would no longer be considered diagnostic, and an additional or modified EEWP would be required. Troubleshooting does not inherently mean that energized work is justified. A continuity measurement may be an alternative to energized testing.

Note that 130.2(B)(3)(2), (B)(3)(3), and (B)(3)(4) are limited to staying outside the restricted approach boundary. If the boundary is crossed for the performance of any of the tasks, then an EEWP is required.

130.3 Working While Exposed to Electrical Hazards.

The primary protective strategy must be to establish an electrically safe work condition (ESWC), which is a form of the risk control of administration (the use of procedures including lockout/tagout) from the hierarchy of risk controls to achieve elimination of the hazard. [See 110.1(H)(3) and associated commentary regarding the hierarchy of risk controls.] After this strategy is executed, all electrical energy has been removed from all conductors and circuit parts to which the employee could be exposed. After the ESWC has been established, no PPE is required, and unqualified persons are permitted to execute the remainder of the work. The only exception to this requirement is where working on exposed energized electrical conductors or circuit parts can be justified as described under one of the conditions listed 130.2(A).

Employers are required to provide procedures that prevent injury to employees. Work on exposed conductors that does not take place within an ESWC always exposes employees to potential injury. Even with a company policy to place all equipment into an ESWC prior to work, the point where the ESWC is verified is considered to be energized work. Whether that point is for verification of the ESWC or the energized work is justified, a shock risk assessment and an arc flash risk assessment must be conducted. These assessments are independent of each other. Although an arc flash hazard may not be present where all energized work is performed, energized work typically presents a shock hazard.

Equipment that is considered to be operating normally is generally considered safe, barring extremely unusual circumstances. However, when electrical equipment changes state — such as when equipment is switched from energized to de-energized or a circuit breaker is reset or the equipment does not meet the normal operating conditions — the result might be an initiation of an arcing fault. Depending on the state and condition of the equipment and the circuit protective devices, an employee could be exposed to this arcing fault.

Until the ESWC is established, an unacceptable risk of injury exists and employees must continue to wear protective equipment. There is no way to establish an ESWC without some risk of exposure to a potential hazard. Until the employee is certain that no energy is present, it must be assumed that energy is present. With a proper risk assessment and under the conditions that permit normal operation, establishing an ESWC should remove the hazard before the voltage measurement is made. Although establishing an ESWC must be considered energized work, it should not be exposing the employee to an energized circuit. The ESWC voltage measurement should always be zero. The process is in place to protect the employee if something goes wrong. After the ESWC has been established, it is then possible to remove gear worn to protect from electrical hazards. The approach boundaries no longer exist, and other employees in the vicinity are not put at risk.

Work Involving Electrical Hazards

130.3

> This is in contrast to justified, energized work in which the protective gear must be continuously worn when the employee is within the approach boundaries. The PPE must be worn up until the time the equipment has been placed back into a normal operating condition. In performing the task, the employee is constantly at risk of having an incident occur or at the risk of injury. Without an ESWC, the employer is using the PPE to protect the employee from a known and present hazard while energized work is being performed. Anyone entering the arc flash boundary or a shock protection boundary is put at risk and must be protected.

Safety-related work practices shall be used to safeguard employees from injury while they are exposed to electrical hazards from electrical conductors or circuit parts that are or can become energized. The specific safety-related work practices shall be consistent with the electrical hazards and the associated risk. Appropriate safety-related work practices shall be determined before any person is exposed to the electrical hazards involved by using both shock risk assessment and arc flash risk assessment. Only qualified persons shall be permitted to work on electrical conductors or circuit parts that have not been put into an electrically safe work condition.

> Employers are required to provide procedures that prevent injury to employees. Work that is performed on exposed energized electrical conductors or circuit parts is dangerous. Work conducted on electrical systems not in an electrically safe work condition exposes employees to potential injury. It should be presumed that there is an unacceptable risk of injury from shock or thermal hazards — arc flash, electrical burn, or thermal burn — from exposure to energized conductors and circuit parts, unless the required risk assessment finds otherwise. Both a shock risk assessment (130.4) and an arc flash risk assessment (130.5) are required before any person is permitted to approach the exposed energized electrical conductors or circuit parts.
>
> Employees are often reluctant to question a decision by a supervisor that a work task must be conducted while the circuit remains energized. The employer must demonstrate that de-energizing introduces additional hazards or increased risk. Managers and supervisors tend to be hesitant to accept increased risk of exposure to hazards, particularly if their authorization for employees to work on energized equipment has to be in writing.
>
> The risk assessment procedure must determine whether any conductor will remain energized for the duration of the work task. Exhibit 110.2 illustrates various decision branches and requirement cross references for each type of risk assessment. These risk assessments must answer many questions, including the following:
>
> **Justification**
> - Is energized work justified (i.e., does the alternative present a greater hazard, or is it infeasible for task to be performed de-energized)?
> - What authorization is necessary to justify executing the work task while the exposed conductor(s) is (are) energized?
> - Will energized electrical work impact other work?
> - What measures will be taken to minimize the impact of other work?
>
> **Hazards**
> - What is the potential result of equipment failure (i.e., to the employee, equipment, process, environment)?
> - What is the degree of the shock hazard?
> - What is the degree of the arc flash hazard?
> - Are there other electrical hazards?

Worker Alert

You must fully understand the task at hand. You must make sure you are provided with the applicable safe work practices and procedures before justified, energized work is begun. You should not be improvising procedures while you are performing a justified, energized task.

OSHA Connection

29 CFR 1910.333(a)(2)

Exposed live parts that are not de-energized for reasons of increased or additional hazards or infeasibility require the use of other safety-related work practices to protect employees against contact with energized circuit parts directly with any part of their body or indirectly through some other conductive object.

Risk to employee

- Will the employee be exposed to any of the hazards during the work task?
- Is there a risk of injury to the employee?
- Are there situations where the risk of injury is unacceptable?
- Will other employees be exposed to an electrical hazard because of the work task?

Employee involvement

- What employees are required to be within an approach boundary?
- Is the employee assigned to the task qualified for the specific task on the specific equipment?
- Are unqualified employees necessary?
- Are there special considerations due to a host employer-contract employer relationship?

Employee protection

- Have all protection techniques from the hierarchy of risk controls been considered and used if appropriate?
- What protective equipment is necessary to minimize the employee's exposure to each hazard?

130.4 Shock Risk Assessment.

(A) General. A shock risk assessment shall be performed:

(1) To identify shock hazards
(2) To estimate the likelihood of occurrence of injury or damage to health and the potential severity of injury or damage to health
(3) To determine if additional protective measures are required, including the use of PPE

Shock risk assessment is the process that identifies exposure to the potential electrical shock hazards, estimates the potential severity of a shock injury, estimates the likelihood of occurrence of this injury, then determines if protective measures are required and determines the appropriate protective measure to use. The severity of the injury depends on the current flow through the body, the path it takes, and whether the heart is in a vulnerable point in the cardiac cycle. See commentary to 340.4 for more on the effects of electricity on the human body.

As a person's distance to an exposed energized electrical conductor decreases, the risk of direct contact with the conductor increases. When conducting the shock risk assessment, the employee must determine the voltage of all conductors in the vicinity of the employee's body or of the tool that will be used. The shock approach boundaries provide a trigger for added protection for all employees.

N (B) Additional Protective Measures. If additional protective measures are required, they shall be selected and implemented according to the hierarchy of risk control identified in 110.1(H). When the additional protective measures include the use of PPE, the following shall be determined:

(1) The voltage to which personnel will be exposed
(2) The boundary requirements
(3) The personal and other protective equipment required by this standard to protect against the shock hazard

Worker Alert

You should be aware of other available methods that protect you from injury. The use of PPE should be your employer's last selection after all other protection schemes have been used. If you are not aware whether your employer has used any method other than PPE, you may be able to determine alternate ways to minimize your injury when an incident does occur.

Work Involving Electrical Hazards

130.4(D)

The hierarchy of risk controls is used to address shock mitigation techniques. Arc flash mitigation techniques are addressed in 130.5(C). Some techniques will accomplish both goals.

The hierarchy in 110.1(H)(3) is listed in order of the most effective to the least effective and must be applied in descending order for each risk assessment. Once a hazard has been identified, it first must be determined if the hazard can be eliminated. During the electrical system design stage, methods should be employed to eliminate the hazard in its entirety. In the electrical system design and equipment selection phase, it is easier to utilize the most effective controls of elimination and substitution to limit the risk associated with anticipated justified energized work. In this first context, elimination is removal of a hazard so that it never exists. This removes the potential for human error when interacting with the equipment.

Full elimination of the hazard is often not an option for installed equipment. Although elimination can also be achieved by applying other controls such as administration (establishing an electrically safe work condition), these other controls introduce a potential for human error. Only after all other risk controls have been exhausted should PPE be selected. PPE is considered the least effective and lowest level of risk control for employee protection and should not be the first or only control element used.

> **OSHA Connection**
>
> **29 CFR 1910.132(d)(1)**
> The employer must assess the workplace to determine if hazards are present or are likely to be present. If hazards necessitate the use of PPE, the employer must select and have the employee use PPE that properly fits, as well as communicate selection decisions to the affected employee.

N **(C) Documentation.** The results of the shock risk assessment shall be documented.

Δ **(D) Shock Protection Boundaries.** The shock protection boundaries identified as limited approach boundary and restricted approach boundary shall be applicable where personnel are approaching exposed energized electrical conductors or circuit parts. Table 130.4(D)(a) shall be used for the distances associated with various ac system voltages. Table 130.4(D)(b) shall be used for the distances associated with various dc system voltages.

> Informational Note: In certain instances, the arc flash boundary might be a greater distance from the energized electrical conductors or circuit parts than the limited approach boundary. The shock protection boundaries and the arc flash boundary are independent of each other.

> **OSHA Connection**
>
> **29 CFR 1910.132(d)(2)**
> The employer must verify through a written certification that the required workplace risk assessment was performed. The certification must identify the workplace evaluated, the person certifying that the evaluation was performed, and the date(s) of the risk assessment.

The electrical safety program must include a procedure that provides employees with guidance on required protection when the approach distance is less than the appropriate shock protection boundary. Shock approach boundaries are related to direct contact with energized electrical conductors and circuit parts only and do not consider exposure to arc flash.

There are two shock protection boundaries: the limited approach boundary and the restricted approach boundary. The limited approach boundary is the closest approach distance for an unqualified employee, unless additional protective measures are used. The restricted approach boundary is the closest approach distance for a qualified employee, unless additional protective measures are used. The dimension associated with each of these boundaries depends on the maximum voltage to which an employee might be exposed.

The 600-volt class motor control center (MCC) illustrated in Exhibit 130.2 shows the applicable distance for each shock protection boundary based on this operating voltage. If the conductors are placed in an electrically safe work condition, approach boundaries no longer exist and employees can approach the conductor without risk of injury.

N **TABLE 130.4(D)(a)** Shock Protection Approach Boundaries to Exposed Energized Electrical Conductors or Circuit Parts for Alternating-Current Systems

(1)	(2)	(3)	(4)
	Limited Approach Boundary[b]		Restricted Approach Boundary[b]; Includes Inadvertent Movement Adder
Nominal System Voltage Range, Phase to Phase[a]	Exposed Movable Conductor[c]	Exposed Fixed Circuit Part	
Less than 50 V	Not specified	Not specified	Not specified
50 V–150 V[d]	3.0 m (10 ft 0 in.)	1.0 m (3 ft 6 in.)	Avoid contact
151 V–750 V	3.0 m (10 ft 0 in.)	1.0 m (3 ft 6 in.)	0.3 m (1 ft 0 in.)
751 V–15 kV	3.0 m (10 ft 0 in.)	1.5 m (5 ft 0 in.)	0.7 m (2 ft 2 in.)
15.1 kV–36 kV	3.0 m (10 ft 0 in.)	1.8 m (6 ft 0 in.)	0.8 m (2 ft 9 in.)
36.1 kV–46 kV	3.0 m (10 ft 0 in.)	2.5 m (8 ft 0 in.)	0.8 m (2 ft 9 in.)
46.1 kV–72.5 kV	3.0 m (10 ft 0 in.)	2.5 m (8 ft 0 in.)	1.0 m (3 ft 6 in.)
72.6 kV–121 kV	3.3 m (10 ft 8 in.)	2.5 m (8 ft 0 in.)	1.0 m (3 ft 6 in.)
138 kV–145 kV	3.4 m (11 ft 0 in.)	3.0 m (10 ft 0 in.)	1.2 m (3 ft 10 in.)
161 kV–169 kV	3.6 m (11 ft 8 in.)	3.6 m (11 ft 8 in.)	1.3 m (4 ft 3 in.)
230 kV–242 kV	4.0 m (13 ft 0 in.)	4.0 m (13 ft 0 in.)	1.7 m (5 ft 8 in.)
345 kV–362 kV	4.7 m (15 ft 4 in.)	4.7 m (15 ft 4 in.)	2.8 m (9 ft 2 in.)
500 kV–550 kV	5.8 m (19 ft 0 in.)	5.8 m (19 ft 0 in.)	3.6 m (11 ft 8 in.)
765 kV–800 kV	7.2 m (23 ft 9 in.)	7.2 m (23 ft 9 in.)	4.9 m (15 ft 11 in.)

Notes:
(1) For arc flash boundary, see 130.5(A).
(2) All dimensions are distance from exposed energized electrical conductors or circuit part to employee.
[a]For single-phase systems above 250 volts, select the range that is equal to the system's maximum phase-to-ground voltage multiplied by 1.732.
[b]See definition in Article 100 and text in 130.4(D)(2) and Informative Annex C for elaboration.
[c]*Exposed movable conductors* describes a condition in which the distance between the conductor and a person is not under the control of the person. The term is normally applied to overhead line conductors supported by poles.
[d]This includes circuits where the exposure does not exceed 120 volts nominal.

N **TABLE 130.4(D)(b)** Shock Protection Approach Boundaries to Exposed Energized Electrical Conductors or Circuit Parts for Direct-Current Voltage Systems

(1)	(2)	(3)	(4)
	Limited Approach Boundary		Restricted Approach Boundary; Includes Inadvertent Movement Adder
Nominal Potential Difference	Exposed Movable Conductor*	Exposed Fixed Circuit Part	
Less than 50 V	Not specified	Not specified	Not specified
50 V–300 V	3.0 m (10 ft 0 in.)	1.0 m (3 ft 6 in.)	Avoid contact
301 V–1 kV	3.0 m (10 ft 0 in.)	1.0 m (3 ft 6 in.)	0.3 m (1 ft 0 in.)
1.1 kV–5 kV	3.0 m (10 ft 0 in.)	1.5 m (5 ft 0 in.)	0.5 m (1 ft 5 in.)
5 kV–15 kV	3.0 m (10 ft 0 in.)	1.5 m (5 ft 0 in.)	0.7 m (2 ft 2 in.)
15.1 kV–45 kV	3.0 m (10 ft 0 in.)	2.5 m (8 ft 0 in.)	0.8 m (2 ft 9 in.)
45.1 kV–75 kV	3.0 m (10 ft 0 in.)	2.5 m (8 ft 0 in.)	1.0 m (3 ft 6 in.)
75.1 kV–150 kV	3.3 m (10 ft 8 in.)	3.0 m (10 ft 0 in.)	1.2 m (3 ft 10 in.)
150.1 kV–250 kV	3.6 m (11 ft 8 in.)	3.6 m (11 ft 8 in.)	1.6 m (5 ft 3 in.)
250.1 kV–500 kV	6.0 m (20 ft 0 in.)	6.0 m (20 ft 0 in.)	3.5 m (11 ft 6 in.)
500.1 kV–800 kV	8.0 m (26 ft 0 in.)	8.0 m (26 ft 0 in.)	5.0 m (16 ft 5 in.)

Note: All dimensions are distance from exposed energized electrical conductors or circuit parts to worker.
* *Exposed movable conductor* describes a condition in which the distance between the conductor and a person is not under the control of the person. The term is normally applied to overhead line conductors supported by poles.

Work Involving Electrical Hazards

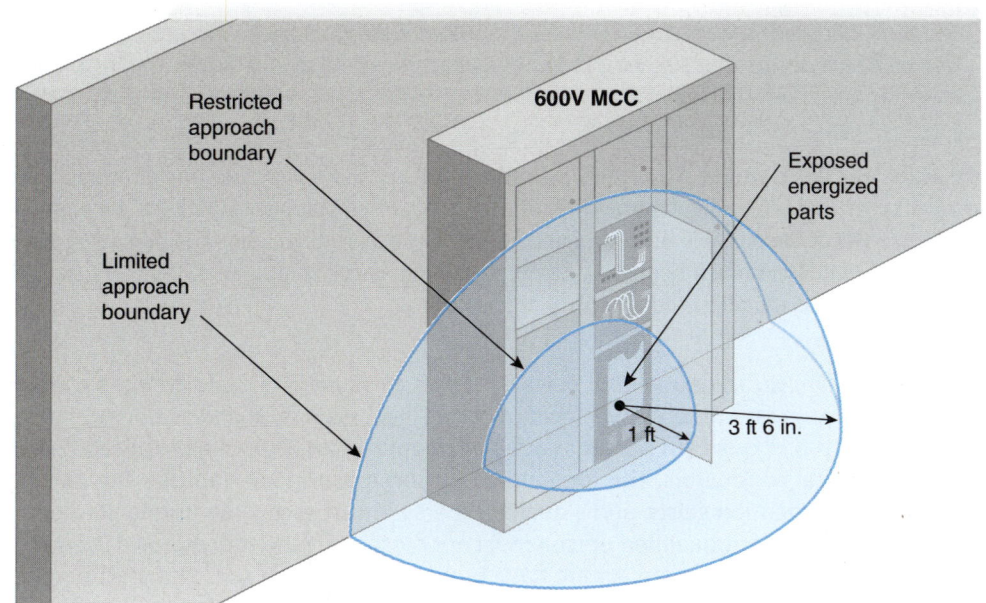

EXHIBIT 130.2

Shock protection boundaries for a 600-volt MCC.

(E) Limited Approach Boundary.

△ **(1) Approach by Unqualified Persons.** Unless permitted by 130.4(E)(3), no unqualified person shall be permitted to approach nearer than the limited approach boundary of energized conductors and circuit parts.

> Unqualified persons have not been trained to recognize and react to risk of injury of shock or electrocution from exposure to potential electrical shock hazards. The limited approach boundary is the approach limit for unqualified persons, unless the conditions of supervision specified in 130.4(E)(3) are met. Only qualified persons should be permitted to be within the space defined by the limited approach boundary. An arc flash boundary may be a greater distance from the energized conductor or circuit part than the limited approach boundary. Arc-rated PPE is required for any employee within the arc flash boundary.

(2) Working at or Close to the Limited Approach Boundary. Where one or more unqualified persons are working at or close to the limited approach boundary, the designated person in charge of the work space where the electrical hazard exists shall advise the unqualified person(s) of the electrical hazard and warn him or her to stay outside of the limited approach boundary.

> Employees who are not associated with an electrical work task could be exposed to an electrical hazard. For instance, a painter could be working in the same room with an exposed energized electrical circuit part. If unqualified persons working near a limited approach boundary cross the shock protection boundary, they are at an elevated risk of injury from exposure to the electrical shock hazards. In this case, the electrical supervisor and the painter's supervisor must establish a communication path so that the painter is made aware of the location of the exposed energized electrical conductor, is advised to stay outside the limited approach boundary, and is informed of how to avoid exposure to any associated electrical hazard(s). Signs or barricades might be necessary.
> If there are exposed energized electrical circuits, there is likely an arc flash boundary. If the arc flash boundary is outside of the limited approach boundary, the unqualified persons must not cross the arc flash boundary unless they are wearing appropriate PPE. Where alerting techniques as identified in 130.7(E) are used — such as safety signs

Handbook for Electrical Safety in the Workplace   2018

and tags, barricades, and attendants — the unqualified persons in the area where the work is being performed also need to know what the alerting techniques mean so that they stay a safe distance away.

> **OSHA Connection**
>
> **29 CFR 1910.333(c)(9)**
> Employees must not perform housekeeping duties at such close distances to live parts that there is a possibility of contact. Adequate safeguards (such as insulating equipment or barriers) must be provided.

Δ **(3) Entering the Limited Approach Boundary.** Where there is a need for an unqualified person(s) to cross the limited approach boundary, a qualified person shall advise the unqualified person(s) of the possible hazards and continuously escort the unqualified person(s) while inside the limited approach boundary. Under no circumstance shall unqualified person(s) be permitted to cross the restricted approach boundary.

In some instances, an unqualified person might be required to perform tasks within the limited approach boundary. If this becomes necessary, a qualified person must ensure that the unqualified person is advised about the location of all exposed energized electrical conductors. The unqualified person must be advised that the risk of shock or electrocution exists, and a qualified person must escort the unqualified person at all times. The unqualified person must not cross the restricted approach boundary under any circumstances. An arc flash boundary may need to be crossed before entering the limited approach boundary. Arc flash PPE is required for any employee within the arc flash boundary.

> **Worker Alert**
>
> The restricted approach boundary for circuit parts operating below 150 volts is that you must avoid contact. No uninsulated object — including your hand — should make contact with exposed energized parts. Many electrocutions occur at this lower voltage level. The use of insulated gloves can minimize the potential for a shock or electrocution due to human error.

Δ **(F) Restricted Approach Boundary.** No qualified person shall approach or take any conductive object closer to exposed energized electrical conductors or circuit parts than the restricted approach boundary set forth in Table 130.4(D)(a) and Table 130.4(D)(b), unless one of the following conditions applies:

(1) The qualified person is insulated or guarded from energized electrical conductors or circuit parts operating at 50 volts or more. Insulating gloves and sleeves are considered insulation only with regard to the energized parts upon which work is performed.

(2) The energized electrical conductors or circuit parts are insulated from the qualified person and from any other conductive object at a different potential.

The restricted approach boundary is the closest approach distance for a qualified person without the use of personal and other shock protective equipment. If it is necessary to cross the restricted approach boundary, the qualified person must take additional precautionary measures. Insulating materials with a defined voltage rating must be placed between the person and the conductor. The insulating material can take several forms. The insulating material can be installed so that the conductor is insulated from possible contact or the employee can be insulated by wearing appropriately rated PPE. In some cases, using more than one protective scheme is desirable. For instance, appropriately rated rubber blankets might be installed to cover one or more conductors, and the employee also might wear appropriate voltage-rated PPE.

This section recognizes that a tool or other object is considered to be an extension of the person's body. If a person is holding an object, the requirements of this section apply to both the person and the object. The effect of these requirements is that the employee (or extended body part) is prevented from being exposed to any difference of a potential 50 volts or more. See 130.7(D)(1) for criteria for employees to use insulated tools or handling equipment when working in the restricted approach boundary.

Exhibit 130.3 shows an employee preparing to open an enclosure. Once the enclosure is opened, the employee will be inside the shock boundaries as well as within the arc flash boundary. In addition, the employee is interacting with the equipment in a manner that increases exposure to an arc flash hazard.

> **OSHA Connection**
>
> **1926.416(a)(1)**
> No employee is permitted to work in proximity to any part of an electric power circuit that could be contacted in the course of work, unless the employee is protected against electric shock by de-energizing the circuit and grounding it or by guarding it effectively by insulation or other means.

Work Involving Electrical Hazards

130.4(F)

EXHIBIT 130.3

Working on equipment inside the protection boundaries. (Courtesy of Salisbury by Honeywell)

The purpose of column 2 of both Table 130.4(D)(a) and Table 130.4(D)(b) is to recognize that an electrical conductor can move. If the conductor is fixed into position, the distance between the employee and the conductor is under the control of the employee. If that distance can vary because the conductor can move (such as a bare overhead conductor or a conductor installed on racks in a manhole), or if the distance can vary because the platform (articulating arm) on which the employee is standing can move, then the distance is not under the employee's control, and column 2 of both tables apply. Column 2 would also apply if a conductor is being disconnected from a fixed part (such as a connection point on an equipment bus) and it is anticipated that the act of disconnection could cause the conductor to swing away from the connection point.

Case Study

130.4(F)

Scenario

Don was a self-employed HVAC technician with a small company that also employed two other technicians. Don had worked in the industry for 42 years. He received a service call from a homeowner who stated that the AC unit at their townhouse would not turn on. With his other technicians already on a call, Don headed to the location himself.

The 220-volt HVAC unit was pad mounted at the rear of the townhouse. Don proceeded directly to the unit. A separate 120-volt receptacle was available nearby for portable tools. The homeowner watched Don flip the power switch several times without the HVAC coming online. Don then proceeded to remove the access panels with a battery operated screw driver. When the homeowner looked out of the window again about 20 minutes later, she saw Don lying on the ground. She rushed outside to check on him but received a shock when she made contact with his body.

The homeowner quickly called 911 and was instructed to open the breaker to the AC unit since she knew the location of the circuit breaker panel. When the EMTs arrived they found Don was unresponsive. One of his hands was near an exposed conductor and his other near the AC unit's metal housing.

Results

Attempts to revive Don failed and he was pronounced dead at arrival at the hospital. It was determined that he suffered heart failure due to the electrocution.

Don's small company could pay the two workers only for the work completed that week. Without Don to run the company, no other work was scheduled and both were unemployed for several months. Each eventually found employment in the same industry at other companies.

The elderly homeowner was admitted to the hospital for observation as a result of trauma experienced from Don's death on her property and from her personal discovery of his body.

(continues)

Analysis

The switch on the HVAC unit was found to be in the "ON" position. It appeared as if the exposed conductor had become separated from the terminal, which may have been the reason for the unit's inability to operate. The likely scenario is that Don was attempting to reinsert the conductor into the terminal block. His left hand was used to brace himself on the grounded metal enclosure while his right hand was being used to insert the conductor into the terminal. While he was inserting the conductor his hand might have slipped onto the exposed (uninsulated) conductor end.

The electrical current from hand-to-hand across Don's chest was sufficient to cause entry and exit wounds on his hands. The wound pattern on his hands indicated that Don had become "hung up" during the process of electrocution. Don might have been conscious but unable to respond when the homeowner first found him. It is likely that current continued to flow through his body until the homeowner opened the branch circuit. The electrical current disrupted Don's heart's ability to function.

Investigation

There was no indication that the tasks performed by Don were necessary while still energized. If an electrically safe work condition (ESWC) had been established, Don would not have died.

A majority of the HVAC systems maintained by Don's company were household units. Interviews with Don's employees revealed that Don did not train his employees in the hazards and risks of performing energized work. Don felt confident in his ability to perform energized work at low voltage and had performed energized tasks repeatedly. Don and his employees had all experienced electric shocks in the past, but shock was not seen as an incident. Electrical shocks were considered to be part of the job. Due to this attitude, shock protection was not felt to be necessary.

OSHA regulations requiring that employees be provided with a safe work environment is not limited to large companies nor is it limited to their facilities. Contract work at a dwelling is covered by the requirements. Don's small HVAC repair company was not exempt from those regulations.

Although recent interest has been with arc flash incidents, shock injuries and electrocution still occur. Previous electric shocks received by Don and his employees should have been a wake-up call for protection from electrocution. Proper incident reporting of these near misses and subsequent improvements to the process may have saved Don's life. Regardless of the work environment, number of employees, or potential for an arc flash, the primary method of preventing electrical injuries must be to establish an ESWC. Don's ignorance of electrical safety requirements and lack of understanding the consequences of his actions made a widow of his wife.

130.5 Arc Flash Risk Assessment.

N **(A) General.** An arc flash risk assessment shall be performed:

(1) To identify arc flash hazards
(2) To estimate the likelihood of occurrence of injury or damage to health and the potential severity of injury or damage to health
(3) To determine if additional protective measures are required, including the use of PPE

Worker Alert

You should be aware of other methods designed to protect you from injury. The use of PPE should be your employer's last selection after all other protection schemes have been used. If you are not aware whether your employer has used any method other than PPE, you may be able to determine alternate ways to minimize your injury when an incident does occur.

Whenever energized electrical conductors or circuit parts are considered to be exposed and an employee is within the limited approach boundary, a potential arc flash hazard is presumed to exist. A potential arc flash hazard can also be presumed to exist when an employee interacts with energized electrical equipment when conductors or circuit parts are not exposed. However, under normal operating conditions the potential for an arc flash hazard is greatly reduced.

Usually, an arc fault event occurs as a result of some movement, such as when a power circuit breaker is racked-out, a conductor springs loose, a tool drops, an animal contacts an energized circuit part, a disconnect is opened or closed, or a starter operates. Most arcing faults are started as a result of human interaction — such as when a person blindly reaches into a cubicle containing energized conductors or circuit parts with a conductive object.

The arc flash risk assessment should be re-evaluated to determine if additional use of the hierarchy of risk controls could be employed to further lower the risk or incident energy prior to determining the necessary PPE. Automatically defaulting to PPE as the level of control utilized would mean that the employer had assumed that no

Work Involving Electrical Hazards

other hierarchy of risk controls could have been employed to lower the incident energy level or to provide additional protection for the employee. The employer would have determined that they would employ the lowest level of control (PPE) for employee protection. PPE should not be the first or only control element used. Properly selected arc-rated PPE limits the severity of an injury but does not necessarily prevent an injury if an incident occurs.

N **(B) Estimate of Likelihood and Severity.** The estimate of the likelihood of occurrence of injury or damage to health and the potential severity of injury or damage to health shall take into consideration the following:

a. The design of the electrical equipment, including its overcurrent protective device and its operating time
b. The electrical equipment operating condition and condition of maintenance

The severity of a potential arc flash injury depends upon various factors, including whether personal and other protective equipment is used, the incident energy level that is impinged upon the body, whether the enclosure is open or not, and most importantly, where the person is standing in relation to the arc flash — that is, whether or not the person is within the arc flash boundary.

N **(C) Additional Protective Measures.** If additional protective measures are required they shall be selected and implemented according to the hierarchy of risk control identified in 110.1(H). When the additional protective measures include the use of PPE, the following shall be determined:

(1) Appropriate safety-related work practices
(2) The arc flash boundary
(3) The PPE to be used within the arc flash boundary

Table 130.5(C) shall be permitted to be used to estimate the likelihood of occurrence of an arc flash event to determine if additional protective measures are required.

The hierarchy of risk controls is used to address arc flash mitigation techniques. Shock mitigation techniques are addressed in 130.4(B). Some techniques will accomplish both goals.

The hierarchy in 110.1(H)(3) is listed in order of the most effective to the least effective and must be applied in descending order for each risk assessment. Once a hazard has been identified, it first must be determined if the hazard can be eliminated. During the electrical system design stage, methods should be employed to eliminate the hazard in its entirety. In the electrical system design and equipment selection phase, it is easier to utilize the most effective controls of elimination and substitution to limit the risk associated with anticipated justified energized work. In this first context, elimination is removal of a hazard so that it never exists. This removes the potential for human error when interacting with the equipment.

Full elimination of the hazard is often not an option for installed equipment. Although elimination can be also be achieved by applying other controls such as administration (establishing an electrically safe work condition), these other controls introduce a potential for human error.

Only after all other risk controls have been exhausted should PPE be selected. Selection of PPE is not the first or only requirement by this section. PPE is considered the least effective and lowest level of risk control for employee protection and should not be the

---

Worker Alert

You should be aware of other methods designed to protect you from injury. The use of PPE should be your employer's last selection after all other protection schemes have been used. If you are not aware whether your employer has used any method other than PPE, you may be able to determine alternate ways to minimize your injury when an incident does occur.

OSHA Connection

29 CFR 1910.132(d)(1)

The employer must assess the workplace to determine if hazards are present or are likely to be present. If hazards necessitate the use of PPE, the employer must select and have the affected employee use PPE that properly fits, as well as communicate selection decisions to the affected employee.

130.5(C)   Article 130

> first or only control element used. An employer must also assure that appropriate work procedures are used by those within the arc flash boundary for the task and equipment involved.
>
> Table 130.5(C) is applicable to both the PPE category and incident energy analysis methods of arc flash risk assessment. An abnormal condition exists when all of the normal operating conditions have not been met. This table does not determine if arc flash PPE is necessary. It aids in determining the likelihood of an arc flash incident occurring for the specific task based on the equipment condition. Only after all other risk controls have been exhausted should PPE be selected. PPE is considered the least effective and lowest level safety of control for employee protection and should not be the first or only control element used.

TABLE 130.5(C)   Estimate of the Likelihood of Occurrence of an Arc Flash Incident for ac and dc Systems

Task	Equipment Condition	Likelihood of Occurrence*
Reading a panel meter while operating a meter switch.	Any	No
Performing infrared thermography and other non-contact inspections outside the restricted approach boundary. This activity does not include opening of doors or covers.		
Working on control circuits with exposed energized electrical conductors and circuit parts, nominal 125 volts ac or dc, or below without any other exposed energized equipment over nominal 125 volts ac or dc, including opening of hinged covers to gain access.		
Examination of insulated cable with no manipulation of cable.		
For dc systems, insertion or removal of individual cells or multi-cell units of a battery system in an open rack.		
For dc systems, maintenance on a single cell of a battery system or multi-cell units in an open rack.		
For ac systems, work on energized electrical conductors and circuit parts, including voltage testing.	Any	Yes
For dc systems, working on energized electrical conductors and circuit parts of series-connected battery cells, including voltage testing.		
Removal or installation of CBs or switches.		
Opening hinged door(s) or cover(s) or removal of bolted covers (to expose bare, energized electrical conductors and circuit parts). For dc systems, this includes bolted covers, such as battery terminal covers.		
Application of temporary protective grounding equipment, after voltage test.		
Working on control circuits with exposed energized electrical conductors and circuit parts, greater than 120 volts.		
Insertion or removal of individual starter buckets from motor control center (MCC).		
Insertion or removal (racking) of circuit breakers (CBs) or starters from cubicles, doors open or closed.		
Insertion or removal of plug-in devices into or from busways.		
Examination of insulated cable with manipulation of cable.		
Working on exposed energized electrical conductors and circuit parts of equipment directly supplied by a panelboard or motor control center.		
Insertion or removal of revenue meters (kW-hour, at primary voltage and current).		
Removal of battery conductive intercell connector covers.		
For dc systems, working on exposed energized electrical conductors and circuit parts of utilization equipment directly supplied by a dc source.		
Opening voltage transformer or control power transformer compartments.		
Operation of outdoor disconnect switch (hookstick operated) at 1 kV through 15 kV.		
Operation of outdoor disconnect switch (gang-operated, from grade) at 1 kV through 15 kV.		

Work Involving Electrical Hazards

TABLE 130.5(C) Continued.

Task	Equipment Condition	Likelihood of Occurrence*
Operation of a CB, switch, contactor, or starter. Voltage testing on individual battery cells or individual multi-cell units. Removal or installation of covers for equipment such as wireways, junction boxes, and cable trays that does not expose bare, energized electrical conductors and circuit parts. Opening a panelboard hinged door or cover to access dead front overcurrent devices. Removal of battery nonconductive intercell connector covers.	Normal	No
Maintenance and testing on individual battery cells or individual multi-cell units in an open rack Insertion or removal of individual cells or multi-cell units of a battery system in an open rack. Arc-resistant switchgear Type 1 or 2 (for clearing times of less than 0.5 sec with a prospective fault current not to exceed the arc-resistant rating of the equipment) and metal enclosed interrupter switchgear, fused or unfused of arc resistant type construction, 1 kV through 15 kV. Insertion or removal (racking) of CBs from cubicles; Insertion or removal (racking) of ground and test device; or Insertion or removal (racking) of voltage transformers on or off the bus.	Abnormal	Yes

Equipment condition considered to be "normal" if all of the following circumstances apply:

(1) The equipment is properly installed in accordance with the manufacturer's recommendations and applicable industry codes and standards.
(2) The equipment is properly maintained in accordance with the manufacturer's recommendations and applicable industry codes and standards.
(3) The equipment is used in accordance with instructions included in the listing and labeling and in accordance with manufacturer's instructions.
(4) Equipment doors are closed and secured.
(5) Equipment covers are in place and secured.
(6) There is no evidence of impending failure such as arcing, overheating, loose or bound equipment parts, visible damage, or deterioration.

*As defined in this standard, the two components of risk are the likelihood of occurrence of injury or damage to health and the severity of injury or damage to health that results from a hazard. Risk assessment is an overall process that involves estimating both the likelihood of occurrence and severity to determine if additional protective measures are required. The estimate of the likelihood of occurrence contained in this table does not cover every possible condition or situation, nor does it address severity of injury or damage to health. Where this table identifies "No" as an estimate of likelihood of occurrence, it means that an arc flash incident is not likely to occur. Where this table identifies "Yes" as an estimate of likelihood of occurrence, it means that additional protective measures are required to be selected and implemented according to the hierarchy of risk control identified in 110.1(H).

Informational Note No. 1: An example of a standard that provides information for arc-resistant switchgear referred to in Table 130.5(C) is IEEE C37.20.7, *Guide for Testing Metal-Enclosed Switchgear Rated Up to 38 kV for Internal Arcing Faults.*

Informational Note No. 2: Improper or inadequate maintenance can result in increased fault clearing time of the overcurrent protective device, thus increasing the incident energy. Where equipment is not properly installed or maintained, PPE selection based on incident energy analysis or the PPE category method might not provide adequate protection from arc flash hazards.

Informational Note No. 3: Both larger and smaller available fault currents could result in higher incident energy. If the available fault current increases without a decrease in the fault clearing time of the overcurrent protective device, the incident energy will increase. If the available fault current decreases, resulting in a longer fault clearing time for the overcurrent protective device, incident energy could also increase.

Informational Note No. 4: The occurrence of an arcing fault inside an enclosure produces a variety of physical phenomena very different from a bolted fault. For example, the arc energy resulting from an arc developed in the air will cause a sudden pressure increase and localized overheating. Equipment and design practices are available to minimize the energy levels and the number of procedures that could expose an employee to high levels of incident energy. Proven designs such as arc-resistant switchgear, remote racking (insertion or removal), remote opening and closing of switching devices, high-resistance grounding of low-voltage and 5000-volt (nominal) systems, current limitation, and specification of covered bus or covered conductors within equipment are available to reduce the risk associated with an arc flash incident. See Informative O for safety-related design requirements.

Informational Note No. 5: For additional direction for performing maintenance on overcurrent protective devices, see Chapter 2, Safety-Related Maintenance Requirements.

Informational Note No. 6: See IEEE 1584, *Guide for Performing Arc Flash Calculations*, for more information regarding incident energy and the arc flash boundary for three-phase systems.

> Regarding Informational Note No. 2, proper maintenance of equipment does not apply only to the equipment that an employee will be performing the task on. Proper maintenance of overcurrent devices is necessary not only for the safe operation of equipment under normal operating conditions, but also for establishing an electrically safe work condition or performing energized work. An employee following a safe work procedure, including the selection of PPE, for an energized task on a properly maintained piece of equipment is put at a greater risk of injury if the upstream overcurrent device has not been maintained. All electrical equipment that is part of a risk assessment, including those that may be remotely located, must be properly maintained.
>
> Electrical equipment is subject to stresses both electrically and environmentally. Maintaining electrical equipment per the manufacturer's instructions or in accordance with consensus-based documents such as NFPA 70B, *Recommended Practice for Electrical Equipment Maintenance*, helps ensure that the equipment operates properly without posing an electrical hazard to employees who interface with the equipment as part of their job task(s).
>
> Informational Note No. 3 deals with the situation where an overcurrent protective device is operating correctly, but the parameters of the circuit in which the device is installed has changed. Under this circumstance, there may be a larger or smaller available short-circuit current, both of which can result in higher available arc flash energies. Where the available short-circuit current increases without a decrease in the opening time of the overcurrent protective device, arc flash energy can increase; and where the available short-circuit current decreases, resulting in a longer clearing time for the overcurrent protective device, arc flash energies can also increase. See also the commentary on 130.7(C)(14)(b).

(D) Documentation. The results of the arc flash risk assessment shall be documented.

> The use of an energized electrical work permit (EEWP), even when it is not required, is one of the best methods for documenting that the required risk assessments have been performed. See Figure J.2 in Informative Annex J for an example of an EEWP.

(E) Arc Flash Boundary.

(1) The arc flash boundary shall be the distance at which the incident energy equals 1.2 cal/cm^2 (5 J/cm^2).

Informational Note: For information on estimating the arc flash boundary, see Informative Annex D.

OSHA Connection

29 CFR 1910.132(d)(2)
The employer must verify through a written certification that the required workplace risk assessment was performed. The certification must identify the workplace evaluated, the person certifying that the evaluation was performed, and the date(s) of the risk assessment.

Work Involving Electrical Hazards

130.5(E)(2)

An arc fault incident can occur as a result of an open air event. However, arc fault events most often occur inside electrical equipment enclosures, and an enclosure can concentrate an arc flash event. Informative Annex D provides information on various methods of estimating the available incident energy and the arc flash boundary. The source documents listed in Table D.1 should be reviewed for the proper use and limitations of the techniques presented. NFPA *70E* does not limit calculation methods to those listed, and other appropriate techniques may be available.

Public consensus is that, should an arc flash occur while an employee is performing a task on justified energized electrical equipment, the employee should be able to survive without permanent physical damage. Testing has concluded that 1.2 cal/cm² is the level at which exposed skin can suffer the onset of a second-degree burn. See the commentary following the term *arc flash hazard* in Article 100 regarding second-degree burns.

Properly rated PPE should limit the employee's injury to a second-degree burn if an arc flash were to occur while performing work within the arc flash boundary. There is no requirement to provide the employee with arc flash protection when the incident energy is below 1.2 cal/cm² since the expected injury from an incident will be survivable and nonpermanent.

> **Worker Alert**
>
> An incident energy of 1.2 cal/cm² is expected to limit your injury to one that is recoverable and nonpermanent. This does not necessarily mean that an injury sustained at this energy level will not result in your hospitalization.

△ **(2)** The arc flash boundary shall be permitted to be determined by Table 130.7(C)(15)(a) or Table 130.7(C)(15)(b) when the requirements of these tables apply.

There are two methods that can be used in an arc flash risk assessment to determine the arc flash boundary. One is the incident energy analysis method, which results in an arc flash boundary at a distance where the incident energy is 1.2 cal/cm². The second is the arc flash PPE category method, which results in an arc flash boundary selected directly from the tables in 130.7(C)(15). The 600-volt class motor control center (MCC) illustrated in Exhibit 130.4 shows the arc flash boundary distance when the risk assessment is conducted using the PPE category method. The shock protection boundaries are also shown for this specific equipment.

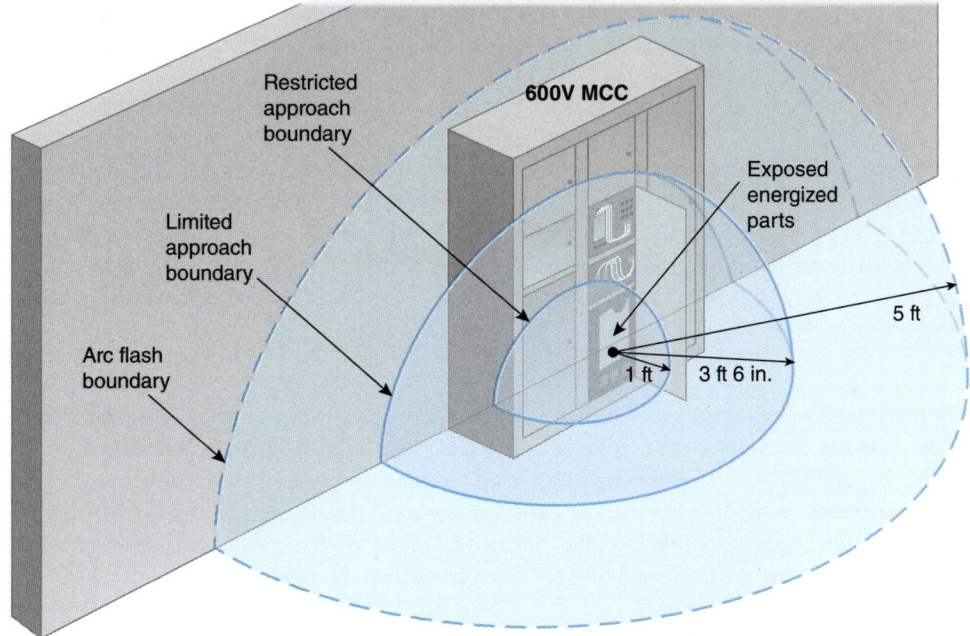

EXHIBIT 130.4

Three approach boundary distances for a 600-volt MCC.

> **Worker Alert**
>
> You should be aware that equipment cannot be evaluated or labeled under both an incident energy and a PPE category method. This type of misunderstanding in the protection requirements can potentially put you at a greater risk of injury.

Δ **(F) Arc Flash PPE.** One of the following methods shall be used for the selection of arc flash PPE:

(1) The incident energy analysis method in accordance with 130.5(G)
(2) The arc flash PPE category method in accordance with 130.7(C)(15)

Either, but not both, methods shall be permitted to be used on the same piece of equipment. The results of an incident energy analysis to specify an arc flash PPE category in Table 130.7(C)(15)(c) shall not be permitted.

> If an employee's body (or part of the employee's body) needs to be within the arc flash boundary in order for the employee to perform a task, an arc flash risk assessment must be performed to determine the amount of incident energy that might be impinged upon the employee and to determine the PPE to be used. The employee then must select and use PPE having a rating at least as high as the predicted incident energy that is available from the energy source. The level of the potential arc flash hazard must be provided in calories per square centimeter (cal/cm^2). There are several methods in which the arc flash risk assessment can be completed. The employer's procedure that defines how to perform the arc flash risk assessment must also specify which method is preferred.
>
> Although there are several methods to conduct an arc flash risk assessment, within NFPA *70E* there are only two methods of selecting the required arc flash PPE. Either the incident energy analysis method or the arc flash PPE category method must be used. NFPA *70E* does not prefer one method over the other, but there are differences in their use and benefits.
>
> Both methods achieve a level of safety for the employee when energized work is justified. Both require that the hierarchy of risk controls be used. Both require the available short-circuit current and fault-clearing time. From there the methods diverge. To use the PPE category method, the equipment must be listed in the table, and the specific parameters for that piece of equipment cannot be exceeded. The incident energy analysis method can be used on any piece of electrical equipment but requires the selection of the most appropriate calculation method for the type of circuit.
>
> Each method has its merits and its limitations. Regardless of the method selected, the reason for selecting one method over the other, or other issues associated with a particular method, the main concern is protecting the employee. NFPA *70E* allows both methods to be used equally. Both may be used in the same facility, but they must not be used on the same piece of equipment.
>
> The availability of arc flash PPE must not be used to justify authorization to conduct energized work. PPE does not prevent an incident from occurring, nor does it necessarily prevent an injury if an incident occurs. Properly selected arc flash PPE may minimize the severity of an injury to one that is recoverable, but the employee may suffer some level of injury. Also, arc flash and shock-protection PPE may not provide protection from an arc blast where the pressure wave is strong enough, for example, to knock the employee off a ladder or into a wall or to eject shrapnel at a velocity high enough to penetrate the body.

(G) Incident Energy Analysis Method. The incident energy exposure level shall be based on the working distance of the employee's face and chest areas from a prospective arc source for the specific task to be performed. Arc-rated clothing and other PPE shall be used by the employee based on the incident energy exposure associated with the specific task. Recognizing that incident energy increases as the distance from the arc flash decreases, additional PPE shall be used for any parts of the body that are closer than the working distance at which the incident energy was determined.

Work Involving Electrical Hazards

130.5(G)

The incident energy analysis method is permitted for any arc flash risk assessment and can be used in lieu of the PPE category method for the specified equipment. It allows for a more precise determination of PPE for a given distance from a specific electrical system or equipment. This method requires an extensive calculation. The incident energy analysis method requires the selection of the most appropriate calculation method for the type of circuit. Although there are several methods listed in Informative Annex D, NFPA 70E does not advocate any specific method of incident energy calculation. Regardless of the calculation method selected, a threshold of 1.2 cal/cm^2 is the limit for the arc flash boundary.

The incident energy analysis predicts the amount of incident energy that might be available from the energy source at the point in the circuit where the work task is to be performed. If the distance between a person and the potential arc source is different from the dimension used by the analysis method, the actual thermal energy might be greater or less than that determined in the analysis. A qualified person will understand that, if the actual working distance is different from what is specified on the label, the PPE specified for the task could be inadequate. In this situation, a qualified person would not proceed with the task because the potential risk of injury has not been evaluated for this unforeseen condition and therefore the work permit is invalid.

Any body parts, such as the hands and arms, might require greater protection than the person's chest and torso and should be protected accordingly. This may require an additional calculation of the incident energy at the distance the hands will be from the energized source. Where arc-rated equipment is used at less than its rating, there can be a substantial increase in the probability of success.

The incident energy analysis shall take into consideration the characteristics of the overcurrent protective device and its fault clearing time, including its condition of maintenance.

The first question is whether the overcurrent protective device has been maintained in accordance with the manufacturer's instructions and applicable industry codes and standards, such as NFPA 70B. It is expected that the device has been verified to be properly installed and the electrical ratings are proper for the installation as part of the maintenance.

The second question is whether there is evidence of impending failure — such as arcing, overheating, loose or bound equipment parts, unusual vibration, unusual smell, visible damage, or deterioration. Where equipment has not been properly installed, maintained, and rated, or where there a signs of impending failure, an overcurrent protective device may fail to clear a fault or fail to clear the fault in accordance with the manufacturer's published time–current characteristic curve. Under this particular circumstance, the PPE selection based on the arc flash hazard label may not provide adequate protection of the employee from the arc flash hazard.

One of the generally accepted methods for estimating total clearing time for an overcurrent protective device where arcing currents are involved is to determine the estimated arcing current and then to plot that arcing current on the protective device's time–current characteristic curve, thereby determining its tripping time. Where power circuit breakers are involved, the device opening time needs to be added to the tripping time determined from the time–current characteristic curve for the device to obtain the total fault clearing time. Manufacturers of overcurrent devices can provide the time-current curves for their devices. See Exhibit 130.5 for a representative time–current curve of a circuit breaker with overload protection, short-time delay, and instantaneous trip override.

EXHIBIT 130.5

Circuit breaker time–current curve. (Courtesy of IAEI)

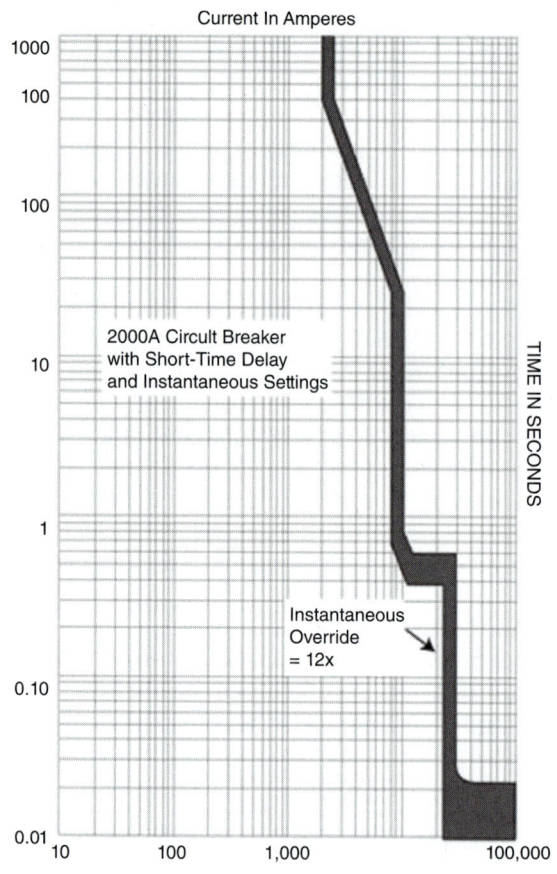

The incident energy analysis shall be updated when changes occur in the electrical distribution system that could affect the results of the analysis. The incident energy analysis shall also be reviewed for accuracy at intervals not to exceed 5 years.

NFPA *70E* does not define what is meant by a change to the electrical distribution system. Where there is exposure to a possible arc flash hazard, a change could be interpreted to mean when the data on the arc flash hazard equipment label is no longer applicable or when new equipment is added that requires an arc flash label.

In some facilities the electrical distribution system changes infrequently, while in others it can change constantly. A modification that causes a new risk assessment to be required does not have to be a change of conditions on the premises itself. It could result from changes made by the utility company to its electrical distribution system supplying the premises, resulting in a change to the available fault current to the facility.

The requirement to review the arc flash risk assessment is not a requirement to have an entire study conducted. If there are no changes to the system, such as circuit breaker, conductor, or utility transformer replacement, and the installed equipment has been properly maintained, the review may just be verification of the facts that led to the original assessment result.

Work Involving Electrical Hazards

130.5(G)

Table 130.5(G) identifies the arc-rated clothing and other PPE requirements of Article 130 and shall be permitted to be used with the incident energy analysis method of selecting arc flash PPE.

Informational Note: For information on estimating the incident energy, see Informative Annex D. For information on selection of arc-rated clothing and other PPE, see Informative Annex H.

N **TABLE 130.5(G)** Selection of Arc-Rated Clothing and Other PPE When the Incident Energy Analysis Method Is Used

---

Incident energy exposures equal to 1.2 cal/cm² up to 12 cal/cm²
Arc-rated clothing with an arc rating equal to or greater than the estimated incident energy[a]
Long-sleeve shirt and pants or coverall or arc flash suit (SR)
Arc-rated face shield and arc-rated balaclava or arc flash suit hood (SR)[b]
Arc-rated outerwear (e.g., jacket, parka, rainwear, hard hat liner) (AN)
Heavy-duty leather gloves, arc-rated gloves, or rubber insulating gloves with leather protectors (SR)[c]
Hard hat
Safety glasses or safety goggles (SR)
Hearing protection
Leather footwear

Incident energy exposures greater than 12 cal/cm²
Arc-rated clothing with an arc rating equal to or greater than the estimated incident energy[a]
Long-sleeve shirt and pants or coverall or arc flash suit (SR)
Arc-rated arc flash suit hood
Arc-rated outerwear (e.g., jacket, parka, rainwear, hard hat liner) (AN)
Arc-rated gloves or rubber insulating gloves with leather protectors (SR)[c]
Hard hat
Safety glasses or safety goggles (SR)
Hearing protection
Leather footwear

SR: Selection of one in group is required.
AN: As needed.
[a]Arc ratings can be for a single layer, such as an arc-rated shirt and pants or a coverall, or for an arc flash suit or a multi-layer system if tested as a combination consisting of an arc-rated shirt and pants, coverall, and arc flash suit.
[b]Face shields with a wrap-around guarding to protect the face, chin, forehead, ears, and neck area are required by 130.7(C)(10)(c). Where the back of the head is inside the arc flash boundary, a balaclava or an arc flash hood shall be required for full head and neck protection.
[c]Rubber insulating gloves with leather protectors provide arc flash protection in addition to shock protection. Higher class rubber insulating gloves with leather protectors, due to their increased material thickness, provide increased arc flash protection.

Table 130.5(G) was previously numbered Table H.3(b). There is no requirement to provide the employee with arc flash protection when the incident energy is below 1.2 cal/cm² since the expected injury from an incident will be survivable and nonpermanent. However, it is not prohibited to provide protection for the employee from incident energies below this survivable limit.

Note that heavy-duty leather gloves or leather protectors worn over the rubber gloves are included as arc flash protection. Leather materials are typically not arc flash rated. However, heavy-duty leather gloves made entirely of leather with a minimum thickness of 0.03 in. (0.7 mm) that are unlined or lined with nonflammable, nonmelting fabrics have been shown to have arc thermal performance values (ATPV) in excess of

130.5(H)   Article 130

10 cal/cm². Leather protectors worn over rubber insulating gloves provide additional arc flash protection for the hands. Before opting for leather gloves or protectors instead of arc-rated gloves, it is necessary to determine that the leather gloves will provide adequate protection from the anticipated incident energy.

When using the incident energy analysis method, the selection of PPE must also comply with the requirements of 130.7(C).

(H) Equipment Labeling. Electrical equipment such as switchboards, panelboards, industrial control panels, meter socket enclosures, and motor control centers that are in other than dwelling units and that are likely to require examination, adjustment, servicing, or maintenance while energized shall be marked with a label containing all the following information:

> Equipment that will be the point of verification of the electrically safe work condition (ESWC) or equipment that is justified to be worked on while energized should carry this label. The information on the label is vital for employees performing tasks where exposure to electrical hazards is possible. The label examples in Exhibit 130.6 illustrate two possible configurations. The example on the left (a) is for equipment evaluated using the incident energy analysis method, and the example on the right (b) is for equipment evaluated using the PPE category method. The information on the label should primarily be used for the establishment of an ESWC. Equipment labeling is not a carte blanche allowance to perform energized work. Energized work must be justified regardless of the presence of the label.
>
> The employee should not be expected to calculate an incident energy value or to determine whether a job complies with the arc flash PPE category method. However, the employee should be capable of reading and interpreting the information included on an arc flash hazard label. It is the employer's responsibility to provide employees performing work tasks with the information they need to work safely. Part of this is ensuring that arc flash hazard labels are in place and that the employee has the information necessary to select the appropriate PPE.
>
> Without proper equipment maintenance, the affixed label may be invalid. Qualified persons should understand the maintenance program for the energized equipment

> **Worker Alert**
>
> You must understand that the PPE necessary to protect you — as stated on the equipment label — is typically based on the working distance. If any part of your body will be closer than the working distance, an additional level of protection is necessary for those body parts. This information should be available on the energized electrical work permit.

EXHIBIT 130.6

Representative warning labels.

⚠ WARNING

ARC FLASH HAZARD

Nominal system voltage _____

Arc flash boundary _____

Available incident energy _____

Working distance _____

Minimum arc rating of clothing _____

⚠ WARNING

ARC FLASH HAZARD

Nominal system voltage _____

Arc flash boundary _____

Working distance _____

PPE category _____

Work Involving Electrical Hazards

> they are working on as well as that of the protective devices that were used to determine the label parameters. Without proper maintenance, unexpected hazards could be present in the equipment, or the PPE specified could not provide protection for the actual incident energy exposure due to an inoperable circuit breaker. Label information without a maintenance program places employees at risk of injury.
>
> NFPA *70E* does not require that homeowners install field-marked arc flash hazard labels on the equipment installed on their premises. However, any employee (contractor) performing justified energized work in dwelling units where electrical conductors and circuits are exposed is subject to a possible injury. The lack of a labeling requirement for dwellings is not permission for energized work to be performed at these locations. Employees within dwellings and their employers are not exempt from the requirements of NFPA *70E*. A shock risk assessment and an arc flash risk assessment must be performed if energized work within a dwelling is to be justified.

(1) Nominal system voltage
(2) Arc flash boundary
(3) At least one of the following:
   a. Available incident energy and the corresponding working distance, or the arc flash PPE category in Table 130.7(C)(15)(a) or Table 130.7(C)(15)(b) for the equipment, but not both
   b. Minimum arc rating of clothing
   c. Site-specific level of PPE

Exception No. 1: Unless changes in electrical distribution system(s) render the label inaccurate, labels applied prior to the effective date of this edition of the standard shall be acceptable if they complied with the requirements for equipment labeling in the standard in effect at the time the labels were applied.

Exception No. 2: In supervised industrial installations where conditions of maintenance and engineering supervision ensure that only qualified persons monitor and service the system, the information required in 130.5(H)(1) through 130.5(H)(3) shall be permitted to be documented in a manner that is readily available to persons likely to perform examination, servicing, maintenance, and operation of the equipment while energized.

Worker Alert

You should be aware that equipment labeled with an incident energy should not be also labeled with a PPE category. A misunderstanding in the protection requirements can potentially put you at a greater risk of injury.

> All equipment labels must include the nominal system voltage, the arc flash boundary, and at least one of the four items listed in 130.5(H)(3). An incident energy and a PPE category should not be on the same piece of equipment. Only one method of risk assessment may be applied to a piece of equipment. The PPE category tables are not applicable to an incident energy analysis.
>
> By providing the calculated incident energy in 130.5(H)(3)(a), an employee can select equipment rated at least for the same energy level. Using the PPE category method [also in 130.5(H)(3)(a)] allows PPE to be selected by Table 130.7(C)(15)(c). Note that some manufacturers may label PPE equipment by category number rather than incident energy. Equipment may be labeled with a minimum arc rating for the PPE [in 130.5(H)(3)(b)]. This arc rating may be at any level above that required by the arc flash risk assessment. Site-specific PPE [in 130.5(H)(3)(c)] can be designated by anything determined by the facility. For example, HRC2 or BLUE could be a site-specific designation for 8 cal/cm^2-rated equipment.
>
> It is advantageous to specify or select arc-rated equipment that will be exposed to less than its rating during a fault. The testing of arc-rated clothing is based on a 50 percent probability of success. Exceeding the minimum requirement can substantially increase in the probability of success.

The method of calculating and the data to support the information for the label shall be documented. The data shall be reviewed for accuracy at intervals not to exceed 5 years. Where the review of the data identifies a change that renders the label inaccurate, the label shall be updated.

The owner of the electrical equipment shall be responsible for the documentation, installation, and maintenance of the marked label.

130.6 Other Precautions for Personnel Activities.

(A) Alertness.

(1) When Electrical Hazards Might Exist. Employees shall be instructed to be alert at all times when they are working within the limited approach boundary of energized electrical conductors or circuit parts operating at voltages equal to or greater than 50 volts and in work situations when electrical hazards might exist.

> Human factors are generally recognized as one of the leading causes of injuries. An employee conducting work is typically solely responsible for their actions. After employees have gone through training, been qualified for the task, and been given procedures, it is their personal actions or lack thereof that will impact their safety. Alertness, as used in this section, is attentiveness to self, others, and the situation.

(2) When Impaired. Employees shall not be permitted to work within the limited approach boundary of energized electrical conductors or circuit parts operating at voltages equal to or greater than 50 volts, or where other electrical hazards exist, while their alertness is recognizably impaired due to illness, fatigue, or other reasons.

> Human factors are generally recognized as one of the leading causes of injuries, and an impaired employee may be unable to perform the task at hand safely. Employers and employees must realize that an illness or fatigue from extended hours may put the employee at risk. The employer has a duty to observe the physical and mental condition of the employees. At the time of the job briefing, the person in charge must evaluate whether any employee is impaired for any reason. It may be advantageous to reschedule the work rather than put the employee at undue risk. No employee should be compelled to rush to complete a task or work when impaired. Doing so can place the qualified person at a risk that was not considered by the energized work permit.

(3) Changes in Scope. Employees shall be instructed to be alert for changes in the job or task that could lead the person outside of the electrically safe work condition or expose the person to additional hazards that were not part of the original plan.

> When the job briefing is given, employees must be instructed about the details and limits of the expected work task. A change in the condition or work environment that was not a part of the original plan might result in unanticipated exposure to an electrical hazard. A seemingly minor deviation from the work plan could drastically alter the shock assessment or arc flash assessment, or it could require the employee to perform a task for which they are not qualified. For example, closing a switch rather than conducting the planned voltage measurements may introduce an unanticipated hazard. Employees should be trained to stop work when there is any deviation from the planned task. Work should not proceed until a new job plan or work permit has been provided. A new risk assessment may be necessary prior to performing the new task.

Worker Alert

It is solely your responsibility to remain alert and attentive while conducting an energized task. You should not be distracted by cell phones, by other persons, or by other tasks occurring around you.

Worker Alert

You are uniquely qualified to determine impairments that may prevent you from safely performing an assigned task. You must recognize when you feel ill or are fatigued by an extended shift and acknowledge that continuing in this condition could put you or others around you at risk.

Worker Alert

You may not realize until you are at the equipment that the assigned task as documented in the energized work permit is not correct. You may also be approached during the assigned task to perform another undocumented task. In either case, changes from the original plan can put you at an increased risk of injury.

Work Involving Electrical Hazards

130.6(E)(1)

(B) Blind Reaching. Employees shall be instructed not to reach blindly into areas that might contain exposed energized electrical conductors or circuit parts where an electrical hazard exists.

> The employee must be able to see the location where the task will be conducted. There is no way to assume that the task can be safely performed if employees are unable to see what they are doing. The use of a mirror to see behind an obstruction is also considered blind reaching.

(C) Illumination.

(1) General. Employees shall not enter spaces where electrical hazards exist unless illumination is provided that enables the employees to perform the work safely.

> The employer should ensure that adequate lighting is provided to perform the work safely. Adequate lighting also should be included in the risk assessment procedure. Additional illumination could be required due to darkness of a face shield. Prior to start of work, the work area should be viewed wearing the face shield to determine if additional illumination is necessary.
>
> The work permit should specify the type of additional lighting required to safely perform a task. For example, if the required fixed temporary lighting necessary to perform the task is not available, work should not begin until it is in place. The improvised use of a flashlight would alter the work plan and could introduce risks to employees that were not anticipated. Work should not be performed until appropriate and sufficient lighting specified on the work permit is available.

(2) Obstructed View of Work Area. Where lack of illumination or an obstruction precludes observation of the work to be performed, employees shall not perform any task within the limited approach boundary of energized electrical conductors or circuit parts operating at voltages equal to or greater than 50 volts or where an electrical hazard exists.

> The primary objective is that the employees are able see what they are working on. An obstruction could be a barrier installed by the equipment manufacturer to protect specific points within the equipment or a barrier that has been installed to isolate an energized component. View of the work area could also be obstructed by the installation location of the equipment or by equipment that was not installed with the appropriate amount of required working space.

(D) Conductive Articles Being Worn. Conductive articles of jewelry and clothing (such as watchbands, bracelets, rings, key chains, necklaces, metalized aprons, cloth with conductive thread, metal headgear, or metal frame glasses) shall not be worn within the restricted approach boundary or where they present an electrical contact hazard with exposed energized electrical conductors or circuit parts.

(E) Conductive Materials, Tools, and Equipment Being Handled.

(1) General. Conductive materials, tools, and equipment that are in contact with any part of an employee's body shall be handled in a manner that prevents unintentional contact with energized electrical conductors or circuit parts. Such materials and equipment shall include, but are not limited to, long conductive objects, such as ducts, pipes and tubes, conductive hose and rope, metal-lined rules and scales, steel tapes, pulling lines, metal scaffold parts, structural members, bull floats, and chains.

Worker Alert

You should not attempt to pick up a nut, bolt, or tool that has fallen into equipment — even if it is visible. Retrieving a dropped item inches away from the assigned task location may be a new task that presents additional hazards and greater risk of injury. You need to address all hazards and associated risks before deviating from the issued work permit.

OSHA Connection

29 CFR 1910.333(c)(4)(ii)

Employees must not perform tasks near exposed energized parts where lack of illumination or an obstruction prevents their observation of the work. Employees must not reach blindly into areas.

Worker Alert

You must make sure that you remove conductive articles. Even if your chest is outside the restricted approach boundary, a loose necklace could bridge the distance from the energized part to your neck, leading to an electrocution.

> Long objects that are difficult to control, such as ladders, should be handled by assigning an employee to each end of the object. This work practice allows the object to be handled safely without crossing the limited approach boundary. Conductive fish tapes should not be used for a work task associated with an exposed energized electrical conductor or circuit part.

(2) Approach to Energized Electrical Conductors and Circuit Parts. Means shall be employed to ensure that conductive materials approach exposed energized electrical conductors or circuit parts no closer than that permitted by 130.2.

(F) Confined or Enclosed Work Spaces. When an employee works in a confined or enclosed space (such as a manhole or vault) that contains exposed energized electrical conductors or circuit parts operating at voltages equal to or greater than 50 volts or where an electrical hazard exists, the employer shall provide, and the employee shall use, protective shields, protective barriers, or insulating materials as necessary to avoid inadvertent contact with these parts and the effects of the electrical hazards.

> Confined spaces are areas that are not necessarily designed for people but are large enough for employees to enter and perform certain tasks. Another characteristic of a confined space is limited or restricted means for entry or exit. A large equipment housing is an example of a confined space that could contain exposed energized electrical conductors or circuit parts.
>
> Confined spaces might contain a hazardous atmosphere — due to toxic gases, low oxygen, flammability, or excessive heat — that could expose an employee to a life-threatening situation. Ventilation, emergency evacuation, and atmospheric testing should be included in the risk assessment procedure. If the assessment determines that the risks could be reduced to an acceptable level by installing barriers, shields, or other isolating devices, the task can be performed, provided all hazards identified in the risk assessment procedure are mitigated.

(G) Doors and Hinged Panels. Doors, hinged panels, and the like shall be secured to prevent their swinging into an employee and causing the employee to contact exposed energized electrical conductors or circuit parts operating at voltages equal to or greater than 50 volts or where an electrical hazard exists if movement of the door, hinged panel, and the like is likely to create a hazard.

(H) Clear Spaces. Working space required by other codes and standards shall not be used for storage. This space shall be kept clear to permit safe operation and maintenance of electrical equipment.

> The space must not be used for storage of any items including portable equipment on rollers, hand carts, and other easily removed items.

(I) Housekeeping Duties. Employees shall not perform housekeeping duties inside the limited approach boundary where there is a possibility of contact with energized electrical conductors or circuit parts, unless adequate safeguards (such as insulating equipment or barriers) are provided to prevent contact. Electrically conductive cleaning materials (including conductive solids such as steel wool, metalized cloth, and silicone carbide, as well as conductive liquid solutions) shall not be used inside the limited approach boundary unless procedures to prevent electrical contact are followed.

Work Involving Electrical Hazards

130.6(L)

> It is important to understand that the limited approach boundary only exists where there are exposed energized electrical conductors and circuit parts. This requirement does not apply where mitigation strategies have been employed to prevent employees from accidentally contacting exposed electrical conductors and circuit parts. Arc-rated PPE is necessary if housekeeping duties are being performed within the arc flash boundary.

(J) Occasional Use of Flammable Materials. Where flammable materials are present only occasionally, electric equipment capable of igniting them shall not be permitted to be used, unless measures are taken to prevent hazardous conditions from developing. Such materials shall include, but are not limited to, flammable gases, vapors, or liquids, combustible dust, and ignitible fibers or flyings.

> Informational Note: Electrical installation requirements for locations where flammable materials are present on a regular basis are contained in *NFPA 70, National Electrical Code*.

> Many cleaning materials and the propellant used in some spray cans are flammable. Liquids sometimes vaporize readily and flow into recesses and crevices of electrical equipment. An electrical arc caused by the operation of the equipment could ignite any vapor that remains.

(K) Anticipating Failure. When there is evidence that electric equipment could fail and injure employees, the electric equipment shall be de-energized, unless the employer can demonstrate that de-energizing introduces additional hazards or increased risk or is infeasible because of equipment design or operational limitation. Until the equipment is de-energized or repaired, employees shall be protected from hazards associated with the impending failure of the equipment by suitable barricades and other alerting techniques necessary for safety of the employees.

> Informational Note: See 130.7(E) for alerting techniques.

> Electrical equipment frequently offers indications that failure is impending, and employees should be trained to recognize these indications. Indications of impending failure can include hot enclosures, unusual noises or sounds, warning lights, and unfamiliar smells. If any of these indications is observed, normal operation of the equipment should not be permitted or attempted. The equipment must be isolated through the use of barricades or similar protective measures to protect employees against accidental contact with the equipment while in failure mode. After the equipment has been isolated, it should be de-energized from a remote location. Disconnecting means located in the equipment should not be operated unless the employee is protected from the effects of equipment failure.

Worker Alert

When you interact with equipment that is in a state of impending failure, you are put at risk of injury even when attempting to operate the equipment as designed. You must be able to recognize the failure mode of equipment that you interact with in order to prevent injury during its normal operation.

(L) Routine Opening and Closing of Circuits. Load-rated switches, circuit breakers, or other devices specifically designed as disconnecting means shall be used for the opening, reversing, or closing of circuits under load conditions. Cable connectors not of the load-break type, fuses, terminal lugs, and cable splice connections shall not be permitted to be used for such purposes, except in an emergency.

> When non–load-break-rated devices are used to break electrical load currents in an emergency situation, the party breaking the load needs to be aware of the risk of injury from exposure to potential electrical hazards.

> **OSHA Connection**
>
> **29 CFR 1910.334(b)(2)**
>
> The circuit must not be manually re-energized until it has been determined that the equipment and circuit can be safely energized.

(M) Reclosing Circuits After Protective Device Operation. After a circuit is de-energized by the automatic operation of a circuit protective device, the circuit shall not be manually re-energized until it has been determined that the equipment and circuit can be safely energized. The repetitive manual reclosing of circuit breakers or re-energizing circuits through replaced fuses shall be prohibited. When it is determined from the design of the circuit and the overcurrent devices involved that the automatic operation of a device was caused by an overload rather than a fault condition, examination of the circuit or connected equipment shall not be required before the circuit is re-energized.

> If an overcurrent device (such as a fuse or circuit breaker) operates, it can be assumed that the rated current has been exceeded or that a short circuit or ground-fault condition exists. Reclosing a circuit into a short circuit or ground fault could have a disastrous result and must be avoided. The cause of the device operation must be determined before reclosing the circuit.

△ **(N) Safety Interlocks.** Only qualified persons following the requirements for working inside the restricted approach boundary as covered by 130.4(D) shall be permitted to defeat or bypass an electrical safety interlock over which the person has sole control, and then only temporarily while the qualified person is working on the equipment. The safety interlock system shall be returned to its operable condition when the work is completed.

130.7 Personal and Other Protective Equipment.

> **OSHA Connection**
>
> **29 CFR 1910.132(f)(1)**
>
> The employer must provide training to each employee required to use PPE. The employee must be trained to know when PPE is necessary; what PPE is necessary; how to properly don, doff, adjust, and wear PPE; the limitations of the PPE; and, the proper care, maintenance, useful life, and disposal of the PPE.

> Regardless of the method used to determine the PPE rating that is required, the requirements of 130.7 apply.
>
> Even when energized work is justified, the decision to default to PPE as the primary protection method for the safe work practice means that the employer has assumed that no other hierarchy of risk control could be utilized to lower the incident energy level or to provide additional protection for the employee. Without considering these other controls, the employer would have determined that it will utilize the lowest level of control (PPE) for employee protection. The most effective level of control is elimination of the hazard.
>
> PPE does not prevent an injury if an incident occurs. Note that using arc-rated PPE at its rating provides only a 50 percent probability of protection from a second-degree burn. Properly selected arc flash PPE may minimize the severity of an injury to one that is recoverable, but the employee may still suffer some level of injury.
>
> PPE also does not have an arc blast rating; it is only rated for arc flash and/or shock protection. PPE also does not protect from blunt force trauma. Arc flash and shock-protection PPE may not provide protection from an arc blast where, for example, the pressure wave is strong enough to knock the employee off a ladder or into a wall, to project a door or panel into the employee, or to eject shrapnel at a velocity high enough to penetrate the body.

> **Worker Alert**
>
> If your employer exposes you to electrical hazards with risk of injury during the work day, your employer is required to provide you with the necessary protective equipment.

(A) General. Employees exposed to electrical hazards when the risk associated with that hazard is not adequately reduced by the applicable electrical installation requirements shall be provided with, and shall use, protective equipment that is designed and constructed for the specific part of the body to be protected and for the work to be performed.

> Personal and other protective equipment is normally fabricated to provide protection from a particular electrical hazard for a particular body part, but it may also provide protection from another electrical hazard. A classic example is the use of rubber insulated

Work Involving Electrical Hazards

gloves and leather protectors that provide shock protection for the hands and forearms that are also considered to provide some degree of arc flash protection for the hands and forearms.

The performance of a proper analysis involves identifying each electrical hazard involved, the body parts that are within the specific protection boundary, and the severity of the hazard where the body part is to be located and comparing the level of the hazard with the protection offered by the PPE selected. Where an employee's face (but not the back of the head) is going to be within the arc flash boundary, a hard hat and face shield combination that is rated for the anticipated available incident energy level is required. Where the whole head is going to be within the arc flash boundary, a properly rated arc flash hood, or hard hat and face shield combination with arc-rated balaclava, is required. When the back of the head is within the arc flash boundary, it has to be properly protected, as with any other body part.

The employee is to be provided with the appropriate PPE. Since the employer is typically responsible for the enforcement of NFPA *70E*, supplying appropriate PPE not only means providing properly rated PPE for the planned task but also verifying that the PPE supplied is in compliance with the applicable protective equipment standards listed in Informational Tables 130.7(C)(14) and 130.7(G). Verification that issued PPE complies with industry consensus standards is paramount to providing protection for the employee in the event of a shock or arc flash incident. Equipment that has not been adequately tested may not provide the expected protection of the employee and in some cases may increase the severity of the injury to the employee during an incident.

A garment label may not be sufficient to confirm that the required tests have been conducted on the equipment. Some standards evaluate fabric only, not the final product (i.e., shirt, pants) that is made of the fabric. A separate standard may be necessary to address the testing of the final product. It is the employer's responsibility to confirm that the correct standard has been used to determine the protective rating for purchased PPE. See 130.7(C)(14).

> Informational Note: The PPE requirements of 130.7 are intended to protect a person from arc flash and shock hazards. While some situations could result in burns to the skin, even with the protection selected, burn injury should be reduced and survivable. Due to the explosive effect of some arc events, physical trauma injuries could occur. The PPE requirements of 130.7 do not address protection against physical trauma other than exposure to the thermal effects of an arc flash.

The PPE required by NFPA *70E* is designed to protect from shock and thermal injuries. Protection from other injuries may not be accomplished by this PPE. An employer who authorizes energized work must determine the method of protection the employee will use for these other potential injuries. During an arcing fault, electrical energy is converted into various forms of energy. Electrical energy can vaporize metal, which can change from solid state to gas vapor in an expanding plasma ball with explosive, concussive force. When copper vaporizes, it expands by a factor of 67,000 times in volume and can create a superheated plasma.

Arc temperatures can reach as high as 19,500°C (35,000°F) and create molten metal, aluminum, or copper vapor or superheated air. The threshold for a second-degree burn is 80°C (175°F) for 0.1 seconds, and the threshold for a third-degree burn is 96°C (205°F) for 0.1 seconds. Eye damage can result from the radiation associated with the intense light.

Unprotected eardrums can rupture from the generated pressure of an arc flash event. Eardrum rupture can occur at a threshold as low as 34,475 Pa (720 lb/ft^2) or from a pressure differential of as low as 5 psi across the eardrum. Sound levels can exceed 160 dB. Short-term exposure to 140 dB can cause permanent hearing damage. Pressure levels from an event can be over 2000 psf. Lung damage occurs at a threshold of 82,737 to 103,421 Pa (1728 to 2160 lb/ft^2). Shrapnel can reach speeds in excess of 1100 kph

(700 mph). Objects and personnel can be flung across a room, from a ladder, or out of the bucket of a bucket truck.

The primary method required to protect employees is that the equipment be in an electrically safe work condition. Although NFPA *70E* does not specify a limit to the level of incident energy that a protected employee is permitted to be subjected to, the employer should understand that other injuries not addressed by the standard are possible. In addition to the thermal energy generated from an arc flash event, an arcing fault can generate a significant pressure wave. The level of a pressure wave is related to the amount of arcing current that is generated. There is an equation identified in the commentary on Informative Annex K, but it has not been generally adopted. Therefore, the degree of the pressure wave, and possible results from it, are not currently considered to be predictable with reasonable reliability.

> **OSHA Connection**
>
> **29 CFR 1910.132(b)**
> The employer is responsible for assuring the adequacy, including proper maintenance, and sanitation of any protective equipment employees provide for their own use.

Δ **(B) Care of Equipment.** Protective equipment shall be maintained in a safe, clean, and reliable condition and in accordance with manufacturers' instructions. The protective equipment shall be visually inspected before each use. Protective equipment shall be stored in a manner to prevent damage from physically damaging conditions and from moisture, dust, or other deteriorating agents.

> Informational Note: Specific requirements for periodic testing of electrical protective equipment are given in 130.7(C)(14) and 130.7(G).

Adherence to the manufacturer's instructions as well as the guidance and requirements contained in consensus standards assures that personal and other protective equipment is kept in a suitable condition and ready for use when needed.

Personal and other protective equipment has a lifespan that can include many use cycles, such as donning and doffing, cleaning, and laundering. To ensure that protective equipment is maintained in a reliable condition ready for use and will be effective when needed, it must be cared for and inspected at regular intervals and prior to use. Specific guidance regarding the care and laundering of some of the various types of protective equipment may be found in the national consensus standards listed in Informative Annex A.3.2.

Guidance on commercial and home laundering can be found in ASTM F1449, *Standard Guide for Industrial Laundering of Flame, Thermal, and Arc Resistant Clothing,* and ASTM F2757, *Standard Guide for Home Laundering Care and Maintenance of Flame, Thermal and Arc Resistant Clothing.* These standards may be helpful in determining the types of cleaning agents to be used, whether bleach-type additives can be used, and which cleaning processes and procedures are allowed to be used, including the temperature of the water. The employer needs to determine whether commercial or home laundering is to be used. If arc-rated PPE is to be shared, sanitary considerations need to be addressed, such as cleaning between each use.

(C) Personal Protective Equipment (PPE).

(1) General. When an employee is working within the restricted approach boundary, the worker shall wear PPE in accordance with 130.4. When an employee is working within the arc flash boundary, he or she shall wear protective clothing and other PPE in accordance with 130.5. All parts of the body inside the arc flash boundary shall be protected.

(2) Movement and Visibility. When arc-rated clothing is worn to protect an employee, it shall cover all ignitible clothing and shall allow for movement and visibility.

> **Worker Alert**
>
> You should confirm that the equipment provided by your employer will protect all your body parts that may be subjected to an injury during the assigned task. You should be provided with the necessary protection before beginning the assigned task.

Work Involving Electrical Hazards   130.7(C)(6)

> Rehearsing a work task on similar equipment in an electrically safe work condition while wearing PPE is one way to determine if PPE is non-restricting.

△ **(3) Head, Face, Neck, and Chin (Head Area) Protection.** Employees shall wear nonconductive head protection wherever there is a danger of head injury from electric shock or burns due to contact with energized electrical conductors or circuit parts or from flying objects resulting from electrical explosion. Employees shall wear nonconductive protective equipment for the face, neck, and chin whenever there is a danger of injury from exposure to electric arcs or flashes or from flying objects resulting from electrical explosion. If employees use hairnets or beard nets, or both, these items must be arc rated.

Informational Note: See 130.7(C)(10)(b) and (c) for arc flash protective requirements.

(4) Eye Protection. Employees shall wear protective equipment for the eyes whenever there is danger of injury from electric arcs, flashes, or from flying objects resulting from electrical explosion.

> Safety glasses or goggles protect the eyes from impact that exceeds the protection offered by face shields and hood windows. Face shields or hoods in accordance with ANSI/ISEA Z87.1-2015, *American National Standard for Occupational and Educational Personal Eye and Face Protection Devices*, are considered as a "secondary eye protective device" that must be used with a "primary eye protective device" (spectacle or goggle) underneath.

(5) Hearing Protection. Employees shall wear hearing protection whenever working within the arc flash boundary.

> Ear canal inserts are the form of hearing protection recognized in NFPA *70E*. They interfere less with the proper fit and application of other PPE intended to protect the head and face. Hearing protection should not adversely impact the performance of other items of PPE. For example, ear muffs worn over a balaclava may not only present additional flammable material but may not provide the necessary hearing protection. Likewise, ear muffs worn under a balaclava may stretch the fabric beyond its ability to withstand an incident exposure or may affect the snug fit necessary to provide adequate protection.

(6) Body Protection. Employees shall wear arc-rated clothing wherever there is possible exposure to an electric arc flash above the threshold incident energy level for a second degree burn [$1.2\ cal/cm^2$ ($5\ J/cm^2$)].

> The arc flash boundary is the "approach limit from an arc source at which incident energy equals $1.2\ cal/cm^2$." Based on research, this level of thermal energy can result in a second-degree burn. Employees exposed to greater than $1.2\ cal/cm^2$ need to wear arc-rated clothing for protection from the thermal effects of an arcing event.
>
> Although protection from an arc flash incident is not specified where the incident energy is less than $1.2\ cal/cm^2$, this does not mean that a survivable burn should be considered acceptable. This standard is the minimum necessary to provide an employee involved in an arc flash incident with a chance to return home at the end of the day. The primary method used to protect employees is by placing the equipment in an electrically safe work condition regardless of amount of incident energy present.

OSHA Connection

29 CFR 1910.335(a)(1)(i)
Employees must be provided with, and must use, protective equipment that is appropriate for the specific parts of the body to be protected and for the work to be performed.

Worker Alert

Ear canal inserts are the preferred hearing protection for your ears.

Worker Alert

Although protection from a burn is not required below $1.2\ cal/cm^2$, you may opt to protect yourself from an injury that, while not life threating, may be painful.

Handbook for Electrical Safety in the Workplace   2018

> An employer defaulting to PPE as the safe work practice has assumed that no other hierarchy of risk controls could be employed to lower the incident energy level or to provide additional protection for the employee. The employer would have determined that they will employ the lowest level of control (PPE) for employee protection. The most effective method of control is elimination of the hazard. Under no circumstance should the ability to wear PPE be used to justify energized work. An arc flash incident and subsequent injury is not prevented by the use of PPE.

△ **(7) Hand and Arm Protection.** Hand and arm protection shall be provided in accordance with 130.7(C)(7)(a), (b), and (c).

   (a) *Shock Protection.* Employees shall wear rubber insulating gloves with leather protectors where there is a danger of hand injury from electric shock due to contact with exposed energized electrical conductors or circuit parts. Employees shall wear rubber insulating gloves with leather protectors and rubber insulating sleeves where there is a danger of hand and arm injury from electric shock due to contact with exposed energized electrical conductors or circuit parts. Rubber insulating gloves shall be rated for the voltage for which the gloves will be exposed.

   Rubber insulating gloves shall be permitted to be used without leather protectors, under the following conditions:

   (1) There shall be no activity performed that risks cutting or damaging the glove.
   (2) The rubber insulating gloves shall be electrically retested before reuse.
   (3) The voltage rating of the rubber insulating gloves shall be reduced by 50 percent for class 00 and by one whole class for classes 0 through 4.

   (b) *Arc Flash Protection.* Hand and arm protection shall be worn where there is possible exposure to arc flash burn. The apparel described in 130.7(C)(10)(d) shall be required for protection of hands from burns. Arm protection shall be accomplished by the apparel described in 130.7(C)(6).

> Where the hands and arms are closer than the working distance, a greater level of protection is required. This may require an additional determination of the incident energy at the hand position during the task or arc rating of PPE for the body parts that are nearer to the energized parts. Sleeves must not be shortened or rolled up, exposing skin or flammable undergarments. Voltage-rated gloves with heavy-duty leather protectors have been shown to provide arc flash protection up to 10 cal/cm².

   (c) *Maintenance and Use.* Electrical protective equipment shall be maintained in a safe, reliable condition. Insulating equipment shall be inspected for damage before each day's use and immediately following any incident that can reasonably be suspected of having caused damage. Insulating gloves shall be given an air test, along with the inspection. Electrical protective equipment shall be subjected to periodic electrical tests. Test voltages shall be in accordance with applicable state, federal, or local codes and standards. The maximum intervals between tests shall not exceed that specified in Table 130.7(C)(7).

OSHA Connection
29 CFR 1910.137(c)(2)(xii)
The employer must certify that protective equipment has been tested. The certification must identify the equipment that passed the test and the date it was tested.

> Informational Note: See OSHA 29 CFR 1910.137; ASTM F478, *Standard Specification for In-Service Care of Insulating Line Hose and Covers*; ASTM F479, *Standard Specification for In-Service Care of Insulating Blankets*; and ASTM F496, *Standard Specification for In-Service Care of Insulating Gloves and Sleeves*, which contain information related to in-service and testing requirements for rubber insulating equipment.

Manufacturers of arc-rated clothing and other arc-rated protective equipment provide instructions for cleaning and care of their products. The electrical safety program must

Work Involving Electrical Hazards

130.7(C)(9)

describe the maintenance and cleaning process or processes that ensure the integrity of the apparel. Employees should inspect their arc-rated clothing and ensure that the apparel is not soiled with a flammable contaminant. Company logos and patches attached to arc-rated clothing must also be of arc-rated material.

▲ TABLE 130.7(C)(7) *Rubber Insulating Equipment, Maximum Test Intervals*

Rubber Insulating Equipment	When to Test
Blankets	Before first issue; every 12 months thereafter*
Covers	If insulating value is suspect
Gloves	Before first issue; every 6 months thereafter*
Line hose	If insulating value is suspect
Sleeves	Before first issue; every 12 months thereafter*

*New insulating equipment is not permitted to be placed into service unless it has been electrically tested within the previous 12 months. Insulating equipment that has been issued for service is not new and is required to be retested in accordance with the intervals in this table.

(8) Foot Protection. Where insulated footwear is used as protection against step and touch potential, dielectric footwear shall be required. Insulated soles shall not be used as primary electrical protection.

> Informational Note: Electrical Hazard footwear meeting ASTM F2413, *Standard Specification for Performance Requirements for Protective (Safety) Toe Cap Footwear*, can provide a secondary source of electric shock protection under dry conditions.

The integrity of the insulating quality of footwear with insulated soles cannot be easily determined after they have been worn in a work environment. Electrical hazard (EH) rated footwear with insulated soles must not serve as the primary protection from touch and step potential.

▲ **(9) Factors in Selection of Protective Clothing.** Clothing and equipment that provide worker protection from shock and arc flash hazards shall be used. If arc-rated clothing is required, it shall cover associated parts of the body as well as all flammable apparel while allowing movement and visibility.

Clothing and equipment required for the degree of exposure shall be permitted to be worn alone or integrated with flammable, nonmelting apparel. Garments that are not arc rated shall not be permitted to be used to increase the arc rating of a garment or of a clothing system.

> Informational Note: Protective clothing includes shirts, pants, coveralls, jackets, and parkas worn routinely by workers who, under normal working conditions, are exposed to momentary electric arc and related thermal hazards. Arc-rated rainwear worn in inclement weather is included in this category of clothing.

In order for the equipment to provide protection for an employee conducting justified energized electrical work, the equipment must be capable of withstanding the conditions presented by an incident. Shock protection PPE is typically used to insulate the employee from an exposure to a specific maximum voltage level. Arc flash PPE is typically used to limit the probability and severity of a thermal injury when an employee is exposed to a specific maximum incident energy arc flash. The employer is responsible for providing equipment capable of protecting the employee who is put at risk of an

---

OSHA Connection

29 CFR 1910.132(d)(1))
The employer must assess the workplace to determine if hazards are present or are likely to be present. If hazards necessitate the use of PPE, the employer must select and have the affected employee use PPE that properly fits, as well as communicate selection decisions to the affected employee.

Worker Alert

You are permitted to wear flammable garments — not meltable garments — under PPE. Compliant PPE has a 50 percent probability of exposing you to an energy level that may cause a second-degree burn. This energy level should not ignite flammable underlayers.

Worker Alert

Any gear or equipment worn over the PPE specified on the energized work permit must also be arc rated. Similar equipment may be available at the work site. It is ultimately your responsibility to ensure that the fall harness, hi-vis vest, or other gear you will be using is arc rated.

EXHIBIT 130.7

Arc-rated harness. (Courtesy of Salisbury by Honeywell)

injury during energized work. Verification by test is generally the only reliable method of determining that a material is capable of functioning as expected. The employer must verify that issued PPE meets the applicable consensus standard. See Informational Table 130.7(C)(14).

(a) *Layering.* Nonmelting, flammable fiber garments shall be permitted to be used as underlayers in conjunction with arc-rated garments in a layered system. If nonmelting, flammable fiber garments are used as underlayers, the system arc rating shall be sufficient to prevent breakopen of the innermost arc-rated layer at the expected arc exposure incident energy level to prevent ignition of flammable underlayers. Garments that are not arc rated shall not be permitted to be used to increase the arc rating of a garment or of a clothing system.

> Informational Note: A typical layering system might include cotton underwear, a cotton shirt and trouser, and an arc-rated coverall. Specific tasks might call for additional arc-rated layers to achieve the required protection level.

The layering being addressed is not only the layering of arc-rated PPE to increase the arc rating of the system but the layering of clothing worn under arc-rated PPE.

Layering can increase the overall protective characteristics of arc-rated clothing. Air is a good thermal insulator. Wearing multiple layers of clothing traps air in between the clothing layers. The layering effect tends to improve the thermal insulating efficiency of the protective system. However, the increase in efficiency does not necessarily increase the arc rating of the protective clothing system.

The combined rating of two arc-rated garments is not linear. Combination systems have to be tested, and the rating of the system cannot be determined by simply adding the arc rating of the two garments together.

(b) *Outer Layers.* Garments worn as outer layers over arc-rated clothing, such as jackets or rainwear, shall also be made from arc-rated material.

Flammable garments such as jackets, rainwear, or protective gear such as a harness worn over arc-rated clothing can act as a flame source themselves. This provides a heat source for the arc-rated clothing underneath, which potentially exceeds the insulating capacity of the arc-rated clothing, exposing the user to sufficient thermal energy to cause a burn injury. An arc-rated fall protection harness is shown in Exhibit 130.7.

Arc-rated rainwear made from arc-rated material that will enhance protection against an arc flash will be certified to ASTM F1506, *Standard Performance Specification for Flame Resistant and Arc Rated Textile Materials for Wearing Apparel for Use by Electrical Workers Exposed to Momentary Electric Arc and Related Thermal Hazards,* and bear an arc rating.

(c) *Underlayers.* Meltable fibers such as acetate, nylon, polyester, polypropylene, and spandex shall not be permitted in fabric underlayers.

Exception: An incidental amount of elastic used on nonmelting fabric underwear or socks shall be permitted.

> Informational Note No. 1: Arc-rated garments (e.g., shirts, trousers, and coveralls) worn as underlayers that neither ignite nor melt and drip in the course of an exposure to electric arc and related thermal hazards generally provide a higher system arc rating than nonmelting, flammable fiber underlayers.

Work Involving Electrical Hazards

130.7(C)(10)(a)

Informational Note No. 2: Arc-rated underwear or undergarments used as underlayers generally provide a higher system arc rating than nonmelting, flammable fiber underwear or undergarments used as underlayers.

> Significant injuries can occur when fabrics melt onto an employee's skin. Arc-rated PPE does not necessarily prevent the passage of thermal energy to the employee. However, properly rated PPE should limit the thermal energy level impinged on the employee's body to one that does not cause worse than a second-degree burn. This energy level may be sufficient to melt undergarments onto the employee's skin. Therefore, undergarments must be made of nonmelting material. However, an incidental quantity of these fabrics, such as those used in the elastic bands in underwear, is permitted. There may be some additional benefits to wearing arc-rated undergarments.

(d) *Coverage.* Clothing shall cover potentially exposed areas as completely as possible. Shirt and coverall sleeves shall be fastened at the wrists, shirts shall be tucked into pants, and shirts, coveralls, and jackets shall be closed at the neck.

> Arc-rated clothing must completely cover all body areas that are within the arc flash boundary. Shirt sleeves must be fastened at the wrists, and the top button of shirts and/or jackets must be fastened to minimize the chance that heated air could reach below the arc-rated clothing. Shirt sleeves should fit under the gauntlet of the protective gloves to minimize the chance that thermal energy could enter under the shirt sleeves.

(e) *Fit.* Tight-fitting clothing shall be avoided. Loose-fitting clothing provides additional thermal insulation because of air spaces. Arc-rated apparel shall fit properly such that it does not interfere with the work task.

> The fit of arc-rated clothing is important to the safety of the employee. Heat is conducted through the material when the surface of arc-rated clothing is heated. This conducted heat energy could result in a burn if the arc-rated clothing is touching skin. Arc-rated clothing must fit loosely to provide additional thermal insulation. However, arc-rated clothing must not be so loose that it interferes with the employee's movements. Men's and women's PPE is available. See Exhibit 130.8 for examples of arc-rated clothing sized specifically for women.

(f) *Interference.* The garment selected shall result in the least interference with the task but still provide the necessary protection. The work method, location, and task could influence the protective equipment selected.

> The plan for the work task must define the protective garments to be worn by the employee. As the plan is developed, the location and position of the employee must be considered to provide the best chance that the PPE does not interfere with the employee's movements during the work task. Doing a dry run of the task while wearing PPE will identify whether there are PPE restrictions for the task.

(10) Arc Flash Protective Equipment.

(a) *Arc Flash Suits.* Arc flash suit design shall permit easy and rapid removal by the wearer. The entire arc flash suit, including the hood's face shield, shall have an arc rating that is suitable for the arc flash exposure. When exterior air is supplied into the hood, the air hoses and pump housing shall be either covered by arc-rated materials or constructed of nonmelting and nonflammable materials.

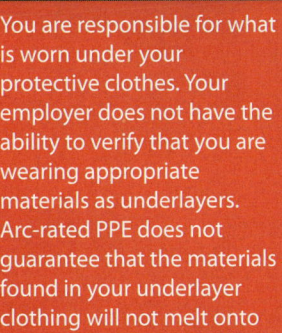

Worker Alert

You are responsible for what is worn under your protective clothes. Your employer does not have the ability to verify that you are wearing appropriate materials as underlayers. Arc-rated PPE does not guarantee that the materials found in your underlayer clothing will not melt onto your skin during an incident.

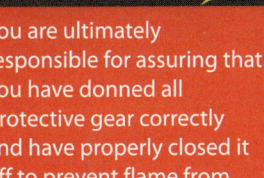

Worker Alert

You are ultimately responsible for assuring that you have donned all protective gear correctly and have properly closed it off to prevent flame from entering during an incident.

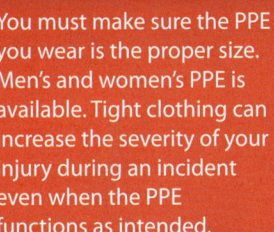

Worker Alert

You must make sure the PPE you wear is the proper size. Men's and women's PPE is available. Tight clothing can increase the severity of your injury during an incident even when the PPE functions as intended.

EXHIBIT 130.8

Arc-rated clothing specially sized for women. (Courtesy of Workrite Uniform)

The protection provided by an arc flash suit is comprised of more than the arc rating of the fabric or the fabric system. The design and construction of the suit is of great importance. A poorly or improperly designed suit may provide for the easy passage of energy through the holes or ports in the garment, thus bypassing the protection offered by the fabric.

Care must be taken if an older arc flash suit is still in use. In the past, suits were rated to the greater protection offered by the double layers of fabric on the chest — not by the lesser rating of the single layer of fabric on the arms and back. Protection adequate for the incident energy must be provided for all body parts within the arc flash boundary.

An arc flash suit must be evaluated as a complete system. A suit is not a combination of individual components that have not been evaluated as a whole. Exhibit 130.9 shows an employee in a 40 cal/cm² arc flash suit with other necessary PPE for the assigned task. An arc flash suit does not provide protection for an employee's hands and feet, which must also be covered by adequate arc fault protective equipment, also as shown in the exhibit.

(b) *Head Protection.*

(1) An arc-rated hood or an arc-rated balaclava with an arc-rated face shield shall be used when the back of the head is within the arc flash boundary.
(2) An arc-rated hood shall be used when the anticipated incident energy exposure exceeds 12 cal/cm² (50.2 J/cm²).

Complete protection for the head is required when the entire head is within the arc flash boundary. The combination of an arc-rated face shield and balaclava is different from a full arc-rated hood as shown in Exhibit 130.10.

Worker Alert

You must understand the working distance and arc flash boundary on the label. You should be aware of the proximity of your head to these boundaries. If during the performance of the assigned task your head is closer to the equipment than what was planned, there is a greater risk of injury.

Work Involving Electrical Hazards

EXHIBIT 130.9

A 40 cal/cm² arc flash suit. (Courtesy of Oberon Company)

EXHIBIT 130.10

Arc-rated face shield and balaclava (left) and an arc-rated hood (right). (Courtesy of Salisbury by Honeywell)

(c) *Face Protection.* Face shields shall have an arc rating suitable for the arc flash exposure. Face shields with a wrap-around guarding to protect the face, chin, forehead, ears, and neck area shall be used. Face shields without an arc rating shall not be used. Eye protection (safety glasses or goggles) shall always be worn under face shields or hoods.

Informational Note: Face shields made with energy-absorbing formulations that can provide higher levels of protection from the radiant energy of an arc flash are available, but these shields are tinted and can reduce visual acuity and color perception. Additional illumination of the task area might be necessary when these types of arc-protective face shields are used.

It is critical that the face and head be protected from the potential thermal energy exposure determined the by risk assessment. ASTM F2178, *Standard Test Method for Determining the Arc Rating and Standard Specification for Eye or Face Protective Products,* dictates that the arc rating of an arc flash face shield or hood is not the lesser rating of the window and the fabric. It mandates that a manufacturer conduct testing on its product as it is sold to the marketplace, since the shape and design of the hood and face shield often has more to do with the performance of the product than the fabric and plastic qualities.

The light transmission and clarity of colors visible through arc flash face shields and hood windows have dramatically improved. However, many have a green tint that can negatively impact visibility and color perception. Additional illumination may be required to enhance the employee's ability to see the task to be performed.

Face shields or hoods in accordance with ANSI/ISEA Z87.1, *American National Standard for Occupational and Educational Eye and Face Protection*, are considered as a "secondary eye protective device" that must be used with a "primary eye protective device" (spectacle or goggle) underneath. Marking of the face shield in Exhibit 130.11 indicates that the shield itself is not shatterproof and additional protection is necessary.

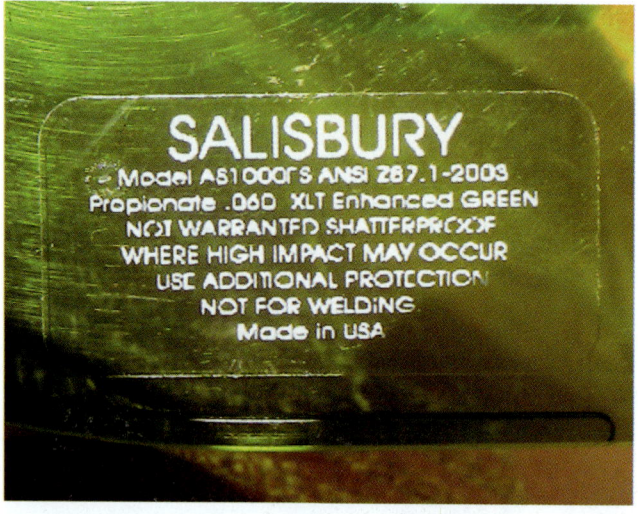

EXHIBIT 130.11

Face shield indicating need for additional impact protection for the eyes.

> **Worker Alert**
>
> Heavy-duty leather gloves have not been determined to limit injury when subjected to incident energies above 10 cal/cm². You should be provided with arc-rated gloves if the ability of leather gloves to provide protection is questionable. Note that equipment marked with an incident energy below 10 cal/cm² at a working distance may have a higher incident energy at your hand position.

(d) *Hand Protection.*

(1) Heavy-duty leather gloves or arc-rated gloves shall be worn where required for arc flash protection.

Informational Note: Heavy-duty leather gloves are made entirely of leather with minimum thickness of 0.03 in. (0.7 mm) and are unlined or lined with nonflammable, nonmelting fabrics.

Work Involving Electrical Hazards

130.7(C)(10)

Heavy-duty leather gloves meeting this requirement have been shown to have ATPV values in excess of 10 cal/cm² (41.9 J/cm²).

(2) Where insulating rubber gloves are used for shock protection, leather protectors shall be worn over the rubber gloves.

Informational Note: The leather protectors worn over rubber insulating gloves provide additional arc flash protection for the hands for arc flash protection exposure.

Generally, an arc flash risk assessment is based on an exposure distance of 18 or 36 inches. The thermal exposure to the hands will likely be much greater since they are often closer to the hazard than the body. Additional thermal protection for the hands is necessary in this case, which may also include equipment labeled at or below 1.2 cal/cm². This may require an additional determination of the incident energy at the hand position during the task or of the arc rating of PPE for the body parts that are nearer to the energized parts.

Leather materials are typically not arc flash rated. However, heavy-duty leather gloves made entirely of leather with a minimum thickness of 0.03 inch that is unlined or lined with nonflammable, nonmelting fabrics have been shown to have arc thermal performance values (ATPV) in excess of 10 cal/cm². Care should be taken when evaluating the arc rating of rubber gloves in conjunction with leather protectors. Because of the wide variation in the thickness of leather protectors, correlation of the test value could prove difficult. Before opting for leather gloves or protectors rather than arc-rated gloves, it is necessary to determine that they will provide adequate protection of the employee from the anticipated incident energy. Exhibit 130.12 shows heavy-duty leather protectors over insulated gloves.

Rehearsal of the work task while wearing layers of hand protection will determine if the dexterity for the task is sufficient. If the hands are being protected against only exposure to an arc flash, then heavy-duty leather gloves or arc-rated gloves can be used without voltage-rated rubber gloves.

(e) *Foot Protection.* Heavy-duty leather footwear or dielectric footwear or both provide some arc flash protection to the feet and shall be used in all exposures greater than 4 cal/cm² (16.75 J/cm²).

Footwear with an arc rating is not available. Normally, the employee's feet are less exposed than the hands or head due to the proximity of most tasks. However, employees should not wear footwear made from lightweight materials or from materials that are flammable or may melt and drip. In most cases, heavy-duty leather work shoes are satisfactory.

Dielectric overshoes, as shown in Exhibit 130.13, may be used over heavy-duty footwear.

EXHIBIT 130.12

Leather protectors over insulated gloves. (Courtesy of Salisbury by Honeywell)

EXHIBIT 130.13

Dielectric overshoes. (Courtesy of Salisbury by Honeywell)

△ **(11) Clothing Material Characteristics.** Arc-rated clothing shall meet the requirements described in 130.7(C)(12) and 130.7(C)(14).

> Informational Note No. 1: Arc-rated materials, such as flame-retardant-treated cotton, meta-aramid, para-aramid, and poly-benzimidazole (PBI) fibers, provide thermal protection. These materials can ignite but will not continue to burn after the ignition source is removed. Arc-rated fabrics can reduce burn injuries during an arc flash exposure by providing a thermal barrier between the arc flash and the wearer.
>
> Informational Note No. 2: Non–arc-rated cotton, polyester-cotton blends, nylon, nylon-cotton blends, silk, rayon, and wool fabrics are flammable. Fabrics, zipper tapes, and findings made of these materials can ignite and continue to burn on the body, resulting in serious burn injuries.
>
> Informational Note No. 3: Rayon is a cellulose-based (wood pulp) synthetic fiber that is a flammable but nonmelting material.

Clothing consisting of fabrics, zipper tapes, and findings made from flammable synthetic materials that melt at temperatures below 315°C (600°F), such as acetate, acrylic, nylon, polyester, polyethylene, polypropylene, and spandex, either alone or in blends, shall not be used.

> Informational Note: These materials melt as a result of arc flash exposure conditions, form intimate contact with the skin, and aggravate the burn injury.

Exception: Fiber blends that contain materials that melt, such as acetate, acrylic, nylon, polyester, polyethylene, polypropylene, and spandex, shall be permitted if such blends in fabrics are arc rated and do not exhibit evidence of melting and dripping during arc testing.

> Informational Note: ASTM F1959/F1959M, *Standard Test Method for Determining the Arc Rating of Materials for Clothing*, and ASTM F1506, *Standard Performance Specification for Flame Resistant and Arc Rated Textile Materials for Wearing Apparel for Use by Electrical Workers Exposed to Momentary Electric Arc and Related Thermal Hazards*, contain information on test methods used to determine the arc rating of fabrics.

△ **(12) Clothing and Other Apparel Not Permitted.** Clothing and other apparel (such as hard hat liners and hair nets) made from materials that do not meet the requirements of 130.7(C)(11) regarding melting or made from materials that do not meet the flammability requirements shall not be permitted to be worn.

> Informational Note: Some flame-resistant fabrics, such as non-flame-resistant modacrylic and non-durable flame-retardant treatments of cotton, are not recommended for industrial electrical or utility applications.

Apparel made from materials that are not arc rated must not be worn. For instance, hair nets, ear warmers, or head covers could melt onto an employee's hair and head unless they are made of arc-rated material.

Exception No. 1: Nonmelting, flammable (non–arc-rated) materials shall be permitted to be used as underlayers to arc-rated clothing, as described in 130.7(C)(11).

Exception No. 2: Where the work to be performed inside the arc flash boundary exposes the worker to multiple hazards, such as airborne contaminants, and the risk assessment identifies that the level of protection is adequate to address the arc flash hazard, non–arc-rated PPE shall be permitted.

Work Involving Electrical Hazards

130.7(C)(13)

(13) Care and Maintenance of Arc-Rated Clothing and Arc-Rated Arc Flash Suits.

(a) *Inspection.* Arc-rated apparel shall be inspected before each use. Work clothing or arc flash suits that are contaminated or damaged to the extent that their protective qualities are impaired shall not be used. Protective items that become contaminated with grease, oil, or flammable liquids or combustible materials shall not be used.

> Any flammable soiling or contamination on the surface of the arc-rated clothing can reduce or even void the arc rating of the apparel. The clothing must also be free from tears, cuts, or rips. Garments that are not suitable for use must be removed from service. If corrections can be made, such as laundering or repair using appropriate techniques, the garment can be returned to service; otherwise, the garment should be disposed of.

Worker Alert

PPE is the last line of defense preventing a permanent injury or your death. You should take great care in inspecting, maintaining, and storing the PPE that is intended to save your life if an incident occurs.

(b) *Manufacturer's Instructions.* The garment manufacturer's instructions for care and maintenance of arc-rated apparel shall be followed.

> The manufacturer's laundry care instructions are a required element of the labeling of any arc flash garment, per ASTM F1506, *Standard Performance Specification for Flame Resistant and Arc Rated Textile Materials for Wearing Apparel for Use by Electrical Workers Exposed to Momentary Electric Arc and Related Thermal Hazards.* Improper laundering or failure to follow the instruction provided by the manufacturer may diminish the longevity of the product's useful life and reduce the product's protective qualities.

(c) *Storage.* Arc-rated apparel shall be stored in a manner that prevents physical damage; damage from moisture, dust, or other deteriorating agents; or contamination from flammable or combustible materials.

> For the protective clothing to perform as intended, it must be protected when in use and in storage. Contaminants such as grease and oil must be avoided, since contamination reduces the thermal protection provided by the clothing. Exposure to flammable materials also must be avoided.

(d) *Cleaning, Repairing, and Affixing Items.* When arc-rated clothing is cleaned, manufacturer's instructions shall be followed to avoid loss of protection. When arc-rated clothing is repaired, the same arc-rated materials used to manufacture the arc-rated clothing shall be used to provide repairs.

Informational Note No. 1: Additional guidance is provided in ASTM F1506, *Standard Performance Specification for Flame Resistant and Arc Rated Textile Materials for Wearing Apparel for Use by Electrical Workers Exposed to Momentary Electric Arc and Related Thermal Hazards,* when trim, name tags, logos, or any combination thereof are affixed to arc-rated clothing.

Informational Note No. 2: Additional guidance is provided in ASTM F1449, *Standard Guide for Industrial Laundering of Flame, Thermal, and Arc Resistant Clothing,* and ASTM F2757, *Standard Guide for Home Laundering Care and Maintenance of Flame, Thermal, and Arc Resistant Clothing.*

> Manufacturers provide cleaning instructions for their products used for thermal protection. These instructions should be followed closely to ensure that the performance of the garment is not compromised. Company logos, replacement garment closures (zippers), and the sewing thread used to attach them may affect the arc rating of the PPE.

130.7(C)(14)
Article 130

△ (14) Standards for Personal Protective Equipment (PPE).

(a) General. PPE shall conform to applicable state, federal, or local codes and standards.

Informational Note No.1: The standards listed in Table 130.7(C)(14), which is part of this Informational Note, are examples of standards that contain information on the care, inspection, testing, and manufacturing of PPE.

Informational Note No.2: Non–arc-rated or flammable fabrics are not covered by any of the standards in Table 130.7(C)(14), Informational Note. See 130.7(C)(11) and 130.7(C)(12).

> Informational Table 130.7(C)(14) encompasses only protective equipment that is normally considered as PPE. The employer is required by 130.7(A) to provide the appropriate PPE to the employee. The PPE is required by this section to conform to the appropriate standard. Therefore, it is the employer's responsibility to determine that the PPE supplied to the employee is in compliance with the applicable standard.

TABLE 130.7(C)(14) Informational Note: Standards For Personal Protective Equipment

Subject	Document Title	Document Number
Apparel — Arc Rated	Standard Performance Specification for Flame Resistant and Arc Rated Textile Materials for Wearing Apparel for Use by Electrical Workers Exposed to Momentary Electric Arc and Related Thermal Hazards	ASTM F1506
	Standard Guide for Industrial Laundering of Flame, Thermal, and Arc Resistant Clothing	ASTM F1449
	Standard Guide for Home Laundering Care and Maintenance of Flame, Thermal and Arc Resistant Clothing	ASTM F2757
Aprons — Insulating	Standard Specification for Electrically Insulating Aprons	ASTM F2677
Eye and Face Protection — General	Eye and Face Protection — General Occupational and Educational Professional Eye and Face Protection Devices	ANSI/ISEA Z87.1
Face — Arc Rated	Standard Test Method for Determining the Arc Rating and Standard Specification for Personal Eye or Face Protective Products	ASTM F2178
Fall Protection	Standard Specification for Personal Climbing Equipment	ASTM F887
Footwear — Dielectric Specification	Standard Specification for Dielectric Footwear	ASTM F1117
Footwear — Dielectric Test Method	Standard Test Method for Determining Dielectric Strength of Dielectric Footwear	ASTM F1116
Footwear — Standard Performance Specification	Standard Specification for Performance Requirements for Protective (Safety) Toe Cap Footwear	ASTM F2413
Footwear — Standard Test Method	Standard Test Methods for Foot Protections	ASTM F2412
Gloves — Arc Rated	Standard Test Method for Determining Arc Ratings of Hand Protective Products Developed and Used for Electrical Arc Flash Protection	ASTM F2675/F2675M
Gloves — Leather Protectors	Standard Specification for Leather Protectors for Rubber Insulating Gloves and Mittens	ASTM F696
Gloves — Rubber Insulating	Standard Specification for Rubber Insulating Gloves	ASTM D120
Gloves and Sleeves — In-Service Care	Standard Specification for In-Service Care of Insulating Gloves and Sleeves	ASTM F496
Head Protection — Hard Hats	Industrial Head Protection	ANSI/ISEA Z89.1
Rainwear — Arc Rated	Standard Specification for Arc and Flame Resistant Rainwear	ASTM F1891
Rubber Protective Products — Visual Inspection	Standard Guide for Visual Inspection of Electrical Protective Rubber Products	ASTM F1236
Sleeves — Insulating	Standard Specification for Rubber Insulating Sleeves	ASTM D1051

Work Involving Electrical Hazards

130.7(C)(14)

(b) *Conformity Assessment.* All suppliers or manufacturers of PPE shall demonstrate conformity with an appropriate product standard by one of the following methods:

(1) Self-declaration with a Supplier's Declaration of Conformity
(2) Self-declaration under a registered quality management system and product testing by an accredited laboratory and a Supplier's Declaration of Conformity
(3) Certification by an accredited independent third-party certification organization

Informational Note: Examples of a process for conformity assessment to an appropriate product standard can be found in ANSI/ISEA 125, *American National Standard for Conformity Assessment of Safety and Personal Protective Equipment.* See Informative Annex H.4.

Previous editions of NFPA *70E* did not contain a requirement that the manufacturer of PPE have the equipment evaluated to applicable standards, only that PPE conform to standards. Section 130.7(C)(14)(b) is not a requirement that the manufacturer of PPE have its equipment evaluated for conformance to any standard. The requirement states only that the manufacturer be able to provide a claim as such. The effectiveness of protective equipment may not be evident until that equipment is called upon to perform its safety function. An employer must not supply their employees with substandard, counterfeit, or inappropriate PPE. Such gear may actually increase the injury to the employee when an incident occurs.

As with past NFPA *70E* editions, this section places the responsibility of determining compliance to the appropriate standard with the employer, purchaser, or person providing PPE to employees.

Delivery of one of these conformity methods to the purchaser of PPE does not absolve the employer from determining the validity of the claim. The employer must be competent to determine the standard applicable to the purchased equipment, the correctness of the claim, and the validity of the test results. It may be necessary for the purchaser to specify exactly which standards the purchased equipment must comply with.

Within the European Union (EU), and in some other locations, the Declaration of Conformity (DoC) is a legal document declaring that the equipment complies with the specific laws of the governing country. The individual signing that DoC resides within the EU. The signatory of that DoC is liable if the equipment leads to or is involved in an incident, and their residence within the EU allows for them to be formally charged.

In contrast, in 130.7(C)(14)(b)(1) the supplier's DoC is a variation of the system used in the EU. However, this DoC is not tied to a legal system and has no external oversight. It is the employer's responsibility to determine the validity of the declaration.

The accredited laboratory in 130.7(C)(14)(b)(2) is not necessarily an independent testing laboratory. Many companies are registered under the ISO 9000 series of standards for management systems. These companies may have an on-site laboratory to conduct evaluations and testing of their products by company employees.

130.7(C)(14)(b)(3) is testing to the applicable standards by an independent organization. Within the United States, OSHA has a process for accrediting organizations for performing evaluations using specific standards. Within NFPA *70E*, equipment evaluated under this system is considered to be listed.

An employer may not be competent in determining that purchased equipment complies with the applicable standard or that information provided demonstrates proper compliance. Often in order to facilitate acceptance of the equipment, listed equipment is employed even when a standard, such as NFPA *70E*, does not require listing.

Case Study

130.7(C)(14)

Scenario

Ian was an electrician for an electrical contracting firm. He arrived at a work site to conduct tasks assigned by the host employer. A documented meeting was held between the two. The host employer provided information on the electrical hazards within the equipment and documentation regarding the risk assessments for the equipment and tasks.

The initial task was to be voltage measurement in a 600-volt motor control center. The risk assessment provided by the host employer and equipment label indicated an incident energy of 5.1 cal/cm^2 at a distance of 18 inches. Ian donned the 8 cal/cm^2 PPE that was provided by his employer. During the act of measuring the terminal voltage an arc flash occurred. It was not determined what had initiated the incident. Ian was nonresponsive when the plant supervisor found him with his PPE severely damaged. Ian was rushed to the hospital.

Results

Ian sustained third-degree burns over nearly 60 percent of his body. The injury was so severe that he died 3 weeks later.

Analysis

Investigation after the incident determined that both the risk assessment provided to Ian as well as the information on the equipment label were appropriate for the task. Inspection of the label on his arc-rated PPE indicated a rating of 8 cal/cm^2 presumably based on the specified testing standards. The work procedure was deemed to be sufficient.

From the label information it was determined that the arc rating of the PPE had not been properly evaluated, and the PPE was not capable of withstanding the incident energy exposure. It is unclear if the inappropriate PPE exacerbated Ian's injury.

Ian's employer missed its responsibility to protect him from the electrical hazards present for his assigned tasks. Ian's employer may not have had the qualifications necessary to determine that the PPE issued to him was appropriate or capable of providing the protection necessary to save his life.

Relevant NFPA *70E* Requirements

If Ian's employer had followed the requirements of NFPA *70E*, Ian might not have been killed. Some of the requirements his employer had missed include the following:

- Provide employees with PPE [130.7(A)].
- PPE used must provide protection of the employee [130.7(C)(9)].
- PPE must conform to applicable standards [130.7(C)(14)(a)].

(c) *Marking.* All suppliers or manufacturers of PPE shall provide the following information on the personal protective equipment, on the smallest unit container, or contained within the manufacturer's instructions:

(1) Name of manufacturer
(2) Product performance standards to which the product conforms
(3) Arc rating where appropriate for the equipment
(4) One or more identifiers such as model, serial number, lot number, or traceability code
(5) Care instructions

> PPE labels are often the first indication of proper compliance to the appropriate standard. The employer must understand the marking required by a specific standard and the differences between similar standards. For example, one standard may apply to the general flame- or arc-resistance testing of a fabric. When this fabric is used to manufacturer an arc-rated suit, compliance does not rely on the fabric testing but with testing addressed in the standard for the entire suit, including zipper, buttons, logos, thread, face shield, and so forth. The correct standard must be referenced on the label.
>
> The employer must also be able to identify markings that indicate equipment has not been properly evaluated. For example, no PPE should be labeled as "NFPA approved" or as complying with NFPA *70E*.

Work Involving Electrical Hazards

(15) Arc Flash PPE Category Method. The requirements of 130.7(C)(15) shall apply when the arc flash PPE category method is used for the selection of arc flash PPE.

> If the arc flash risk assessment is conducted using the incident energy calculation method, the tables referenced in 130.7(C)(15)(a) and (C)(15)(b) are not permitted to be used to determine the required PPE.
>
> When conducting the arc flash risk assessment using the PPE category method, the tables must be used in the following sequence:
>
> 1. It must be determined if an arc flash is likely for the tasks specified in Table 130.5(C).
> 2. If an arc flash is likely, the hierarchy of risk controls in 110.1(H) must be exhausted before determining necessary PPE.
> 3. When PPE will be employed as a risk control, the level of PPE necessary must be determined from either Table 130.7(C)(15)(a) for ac systems or Table 130.7(C)(15)(b) for open-air dc systems.
> 4. Table 130.7(C)(15)(c) must then be used to determine the personal equipment needed to achieve the required PPE category.

It cannot be overstated that the use of the arc flash PPE category method requires strict adherence to the tables. This not only includes the specific equipment listed but also the electrical parameters on the table. This method does not require that extensive calculations be conducted — it provides a simple method for determining PPE for the equipment listed on the tables. The method does not allow for lower PPE categories to be selected for electrical circuit parameters that are lower than the table values. There is no interpolation of the table. The application of the tables is either a "go" or "no go."

The arc flash PPE category method cannot be used if the proposed task or the equipment type is not listed in the tables. Also, the arc flash PPE category method cannot be used if the electrical equipment is in the table but with electrical parameters that exceed any specified value. These cases would require that the incident energy analysis method be used.

As with any standard, the requirements included in the arc flash PPE category method tables are minimum requirements only. The user of this standard may determine that arc flash PPE is required for a task even where the table indicates it is not. It is permissible to require arc flash PPE rated above that required by this minimum standard. Where arc-rated equipment is used at less than its rating, there can be a substantial increase in the probability of success.

It is inappropriate to utilize the PPE category method as justification for authorizing energized work. The tables are devised to protect employees in instances in which placing equipment into an electrically safe work condition is either infeasible or creates a greater hazard. Justifying energized work under the assumption that it is safe to do so because of the PPE category tables exposes employees to undue hazards and an unnecessary risk of injury.

If the distance between a person and the potential arc source is different from the dimension specified in the table, the actual thermal energy might be greater or less than that anticipated by the PPE category method. A qualified person will understand that, if the actual working distance is different than that specified on the table and subsequently the label, the PPE specified for the task could be inadequate. A qualified person would not proceed with the task because the potential risk of injury has not been evaluated for this unforeseen condition, which makes the work permit invalid.

Any body parts, such as the hands and arms, might require greater protection than the person's chest and torso. These parts of the body should be protected accordingly. Where arc-rated equipment is used at less than its rating, there can be a substantial increase in the probability of success.

(a) *Alternating Current (ac) Equipment.* When the arc flash risk assessment performed in accordance with 130.5 indicates that arc flash PPE is required and the arc flash PPE category method is used for the selection of PPE for ac systems in lieu of the incident energy analysis of 130.5(E)(1), Table 130.7(C)(15)(a) shall be used to determine the arc flash PPE category. The estimated maximum available fault current, maximum fault-clearing times, and minimum working distances for various ac equipment types or classifications are listed in Table 130.7(C)(15)(a). An incident energy analysis shall be required in accordance with 130.5 for the following:

(1) Power systems with greater than the estimated maximum available fault current
(2) Power systems with longer than the maximum fault clearing times
(3) Less than the minimum working distance

> The arc flash PPE categories tables are only applicable when using the arc flash PPE category method. They do not apply to evaluation conducted using the incident energy analysis method.
>
> A determination of whether the arc flash PPE category method is applicable involves deciding whether or not the available fault current and total fault clearing time fall within the maximum available short-circuit current and fault clearing times parameters, which are indicated in the applicable equipment classification (category) for Table 130.7(C)(15)(a) for ac systems and Table 130.7(C)(15)(b) for dc systems. If the task is not listed in Table 130.5(C), then an incident energy analysis is required. If the equipment type is not listed or if the determined values for working distance, available fault current, or total fault clearing time are outside of the parameters given in Table 130.7(C)(15)(a), then an incident energy analysis is required. There is no interpolation of the parameters. The application of the tables is either a "go" or "no go."

(b) *Direct Current (dc) Equipment.* When the arc flash risk assessment performed in accordance with 130.5 indicates that arc flash PPE is required and the arc flash PPE category method is used for the selection of PPE for dc systems in lieu of the incident energy analysis of 130.5(E)(1), Table 130.7(C)(15)(b) shall be used to determine the arc flash PPE category. The estimated maximum available fault current, maximum arc duration, and working distances for dc equipment are listed in 130.7(C)(15)(b). An incident energy analysis shall be required in accordance with 130.5 for the following:

(1) Power systems with greater than the estimated maximum available fault current
(2) Power systems with longer than the maximum arc duration
(3) Less than the minimum working distance

Informational Note No.1: The arc flash PPE category of the protective clothing and equipment is generally based on determination of the estimated exposure level.

Informational Note No.2: In most cases, closed doors do not provide enough protection to eliminate the need for PPE in situations in which the state of the equipment is known to readily change (e.g., doors open or closed, rack in or rack out).

> The arc flash PPE categories tables are only applicable when using the arc flash PPE category method. They do not apply to evaluations conducted using the incident energy analysis method.

Work Involving Electrical Hazards 130.7(C)(15)

A determination of whether the arc flash PPE category method is applicable involves deciding whether or not the available fault current and arc-duration fall within the maximum available short-circuit current and arc-duration parameters, which are indicated in the applicable equipment classification (category) for Table 130.7(C)(15)(a) for ac systems and Table 130.7(C)(15)(b) for dc systems. If the task is not listed in Table 130.5(C), then an incident energy analysis is required. If the equipment type is not listed or if the determined values for working distance, available fault current, or arc duration are outside of the parameters given in Table 130.7(C)(15)(b), then an incident energy analysis is required. There is no interpolation of the parameters. The application of the tables is either a "go" or "no go."

(c) *Protective Clothing and Personal Protective Equipment (PPE).* Once the arc flash PPE category has been identified from Table 130.7(C)(15)(a) or Table 130.7(C)(15)(b), Table 130.7(C)(15)(c) shall be used to determine the required PPE for the task. Table 130.7(C)(15)(c) lists the requirements for PPE based on arc flash PPE categories 1 through 4. This clothing and equipment shall be used when working within the arc flash boundary.

> Informational Note No. 1: See Informative Annex H for a suggested simplified approach to ensure adequate PPE for electrical workers within facilities with large and diverse electrical systems.

An employer might implement a procedure that defines a general requirement for employees to wear a minimum level of protective clothing. The procedure could define a secondary level of protection that is easily recognized by employees and, still, a third level of protection that is required in special situations. Two key factors in this type of requirement are that the protection is adequate for the greatest exposure for each level of protective clothing and that each employee can recognize when a higher level of protection is necessary to wear.

> Informational Note No. 2: The PPE requirements of this section are intended to protect a person from arc flash hazards. While some situations could result in burns to the skin, even with the protection described in Table 130.7(C)(15)(c), burn injury should be reduced and survivable. Due to the explosive effect of some arc events, physical trauma injuries could occur. The PPE requirements of this section do not address protection against physical trauma other than exposure to the thermal effects of an arc flash.

The wearing of arc-rated clothing and protective equipment reduces the chance of thermal injury from an arc flash event. However, because of the nature of an arcing fault, determining the degree of each hazard associated with an arcing fault can be difficult. There currently is no consensus method for determining the pressure wave associated with an arc blast from an arc flash event.

> Informational Note No. 3: The arc rating for a particular clothing system can be obtained from the arc-rated clothing manufacturer.

The combined rating of arc-rated garments is not linear and can only be determined through testing. In order to have a combined rating, both garments must be arc rated. Combination systems have to be tested, and the overall rating of the system cannot be determined by simply adding the arc rating of the garments together.

OSHA Connection

29 CFR 1910.132(d)(1)
The employer must assess the workplace to determine if hazards are present or are likely to be present. If hazards necessitate the use of PPE, the employer must select and have each affected employee use PPE that properly fits, as well as communicate selection decisions to the affected employee.

TABLE 130.7(C)(15)(a) Arc-Flash PPE Categories for Alternating Current (ac) Systems

Equipment	Arc-Flash PPE Category	Arc-Flash Boundary
Panelboards or other equipment rated 240 volts and below Parameters: Maximum of 25 kA available fault current; maximum of 0.03 sec (2 cycles) fault clearing time; minimum working distance 455 mm (18 in.)	1	485 mm (19 in.)
Panelboards or other equipment rated greater than 240 volts and up to 600 volts Parameters: Maximum of 25 kA available fault current; maximum of 0.03 sec (2 cycles) fault clearing time; minimum working distance 455 mm (18 in.)	2	900 mm (3 ft)
600-volt class motor control centers (MCCs) Parameters: Maximum of 65 kA available fault current; maximum of 0.03 sec (2 cycles) fault clearing time; minimum working distance 455 mm (18 in.)	2	1.5 m (5 ft)
600-volt class motor control centers (MCCs) Parameters: Maximum of 42 kA available fault current; maximum of 0.33 sec (20 cycles) fault clearing time; minimum working distance 455 mm (18 in.)	4	4.3 m (14 ft)
600-volt class switchgear (with power circuit breakers or fused switches) and 600-volt class switchboards Parameters: Maximum of 35 kA available fault current; maximum of up to 0.5 sec (30 cycles) fault clearing time; minimum working distance 455 mm (18 in.)	4	6 m (20 ft)
Other 600-volt class (277 volts through 600 volts, nominal) equipment Parameters: Maximum of 65 kA available fault current; maximum of 0.03 sec (2 cycles) fault clearing time; minimum working distance 455 mm (18 in.)	2	1.5 m (5 ft)
NEMA E2 (fused contactor) motor starters, 2.3 kV through 7.2 kV Parameters: Maximum of 35 kA available fault current; maximum of up to 0.24 sec (15 cycles) fault clearing time; minimum working distance 910 mm (36 in.)	4	12 m (40 ft)
Metal-clad switchgear, 1 kV through 15 kV Parameters: Maximum of 35 kA available fault current; maximum of up to 0.24 sec (15 cycles) fault clearing time; minimum working distance 910 mm (36 in.)	4	12 m (40 ft)
Arc-resistant switchgear 1 kV through 15 kV [for clearing times of less than 0.5 sec (30 cycles) with an available fault current not to exceed the arc-resistant rating of the equipment], and metal-enclosed interrupter switchgear, fused or unfused of arc-resistant-type construction, 1 kV through 15 kV Parameters: Maximum of 35 kA available fault current; maximum of up to 0.24 sec (15 cycles) fault clearing time; minimum working distance 910 mm (36 in.)	N/A (doors closed) 4 (doors open)	N/A (doors closed) 12 m (40 ft)
Other equipment 1 kV through 15 kV Parameters: Maximum of 35 kA available fault current; maximum of up to 0.24 sec (15 cycles) fault clearing time; minimum working distance 910 mm (36 in.)	4	12 m (40 ft)

Note: For equipment rated 600 volts and below and protected by upstream current-limiting fuses or current-limiting circuit breakers sized at 200 amperes or less, the arc flash PPE category can be reduced by one number but not below arc flash PPE category 1.

Informational Note to Table 130.7(C)(15)(a): The following are typical fault clearing times of overcurrent protective devices:

(1) 0.5 cycle fault clearing time is typical for current limiting fuses when the fault current is within the current limiting range.
(2) 1.5 cycle fault clearing time is typical for molded case circuit breakers rated less than 1000 volts with an instantaneous integral trip.
(3) 3.0 cycle fault clearing time is typical for insulated case circuit breakers rated less than 1000 volts with an instantaneous integral trip or relay operated trip.
(4) 5.0 cycle fault clearing time is typical for relay operated circuit breakers rated 1 kV to 35 kV when the relay operates in the instantaneous range (i.e., "no intentional delay").
(5) 20 cycle fault clearing time is typical for low-voltage power and insulated case circuit breakers with a short time fault clearing delay for motor inrush.

Work Involving Electrical Hazards

130.7(C)(15)

(6) 30 cycle fault clearing time is typical for low-voltage power and insulated case circuit breakers with a short time fault clearing delay without instantaneous trip.

Informational Note No. 1: See Table 1 of IEEE 1584TM, *Guide for Performing Arc Flash Hazard Calculations*, for further information regarding Notes b through d.

Informational Note No. 2: An example of a standard that provides information for arc-resistant switchgear referred to in Table 130.7(C)(15)(a) is IEEE C37.20.7, *Guide for Testing Metal-Enclosed Switchgear Rated Up to 38 kV for Internal Arcing Faults*.

TABLE 130.7(C)(15)(b) Arc-Flash PPE Categories for Direct Current (dc) Systems

Equipment	Arc-Flash PPE Category	Arc-Flash Boundary
Storage batteries, dc switchboards, and other dc supply sources Parameters: Greater than or equal to 100 V and less than or equal to 250 V Maximum arc duration and minimum working distance: 2 sec @ 455 mm (18 in.)		
Available fault current less than 4 kA	2	900 mm (3 ft)
Available fault current greater than or equal to 4 kA and less than 7 kA	2	1.2 m (4 ft)
Available fault current greater than or equal to 7 kA and less than 15 kA	3	1.8 m (6 ft)
Storage batteries, dc switchboards, and other dc supply sources Parameters: Greater than 250 V and less than or equal to 600 V Maximum arc duration and minimum working distance: 2 sec @ 455 mm (18 in.)		
Available fault current less than 1.5 kA	2	900 mm (3 ft)
Available fault current greater than or equal to 1.5 kA and less than 3 kA	2	1.2 m (4 ft)
Available fault current greater than or equal to 3 kA and less than 7 kA	3	1.8 m (6 ft.)
Available fault current greater than or equal to 7 kA and less than 10 kA	4	2.5 m (8 ft)

Notes

(1) Apparel that can be expected to be exposed to electrolyte must meet both of the following conditions:
   (a) Be evaluated for electrolyte protection

   Informational Note: ASTM F1296, *Standard Guide for Evaluating Chemical Protective Clothing*, contains information on evaluating apparel for protection from electrolyte.

   (b) Be arc-rated

   Informational Note: ASTM F1891, *Standard Specifications for Arc Rated and Flame Resistant Rainwear*, contains information on evaluating arc-rated apparel.

(2) A two-second arc duration is assumed if there is no overcurrent protective device (OCPD) or if the fault clearing time is not known. If the fault clearing time is known and is less than 2 seconds, an incident energy analysis could provide a more representative result.

Informational Note No. 1: When determining available fault current, the effects of cables and any other impedances in the circuit should be included. Power system modeling is the best method to determine the available short-circuit current at the point of the arc. Battery cell short-circuit current can be obtained from the battery manufacturer. See Informative Annex D.5 for the basis for table values and alternative methods to determine dc incident energy. Methods should be used with good engineering judgment.

Informational Note No. 2: The methods for estimating the dc arc-flash incident energy that were used to determine the categories for this table are based on open-air incident energy calculations. Open-air calculations were used because many battery systems and other dc process systems are in open areas or rooms. If the specific task is within an enclosure, it would be prudent to consider additional PPE protection beyond the value shown in this table. Research with ac arc flash has shown a multiplier of as much as 3× for arc-in-a-box [508 mm (20 in.) cube] versus open air. Engineering judgment is necessary when reviewing the specific conditions of the equipment and task to be performed, including the dimensions of the enclosure and the working distance involved.

> The arc flash PPE category method is only suitable for use where open-air arcs are involved, such as those found in many battery systems or other dc process systems that are in open areas or rooms. The arc flash PPE category method does not cover arc-in-a-box type situations where the incident energy is focused and a multiplier effect is involved.

TABLE 130.7(C)(15)(c) Personal Protective Equipment (PPE)

> Table 130.7(C)(15)(c) is not applicable to evaluations conducted using the incident energy analysis method. For arc flash PPE clothing requirements for the incident energy analysis method, see 130.5(G) and 130.7(C)(1) though (C)(14).

Arc-Flash PPE Category	PPE
1	**Arc-Rated Clothing, Minimum Arc Rating of 4 cal/cm² (16.75 J/cm²)[a]**
	Arc-rated long-sleeve shirt and pants or arc-rated coverall
	Arc-rated face shield[b] or arc flash suit hood
	Arc-rated jacket, parka, rainwear, or hard hat liner (AN)
	Protective Equipment
	Hard hat
	Safety glasses or safety goggles (SR)
	Hearing protection (ear canal inserts)[c]
	Heavy-duty leather gloves[d]
	Leather footwear (AN)
2	**Arc-Rated Clothing, Minimum Arc Rating of 8 cal/cm² (33.5 J/cm²)[a]**
	Arc-rated long-sleeve shirt and pants or arc-rated coverall
	Arc-rated flash suit hood or arc-rated face shield[b] and arc-rated balaclava
	Arc-rated jacket, parka, rainwear, or hard hat liner (AN)
	Protective Equipment
	Hard hat
	Safety glasses or safety goggles (SR)
	Hearing protection (ear canal inserts)[c]
	Heavy-duty leather gloves[d]
	Leather footwear
3	**Arc-Rated Clothing Selected so That the System Arc Rating Meets the Required Minimum Arc Rating of 25 cal/cm² (104.7 J/cm²)[a]**
	Arc-rated long-sleeve shirt (AR)
	Arc-rated pants (AR)
	Arc-rated coverall (AR)
	Arc-rated arc flash suit jacket (AR)
	Arc-rated arc flash suit pants (AR)
	Arc-rated arc flash suit hood
	Arc-rated gloves[d]
	Arc-rated jacket, parka, rainwear, or hard hat liner (AN)
	Protective Equipment
	Hard hat
	Safety glasses or safety goggles (SR)
	Hearing protection (ear canal inserts)[c]
	Leather footwear

Work Involving Electrical Hazards

TABLE 130.7(C)(15)(c) Continued.

Arc-Flash PPE Category	PPE
4	**Arc-Rated Clothing Selected so That the System Arc Rating Meets the Required Minimum Arc Rating of 40 cal/cm² (167.5 J/cm²)**[a]
	Arc-rated long-sleeve shirt (AR)
	Arc-rated pants (AR)
	Arc-rated coverall (AR)
	Arc-rated arc flash suit jacket (AR)
	Arc-rated arc flash suit pants (AR)
	Arc-rated arc flash suit hood
	Arc-rated gloves[c]
	Arc-rated jacket, parka, rainwear, or hard hat liner (AN)
	Protective Equipment
	Hard hat
	Safety glasses or safety goggles (SR)
	Hearing protection (ear canal inserts)[c]
	Leather footwear

AN: As needed (optional). AR: As required. SR: Selection required.
[a] Arc rating is defined in Article 100.
[b] Face shields are to have wrap-around guarding to protect not only the face but also the forehead, ears, and neck, or, alternatively, an arc-rated arc flash suit hood is required to be worn.
[c] Other types of hearing protection are permitted to be used in lieu of or in addition to ear canal inserts provided they are worn under an arc-rated arc flash suit hood.
[d] If rubber insulating gloves with leather protectors are used, additional leather or arc-rated gloves are not required. The combination of rubber insulating gloves with leather protectors satisfies the arc flash protection requirement.

> The arc-rated clothing and protective equipment shown in Table 130.7(C)(15)(c) are only to be used with Table 130.7(C)(15)(a) for ac systems and Table 130.7(C)(15)(b) for dc systems. Table 130.7(C)(15)(c) is not to be used to select PPE as a result of an incident energy calculation. The PPE listed in these tables protect only from an arc flash hazard. Arc-rated clothing is available in many constructions, and arc flash PPE rated in cal/cm² is suitable for that incident energy level. Table 130.7(C)(15)(c) suggests acceptable combinations of clothing items to achieve a desired arc flash PPE category. Other combinations are possible.
>
> Table 130.7(C)(15)(c) provides general information that can help an employee understand the process for selecting clothing based on an arc flash PPE category designation, but it does not describe any required combination or construction of a protective system. The manufactured system can differ from what is described in the table; the clothing manufacturer needs to be consulted. See Informational Note No. 3 to 130.7(C)(15)(c).

(D) Other Protective Equipment.

(1) Insulated Tools and Equipment. Employees shall use insulated tools or handling equipment, or both, when working inside the restricted approach boundary of exposed energized electrical conductors or circuit parts where tools or handling equipment might make unintentional contact. Insulated tools shall be protected from damage to the insulating material.

Informational Note: See 130.4(D), Shock Protection Boundaries.

(a) *Requirements for Insulated Tools.* The following requirements shall apply to insulated tools:

(1) Insulated tools shall be rated for the voltages on which they are used.
(2) Insulated tools shall be designed and constructed for the environment to which they are exposed and the manner in which they are used.
(3) Insulated tools and equipment shall be inspected prior to each use. The inspection shall look for damage to the insulation or damage that can limit the tool from performing its intended function or could increase the potential for an incident (e.g., damaged tip on a screwdriver).

When working inside the restricted approach boundary, employees must select and follow work procedures, which include the use of insulated tools. The term *insulated* means that the tool manufacturer has assigned a voltage rating to the insulating material. Qualified persons are expected to be competent to inspect an insulated tool for potential damage. Qualified persons also must be able to determine whether the voltage rating remains intact.

Exhibit 130.14 shows marked insulated tools. Only tools with a defined voltage rating are considered to be insulated. It is important for employees to look for the markings on the tool before using it. Tools with unmarked rubber grips and plastic handles must not be used in lieu of a properly rated tool.

EXHIBIT 130.14

Examples of insulated tools. (Courtesy of Bobby Gray)

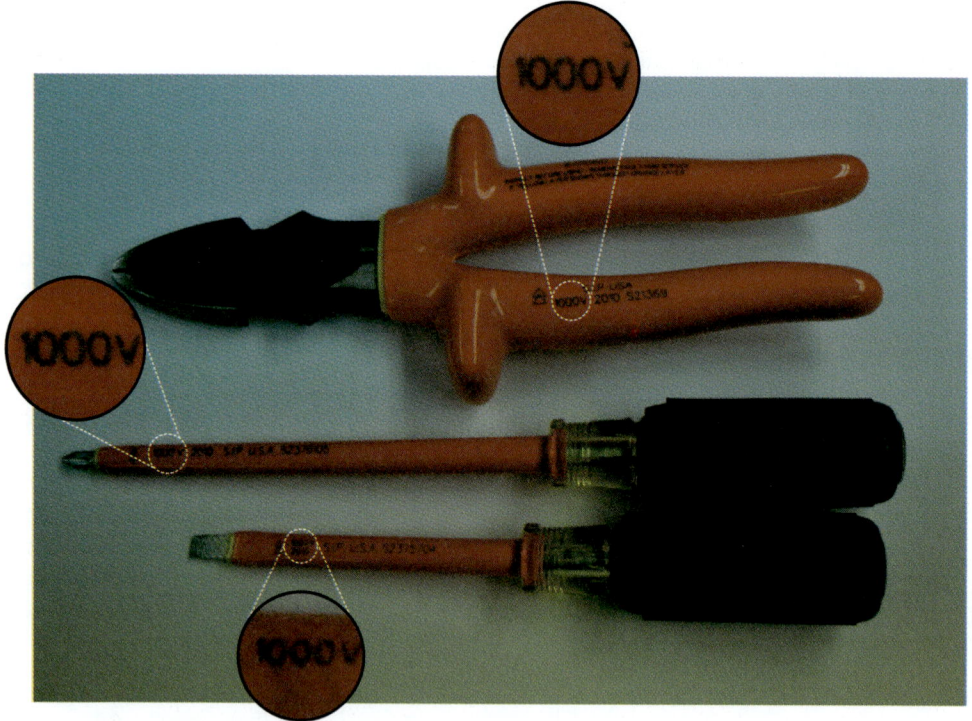

(b) *Fuse or Fuseholder Handling Equipment.* Fuse or fuseholder handling equipment, insulated for the circuit voltage, shall be used to remove or install a fuse if the fuse terminals are energized.

Replacing fuses live is energized work and, as such, must be justified.

(c) *Ropes and Handlines.* Ropes and handlines used within the limited approach boundary shall be nonconductive.

> Where ropes and handlines are used around energized conductors and circuit parts, they must be made of nonconductive material to protect employees from potential shock hazards.

(d) *Fiberglass-Reinforced Plastic Rods.* Fiberglass-reinforced plastic rod and tube used for live-line tools shall meet the requirements of applicable portions of electrical codes and standards dealing with electrical installation requirements.

Informational Note: For further information concerning electrical codes and standards dealing with installation requirements, refer to ASTM F711, *Standard Specification for Fiberglass-Reinforced Plastic (FRP) Rod and Tube Used in Live Line Tools.*

(e) *Portable Ladders.* Portable ladders shall have nonconductive side rails when used within the limited approach boundary or where the employee or ladder could contact exposed energized electrical conductors or circuit parts. Nonconductive ladders shall meet the requirements of applicable state, federal, or local codes and standards.

Informational Note: The standards listed in Table 130.7(G), Informational Note are examples of standards that contain information on portable ladders.

> The use of ladders with conductive side rails in the vicinity of exposed energize conductors or circuit parts creates an unacceptable risk of injury from an electric shock. It may also create an unacceptable risk of injury from a potential arc flash hazard, depending on the circumstances.

(f) *Protective Shields.* Protective shields, protective barriers, or insulating materials shall be used to protect each employee from shock, burns, or other electrically related injuries while an employee is working within the limited approach boundary of energized conductors or circuit parts that might be unintentionally contacted or where dangerous electric heating or arcing might occur. When normally enclosed energized conductors or circuit parts are exposed for maintenance or repair, they shall be guarded to protect unqualified persons from contact with the energized conductors or circuit parts.

> The use of these protective techniques is necessary to protect the employee from injuries from potential exposure to electrical hazards. Generally, protective shields, protective barriers, and insulating material are not considered to be full protection from an arc flash event. Anyone within the arc flash boundary must use appropriate arc flash personal and other protective equipment to be effectively protected from a potential arc flash event.
>
> When qualified persons are performing tasks within the restricted approach boundary and unqualified persons are allowed within the limited approach boundary, the energized conductors and circuit parts are to be guarded to protect the unqualified persons from contacting them and thereby initiating an event. For equipment to be considered guarded, the unqualified person must be isolated from, kept away from, or protected from the energized conductors or circuit parts.

(g) *Rubber Insulating Equipment.* Rubber insulating equipment used for protection from unintentional contact with energized conductors or circuit parts shall meet the requirements of applicable state, federal, or local codes and standards.

Informational Note: The standards listed in Table 130.7(G), Informational Note are examples of standards that contain information on rubber insulating equipment.

(h) *Voltage-Rated Plastic Guard Equipment.* Plastic guard equipment for protection of employees from unintentional contact with energized conductors or circuit parts, or for protection of employees or energized equipment or material from contact with ground, shall meet the requirements of applicable state, federal, or local codes and standards.

Informational Note: The standards listed in Table 130.7(G), Informational Note are examples of standards that contain information on voltage-rated plastic guard equipment.

(i) *Physical or Mechanical Barriers.* Physical or mechanical (field-fabricated) barriers shall be installed no closer than the limited approach boundary distance given in Table 130.4(D)(a) and Table 130.4(D)(b). While the barrier is being installed, the limited approach boundary distance specified in Table 130.4(D)(a) and Table 130.4(D)(b) shall be maintained, or the energized conductors or circuit parts shall be placed in an electrically safe work condition.

(E) Alerting Techniques.

> People who are not involved in the work task can be exposed to an electrical hazard when the work task is being executed. People must be provided with a warning that an electrical hazard exists to avoid unnecessary exposure to electrical hazards.

(1) Safety Signs and Tags. Safety signs, safety symbols, or tags shall be used where necessary to warn employees about electrical hazards that might endanger them. Such signs and tags shall meet the requirements of applicable state, federal, or local codes and standards.

Informational Note No. 1: Safety signs, tags, and barricades used to identify energized "look-alike" equipment can be employed as an additional preventive measure.

Informational Note No. 2: The standards listed in Table 130.7(G), Informational Note are examples of standards that contain infomation on safety signs and tags.

(2) Barricades. Barricades shall be used in conjunction with safety signs where it is necessary to prevent or limit employee access to work areas containing energized conductors or circuit parts. Conductive barricades shall not be used where it might increase the likelihood of exposure to an electrical hazard. Barricades shall be placed no closer than the limited approach boundary given in Table 130.4(D)(a) and Table 130.4(D)(b). Where the arc flash boundary is greater than the limited approach boundary, barricades shall not be placed closer than the arc flash boundary.

> Barricades are not intended to prevent approach to an area. Instead, a barricade is intended to act as a warning device. When installed, the barricade should enclose the area containing the electrical hazard. The barricade must not be closer to the exposed energized electrical conductor or circuit part than the limited approach boundary. The barricade should be placed so as not to impede the exit of employees within the boundary. See Exhibit 130.15 for an example of a barricade.

Worker Alert

The placement of barriers and barricades will often be your duty as part of performing the task. The limited approach boundary distance will not be found on an equipment label — it should be on the energized work permit. If the task does not require a work permit, you must be capable of determining the distance from the appropriate table.

Work Involving Electrical Hazards 130.7(G)

EXHIBIT 130.15

Barricade used to keep unqualified persons from an area. (Courtesy of The T-CAP / www.TheTCap.com)

(3) Attendants. If signs and barricades do not provide sufficient warning and protection from electrical hazards, an attendant shall be stationed to warn and protect employees. The primary duty and responsibility of an attendant providing manual signaling and alerting shall be to keep unqualified employees outside a work area where the unqualified employee might be exposed to electrical hazards. An attendant shall remain in the area as long as there is a potential for employees to be exposed to the electrical hazards.

> The attendant should have no other duty than to deliver the warning.

N (4) Cutting, Removing, or Rerouting of Conductors. Where conductors are de-energized in order to cut, remove, or reroute them and conductor terminations are not within sight, such as where they are in a junction or pull box, additional steps to verify absence of voltage or identify the conductors shall be taken prior to cutting, removing, or rerouting the conductors.

> Informational Note: Additional steps to be taken include, but are not limited to, remotely spiking the conductors and pulling the conductors to visually verify movement. Nonshielded conductors could be additionally verified with a noncontact test instrument, and shielded conductors could be verified with devices to identify the conductors.

△ (F) Look-Alike Equipment. Where work performed on equipment that is de-energized and placed in an electrically safe condition exists in a work area with other energized equipment that is similar in size, shape, and construction, one of the alerting methods in 130.7(E)(1), (2), or (3) shall be employed to prevent the employee from entering look-alike equipment.

> Similar electrical equipment is likely to exist in the same physical area when an installation involves multiple similar processes. Often the only visible difference is the equipment labels. Employees must be aware that equipment similar to the one that is being maintained exists. Employees should consider installing some temporary identifying mark to reduce the chance of opening the wrong equipment.

(G) Standards for Other Protective Equipment. Other protective equipment required in 130.7(D) shall conform to the applicable state, federal, or local codes and standards.

> Informational Note: The standards listed in Table 130.7(G), which is part of this Informational Note, are examples of standards that contain information on other protective equipment.

Informational Table 130.7(G) identifies standards that define requirements for specific protective equipment. All equipment listed in the table impacts safe work procedures that a qualified person should implement. In order to provide protection for an employee conducting justified energized electrical work, the equipment must be capable of withstanding the conditions presented by an incident. Shock protection PPE is typically used to insulate the employee from an exposure to a specific maximum voltage level. Arc flash PPE is typically used to limit the probability and severity of a thermal injury when an employee is exposed to a specific maximum incident energy arc flash. Verification by test is generally the only reliable method of determining that a material is capable of functioning as expected.

The employer is required by 130.7(A) to provide the appropriate PPE to the employee, and the provided protective equipment is required by this section to conform to the appropriate standard. The employer, who is often considered the authority having jurisdiction (AHJ) within the scope of this standard, is responsible for providing equipment capable of protecting the employee who is put at risk of an injury during energized work. The employer must verify that issued equipment meets the applicable consensus standard. Section 130.7(C)(14)(b) provides three methods that may assist an employer in determining compliance with an appropriate standard. The employer is responsible for determining the validity of any stated compliance by a PPE manufacturer. An employer may not be competent in determining that purchased equipment complies with the applicable standard or that information provided demonstrates compliance. Often in order to facilitate acceptance of the equipment, listed equipment is employed even when a standard, such as NFPA *70E*, does not require listing.

△ TABLE 130.7(G) *Informational Note: Standards on Other Protective Equipment*

Subject	Document	Document Number
Arc Protective Blankets	Standard Test Method for Determining the Protective Performance of an Arc Protective Blanket for Electric Arc Hazards	ASTM F2676
Blankets	Standard Specification for Rubber Insulating Blankets	ASTM D1048
Blankets — In-service Care	Standard Specification for In-Service Care of Insulating Blankets	ASTM F479
Covers	Standard Specification for Rubber Covers	ASTM D1049
Fiberglass Rods — Live Line Tools	Standard Specification for Fiberglass-Reinforced Plastic (FRP) Rod and Tube Used in Live Line Tools	ASTM F711
Insulated Hand Tools	Standard Specification for Insulated and Insulating Hand Tools	ASTM F1505
Ladders	American National Standard for Ladders — Wood — Safety Requirements	ANSI/ASC A14.1
	American National Standard for Ladders — Fixed — Safety Requirements	ANSI/ASC A14.3
	American National Standard Safety Requirements for Job Made Ladders	ANSI ASC A14.4
	American National Standard for Ladders-Portable Reinforced Safety Requirements	ANSI ASC A14.5
Line Hose	Standard Specification for Rubber Insulating Line Hoses	ASTM D1050
Line Hose and Covers — In-service Care	Standard Specification for In-Service Care of Insulating Line Hose and Covers	ASTM F478
Plastic Guard	Standard Test Methods and Specifications for Electrically Insulating Plastic Guard Equipment for Protection of Workers	ASTM F712
Sheeting	Standard Specification for PVC Insulating Sheeting	ASTM F1742
	Standard Specification for Rubber Insulating Sheeting	ASTM F2320
Safety Signs and Tags	Series of Standards for Safety Signs and Tags	ANSI Z535
Shield Performance on Live Line Tool	Standard Test Method for Determining the Protective Performance of a Shield Attached on Live Line Tools or on Racking Rods for Electric Arc Hazards	ASTM F2522
Temporary Protective Grounds — In-service Testing	Standard Specification for In-Service Test Methods for Temporary Grounding Jumper Assemblies Used on De-energized Electric Power Lines and Equipment	ASTM F2249
Temporary Protective Grounds — Test Specification	Standard Specification for Temporary Protective Grounds to Be Used on De-energized Electric Power Lines and Equipment	ASTM F855

Work Involving Electrical Hazards

130.8(C)

> Informational Table 130.7(G) encompasses only protective equipment that is normally considered as PPE. For instance, voltmeters provide information that enables employees to protect themselves from electrical shock, but because they are not generally considered PPE, voltmeters are not covered in the table.

130.8 Work Within the Limited Approach Boundary or Arc Flash Boundary of Overhead Lines.

> In most cases, overhead conductors are guarded by being elevated so that they are not subject to incidental contact. When working on an overhead conductor, employees are likely to be supported by an elevated or articulating platform or by a permanently installed platform or deck. When using such support methods, employees may have difficulty escaping from an arc flash or avoiding direct contact with energized conductors. These factors must be considered in the risk assessment and emphasize the need for an emergency recovery plan.

(A) Uninsulated and Energized. Where work is performed in locations containing uninsulated energized overhead lines that are not guarded or isolated, precautions shall be taken to prevent employees from contacting such lines directly with any unguarded parts of their body or indirectly through conductive materials, tools, or equipment. Where the work to be performed is such that contact with uninsulated energized overhead lines is possible, the lines shall be de-energized and visibly grounded at the point of work or suitably guarded.

> Electrical conductors that are not insulated for the circuit voltage have the same potential for shock and electrocution as do conductors that are completely bare. Some overhead conductors have a covering as protection from environmental degradation, but the covering has no insulation rating.
>
> Exhibit 130.16(a) illustrates the operation of equipment in close proximity of overhead power lines. Equipment such as a crane, with the capability of reaching overhead power lines, presents a shock hazard to the equipment operator and to employees who are working in the vicinity of the equipment. Qualified persons must observe and comply with the approach boundaries identified in Table 130.4(D)(a) for ac systems or Table 130.4(D)(b) for dc systems. While the employee is at ground level, the overhead bare conductors are adequately isolated from contact. When the bucket approaches the conductors, the possibility of contact with the bare conductors is greatly increased, and the conductors need to be de-energized and visibly grounded. Exhibit 130.16(b) shows signage indicating that equipment booms should be kept a safe distance away from overhead power lines. See 130.8(F) regarding elevated equipment.
>
> Employees should not work near overhead conductors unless they are protected from unintentional contact with the conductors. Personnel carrying conduits, pipes, ladders, and other long objects must exercise caution to avoid entering the space defined by the limited approach boundary. When long objects are moved, employees should be assigned to each end of the object to maintain control of both ends.

(B) Determination of Insulation Rating. A qualified person shall determine if the overhead electrical lines are insulated for the lines' operating voltage.

(C) De-energizing or Guarding. If the lines are to be de-energized, arrangements shall be made with the person or organization that operates or controls the lines to de-energize them and visibly ground them at the point of work. If arrangements are made to use protective measures, such as guarding, isolating, or insulation, these precautions shall prevent each employee

EXHIBIT 130.16

(a) A crane operating in close proximity to energized overhead power lines. (Courtesy of FEMA, photo by George Armstrong) (b) Signage warning against contact with overhead power lines.

from contacting such lines directly with any part of his or her body or indirectly through conductive materials, tools, or equipment.

> The operation and maintenance of transmission and distribution lines is often the responsibility of a utility. The person responsible for operation and maintenance of the affected conductors must be consulted and directly involved in de-energizing and grounding the overhead conductors.
>
> Suitable guards should be installed to prevent accidental contact with the overhead lines. However, to eliminate the chance of unintentional contact, the guards must be of sufficient strength to control the approach or any possible movement of the person or object. In most instances, line hose is not satisfactory to prevent unintentional contact.
>
> Safety grounds, as shown in Exhibit 120.14, must be installed in a manner that provides an equipotential zone for the work area. An equipotential zone is an area in which no (or unperceivable) voltage differences exist between exposed conductive surfaces that an employee might come in contact with while performing the task. Other conductors in the immediate vicinity of the work area that could be contacted must be guarded from potential contact.

(D) Employer and Employee Responsibility. The employer and employee shall be responsible for ensuring that guards or protective measures are satisfactory for the conditions. Employees shall comply with established work methods and the use of protective equipment.

Work Involving Electrical Hazards

130.8(F)(1)

Employers are responsible for providing the electrical safety program, and employees are responsible for implementing the requirements of the program. Both employers and employees are responsible for ensuring that any installed guards are adequate for the conditions. The employer and employee must work together to make sure that effective procedures exist and that they are applied stringently and reviewed frequently.

(E) Approach Distances for Unqualified Persons. When unqualified persons are working on the ground or in an elevated position near overhead lines, the location shall be such that the employee and the longest conductive object the employee might contact do not come closer to any unguarded, energized overhead power line than the limited approach boundary in Table 130.4(D)(a), column 2 or Table 130.4(D)(b), column 2.

The approach distance for unqualified persons remains the same, regardless of the installation method for the conductor(s). The limited approach distance depends on whether the distance between the conductor and the employee is under the employee's control.

If the supporting platform can move, as would be the case for an articulating platform, column 2 of both Table 130.4(D)(a) and Table 130.4(D)(b) applies. If the conductor is supported on a messenger or similar support method, the conductor can move as the wind blows, and therefore the distance between the employee and the conductor is not under the employee's control, and column 2 still applies. If the overhead conductor is fixed into position, as is the case with solid bus conductors, and the employee is standing on a fixed platform or scaffold, the employee has control of the distance between himself or herself and the conductor, and column 3 applies.

> Informational Note: Objects that are not insulated for the voltage involved should be considered to be conductive.

Some conductors have a covering that is intended to serve as protection from the effects of the environment. This covering is not insulating material and generally has no established voltage rating. Weatherproof conductors must be considered to be uninsulated.

(F) Vehicular and Mechanical Equipment.

(1) Elevated Equipment. Where any vehicle or mechanical equipment structure will be elevated near energized overhead lines, it shall be operated so that the limited approach boundary distance of Table 130.4(D)(a), column 2 or Table 130.4(D)(b), column 2, is maintained. However, under any of the following conditions, the clearances shall be permitted to be reduced:

The limited approach boundary given in column 2 of both Table 130.4(D)(a) and Table 130.4(D)(b) defines the closest dimension that any vehicle or mechanical equipment structure can be elevated to an exposed energized overhead conductor, unless conditions defined in this section permit closer approach. Distances can be difficult to estimate when standing on the ground or sitting in the seat of a crane or other mobile equipment.

(1) If the vehicle is in transit with its structure lowered, the limited approach boundary to overhead lines in Table 130.4(D)(a), column 2 or Table 130.4(D)(b), column 2, shall be permitted to be reduced by 1.83 m (6 ft). If insulated barriers, rated for the voltages involved, are installed and they are not part of an attachment to the vehicle, the clearance shall be permitted to be reduced to the design working dimensions of the insulating barrier.

> Any elevating structure of a vehicle, such as a boom or dump truck bed, must be in the resting position. The limited approach boundary cannot be reduced if such structures are not in a resting position.

(2) If the equipment is an aerial lift insulated for the voltage involved, and if the work is performed by a qualified person, the clearance (between the uninsulated portion of the aerial lift and the power line) shall be permitted to be reduced to the restricted approach boundary given in Table 130.4(D)(a), column 4 or Table 130.4(D)(b), column 4.

> When qualified persons are supported by an aerial lifting device, such as a truck boom that is fully insulated from contact with earth, the minimum unprotected approach distance is defined as the restricted approach boundary given in column 4 of both Table 130.4(D)(a) and Table 130.4(D)(b). The qualified person should have received training in the operation of the aerial lifting device in addition to all other required training.

△ **(2) Equipment Contact.** Employees standing on the ground shall not contact the vehicle or mechanical equipment or any of its attachments unless either of the following conditions apply:

(1) The employee is using protective equipment rated for the voltage.
(2) The equipment is located so that no uninsulated part of its structure (that portion of the structure that provides a conductive path to employees on the ground) can come closer to the line than permitted in 130.8(F)(1).

> Although equipment contact with overhead conductors could be several feet away from the employee, they might provide the conductive path to earth when touching the equipment with unprotected hands or another body part. Handlines and tag lines sometimes serve as the point of contact for a person.
>   Employees who are outside the equipment that is in contact with an energized conductor have greater exposure to electrocution than those who are inside the equipment cab. Employees could be exposed to electrocution by step potential if they are standing on the ground near equipment that makes contact with an overhead line.
>   A barricade should be erected around the physical area to surround equipment that could contact an overhead line and should not permit approach closer than the limited approach boundary. Signs should be installed to warn people to stay out of the area.

(3) Equipment Grounding. If any vehicle or mechanical equipment capable of having parts of its structure elevated near energized overhead lines is intentionally grounded, employees working on the ground near the point of grounding shall not stand at the grounding location whenever there is a possibility of overhead line contact. Additional precautions, such as the use of barricades, dielectric overshoe footwear, or insulation, shall be taken to protect employees from hazardous ground potentials (step and touch potential).

Informational Note: Upon contact of the elevated structure with the energized lines, hazardous ground potentials can develop within a few feet or more outward from the grounded point.

> Some safety programs require mobile equipment to be grounded with a temporary grounding conductor connected to an existing earth ground or a temporary ground

Work Involving Electrical Hazards 130.9

rod. The grounding conductor expands the touch and step potential hazard to include the grounding conductor and the ground rod (or other earth ground connection point). If such a grounding conductor is installed, the employee must not be within the limited approach boundary of any portion of the temporary grounding circuit.

130.9 Underground Electrical Lines and Equipment. Before excavation starts where there exists a reasonable possibility of contacting electrical lines or equipment, the employer shall take the necessary steps to contact the appropriate owners or authorities to identify and mark the location of the electrical lines or equipment. When it has been determined that a reasonable possibility of contacting electrical lines or equipment exists, appropriate safe work practices and PPE shall be used during the excavation.

Marking the location of underground conductors and equipment will help to minimize the possibility of accidental contact with buried electrical conductors during excavation. Safe work practices commensurate with the hazard must be implemented during the excavation.

All underground utilities, including gas, electricity, telephone, and cable TV companies, are members of 811. The call center notifies utility companies of excavation work near their underground installations and directs them to mark the approximate location of underground lines, pipes, and cables. There is a legal obligation in some states for a call to be made to 811 prior to any excavation work. Exhibit 130.17 shows a public service bulletin for the 811 system.

The *NEC* requires that a warning ribbon be placed at 12 inches above underground service conductors that are not encased in concrete.

EXHIBIT 130.17

Public service bulletin for the Call 811 Program. (Courtesy of Common Ground Alliance)

130.10 Cutting or Drilling. Before cutting or drilling into equipment, floors, walls, or structural elements where a likelihood of contacting energized electrical lines or parts exists, the employer shall perform a risk assessment to:

(1) Identify and mark the location of conductors, cables, raceways, or equipment
(2) Create an electrically safe work condition
(3) Identify safe work practices and PPE to be used

CHAPTER 2

Safety-Related Maintenance Requirements

An electrical work environment consists of three interrelated components: installation, maintenance, and safe work practices. Safe work practices are most effective when the installation is code compliant and the equipment is maintained appropriately. The NFPA documents that address each aspect are *NFPA 70®, National Electrical Code®* (*NEC®*); NFPA 70B, *Recommended Practice for Electrical Equipment Maintenance*; and NFPA *70E®, Standard for Electrical Safety in the Workplace®*. Exhibit 200.1 illustrates how these documents are interrelated.

NFPA *70E* considers equipment to be safe for operation if the equipment is installed according to the *NEC* and the manufacturer's instructions and has been maintained in accordance with NFPA 70B in the absence of specific manufacturer's instructions. A deficiency in the installation or maintenance of a system has the potential to adversely impact electrical safety of employees and safe work practices.

EXHIBIT 200.1

Electrical safety standard interaction.

Properly maintained electrical equipment has proven reliable. General maintenance dictates that equipment be maintained in accordance with the manufacturer's instructions and often addresses continued operation of the equipment. Chapter 2 is not a comprehensive maintenance program but does address safety-related maintenance of electrical equipment. A good maintenance program provides for the predictability and reliability necessary for safe operation.

A companion document for NFPA *70E* is NFPA 70B. The purpose of this recommended practice is to reduce hazards to life and property that can result from failure or malfunction of industrial-type electrical systems and equipment. It provides guidance on maintenance practices and on setting up a preventive maintenance program. NFPA 70B applies to preventive maintenance for electrical, electronic, and communication systems and equipment and is not intended to duplicate or supersede instructions that manufacturers normally provide. NFPA *70E* addresses the work practices that should be used during maintenance work.

Article 200 Introduction

Inadequate maintenance can have a negative impact on personal safety. The employer/owner must make sure that equipment is properly maintained. Normal operation of inadequately maintained equipment increases the risk of injury to the equipment operator, not just to the employee performing justified energized maintenance. The risk of equipment failure is reduced when equipment is properly and adequately maintained. A comprehensive electrical equipment maintenance program can increase the reliability of the electrical systems, which avoids electrical outages and malfunctions, and can decrease the exposure of employees to electrical hazards.

Table 130.5(C) requires that the equipment condition, including its maintenance, be taken into consideration for determining the likelihood of an arc flash occurring since a poorly maintained piece of equipment is more prone to failure. Section 130.5(G) requires that an arc flash risk assessment take into consideration the maintenance condition of overcurrent protective devices, because the condition can have an effect on the device's clearing time, thus increasing the incident energy.

△ **200.1 Scope.**

Chapter 2 addresses the requirements that follow.

(1) Chapter 2 covers practical safety-related maintenance requirements for electrical equipment and installations in workplaces as included in 90.2. These requirements identify only that maintenance directly associated with employee safety.

(2) Chapter 2 does not prescribe specific maintenance methods or testing procedures. It is left to the employer to choose from the various maintenance methods available to satisfy the requirements of Chapter 2.

Employers must determine a maintenance strategy and then implement the necessary components of that strategy. Some maintenance is necessary to support the implemented electrical safety program. For information on preventive maintenance programs, see NFPA 70B, *Recommended Practice for Electrical Equipment Maintenance*.

General Maintenance Requirements

205.1

(3) For the purpose of Chapter 2, maintenance shall be defined as preserving or restoring the condition of electrical equipment and installations, or parts of either, for the safety of employees who work where exposed to electrical hazards. Repair or replacement of individual portions or parts of equipment shall be permitted without requiring modification or replacement of other portions or parts that are in a safe condition.

Informational Note: Refer to NFPA 70B, *Recommended Practice for Electrical Equipment Maintenance*; ANSI/NETA MTS, *Standard for Maintenance Testing Specifications for Electrical Power Distribution Equipment and Systems*; and IEEE 3007.2, *IEEE Recommended Practice for the Maintenance of Industrial and Commercial Power Systems*, for guidance on maintenance frequency, methods, and tests.

> Maintenance is often the most neglected component of a strategy to provide a safe work environment. NFPA 70B provides employers with solutions, techniques, and testing intervals for adequate maintenance to maximize the reliability of electrical equipment and systems. It describes electrical maintenance subjects and issues surrounding maintenance of electrical equipment.
>
> NFPA 70B provides information on commissioning and on an effective preventive maintenance program. Commissioning, or acceptance testing, verifies that the equipment functions as intended by the design specification. Acceptance testing generates baseline results that can help to identify equipment deterioration or a change in reliability or safety. Future trend analysis is useful in predicting when equipment failure or an out of tolerance condition will occur and can allow for convenient scheduling of outages.
>
> Most electrical equipment will have a predictable life cycle, and knowing the service life can be crucial in predicting the reliability and safe operation of the equipment. Routine maintenance and maintenance tests can be performed at regular intervals over the service life of equipment or when condition indicators warrant. Maintenance tests help identify changes in overcurrent protective device characteristics and potential failures before they occur. A shutdown can then be scheduled and repairs can be made before equipment damage and with minimum exposure to employees. An alternative method is utilizing reliability-centered maintenance (RCM) techniques. See Chapter 30 of NFPA 70B for further information on RCM.

General Maintenance Requirements

Article 205

> At the time at which it was originally installed, equipment was in a new condition and everything was expected to be in order. Through its use, equipment slowly begins to show signs of wear and tear. Proper maintenance is not just the act of fixing, adjusting, or filling fluids. There is a time aspect that is just as important. Maintenance of a piece of equipment may only be needed every year or two in one installation. That same piece of equipment in another installation may require monthly maintenance to be considered properly maintained.

205.1 Qualified Persons.

Employees who perform maintenance on electrical equipment and installations shall be qualified persons as required in Chapter 1 and shall be trained in, and familiar with, the specific maintenance procedures and tests required.

Worker Alert

You must be qualified to perform maintenance on a specific piece of equipment. Your knowledge of similar equipment or of identical tasks does not equate to your ability to correctly or safely perform maintenance on another piece of equipment.

205.2 Single-Line Diagram.

A single-line diagram, where provided for the electrical system, shall be maintained in a legible condition and shall be kept current.

> Single-line diagrams are one of the best sources of information for locating the electrical hazards that might be encountered at a work site. Therefore, all qualified employees must have the ability to read and understand the single-line diagrams of the systems they work on.
>
> Single-line diagrams are created for different purposes and may display different information. Some single-line diagrams are supplemented by equipment schedules that may or may not be included on the diagram. Some power sources, such as control power for a motor control center, may not be detailed on the single-line diagram. These sources may be detailed on a schematic or elementary diagram or in a panelboard schedule. Exhibit 205.1 shows a simple single-line diagram.

EXHIBIT 205.1

Simple single-line diagram.

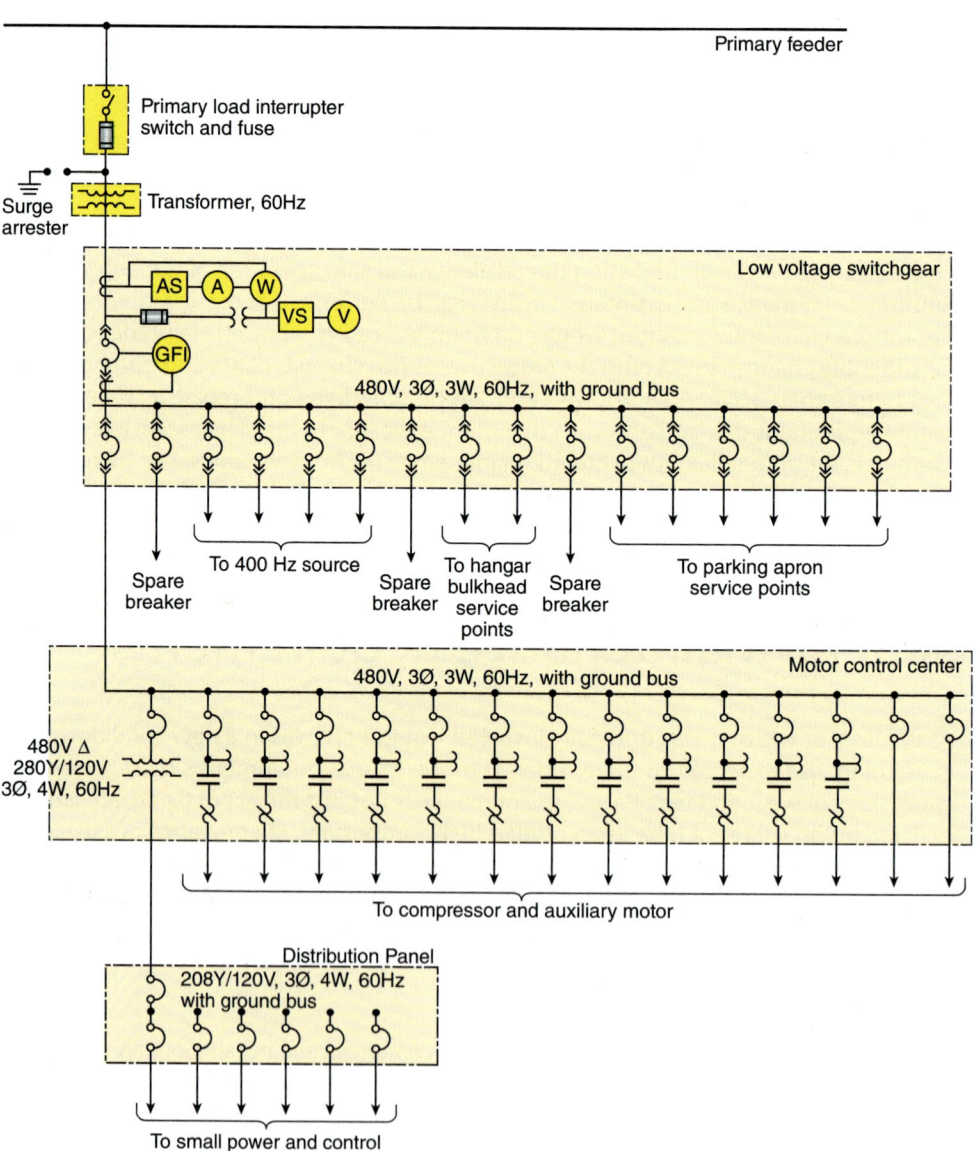

General Maintenance Requirements

205.4

To be useful, the diagrams must be updated and verified. Legible, up-to-date single-line diagrams, along with any necessary supplemental documentation, enable an electrically safe work condition to be implemented. Maintaining these drawings provides valuable information, including the following:

- Sources of power to a specific piece of equipment
- The interrupting capacity of devices at each point in the system
- Possible paths of potential backfeed
- The correct rating for overcurrent devices

205.3 General Maintenance Requirements.

Electrical equipment shall be maintained in accordance with manufacturers' instructions or industry consensus standards to reduce the risk associated with failure. The equipment owner or the owner's designated representative shall be responsible for maintenance of the electrical equipment and documentation.

> Informational Note No. 1: Common industry practice is to apply test or calibration decals to equipment to indicate the test or calibration date and overall condition of equipment that has been tested and maintained in the field. These decals provide the employee immediate indication of last maintenance date and if the tested device or system was found acceptable on the date of test. This local information can assist the employee in the assessment of overall electrical equipment maintenance status.
>
> Informational Note No. 2: Noncontact diagnostic methods in addition to scheduled maintenance activities of electrical equipment can assist in the identification of electrical anomalies.

Equipment that is not maintained or is overly maintained does not only decrease the reliability of the equipment but also presents an increased risk to an employee. A well-established maintenance program will schedule maintenance so that equipment is properly maintained. Chapters 4, 5, and 6 of NFPA 70B, *Recommended Practice for Electrical Equipment Maintenance*, contain recommendations for an effective electrical preventive maintenance program. (See Supplement 2 for excerpts from these NFPA 70B chapters.) The chapters provide a better understanding of benefits that can be derived from a well-administered electrical preventive maintenance program. Deterioration of equipment is normal, and an effective electrical preventive maintenance can delay and predict equipment failure.

Onsite conditions can also affect the required maintenance of equipment. The equipment owner may need to alter the maintenance schedule to address concerns specific to the installation. The equipment manufacturer should be consulted when the recommended maintenance is modified.

205.4 Overcurrent Protective Devices.

Overcurrent protective devices shall be maintained in accordance with the manufacturers' instructions or industry consensus standards. Maintenance, tests, and inspections shall be documented.

> The automatic operation of an overcurrent device should not be assumed to have been the result of a false condition. The system should be investigated to determine the cause of the device's operation before resetting the device.
>
> Following the maintenance schedule defined by the manufacturer or by a consensus standard reduces the risk of failure and the subsequent exposure of employees to electrical hazards such as shock, arc flash, or arc blast. Documents such as NFPA 70B and ANSI/NETA MTS, *Standard for Maintenance Testing Specification*, provide testing and maintenance instructions for some overcurrent devices. ANSI/NEMA AB 4, *Guidelines for*

Worker Alert

Unless the maintenance of overcurrent devices can be proven by documentation, relying on the questionable maintenance of an overcurrent device places you at a greater risk of injury. If you are operating equipment, establishing an electrically safe work condition, or performing justified energized work, you may not be adequately protected from severe injury.

EXHIBIT

An adjustable-trip circuit breaker with a transparent, removable, and sealable cover. (Courtesy of Square D by Schneider Electric)

Worker Alert

You should recognize when there is insufficient space for you to safely perform an assigned task. You should not conduct the task unless sufficient room is provided.

Inspection and Preventive Maintenance of Molded Case Circuit Breakers Used in Commercial and Industrial Applications, provides useful information on the type of maintenance, testing, and inspections that should be documented. See Exhibit 205.2 for an example of an adjustable-trip circuit breaker.

The overcurrent protective device is a critical component for reducing the risk of injury to the employee. Whether the policy is always establishing an electrically safe work condition or some energized electrical work is justified, the overcurrent device is used to determine the required arc flash PPE. Although all maintenance should be documented, the need is specifically stated for overcurrent devices. Any action is generally considered to have not occurred without proper documentation. This especially true if an incident were to occur.

205.5 Spaces About Electrical Equipment.

All working space and clearances required by electrical codes and standards shall be maintained.

> Informational Note: For further information concerning spaces about electrical equipment, see Article 110, Parts II and III, of NFPA 70, *National Electrical Code*.

Adequate working space allows employees to perform tasks without jeopardizing their safety. Sufficient clearance allows for the proper use of tools and equipment while preventing inadvertent contact, which could result in an electrical incident and injury. Exhibit 205.3 illustrates the working space in front of electrical equipment required by *NFPA 70, National Electrical Code (NEC)*. Working spaces must be kept clear. Obstructions — even if temporary, such as with stored equipment — restrict access to and egress from the working space.

The *NEC* general rule for working space is that all equipment be provided with enough space for safe operation and maintenance. The specific working space in the *NEC* is for equipment that warrants justified energized work. This working space may be applied to equipment that will always be in an electrically safe work condition when work is performed. The design layout must consider the possibility that an expected task may require more working space than that specified in the *NEC*.

EXHIBIT 205.3

Working space in front of electrical equipment.

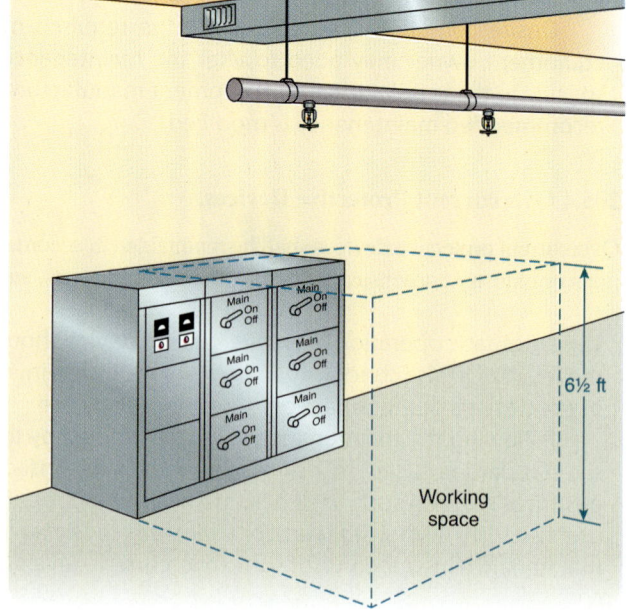

General Maintenance Requirements

205.6 Grounding and Bonding.

Equipment, raceway, cable tray, and enclosure bonding and grounding shall be maintained to ensure electrical continuity.

> The electrical continuity achieved by grounding and bonding enables the fault current to return to the source. During a short-circuit condition, an overcurrent device relies on an effective grounding path to operate as designed. The clearing time might be extended without effective grounding and bonding, thus increasing the amount of incident energy to which an employee could be exposed.

205.7 Guarding of Energized Conductors and Circuit Parts.

Enclosures shall be maintained to guard against unintentional contact with exposed energized conductors and circuit parts and other electrical hazards. Covers and doors shall be in place with all associated fasteners and latches secured.

> Preventing access to energized conductors and circuits is a core concept for employee safety. Energized electrical conductors are required to be guarded against accidental contact, which may be achieved by covering, shielding, enclosing, elevating, or otherwise preventing contact by unauthorized persons or objects. Access to exposed energized electrical components guarded by a locked fence or door can be restricted to only authorized and qualified personnel who have the key. Energized parts should not be exposed to any employee unless safety measures are put in place.

Worker Alert

In order to recognize that a guard is missing, you must first be able to identify equipment that is under a normal operating condition.

205.8 Safety Equipment.

Locks, interlocks, and other safety equipment shall be maintained in proper working condition to accomplish the control purpose.

> Locks and interlocks provide safety for employees by ensuring that only authorized and qualified persons have access to areas that contain exposed energized electrical conductors or circuit parts. They are also used to establish an electrically safe work condition through a lockout/tagout program. An interlocking system may be used to control the flow of electrical power through some systems and to control the sequence of switch operations. Maintaining these locks and interlocks in good working condition helps to minimize exposure to electrical hazards.

205.9 Clear Spaces.

Access to working space and escape passages shall be kept clear and unobstructed.

> Good housekeeping is an important characteristic of a safe work environment. Storage that blocks access or egress or prevents safe work practices must be avoided at all times. The area must not be used for storage, including the storage of movable items such as push carts or trash bins. Maintaining adequate access is essential for an employee to operate the equipment in a safe and efficient manner. The primary intent of providing egress from the area is so that, in the event of an emergency such as an arc flash incident, the employee can escape.

Worker Alert

Clear space is necessary to allow you to quickly leave an area in the event of an incident. Items including tool boxes, parts shipping containers, or hand carts must not be placed in your path of egress.

205.10 Identification of Components.

Identification of components, where required, and safety-related instructions (operating or maintenance), if posted, shall be securely attached and maintained in legible condition.

It is crucial for electrical safety that identification on the single-line diagram is up to date and that it match the identification on the installed equipment. Up-to-date operating or maintenance instructions and necessary warnings are vital to ensure employee safety.

205.11 Warning Signs.

Warning signs, where required, shall be visible, securely attached, and maintained in legible condition.

Warning signs inform both qualified and unqualified employees of potential hazards that might be encountered. They must be clearly visible before examination, adjustment, servicing, or maintenance of the equipment. For example, according to 130.5(H), a warning label for a potential arc flash hazard must provide sufficient information to enable an employee to select appropriate PPE. Other warning signs may be required by installation standards and OSHA regulations.

205.12 Identification of Circuits.

Circuit or voltage identification shall be securely affixed and maintained in updated and legible condition.

Several sections of the *NEC* require that circuit identification be securely affixed to the equipment. *NEC* Section 110.22(A) requires that the purpose of each disconnecting means be indicated unless the purpose is obvious from the arrangement. Section 230.70(B) requires identification of the service disconnecting means. Where a structure is supplied by more than one service, 230.2(E) requires that each service disconnecting means location have a permanent plaque indicating the location of the other disconnecting means.

NEC Section 408.4 details the circuit identification information required for switchgear, switchboards, and panelboards. The circuit identification is to be up to date, accurate, and legible. Mislabeled equipment endangers employees who might assume that they have de-energized the circuit feeding the equipment. However, circuit identification does not remove the employee's responsibility for verifying the absence of voltage when establishing an electrically safe work condition. Regardless of the presence of labels or warnings, the need to perform a risk assessment remains.

205.13 Single and Multiple Conductors and Cables.

Electrical cables and single and multiple conductors shall be maintained free of damage, shorts, and ground that would expose employees to an electrical hazard.

Cables may be exposed after installation. Single and multiple conductors are often installed in raceways or in cable trays. When the cable or conductors are installed in an open cable tray, they should be protected from falling objects that could damage the cable. Temporary protection should be provided when working around exposed cable and conductors so as not to damage the cable.

205.14 Flexible Cords and Cables.

Flexible cords and cables shall be maintained to preserve insulation integrity.

(1) Damaged Cords and Cables. Cords and cables shall not have worn, frayed, or damaged areas that would expose employees to an electrical hazard.

Worker Alert

You are typically the last one available to inspect cords and cables after they have been brought to the work site. Your inspection should occur before the tool or extension cord is plugged into a receptacle. Typically you are also responsible for the routing and protection of the cord during the performance of the task.

Motor Control Centers, and Disconnect Switches

(2) Strain Relief. Strain relief of cords and cables shall be maintained to prevent pull from being transmitted directly to joints or terminals.

(3) Repair and Replacement. Cords and cord caps for portable electrical equipment shall be repaired and replaced by qualified personnel and checked for proper polarity, grounding, and continuity prior to returning to service.

> The transient use of flexible cords and cables increases the possibility for cord and plug damage or interruption of the equipment grounding conductor. Before each use, extension cords must be inspected to ensure that there is no damage [see 110.5(C)]. A damaged ground prong is a common problem with extension cords and cord caps for portable equipment. The ground prong provides the grounding path necessary to mitigate electrical shock or electrocution. Incorrect termination of flexible cords and cables at an enclosure is another common problem. Tension placed on the cable can allow conductors to be exposed and subject the employee to a hazard.
>
> NEC Section 400.9 requires flexible cord to be used only in continuous lengths without splice or tap where initially installed. The repair of hard-service cord and junior hard-service cord 14 AWG and larger is permitted if the conductors are spliced and the completed splice retains the insulation, outer sheath properties, and usage characteristics of the cord being spliced. An in-line repair is not permitted if the cord is reused or reinstalled.
>
> NEC Section 590.6(B)(3) has criteria for an assured equipment grounding conductor program for the temporary use of flexible cords. This written program is continuously enforced at the site by designated persons to ensure that equipment grounding conductors are installed and maintained for all cord sets and equipment connected by cord and plug. The following tests are required before first use on site, when there is evidence of damage, before equipment is returned to service following any repairs, and at intervals not exceeding 3 months:
>
> 1. Test all equipment grounding conductors for electrical continuity.
> 2. Test each receptacle and attachment plug for correct attachment of the equipment grounding conductor.
> 3. Verify that the equipment grounding conductor is connected to its proper terminal.

205.15 Overhead Line Clearances.

For overhead electric lines under the employer's control, grade elevation shall be maintained to preserve no less than the minimum designed vertical and horizontal clearances necessary to minimize risk of unintentional contact.

Article 210

Substations, Switchgear Assemblies, Switchboards, Panelboards, Motor Control Centers, and Disconnect Switches

Worker Alert

Before returning equipment to a normal operating condition and re-energizing, you must account for all nuts, screws, tape, washers, wire pieces, stripped insulation, and any other tools or materials.

210.1 Enclosures.

Enclosures shall be kept free of material that would expose employees to an electrical hazard.

> Housekeeping is a critical action that must be performed before a work task is completed. Materials or tools left in enclosures are a common cause of a fault and can initiate an arc flash event. Employees must remove all extraneous materials and all tools from and around enclosures for electrical safety.

210.2 Area Enclosures.

Fences, physical protection, enclosures, or other protective means, where required to guard against unauthorized access or unintentional contact with exposed energized conductors and circuit parts, shall be maintained.

> Fences and other enclosures should be inspected regularly to ensure that they continue to guard against entry of unauthorized personnel or animals. Gates and doors, especially if equipped with panic hardware, should be checked regularly for security and proper operation. Any defect or damage must be repaired promptly and sufficiently to afford equivalent protection to the initial installation.

210.3 Conductors.

Current-carrying conductors (buses, switches, disconnects, joints, and terminations) and bracing shall be maintained to perform as follows:

(1) Conduct rated current without overheating

> The bundling of conductors affects the ability of those conductors to carry current without overheating. Conductors bundled in wiring methods such as raceways, cable trays, or gutters were calculated for proper ampacity for the number of conductors present at time of installation. Additional conductors placed into these routing methods can affect the safe function of all conductors. Re-evaluation of the ampacity of the new and existing conductors should be conducted prior to the installation of the additional conductors to determine their capacity to dissipate heat.
>
> Discoloration of conductors or terminals is evidence of overheating. Infrared thermography performed while the equipment is operating is one method of investigating overheating. Thermography may be considered a hazardous task depending upon how it is performed. The use of properly installed infrared windows in enclosures is one way to lower the risk associated with infrared scanning. If evidence of overheating is found, the equipment should be de-energized and the problem investigated and repaired in accordance with manufacturer's specifications.

(2) Withstand available fault current

> Short circuits or fault currents present a significant amount of destructive energy that can cause serious damage to electrical equipment and create the potential for serious injury to personnel. The short-circuit current rating of electrical equipment is the amount of current that it can carry safely for a specific period of time before it is damaged. For example, a bus duct may have a short-circuit current rating of 22,000 rms symmetrical amperes for three cycles. It might be damaged if 30,000 amperes were to flow through the bus for three cycles or if 22,000 amperes were to flow for six cycles.

210.4 Insulation Integrity.

Insulation integrity shall be maintained to support the voltage impressed.

Premises Wiring

Temperature extremes, chemical contamination, operating conditions, and aging are common causes that can degrade insulation performance and jeopardize the safety of personnel. Insulation testing performed on a regular basis can be used to indicate if the insulation is deteriorating over time. If the insulation resistance falls below an accepted value or is declining rapidly over a period of time, corrective measures can be taken to prevent damage to equipment and injury to personnel. Degradation of insulation below an acceptable level is a sign of impending failure, and normal operation of the equipment may no longer be a safe task.

210.5 Protective Devices.

Protective devices shall be maintained to adequately withstand or interrupt available fault current.

> Informational Note: Improper or inadequate maintenance can result in increased opening time of the overcurrent protective device, thus increasing the incident energy.

Protective devices are designed to operate within a prescribed range and to disconnect the power to equipment in a timely manner in order to minimize damage to equipment and injury to personnel. If the amount of available fault current increases for any reason — due to a change in upstream components, for example — each protective device must be analyzed to determine if it is adequate for interrupting the new fault current.

When a protective device fails to operate as intended, employees performing normal operation of equipment can be exposed to an injury from a shock or an arcing fault. If the employee is conducting justified energized work and clearing time of the protective device is delayed, an incident energy level greater than anticipated can occur, rendering the employee's selected PPE inadequate.

See Article 225 for further information regarding the maintenance of fuses and circuit breakers.

Worker Alert

Whether you are operating equipment, establishing an electrically safe work condition, or performing justified energized work, you are at a greater risk of injury if protective devices have not been maintained.

Premises Wiring

Article 215

215.1 Covers for Wiring System Components.

Covers for wiring system components shall be in place with all associated hardware, and there shall be no unprotected openings.

In order to protect employees from contact with energized electrical components, all covers and doors must be closed and latched using all fasteners provided with the equipment. All unused openings other than those intended for the operation of equipment or those as part of the design must be closed to afford protection substantially equivalent to the wall of the equipment.

Some panelboards are equipped with a deadfront cover and outer trim. The trim has a hinged door that provides access to the circuit breakers without exposing any live parts. Removing the trim exposes the gutter space. Although the breaker terminals are not visible with the trim removed, they are capable of being inadvertently touched and are considered exposed.

215.2 Open Wiring Protection.

Open wiring protection, such as location or barriers, shall be maintained to prevent unintentional contact.

> A damaged or moved barrier will not provide the protection intended. The protection provided by elevating equipment may be breached if a new means of access, such as a mezzanine, is installed. Protection of open wiring by location in a battery room accessible only to qualified persons is recognized by 110.27(A)(1) of *NFPA 70, National Electrical Code (NEC)*. See Exhibit 215.1.

EXHIBIT 215.1

Open wiring in a restricted access battery room. (Courtesy of International Association of Electrical Inspectors)

215.3 Raceways and Cable Trays.

Raceways and cable trays shall be maintained to provide physical protection and support for conductors.

> Periodic inspection of raceway and cable tray systems will ensure that the systems will function as intended, which is not limited to only providing physical protection and support for conductors. Metal raceway and metal cable tray systems are recognized by the *NEC* as equipment grounding conductors. When these systems are used as an equipment grounding conductor, electrical continuity must be maintained to ensure they have the capacity to conduct safely any fault current likely to be imposed and have sufficiently low impedance to limit the voltage to ground to cause operation of the circuit protective device.

Article 220 Controller Equipment

220.1 Scope.

This article shall apply to controllers, including electrical equipment that governs the starting, stopping, direction of motion, acceleration, speed, and protection of rotating equipment and other power utilization apparatus in the workplace.

A controller can be a remote-controlled magnetic contactor, variable frequency drive, switch, circuit breaker, or device that normally is used to start and stop motors and other apparatus. Stop-and-start stations and similar control circuit components that do not open the power conductors to the motor are not considered to be controllers.

220.2 Protection and Control Circuitry.

Protection and control circuitry used to guard against unintentional contact with exposed energized conductors and circuit parts and to prevent other electrical or mechanical hazards shall be maintained.

Some controller equipment is designed with removable protective components that are used to prevent or minimize exposure to an electrical hazard. If these protective components are removed for repairs or maintenance to the equipment, they must be reinstalled after the task is complete to ensure the continued integrity of the installed components.

Fuses and Circuit Breakers

Article 225

Overcurrent devices play an important role in electrical safety. They protect not only conductors and equipment but also employees. To do this, fuses and circuit breakers must operate within their published time–current characteristic curves safely and correctly. Section 130.5(B) requires that the condition of overcurrent protective devices be taken into consideration for determining the severity of a potential injury to an employee. Section 130.5(G) requires considering the device's condition for an arc flash risk assessment because the condition can have an effect on the device's clearing time. Improper maintenance of these devices places employees who are performing normal operations, establishing an electrically safe work environment, or performing justified energized work at an increased risk of injury. Therefore, adequate maintenance is essential to maintaining a safe work environment.

225.1 Fuses.

Fuses shall be maintained free of breaks or cracks in fuse cases, ferrules, and insulators. Fuse clips shall be maintained to provide adequate contact with fuses. Fuseholders for current-limiting fuses shall not be modified to allow the insertion of fuses that are not current-limiting. Non-current limiting fuses shall not be modified to allow their insertion into current-limiting fuseholders.

Discoloration of fuse terminals and fuse clips could be due to heat from poor contact or corrosion. Fuseholders with rejection features need to be maintained so that they will only accept current-limiting fuses. A fuseholder should never be altered or forced to accept a fuse for which it is not designed. Any damaged fuse should be promptly replaced with an identical fuse. Exhibit 225.1 shows examples of fuses that include a rejection feature to prohibit the installation of non-current-limiting fuses.

Different types of fuses are used throughout an electrical system, and fuses from different manufacturers differ by performance, characteristics, and physical size. Although many fuses might have the same ampere rating, their operating characteristics may differ, making coordination unlikely. Replacement fuses must conform to all requirements

EXHIBIT 225.1

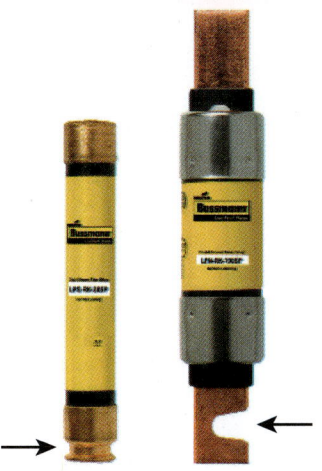

Fuses with a rejection feature. (Courtesy of Eaton, Bussmann Division)

detailed in the electrical hazards risk assessment. For further information on the electrical maintenance of fuses, see Chapter 18 of NFPA 70B, *Recommended Practice for Electrical Equipment Maintenance.*

225.2 Molded-Case Circuit Breakers.

Molded-case circuit breakers shall be maintained free of cracks in cases and cracked or broken operating handles.

Although molded-case circuit breakers can be in service for years and may never be called upon to perform their overload- or short-circuit-tripping functions, they are not "maintenance-free" devices. They require both mechanical and electrical maintenance. Mechanical maintenance consists of inspection and adjustment as needed of mechanical mounting and electrical connections and manual operation of the circuit breaker. Electrical maintenance verifies that the circuit breaker will trip at its desired set point.

Excessive heat in a circuit breaker can cause tripping and an eventual failure. Molded-case circuit breakers should be kept free of external contamination so that internal heat can dissipate normally. A clean circuit breaker enclosure also reduces the potential for arcing between energized conductors and between energized conductors and ground. Loose connections are a common cause of excessive heat, and maintenance should involve checking for loose connections or evidence of overheating. All connections should be maintained in accordance with manufacturers' instructions.

The structural strength of the case is important in withstanding the stresses imposed during fault current operation. Therefore, an inspection should be made for cracks in the case and replacement made if necessary.

Different types of circuit breakers are used throughout an electrical system. Circuit breakers from different manufacturers or those from a different series from the same manufacturer differ by performance and characteristics. Although many circuit breakers might have the same ampere rating, their operating characteristics may differ, making coordination unlikely. Replacement circuit breakers must conform to all requirements detailed in the electrical hazards risk assessment.

Although manual operation of the circuit breaker does not move the mechanical linkages in the tripping mechanisms, it assists in keeping the contacts clean and the lubrication performing properly, which helps assure that the circuit breaker will operate as intended. Some circuit breakers have push-to-trip buttons that should be operated periodically to exercise the tripping mechanical linkages. See Chapter 17 of NFPA 70B and also ANSI/NEMA AB 4, *Guidelines for Inspection and Preventive Maintenance of Molded Case Circuit Breakers Used in Commercial and Industrial Applications,* for more information on electrical maintenance of molded-case circuit breakers.

225.3 Circuit Breaker Testing After Electrical Faults.

Circuit breakers that interrupt faults approaching their interrupting ratings shall be inspected and tested in accordance with the manufacturer's instructions.

Circuit breakers are tested for thousands of manual operations, which is different than a trip due to a fault. Testing of circuit breakers includes higher currents and overloads, but this typically involves a few automatic trips. The type of fault, the energy level present in that fault, and the duration of the fault may all impact the operation of the circuit breaker. A single incident may damage a circuit breaker if pushed beyond its specifications. The manufacturer should be consulted for information regarding the capabilities of a specific circuit breaker.

A high-level fault current can cause damage even when catastrophic failure does not occur. Testing of the device will ensure that the circuit breaker is not damaged and that it will operate at its set point if called upon again. Circuit breakers that encounter high short-circuit currents should receive a thorough inspection and be replaced as necessary.

The result of a circuit breaker not operating within its designed parameters can be disastrous. The incident energy may be increased if the circuit breaker does not trip within its set clearing time. For example, an employee 18 inches from a 20-kA short circuit and 5-cycle tripping time has a potential incident energy exposure of 6.5 cal/cm^2. If the tripping time is increased to 30 cycles, due to improper maintenance or to the circuit breaker being out of calibration, the incident energy is increased to 38.7 cal/cm^2. An employee wearing 8 cal/cm^2 arc flash PPE for the task as specified in the work permit will not be inadequately protected and may suffer substantial injuries or death.

Circuit breakers should have an initial acceptance test and subsequent maintenance testing at recommended intervals. Following the maintenance schedule defined by the manufacturer or by a consensus standard reduces the risk of failure and the subsequent exposure of employees to electrical hazards. NFPA 70B, ANSI/NEMA AB 4, and ANSI/NETA MTS, *Standard for Maintenance Testing Specification*, are documents that can assist an employer in understanding the specific tests and testing intervals required to ensure reliability and safety.

Rotating Equipment

Article 230

230.1 Terminal Boxes.

Terminal chambers, enclosures, and terminal boxes shall be maintained to guard against unintentional contact with exposed energized conductors and circuit parts and other electrical hazards.

Vibration and movement of a motor terminal box could exert pressure on the conductors that are terminated or spliced within it. The terminal box must be securely mounted in place by the complete set of hardware supplied by the manufacturer.

230.2 Guards, Barriers, and Access Plates.

Guards, barriers, and access plates shall be maintained to prevent employees from contacting moving or energized parts.

Inspection and maintenance of rotating equipment and motor guards are necessary to prevent an employee from contacting or becoming entangled in the moving part. Should any guard, barrier, or access plate be removed for repairs or maintenance of the rotating equipment, it must be properly restored to its original integrity.

Article 235 Hazardous (Classified) Locations

> Confined spaces, toxic chemicals, and radiation exposure are often associated with the term *hazardous location*. While each of these may qualify as a hazardous location with the presence of the right type of material, they are not necessarily hazardous locations as defined by *NFPA 70, National Electrical Code (NEC)*. A flammable or combustible concentration of a material must be available in order for a location to be considered hazardous within the scope of the *NEC*.

235.1 Scope.

This article covers maintenance requirements in those areas identified as hazardous (classified) locations.

> Informational Note No. 1: These locations need special types of equipment and installation to ensure safe performance under conditions of proper use and maintenance. It is important that inspection authorities and users exercise more than ordinary care with regard to installation and maintenance. The maintenance for specific equipment and materials is covered elsewhere in Chapter 2 and is applicable to hazardous (classified) locations. Other maintenance will ensure that the form of construction and of installation that makes the equipment and materials suitable for the particular location are not compromised.

> Informational Note No. 2: The maintenance needed for specific hazardous (classified) locations depends on the classification of the specific location. The design principles and equipment characteristics, for example, use of positive pressure ventilation, explosionproof, nonincendive, intrinsically safe, and purged and pressurized equipment, that were applied in the installation to meet the requirements of the area classification must also be known. With this information, the employer and the inspection authority are able to determine whether the installation as maintained has retained the condition necessary for a safe workplace.

> Hazardous locations are required by the *NEC* to be documented. This document often shows the source of the material, process parameters (e.g., temperature, flow, pressure), hazardous location boundaries, and any other pertinent information. Personnel responsible for the design, installation, inspection, operation, and maintenance of electrical equipment are required to have access to this document.
>
> Maintenance personnel must be trained to understand the explosive nature of the material, the type of protection employed, and how equipment maintenance is important to a safe environment. There are 15 different types of protection recognized by the *NEC*, and each prevents ignition of the atmosphere in a different manner. Misunderstanding the protection technique, or applying inappropriate maintenance methods, can be catastrophic.
>
> Troubleshooting equipment in a hazardous location presents a special problem. Most equipment cannot be opened while energized in the presence of explosive or combustible material. Most portable troubleshooting instruments are powered by a battery; however, "battery operated" does not equate to being safe for use in a hazardous location. A spark is likely to occur when the testing device contacts a conductor, and an explosion is possible if an explosive atmosphere exists. The energy available from a single battery is capable of igniting some explosive atmospheres. Before conducting any troubleshooting or maintenance in a hazardous area, it should be determined that an explosive atmosphere does not exist.

Worker Alert

You should not carry flashlights, radios, cell phones, computers, multimeters, or other devices into a hazardous location unless the devices have been evaluated for use in the specific hazardous location.

Hazardous (Classified) Locations

235.2 Maintenance Requirements for Hazardous (Classified) Locations.

Equipment and installations in these locations shall be maintained such that the following criteria are met:

(1) No energized parts are exposed.

Exception to (1): Intrinsically safe and nonincendive circuits.

(2) There are no breaks in conduit systems, fittings, or enclosures from damage, corrosion, or other causes.
(3) All bonding jumpers are securely fastened and intact.
(4) All fittings, boxes, and enclosures with bolted covers have all bolts installed and bolted tight.
(5) All threaded conduit are wrenchtight and enclosure covers are tightened in accordance with the manufacturer's instructions.
(6) There are no open entries into fittings, boxes, or enclosures that would compromise the protection characteristics.
(7) All close-up plugs, breathers, seals, and drains are securely in place.
(8) Marking of luminaires (lighting fixtures) for maximum lamp wattage and temperature rating is legible and not exceeded.
(9) Required markings are secure and legible.

> Equipment maintenance in hazardous locations should be performed only by personnel trained to maintain the special electrical equipment. Employees should be trained to identify and eliminate ignition sources such as high surface temperatures, stored electrical energy, and the buildup of static charges, and to identify the need for special tools, equipment, and tests. These individuals should be familiar with the requirements for the electrical installation of the equipment and protection technique employed. They should understand that, for example, joint compound or tape may weaken an explosionproof fitting during an ignition or may interrupt the required ground path.
>
> Maintenance personnel should be trained to look for cracked viewing windows, missing fasteners, and damaged threads that may affect the integrity of the protection system. All bolts, screws, fittings, and covers must be properly installed. Every missing or damaged fastener must be replaced with those specified by the manufacturer to provide sufficient strength to withstand an internal ignition.
>
> After equipment maintenance is performed, the integrity of the protective scheme that prevents an explosion must be restored. Re-establishing the required air flow for a purged system or sealing a cable within a conduit fitting of an explosionproof system are two examples of restoring the protective scheme.

Worker Alert

You should be aware that fasteners for hazardous location equipment are evaluated for the locations, atmosphere, and chemicals that they are designed to be subjected to. These cover bolts, screws, nuts, and fittings are often a very specific grade of metal selected to withstand internal explosions. You should not substitute these fasteners with any other than those specified by the manufacturer to avoid the potential for a larger explosion to occur.

Article 240 Batteries and Battery Rooms

> Article 480 of *NFPA 70, National Electrical Code (NEC)* applies to installations of stationary storage batteries. The standards that follow are also referenced for the installation of stationary batteries:
>
> - IEEE 484, *Recommended Practice for Installation Design and Installation of Vented Lead-Acid Batteries for Stationary Applications*
> - IEEE 485, *Recommended Practice for Sizing Vented Lead-Acid Storage Batteries for Stationary Applications*
> - IEEE 1145, *Recommended Practice for Installation and Maintenance of Nickel-Cadmium Batteries for Photovoltaic (PV) Systems.*
> - IEEE 1187, *Recommended Practice for Installation Design, and Installation of Valve-Regulated Lead-Acid Batteries for Stationary Applications*
> - IEEE 1375, *IEEE Guide for the Protection of Stationary Battery Systems*
> - IEEE 1578, *Recommended Practice for Stationary Battery Spill Containment and Management*
> - IEEE 1635/ASHRAE 21, *Guide for the Ventilation and Thermal Management of Stationary Battery Installations*

240.1 Ventilation.

When forced or natural ventilation systems are required by the battery system design and are present, they shall be examined and maintained to prevent buildup of explosive mixtures. This maintenance shall include a functional test of any associated detection and alarm systems.

> Informational Note: "Natural ventilation" implies there are no mechanical mechanisms. Maintenance includes activities such as inspection and removal of any obstructions to natural air flow.

> Depending on the battery construction and chemistry, ventilation of the battery room may not be required. A ventilation system is designed to provide for sufficient diffusion and ventilation of gases to prevent the accumulation of an explosive mixture. Mechanical ventilation may not be mandated and ventilation may be achieved by other means. Maintenance of ventilation systems not only includes any electrical system but also maintenance of the associated mechanical systems such as duct work, screens, louvers, and exhaust ports. Where necessary, NFPA 1, *Fire Code*, requires ventilation in accordance with the mechanical code, and either limits the maximum concentration of hydrogen to 1.0 percent of the total volume of the room or requires ventilation at a rate of not less than 1 ft^3/min/ft^2 (5.1 L/sec/m^2) of floor area.

240.2 Eye and Body Wash Apparatus.

Eye and body wash apparatus shall be maintained in operable condition.

> Proper maintenance of eye and body wash apparatus ensures that they supply clean, potable water and that they are in proper working order. A maintenance program should define guidelines for inspection, testing, and maintenance that includes procedures for flushing and flow rate testing.

Portable Electric Tools and Equipment

Article 245

Fixed equipment is typically included in a maintenance program, but portable tools are commonly omitted. The intermittent use of portable tools by many users for a multitude of tasks in various locations often subjects the tools to damage. Electrical shock and electrocution from portable tool use is often the result of improper handling or storage. A facility's electrical safety program must include the maintenance and inspection of portable tools and equipment.

245.1 Maintenance Requirements for Portable Electric Tools and Equipment.

Attachment plugs, receptacles, cover plates, and cord connectors shall be maintained such that the following criteria are met:

(1) There are no breaks, damage, or cracks exposing energized conductors and circuit parts.
(2) There are no missing cover plates.
(3) Terminations have no stray strands or loose terminals.
(4) There are no missing, loose, altered, or damaged blades, pins, or contacts.
(5) Polarity is correct.

> **Worker Alert**
>
> Equipment inspected prior to arriving at the work site may suffer damage in transit. You should always inspect portable tools and flexible cords prior to plugging the equipment into a receptacle. Periodic inspection of portable equipment is also important to help uncover damage or defects from its use.

A visual inspection should be conducted both when a tool is issued and when the tool is returned to the storage area after each use. Employees should be trained to recognize visible defects such as cut, frayed, spliced, or broken cords; cracked or broken attachment plugs; and missing or deformed grounding prongs. Damaged housings, broken switches, and missing parts should also be detected during a visual inspection. Any defect should be reported immediately and the tool removed from service and tagged "Do Not Use" until it is repaired.

Employees should be instructed to report all shocks immediately, no matter how minor, and to cease using the tool. The tool must be immediately removed from service, tagged "Do Not Use," examined, and repaired before further use. Tools that trip GFCI devices must also be removed from service until the cause has been determined and corrected. Also, a record of the GFCI tripping should be given to the next work shift.

Periodic electrical testing of portable electric tools can uncover operating defects. Nonfunctioning and malfunctioning equipment should be returned for repair before continued use. Immediate correction of a defect ensures safe operation, prevents breakdown, and limits more costly repairs.

Personal Safety and Protective Equipment

Article 250

The use of PPE is the last protective measure an employer may specify after exhausting all the other hierarchy of risk control methods for minimizing the risk of employee injury. Since PPE is an employee's final opportunity to avoid severe injury in the event of an incident, employees have a vested interest in maintaining PPE. The condition of the PPE has a direct impact on the employee's well-being. Therefore, employees should take an active role in inspecting and maintaining this special equipment. See 130.7 for additional information and requirements for the selection of PPE.

250.1 Maintenance Requirements for Personal Safety and Protective Equipment.

Personal safety and protective equipment such as the following shall be maintained in a safe working condition:

(1) Grounding equipment
(2) Hot sticks
(3) Rubber gloves, sleeves, and leather protectors
(4) Test instruments
(5) Blanket and similar insulating equipment
(6) Insulating mats and similar insulating equipment
(7) Protective barriers
(8) External circuit breaker rack-out devices
(9) Portable lighting units
(10) Temporary protective grounding equipment
(11) Dielectric footwear
(12) Protective clothing
(13) Bypass jumpers
(14) Insulated and insulating hand tools

This is not an all-inclusive list of PPE that may be used by the employee. To ensure reliability, all equipment must be maintained in accordance with manufacturers' instructions or listings.

250.2 Inspection and Testing of Protective Equipment and Protective Tools.

(A) Visual. Safety and protective equipment and protective tools shall be visually inspected for damage and defects before initial use and at intervals thereafter, as service conditions require, but in no case shall the interval exceed 1 year, unless specified otherwise by the applicable state, federal, or local codes and standards.

Although an inspection of PPE may be conducted at regular intervals, the employee should visually inspect each component immediately before use to verify that no visual defects exist in the equipment. The employee is the last one to inspect the equipment before it may be called upon to prevent a serious injury. See Informational Table 130.7(C)(14) for specific ASTM standards that describe what aspects of the equipment should be included in the visual inspection.

In some instances, such as rubber insulating equipment, the PPE should have a date stamp or other means of identification that indicates when the equipment must be retested. The visual inspection must verify that the equipment has not passed the date in which retesting is required. See Table 130.7(C)(7) for test intervals and the informational note to 130.7(C)(7)(c) for specific ASTM standards for rubber insulating equipment.

(B) Testing. The insulation of protective equipment and protective tools, such as items specified in 250.1(1) through 250.1(14), that is used as primary protection from shock hazards and requires an insulation system to ensure protection of personnel, shall be verified by the appropriate test and visual inspection to ascertain that insulating capability has been retained

> **Worker Alert**
>
> You should take a personal interest in any PPE, including tools, that you use to perform tasks. This equipment is your last line of defense that may prevent serious injury or your death. Poorly maintained gear cannot only initiate an incident but also may increase the severity of your injury.

> **Worker Alert**
>
> Regardless of your employer's inspection program, you should visually inspect all gear prior to use. This serves as a final check of the equipment's potential to prevent a serious injury.

Personal Safety and Protective Equipment

250.3(B)

before initial use, and at intervals thereafter, as service conditions and applicable standards and instructions require, but in no case shall the interval exceed 3 years.

See Informational Note Table 130.7(C)(14) for ASTM standards that describe testing requirements.

250.3 Safety Grounding Equipment.

Temporary protective grounding equipment, safety grounds, and ground sets are terms used to refer to personal protective grounding equipment. Temporary protective grounding equipment is normally constructed with insulated conductors terminated in devices intended for connection to a bare conductor or part. See 120.5(8) for further information regarding the use of this equipment.

Temporary protective grounding equipment should be assigned an identifying mark for record keeping. The identifying mark can be recorded when the equipment is installed on a circuit. After the task has been performed, the equipment can be removed and the identifying mark logged. This will confirm that all temporary protective grounding equipment has been removed prior to re-energizing the circuit.

Some grounding and testing devices are designed to be inserted (racked) into a compartment from which a circuit breaker or disconnect has been removed. These devices can be inserted only into specific spaces. See Exhibit 250.1.

OSHA Connection

29 CFR 1910.137(c)(2) Specific requirements apply to rubber insulating blankets, rubber insulating covers, rubber insulating line hose, rubber insulating gloves, and rubber insulating sleeves. The employer must certify that equipment has been tested. The certification must identify the equipment that passed the test and the date it was tested.

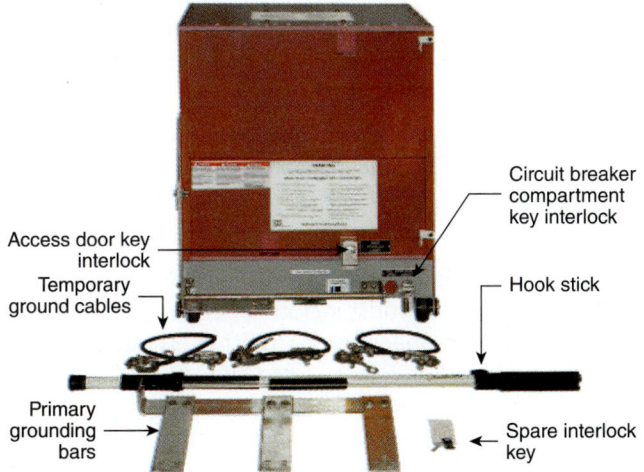

EXHIBIT 250.1

A ground and test device for rack systems. (Courtesy of Schneider Electric)

(A) Visual. Personal protective ground cable sets shall be inspected for cuts in the protective sheath and damage to the conductors. Clamps and connector strain relief devices shall be checked for tightness. These inspections shall be made at intervals thereafter as service conditions require, but in no case shall the interval exceed 1 year.

Temporary protective grounding equipment should be visually inspected before each use.

(B) Testing. Prior to being returned to service, temporary protective grounding equipment that has been repaired or modified shall be tested.

Informational Note: Guidance for inspecting and testing safety grounds is provided in ASTM F2249, *Standard Specification for In-Service Test Methods for Temporary Grounding Jumper Assemblies Used on De-Energized Electric Power Lines and Equipment.*

> Temporary protective grounding equipment must be capable of conducting any available fault current long enough for the overcurrent protection to clear the fault. A destructive test is normally performed when a manufacturer determines the rating of specific devices. However, destructive testing is not an option for equipment that will be used again. For maintenance testing of temporary protective grounding equipment, see ASTM F2249, *Standard Specification for In-Service Test Methods for Temporary Grounding Jumper Assemblies Used on De-Energized Electric Power Lines and Equipment.*

(C) Grounding and Testing Devices. Grounding and testing devices shall be stored in a clean and dry area. Grounding and testing devices shall be properly inspected and tested before each use.

Informational Note: Guidance for testing of grounding and testing devices is provided in Section 9.5 of IEEE C37.20.6, *Standard for 4.76 kV to 38 kV-Rated Ground and Test Devices Used in Enclosures.*

> Grounding and testing devices must not only be visually inspected for defects but also tested before each use. IEEE C37.20.6, *Standard for 4.76 kV to 38 kV-Rated Ground and Test Devices Used in Enclosures*, provides information on integrity tests for grounding and testing devices.

250.4 Test Instruments.

Test instruments and associated test leads used to verify the absence or presence of voltage shall be maintained to assure functional integrity. The maintenance program shall include functional verification as described in 110.4(A)(5).

> Test instruments used in the verification of the absence or presence of voltage are critical to worker safety. The maintenance program must include operation of the test instrument on a known voltage source to verify proper operation of the test instrument, as well as any calibration required within the manufacturer's instructions.

Worker Alert

You should inspect the equipment, including the lead, prior to use. Test leads that are not specifically designed for the piece of equipment must be avoided since they can expose you to risk of electrocution or arc flash injury.

CHAPTER 3

Safety Requirements for Special Equipment

Some facilities use electrical energy in unique ways that differ from most general industries. In some cases, the electrical energy is an integral part of the manufacturing process. In others, the electrical energy is converted to a form that presents unique hazards. When electrical energy is used as a process variable, the general safe work practices defined in Chapter 1 can become unsafe or produce unsafe conditions. Chapter 3 modifies the requirements of Chapter 1 as necessary for use in special situations.

Some workplaces require equipment that is unique. For example, research and development facilities frequently use equipment that exposes employees to unique hazards. General safe work practices might not mitigate that exposure adequately. Chapter 3 permits an employer to comply with appropriate requirements from Chapter 1 by amending requirements that are not appropriate for the specific conditions. Chapter 3 supplements or modifies the safety-related work practices in Chapter 1 with safety requirements for special equipment.

Introduction — Article 300

300.1 Scope.

Chapter 3 covers special electrical equipment in the workplace and modifies the general requirements of Chapter 1.

Chapter 3 covers additional safety-related work practices that are necessary for the practical safeguarding of employees relative to the electrical hazards associated with special equipment and processes that have not been excluded by 90.2(B).

300.2 Responsibility.

The employer shall provide safety-related work practices and employee training. The employee shall follow those work practices.

The employer must define the electrical safety program, and employees must implement the requirements defined in the program. An electrical safety program is most effective when employers and employees work together to accomplish both needs.

Employers are required to provide safety-related work practices and training to employees. They must teach employees to be aware of the actions they take and of the hazards around them. Employers should also instill in employees a sense of self-discipline. They must train employees to perform the tasks, recognize the hazards, understand the potential injury from those hazards, and protect themselves from those hazards.

The employee is responsible for implementing each of these into their work. Although it is the employer that may train, audit, and retrain the employee, it is the employee who will make decisions and take actions that may or may not result in injury. Employees have a responsibility to know their limitations. Only the employee can determine if he or she is truly qualified to safely perform a task on a piece of equipment.

300.3 Organization.

Chapter 3 of this standard is divided into articles. Article 300 applies generally. Article 310 applies to electrolytic cells. Article 320 applies to batteries and battery rooms. Article 330 applies to lasers. Article 340 applies to power electronic equipment. Article 350 applies to research and development (R&D) laboratories.

Each article in Chapter 3 addresses a single unique equipment type or work area, and each article stands alone. Requirements defined in one article apply only to that special equipment type or work area and amend requirements of Chapter 1 for only that purpose.

Article 310 Safety-Related Work Practices for Electrolytic Cells

Article 310 identifies safe work practices that employees should use in electrolytic cell line working zones and the special hazards of working with these ungrounded direct current (dc) systems. A cell line is a series of individual cells that are connected electrically. Generally, the process requires a significant amount of direct current and is ungrounded. See Exhibit 310.1.

Working on an electrolytic cell line is always considered energized electrical work. Each individual cell of an electrolytic cell line is a battery and cannot be de-energized without removing the electrolyte in the vessel. Therefore, establishing an electrically safe work condition is not by itself a viable method for avoiding injury.

EXHIBIT 310.1

An electrolytic cell line. (Photo by David Pace and Michael Petry, Courtesy of Olin Corporation, McIntosh, AL)

Safety-Related Work Practices for Electrolytic Cells

310.1 Scope.

The requirements of this article shall apply to the electrical safety-related work practices used in the types of electrolytic cell areas.

> Informational Note No. 1: See Informative Annex L for a typical application of safeguards in the cell line working zone.
>
> Informational Note No. 2: For further information about electrolytic cells, see *NFPA 70*, *National Electrical Code*, Article 668.

310.2 Definitions.

For the purposes of this article, the definitions that follow shall apply.

Battery Effect. A voltage that exists on the cell line after the power supply is disconnected.

> Informational Note: Electrolytic cells can exhibit characteristics similar to an electrical storage battery and a shock hazard could exist after the power supply is disconnected from the cell line.

Safeguarding. Safeguards for personnel include the consistent administrative enforcement of safe work practices. Safeguards include training in safe work practices, cell line design, safety equipment, PPE, operating procedures, and work checklists.

310.3 Safety Training.

(A) General. The training requirements of this chapter shall apply to employees exposed to electrical hazards in the cell line working zone defined in 110.2 and shall supplement or modify the requirements of 120.5, 130.2, 130.3, and 130.8.

(B) Training Requirements. Employees shall be trained to understand the specific electrical hazards associated with electrical energy on the cell line. Employees shall be trained in safety-related work practices and procedural requirements to provide protection from the electrical hazards associated with their respective job or task assignment.

> Employees who work in the vicinity of the cells and interconnecting bus must be trained to understand the hazards associated with an unintentional grounded condition of either an individual cell or the interconnecting bus. Employees must also understand that the significant magnetic field generated by current flowing in the interconnecting bus might interfere with certain medical devices.

310.4 Employee Training.

(A) Qualified Persons.

(1) Training. Qualified persons shall be trained and knowledgeable in the operation of cell line working zone equipment and specific work methods and shall be trained to avoid the electrical hazards that are present. Such persons shall be familiar with the proper use of precautionary techniques and PPE. Training for a qualified person shall include the following:

(1) Skills and techniques to avoid a shock hazard:
   a. Between exposed energized surfaces, which might include temporarily insulating or guarding parts to permit the employee to work on exposed energized parts
   b. Between exposed energized surfaces and grounded equipment, other grounded objects, or the earth itself, that might include temporarily insulating or guarding parts to permit the employee to work on exposed energized parts

Worker training and qualifications specified in Article 110 are also applicable to cell line work. Employees who work within the area of the dc bus must be trained to understand the unique hazards associated with ungrounded dc voltage. Hand tools that might contact the ungrounded dc bus work must not be grounded.

(2) Method of determining the cell line working zone area boundaries

(2) Qualified Persons. Qualified persons shall be permitted to work within the cell line working zone.

(B) Unqualified Persons.

(1) Training. Unqualified persons shall be trained to identify electrical hazards to which they could be exposed and the proper methods of avoiding the hazards.

(2) In Cell Line Working Zone. When there is a need for an unqualified person to enter the cell line working zone to perform a specific task, that person shall be advised of the electrical hazards by the designated qualified person in charge to ensure that the unqualified person is safeguarded.

310.5 Safeguarding of Employees in the Cell Line Working Zone.

Δ **(A) General.** Operation and maintenance of electrolytic cell lines might require contact by employees with exposed energized surfaces such as buses, electrolytic cells, and their attachments. The approach distances referred to in Table 130.4(C)(a) and Table 130.4(C)(b) shall not apply to work performed by qualified persons in the cell line working zone. Safeguards such as safety-related work practices and other safeguards shall be used to protect employees from injury while working in the cell line working zone. These safeguards shall be consistent with the nature and extent of the related electrical hazards. Safeguards might be different for energized cell lines and de-energized cell lines. Hazardous battery effect voltages shall be dissipated to consider a cell line de-energized.

> Informational Note No. 1: Exposed energized surfaces might not present an electrical hazard. Shock hazards are related to current through the body, producing possible injury or damage to health. Shock severity is a function of many factors, including skin and body resistance, current path through the body, paths in parallel with the body, and system voltage. Arc flash burns and arc blasts are a function of the arcing current and the duration of arc exposure.

> Informational Note No. 2: A cell line or group of cell lines operated as a unit for the production of a particular metal, gas, or chemical compound might differ from other cell lines producing the same product because of variations in the particular raw materials used, output capacity, use of proprietary methods or process practices, or other modifying factors. Detailed standard electrical safety-related work practice requirements could become overly restrictive without accomplishing the stated purpose of Chapter 1.

The limited and restricted approach boundaries do not apply to cell line work zones. However, the cell line work zone must be defined. This is the limit of approach for unqualified persons, and only unqualified persons with a need to cross into this zone are permitted into this zone. An arc flash boundary might be crossed before the cell line work zone is entered. See 310.4(A)(2) regarding cell line work zones.

Employers must institute an electrical safety program that addresses the issues identified in Chapter 1. However, the work practices can be modified as necessary to recognize the different types of exposure to electrical hazards. For instance, because each cell acts like a battery, the employer must define actions that are necessary if an

---

Worker Alert

A greater responsibility of maintaining safety is placed upon you when performing tasks in cell line working zones. The inability to establish an electrically safe work condition and the reliance on work procedures to provide for your safety emphasize the need for human-error-free work.

Safety-Related Work Practices for Electrolytic Cells

> employee needs to contact the dc bus structure. Those procedures must be consistent with the risk associated with the work task. See Informative Annex L for a typical application of safeguards in the cell line working zone.

(B) Signs. Permanent signs shall clearly designate electrolytic cell areas.

(C) Arc Flash Risk Assessment. The requirements of 130.5, Arc Flash Risk Assessment, shall not apply to electrolytic cell line work zones.

> Although the arc flash risk assessment in Article 130 does not apply to cell line work, an arc flash risk assessment is still required. The procedure for conducting the arc flash risk assessment must be specified in the employer's electrical safety program. The risk assessment must include the use of the hierarchy of risk controls. See 110.1(H) regarding the required risk assessment procedure.
>
> Informative Annex D provides information on various methods of estimating the available incident energy and the arc flash boundary. The source documents listed in Table D.1 should be reviewed for the proper use and limitations of the techniques presented. NFPA 70E does not limit calculation methods to those listed, and other appropriate techniques may be available.

Δ (1) General. Each task performed in the electrolytic cell line working zone shall be analyzed for the likelihood of arc flash injury. If there is a likelihood of personal injury, appropriate measures shall be taken to protect persons exposed to the arc flash hazards, including one or more of the following:

(1) Providing appropriate PPE *[see 310.5(D)(2)]* to prevent injury from the arc flash hazard
(2) Altering work procedures to reduce the likelihood of occurrence of an arc flash incident
(3) Scheduling the task so that work can be performed when the cell line is de-energized

> The arc flash risk assessment must include the use of the hierarchy of risk controls. The hierarchy is listed in order of the most effective to the least effective and must be applied in this descending order for each risk assessment. The result of each risk assessment should be evaluated to determine if the hierarchy of controls could be further employed to lower the risk or reduce the hazard. Only after all other risk controls have been exhausted should PPE be selected. PPE is considered the least effective and lowest level safety of control for employee protection and should not be the first or only control element used. See 110.1(H) regarding the necessary elements of a risk assessment.

(2) Routine Tasks. Arc flash risk assessment shall be done for all routine tasks performed in the cell line work zone. The results of the arc flash risk assessment shall be used in training employees in job procedures that minimize the possibility of arc flash hazards. The training shall be included in the requirements of 310.3.

(3) Nonroutine Tasks. Before a nonroutine task is performed in the cell line working zone, an arc flash risk assessment shall be done. If an arc flash hazard is a possibility during nonroutine work, appropriate instructions shall be given to employees involved on how to minimize the risk associated with arc flash.

(4) Arc Flash Hazards. If the likelihood of occurrence of an arc flash hazard exists for either routine or nonroutine tasks, employees shall use appropriate safeguards.

(D) Safeguards. Safeguards shall include one or a combination of the following means.

(1) Insulation. Insulation shall be suitable for the specific conditions, and its components shall be permitted to include glass, porcelain, epoxy coating, rubber, fiberglass, and plastic and, when dry, such materials as concrete, tile, brick, and wood. Insulation shall be permitted to be applied to energized or grounded surfaces.

(2) Personal Protective Equipment (PPE). PPE shall provide protection from electrical hazards. PPE shall include one or more of the following, as determined by authorized management:

(1) Footwear for wet service
(2) Gloves for wet service
(3) Sleeves for wet service
(4) Footwear for dry service
(5) Gloves for dry service
(6) Sleeves for dry service
(7) Electrically insulated head protection
(8) Protective clothing
(9) Eye protection with nonconductive frames
(10) Face shield (polycarbonate or similar nonmelting type)

> The employer is responsible for determining the parts of the body required to be provided with protection. The employer is also responsible for determining the appropriate type of PPE to protect the employee from all identified electrical hazards, including shock and arc flash protection.

(a) *PPE.* Personal and other protective equipment shall be appropriate for conditions, as determined by authorized management.

(b) *Testing of PPE.* PPE shall be verified with regularity and by methods that are consistent with the exposure of employees to electrical hazards.

> All PPE used in cell line work is required to be tested and its ability to provide the necessary protection verified on a regular basis. NFPA *70E* does not specify the testing necessary to determine the continued acceptance of issued PPE. The employer must determine the method used to confirm that PPE maintains the ability to protect the worker. Product testing standards, such as those in Informational Note Table 130.7(G), may provide guidance in determining necessary testing. It is permissible for the PPE to be routinely tested by an organization other than the employer. However, the employer must determine the qualifications and approve the external testing organization.

(3) Barriers. Barriers shall be devices that prevent contact with energized or grounded surfaces that could present an electrical hazard.

(4) Voltage Equalization. Voltage equalization shall be permitted by bonding a conductive surface to an exposed energized surface, either directly or through a resistance, so that there is insufficient voltage to create an electrical hazard.

(5) Isolation. Isolation shall be established by placing equipment or other items in locations such that employees are unable to simultaneously contact exposed conductive surfaces that could present an electrical hazard.

Safety-Related Work Practices for Electrolytic Cells

310.5(D)(12)

(6) Safe Work Practices. Employees shall be trained in safe work practices. The training shall include why the work practices in a cell line working zone are different from similar work situations in other areas of the plant. Employees shall comply with established safe work practices and the safe use of protective equipment.

(a) *Attitude Awareness.* Safe work practice training shall include attitude awareness instruction. Simultaneous contact with energized parts and ground can cause serious electrical shock. Of special importance is the need to be aware of body position where contact may be made with energized parts of the electrolytic cell line and grounded surfaces.

(b) *Bypassing of Safety Equipment.* Safe work practice training shall include techniques to prevent bypassing the protection of safety equipment. Clothing may bypass protective equipment if the clothing is wet. Trouser legs should be kept at appropriate length, and shirt sleeves should be a good fit so as not to drape while reaching. Jewelry and other metal accessories that may bypass protective equipment shall not be worn while working in the cell line working zone.

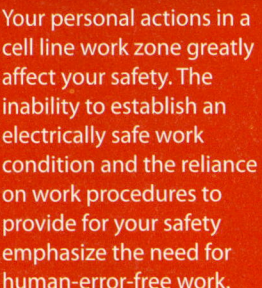

Worker Alert

Your personal actions in a cell line work zone greatly affect your safety. The inability to establish an electrically safe work condition and the reliance on work procedures to provide for your safety emphasize the need for human-error-free work.

(7) Tools. Tools and other devices used in the energized cell line work zone shall be selected to prevent bridging between surfaces at hazardous potential difference.

> Informational Note: Tools and other devices of magnetic material could be difficult to handle in the area of energized cells due to their strong dc magnetic fields.

(8) Portable Cutout-Type Switches. Portable cell cutout switches that are connected shall be considered as energized and as an extension of the cell line working zone. Appropriate procedures shall be used to ensure proper cutout switch connection and operation.

(9) Cranes and Hoists. Cranes and hoists shall meet the requirements of applicable codes and standards to safeguard employees. Insulation required for safeguarding employees, such as insulated crane hooks, shall be periodically tested.

(10) Attachments. Attachments that extend the cell line electrical hazards beyond the cell line working zone shall use one or more of the following:

(1) Temporary or permanent extension of the cell line working zone
(2) Barriers
(3) Insulating breaks
(4) Isolation

(11) Pacemakers and Metallic Implants. Employees with implanted pacemakers, ferromagnetic medical devices, or other electronic devices vital to life shall not be permitted in cell areas unless written permission is obtained from the employee's physician.

> Informational Note: The American Conference of Governmental Industrial Hygienists (ACGIH) and IEEE 463, *Electrical Safety Practices in Electrolytic Cell Line Working Zones*, recommend that persons with implanted pacemakers should not be exposed to magnetic flux densities above 5 gauss.

Employers must take steps to ensure that employees who wear pacemakers and similar electro-medical devices are not exposed to the magnetic fields that normally exist in the cell area.

(12) Testing. Equipment safeguards for employee protection shall be tested to ensure they are in a safe working condition.

310.6 Portable Tools and Equipment.

Informational Note: The order of preference for the energy source for portable hand-held equipment is considered to be as follows:

(1) Battery power
(2) Pneumatic power
(3) Portable generator
(4) Nongrounded-type receptacle connected to an ungrounded source

> Grounded portable tools and equipment must not be used in the area containing the cells or interconnecting bus. Although in normal settings an equipment grounding conductor decreases exposure to an electrical hazard, in cell areas any conductor that is grounded increases exposure to an electrical hazard. All equipment and tools, including pneumatic tools, must be free from any grounding circuit. Pneumatic tools must be fitted with nonconductive hoses.

Δ **(A) Portable Electrical Equipment.** The grounding requirements of 110.5(B) shall not be permitted within an energized cell line working zone. Portable electrical equipment and associated power supplies shall meet the requirements of applicable codes and standards.

(B) Auxiliary Nonelectric Connections. Auxiliary nonelectric connections such as air, water, and gas hoses shall meet the requirements of applicable codes and standards. Pneumatic-powered tools and equipment shall be supplied with nonconductive air hoses in the cell line working zone.

(C) Welding Machines. Welding machine frames shall be considered at cell potential when within the cell line working zone. Safety-related work practices shall require that the cell line not be grounded through the welding machine or its power supply. Welding machines located outside the cell line working zone shall be barricaded to prevent employees from touching the welding machine and ground simultaneously where the welding cables are in the cell line working zone.

(D) Portable Test Equipment. Test equipment in the cell line working zone shall be suitable for use in areas of large magnetic fields and orientation.

Informational Note: Test equipment that is not suitable for use in such magnetic fields could result in an incorrect response. When such test equipment is removed from the cell line working zone, its performance might return to normal, giving the false impression that the results were correct.

Article 320 Safety Requirements Related to Batteries and Battery Rooms

> Article 320 identifies work practices associated with installation and maintenance of batteries containing many cells, such as those used with uninterruptible power supplies (UPS), telecommunications systems, and unit substation dc power supplies.
>
> Working with batteries can expose an employee to both potential shock and arc flash hazards. A person's body might react to contact with dc voltage differently than

Safety Requirements Related to Batteries and Battery Rooms

> from contact with ac voltage (see Commentary Table 340.1). Batteries can also expose an employee to hazards associated with the chemical electrolyte used in the battery. Battery charging can sometimes generate flammable gases, so it is important for the employee to avoid anything that could cause open flame or sparks. The employee must consider exposure to these hazards when selecting work practices and PPE.

320.1 Scope.

This article covers electrical safety requirements for the practical safeguarding of employees while working with exposed stationary storage batteries that exceed 50 volts, nominal.

> Informational Note: For additional information on best practices for safely working on stationary batteries, see the following documents:
>
> (1) NFPA 1, *Fire Code*, Chapter 52, Stationary Storage Battery Systems, 2015
> (2) *NFPA 70, National Electrical Code*, Article 480, Storage Batteries, 2014
> (3) IEEE 450, *IEEE Recommended Practice for Maintenance, Testing, and Replacement of Vented Lead-Acid Batteries for Stationary Applications*, 2010
> (4) IEEE 937, *Recommended Practice for Installation and Maintenance of Lead-Acid Batteries for Photovoltaic Systems*, 2007
> (5) IEEE 1106, *IEEE Recommended Practice for Installation, Maintenance, Testing, and Replacement of Vented Nickel-Cadmium Batteries for Stationary Applications*, 2005 (R 2011)
> (6) IEEE 1184, *IEEE Guide for Batteries for Uninterruptible Power Supply Systems*, 2006 (R 2011)
> (7) IEEE 1188, *IEEE Recommended Practice for Maintenance, Testing, and Replacement of Valve-Regulated Lead-Acid (VRLA) Batteries for Stationary Applications*, 1188a-2014
> (8) IEEE 1657, *Recommended Practice for Personnel Qualifications for Installation and Maintenance of Stationary Batteries*, 2009
> (9) OSHA 29 CFR 1910.305(j)(7), "Storage batteries"
> (10) OSHA 29 CFR 1926.441, "Batteries and battery charging"
> (11) DHHS (NIOSH) Publication No. 94-110, *Applications Manual for the Revised NIOSH Lifting Equation*, 1994
> (12) IEEE/ASHRAE 1635, *Guide for the Ventilation and Thermal Management of Batteries for Stationary Applications*, 2012

320.2 Definitions.

For the purposes of this article definitions that follow shall apply.

Authorized Personnel. The person in charge of the premises, or other persons appointed or selected by the person in charge of the premises who performs certain duties associated with stationary storage batteries.

Battery. A system consisting of two or more electrochemical cells connected in series or parallel and capable of storing electrical energy received and that can give it back by reconversion.

Battery Room. A room specifically intended for the installation of batteries that have no other protective enclosure.

Cell. The basic electrochemical unit, characterized by an anode and a cathode used to receive, store, and deliver electrical energy.

Electrolyte. A solid, liquid, or aqueous immobilized liquid medium that provides the ion transport mechanism between the positive and negative electrodes of a cell.

Nominal Voltage. The value assigned to a cell or battery of a given voltage class for the purpose of convenient designation; the operating voltage of the cell or system may vary above or below this value.

Pilot Cell. One or more cells chosen to represent the operating parameters of the entire battery (sometimes called "temperature reference" cell).

Prospective Short-Circuit Current. The highest level of fault current that could theoretically occur at a point on a circuit. This is the fault current that can flow in the event of a zero impedance short circuit and if no protection devices operate.

> Informational Note: Some batteries have built-in management devices to limit maximum short-circuit current. The determination of the prospective short-circuit current for these batteries assumes that the internal battery management system protection devices are operable.

Valve-Regulated Lead Acid (VRLA) Cell. A lead-acid cell that is sealed with the exception of a valve that opens to the atmosphere when the internal pressure in the cell exceeds atmospheric pressure by a pre-selected amount, and that provides a means for recombination of internally generated oxygen and the suppression of hydrogen gas evolution to limit water consumption.

Vented Cell. A type of cell in which the products of electrolysis and evaporation are allowed to escape freely into the atmosphere as they are generated. (Also called "flooded cell.")

320.3 Safety Procedures.

(A) General Safety Hazards.

N **(1) Energy Thresholds.** Energy exposure levels shall not exceed those identified in the following list unless appropriate controls are implemented:

(1) AC: 50 volts and 5 milliamperes
(2) DC: 100 volts

> Informational Note: This information is extracted from the Department of Energy (DOE) Electrical Safety Handbook, DOE-HDBK-1092.

> **OSHA Connection**
> 29 CFR 1910.333(a)(1)
> Live parts that operate at 50 volts or above must be de-energized. Compliance with this regulation may not be met where 100 volts is used as the energy exposure limit.

> Although the dc threshold for the potential for an electrical shock is 50 volts in Article 130, Article 320 allows an increase of the threshold to 100 volts. The employer must implement the hierarchy of risk controls as well as define the safe work practices for each scheduled task when 100 volts or greater is present.
> Environmental conditions, such as a wet environment, may warrant a lower dc threshold. Cut human skin can decrease the voltage level necessary to injure a worker.

(2) Battery Risk Assessment. Prior to any work on a battery system, a risk assessment shall be performed to identify the chemical, electrical shock, and arc flash hazards and assess the risks associated with the type of tasks to be performed.

> Batteries are sources of energy. Therefore, isolating the source of voltage from a cell is not possible. Working on a battery system is always considered energized electrical work.

Safety Requirements Related to Batteries and Battery Rooms

> Unlike Article 310 for electrolytic cells, Article 320 does not waive the risk assessments outlined in Article 130. The procedure for conducting the arc flash risk assessment must be specified in the employer's electrical safety program. The risk assessment must include the use of the hierarchy of risk controls. The hierarchy is listed in order of the most effective to the least effective and must be applied in this descending order for each risk assessment. The result of each risk assessment should be evaluated to determine if the hierarchy of controls could be further employed to lower the risk or reduce the hazard. Only after all other risk controls have been exhausted should PPE be selected. PPE is considered the least effective and lowest level safety of control for employee protection and should not be the first or only control element used. See 110.1(H) regarding the necessary elements of a risk assessment.
>
> Risk associated with batteries can be mitigated starting with the system design. For example, a battery system could be designed to allow the battery to be partitioned into low-voltage segments before work is conducted on it. Other system design mitigation methods include widely separating the positive and negative conductors and installing insulated covers on battery intercell connector bus bars or terminals.
>
> Either the PPE category or incident energy analysis method may be used for the arc flash risk assessment. Informative Annex D provides information on various methods of estimating the available incident energy and the arc flash boundary. The source documents listed in Table D.1 should be reviewed for the proper use and limitations of the techniques presented. NFPA *70E* does not limit calculation methods to those listed, and other appropriate techniques may be available.
>
> Exhibit 320.1 illustrates how a risk assessment of a battery system for the various types of hazards (shock, chemical, arc flash, and thermal) might be conducted. It also illustrates how the likely exposure (risk) depends on the type of task being performed. The same process could be applied to other types of systems. This figure is for illustrative purposes and may not apply to a specific installation or electrical safety program. The illustration does not absolve the user of their responsibility to read, understand, and properly apply the requirements.

(3) Battery Room or Enclosure Requirements.

(a) *Personnel Access to Energized Batteries.* Each battery room or battery enclosure shall be accessible only to authorized personnel.

(b) *Illumination.* Employees shall not enter spaces containing batteries unless illumination is provided that enables the employees to perform the work safely.

> Informational Note: Battery terminals are normally exposed and pose possible shock hazard. Batteries are also installed in steps or tiers that can cause obstructions.

(4) Apparel. Personnel shall not wear electrically conductive objects such as jewelry while working on a battery system.

(5) Abnormal Battery Conditions. Instrumentation that provides alarms for early warning of abnormal conditions of battery operation, if present, shall be tested annually.

> Informational Note: Battery monitoring systems typically include alarms for such conditions as overvoltage, undervoltage, overcurrent, ground fault, and overtemperature. The type of conditions monitored will vary depending upon the battery technology. One source of guidance on monitoring battery systems is IEEE 1491, *Guide for the Selection and Use of Battery Monitoring Equipment in Stationary Applications.*

EXHIBIT 320.1

Risk assessment of a battery system.

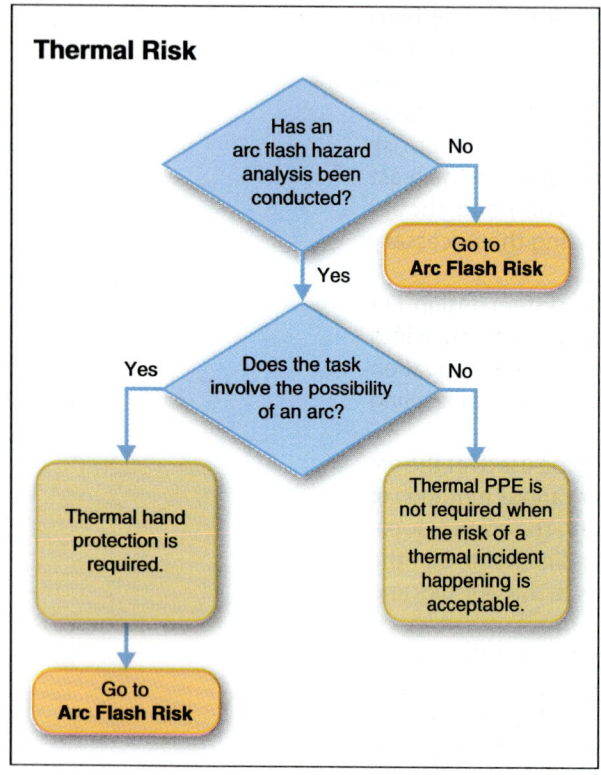

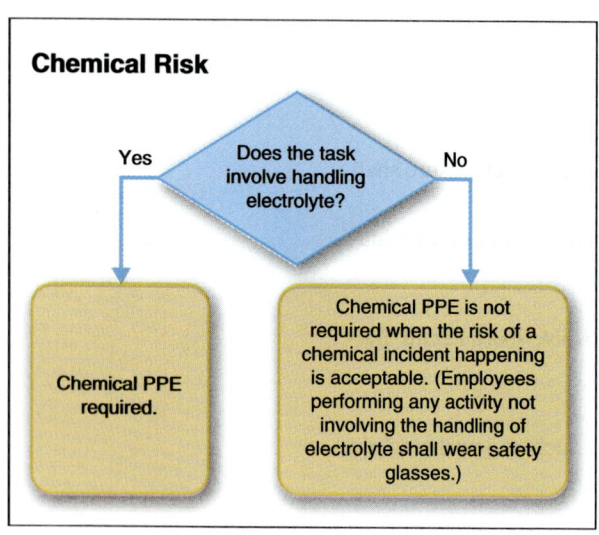

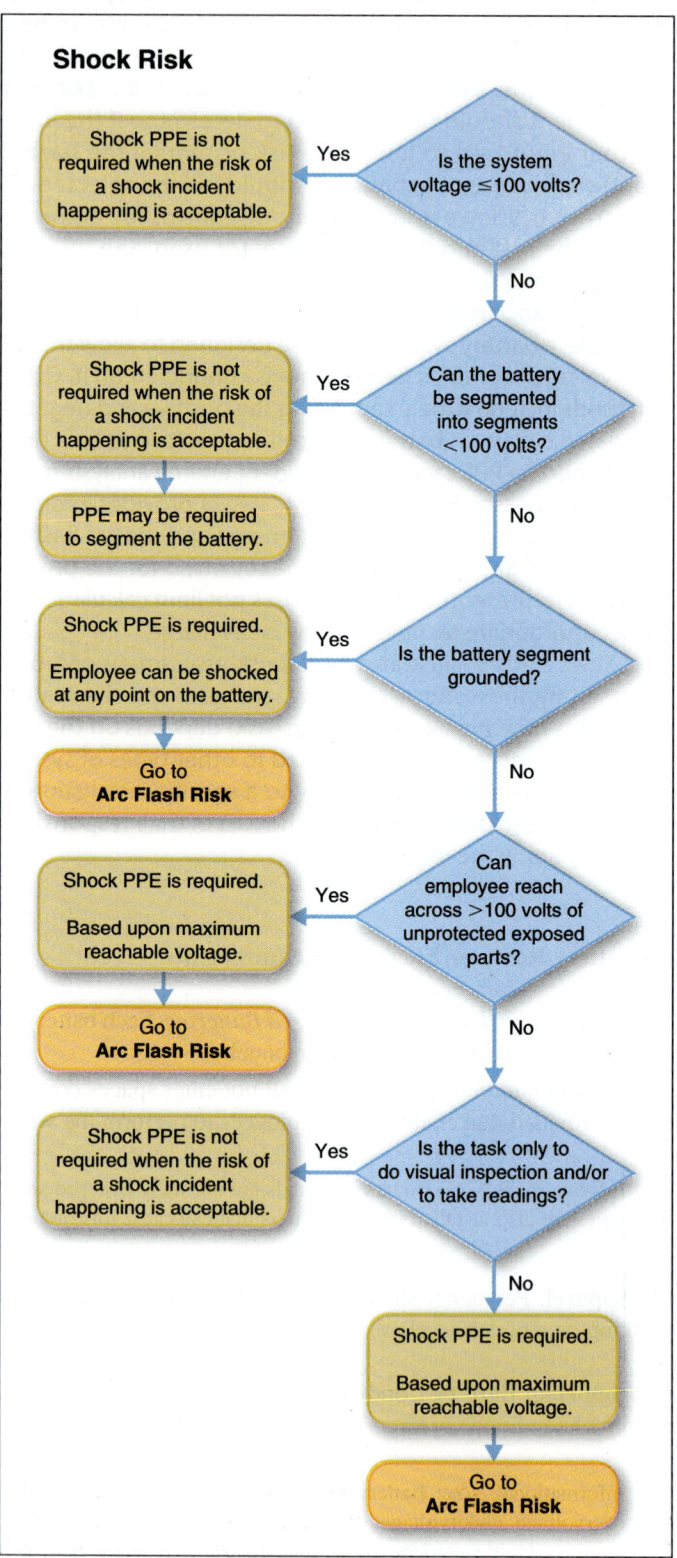

See next page for **Arc Flash Risk**.

Safety Requirements Related to Batteries and Battery Rooms — 320.3(A)(6)

EXHIBIT 320.1 (continued)

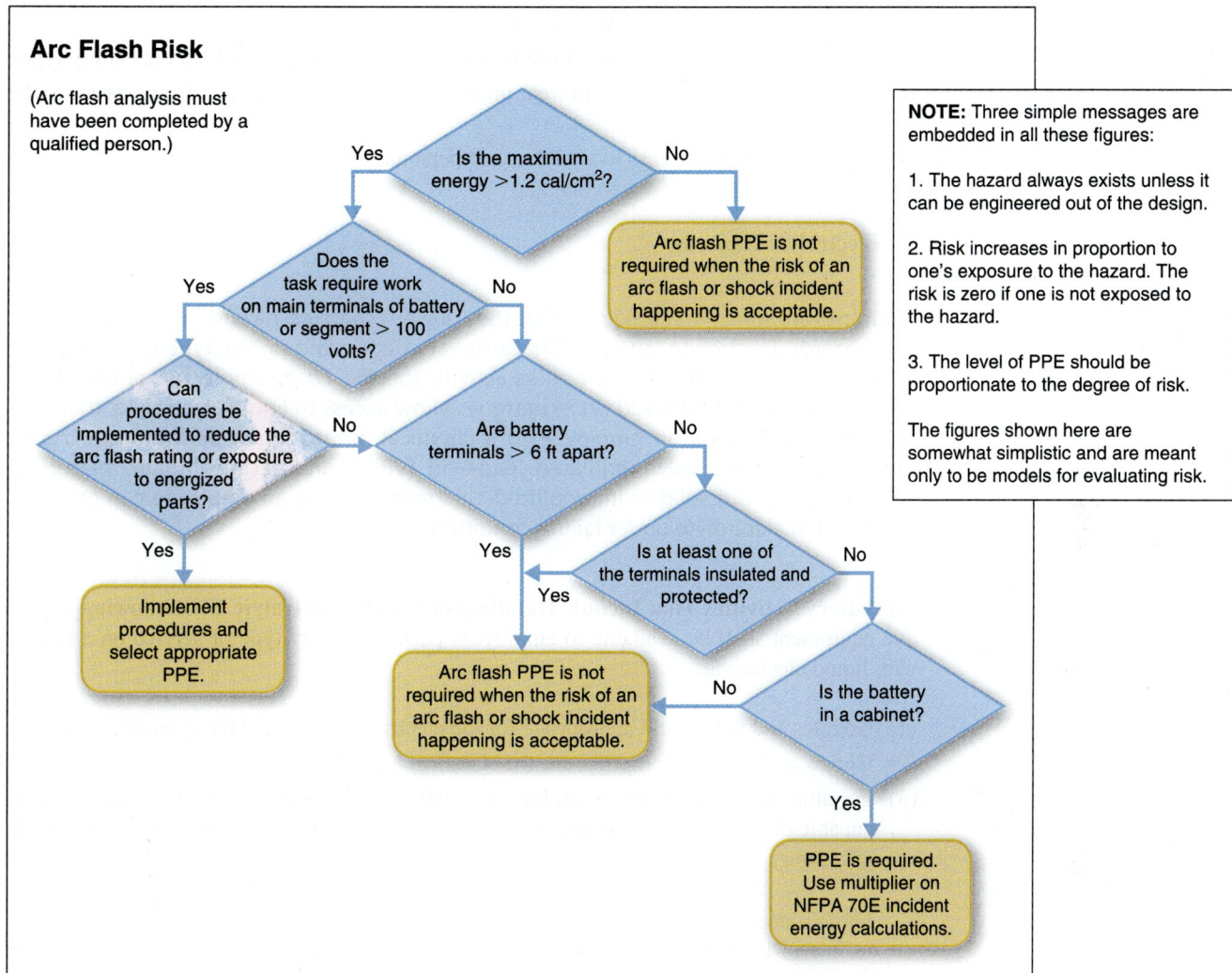

(6) **Warning Signs.** The following warning signs or labels shall be posted in appropriate locations:

(1) Electrical hazard warnings indicating the shock hazard due to the battery voltage and the arc flash hazard due to the prospective short-circuit current, and the thermal hazard.

Informational Note No.1: Because internal resistance, prospective short-circuit current, or both are not always provided on battery container labels or data sheets, and because many variables can be introduced into a battery layout, the battery manufacturer should be consulted for accurate data. Variables can include, but are not limited to, the following:

   (1) Series connections
   (2) Parallel connections
   (3) Charging methodology
   (4) Temperature
   (5) Charge status
   (6) Dc distribution cable size and length

Informational Note No. 2: See 130.5(D) for requirements for equipment labeling.

(2) Chemical hazard warnings, applicable to the worst case when multiple battery types are installed in the same space, indicating the following:
   a. Potential presence of explosive gas (when applicable to the battery type)
   b. Prohibition of open flame and smoking
   c. Danger of chemical burns from the electrolyte (when applicable to the battery type)
(3) Notice for personnel to use and wear protective equipment and apparel appropriate to the hazard for the battery
(4) Notice prohibiting access to unauthorized personnel

(B) Electrolyte Hazards.

> Batteries are somewhat unique in that they present chemical hazards as well as electrical hazards. Electrolyte (chemical) hazards vary depending on the type of battery, so the risk is product-specific as well as activity-specific. For example, nickel-cadmium (NiCd) and vented lead-acid (VLA) batteries allow access to liquid electrolyte, thereby potentially exposing an employee to a chemical hazard when performing certain tasks. By contrast, valve-regulated lead-acid (VRLA) and certain lithium batteries are designed with solid or immobilized electrolyte so that an employee can only be exposed to electrolyte under failure conditions.

(1) Battery Activities That Include Handling of Liquid Electrolyte. The following protective equipment shall be available to employees performing any type of service on a battery with liquid electrolyte:

(1) Goggles and face shield appropriate for the electrical hazard and the chemical hazard
(2) Gloves and aprons appropriate for the chemical hazards
(3) Portable or stationary eye wash facilities and equipment within the work area that are capable of drenching or flushing of the eyes and body for the duration necessary to mitigate injury from the electrolyte hazard.

Informational Note: Guidelines for the use and maintenance of eye wash facilities for vented batteries in nontelecom environments can be found in ANSI/ISEA Z358.1, *American National Standard for Emergency Eye Wash and Shower Equipment*.

> These requirements only apply if electrolyte is being handled, which is possible only with batteries utilizing free-flowing liquid electrolyte. Activities in which "electrolyte is being handled" would include acid adjustment, removal of excess electrolyte, or cleanup of an electrolyte leak or spill. Most battery maintenance activities do not involve handling of electrolyte, so the requirement for safety glasses in 320.3(B)(2) would apply.

△ **(2) Activities That Do Not Include Handling of Electrolyte.** Employees performing any activity not involving the handling of electrolyte shall wear safety glasses.

Informational Note: Battery maintenance activities usually do not involve handling electrolyte. Batteries with solid electrolyte (such as most lithium batteries) or immobilized electrolyte (such as valve-regulated lead acid batteries) present little or no electrolyte hazard. Most modern density meters expose a worker to a quantity of electrolyte too minute to be considered hazardous, if at all. Such work would not be considered handling electrolyte. However, if specific gravity readings

Safety Requirements Related to Batteries and Battery Rooms   320.3(D)

are taken using a bulb hydrometer, the risk of exposure is higher — this could be considered to be handling electrolyte, and the requirements of 320.3(B)(1) would apply.

(C) Testing, Maintenance, and Operation.

(1) Direct-Current Ground-Fault Detection. Ground-fault detection shall be based on the type of dc grounding systems utilized.

> Informational Note: Not all battery systems have dc ground-fault detection systems. For personnel safety reasons, it is important to understand the grounding methodology being used and to determine the appropriate manner of detecting ground faults. If an unintended ground develops within the system (e.g., dirt and acid touching the battery rack), it can create a short circuit that could cause a fire. Commonly used dc grounding systems include, but are not limited to, the following:
>
> (1) Type 1. An ungrounded dc system, in which neither pole of the battery is connected to ground. If an unintentional ground occurs at any place in the battery, an increased potential would exist, allowing fault current to flow between the opposite end of the battery and the ground. An ungrounded dc system is typically equipped with an alarm to indicate the presence of a ground fault.
>
> (2) Type 2. A solidly grounded dc system, in which either the most positive or most negative pole of the battery is connected directly to ground. If an unintentional ground occurs, it introduces a path through which fault current can flow. A ground detection system is not typically used on this type of grounded system.
>
> (3) Type 3. A resistance grounded dc system, which is a variation of a Type 1 system, in which the battery is connected to ground through a resistance. Detection of a change in the resistance typically enables activation of a ground-fault alarm. Introducing an unintentional ground at one point of the battery could be detected and alarmed. A second unintentional ground at a different point in the battery would create a path for short-circuit current to flow.
>
> (4) Type 4. A solidly grounded dc system, either at the center point or at another point to suit the load system. If an unintentional ground occurs on either polarity, it introduces a path through which short circuit current can flow. A ground detection system is not typically used on this type of grounded system.

> The employee must know the type of grounding employed in order to understand the type of dc ground-fault detection required. The informational note describes four different battery grounding types. Some types will normally have ground-fault detection, whereas in others a ground-fault detector would be useless or could even create a safety hazard.

(2) Tools and Equipment.

(a) Tools and equipment for work on batteries shall be equipped with handles listed as insulated for the maximum working voltage.

(b) Battery terminals and all electrical conductors shall be kept clear of unintended contact with tools, test equipment, liquid containers, and other foreign objects.

(c) Nonsparking tools shall be required when the risk assessment required by 110.1(H) justifies their use.

(D) Cell Flame Arresters and Cell Ventilation. When present, battery cell ventilation openings shall be unobstructed. Cell flame arresters shall be inspected for proper installation and unobstructed ventilation and shall be replaced when necessary in accordance with the manufacturer's instructions.

Article 330 Safety-Related Work Practices: Lasers

330.1 Scope.

This article applies to safety-related work practices for maintaining lasers and their associated equipment.

> Informational Note No. 1: For recommendations on laser safety requirements for laser use, see ANSI Z136.1, Standard for Safe Use of Lasers.
>
> Informational Note No. 2: For laser product requirements for laser manufacturers, see 21 CFR Part 1040, "Performance Standards for Light-Emitting Products," Sections 1040.10 "Laser products" and 1040.11, "Specific purpose laser products."

Article 330 is limited to tasks necessary to maintain a laser system in the laboratory or in the workshop. It does not cover the general application and use of lasers in the workplace. Employees who work with lasers might be exposed to hazards associated with the laser output in addition to the electrical hazards associated with the equipment.

△ 330.2 Definitions.

For the purposes of this article, the following definitions shall apply.

N Field Evaluated. A thorough evaluation of nonlisted or modified equipment in the field that is performed by persons or parties acceptable to the authority having jurisdiction.

> Informational Note: The evaluation approval ensures that the equipment meets appropriate codes and standards or is similarly found suitable for a specified purpose.

Laser. A device that produces radiant energy at wavelengths between 180 nm (nanometer) and 1 mm (millimeter) predominantly by controlled stimulated emission. Laser radiation can be highly coherent temporally, spatially, or both.

△ Laser Energy Source. Any device intended for use in conjunction with a laser to supply energy for the excitation of electrons, ions, or molecules.

Laser Radiation. All electromagnetic radiation emitted by a laser or laser system between 180 nm (nanometers) and 1 mm (millimeters) that is produced as a result of a controlled stimulated emission.

Laser System. A laser in combination with an appropriate laser energy source with or without additional incorporated components.

> There are two classification systems in use, the FDA laser regulations and the international standard IEC 60825, *Safety of Laser Products*. At this time the FDA and IEC 60825 laser classification systems are not fully harmonized. Laser systems are classified by output power and wavelength. The classifications described by physical hazard are as follows:
>
> - *Class 1 laser system* — Incapable of producing damaging radiation levels during operation. Class 1 systems may contain laser sources of a higher class but are

Safety-Related Work Practices: Lasers 330.4(A)

> intrinsically safe when used as intended. Examples are found in DVD players and laser printers.
> - *Class 1M laser system* — Incapable of producing hazardous exposure conditions during normal operation unless the beam is viewed with an optical instrument.
> - *Class 2 laser system (Class 2 and 2M)* — Emits in the visible portion of the spectrum (0.4 μm to 0.7 μm) and eye protection is normally afforded by the aversion response (blinking reflex). Examples of Class 2 systems are found in laser pointers and some point-of-sale scanners.
> - *Class 3 laser system (Class 3R and Class 3B)* — Hazardous if viewed directly but is considered safe if handled carefully and with restricted beam viewing. Examples of Class 3 lasers are found inside DVD writers.
> - *Class 4 laser system* — Can burn the skin or cause permanent eye damage as a result of direct, diffuse, or indirect beam viewing. May ignite combustible materials. Class 4 lasers are typically limited to industrial, scientific, military, and medical use.

N **Protective Barrier.** Prevents user access to a hazardous voltage, current, or stored energy area.

N **330.3 Hazardous Energy.**

N **(A) Voltage and Current.** For the purpose of this section, hazardous voltage and current for ac systems is considered greater than or equal to 50 volts ac and 5 mA. For dc systems, hazardous voltage or current is considered greater than or equal to 100 volts dc and 40 mA.

> Although the dc threshold for the potential for an electrical shock is 50 volts in Article 130, Article 330 allows an increase of the threshold to 100 volts. However, unlike other NFPA *70E* articles addressing dc systems, Article 330 also limits the current to 40 mA. The employer must implement the hierarchy of risk controls as well as define the safe work practices for each scheduled task when 100 volts or greater is present.
>
> Environmental conditions, such as a wet environment, may warrant a lower dc threshold. Cut human skin can decrease the voltage level necessary to injure a worker.

OSHA Connection

29 CFR 1910.333(a)(1)
Live parts that operate at 50 volts or above must be de-energized. Compliance with this regulation may not be met where 100 volts is used as the energy exposure limit.

N **(B) Stored Energy.** For the purpose of this article, hazardous stored energy is considered greater than or equal to 0.25 joules at 400 volts or greater, or 1 joule at greater than 100 volts up to 400 volts.

> These energy levels are not incident energy levels. These levels are the limit of energy that a system may have without being considered a hazard. This is independent of the hazardous voltage and current levels in 330.3(A).

330.4 Electrical Safety Training.

(A) Personnel to Be Trained. Employers shall provide training for all personnel who work on or are near lasers or laser systems with user-accessible hazardous voltage, current, or stored energy (e.g., flashlamp-pumped lasers).

OSHA Connection

OSHA regulations refer to ANSI Z136.1, *Safe Use of Lasers*, as a consensus standard on the subject. In addition to providing a laser safety program consisting of policies, procedures, and training to employees, it is recommended that the employer appoint a laser safety officer for facilities that use Class 3B and Class 4 lasers.

> Although NFPA *70E* addresses the electrical hazards associated with maintaining laser systems, understanding the laser class is essential to addressing safety issues. Although any class of laser may be found in the laboratory or workshop, many are not considered to be hazardous under normal operation or viewing. See the commentary following the definition of *Laser System* in 330.2 above.
>
> The ANSI Z136 series addresses hazards and associated regulatory information in detail. The hazards are also addressed by the IEC 60825 series. The ANSI series contains

nine ANSI standards for lasers. The following documents are applicable to facilities addressed by Article 330:

- ANSI Z136.1-2014, *American National Standard for Safe Use of Lasers*
- ANSI Z136.4-2010, *Recommended Practice for Laser Safety Measurements for Hazard Evaluation*
- ANSI Z136.5-2000, *American National Standard for Safe Use of Lasers in Educational Institutions*
- ANSI Z136.6-2005, *American National Standard for Safe Use of Lasers Outdoors*
- ANSI Z136.8-2012, *American National Standard for Safe Use of Lasers in Research, Development, or Testing*

(B) Electrical Safety Training for Work on or with Lasers. Training in electrical safe work practices shall include, but is not limited to, the following:

(1) Chapter 1 electrical safe work practices
(2) Electrical hazards associated with laser equipment
(3) Stored energy hazards, including capacitor bank explosion potential
(4) Ionizing radiation
(5) X-ray hazards from high-voltage equipment (>5 kV)
(6) Assessing the listing status of electrical equipment and the need for field evaluation of nonlisted equipment

> Great care is needed when working with the various types of laser systems, and electrical safety training is paramount. Lasers that are electrically powered can be hazardous due to their radiation as well as their power sources. High-energy density batteries, generators, ultracapacitors, and associated power distribution panels present potential shock, arc flash, and fire hazards. Some source batteries are megajoule systems. A typical welding laser will have a prime power source of 50 kVA to 100 kVA, with larger systems approaching 500 kVA. Large systems are often water cooled, so wet environments might be present as well. These units can be mobile units powered by diesel generators.

330.5 Safeguarding of Persons from Electrical Hazards Associated with Lasers and Laser Systems.

N (A) Temporary Guarding. Temporary guarding (e.g., covers, protective insulating barriers) shall be used to limit exposure to any electrical hazard when the permanent laser enclosure covers are removed for maintenance and testing.

N (B) Work Requiring an Electrically Safe Work Condition. Work that might expose employees to electrical hazards shall be performed with the equipment in an electrically safe work condition in accordance with 120.1, 120.2, and 130.2.

> Work that is performed on exposed energized electrical conductors or circuit parts is dangerous. The requirement in NFPA *70E* and OSHA regulations is that first and foremost employees must work with equipment de-energized and in an electrically safe work condition (ESWC) unless operated under a normal condition. Therefore the primary protective strategy must be to establish an ESWC. After this strategy is executed, all electrical energy has been removed from all conductors and circuit parts to which the employee could be exposed.

Safety-Related Work Practices: Power Electronic Equipment

> Although Chapter 1 addresses shock hazards, arc flash hazards, and the limited conditions that permit justified energized work, Article 330 includes additional hazard limits in 330.3. If the specified voltage, current, or energy levels are exceeded by the laser system, the primary safe work practice must also be to establish an ESWC.

N **(C) Energized Electrical Testing.** Energized electrical testing, troubleshooting, and voltage testing shall not require an energized work permit in accordance with 130.2(B)(3).

N **(D) Warning Signs and Labels.** Electrical safety warning signs and labels shall be posted as applicable on electrical equipment doors, covers, and protective barriers. The warning signs and labels shall adequately warn of the hazard using effective words, colors, and symbols. These signs and labels shall be permanently affixed to the equipment and shall be of sufficient durability to withstand the environment involved.

N **(E) Listing.** Laser system electrical equipment shall be listed or field evaluated prior to use.

> **OSHA Connection**
> 29 CFR 1926.54(d)
> Areas in which lasers are used must be posted with standard laser warning placards. The warning signs should comply with ANSI Z535, *Series of Standards for Safety Signs and Tags*.

330.6 Responsibility for Electrical Safety.

All persons with access to hazardous voltage, current, or stored energy shall be responsible for the following:

(1) Obtaining authorization for work with or on hazardous electrical equipment in lasers and laser systems
(2) Use of Chapter 1 safety-related work practices
(3) Reporting laser equipment failures, accidents, inadequate barriers, and inadequate signage to the employer

Article 340

Safety-Related Work Practices: Power Electronic Equipment

> Chapter 1 applies to electrical equipment that operates at frequencies normally supplied for consumer use. The reaction of the human body to current flow changes as the frequency increases or decreases. When a frequency reaches the microwave band, joule heating can result in internal burns.
> Employees who work on or with equipment within the scope of Article 340 must be qualified to perform tasks using the specific electronic equipment. They must be trained to understand the unique hazards associated with the specific equipment and how to avoid exposure to those hazards.

340.1 Scope.

This article shall apply to safety-related work practices around power electronic equipment, including the following:

(1) Electric arc welding equipment
(2) High-power radio, radar, and television transmitting towers and antennas
(3) Industrial dielectric and radio frequency (RF) induction heaters

(4) Shortwave or RF diathermy devices
(5) Process equipment that includes rectifiers and inverters such as the following:
   a. Motor drives
   b. Uninterruptible power supply systems
   c. Lighting controllers

> Informational Note: The following standards provide specific guidance for safety-related work practices around power electronic equipment: International Electrotechnical Commission IEC 60479-1, *Effects of Current on Human Beings and Livestock, Part 1: General Aspects*, and the International Commission on Radiological Protection (ICRP) Publication 33, *Protection Against Ionizing Radiation from External Sources Used in Medicine*.

Article 340 includes some common types of equipment that are found on construction sites or at industrial or commercial facilities. It also includes some types of equipment that are not as common. This list is not all-inclusive. For example, photovoltaic, fuel cell, and wind systems used for the generation of electricity generally incorporate power electronic devices (power converters).

340.2 Definition.

For the purposes of this article, the definition that follows shall apply.

Radiation Worker. A person who is required to work in electromagnetic fields, the radiation levels of which exceed those specified for nonoccupational exposure.

340.3 Application.

The purpose of this article is to provide guidance for safety personnel in preparing specific safety-related work practices within their industry.

340.4 Hazards Associated with Power Electronic Equipment.

The employer and employees shall be aware of the hazards associated with the following:

(1) High voltages within the power supplies
(2) Radio frequency energy–induced high voltages
(3) Effects of RF fields in the vicinity of antennas and antenna transmission lines, which can introduce electrical shock and burns
(4) Ionizing (X-radiation) hazards from magnetrons, klystrons, thyratrons, cathode-ray tubes, and similar devices
(5) Nonionizing RF radiation hazards from the following:
   a. Radar equipment
   b. Radio communication equipment, including broadcast transmitters
   c. Satellite–earth-transmitters
   d. Industrial scientific and medical equipment
   e. RF induction heaters and dielectric heaters
   f. Industrial microwave heaters and diathermy radiators

Commentary Table 340.1 contains quantitative data on the physiological effects of current on the human body.

Safety-Related Work Practices: Power Electronic Equipment

COMMENTARY TABLE 340.1 Quantitative Effects of Electric Current on Humans (Average Data)

	Current (mA)					
	Direct Current (mA)		Alternating Current (mA)			
	DC		60 Hz		10 kHz	
Effects	150 lbs	115 lbs	150 lbs	115 lbs	150 lbs	115 lbs
Slight sensation on hand	1	0.6	0.4	0.3	7	5
Perception threshold, median	5.2	3.5	1.1	0.7	12	8
Shock — not painful and no loss of muscular control	9	6	1.8	1.2	17	11
Painful shock — muscular control lost by 0.5%	62	41	9	6	55	37
Painful shock — let-go threshold, median	76	51	16	10.5	75	50
Painful and severe shock — breathing difficult, muscular control lost by 99.5%	90	60	23	15	94	63
Possible ventricular fibrillation:						
Three-second shocks	500	500	100	100		
Short shocks (T in seconds)			$165/(\sqrt{T})$	$165/(\sqrt{T})$		
High-voltage surges (Energy in joules, i.e., watt-seconds)	50 J	50 J	13.6 J	13.6 J		

Notes:

Derived from "Deleterious Effects of Electric Shock," Charles F. Dalziel, p. 24. Presented at a meeting of experts on electrical accidents and related matters, sponsored by the International Labour Office, World Health Office and International Electrotechnical Commission, Geneva, Switzerland, October 23–31, 1961. Refer to the study for definitions and details.

The data in the preceding table are based on limited experiments conducted on human subjects and animals in 1961. These figures may not be fully dependable due to lack of additional information and normal physiological differences between individuals. Electric current should probably be considered fatal at current values lower than indicated. From the *Health and Safety Manual*, LBNL/PPUB-3000, Environmental, Health and Safety (EH&S) Division of Lawrence Berkley National Laboratory, operated by the University of California for the U.S. Department of Energy, from experimental data derived from 115 subjects, information is as follows:

- The average threshold of perception of dc current in a 150 lb person (average healthy young male) is 5 mA.
- The threshold varies considerably from 2 mA to 10 mA dc.
- The average threshold for 60 Hz ac current in the 150 lb person is 1 mA.
- The threshold of perception increases with frequency so that at 100 kHz it is 150 mA (0.15 A).
- The threshold for a 115 lb person (average healthy young female) is around two-thirds of that for the 150 lb person (average healthy young male).

Power electronic equipment commonly holds stored electrical energy. Filter boards and power boards in the equipment contain capacitors that could store energy in addition to the stored energy in the bus capacitors. Electromagnetic interference (EMI) filters must be discharged prior to servicing to prevent electric shock or arc flash hazard. The equipment in Exhibit 340.1 requires a 15-minute waiting period before the enclosure is opened in order to allow time for stored energy to discharge and carries a reminder to verify the lack of voltage. Time itself must not be relied upon for depletion of stored energy. Before accessing the interior of an uninterruptible power supply (UPS) unit, care must be exercised to ensure that each source of input and output power has been electrically or physically isolated. Batteries or capacitors located within the UPS unit might still be charged even after all apparent voltage sources have been isolated or confirmed to be de-energized.

EXHIBIT 340.1

Equipment requiring dissipation of stored energy. (Courtesy of Schneider Electric)

340.5 Specific Measures for Personnel Safety.

(A) Employer Responsibility. The employer shall be responsible for the following:

(1) Proper training and supervision by properly qualified personnel, including the following:
   a. Identification of associated hazards
   b. Strategies to reduce the risk associated with the hazards
   c. Methods of avoiding or protecting against the hazard
   d. Necessity of reporting any incident that resulted in, or could have resulted in, injury or damage to health
(2) Properly installed equipment
(3) Proper access to the equipment
(4) Availability of the correct tools for operation and maintenance
(5) Proper identification and guarding of dangerous equipment
(6) Provision of complete and accurate circuit diagrams and other published information to the employee prior to the employee starting work (The circuit diagrams should be marked to indicate the components that present an electrical hazard.)
(7) Maintenance of clear and clean work areas around the equipment to be worked on
(8) Provision of adequate and proper illumination of the work area

(B) Employee Responsibility. The employee shall be responsible for the following:

(1) Understanding the hazards associated with the work
(2) Being continuously alert and aware of the possible hazards
(3) Using the proper tools and procedures for the work
(4) Informing the employer of malfunctioning protective measures, such as faulty or inoperable enclosures and locking schemes

(5) Examining all documents provided by the employer relevant to the work to identify the location of components that present an electrical hazard
(6) Maintaining good housekeeping around the equipment and work space
(7) Reporting any incident that resulted in, or could have resulted in, injury or damage to health
(8) Using and appropriately maintaining the PPE and tools required to perform the work safely

> Servicing damaged equipment may present additional hazards not associated with servicing properly functioning equipment. For example, stored energy in damaged equipment may not discharge as intended. High earth leakage currents to the equipment chassis or enclosure can occur if the equipment grounding system is damaged or improperly installed. Testing for the presence of voltage is necessary even after waiting the prescribed time.

Safety-Related Work Requirements: Research and Development Laboratories

Article 350

> Article 350 addresses unique conditions that might exist in laboratory and research areas. Electrical installations in laboratory or research areas often contain custom or specially designed electrical equipment that may have unique electrical safety–related requirements.

350.1 Scope.

The requirements of this article shall apply to the electrical installations in those areas, with custom or special electrical equipment, designated by the facility management for research and development (R&D) or as laboratories.

> This article covers all laboratory facilities, including those that exist in educational facilities. Research and development facilities, including those associated with institutions of higher learning, are also covered.

350.2 Definitions.

For the purposes of this article, the definitions that follow shall apply.

Competent Person. A person who meets all the requirements of *qualified person*, as defined in Article 100 in Chapter 1 of this standard and who, in addition, is responsible for all work activities or safety procedures related to custom or special equipment and has detailed knowledge regarding the exposure to electrical hazards, the appropriate control methods to reduce the risk associated with those hazards, and the implementation of those methods.

Field Evaluated. A thorough evaluation of nonlisted or modified equipment in the field that is performed by persons or parties acceptable to the authority having jurisdiction. The evaluation approval ensures that the equipment meets appropriate codes and standards, or is similarly found suitable for a specified purpose.

> Equipment in laboratory or research areas is often custom designed. A consensus product standard covering the special equipment might not be issued. Also, submitting the one-off piece of equipment to a formal listing process may not be necessary because the equipment is not available for sale or use outside of the company for which it is designed. Field evaluation of the custom equipment ensures that it is suitable for employee use within the intended application.

Laboratory. A building, space, room, or group of rooms intended to serve activities involving procedures for investigation, diagnostics, product testing, or use of custom or special electrical components, systems, or equipment.

Research and Development (R&D). An activity in an installation specifically designated for research or development conducted with custom or special electrical equipment.

350.3 Applications of Other Articles.

The electrical system for R&D and laboratory applications shall meet the requirements of the remainder of this document, except as amended by Article 350.

> Informational Note: Examples of these applications include low-voltage–high-current power systems; high-voltage–low-current power systems; dc power supplies; capacitors; cable trays for signal cables and other systems, such as steam, water, air, gas, or drainage; and custom-made electronic equipment.

350.4 Electrical Safety Authority (ESA).

Each laboratory or R&D system application shall be permitted to assign an ESA to ensure the use of appropriate electrical safety-related work practices and controls. The ESA shall be permitted to be an electrical safety committee, engineer, or equivalent qualified individual. The ESA shall be permitted to delegate authority to an individual or organization within their control.

N **(A) Responsibility.** The ESA shall act in a manner similar to an authority having jurisdiction for R&D electrical systems and electrical safe work practices.

N **(B) Qualifications.** The ESA shall be competent in the following:

(1) The requirements of this standard
(2) Electrical system requirements applicable to the R&D laboratories

N 350.5 Specific Measures and Controls for Personnel Safety.

Each laboratory or R&D system application shall designate a competent person as defined in this article to ensure the use of appropriate electrical safety-related work practices and controls.

Safety-Related Work Requirements

> As required in Chapter 1, the employer must provide written procedures or other instructions of the electrical safety program for the unique conditions encountered in laboratory and research areas. A competent person — not just qualified — is required to oversee the laboratory to ensure that employees follow the procedures.

(A) Job Briefings. Job briefings shall be performed in accordance with 110.1(I).

Exception: Prior to starting work, a brief discussion shall be permitted if the task and hazards are documented and the employee has reviewed applicable documentation and is qualified for the task.

(B) Personnel Protection. Safety-related work practices shall be used to safeguard employees from injury while they are exposed to electrical hazards from exposed electrical conductors or circuit parts that are or can become energized. The specific safety-related work practices shall be consistent with the electrical hazard(s) and the associated risk. For calibration and adjustment of equipment as it pertains to sensors, motor controllers, control hardware, and other devices that need to be installed inside equipment or control cabinet, surrounded by electrical hazards, the ESA shall define the required PPE based on the risk and exposure.

Use of electrical insulating blankets, covers, or barriers shall be permitted to prevent inadvertent contact to exposed terminals and conductors. Insulated/nonconductive adjustment and alignment tools shall be used where feasible.

350.6 Approval Requirements.

The equipment or systems used in the R&D area or in the laboratory shall be listed or field evaluated prior to use.

> Informational Note: Laboratory and R&D equipment or systems can pose unique electrical hazards that might require mitigation. Such hazards include ac and dc, low voltage and high amperage, high voltage and low current, large electromagnetic fields, induced voltages, pulsed power, multiple frequencies, and similar exposures.

> This requirement is not intended to be applied to equipment under development. Unique equipment is often necessary to conduct research or to evaluate items under development, and listing of the equipment is often not possible. This equipment is permitted to be field evaluated (see the definition of *Field Evaluated* in 350.2) by a party acceptable to the authority having jurisdiction. The use of custom-made equipment does not remove the employer's responsibility for providing electrical safety–related work practices.

350.7 Custom Built, Non-Listed Research Equipment, 1000 Volts or less AC or DC.

(A) Equipment Marking and Documentation.

(1) Marking. Marking of equipment shall be required for, but not limited to, equipment fabricated, designed, or developed for research testing and evaluation of electrical systems. Marking shall sufficiently list all voltages entering and leaving control cabinets, enclosures, and equipment.

Caution, Warning, or Danger labels shall be affixed to the exterior describing specific hazards and safety concerns.

> Informational Note: Refer to ANSI Z535, *Series of Standards for Safety Signs and Tags*, for more information on precautionary marking of electrical systems or equipment.

N (2) Documentation. Sufficient documentation shall be provided and readily available to personnel that install, operate, and maintain equipment that describes operation, shutdown, safety concerns, and nonstandard installations.

Schematics, drawings, and bill of materials describing power feeds, voltages, currents, and parts used for construction, maintenance, and operation of the equipment shall be provided.

N (3) Shutdown Procedures. Safety requirements and emergency shutdown procedures of equipment shall include lockout/tagout (LOTO) requirements. If equipment-specific LOTO is required, then documentation outlining this procedure and PPE requirements shall be made readily available.

N (4) Specific Hazards. Specific hazards, other than electrical, associated with research equipment shall be documented and readily available.

N (5) Approvals. Drawings, standard operational procedures, and equipment shall be approved by the ESA on site before initial start up. Assembly of equipment shall comply with national standards where applicable unless research application requires exceptions. Equipment that does not meet the applicable standards shall be required to be approved by the ESA. Proper safety shutdown procedures and PPE requirements shall be considered in the absence of grounding and/or bonding.

N (B) Tools, Training, and Maintenance. Documentation shall be provided if special tools, unusual PPE, or other equipment is necessary for proper maintenance and operation of equipment. The ESA shall make the determination of appropriate training and qualifications required to perform specific tasks.

N 350.8 Custom Built, Unlisted Research Equipment, >1000 V AC or DC.

Installations shall comply with all requirements of 350.7.

In the event that research equipment requires PPE beyond what is commercially available, the ESA shall determine safe work practices and PPE to be used.

N 350.9 Energy Thresholds.

Energy exposure levels shall not exceed those identified in the following list unless appropriate controls are implemented as approved by the ESA:

(1) AC: 50-Volts and 5 milliamperes.
(2) DC: 100-Volts and 40 milliamperes.
(3) Capacitive systems:
   a. 100-Volts and 100 Joules of stored energy
   b. 400-Volts and 1.0 Joule of stored energy
   c. 0.25 Joules of stored energy

Informational Note: This information is extracted from the Department of Energy (DOE) Electrical Safety Handbook, DOE-HDBK-1092.

> **OSHA Connection**
> 29 CFR 1910.333(a)(1)
> Live parts that operate at 50 volts or above must be de-energized. Compliance with this regulation may not be met where 100 volts is used as the energy exposure limit.

> Although the dc threshold for the potential for an electrical shock is 50 volts in Article 130, Article 350 allows an increase of the threshold to 100 volts. However, unlike other NFPA *70E* articles addressing dc systems, Article 350 also limits the current to 40 mA.

Safety-Related Work Requirements

> These energy levels in 350.9(3) are not incident energy levels. These levels are the limit of energy that a system may have without being considered a hazard. This is independent of the hazardous voltage and current levels in 350.9(1) and 350.9(2).

N 350.10 Establishing an Electrically Safe Work Condition.

Energized electrical conductors and circuit parts shall be put into an electrically safe work condition before an employee performs work.

Exception: At the discretion of the ESA, alternative methods of ensuring worker safety shall be permitted to be employed for the following conditions:

(1) *Minor tool changes and adjustments, and other normal production operations that are routine, repetitive, or sequential and integral to the use of the equipment for production*
(2) *Minor changes to the unit under test and other minor servicing activities, to include the activities listed under 350.10 Exception condition (1), that take place during research and development*
(3) *Work on cord-and-plug-connected equipment for which exposure to the hazards of unexpected energization or start up is controlled by the following:*
   a. *Unplugging the equipment from the energy source*
   b. *The employee performing the work maintaining exclusive control of the plug*

> Work that is performed on exposed energized electrical conductors or circuit parts is dangerous. The requirement in NFPA *70E* and OSHA regulations is that, first and foremost, employees must work with equipment de-energized and in an electrically safe work condition (ESWC) unless operated under a normal condition. Therefore, the primary protective strategy must be to establish an ESWC. After this strategy is executed, all electrical energy has been removed from all conductors and circuit parts to which the employee could be exposed.
>
> The requirements of Chapter 3 can modify the requirements of Chapter 1. Although Chapter 1 addresses shock hazards, arc flash hazards, and the limited conditions that permit justified energized work, Article 350 includes additional hazard limits in 350.9. If the specified voltage, current, or energy levels are exceeded by the system, the primary safe work practice must also be to establish an ESWC. The explicit exception to establishing an ESWC is the sole allowance for justified energized work in a research and development laboratory. The exceptions in 130.2(A) do not apply.

INFORMATIVE ANNEX A

Informative Publications

> Informative Annex A identifies important publications that provide additional information to assist the user in understanding and applying the requirements of NFPA *70E*. This informative annex provides further information about the publisher and edition of the documents referenced in the Informational Notes. These documents are for informational purposes only.
>
> The state of electrical safety is constantly moving forward. Existing documents are either deleted or revised periodically, while new documents are issued. The user of NFPA *70E* is encouraged to verify that the referenced document is the latest published edition since the document's issue cycle may be different from that of NFPA *70E*.

△ A.1 General.

The following documents or portions thereof are referenced within this standard for informational purposes only and are thus not part of the requirements of this document.

A.2 NFPA Publications.

National Fire Protection Association, 1 Batterymarch Park, Quincy, MA 02169-7471.
NFPA 70®, *National Electrical Code*®, 2017 edition.
NFPA 1, *Fire Code*, 2018 edition.
NFPA 70B, *Recommended Practice for Electrical Equipment Maintenance*, 2016 edition.
NFPA 79, *Electrical Standard for Industrial Machinery*, 2015 edition.

A.3 Other Publications.

△ **A.3.1 ANSI Publications.** American National Standards Institute, Inc., 25 West 43rd Street, 4th Floor, New York, NY 10036.

ANSI/ASC A14.1, *American National Standard for Ladders — Wood — Safety Requirements*, 2007.
ANSI/ASC A14.3, *American National Standard for Ladders — Fixed — Safety Requirements*, 2008.
ANSI/ASC A14.4, *American National Standard Safety Requirements for Job-Made Wooden Ladders*, 2009.
ANSI/ASC A14.5, *American National Standard for Ladders — Portable Plastic Reinforced — Safety Requirements*, 2007.
ANSI Z87.1, *American National Standard for Occupational and Educational Eye and Face Protection*, 2015.
ANSI Z89.1, *American National Standard for Head Protection*, 2014.

ANSI Z535, *Series of Standards for Safety Signs and Tags*, 2011.

ANSI/AIHA Z10, *American National Standard for Occupational Health and Safety Management Systems*, 2012.

ANSI/ASSE Z244.1, *Control of Hazardous Energy — Lockout/Tagout and Alternative Methods*, 2003 (R 2008).

ANSI C84.1, *Electric Power Systems and Equipment — Voltage Ratings (60 Hz)*, 2011.

ANSI/ISO 14001, *Environmental Management Systems — Requirements with Guidance for Use*, 2004/Corrigendum 1, 2009.

ANSI/NETA MTS, *Standard for Maintenance Testing Specifications for Electrical Power Distribution Equipment and Systems*, 2011.

A.3.2 ASTM Publications. ASTM International, 100 Barr Harbor Drive, P.O Box C700, West Conshohocken, PA 19428-2959.

ASTM D120, *Standard Specification for Rubber Insulating Gloves*, 2014a.

ASTM D1048, *Standard Specification for Rubber Insulating Blankets*, 2014.

ASTM D1049, *Standard Specification for Rubber Insulating Covers*, 1998 (R 2010).

ASTM D1050, *Standard Specification for Rubber Insulating Line Hoses*, 2005 (R 2011).

ASTM D1051, *Standard Specification for Rubber Insulating Sleeves*, 2014a.

ASTM F478, *Standard Specification for In-Service Care of Insulating Line Hose and Covers*, 2014a.

ASTM F479, *Standard Specification for In-Service Care of Insulating Blankets*, 2006 (R 2011).

ASTM F496, *Standard Specification for In-Service Care of Insulating Gloves and Sleeves*, 2014a.

ASTM F696, *Standard Specification for Leather Protectors for Rubber Insulating Gloves and Mittens*, 2006 (R 2011).

ASTM F711, *Standard Specification for Fiberglass-Reinforced Plastic (FRP) Rod and Tube Used in Live Line Tools*, 2002 (R 2013).

ASTM F712, *Standard Test Methods and Specifications for Electrically Insulating Plastic Guard Equipment for Protection of Workers*, 2006 (R 2011).

ASTM F855, *Standard Specification for Temporary Protective Grounds to Be Used on De-energized Electric Power Lines and Equipment*, 2015.

ASTM F887, *Standard Specification for Personal Climbing Equipment*, 2013.

ASTM F1116, *Standard Test Method for Determining Dielectric Strength of Dielectric Footwear*, 2014a.

ASTM F1117, *Standard Specification for Dielectric Footwear*, 2003 (R 2013).

ASTM F1236, *Standard Guide for Visual Inspection of Electrical Protective Rubber Products*, 2015.

ASTM F1296, *Standard Guide for Evaluating Chemical Protective Clothing*, 2015.

ASTM F1449, *Standard Guide for Industrial Laundering of Flame, Thermal, and Arc Resistant Clothing*, 2015.

ASTM F1505, *Standard Specification for Insulated and Insulating Hand Tools*, 2015.

ASTM F1506, *Standard Performance Specification for Flame Resistant and Arc Rated Textile Materials for Wearing Apparel for Use by Electrical Workers Exposed to Momentary Electric Arc and Related Thermal Hazards*, 2015.

ASTM F1742, *Standard Specification for PVC Insulating Sheeting*, 2003 (R 2011).

ASTM F1891, *Standard Specification for Arc and Flame Resistant Rainwear*, 2012.

ASTM F1959/F1959M, *Standard Test Method for Determining the Arc Rating of Materials for Clothing*, 2014.

ASTM F2178, *Standard Test Method for Determining the Arc Rating and Standard Specification for Eye or Face Protective Products*, 2012.

ASTM F2249, *Standard Specification for In-Service Test Methods for Temporary Grounding Jumper Assemblies Used on De-Energized Electric Power Lines and Equipment*, 2003 (R 2015).

ASTM F2412/F2320, *Standard Specification for Rubber Insulating Sheeting*, 2011.

Informative Publications

ASTM F2412, *Standard Test Methods for Foot Protections*, 2011.
ASTM F2413, *Standard Specification for Performance Requirements for Protective (Safety) Toe Cap Footwear*, 2011.
ASTM F2522, *Standard Test Method for Determining the Protective Performance of a Shield Attached on Live Line Tools or on Racking Rods for Electric Arc Hazards*, 2012.
ASTM F2675/F2675M, *Test Method for Determining Arc Ratings of Hand Protective Products Developed and Used for Electrical Arc Flash Protection*, 2013.
ASTM F2676, *Standard Test Method for Determining the Protective Performance of an Arc Protective Blanket for Electric Arc Hazards*, 2009.
ASTM F2677, *Standard Specification for Electrically Insulating Aprons*, (R 2013).
ASTM F2757, *Standard Guide for Home Laundering Care and Maintenance of Flame, Thermal and Arc Resistant Clothing*, 2016.

A.3.3 ICRP Publications. International Commission on Radiological Protection, SE-171 16 Stockholm, Sweden.

ICRP Publication 33, *Protection Against Ionizing Radiation from External Sources Used in Medicine*, March 1982.

A.3.4 IEC Publications. International Electrotechnical Commission, 3, rue de Varembé, P.O. Box 131, CH-1211 Geneva 20, Switzerland.

IEC TS 60479-1, *Effects of Current on Human Beings and Livestock Part 1: General Aspects*, 2016.
IEC 60204-1 ed 5.1 Consol. with am 1, *Safety of Machinery — Electrical Equipment of Machines — Part 1: General Requirements*, 2009.

A.3.5 IEEE Publications. Institute of Electrical and Electronics Engineers, IEEE Operations Center, 445 Hoes Lane, P. O. Box 1331, Piscataway, NJ 08855-1331.

IEEE C37.20.7, *Guide for Testing Metal-Enclosed Switchgear Rated up to 38 kV for Internal Arcing Faults*, 2007/Corrigendum 1, 2010.
ANSI/IEEE C2, *National Electrical Safety Code*, 2012, 2017.
ANSI/IEEE C 37.20.6, *Standard for 4.76 kV to 38 kV Rated Ground and Test Devices Used in Enclosures*, 2007.
IEEE 4, *Standard Techniques for High Voltage Testing*, 2013.
IEEE 450, *IEEE Recommended Practice for Maintenance, Testing, and Replacement of Vented Lead-Acid Batteries for Stationary Applications*, 2010.
IEEE 516, *Guide for Maintenance Methods on Energized Power Lines*, 2009.
IEEE 937, *Recommended Practice for Installation and Maintenance of Lead-Acid Batteries for Photovoltaic Systems*, 2007.
IEEE 946, *IEEE Recommended Practice for the Design of DC Auxiliary Power Systems for Generating Systems*, 2004.
IEEE 1106, *IEEE Recommended Practice for Installation, Maintenance, Testing, and Replacement of Vented Nickel-Cadmium Batteries for Stationary Applications*, 2010.
IEEE 1184, *IEEE Guide for Batteries for Uninterruptible Power Supply Systems*, 2006.
IEEE 1187, *Recommended Practice for Installation Design and Installation of Valve-Regulated Lead-Acid Storage Batteries for Stationary Applications*, 2002.
IEEE 1188, *IEEE Recommended Practice for Maintenance, Testing, and Replacement of Valve-Regulated Lead-Acid (VRLA) Batteries for Stationary Applications*, 2005 (R 2010).
IEEE 1491, *IEEE Guide for Selection and Use of Battery Monitoring Equipment in Stationary Applications*, 2012.
IEEE 1584™, *Guide for Performing Arc Flash Hazard Calculations*, 2002.
IEEE 1584a™, *Guide for Performing Arc Flash Hazard Calculations, Amendment 1*, 2004.

IEEE 1584b™, *Guide for Performing Arc Flash Hazard Calculations — Amendment 2: Changes to Clause 4*, 2011.

IEEE 1657, *Recommended Practice for Personnel Qualifications for Installation and Maintenance of Stationary Batteries*, 2009.

IEEE 3007.1, *IEEE Recommended Practice for the Operation and Management of Industrial and Commercial Power Systems*, 2010.

IEEE 3007.2, *IEEE Recommended Practice for the Maintenance of Industrial and Commercial Power Systems*, 2010.

IEEE 3007.3, *IEEE Recommended Practice for Electrical Safety in Industrial and Commercial Power Systems*, 2012.

Anderson, W. E., "Risk Analysis Methodology Applied to Industrial Machine Development," *IEEE Transactions on Industrial Applications*, Vol. 41, No. 1, January/February 2005, pp. 180–187.

Ammerman, R. F., Gammon, T., Sen, P. K., and Nelson, J. P., "DC-Arc Models and Incident-Energy Calculations," *IEEE Transactions on Industrial Applications*, Vol. 46, No. 5, 2010.

Doan, D. R, "Arc Flash Calculations for Exposures to DC Systems," *IEEE Transactions on Industrial Applications*, Vol 46, No. 6, 2010.

Doughty, R. L., T. E. Neal, and H. L. Floyd II, "Predicting Incident Energy to Better Manage the Electric Arc Hazard on 600 V Power Distribution Systems," Record of Conference Papers IEEE IAS 45th Annual Petroleum and Chemical Industry Conference, September 28–30, 1998.

Lee, R., "The Other Electrical Hazard: Electrical Arc Flash Burns," *IEEE Trans. Applications*, Vol. 1A-18, No. 3, May/June 1982.

A.3.6 British Standards Institute, Occupational Health and Safety Assessment Series (OHSAS) Project Group Publications. British Standards Institute, American Headquarters, 12110 Sunset Hills Road, Suite 200, Reston VA 20190-5902.

BS OSHAS 18001, *Occupational Health and Safety Management Systems*, 2007.

A.3.7 CSA Publications. Canadian Standards Association, 5060 Spectrum Way, Mississauga, ON L4W 5N6, Canada.

CAN/CSA Z462, *Workplace Electrical Safety*, 2012.
CAN/CSA Z1000, *Occupational Health and Safety Management*, 2006 (R 2011).

A.3.8 ISA Publications. Instrumentation, Systems, and Automation Society, 67 Alexander Drive, Research Triangle Park, NC 27709.

ANSI/ISA 61010-1, *Safety Requirements for Electrical Equipment for Measurement, Control, and Laboratory Use, Part 1: General Requirements*, 2007.

A.3.9 ISEA Publications. International Safety Equipment Association, 1901 North Moore Street, Arlington, VA 22209-1762.

ANSI/ISEA Z358.1, *American National Standard for Emergency Eye Wash and Shower Equipment*, 2009.

A.3.10 ISO Publications. International Organization for Standardization, 1, Ch. de la Voie-Creuse, Case postale 56, CH-1211 Geneva 20, Switzerland.

ISO 14001, *Environmental Management Systems — Requirements with Guidance for Use*, 2004.

Informative Publications

N A.3.11 NIOSH Publications. National Institute for Occupational Safety and Health, Centers for Disease Control and Prevention, 1600 Clifton Road, Atlanta, GA 30333.

DHHS (NIOSH) Publication No. 94-110, *Applications Manual for the Revised NIOSH Lifting Equation*, 1994.

N A.3.12 UL Publications. Underwriters Laboratories Inc., 333 Pfingsten Road, Northbrook, IL 60062-2096.

ANSI/UL 943, *Standard for Ground-Fault Circuit Interrupters*, 2006 (R 2012).

N A.3.13 Government Publications. U.S. Government Publishing Office, 732 North Capitol Street, NW, Washington, DC 20401-0001.

Title 29, Code of Federal Regulations, Part 1910, "Occupational Safety and Health Standards", Subpart S, "Electrical," 1910.137, "Personal Protective Equipment", and 1910.305(j)(7), "Storage Batteries"; and Part 1926, "Safety and Health Regulations for Construction", Subpart K, "Electrical," 1926.441, Batteries and Battery Charging.
Department of Energy, DOE Handbook Electrical Safety, DOE – HDBK- 1092 – 2013.

N A.3.14 Other Publications. "DC Arc Hazard Assessment Phase II," Copyright Material, Kinectrics Inc., Report No. K-012623-RA-0002-R00.

INFORMATIVE ANNEX B

Reserved

In the 2018 edition of NFPA *70E®, Standard for Electrical Safety in the Workplace®*, Informative Annex B is reserved for future use.

INFORMATIVE ANNEX C

Limits of Approach

This informative annex is not a part of the requirements of this NFPA document but is included for informational purposes only.

> Informative Annex C provides information to illustrate approach boundaries. The information is intended to provide suggestions regarding workers' safe approach to each limit. The approach limits trigger the need for greater control of work performed inside that approach limit.

C.1 Preparation for Approach.

Observing a safe approach distance from exposed energized electrical conductors or circuit parts is an effective means of maintaining electrical safety. As the distance between a person and the exposed energized conductors or circuit parts decreases, the potential for electrical incident increases.

C.1.1 Unqualified Persons, Safe Approach Distance. Unqualified persons are safe when they maintain a distance from the exposed energized conductors or circuit parts, including the longest conductive object being handled, so that they cannot contact or enter a specified air insulation distance to the exposed energized electrical conductors or circuit parts. This safe approach distance is the limited approach boundary. Further, persons must not cross the arc flash boundary unless they are wearing appropriate personal protective clothing and are under the close supervision of a qualified person. Only when continuously escorted by a qualified person should an unqualified person cross the limited approach boundary. Under no circumstance should an unqualified person cross the restricted approach boundary, where special shock protection techniques and equipment are required.

> According to 130.3, safety-related work practices must be used to safeguard employees from injury when the risk of exposure to electrical hazards or potential electrical hazards is unacceptable, and the work practices must be consistent with the nature and extent of the hazard. These work practices are used to protect employees from the risk associated with the four conditions of electrical hazards: arc flash, arc blast, thermal burn, and electrical shock.
>
> The restricted and limited approach boundaries only address the potential for electric shock or electrocution. An unqualified worker within the limited approach boundary may be at risk of an arc flash injury even when under the close supervision of, or while continuously escorted by, a qualified person. Any person must not be allowed to cross the arc flash boundary without first receiving the specific safety-related training to understand the hazard(s) involved and the appropriate use of the necessary PPE.

C.1.2 Qualified Persons, Safe Approach Distance.

C.1.2.1 Determine the arc flash boundary and, if the boundary is to be crossed, appropriate arc-rated protective equipment must be utilized.

C.1.2.2 For a person to cross the limited approach boundary and enter the limited space, a person should meet the following criteria:

(1) Be qualified to perform the job/task
(2) Be able to identify the hazards and associated risks with the tasks to be performed

C.1.2.3 To cross the restricted approach boundary and enter the restricted space, qualified persons should meet the following criteria:

(1) As applicable, have an energized electrical work permit authorized by management.
(2) Use personal protective equipment (PPE) that is rated for the voltage and energy level involved.
(3) Minimize the likelihood of bodily contact with exposed energized conductors and circuit parts from inadvertent movement by keeping as much of the body out of the restricted space as possible and using only protected body parts in the space as necessary to accomplish the work.
(4) Use insulated tools and equipment.

(See *Figure C.1.2.3*.)

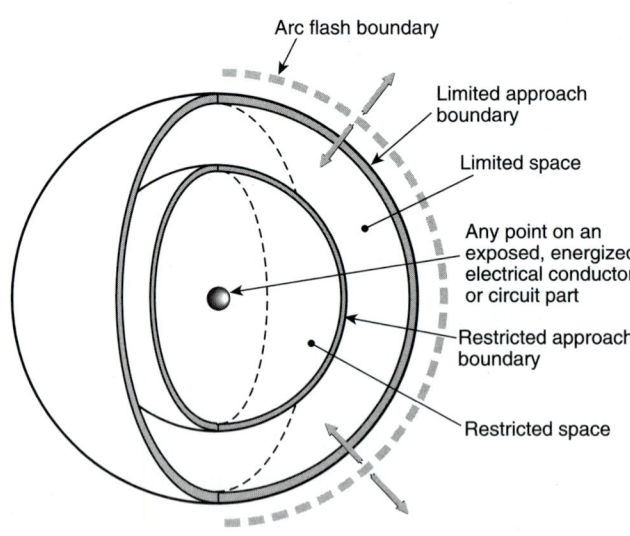

△ **FIGURE C.1.2.3** Limits of Approach.

Exhibit C.1 illustrates the three approach boundary distances for a 600-volt motor control center (MCC) when the risk assessment is conducted using the PPE category method.

Limits of Approach

EXHIBIT C.1

Three approach boundary distances for 600-volt MCC.

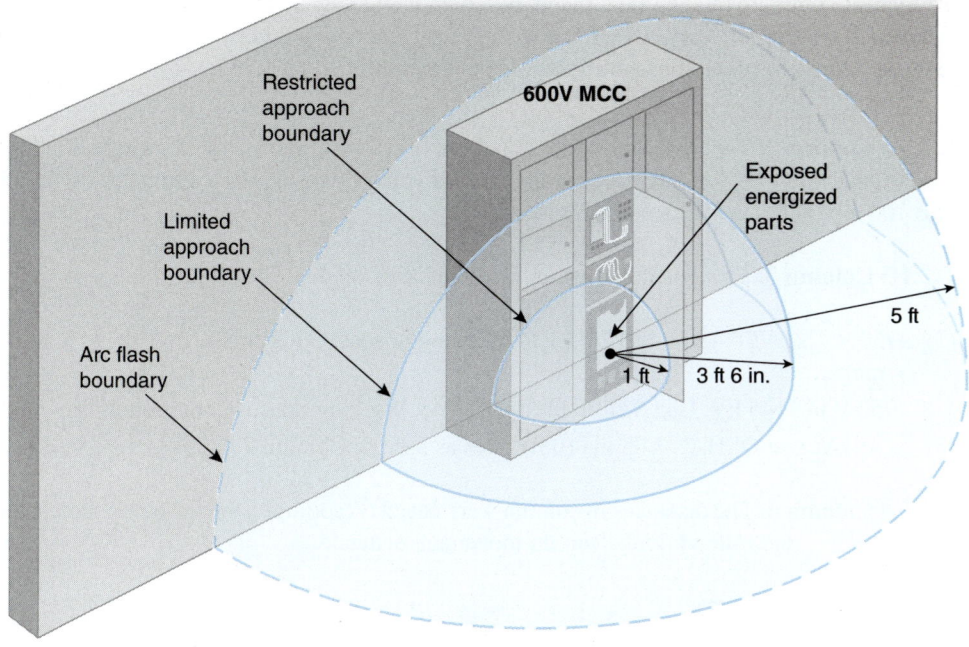

C.2 Basis for Distance Values in Tables 130.4(D)(a) and 130.4(D)(b).

The information contained in Tables 130.4(D)(a) and 130.4(D)(b) is derived from various sources. Section C.2 explains how the table distances were selected.

C.2.1 General Statement. Columns 2 through 5 of Table 130.4(D)(a) and Table 130.4(D)(b) show various distances from the exposed energized electrical conductors or circuit parts. They include dimensions that are added to a basic minimum air insulation distance. Those basic minimum air insulation distances for voltages 72.5 kV and under are based on IEEE 4, *Standard Techniques for High Voltage Testing*, Appendix 2B; and voltages over 72.5 kV are based on IEEE 516, *Guide for Maintenance Methods on Energized Power Lines*. The minimum air insulation distances that are required to avoid flashover are as follows:

(1) ≤300 V: 1 mm (0 ft 0.03 in.)
(2) >300 V to ≤750 V: 2 mm (0 ft 0.07 in.)
(3) >750 V to ≤2 kV: 5 mm (0 ft 0.19 in.)
(4) >2 kV to ≤15 kV: 39 mm (0 ft 1.5 in.)
(5) >15 kV to ≤36 kV: 161 mm (0 ft 6.3 in.)
(6) >36 kV to ≤48.3 kV: 254 mm (0 ft 10.0 in.)
(7) >48.3 kV to ≤72.5 kV: 381 mm (1 ft 3.0 in.)
(8) >72.5 kV to ≤121 kV: 640 mm (2 ft 1.2 in.)
(9) >138 kV to ≤145 kV: 778 mm (2 ft 6.6 in.)
(10) >161 kV to ≤169 kV: 915 mm (3 ft 0.0 in.)
(11) >230 kV to ≤242 kV: 1.281 m (4 ft 2.4 in.)
(12) >345 kV to ≤362 kV: 2.282 m (7 ft 5.8 in.)
(13) >500 kV to ≤550 kV: 3.112 m (10 ft 2.5 in.)
(14) >765 kV to ≤800 kV: 4.225 m (13 ft 10.3 in.)

C.2.1.1 Column 1. The voltage ranges have been selected to group voltages that require similar approach distances based on the sum of the electrical withstand distance and an inadvertent movement factor. The value of the upper limit for a range is the maximum voltage for the highest nominal voltage in the range, based on ANSI C84.1, *Electric Power Systems and Equipment—Voltage Ratings (60 Hz)*. For single-phase systems, select the range that is equal to the system's maximum phase-to-ground voltage multiplied by 1.732.

C.2.1.2 Column 2. The distances in column 2 are based on OSHA's rule for unqualified persons to maintain a 3.05 m (10 ft) clearance for all voltages up to 50 kV (voltage-to-ground), plus 100 mm (4.0 in.) for each 10 kV over 50 kV.

C.2.1.3 Column 3. The distances in column 3 are based on the following:

(1) ≤750 V: Use *NEC* Table 110.26(A)(1), Working Spaces, Condition 2, for the 151 V to 600 V range.
(2) >750 V to ≤145 kV: Use *NEC* Table 110.34(A), Working Space, Condition 2.
(3) >145 kV: Use OSHA's 3.05 m (10 ft) rules as used in Column 2.

C.2.1.4 Column 4. The distances in column 4 are based on adding to the flashover dimensions shown in C.2.1 the following inadvertent movement distance:

≤300 V: Avoid contact.

Based on experience and precautions for household 120/240-V systems:

>300 V to ≤750 V: Add 304.8 mm (1 ft 0 in.) for inadvertent movement.

These values have been found to be adequate over years of use in ANSI/IEEE C2, *National Electrical Safety Code*, in the approach distances for communication workers.

>72.5 kV: Add 304.8 mm (1 ft 0 in.) for inadvertent movement.

These values have been found to be adequate over years of use in ANSI/IEEE C2, *National Electrical Safety Code*, in the approach distances for supply workers.

INFORMATIVE ANNEX D

Incident Energy and Arc Flash Boundary Calculation Methods

This informative annex is not a part of the requirements of this NFPA document but is included for informational purposes only.

Informative Annex D illustrates how the arc flash boundary and incident energy might be calculated. These examples are not intended to limit the choice of calculation methods; the method chosen should be applicable to the situation. All the publicly known methods of calculating the arc flash incident energy and arc flash boundary produce results that are estimates of the actual values. The thermal hazard associated with an arcing fault is very complex, with many variable attributes having an impact on the calculation.

NFPA and IEEE (Institute of Electrical and Electronic Engineers) have issued the "IEEE/NFPA Arc Flash Phenomena Collaborative Research Project" report (March 2, 2017). This project produced data to further understand arc flash phenomena, as well as data on the non-thermal effects of arc blast.

The arc flash hazard is not limited to three-phase systems. Single-phase systems can also present an arc flash hazard and must be considered. The Annex D calculation examples do not specifically address single-phase systems. For example, the IEEE 1584, *Guide for Performing Arc Flash Hazard Calculations*, theoretically derived model is intended for use with applications where faults escalate to three-phase faults. However, it may be used where single-phase systems are encountered, but the result will likely be conservative.

NFPA *70E* does not place an upper limit to the level of incident energy an employee may be exposed to during a justified energized task. Employees who might be exposed to an arcing fault must wear arc-rated clothing or use other equipment to avoid a severe thermal injury. Protecting employees from the thermal effects of an arcing fault does not necessarily protect them from injury. An arcing fault exhibits characteristics of other hazards. For instance, the arc may generate a significant pressure wave. An employee could be injured by the pressure differential developed between the outside and inside of the body. The calculations illustrated in this informative annex do not determine the pressure wave value. Currently, there are no standards available that address worker protection from the effects of any pressure wave, shrapnel, and so forth.

D.1 Introduction.

Informative Annex D summarizes calculation methods available for calculating arc flash boundary and incident energy. It is important to investigate the limitations of any methods to be used. The limitations of methods summarized in Informative Annex D are described in Table D.1.

> Table D.1 identifies the source for and limitations of the methods of performing calculations to determine arc flash boundary and incident energy that are demonstrated in Annex D. The table identifies which section of Informative Annex D covers each calculation method.

TABLE D.1 Limitation of Calculation Methods

Section	Source	Limitations/Parameters
D.2	Lee, "The Other Electrical Hazard: Electrical Arc Flash Burns"	Calculates incident energy and arc flash boundary for arc in open air; conservative over 600 V and becomes more conservative as voltage increases
D.3	Doughty, et al., "Predicting Incident Energy to Better Manage the Electrical Arc Hazard on 600 V Power Distribution Systems"	Calculates incident energy for three-phase arc on systems rated 600 V and below; applies to short-circuit currents between 16 kA and 50 kA
D.4	IEEE 1584, *Guide for Performing Arc Flash Calculations*	Calculates incident energy and arc flash boundary for: 208 V to 15 kV; three-phase; 50 Hz to 60 Hz; 700 A to 106,000 A short-circuit current; and 13 mm to 152 mm conductor gaps
D.5	Doan, "Arc Flash Calculations for Exposure to DC Systems"	Calculates incident energy for dc systems rated up to 1000 V dc

D.2 Ralph Lee Calculation Method.

D.2.1 Basic Equations for Calculating Arc Flash Boundary Distances. The short-circuit symmetrical ampacity, I_{sc}, from a bolted three-phase fault at the transformer terminals is calculated with the following formula:

$$I_{sc} = \{[MVA\,Base \times 10^6] \div [1.732 \times V]\} \times \{100 \div \%Z\} \quad \text{[D.2.1(a)]}$$

where I_{sc} is in amperes, V is in volts, and $\%Z$ is based on the transformer MVA.

A typical value for the maximum power, P (in MW) in a three-phase arc can be calculated using the following formula:

$$P = [\text{maximum bolted fault, in } MVA_{bf}] \times 0.707^2 \quad \text{[D.2.1(b)]}$$

$$P = 1.732 \times V \times I_{sc} \times 10^{-6} \times 0.707^2 \quad \text{[D.2.1(c)]}$$

The arc flash boundary distance is calculated in accordance with the following formulae:

$$D_c = [2.65 \times MVA_{bf} \times t]^{\frac{1}{2}} \quad \text{[D.2.1(d)]}$$

$$D_c = [53 \times MVA \times t]^{\frac{1}{2}} \quad \text{[D.2.1(e)]}$$

where:

D_c = distance in feet of person from arc source for a just curable burn (that is, skin temperature remains less than 80°C).

Incident Energy and Arc Flash Boundary Calculation Methods

MVA_{bf} = bolted fault MVA at point involved.
MVA = MVA rating of transformer. For transformers with MVA ratings below 0.75 MVA, multiply the transformer MVA rating by 1.25.
t = time of arc exposure in seconds.

The clearing time for a current-limiting fuse is approximately 1/4 cycle or 0.004 second if the arcing fault current is in the fuse's current-limiting range. The clearing time of a 5-kV and 15-kV circuit breaker is approximately 0.1 second or 6 cycles if the instantaneous function is installed and operating. This can be broken down as follows: actual breaker time (approximately 2 cycles), plus relay operating time of approximately 1.74 cycles, plus an additional safety margin of 2 cycles, giving a total time of approximately 6 cycles. Additional time must be added if a time delay function is installed and operating.

The formulas used in this explanation are from Ralph Lee, "The Other Electrical Hazard: Electrical Arc Flash Burns," in *IEEE Trans. Industrial Applications*. The calculations are based on the worst-case arc impedance. (See Table D.2.1.)

TABLE D.2.1 Flash Burn Hazard at Various Levels in a Large Petrochemical Plant

(1)	(2)	(3)	(4)	(5)	(6)	(7)	
Bus Nominal Voltage Levels	System (MVA)	Transformer (MVA)	System or Transformer (% Z)	Short-Circuit Symmetrical (A)	Clearing Time of Fault (cycles)	Arc Flash Boundary Typical Distance*	
						SI	U.S.
230 kV	9000		1.11	23,000	6.0	15 m	49.2 ft
13.8 kV	750		9.4	31,300	6.0	1.16 m	3.8 ft
Load side of all 13.8-V fuses	750		9.4	31,300	1.0	184 mm	0.61 ft
4.16 kV		10.0	5.5	25,000	6.0	2.96 m	9.7 ft
4.16 kV		5.0	5.5	12,600	6.0	1.4 m	4.6 ft
Line side of incoming 600-V fuse		2.5	5.5	44,000	60.0–120.0	7 m–11 m	23 ft–36 ft
600-V bus		2.5	5.5	44,000	0.25	268 mm	0.9 ft
600-V bus		1.5	5.5	26,000	6.0	1.6 m	5.4 ft
600-V bus		1.0	5.57	17,000	6.0	1.2 m	4 ft

*Distance from an open arc to limit skin damage to a curable second degree skin burn [less than 80°C (176°F) on skin] in free air.

D.2.2 Single-Line Diagram of a Typical Petrochemical Complex. The single-line diagram (see Figure D.2.2) illustrates the complexity of a distribution system in a typical petrochemical plant.

D.2.3 Sample Calculation. Many of the electrical characteristics of the systems and equipment are provided in Table D.2.1. The sample calculation is made on the 4160-volt bus 4A or 4B. Table D.2.1 tabulates the results of calculating the arc flash boundary for each part of the system. For this calculation, based on Table D.2.1, the following results are obtained:

(1) Calculation is made on a 4160-volt bus.
(2) Transformer MVA (and base MVA) = 10 MVA.
(3) Transformer impedance on 10 MVA base = 5.5 percent.
(4) Circuit breaker clearing time = 6 cycles.

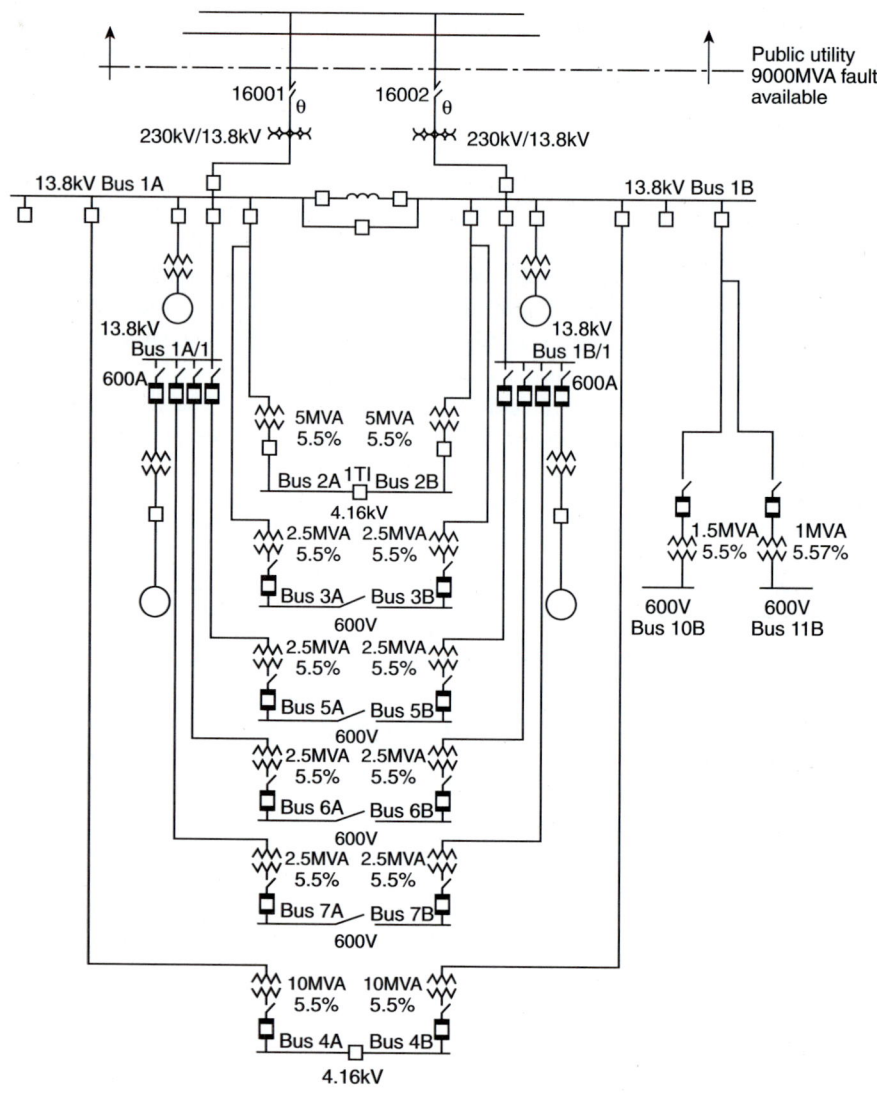

FIGURE D.2.2 *Single-Line Diagram of a Typical Petrochemical Complex*

Using Equation D.2.1(a), calculate the short-circuit current:

$$I_{sc} = \{[MVA\,Base \times 10^6] \div [1.732 \times V]\} \times \{100 \div \%Z\}$$
$$= \{[10 \times 10^6] \div [1.732 \times 4160]\} \times \{100 \div 5.5\}$$
$$= 25{,}000 \text{ amperes}$$

Using Equation D.2.1(b), calculate the power in the arc:

$$P = 1.732 \times 4160 \times 25{,}000 \times 10^{-6} \times 0.707^2$$
$$= 91 \text{ MW}$$

Using Equation D.2.1(d), calculate the second degree burn distance:

$$D_c = \{2.65 \times [1.732 \times 25{,}000 \times 4160 \times 10^{-6}] \times 0.1\}^{\frac{1}{2}}$$
$$= 6.9 \text{ or } 7.00 \text{ ft}$$

Incident Energy and Arc Flash Boundary Calculation Methods

Or, using Equation D.2.1(e), calculate the second degree burn distance using an alternative method:

$$D_c = [53 \times 10 \times 0.1]^{1/2}$$
$$= 7.28 \text{ ft}$$

D.2.4 Calculation of Incident Energy Exposure Greater Than 600 V for an Arc Flash Hazard Analysis. The equation that follows can be used to predict the incident energy produced by a three-phase arc in open air on systems rated above 600 V. The parameters required to make the calculations follow.

(1) The maximum bolted fault, three-phase short-circuit current available at the equipment.
(2) The total protective device clearing time (upstream of the prospective arc location) at the maximum short-circuit current. If the total protective device clearing time is longer than 2 seconds, consider how long a person is likely to remain in the location of the arc flash. It is likely that a person exposed to an arc flash will move away quickly if it is physically possible, and 2 seconds is a reasonable maximum time for calculations. A person in a bucket truck or a person who has crawled into equipment will need more time to move away. Sound engineering judgment must be used in applying the 2-second maximum clearing time, since there could be circumstances where an employee's egress is inhibited.
(3) The distance from the arc source.
(4) Rated phase-to-phase voltage of the system.

$$E = \frac{793 \times F \times V \times t_A}{D^2} \qquad [\text{D.2.4(4)}]$$

where:

E = incident energy, cal/cm^2
F = bolted fault short-circuit current, kA
V = system phase-to-phase voltage, kV
t_A = arc duration, sec
D = distance from the arc source, in.

This discussion expands on the concept of the reaction time of a human during an incident. The human reaction time is a composite of many factors. When using exposure time as a basis for calculating incident energy, each factor needs to be studied because each has its own eccentricities.

REACTION TIME

Reaction time is a complicated subject. Often reaction times are used without a good comprehension of where the numbers derive from, how they were acquired, or the variables that shaped them. A reaction time of 1.5 seconds is commonly quoted by experts in regard to automobile accidents. In regard to arc flash incidents, 2 seconds is a reasonable maximum time to use in calculating the arc flash incident energy, provided the employee's egress is not inhibited. If the total clearing time of the upstream overcurrent protective device is greater than 2 seconds or egress is restricted, then additional time may be needed to exit the arc flash boundary.

Sound engineering judgment must be used in determining if the 2-second exposure time is applicable. Reaction time can be broken down into different components or categories, such as perception, decision, and motor response times, each having fairly dissimilar properties.

MENTAL PROCESSING TIME

Mental processing time is the length of time an employee takes to recognize that an event has happened (perception time) and to decide upon a response (decision time). For example, it might be the time it takes an employee to realize that an arc flash event is underway and decide what action to take. Perception and decision time can be further broken down into subcategories in order to better understand the hazard response.

Perception time. Perception time can be broken down into the following two subcategories:

- *Sensation time.* The time it takes to detect the sensory input from an event is the sensation time. The greater the signal intensity, the better the visibility and the faster the reaction time. Since reaction times can be faster for acoustic signals than for visual signals, the sound wave associated with an arc blast might lead to a faster response time.
- *Recognition time.* The time needed to understand the meaning of the event is the recognition time. In some cases an extremely fast automatic response may kick in, while in others a controlled response, which can take substantial time, may happen. Therefore, training can help to decrease the response time.

Decision time. Decision time can be broken down into the following two subcategories:

- *Situational awareness time.* The time it takes to recognize and interpret the event, extract its meaning, and possibly extrapolate it into the future is the situational awareness time. Again, practice or rehearsal might decrease response time.
- *Response selection time.* The time needed to determine which reaction to make and to mentally encode the movement is the response selection time. Generally, response selection time slows when more than one event is perceived or when more than one response is possible (that is, when choice is involved). As with other categories here, practice or rehearsal might decrease response time.

Additional factors. The following factors might also have an impact on response time to an event:

- *Movement time.* A number of factors affect movement time, such as the number of exit passageways, length of the passageways, and any obstacles that might be in the way. As a general rule, the greater the complexity of the movement, the longer it takes; yet practice or rehearsal in general can lower movement times. An emotional stimulus can accelerate gross motor movements but inhibit fine detail movement.
- *Expectation.* If an event is expected, practiced for, and rehearsed, it may be possible to get the reaction time down to around 1.4 seconds when the movement time is around 0.7 seconds. Reaction time for an unexpected event could be around 1.75 seconds, including 0.7 seconds of travel time. Extra time is needed to interpret and decide on an appropriate response where the event is a complete surprise. In this case a best estimate might be around 2.0 seconds, including 1.2 seconds for perception and decision and 0.8 seconds for movement. It may be necessary to study the situation to determine the appropriate reaction time.
- *Other factors.* Factors such as perceived urgency, the complexity of the task, whether the employee is holding tools, age, and gender can affect the overall response time to an event. The more complex an employee's task when an event happens, the longer the anticipated response time.

Incident Energy and Arc Flash Boundary Calculation Methods

MINIMIZING EXPOSURE

Overcurrent protective device operating time depends on whether the device is current limiting or not. Depending on the available fault current, an overcurrent protective device might be expected to extinguish an arcing current in anywhere from ¼ cycle to 30 cycles. Employees cannot outrun an arc flash event or minimize their exposure time for such short intervals, but they might be able to minimize their time inside the arc flash boundary when extended tripping times are involved.

Where the tripping time of the overcurrent protective device is longer than the reaction time of the employee, the employee may be able to increase his or her distance from the arcing event or exit the arc flash boundary. Doubling the distance between the source of an arc flash event and the employee decreases the incident energy level by around four (it is an inverse square type of relationship).

If the overcurrent protective device takes longer than 2 seconds to trip in response to an arcing current, consideration should be given to how long a person is likely to remain within the arc flash boundary. The physical layout needs to be considered when exposure time is used to calculate the incident energy level. Anticipated exposure time might have to be increased where a narrow aisle is the only means of egress. Other factors to consider include whether it is possible for an employee to get stuck in a position and not escape within the anticipated exposure time; whether the employee has studied the exit routes; whether the event is in an enclosed area or an outside switchyard; and whether the employee is in a bucket, aerial lift, or on a ladder. Field staff should evaluate and verify that, in the event of arc flash, they can exit the arc flash boundary within the exposure time assumed.

This discussion demonstrates the basic principles and thought processes involved when using exposure time as a basis for calculating incident energy. Each type of reaction time needs to be studied because each type of reaction has its own eccentricities.

D.3 Doughty Neal Paper.

D.3.1 Calculation of Incident Energy Exposure. The following equations can be used to predict the incident energy produced by a three-phase arc on systems rated 600 V and below. The results of these equations might not represent the worst case in all situations. It is essential that the equations be used only within the limitations indicated in the definitions of the variables shown under the equations. The equations must be used only under qualified engineering supervision.

> Informational Note: Experimental testing continues to be performed to validate existing incident energy calculations and to determine new formulas.

The parameters required to make the calculations follow.

(1) The maximum bolted fault, three-phase short-circuit current available at the equipment and the minimum fault level at which the arc will self-sustain. (Calculations should be made using the maximum value, and then at lowest fault level at which the arc is self-sustaining. For 480-volt systems, the industry accepted minimum level for a sustaining arcing fault is 38 percent of the available bolted fault, three-phase short-circuit current. The highest incident energy exposure could occur at these lower levels where the overcurrent device could take seconds or minutes to open.)

(2) The total protective device clearing time (upstream of the prospective arc location) at the maximum short-circuit current, and at the minimum fault level at which the arc will sustain itself.

(3) The distance of the worker from the prospective arc for the task to be performed.

Typical working distances used for incident energy calculations are as follows:

(1) Low voltage (600 V and below) MCC and panelboards — 455 mm (18 in.)
(2) Low voltage (600 V and below) switchgear — 610 mm (24 in.)
(3) Medium voltage (above 600 V) switchgear — 910 mm (36 in.)

D.3.2 Arc in Open Air. The estimated incident energy for an arc in open air is as follows:

$$E_{MA} = 5217 D_A^{-1.9593} t_A \begin{bmatrix} 0.0016F^2 \\ -0.0076F \\ +0.8938 \end{bmatrix} \quad \text{[D.3.2(a)]}$$

where:

E_{MA} = maximum open arc incident energy, cal/cm²
D_A = distance from arc electrodes, in. (for distances 18 in. and greater)
t_A = arc duration, sec
F = short-circuit current, kA (for the range of 16 kA to 50 kA)

Sample Calculation: Using Equation D.3.2(a), calculate the maximum open arc incident energy, cal/cm², where D_A = 18 in., t_A = 0.2 second, and F = 20 kA.

$$E_{MA} = 5271 D_A^{-1.9593} t_A \begin{bmatrix} 0.0016F^2 - 0.0076F \\ +0.8938 \end{bmatrix} \quad \text{[D.3.2(b)]}$$

$$= 5271 \times .0035 \times 0.2 \times [0.0016 \times 400 - 0.0076 \times 20 + 0.8938]$$

$$= 3.69 \times [1.381]$$

$$= 21.33 \, \text{J/cm}^2 \, (5.098 \, \text{cal/cm}^2)$$

D.3.3 Arc in a Cubic Box. The estimated incident energy for an arc in a cubic box (20 in. on each side, open on one end) is given in the equation that follows. This equation is applicable to arc flashes emanating from within switchgear, motor control centers, or other electrical equipment enclosures.

$$E_{MB} = 1038.7 D_B^{-1.4738} t_A \begin{bmatrix} 0.0093F^2 \\ -0.3453F \\ +5.9675 \end{bmatrix} \quad \text{[D.3.3(a)]}$$

where:

E_{MB} = maximum 20 in. cubic box incident energy, cal/cm²
D_B = distance from arc electrodes, in. (for distances 18 in. and greater)
t_A = arc duration, sec
F = short-circuit current, kA (for the range of 16 kA to 50 kA)

Sample Calculation: Using Equation D.3.3(a), calculate the maximum 20 in. cubic box incident energy, cal/cm², using the following:

(1) D_B = 18 in.
(2) t_A = 0.2 sec
(3) F = 20 kA

Incident Energy and Arc Flash Boundary Calculation Methods

$$E_{MB} = 1038.7 D_B^{-1.4738} t_A \begin{bmatrix} 0.0093 F^2 - 0.3453 F \\ +5.9675 \end{bmatrix} \quad \text{[D.3.3(b)]}$$

$$= 1038 \times 0.0141 \times 0.2 \begin{bmatrix} 0.0093 \times 400 - 0.3453 \times 20 \\ +5.9675 \end{bmatrix}$$

$$= 2.928 \times [2.7815]$$

$$= 34.1 \text{ J/cm}^2 \left(8.144 \text{ cal/cm}^2\right)$$

D.3.4 Reference. The equations for this section were derived in the IEEE paper by R. L. Doughty, T. E. Neal, and H. L. Floyd, II, "Predicting Incident Energy to Better Manage the Electric Arc Hazard on 600 V Power Distribution Systems."

D.4 IEEE 1584 Calculation Method.

D.4.1 Basic Equations for Calculating Incident Energy and Arc Flash Boundary. This section provides excerpts from IEEE 1584-2002, *IEEE Guide for Performing Arc Flash Hazard Calculations*, for estimating incident energy and arc flash boundaries based on statistical analysis and curve fitting of available test data. An IEEE working group produced the data from tests it performed to produce models of incident energy.

The complete data, including a spreadsheet calculator to solve the equations, can be found in the IEEE 1584-2002, *Guide for Performing Arc Flash Hazard Calculations*. Users are encouraged to consult the latest version of the complete document to understand the basis, limitation, rationale, and other pertinent information for proper application of the standard. It can be ordered from the IEEE Standards Store, 6300 Interfirst Drive, Ann Arbor, MI 48108.

> Since IEEE periodically revises its documents, a prudent action for the NFPA *70E* user would be to consult the latest adopted version or amendment of IEEE 1584.

D.4.1.1 System Limits. An equation for calculating incident energy can be empirically derived using statistical analysis of raw data along with a curve-fitting algorithm. It can be used for systems with the following limits:

(1) 0.208 kV to 15 kV, three-phase
(2) 50 Hz to 60 Hz
(3) 700 A to 106,000 A available short-circuit current
(4) 13 mm to 152 mm conductor gaps

For three-phase systems in open-air substations, open-air transmission systems, and distribution systems, a theoretically derived model is available. This theoretically derived model is intended for use with applications where faults escalate to three-phase faults. Where such an escalation is not possible or likely, or where single-phase systems are encountered, this equation will likely provide conservative results.

D.4.2 Arcing Current. To determine the operating time for protective devices, find the predicted three-phase arcing current.

For applications with a system voltage under 1 kV, solve Equation D.4.2(a) as follows:

$$\lg I_a = K + 0.662 \lg I_{bf} + 0.0966 V \quad \text{[D.4.2(a)]}$$
$$+ 0.000526 G + 0.5588 V \left(\lg I_{bf} \right)$$
$$- 0.00304 G \left(\lg I_{bf} \right)$$

where:

lg = the $\log_{10}$
I_a = arcing current, kA
K = −0.153 for open air arcs; −0.097 for arcs-in-a-box
I_{bf} = bolted three-phase available short-circuit current (symmetrical rms), kA
V = system voltage, kV
G = conductor gap, mm *(see Table D.4.2)*

For systems greater than or equal to 1 kV, use Equation D.4.2(b):

$$\lg I_a = 0.00402 + 0.983 \lg I_{bf} \qquad [\text{D.4.2(b)}]$$

This higher voltage formula is used for both open-air arcs and for arcs-in-a-box. Convert from lg:

$$I_a = 10^{\lg I_a} \qquad [\text{D.4.2(c)}]$$

Use 0.85 I_a to find a second arc duration. This second arc duration accounts for variations in the arcing current and the time for the overcurrent device to open. Calculate the incident energy using both arc durations (I_a and 0.85 I_a), and use the higher incident energy.

TABLE D.4.2 Factors for Equipment and Voltage Classes

System Voltage (kV)	Type of Equipment	Typical Conductor Gap (mm)	Distance Exponent Factor x
0.208–1	Open air	10–40	2.000
	Switchgear	32	1.473
	MCCs and panels	25	1.641
	Cables	13	2.000
>1–5	Open air	102	2.000
	Switchgear	13–102	0.973
	Cables	13	2.000
>5–15	Open air	13–153	2.000
	Switchgear	153	0.973
	Cables	13	2.000

D.4.3 Incident Energy at Working Distance — Empirically Derived Equation. To determine the incident energy using the empirically derived equation, determine the $\log_{10}$ of the normalized incident energy. The following equation is based on data normalized for an arc time of 0.2 second and a distance from the possible arc point to the person of 610 mm:

$$\lg E_n = k_1 + k_2 + 1.081 \lg I_a + 0.0011 G \qquad [\text{D.4.3(a)}]$$

where:

E_n = incident energy, normalized for time and distance, J/cm²
k_1 = −0.792 for open air arcs
    = −0.555 for arcs-in-a-box

Incident Energy and Arc Flash Boundary Calculation Methods

k_2 = 0 for ungrounded and high-resistance grounded systems
  = −0.113 for grounded systems
G = conductor gap, mm (see Table D.4.2)

Then,

$$E_n = 10^{\lg E_n} \qquad [D.4.3(b)]$$

Converting from normalized:

$$E = 4.184 C_f E_n \left(\frac{t}{0.2}\right)\left(\frac{610^x}{D^x}\right) \qquad [D.4.3(c)]$$

where:

E = incident energy, J/cm².
C_f = calculation factor
  = 1.0 for voltages above 1 kV.
  = 1.5 for voltages at or below 1 kV.
E_n = incident energy normalized.
t = arcing time, sec.
x = distance exponent from Table D.4.2.
D = distance, mm, from the arc to the person (working distance). See Table D.4.3 for typical working distances.

TABLE D.4.3 Typical Working Distances

Classes of Equipment	Typical Working Distance* (mm)
15-kV switchgear	910
5-kV switchgear	910
Low-voltage switchgear	610
Low-voltage MCCs and panelboards	455
Cable	455
Other	To be determined in field

* Typical working distance is the sum of the distance between the worker and the front of the equipment and the distance from the front of the equipment to the potential arc source inside the equipment.

If the arcing time, t, in Equation D.4.3(c) is longer than 2 seconds, consider how long a person is likely to remain in the location of the arc flash. It is likely that a person exposed to an arc flash will move away quickly if it is physically possible, and 2 seconds is a reasonable maximum time for calculations. Sound engineering judgment should be used in applying the 2-second maximum clearing time, because there could be circumstances where an employee's egress is inhibited. For example, a person in a bucket truck or a person who has crawled into equipment will need more time to move away.

D.4.4 Incident Energy at Working Distance — Theoretical Equation. The following theoretically derived equation can be applied in cases where the voltage is over 15 kV or the gap is outside the range:

$$E = 2.142 \times 10^6 \, VI_{bf}\left(\frac{t}{D^2}\right) \qquad [D.4.4]$$

where:

E = incident energy, J/cm²
V = system voltage, kV
I_{bf} = available three-phase bolted fault current
t = Arcing time, sec
D = distance (mm) from the arc to the person (working distance)

For voltages over 15 kV, arcing fault current and bolted fault current are considered equal.

D.4.5 Arc Flash Boundary. The arc flash boundary is the distance at which a person is likely to receive a second degree burn. The onset of a second degree burn is assumed to be when the skin receives 5.0 J/cm² of incident energy.

For the empirically derived equation,

$$D_B = \left[4.184 C_f E_n \left(\frac{t}{0.2} \right) \left(\frac{610^x}{E_B} \right) \right]^{\frac{1}{x}} \quad \text{[D.4.5(a)]}$$

For the theoretically derived equation,

$$D_B = \sqrt{2.142 \times 10^6 \, V I_{bf} \left(\frac{t}{E_B} \right)} \quad \text{[D.4.5(b)]}$$

where:

D_B = distance (mm) of the arc flash boundary from the arcing point
C_f = calculation factor
  = 1.0 for voltages above 1 kV
  = 1.5 for voltages at or below 1 kV
E_n = incident energy normalized
t = time, sec
x = distance exponent from Table D.4.2
E_B = incident energy in J/cm² at the distance of the arc flash boundary
V = system voltage, kV
I_{bf} = bolted three-phase available short-circuit current

Informational Note: These equations could be used to determine whether selected personal protective equipment (PPE) is adequate to prevent thermal injury at a specified distance in the event of an arc flash.

D.4.6 Current-Limiting Fuses. The formulas in this section were developed for calculating arc flash energies for use with current-limiting Class L and Class RK1 fuses. The testing was done at 600 V and at a distance of 455 mm, using commercially available fuses from one manufacturer. The following variables are noted:

I_{bf} = available three-phase bolted fault current (symmetrical rms), kA
E = incident energy, J/cm²

(A) Class L Fuses 1601 A through 2000 A. Where I_{bf} < 22.6 kA, calculate the arcing current using Equation D.4.2(a), and use time-current curves to determine the incident energy using Equations D.4.3(a), D.4.3(b), and D.4.3(c).

Where 22.6 kA $\leq I_{bf} \leq$ 65.9 kA,

$$E = 4.184(-0.1284 I_{bf} + 32.262) \qquad \text{[D.4.6(a)]}$$

Where 65.9 kA $< I_{bf} \leq$ 106 kA,

$$E = 4.184(-0.5177 I_{bf} + 57.917) \qquad \text{[D.4.6(b)]}$$

Where $I_{bf} >$ 106 kA, contact the manufacturer.

(B) Class L Fuses 1201 A through 1600 A. Where $I_{bf} <$ 15.7 kA, calculate the arcing current using Equation D.4.2(a), and use time-current curves to determine the incident energy using Equations D.4.3(a), D.4.3(b), and D.4.3(c).

Where 15.7 kA $\leq I_{bf} \leq$ 31.8 kA,

$$E = 4.184(-0.1863 I_{bf} + 27.926) \qquad \text{[D.4.6(c)]}$$

Where 44.1 kA $\leq I_{bf} \leq$ 65.9 kA,

$$E = 12.3 \text{ J/cm}^2 \, (2.94 \text{ cal/cm}^2) \qquad \text{[D.4.6(d)]}$$

Where 65.9 kA $< I_{bf} \leq$ 106 kA,

$$E = 4.184(-0.0631 I_{bf} + 7.0878) \qquad \text{[D.4.6(e)]}$$

Where $I_{bf} >$ 106 kA, contact the manufacturer.

(C) Class L Fuses 801 A through 1200 A. Where $I_{bf} <$ 15.7 kA, calculate the arcing current using Equation D.4.2(a), and use time-current curves to determine the incident energy per Equations D.4.3(a), D.4.3(b), and D.4.3(c).

Where 15.7 kA $\leq I_{bf} \leq$ 22.6 kA,

$$E = 4.184(-0.1928 I_{bf} + 14.226) \qquad \text{[D.4.6(f)]}$$

Where 22.6 kA $< I_{bf} \leq$ 44.1 kA,

$$E = 4.184 \begin{pmatrix} 0.0143 I_{bf}^2 - 1.3919 I_{bf} \\ +34.045 \end{pmatrix} \qquad \text{[D.4.6(g)]}$$

Where 44.1 kA $< I_{bf} \leq$ 106 kA,

$$E = 1.63 \qquad \text{[D.4.6(h)]}$$

Where $I_{bf} >$ 106 kA, contact the manufacturer.

(D) Class L Fuses 601 A through 800 A. Where $I_{bf} <$ 15.7 kA, calculate the arcing current using Equation D.4.2(a), and use time-current curves to determine the incident energy using Equations D.4.3(a), D.4.3(b), and D.4.3(c).

Where 15.7 kA $\leq I_{bf} \leq$ 44.1 kA,

$$E = 4.184(-0.0601 I_{bf} + 2.8992) \qquad \text{[D.4.6(i)]}$$

Where 44.1 kA < I_{bf} ≤ 106 kA,

$$E = 1.046 \qquad [D.4.6(j)]$$

Where I_{bf} > 106 kA, contact the manufacturer.

(E) Class RK1 Fuses 401 A through 600 A. Where I_{bf} < 8.5 kA, calculate the arcing current using Equation D.4.2(a), and use time-current curves to determine the incident energy using Equations D.4.3(a), D.4.3(b), and D.4.3(c).

Where 8.5 kA ≤ I_{bf} ≤ 14 kA,

$$E = 4.184\left(-3.0545 I_{bf} + 43.364\right) \qquad [D.4.6(k)]$$

Where 14 kA < I_{bf} ≤ 15.7 kA,

$$E = 2.510 \qquad [D.4.6(l)]$$

Where 15.7 kA < I_{bf} ≤ 22.6 kA,

$$E = 4.184\left(-0.0507 I_{bf} + 1.3964\right) \qquad [D.4.6(m)]$$

Where 22.6 kA < I_{bf} ≤ 106 kA,

$$E = 1.046 \qquad [D.4.6(n)]$$

Where I_{bf} > 106 kA, contact the manufacturer.

(F) Class RK1 Fuses 201 A through 400 A. Where I_{bf} < 3.16 kA, calculate the arcing current using Equation D.4.2(a), and use time-current curves to determine the incident energy using Equations D.4.3(a), D.4.3(b), and D.4.3(c).

Where 3.16 kA ≤ I_{bf} ≤ 5.04 kA,

$$E = 4.184\left(-19.053 I_{bf} + 96.808\right) \qquad [D.4.6(o)]$$

Where 5.04 kA < I_{bf} ≤ 22.6 kA,

$$E = 4.184\left(-0.0302 I_{bf} + 0.9321\right) \qquad [D.4.6(p)]$$

Where 22.6 kA < I_{bf} ≤ 106 kA,

$$E = 1.046 \qquad [D.4.6(q)]$$

Where I_{bf} > 106 kA, contact the manufacturer.

(G) Class RK1 Fuses 101 A through 200 A. Where I_{bf} < 1.16 kA, calculate the arcing current using Equation D.4.2(a), and use time-current curves to determine the incident energy using Equations D.4.3(a), D.4.3(b), and D.4.3(c).

Where 1.16 kA ≤ I_{bf} ≤ 1.6 kA,

$$E = 4.184\left(-18.409 I_{bf} + 36.355\right) \qquad [D.4.6(r)]$$

Incident Energy and Arc Flash Boundary Calculation Methods

Where 1.6 kA $< I_{bf} \leq$ 3.16 kA,

$$E = 4.184\left(-4.2628 I_{bf} + 13.721\right) \qquad [\text{D.4.6(s)}]$$

Where 3.16 kA $< I_{bf} \leq$ 106 kA,

$$E = 1.046 \qquad [\text{D.4.6(t)}]$$

Where $I_{bf} >$ 106 kA, contact the manufacturer.

(H) Class RK1 Fuses 1 A through 100 A. Where $I_{bf} <$ 0.65 kA, calculate the arcing current using Equation D.4.2(a), and use time-current curves to determine the incident energy using Equations D.4.3(a), D.4.3(b), and D.4.3(c).

Where 0.65 kA $\leq I_{bf} \leq$ 1.16 kA,

$$E = 4.184\left(-11.176 I_{bf} + 13.565\right) \qquad [\text{D.4.6(u)}]$$

Where 1.16 kA $< I_{bf} \leq$ 1.4 kA,

$$E = 4.184\left(-1.4583 I_{bf} + 2.2917\right) \qquad [\text{D.4.6(v)}]$$

Where 1.4 kA $< I_{bf} \leq$ 106 kA,

$$E = 1.046 \qquad [\text{D.4.6(w)}]$$

Where $I_{bf} >$ 106 kA, contact the manufacturer.

D.4.7 Low-Voltage Circuit Breakers. The equations in Table D.4.7 can be used for systems with low-voltage circuit breakers. The results of the equations will determine the incident energy and arc flash boundary when I_{bf} is within the range as described. Time-current curves for the circuit breaker are not necessary within the appropriate range.

When the bolted fault current is below the range indicated, calculate the arcing current using Equation D.4.2(a), and use time-current curves to determine the incident energy using Equations D.4.3(a), D.4.3(b), and D.4.3(c).

The range of available three-phase bolted fault currents is from 700 A to 106,000 A. Each equation is applicable for the following range:

$$I_1 < I_{bf} < I_2$$

where:

I_1 = minimum available three-phase, bolted, short-circuit current at which this method can be applied. I_1 is the lowest available three-phase, bolted, short-circuit current level that causes enough arcing current for instantaneous tripping to occur, or, for circuit breakers with no instantaneous trip, that causes short-time tripping to occur.
I_2 = interrupting rating of the circuit breaker at the voltage of interest.

To find I_1, the instantaneous trip (I_t) of the circuit breaker must be found. I_t can be determined from the time-current curve, or it can be assumed to be 10 times the rating of the circuit breaker for circuit breakers rated above 100 amperes. For circuit breakers rated 100 amperes and below, a value of I_t = 1300 A can be used. When short-time delay is utilized, I_t is the short-time pickup current.

TABLE D.4.7 Incident Energy and Arc Flash Protection Boundary by Circuit Breaker Type and Rating

Rating (A)	Breaker Type	Trip Unit Type	480 V and Lower		575 V–600 V	
			Incident Energy (J/cm²)[a]	Arc Flash Boundary (mm)[a]	Incident Energy (J/cm²)[a]	Arc Flash Boundary (mm)[a]
100–400	MCCB	TM or M	$0.189\, I_{bf} + 0.548$	$9.16\, I_{bf} + 194$	$0.271\, I_{bf} + 0.180$	$11.8\, I_{bf} + 196$
600–1200	MCCB	TM or M	$0.223\, I_{bf} + 1.590$	$8.45\, I_{bf} + 364$	$0.335\, I_{bf} + 0.380$	$11.4\, I_{bf} + 369$
600–1200	MCCB	E, LI	$0.377\, I_{bf} + 1.360$	$12.50\, I_{bf} + 428$	$0.468\, I_{bf} + 4.600$	$14.3\, I_{bf} + 568$
1600–6000	MCCB or ICCB	TM or E, LI	$0.448\, I_{bf} + 3.000$	$11.10\, I_{bf} + 696$	$0.686\, I_{bf} + 0.165$	$16.7\, I_{bf} + 606$
800–6300	LVPCB	E, LI	$0.636\, I_{bf} + 3.670$	$14.50\, I_{bf} + 786$	$0.958\, I_{bf} + 0.292$	$19.1\, I_{bf} + 864$
800–6300	LVPCB	E, LS[b]	$4.560\, I_{bf} + 27.230$	$47.20\, I_{bf} + 2660$	$6.860\, I_{bf} + 2.170$	$62.4\, I_{bf} + 2930$

MCCB: Molded-case circuit breaker.
TM: Thermal-magnetic trip units.
M: Magnetic (instantaneous only) trip units.
E: Electronic trip units have three characteristics that may be used separately or in combination: L: Long time, S: Short time, I: Instantaneous.
ICCB: Insulated-case circuit breaker.
LVPCB: Low-voltage power circuit breaker.
[a] I_{bf} is in kA; working distance is 455 mm (18 in.).
[b] Short-time delay is assumed to be set at maximum.

The corresponding bolted fault current, I_{bf}, is found by solving the equation for arc current for box configurations by substituting I_t for arcing current. The 1.3 factor in Equation D.4.7(b) adjusts current to the top of the tripping band.

$$\lg(1.3 I_t) = 0.084 + 0.096V + 0.586\left(\lg I_{bf}\right) + 0.559V\left(\lg I_{bf}\right) \qquad [D.4.7(a)]$$

At 600 V,

$$\lg I_1 = 0.0281 + 1.09 \lg(1.3 I_t) \qquad [D.4.7(b)]$$

At 480 V and lower,

$$\lg I_1 = 0.047 + 1.17 \lg(1.3 I_t) \qquad [D.4.7(c)]$$

$$I_{bf} = I_1 = 10^{\lg I_1} \qquad [D.4.7(d)]$$

D.4.8 References. The complete data, including a spreadsheet calculator to solve the equations, can be found in IEEE 1584, *Guide for Performing Arc Flash Hazard Calculations*. IEEE publications are available from the Institute of Electrical and Electronics Engineers, 445 Hoes Lane, P.O. Box 1331, Piscataway, NJ 08855-1331, USA (http://standards.ieee.org/).

D.5 Direct-Current Incident Energy Calculations.

D.5.1 Maximum Power Method. The following method of estimating dc arc flash incident energy that follows was published in the *IEEE Transactions on Industry Applications (see reference 2, which follows)*. This method is based on the concept that the maximum power possible in a dc arc will occur when the arcing voltage is one-half the system voltage. Testing completed for Bruce Power *(see reference 3, which follows)* has shown that this calculation is conservatively high in estimating the arc flash value. This method applies to dc systems rated up to 1000 V.

Incident Energy and Arc Flash Boundary Calculation Methods

$$I_{arc} = 0.5 \times I_{bf}$$ [D.5.1]

$$IE_m = 0.01 \times V_{sys} \times I_{arc} \times T_{arc} / D^2$$

where:

I_{arc} = arcing current amperes
I_{bf} = system bolted fault current amperes
IE_m = estimated dc arc flash incident energy at the maximum power point cal/cm^2
V_{sys} = system voltage volts
T_{arc} = arcing time sec
D = working distance cm

For exposures where the arc is in a box or enclosure, it would be prudent to consider additional PPE protection beyond the values shown in Table 130.7(C)(15)(b).

> This maximum power method to calculate the arc flash incident energy for a direct current power source uses principles similar to those used by Ralph Lee in his paper, "The Other Electrical Hazard: Electrical Arc Blast Burns," in *IEEE Transactions on Industrial Applications*, Volume 1A-18, Issue 3, page 246, 1987.
>
> Without having a full appreciation of the intricacies involved, it is possible to misapply the maximum power method equations. Key to the use of the method is the appropriate determination of arcing time. Under transient conditions, such as at the initiation of an arcing fault, the current in a dc circuit does not change instantaneously. The rate of change is dependent on the L/R time constant of the circuit. The longer the time constant, the longer the circuit will take to reach its new steady state value. The rms current value during this period of time is dependent on the time constant. For devices that trip in response to rms current values, the L/R time constant can affect the total clearing time of the overcurrent protective device used to protect the circuit. The manufacturer of the overcurrent protective device may need to be contacted to obtain an appropriate time–current characteristic curve.

D.5.2 Detailed Arcing Current and Energy Calculations Method. A thorough theoretical review of dc arcing current and energy was published in the *IEEE Transactions on Industry Applications*. Readers are advised to refer to that paper *(see reference 1)* for those detailed calculations.

References:

1. "DC-Arc Models and Incident-Energy Calculations," Ammerman, R.F.; et al.; *IEEE Transactions on Industry Applications*, Vol. 46, No.5.
2. "Arc Flash Calculations for Exposures to DC Systems," Doan, D.R., *IEEE Transactions on Industry Applications*, Vol. 46, No.6.
3. "DC Arc Hazard Assessment Phase II", Copyright Material, Kinectrics Inc., Report No. K-012623-RA-0002-R00.

D.5.3 Short Circuit Current. The determination of short circuit current is necessary in order to use Table 130.7(C)(15)(b). The arcing current is calculated at 50 percent of the dc short-circuit value. The current that a battery will deliver depends on the total impedance of the short-circuit path. A conservative approach in determining the short-circuit current that the battery will deliver at 25°C is to assume that the maximum available short-circuit current is 10 times the 1 minute ampere rating (to 1.75 volts per cell at 25°C and the specific gravity of 1.215) of the battery. A more accurate value for the short-circuit current for the specific application can be obtained from the battery manufacturer.

References:

1. IEEE 946, *Recommended Practice for the Design of DC Auxiliary Powers Systems for Generating Stations.*

INFORMATIVE ANNEX E

Electrical Safety Program

This informative annex is not a part of the requirements of this NFPA document but is included for informational purposes only.

> Informative Annex E provides information that could be used as the groundwork for an electrical safety program.

(See 110.1, Electrical Safety Program.)

E.1 Typical Electrical Safety Program Principles.

Electrical safety program principles include, but are not limited to, the following:

(1) Inspecting and evaluating the electrical equipment
(2) Maintaining the electrical equipment's insulation and enclosure integrity
(3) Planning every job and document first-time procedures
(4) De-energizing, if possible *(see 120.5)*
(5) Anticipating unexpected events
(6) Identifying the electrical hazards and reduce the associated risk
(7) Protecting employees from shock, burn, blast, and other hazards due to the working environment
(8) Using the right tools for the job
(9) Assessing people's abilities
(10) Auditing the principles

E.2 Typical Electrical Safety Program Controls.

Electrical safety program controls can include, but are not limited to, the following:

(1) The employer develops programs and procedures, including training, and the employees apply them.
(2) Employees are to be trained to be qualified for working in an environment influenced by the presence of electrical energy.
(3) Procedures are to be used to identify the electrical hazards and to develop job safety plans to eliminate those hazards or to control the associated risk for those hazards that cannot be eliminated.

(4) Every electrical conductor or circuit part is considered energized until proved otherwise.
(5) De-energizing an electrical conductor or circuit part and making it safe to work on is, in itself, a potentially hazardous task.
(6) Tasks to be performed within the limited approach boundary or arc flash boundary of exposed energized electrical conductors and circuit parts are to be identified and categorized.
(7) Precautions appropriate to the working environment are to be determined and taken.
(8) A logical approach is to be used to determine the associated risk of each task.

E.3 Typical Electrical Safety Program Procedures.

Electrical safety program procedures can include, but are not limited to determination and assessment of the following:

(1) Purpose of task
(2) Qualifications and number of employees to be involved
(3) Identification of hazards and assessment of risks of the task
(4) Limits of approach
(5) Safe work practices to be used
(6) Personal protective equipment (PPE) involved
(7) Insulating materials and tools involved
(8) Special precautionary techniques
(9) Electrical single-line diagrams
(10) Equipment details
(11) Sketches or photographs of unique features
(12) Reference data

INFORMATIVE ANNEX F

Risk Assessment and Risk Control

This informative annex is not a part of the requirements of this NFPA document but is included for informational purposes only.

> This informative annex deals with risk assessment and risk control. Risk assessment is composed of risk estimation and risk evaluation. Risk control incorporates a hierarchy of controls from the highest level to the lowest level of controls in order to reduce the risk to an acceptable level for the task at hand. The procedure involves an iterative process of risk reduction until an acceptable risk level is attained.
>
> Electrical safety issues (not health issues) are the focus of this standard. However, from an overall safety point of view, both health and safety issues are important. Electrical safety issues need to be assessed and prioritized. Electrical safety issues include the potential electrical hazards of electrical shock, arc flash, arc blast, and burns from hot electrical equipment associated with a particular task, risks associated with the hazards, electrical safety management system deficiencies, the opportunities for improvement, and the appropriate PPE necessary for the assigned task.

N F.1 Introduction to Risk Management.

> In a general sense, risk can be described as the potential that a chosen action or inaction will lead to some type of loss or injury. For the purpose of electrical safety, risk is defined as a combination of the likelihood of occurrence of injury and the severity of injury that results from a hazard. The type of injury (either direct or indirect) can be caused by contact with exposed energized circuit parts or can be caused when an arc flash occurs.
>
> Risk assessment is a step in a risk management procedure that involves risk estimation and risk evaluation. Risk assessment is the determination of a value of risk related to an actual situation involving a recognized hazard. Two basic approaches to risk assessment — the hazard-based approach and the task-based approach — are briefly addressed in Sections F.4 and F.5. There are many techniques that may be used for conducting a risk assessment. Section F.6 explains three possible methods.

Risk management is the logical, systematic process used to manage the risk associated with any activity, process, function, or product including safety, the environment, quality, and finance. The risk management process and principles can be used by organizations of any type or size.

The following risk management principles can readily be applied to electrical safety. Risk management:

(1) Is an integral part of all organizational processes and decision making
(2) Is systematic, structured, and timely

(3) Is based on the best available information
(4) Takes human and cultural factors into account
(5) Is dynamic, iterative, and responsive to change
(6) Facilitates continual improvement of the organization

Informational Note: For more information on risk management principles see ISO 31000:2009, *Risk Management — Principles and Guidelines*.

The risk management process includes the following:

(1) Communication and consultation
(2) Establishing the risk assessment context and objectives
(3) Risk assessment
(4) Risk treatment
(5) Recording and reporting the risk assessment results and risk treatment decisions
(6) Monitoring and reviewing risks

Risk assessment is the part of risk management that involves the following:

(1) Identifying sources of risk
(2) Analyzing the sources of risk to estimate a level of risk
(3) Evaluating the level of risk to determine if risk treatment is required

(See *Figure F.1*.)

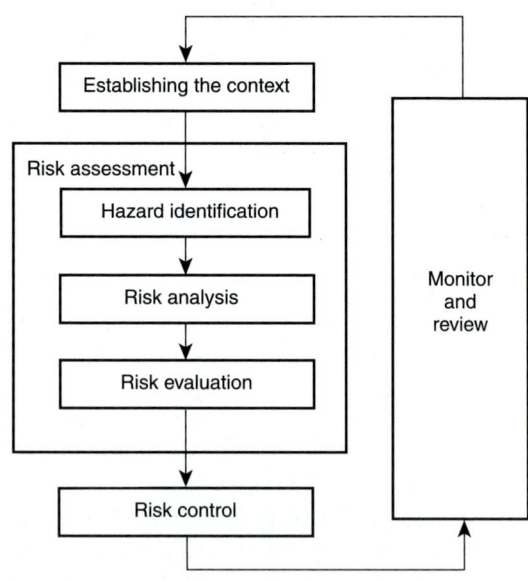

FIGURE F.1 *Risk Management Process (Adapted from ISO 31000 figure 3).*

For risk to be properly assessed, the situation must be placed into a specific context and the objective defined. A risk assessment may be different if the objective is arc flash protection rather than shock protection. An exposed hazard introduces a risk of injury. If employees are not permitted to enter the room, there is no risk of personal injury. If employees are permitted into that room, the risk of personal injury is greatly increased. However, not all tasks in proximity to that hazard may pose an additional increased risk of injury. Without context or objective, the risk assessment is incomplete.

Risk Assessment and Risk Control

N F.1.1 Occupational Health and Safety (OHS) Risk Management. The same logical, systematic process and the same principles apply to risk management in the OHS sphere of activity. However, it is more focused and the terminology more narrowly defined, as follows:

(1) The OHS objective is freedom from harm (i.e., injury or damage to health).
(2) Sources of risk are referred to as hazards.
(3) Analyzing and estimating the level of risk is a combination of the estimation of the likelihood of the occurrence of harm and the severity of that harm.
(4) The level of risk is evaluated to determine if it is reasonable to conclude that freedom from harm can be achieved or if further risk treatment is required.
(5) Risk treatment is referred to as risk control.

Therefore, OHS risk assessment involves the following:

(1) Hazard identification: Find, list, and characterize hazards.
(2) Risk analysis: Sources, causes, and potential consequences are analyzed to determine the following:
   a. The likelihood that harm might result
   b. The potential severity of that harm
   c. Estimate the level of risk
(3) Risk evaluation: The level of risk is evaluated to determine if the objective of freedom from harm can reasonably be met by the risk control that is in place or is further risk control required?

> Users of NFPA *70E* will likely follow their own version of the occupational health and safety (OHS) risk management system to conduct the required shock and arc flash risk assessments.
>
> **Step 1: Hazard Identification**
>
> Hazard identification is possibly the simplest step in the process. What a possible source of injury is to an employee from an electrical safety context is typically obvious. NFPA *70E* currently addresses only two hazards directly — electric shock and arc flash burn. As part of the risk assessment, it is necessary to address all electrical hazards. The definition of *electrical hazard* in Article 100 includes any of the following: electric shock, arc flash burn, thermal burn, or arc blast. Other known hazards include flying parts, molten metal, intense light, poisonous oxides, and generated pressure waves (blasts).
>
> **Step 2: Risk Analysis**
>
> The second step is more difficult to define. The risk related to an identified hazard is composed of the severity of the possible injury and the likelihood of occurrence of that injury. A qualitative rather than quantitative approach may be necessary to estimate the likelihood of harm, the severity of the injury, and the level of risk associated with the hazard. Often, three factors are estimated independently and used to determine the likelihood of the occurrence of harm. These independent factors are as follows:
>
> 1. The frequency and duration of the exposure
> 2. The likelihood of occurrence of the hazardous event
> 3. The likelihood of avoiding or limiting the injury

The occurrence of a hazardous event influences the likelihood of the occurrence of injury. The possibility of the hazardous event occurring should address the likelihood of the event materializing during the use or foreseeable misuse, or both, of the electrical system. Foreseeable characteristics of human behavior that may impact the likelihood of an occurrence are stress (e.g., due to time constraints, work task, perceived damage limitation) and lack of awareness of information relevant to the hazard. Human behavior will be influenced by factors such as skills, training, experience, and complexity of the equipment or the process.

Subjectivity may have a substantial impact on the result of the risk assessment. The use of subjective information should be minimized as far as reasonably practicable. When determining the likelihood of the occurrence of a hazardous event, it might be helpful to ask the types of questions that follow. These questions are not intended to be a complete or accurate list of the actual questions that should be asked or investigations undertaken.

1. Does the equipment meet the necessary normal operating conditions?
2. At what point in its rated life is the equipment?
3. Have all connections been verified to be appropriately tightened (torqued) in accordance with the manufacturer's requirements or appropriate industry standard?
4. Is any component, device, or equipment loose or damaged?
5. Does the enclosure have all of its bolts and screws installed?
6. Does the equipment have ventilation openings?
7. Is the enclosure arc rated?
8. Are there openings in the enclosure that rodents or other vermin could enter?
9. Has the enclosure been examined for moisture, dust, dirt, soot, or grease?
10. What action may an employee take?
11. What error may an employee make?

The following are circuit breaker (CB) condition questions:

12. Has the right type been used?
13. Has it been applied within its marked rating?
14. Have the proper conductor types and sizes been used?
15. What is the ampere rating involved?
16. Has the CB periodically been operated in accordance with the manufacturer's instructions or in accordance with standard(s) requirements?
17. Has a calibration sampling program been instituted?
18. Has the CB interrupted high-fault currents or repeatedly interrupted fault currents?
19. Has the operating temperature been checked under normal use conditions?
20. Have insulation resistance and/or individual pole resistance (millivolt drop) tests been performed?
21. Have inverse-time and/or instantaneous overcurrent trip tests been conducted?
22. Has a rated hold-in test been conducted?
23. Have any accessory devices involved with the CB been tested?
24. Have the surfaces been examined for evidence of overheating, blistering, cracks, dust, dirt, soot, grease, or moisture?
25. Have all electrical connections been verified to be clean and secure?
26. Is there any discoloration or flaking of external metal parts, or melting or blistering of adjacent wire insulation?
27. If the CB has interchangeable trip units, have the trip units been visually checked for overheating or looseness?

Risk Assessment and Risk Control

The likelihood of avoiding injury may be estimated by taking into account aspects of the electrical system design and its intended application that can help to avoid or limit the injury from a hazard. The following are examples:

1. Sudden or gradual appearance of the hazardous event
2. Spatial possibility to withdraw from the hazard
3. Nature of the component or system — for example, the use of touch-safe components, which reduce the likelihood of contact with energized parts
4. Likelihood of recognition of a hazard

Severity of injuries can be estimated by taking into account reversible injuries, irreversible injuries, and death.

Step 3. Risk Evaluation

Risk evaluation is a determination if risk control methods can satisfactorily protect the employee from harm. Once the risk has been estimated prior to the application of protective measures, all practicable efforts must be made to reduce the risk of injury. Careful consideration of failure modes is an important part of risk reduction. Care should be taken to ensure that both technical and behavioral failures, which could result in ineffective risk reduction, are taken into account during the risk reduction stage of the risk assessment.

Situations in which hazard elimination cannot be attained typically require a balanced approach in order to reduce the likelihood of injury. For example, the effective control of access to an electrical system requires the use of barriers, awareness placards, safe operating instructions, qualification and training, and PPE, as well as initial and refresher or periodic training for all affected personnel in the area. Engineering controls alone are not sufficient to reduce the remaining risk to a tolerable level. Often, all six levels of risk controls in Table F.3 must be implemented in some form to achieve an adequate risk reduction strategy.

Once the assessment has been completed and protective measures have been determined, it is imperative to ensure that the protective measures are implemented prior to initiating the electrical work. While this procedure might not result in a reduction of the PPE required, it could improve the understanding of the properties of the hazards associated with a task to a greater extent and thus allow for improvement in the implementation of the protective measures that have been selected.

N F.2 Relationship to Occupational Health and Safety Management System (OHSMS).

As discussed in Annex P, the most effective application of the requirements of this standard can be achieved within the framework of an OHSMS. Using a management system provides a methodical approach to health and safety by means of goal setting, planning, and performance measurement.

Risk management shares the six management system process elements of the following:

(1) Leadership. If any venture is to succeed it needs to be sponsored at the highest levels of the organization.
(2) Policy. The organization should articulate its vision and establish relevant, attainable goals.
(3) Plan. A plan is developed in line with the organization's vision and to achieve its goals. The plan must include mechanisms to measure and monitor the success of the plan.
(4) Do. The plan is executed.

(5) Check (Monitor). The success of the plan in achieving the organization's goals is continuously monitored.

(6) Act (Review). The measuring and monitoring results are compared to the organization's goals for the purposes of reviewing and revising goals and plans to improve performance.

As noted in F.1, risk management is iterative. The repeating nature of the management system plan-do-check-act (PDCA) cycle is intended to promote continuous improvement in health and safety performance.

Risk assessment fits into the "plan" and "do" stages of the PDCA cycle, as follows:

(1) Planning: Information used during the planning stage comes from sources that can include workplace inspections, incident reports, and risk assessments.
(2) Do: Risk assessment is an ongoing activity.

N F.3 Hierarchy of Risk Control.

The purpose of specifying and adhering to a hierarchy of risk control methods is to identify the most effective individual or combination of preventive or protective measures to reduce the risk associated with a hazard. Each risk control method is considered less effective than the one before it. Table F.3 lists the hierarchy of risk control identified in this and other safety standards and provides examples of each.

TABLE F.3 The Hierarchy of Risk Control Methods

Risk Control Method	Examples
(1) Elimination	Conductors and circuit parts in an electrically safe working condition
(2) Substitution	Reduce energy by replacing 120 V control circuitry with 24 Vac or Vdc control circuitry
(3) Engineering controls	Guard energized electrical conductors and circuit parts to reduce the likelihood of electrical contact or arcing faults
(4) Awareness	Signs alerting of the potential presence of hazards
(5) Administrative controls	Procedures and job planning tools
(6) PPE	Shock and arc flash PPE

Although it can never be entirely eliminated, risk can be significantly reduced through the application of the hierarchy of risk controls. Whenever the residual risk is unacceptable, additional safety measures must be taken to reduce the risk to an acceptable level.

The hierarchy is listed in order of the most effective to the least effective and must be applied in this descending order for each risk assessment. Once a hazard has been identified, it first must be determined if the hazard can be eliminated. During the electrical system design stage, methods should be employed to eliminate the hazard in its entirety. In the electrical system design and equipment selection phase, it is easier to utilize the most effective controls of elimination and substitution to limit the risk associated with anticipated justified energized work. In this first context, elimination is the removal of a hazard so that it does not exist. This removes the potential for human error when interacting with the equipment.

Elimination of the hazard is often not an option for available or installed electrical equipment. Although elimination also can be achieved by applying other controls such as through establishing an electrically safe work condition, these other controls introduce a potential for human error. Therefore, the initial attempt should be full elimination of the hazard or substitution of equipment to minimize the hazard.

The result of each risk assessment should be evaluated to determine if the hierarchy of controls could be further employed to lower the risk or reduce the hazard. Exhibit F.1

Risk Assessment and Risk Control

illustrates the iterative process of applying the hierarchy of risk controls. Each step is evaluated and controls reapplied as necessary until the risk of injury is reduced to an acceptable level. Only after all other risk controls have been exhausted should PPE be selected. PPE is considered the least effective and lowest level of safety of control for employee protection and should not be the first or only control element used.

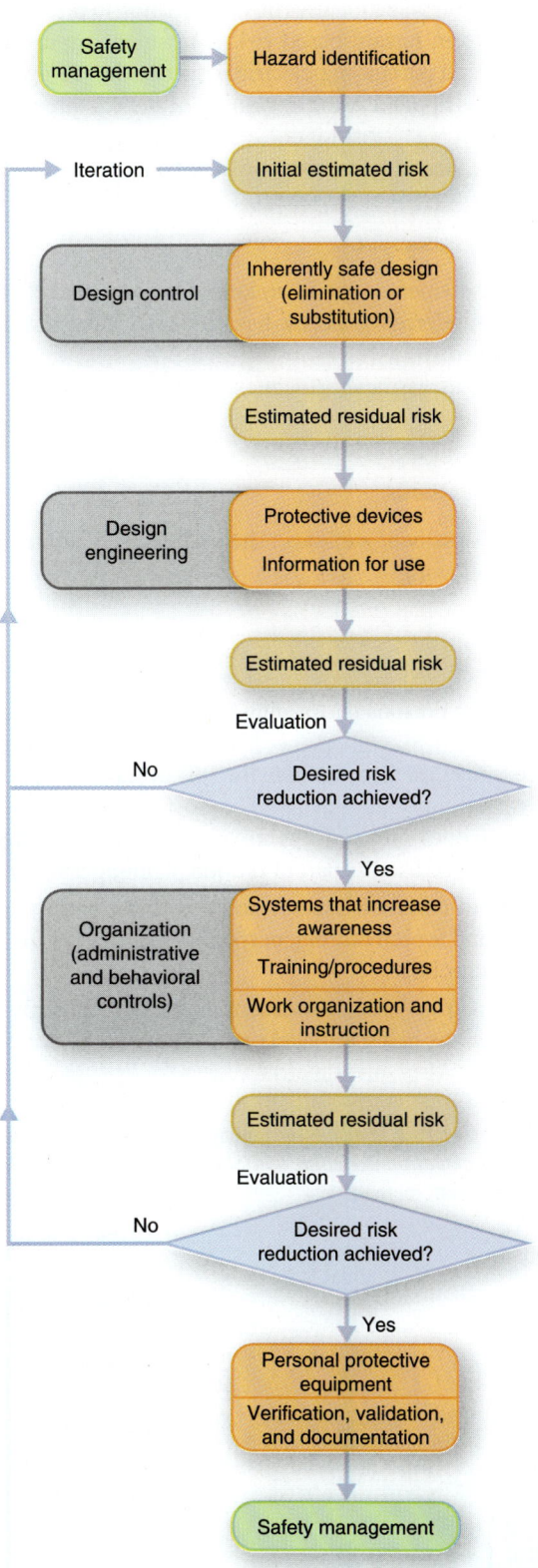

EXHIBIT F.1

Risk assessment process.

F.4 Hazard-Based Risk Assessment.

In a hazard-based risk assessment, workplace hazards are identified and characterized for materials, processes, the worksite, and the environment. Activities that might be affected by those hazards are identified. The risk associated with each activity is analyzed for likelihood of harm and severity of harm. An organization uses this information to prioritize risk reduction decisions.

The information from hazard-based risk assessments is useful to organizations when designing, specifying, and purchasing electrical distribution equipment. Risk control is much more effective when it is applied at the beginning of the equipment or process lifecycle. Risk can be reduced by specifying "substitution" and "engineering" risk control methods that affect the likelihood of occurrence of harm or severity of harm.

F.5 Task-Based Risk Assessment.

In a task-based risk assessment, a job is broken down into discrete tasks. Hazards are identified for each task (often referred to as task-hazard pairs). The risk associated with each hazard is analyzed and evaluated.

The task-based risk assessment is the most commonly used when performing a field level risk assessment.

F.6 Risk Assessment Methods.

There are many risk assessment methods. The method or combination of methods should be chosen based on the following:

(1) The application
(2) The desired result
(3) The skill level of the persons performing the assessment

Some risk assessment methods include the following:

(1) Brainstorming. An open group discussion regarding hazards, the associated risk, and risk control methods can be used as part of pre-job planning and during a job briefing session.
(2) Checklists. A list of common hazards and possible control methods is a useful tool for pre-job planning and for job briefing purposes. See Annex I for an example of a job briefing and planning checklist.
(3) Risk assessment matrix. A risk assessment matrix is commonly used to quantify levels of risk. The matrix can be in a multilevel or a simple two-by-two format. See Figure F.6 for an example of a risk assessment matrix.

Informational Note: See ISO 31010, Risk management — *Risk assessment techniques*, and ANSI/AIHA Z10-2012, *Occupational Health and Safety Management Systems*, for further information regarding risk assessment methods.

Risk Assessment and Risk Control

Likelihood of Occurrence of Harm	Severity of Harm	
	Energy ≤ [Selected Threshold]	Energy > [Selected Threshold]
Improbable	Low	Low
Possible	Low	High

Legend

Likelihood of Occurrence of Harm
Improbable: Source of harm is adequately guarded to avoid contact with hazardous energy

Possible: Source of harm is not adequately guarded to avoid contact with hazardous energy

Severity of Harm
Energy ≤ [Selected Threshold]: Level of hazardous energy insufficient to cause harm

Energy > [Selected Threshold]: Level of hazardous energy insufficient to cause harm

Risk Evaluation
Identify the risk controls in place and evaluate the effectiveness of the controls. Prioritize actions taken to control risk based on the level of risk as follows:

Low: Risk Acceptable — Further risk control discretionary

High: Risk Unacceptable — Further risk control required before proceeding

△ **FIGURE F.6** *Example of a Qualitative Two-by-Two Risk Assessment Matrix.*

Several methods are available for qualitatively estimating risk, such as risk assessment matrices, risk ranking, or risk scoring systems. Sample risk assessment matrices are shown in Figure F.6 and Exhibit F.2. A matrix is an ordered presentation of data in a display of rows and columns that defines the cells of the array. A risk assessment matrix is a simple table that groups risk based on severity and likelihood. It can be used to assess the need for remedial action, such as the use of PPE for a given task, and to prioritize safety issues.

The risk assessment matrix that appears in Figure F.6 displays the two factors that have to be considered when evaluating risk: likelihood of the occurrence of harm and the severity of the injury that can result. The columns and rows must then be assigned values such as low and high. A matrix will become cumbersome if too many columns and rows are used, and it will fail to impart the necessary information if too few are used. Practically speaking, the maximum number of categories for a useful matrix is five. Figure F.6 uses two for the rows (improbable and probable) and two for the columns (first energy level and second energy level).

The risk assessment matrices in this informational annex and associated commentary are only illustrations of aids that can be useful in prioritizing and in determining remedial actions that should be considered and taken. There are many different risk assessment matrices available, such as ANSI/AIHA Z10, *American National Standard for Occupational Safety and Health Management Systems*, which displays a different presentation than those presented here.

Likelihood of Occurrence of Arc Flash Event and Circuit Breaker Operation

Experience has shown that the likelihood of an arc flash event increases as people interact with electrical equipment and that some types of interactions with electrical equipment increase the likelihood of an arc flash event happening more than others. Turning on a circuit breaker (CB) may increase the likelihood of an arc flash event more than turning off a CB, for instance. CBs housed in electrical equipment enclosures that have been properly installed, applied within their ratings, and properly maintained have a lower likelihood of causing an arc flash event than those that have not. Additionally, it is more likely that the actual incident energy level of a maintained CB will be approximately the calculated level. It is known that incident energy level available affects the seriousness of the harm — the greater the incident energy level, the more harm that can be expected.

The risk of injury largely depends on the amount of energy available to the breaker, how old it is, how well it is maintained, and the task that is to be performed, among other factors. For example, there will be little risk when simply operating (turning on and off) a well-maintained breaker in a dwelling with a 240-volt service and 10,000 amperes available. In contrast, a commercial building with an equally well-maintained breaker with 40,000 amperes available poses greater risk.

Example: Circuit Breaker Operation While Energized

One example illustrates the use of a risk register and the other the use of a risk assessment matrix. The examples should not be relied upon for any particular installation. They are simply meant to demonstrate the thinking process required to perform a risk assessment based on the principles included in Informative Annex F.

Background Facts. Using a selected risk register and a risk assessment matrix, an electrical safety committee is analyzing two task scenarios to determine if additional safety controls are required. The first task scenario is the operation (turning on and off) of a 1600-ampere CB at a main 480Y/277-volt, non-arc-rated switchboard in a building where the short-circuit current is calculated to be 35,000 amperes. The second task scenario is the operation (turning on and off) of a 20-ampere HID CB in a 480Y/277-volt lighting panelboard where the short-circuit current is 25,000 amperes. In both cases, the electrical equipment is under normal operating conditions, the equipment is within its rated life, a damp environment is not involved, and the CBs are operated while the equipment is in a dead front configuration.

The switchboard has an incident energy level of 31 cal/cm^2, and the lighting panelboard has an incident energy level of 5.8 cal/cm^2. The 1,600-ampere switchboard CB is operated twice a year when maintenance is scheduled for the facility, and the 20-ampere HID CB is operated twice a day to turn on and turn off the lighting. Of the possible electrical hazards, only a risk assessment for the arc flash hazard will be performed.

Analysis Using Risk Register. Scenario 1 illustrates the risk evaluation of the 1600-ampere CB in the switchboard, and Scenario 2 illustrates the 20-ampere CB in the panelboard. The following tables selected by the safety committee are applicable to these evaluations.

Scenario 1: The switchboard is not arc rated and the incident energy level is 31 cal/cm^2, therefore the severity selected from Commentary Table F.1 is 6. The CB is operated twice a year, so the frequency and duration of exposure from Commentary Table F.2 is determined to be 3. The likelihood of a hazardous event occurring is considered to be negligible due to the proper application of the CB and switchboard, and the value selected from Commentary Table F.3 is 1. Finally, since it is not anticipated that in every case the switchboard enclosure would be breached should an arc flash event occur while operating the CB, the likelihood of avoiding or limiting injury is rare, and the value is selected to be 3 from Commentary Table F.4.

Risk Assessment and Risk Control

COMMENTARY TABLE F.1   *Severity of the Possible Injury (Se) Classification*

Severity of Injury	Se Value
Irreversible — trauma, death	8
Permanent — skeletal damage, blindness, hearing loss, third-degree burns	6
Reversible — minor impact, hearing damage, second-degree burns	3
Reversible — minor laceration, bruises, first-degree burns	1

COMMENTARY TABLE F.2   *Frequency and Duration of Exposure (Fr) Classification*

Frequency of Exposure	Fr Value
≥ 1 per hour	5
< 1 per hour to ≥ 1 per day	5
< 1 per day to ≥ 1 every 2 weeks	4
< 1 every 2 weeks to ≥ 1 per year	3
< 1 per year	2

COMMENTARY TABLE F.3   *Likelihood of a Hazardous Event (Pr) Classification*

Likelihood of a Hazardous Event	Pr Value
Very high	5
Likely	4
Possible	3
Rare	2
Negligible	1

COMMENTARY TABLE F.4   *Likelihood of Avoiding or Limiting Injury (Av) Classification*

Likelihood of Avoiding or Limiting Injury	Av Value
Impossible	5
Rare	3
Probable	1

Scenario 2: Should an arc flash incident occur, it is assumed that at 8 cal/cm² or less, the integrity of the lighting panelboard will not be breached. Based on an incident energy of 5.8 cal/cm², the severity of injury is selected to be 1 from Commentary Table F.1. Based on the CB being operated twice per day, the frequency and duration of exposure from Commentary Table F.2 is determined to be 5. For the same reason as for the 1600-ampere switchboard CB, the likelihood of an incident is selected to be 1 from Commentary Table F.3. Finally, since it is assumed that the enclosure integrity remains intact, the likelihood of avoiding or limiting injury is considered to be probable and is selected to be 1 from Commentary Table F.4.

The completed risk register is displayed as Commentary Table F.5. After evaluation, the electrical safety committee has determined that a risk score higher than 10 requires consideration of additional safety controls. However, for the given scenarios and installed equipment, only administrative controls and PPE from the hierarchy of controls are to be implemented. Therefore, based on their analysis, the committee has determined that the use of PPE is required when operating the 1600-ampere CB and that the use of PPE is not required when operating the 20-ampere HID lighting panelboard CB.

COMMENTARY TABLE F.5 Risk Register for Example Scenario 1 (1600-A SWB CB) and Scenario 2 (20-A HID Lighting Panelboard CB)

Scenario No.	Hazard	Severity Se (Commentary Table F.1)	Likelihood of Occurrence of Harm Fr (Commentary Table F.2)	Pr (Commentary Table F.3)	Av (Commentary Table F.4)	Po (Fr + Pr + Av)	Risk Score Se × Po
1	Arc flash	6	3	1	3	7	42
2	Arc flash	1	5	1	1	7	7

Analysis Using Risk Assessment Matrix. The electrical safety committee included incident energy levels in their selected risk assessment matrix (Exhibit F.2) based on their assumption that incident energy levels less than or equal to 8 cal/cm² will not breach the integrity of the enclosure. Further, they have determined that the likelihood of occurrence of an arc flash event based on their equipment being properly selected, installed, and maintained is unlikely. Scenario 1 illustrates the risk evaluation of the 1600-ampere CB in the switchboard, and Scenario 2 illustrates the 20-ampere CB in the panelboard.

EXHIBIT F.2

Risk assessment matrix

Likelihood of occurrence in period	Severity of the injury (consequences)				
	Slight	Minor	Medium	Critical	Catastrophic
cal/cm²	<1.2	≥1.2 to ≤8		>8 to ≤40	>40
Unlikely					
Seldom					
Occasional					
Likely					
Definite					

Notes:
1. Extreme equals 25 through 15.
2. High equals 12 through 9.
3. Moderate equals 8 through 4.
4. Low equals 3 through 1.

Since the incident energy level in Scenario 1 is greater than 8 cal/cm² and less than 40 cal/cm² and the likelihood of an incident is considered unlikely, the risk is color-coded yellow and is assumed to be moderate. Therefore, based on their analysis, the committee recommends that the additional controls indicated in Commentary Table F.6 be considered by management.

For Scenario 2, the risk assessment level is determined to be low (color code green), since the incident energy level is greater than 4 cal/cm² and less than or equal to 8 cal/cm² and the likelihood of an incident is considered unlikely. The electrical safety committee recommends that the existing controls remain in place as detailed in Commentary Table F.6.

Risk Assessment and Risk Control

COMMENTARY TABLE F.6 *Definition of Terms and Risk Categories for Use in Risk Assessment Matrix*

Likelihood (Probability) of Occurrence

Definite	Almost certain of happening
Likely	Can happen at any time
Occasional	Occurs sporadically, from time to time
Seldom	Remote possibility; could happen sometime; most likely will not happen
Unlikely	Rare and exceptional for all practical purposes; can assume it will not happen

Severity of Injury

Catastrophic	Death or permanent total disability
Critical	Permanent partial disability or temporary total disability 3 months or longer
Medium	Medical treatment and lost work injury
Minor	Minor medical treatment possible
Slight	First aid or minor treatment

Risk and Risk Controls

Extreme (Color code red)	Intolerable risk
	    Do not proceed
	    Immediately introduce further controls
	    Detailed action and plan required

High (Color code orange)	Unsupportable risk
	    Review and introduce additional controls
	    Requires senior management attention

Moderate (Color code yellow)	Tolerable risk
	    Incorporates some level of risk that is unlikely to occur
	    Specific management responsibility
	    Consider additional controls
	    Take remedial action at appropriate time

Low (Color code green)	Supportable risk
	    Monitor and maintain controls in place
	    Manage by routine
	    Procedures
	    Little or no impact

Sample Lockout/Tagout Program

INFORMATIVE ANNEX G

This informative annex is not a part of the requirements of this NFPA document but is included for informational purposes only.

Informative Annex G illustrates how a lockout/tagout program might be published. An employer could "fill in the blanks" and publish the resulting program for his or her organization. See Supplement 3 for another safety procedure example, which illustrates the types of information that should comprise a typical safety procedure.

Lockout is the preferred method of controlling personnel exposure to electrical energy hazards. Tagout is an alternative method that is available to employers. The sample program and procedures that follow are provided to assist employers in developing a lockout/tagout program and procedures that meet the requirements of Article 120 of *NFPA* 70E. The sample program and procedures can be used for a simple lockout/tagout or as part of a complex lockout/tagout. A more comprehensive procedure will need to be developed, documented, and used for the complex lockout/tagout.

LOCKOUT/TAGOUT PROGRAM
FOR [COMPANY NAME]
OR
TAGOUT PROGRAM FOR [COMPANY NAME]

1.0 Purpose.

This procedure establishes the minimum requirements for lockout/tagout of electrical energy sources. It is to be used to ensure that conductors and circuit parts are disconnected from sources of electrical energy, locked (tagged), and tested before work begins where employees could be exposed to dangerous conditions. Sources of stored energy, such as capacitors or springs, shall be relieved of their energy, and a mechanism shall be engaged to prevent the reaccumulation of energy.

2.0 Responsibility.

All employees shall be instructed in the safety significance of the lockout/tagout procedure. All new or transferred employees and all other persons whose work operations are or might be in the area shall be instructed in the purpose and use of this procedure. *[Name(s) of the person(s) or the job title(s) of the employee(s) with responsibility]* shall ensure that appropriate personnel receive instructions on their roles and responsibilities. All persons installing a lockout/tagout device shall sign their names and the date on the tag *[or state how the name of the individual or person in charge will be available]*.

3.0 Preparation for Lockout/Tagout.

3.1 Review current diagrammatic drawings (or their equivalent), tags, labels, and signs to identify and locate all disconnecting means to determine that power is interrupted by a physical break and not de-energized by a circuit interlock. Make a list of disconnecting means to be locked (tagged).

3.2 Review disconnecting means to determine adequacy of their interrupting ability. Determine if it will be possible to verify a visible open point, or if other precautions will be necessary.

3.3 Review other work activity to identify where and how other personnel might be exposed to electrical hazards. Review other energy sources in the physical area to determine employee exposure to those sources of other types of energy. Establish energy control methods for control of other hazardous energy sources in the area.

3.4 Provide an adequately rated test instrument to test each phase conductor or circuit part to verify that they are de-energized *(see Section G.11.3)*. Provide a method to determine that the test instrument is operating satisfactorily.

3.5 Where the possibility of induced voltages or stored electrical energy exists, call for grounding the phase conductors or circuit parts before touching them. Where it could be reasonably anticipated that contact with other exposed energized conductors or circuit parts is possible, call for applying ground connecting devices.

⚠ 4.0 Simple Lockout/Tagout.

The simple lockout/tagout procedure will involve G.1.0 through G.3.0, G.5.0 through G.9.0, and G.11.0 through G.13.0.

5.0 Sequence of Lockout/Tagout System Procedures.

5.1 The employees shall be notified that a lockout/tagout system is going to be implemented and the reason for it. The qualified employee implementing the lockout/tagout shall know the disconnecting means location for all sources of electrical energy and the location of all sources of stored energy. The qualified person shall be knowledgeable of hazards associated with electrical energy.

5.2 If the electrical supply is energized, the qualified person shall de-energize and disconnect the electric supply and relieve all stored energy.

5.3 Wherever possible, the blades of disconnecting devices should be visually verified to be fully opened, or draw-out type circuit breakers should be verified to be completely withdrawn to the fully disconnected position.

5.4 Lockout/tagout all disconnecting means with lockout/tagout devices.

> Informational Note: For tagout, one additional safety measure must be employed, such as opening, blocking, or removing an additional circuit element.

5.5 Attempt to operate the disconnecting means to determine that operation is prohibited.

Sample Lockout/Tagout Program

⚠ **5.6** A test instrument shall be used. *(See G.11.3.)* Inspect the instrument for visible damage. Do not proceed if there is an indication of damage to the instrument until an undamaged device is available.

5.7 Verify proper instrument operation on a known source of voltage and then test for absence of voltage.

5.8 Verify proper instrument operation on a known source of voltage after testing for absence of voltage.

5.9 Where required, install a grounding equipment/conductor device on the phase conductors or circuit parts, to eliminate induced voltage or stored energy, before touching them. Where it has been determined that contact with other exposed energized conductors or circuit parts is possible, apply ground connecting devices rated for the available fault duty.

5.10 The equipment, electrical source, or both are now locked out (tagged out).

6.0 Restoring the Equipment, Electrical Supply, or Both to Normal Condition.

6.1 After the job or task is complete, visually verify that the job or task is complete.

6.2 Remove all tools, equipment, and unused materials and perform appropriate housekeeping.

6.3 Remove all grounding equipment/conductors/devices.

6.4 Notify all personnel involved with the job or task that the lockout/tagout is complete, that the electrical supply is being restored, and that they are to remain clear of the equipment and electrical supply.

6.5 Perform any quality control tests or checks on the repaired or replaced equipment, electrical supply, or both.

6.6 Remove lockout/tagout devices. The person who installed the devices is to remove them.

6.7 Notify the owner of the equipment, electrical supply, or both, that the equipment, electrical supply, or both are ready to be returned to normal operation.

6.8 Return the disconnecting means to their normal condition.

7.0 Procedure Involving More Than One Person.

For a simple lockout/tagout and where more than one person is involved in the job or task, each person shall install his or her own personal lockout/tagout device.

8.0 Procedure Involving More Than One Shift.

When the lockout/tagout extends for more than one day, it shall be verified that the lockout/tagout is still in place at the beginning of the next day. When the lockout/tagout is continued on successive shifts, the lockout/tagout is considered to be a complex lockout/tagout.

For a complex lockout/tagout, the person in charge shall identify the method for transfer of the lockout/tagout and of communication with all employees.

9.0 Complex Lockout/Tagout.

A complex lockout/tagout plan is required where one or more of the following exist:

(1) Multiple energy sources (more than one)
(2) Multiple crews
(3) Multiple crafts
(4) Multiple locations
(5) Multiple employers
(6) Unique disconnecting means
(7) Complex or particular switching sequences
(8) Lockout/tagout for more than one shift; that is, new shift workers

9.1 All complex lockout/tagout procedures shall require a written plan of execution. The plan shall include the requirements in G.1.0 through G.3.0, G.5.0, G.6.0, and G.8.0 through G.12.0.

9.2 A person in charge shall be involved with a complex lockout/tagout procedure. The person in charge shall be at the procedure location.

9.3 The person in charge shall develop a written plan of execution and communicate that plan to all persons engaged in the job or task. The person in charge shall be held accountable for safe execution of the complex lockout/tagout plan. The complex lockout/tagout plan must address all the concerns of employees who might be exposed, and they must understand how electrical energy is controlled. The person in charge shall ensure that each person understands the electrical hazards to which they are exposed and the safety-related work practices they are to use.

9.4 All complex lockout/tagout plans identify the method to account for all persons who might be exposed to electrical hazards in the course of the lockout/tagout.
One of the following methods is to be used:

(1) Each individual shall install his or her own personal lockout or tagout device.
(2) The person in charge shall lock his/her key in a lock box.
(3) The person in charge shall maintain a sign-in/sign-out log for all personnel entering the area.
(4) Another equally effective methodology shall be used.

9.5 The person in charge can install locks/tags or direct their installation on behalf of other employees.

9.6 The person in charge can remove locks/tags or direct their removal on behalf of other employees, only after all personnel are accounted for and ensured to be clear of potential electrical hazards.

9.7 Where the complex lockout/tagout is continued on successive shifts, the person in charge shall identify the method for transfer of the lockout and the method of communication with all employees.

10.0 Discipline.

10.1 Knowingly violating the requirements of this program will result in [*state disciplinary actions that will be taken*].

Sample Lockout/Tagout Program

10.2 Knowingly operating a disconnecting means with an installed lockout device (tagout device) will result in [*state disciplinary actions to be taken*].

11.0 Equipment.

11.1 Locks shall be [*state type and model of selected locks*].

11.2 Tags shall be [*state type and model to be used*].

11.3 The test instrument(s) to be used shall be [*state type and model*].

12.0 Review.

This program was last reviewed on [date] and is scheduled to be reviewed again on [date] (not more than 1 year from the last review).

13.0 Lockout/Tagout Training.

Recommended training can include, but is not limited to, the following:

(1) Recognition of lockout/tagout devices
(2) Installation of lockout/tagout devices
(3) Duty of employer in writing procedures
(4) Duty of employee in executing procedures
(5) Duty of person in charge
(6) Authorized and unauthorized removal of locks/tags
(7) Enforcement of execution of lockout/tagout procedures
(8) Simple lockout/tagout
(9) Complex lockout/tagout
(10) Use of single-line and diagrammatic drawings to identify sources of energy
(11) Alerting techniques
(12) Release of stored energy
(13) Personnel accounting methods
(14) Temporary protective grounding equipment needs and requirements
(15) Safe use of test instruments

Guidance on Selection of Protective Clothing and Other Personal Protective Equipment (PPE)

INFORMATIVE ANNEX H

This informative annex is not a part of the requirements of this NFPA document but is included for informational purposes only.

Informative Annex H provides guidance on the selection of clothing and PPE, regardless of whether the arc flash PPE category method or the incident energy method is used to perform an arc flash risk assessment. This annex also provides guidance for the selection of shock protective equipment.

Δ H.1 Arc-Rated Clothing and Other Personal Protective Equipment (PPE) for Use with Arc Flash PPE Categories.

Table 130.5(C), Table 130.7(C)(15)(a), Table 130.7(C)(15)(b), and Table 130.7(C)(15)(c) provide guidance for the selection and use of PPE when using arc flash PPE categories.

Δ H.2 Simplified Two-Category Clothing Approach for Use with Table 130.7(C)(15(a), Table 130.7(C)(15)(b), and Table 130.7(C)(15)(c).

The use of Table H.2 is a simplified approach to provide minimum PPE for electrical workers within facilities with large and diverse electrical systems. The clothing listed in Table H.2 fulfills the minimum arc-rated clothing requirements of Table 130.7(C)(15)(a), Table 130.7(C)(15)(b), and Table 130.7(C)(15)(c). The clothing systems listed in this table should be used with the other PPE appropriate for the arc flash PPE category *[see Table 130.7(C)(15)(c)]*. The notes to Table 130.7(C)(15)(a), Table 130.7(C)(15)(b), and Table 130.7(C)(15)(c) must apply as shown in those tables.

After an employer develops and publishes a procedure that describes how thermal protection is determined based on the use of the arc flash PPE categories method, the employer must develop a system that enables the procedure requirements to be administered efficiently and effectively. Section H.2 illustrates one method that enables a PPE program to be efficiently and effectively administered where the arc flash PPE category method has been selected for performing an arc flash risk assessment.

◬ **TABLE H.2** *Simplified Two-Category, Arc-Rated Clothing System*

Clothing[a]	Applicable Tasks
Everyday Work Clothing Arc-rated long-sleeve shirt with arc-rated pants (minimum arc rating of 8) *or* Arc-rated coveralls (minimum arc rating of 8)	Situations where a risk assessment indicates that PPE is required and where Table 130.7(C)(15)(a) and Table 130.7(C)(15)(b) specify arc flash PPE category 1 or 2[b]
Arc Flash Suit A total clothing system consisting of arc-rated shirt and pants and/or arc-rated coveralls and/or arc flash coat and pants (clothing system minimum arc rating of 40)	Situations where a risk assessment indicates that PPE is required and where Table 130.7(C)(15)(a) and Table 130.7(C)(15)(b) specify arc flash PPE category 3 or 4[b]

[a] Note that other PPE listed in Table 130.7(C)(15)(c), which include arc-rated face shields or arc flash suit hoods, arc-rated hard hat liners, safety glasses or safety goggles, hard hats, hearing protection, heavy-duty leather gloves, rubber insulating gloves, and leather protectors, could be required. The arc rating for a garment is expressed in cal/cm^2.

[b] The estimated available fault current capacities and fault clearing times or arcing durations are listed in the text of Table 130.7(C)(15)(a) and Table 130.7(C)(15)(b). For power systems with greater than the estimated available fault current capacity or with longer than the assumed fault clearing times, Table H.2 cannot be used and arc flash PPE must be determined and selected by means of an incident energy analysis in accordance with 130.5(G).

◬ **H.3 Arc-Rated Clothing and Other Personal Protective Equipment (PPE) for Use with Risk Assessment of Electrical Hazards.**

Table H.3 provides a summary of specific sections within the NFPA *70E* standard describing PPE for electrical hazards.

> Even when using the arc flash PPE category method, the sections identified in Table H.3 should be reviewed to ensure that appropriate PPE is being used to protect employees from the electrical hazards identified for the task involved. This table does not include any clothing below 1.2 cal/cm^2. There are no requirements to provide the employee with arc flash protection below this incident energy, since an injury from an incident is expected to be survivable and nonpermanent.
>
> Former Table H.3(b), Guidance on Selection of Arc-Rated Clothing and Other PPE When the Incident Energy Exposure is Determined, has been relocated to Article 130 as Table 130.5(D), Selection of Arc-Rated Clothing and Other PPE When the Incident Energy Analysis Method Is Used.

◬ **TABLE H.3** *Summary of Specific Sections Describing PPE for Electrical Hazards*

Shock Hazard PPE	Applicable Section(s)
Rubber insulating gloves and leather protectors, unless the requirements of ASTM F496 are met	130.7(C)(7)(a)
Rubber insulating sleeves as needed	130.7(C)(7)(a)
Class G or E hard hat as needed	130.7(C)(3)
Safety glasses or goggles as needed	130.7(C)(4)
Dielectric overshoes as needed	130.7(C)(8)

Guidance on Selection of Protective Clothing and Other PPE

TABLE H.3 *Summary of Specific Sections Describing PPE for Electrical Hazards (Continued)*

Shock Hazard PPE	Applicable Section(s)
Incident Energy Exposures Greater than or Equal to 1.2 cal/cm² (5 J/cm²)	
Clothing: Arc-rated clothing system with an arc rating appropriate to the anticipated incident energy exposure	130.7(C)(1), 130.7(C)(2), 130.7(C)(6), 130.7(C)(9)(d)
Clothing underlayers (when used): Arc-rated or nonmelting untreated natural fiber	130.7(C)(9)(c), 130.7(C)(11), 130.7(C)(12)

Gloves:
  Exposures greater than or equal to 1.2 cal/cm² (5 J/cm²) and less than or equal to 8 cal/cm² (33.5 J/cm²): heavy-duty leather gloves
  Exposures greater than 8 cal/cm² (33.5 J/cm²): rubber insulating gloves with their leather protectors or arc-rated gloves
	130.7(C)(7)(b),
	130.7(C)(10)(d)

Hard hat: Class G or E	130.7(C)(1), 130.7(C)(3)

Face shield:
  Exposures greater than or equal to 1.2 cal/cm² (5 J/cm²) and less than or equal to 12 cal/cm² (50.2 J/cm²): Arc-rated face shield that covers the face, neck, and chin and an arc-rated balaclava or an arc-rated arc flash suit hood
  Exposures greater than 12 cal/cm² (50.2 J/cm²): arc-rated arc flash suit hood
	130.7(C)(1),
	130.7(C)(3),
	130.7(C)(10)(a),
	130.7(C)(10)(b),
	130.7(C)(10)(c)

Safety glasses or goggles	130.7(C)(4), 130.7(C)(10)(c)
Hearing protection	130.7(C)(5)

Footwear:
  Exposures less than or equal to 4 cal/cm² (16.75 J/cm²): Heavy-duty leather footwear (as needed)
  Exposures greater than 4 cal/cm² (16.75 J/cm²): Heavy-duty leather footwear
	130.7(C)(10)(e)

N H.4 Conformity Assessment of Personal Protective Equipment (PPE).

Annex A references performance standards for items of PPE. Conformance to these standards is intended to provide employees with appropriate PPE to ensure that any residual risk associated with their duties remains at an acceptable level. As with past NFPA *70E* editions, the responsibility of verifying conformance to the appropriate standard is with the employer, purchaser, or person providing PPE to employees.

Section H.4 adds a system of conformity assessment that can augment an employer's PPE approval process. ANSI/ISEA 125, *American National Standard for Conformity Assessment of Safety and Personal Protective Equipment*, is referenced as the standard for the conformity assessment methodology and provides three levels of conformity assessment ranging from supplier self-declaration to independent third-party certification. In accordance with 130.7(C)(14), the level of conformity assessment for any

> particular PPE item is determined by the manufacturer or can be mandated by the purchaser.

N H.4.1 Introduction. Section 130.7(C)(14) requires personal protective equipment (PPE) provided by a supplier or manufacturer to conform to appropriate product standards by one of three methods. Additional information for these conformity assessment methods can be found within ANSI/ISEA 125, *American National Standard for Conformity Assessment of Safety and Personal Protective Equipment*. ANSI/ISEA 125 establishes criteria for conformity assessment of safety and PPE that is sold with claims of compliance with product performance standards. ANSI/ISEA 125 contains provisions for data collection, product verification, conformation of quality and manufacturing production control, and roles and responsibilities of suppliers, testing organizations, and third-party certification organizations.

> Delivery of a conformity method to the purchaser of PPE does not absolve the employer from determining the validity of the claim. The employer must be competent to determine the standard applicable to the purchased equipment, the correctness of the claim, and the validity of the test results. It may be necessary for the purchaser to specify exactly which standards the equipment must comply with.

N H.4.2 Level of Conformity. ANSI/ISEA 125 provides for three different levels of conformity assessment: Level 1, Level 2, and Level 3.

Level 1 conformity is where the supplier or manufacturer is making a self-declaration that a product meets all of the requirements of the standard(s) to which conformance is claimed. A supplier Declaration of Conformity for each product is required to be made available for examination upon request.

Level 2 conformity is where the supplier or manufacturer is making a self-declaration that a product meets all of the requirements of the standard(s) to which conformance is claimed, the supplier or manufacturer has a registered ISO 9001 Quality Management System or equivalent quality management system, and all testing has been carried out by an ISO 17025 accredited testing laboratory. A supplier Declaration of Conformity for each product is required to be made available for examination upon request.

Level 3 conformity is where the products are certified by an ISO 17065 accredited independent third-party certification organization (CO). All product testing is directed by the CO, and all changes to the product must be reviewed and retested if necessary. Compliant products are issued a Declaration of Conformity by the CO and products are marked with the CO's mark or label.

N H.4.3 Equivalence. While there are three levels of conformity assessment described in ANSI/ISEA 125, the levels are not to be considered as equivalent. Users are cautioned that the level of rigor required to demonstrate conformity should be based on the potential safety and health consequence of using a product that does not meet a stated performance standard. A higher potential safety and health consequence associated with the use of a noncompliant product should necessitate a higher level of conformity assessment.

> When employees are put at risk of injury through authorization by their employer to conduct energized work, PPE is the last line of defense available to limit their injury or prevent their death. The effectiveness of protective equipment may not be evident until that equipment is called upon to perform its safety function. An employer must not supply its employees with substandard, counterfeit, or

Guidance on Selection of Protective Clothing and Other PPE

inappropriate PPE. Such gear may actually increase the severity of an injury to the employee if an incident occurs.

A Level 1 conformity is a variation of the supplier's Declaration of Conformity (DoC) system used in the European Union (EU). Within the EU, and in some other locations, the DoC is a legal document declaring that the equipment complies with the specific laws of the governing country. However, a Level 1 conformity is not tied to a legal system and has no external oversight. It is the employer's responsibility to determine the validity of the declaration.

The accredited laboratory in a Level 2 conformity is not necessarily an independent testing laboratory. Many companies are registered under the ISO 9000 series of standards for management systems. These companies may have an on-site laboratory to conduct evaluations and testing of their products by company employees. It is the employer's responsibility to determine the validity of the declaration.

Level 3 conformity is testing to the applicable standards by an independent organization. Within the United States, OSHA has a process for accrediting organizations for performing evaluations using specific standards. Within NFPA *70E*, equipment evaluated under this system is considered to be listed. It is the employer's responsibility to determine the validity of the declaration.

N H.4.4 Supplier's Declaration of Conformity. A Declaration of Conformity should be issued by the supplier and made available for examination upon request from a customer, user, or relevant authority. The Declaration of Conformity should, at a minimum:

(1) List the supplier name and address.
(2) Include a product model number or other identification details.
(3) List the product performance standard or standards (designation and year) to which conformance is claimed.
(4) Include a statement of attestation.
(5) Be dated, written on supplier letterhead, and signed by an authorized representative. The name and title of the authorized representative should also be printed.

Additional information should include:

(1) The level of conformity followed
(2) Whether the ISO 17025 testing facility is an independent or in-house laboratory (owned or partially owned by an entity within the supplier's corporate structure or within the manufacturing stream for the applicable product, including subcontractors and sub-suppliers)
(3) Reference to the test report (title, number, date, etc.) that serves as the basis of determining conformity

For an example of a Supplier's Declaration of Conformity see Figure H.4.4.

```
        Supplier's Declaration of Conformity
No. _____
Issuer's name: _____
Issuer's address: _____
Object of the declaration: _____
_____
_____

The object of the declaration described above is in conformity with the
following documents:
Documents No.      Title              Edition/Date of issue
_____   _____       _____
_____   _____       _____
_____   _____       _____

Additional information:
_____
_____
_____

Signed for and on behalf of:
_____
_____

Place and date of issue
_____

(Name, function)    (Signature or equivalent authorized by the issuer)
```

FIGURE H.4.4 *Supplier's Declaration of Conformity.*

N H.4.5 References. ANSI/ISEA contains detailed information and guidance on the application of the different conformity assessment levels. Copies of ANSI/ISEA 125 are available free of charge by e-mailing the International Safety Equipment Association at: ISEA@Safetyequipment.org and requesting a complimentary copy.

INFORMATIVE ANNEX I

Job Briefing and Planning Checklist

This informative annex is not a part of the requirements of this NFPA document but is included for informational purposes only.

> The employer is required by 110.1(A) to implement and document an overall electrical safety program (ESP). Job briefings must be included as one of the ESP elements. Before starting each job, the employee in charge must conduct a job briefing with the employees involved. The briefing must cover such subjects as hazards associated with the job, work procedures involved, special precautions, energy source controls, PPE requirements, and the information on the energized electrical work permit. The job briefing needs to be performed before the work tasks are started.
>
> This form contains examples of subjects that should be discussed when the job briefing is held. This form is not intended to be an all-inclusive list of subjects that should be considered. Other subjects may need to be included based on the specific circumstances. The purpose of the checklist in Figure I.1 is to help facilitate the conversation.

I.1 Job Briefing and Planning Checklist.

Figure I.1 illustrates considerations for a job briefing and planning checklist.

Identify
- ❏ Hazards
- ❏ Voltage levels involved
- ❏ Skills required
- ❏ Any "foreign" (secondary source) voltage source
- ❏ Any unusual work conditions
- ❏ Number of people needed to do the job
- ❏ Shock protection boundaries
- ❏ Available incident energy
- ❏ Potential for arc flash (Conduct an arc flash risk assessment.)
- ❏ Arc flash boundary
- ❏ Any evidence of impending failure?

Ask
- ❏ Can the equipment be de-energized?
- ❏ Are backfeeds of the circuits to be worked on possible?
- ❏ Is an energized electrical work permit required?
- ❏ Is a standby person required?
- ❏ Is the equipment properly installed and maintained?

Check
- ❏ Job plans
- ❏ Single-line diagrams and vendor prints
- ❏ Status board
- ❏ Information on plant and vendor resources is up to date
- ❏ Safety procedures
- ❏ Vendor information
- ❏ Individuals are familiar with the facility

Know
- ❏ What the job is
- ❏ Who else needs to know — Communicate!
- ❏ Who is in charge

Think
- ❏ About the unexpected event . . . What if?
- ❏ Lock — Tag — Test — Try
- ❏ Test for voltage — FIRST
- ❏ Use the right tools and equipment, including PPE
- ❏ Install and remove temporary protective grounding equipment
- ❏ Install barriers and barricades
- ❏ What else . . . ?

Prepare for an emergency
- ❏ Is the standby person CPR/AED trained?
- ❏ Is the required emergency equipment available? Where is it?
- ❏ Where is the nearest telephone?
- ❏ Where is the fire alarm?
- ❏ Is confined space rescue available?
- ❏ What is the exact work location?
- ❏ How is the equipment shut off in an emergency?
- ❏ Are the emergency telephone numbers known?
- ❏ Where is the fire extinguisher?
- ❏ Are radio communications available?
- ❏ Is an AED available?

△ *FIGURE I.1 Sample Job Briefing and Planning Checklist.*

Energized Electrical Work Permit

INFORMATIVE ANNEX J

This informative annex is not a part of the requirements of this NFPA document but is included for informational purposes only.

> Under both NFPA *70E* and OSHA regulations, work is required to be performed in a verified de-energized state (electrical safe work condition), unless energized work can be justified. There are only three conditions given in 130.2(A) under which energized work is permitted.
>
> If an employee will be exposed to an electrical hazard during justified energized electrical work, the hierarchy of risk controls must be employed to lower the incident energy level or to provide additional protection for the employee prior to the start of the task. The use of PPE is considered the least effective form of risk control available, and it must not be the first or only control method used to protect the employee.
>
> Once energized electrical work is properly justified, the hierarchy of risk controls has been employed, and the justified work can safely be conducted, the elements of a work permit required by 130.2(B)(2) are provided on this energized work permit form. The format of this work permit example is not fixed by requirement, although many employers have used this template successfully.
>
> The purpose of a work permit is to ensure that people in responsible positions are involved in the decision whether or not to accept the increased risk of injury to the employee assigned the energized electrical task. An additional benefit of the work permit is that its review might initiate a decision to perform the work de-energized.

J.1 Energized Electrical Work Permit Sample.

Figure J.1 illustrates considerations for an energized electrical work permit.

J.2 Energized Electrical Work Permit.

Figure J.2 illustrates items to consider when determining the need for an energized electrical work permit.

ENERGIZED ELECTRICAL WORK PERMIT

PART I: TO BE COMPLETED BY THE REQUESTER:

Job/Work Order Number _____

(1) Description of circuit/equipment/job location: _____

(2) Description of work to be done: _____

(3) Justification of why the circuit/equipment cannot be de-energized or the work deferred until the next scheduled outage: _____

Requester/Title _____ Date _____

PART II: TO BE COMPLETED BY THE ELECTRICALLY QUALIFIED PERSONS *DOING* THE WORK:

Check when complete ☐

(1) Detailed description of the job procedures to be used in performing the above detailed work: _____

(2) Description of the safe work practices to be employed: _____ ☐

(3) Results of the shock risk assessment: _____
    (a) Voltage to which personnel will be exposed ☐
    (b) Limited approach boundary ☐
    (c) Restricted approach boundary ☐
    (d) Necessary shock, personal, and other protective equipment to safely perform assigned task ☐

(4) Results of the arc flash risk assessment: _____
    (a) Available incident energy at the working distance or arc flash PPE category ☐
    (b) Necessary arc flash personal and other protective equipment to safely perform the assigned task ☐
    (c) Arc flash boundary ☐

(5) Means employed to restrict the access of unqualified persons from the work area: _____ ☐

(6) Evidence of completion of a job briefing, including discussion of any job-related hazards: _____ ☐

(7) Do you agree the above-described work can be done safely? ☐ Yes ☐ No (If *no*, return to requester.)

Electrically Qualified Person(s) _____ Date _____

Electrically Qualified Person(s) _____ Date _____

PART III: APPROVAL(S) TO PERFORM THE WORK WHILE ELECTRICALLY ENERGIZED:

Manufacturing Manager _____ Maintenance/Engineering Manager _____

Safety Manager _____ Electrically Knowledgeable Person _____

General Manager _____ Date _____

Note: Once the work is complete, forward this form to the site Safety Department for review and retention.

© 2017 National Fire Protection Association   NFPA 70E

FIGURE J.1 *Sample Permit for Energized Electrical Work.*

Energized Electrical Work Permit

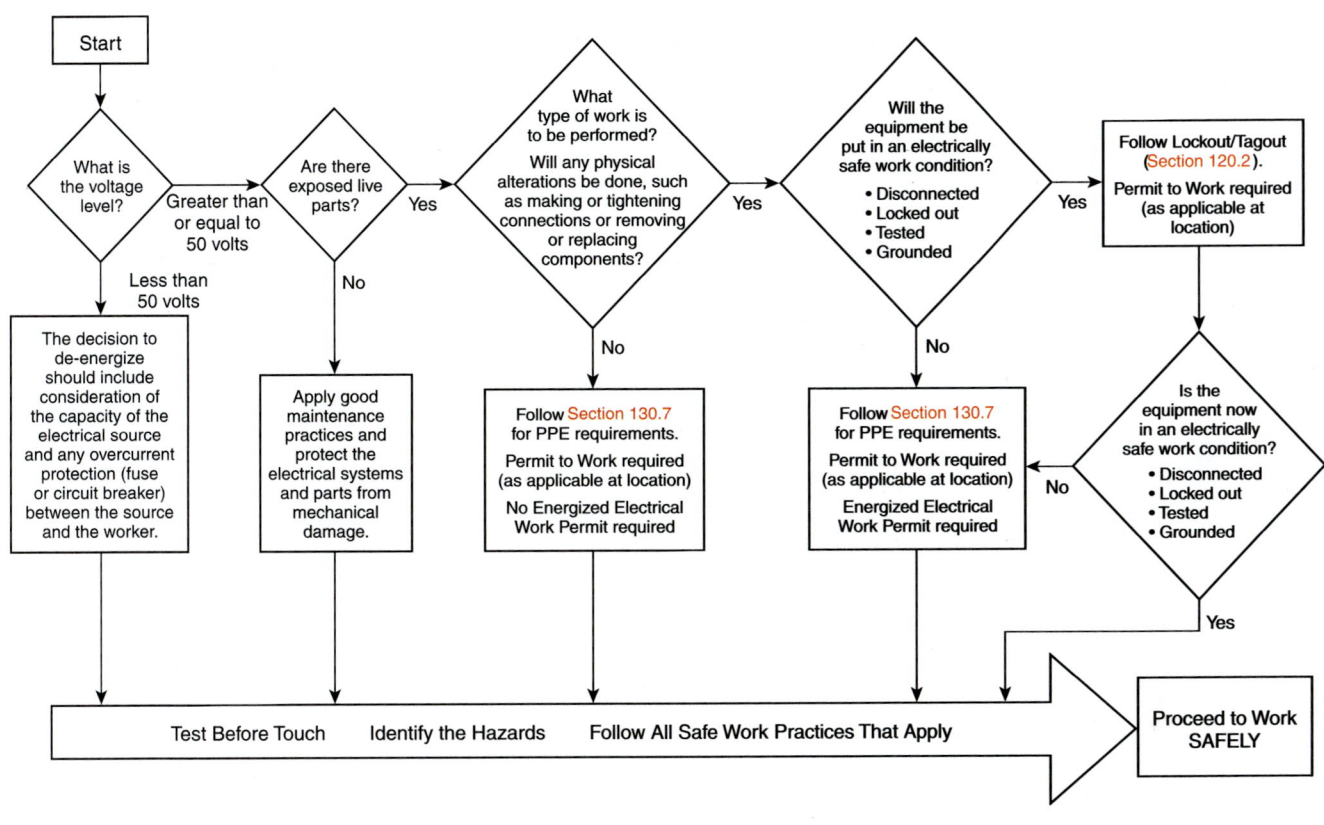

FIGURE J.2 *Energized Electrical Work Permit Flow Chart.*

INFORMATIVE ANNEX K

General Categories of Electrical Hazards

This informative annex is not a part of the requirements of this NFPA document but is included for informational purposes only.

> **Informative Annex K** provides an abbreviated discussion of known electrical hazards. Critical information is provided for an employee to use in support of an improved electrical safety program.

K.1 General.

Electrical injuries represent a serious workplace health and safety issue to electrical and non-electrical workers. Data from the U.S. Bureau of Labor Statistics (BLS) indicate that there were nearly 6000 fatal electrical injuries to workers in the United States from 1992 through 2012. BLS data also indicate that there were 24,100 non-fatal electrical injuries from 2003 through 2012. From 1992 to 2013, the number of fatal workplace electrical injuries has fallen steadily and dramatically from 334 in 1992 to 139 in 2013. However, the trend with non-fatal electrical injuries is less consistent. Between 2003 and 2009, non-fatal injury totals ranged from 2390 in 2003 to 2620 in 2009, with a high of 2950 injuries in 2005. Non-fatal injury totals between 2010 through 2012 were the lowest over this 10-year period, with 1890 non-fatal injuries in 2010, 2250 in 2011, and 1700 in 2012.

There are two general categories of electrical injury: electrical shock and electrical burns. Electrical burns can be further subdivided into burns caused by radiant energy (arc burns), burns caused by exposure to ejected hot gases and materials (thermal burns), and burns caused by the conduction of electrical current through body parts (conduction burns). In addition, hearing damage can occur from acoustic energy, and traumatic injury can be caused by toxic gases and pressure waves associated with an arcing event.

About 98 percent of fatal occupational electrical injuries are electrical shock injuries. A corporate case study examining electrical injury reporting and safety practices found that 40 percent of electrical incidents involved 250 volts or less and were indicative of a misperception of electrical safety as a high-voltage issue. In addition, electrical incidents once again were found to involve a large share of non-electrical workers, with approximately one-half of incidents involving workers from outside electrical crafts. Research of electrical fatalities in construction found that the highest proportion of fatalities occurred in establishments with 10 or fewer employers and pointed out that smaller employers could have fewer formal training requirements and less structured training in safety practices.

> Electrical workers are exposed to risk of injury not only by electrical hazards but also by other hazards. A risk assessment should address all potential hazards. **Commentary**

Table K.1 lists fatalities by employment according to the Bureau of Labor Statistics (BLS) from 2003 to 2015.

COMMENTARY TABLE K.1 Number of Fatalities by Employment, 2003 to 2015

Occupation	Number of Fatalities
Electricians	1054
Electrician helpers	43
Electrical contractors and other wiring installation contractors	972
Residential electrical contractors and other wiring installation contractors	105
Nonresidential electrical contractors and other wiring installation contractors	346
Electrical power generation, transmission, and distribution	447
Electric power-line installers and repairers	386
Electrical and electronic equipment mechanics, installers, and repairers	385

△ K.2 Electric Shock.

Over 40 percent of all electrical fatalities in the U.S. involved overhead power line contact. This includes overhead power line fatalities from direct contact by a worker, contact through hand-carried objects, and contact through machines and vehicles. Comparing the ratio of total electrical fatalities to total electrical injuries (fatal and nonfatal), it was noticed that electrical injuries are more often fatal than many other injury categories. For example, from 2003 to 2009 there were 20,033 electrical injuries of which 1573 were fatalities. One worker died for every 12.74 electrical injuries. For the same period there were 1,718,219 fall injuries of which 5279 were fatalities — one worker died for every 325 injuries.

Of those, 1573 were electrical fatalities. A more detailed look at the demographics for 168 electrical fatalities in 2009 showed that 99 percent of deaths were the result of electrocution, and 70 percent occurred while the worker was performing a constructing, repairing, or cleaning activity.

Protection against electric shock exposure and incidents was the original mission of NFPA *70E*. Establishing an electrically safe work condition is the desired approach to mitigating electric shock exposure, but where tasks are permitted on energized electrical conductors and circuit parts, the requirements in Article 130 provide protection strategies that allow an employee to safely work on energized electrical equipment.

Although 130.2(A)(3) establishes 50 volts and higher as the threshold at which shock protection for personnel is required, voltages lower than 50 volts can be hazardous under certain conditions. Wet, damp, and submersed conditions lower the body resistance to electric current, and voltages lower than 50 volts in these conditions are potentially dangerous. The lower voltage levels may not necessarily pose an injurious electric shock hazard, but the effects of electric current on muscular control can be dangerous to an employee who might be partially or completely immersed in a body of water. Swimming pool maintenance is an activity that could pose this threat to an employee.

The Bureau of Labor Statistics (BLS) documents that exposure to electricity accounted for 2498 fatalities from 2003 to 2015. For the period of 2011 to 2015, electrocutions by occupation are shown in Commentary Table K.2. Electrical employees are not the only employees being fatally injured by electricity in the workplace. Employees in nonelectrical occupations, such as production line workers and groundskeepers, who do not expect to be exposed to electrical hazards, are being fatally injured through exposure to electrical current during the course of conducting their assigned tasks.

General Categories of Electrical Hazards

The need for contract employers to establish safe work practices is evident by the BLS-documented 231 electrical exposure fatalities at private residences, which are covered workplaces under NFPA *70E* and OSHA. For comparison, 229 fatalities occurred in industrial premises for the same 2011 to 2015 period.

BLS-documented fatalities by voltage level are shown in Commentary Table K.3. Commentary Table K.4 lists the number of fatalities by electrical part. Note that from 2011 to 2015, batteries have accounted for three fatalities and flexible cords for 90 fatalities.

Additional data and information regarding electrical safety can be found in the resource library of the Electrical Safety Foundation International (ESFI) at www.esfi.org.

COMMENTARY TABLE K.2 *Number of Fatalities from Contact with Electricity by Occupation, 2011 to 2015*

Occupation	Number of Fatalities
Construction and extraction	346
Installation, maintenance, and repair	164
Building and grounds cleaning and maintenance	84
Management	55
Production	36
Transportation and material moving	33

COMMENTARY TABLE K.3 *Electrical Fatalities by Voltage Level, 2011 to 2015*

Activity	Number of Fatalities
Exposure to electricity, 220 volts or less	156
Exposure to electricity, greater than 220 volts	548

COMMENTARY TABLE K.4 *Electrical Fatalities by Equipment, 2003 to 2015*

Electric Part	Number of Fatalities
All electric parts	2559
• Power lines, transformers, converters	1483
• Electrical wiring	536
• Switchboards, switches, fuses	137
• Generators	88
• Power cords, electrical cords, extension cords (2011–2015)	90
• Batteries, other than automotive (2011–2015)	3

K.3 Arc Flash.

In the recently issued 29 CFR Subpart V, OSHA identified 99 injuries that involved burns from arcs from energized equipment faults or failures, resulting in 21 fatalities and 94 hospitalized injuries for the period January 1991 through December 1998.

Based on this data, OSHA estimated that an average of at least eight burn injuries from arcs occur each year involving employees doing work covered by OSHA rules, leading to 12 non-fatal injuries and two fatalities per year. Of the reports indicating the extent of the burn injury, 75 percent reported third-degree burns.

During the period involved, Federal OSHA only required non-fatal injuries to be reported when there were three or more workers hospitalized. OSHA found that there were six injuries for every fatality in California, which requires the reporting of every hospitalized injury.

Using that data, OSHA estimated that would be at least 36 injuries to every fatality, and probably many more. Also, many non-fatal electric shocks involve burns from associated electric arcs.

Starting January 1, 2015, Federal OSHA requires every hospitalized injury to be reported.

The Bureau of Labor Statistics (BLS) database does not indicate fatalities due to an "arc flash." However, during the 2011 to 2015 period, electrical burns accounted for 17 fatalities. While 11 burn fatalities were associated with third- and fourth-degree burns, one fatality was associated with a second-degree burn.

△ K.4 Arc Blast.

The tremendous temperatures of the arc cause the explosive expansion of both the surrounding air and the metal in the arc path. For example, copper expands by a factor of 67,000 times when it turns from a solid to a vapor. The danger associated with this expansion is one of high pressures, sound, and shrapnel. The high pressures can easily exceed hundreds or even thousands of pounds per square foot, knocking workers off ladders, rupturing eardrums, and collapsing lungs. Finally, material and molten metal are expelled away from the arc at speeds exceeding 1120 km/hr (700 mph), fast enough for shrapnel to completely penetrate the human body.

Protection against the arc flash hazards described in Section K.3 is to help prevent employees from receiving incurable burns. Extremely dangerous concussive forces, sound, and shrapnel can occur in arc blast events. Although arc-rated garments are available, they are not intended to provide arc blast protection.

Arc terminal temperature is estimated to be in excess of 35,000°F (19,430°C). The plasma of vaporizing metal has a temperature of 23,000°F (12,760°C). For comparison, an atomic bomb after 0.3 seconds reaches only 12,600°F (6980°C), and the surface of the sun is only 10,000°F (5540°C). The superheating of the air during an arcing incident creates an acoustic wave similar to the generation of thunder by lightning.

The acoustic and pressure waves from arcs are developed from the expansion of boiling metal and the superheating of air by the arc passing through it. Vaporizing copper expands 67,000 times in volume, whereas water expands 1670 times while becoming steam. This expansion accounts for the expulsion of molten metal droplets from the arc, which can be thrust up to distances around 10 ft (3 m). This pressure generates ionized vapor (plasma) outward from the arc for distances that are proportional to the arc power. Fifty-three kilowatts of power will vaporize 0.05 in.^{3} (0.328 cm^3) of copper into 3350 in.^{3} (54,907 cm^3) of vapor, and 1 in.^{3} (16.39 cm^3) vaporizes into 1.44 yd^3 (1.098 m^3).

Before the hot vapor forming an arc starts to cool, it combines with oxygen in the air to become an oxide of the metal vapor. It solidifies as it cools and becomes minute particles that appear as smoke — copper and iron are black, and aluminum is grey. These particles are poisonous if inhaled, are quite hot, and will cling to any surface they touch.

Arc blasts have propelled large objects — personnel, switchboard doors, and bus bars — several feet at high rates of speed. Arc blasts can provide enough pressure to collapse lungs and rupture eardrums if hearing protection is not used.

Ralph H. Lee, in his paper "Pressures Developed by Arcs" (*IEEE Transactions on Industry Applications*, Volume 1A-23, No. 4, pp. 760–764, July/August 1987), provides information regarding arc blast pressures. The following equation from Lee's paper can be used to estimate the arc blast pressure. However, it should be noted that this equation has not been generally adopted and additional testing is required.

General Categories of Electrical Hazards

$$P = (11.5 \times I_a)/D^{0.9}$$

where:
P = pressure (lb/ft²)
I_a = arcing current (kA)
D = distance from the center of the arc (ft)

From this equation, the pressure from a 100 kA arc can reach around 400 lb/ft² (1950 kg/m²) at a distance of 3.3 ft (1 m). A 25 kA arc at a distance of 2 ft (0.6 m) can produce a pressure of around 160 lb/ft² (780 kg/m²). The average man's upper body projects about 2.2 ft² (0.2 m²) of body area. The 25 kA arc at 2 ft (0.6 m) is sufficient to place a total pressure of about 352 lb (2.2 ft² × 160 lb/ft²) on the average man's chest.

N K.5 Other Information.

For additional information, the following documents are available:

Occupational Injuries From Electrical Shock and Arc Flash Events Final Report, by Richard Campbell, and David Dini, Sponsored by The Fire Protection Research Foundation, Quincy, MA

Occupational Electrical Injuries in the US, 2003–2009, by James Cawley and Brett C. Banner, ESFI

Technical paper ESW 2012-24 presented at IEEE ESW conference, *Arc Flash Hazards, Incident Energy, PPE Ratings and Thermal Burn Injury — A Deeper Look*, by Tammy Gammon, Wei-Jen Lee, and Ben Johnson

Technical Paper ESW 2015-17 presented at IEEE ESW conference, OSHA Subpart V, *Electric Power and Distribution*, April 11, 2014

INFORMATIVE ANNEX L

Typical Application of Safeguards in the Cell Line Working Zone

This informative annex is not a part of the requirements of this NFPA document but is included for informational purposes only.

Informative Annex L discusses and illustrates the application of typical safeguards in a process area associated with a dc electrical system that cannot be de-energized.

L.1 Application of Safeguards.

This informative annex permits a typical application of safeguards in electrolytic areas where electrical hazards exist. Take, for example, an employee working on an energized cell. The employee uses manual contact to make adjustments and repairs. Consequently, the exposed energized cell and grounded metal floor could present an electrical hazard. Safeguards for this employee can be provided in the following ways:

(1) Protective boots can be worn that isolate the employee's feet from the floor and that provide a safeguard from the electrical hazard.
(2) Protective gloves can be worn that isolate the employee's hands from the energized cell and that provide a safeguard.
(3) If the work task causes severe deterioration, wear, or damage to personal protective equipment (PPE), the employee might have to wear both protective gloves and boots.
(4) A permanent or temporary insulating surface can be provided for the employee to stand on to provide a safeguard.
(5) The design of the installation can be modified to provide a conductive surface for the employee to stand on. If the conductive surface is bonded to the cell, a safeguard will be provided by voltage equalization.
(6) Safe work practices can provide safeguards. If protective boots are worn, the employee should not make long reaches over energized (or grounded) surfaces such that his or her elbow bypasses the safeguard. If such movements are required, protective sleeves, protective mats, or special tools should be used. Training on the nature of electrical hazards and proper use and condition of safeguards is, in itself, a safeguard.
(7) The energized cell can be temporarily bonded to ground.

L.2 Electrical Power Receptacles.

Power supply circuits and receptacles in the cell line area for portable electric equipment should meet the requirements of 668.21 of *NFPA 70*, *National Electrical Code*. However, it is recommended that receptacles for portable electric equipment not be installed in electrolytic cell areas and that only pneumatic-powered portable tools and equipment be used.

> Section 668.21 of *NFPA 70*®, *National Electrical Code*® (*NEC*®), addresses circuit isolation, receptacle configuration, and marking requirements for circuits supplying power to ungrounded receptacles for hand-held, cord-connected equipment in the cell line.

Layering of Protective Clothing and Total System Arc Rating

INFORMATIVE ANNEX M

This informative annex is not a part of the requirements of this NFPA document but is included for informational purposes only.

Informative Annex M discusses how layering of protective clothing can impact the overall rating of the layered protection. The total arc rating of a layered clothing system is to be determined by testing the multilayer system as it would be worn in the field. The total system arc rating cannot be determined simply by adding together the arc ratings of the individual layers. Exhibit M.1 shows an arc-rated PPE system of clothing.

When layers of clothing are worn, some air space is captured between the layers. Air is a good thermal insulator and modifies the protective nature of the sum of the protective clothing. The resulting protection offered by the layers of clothing can be greater or less than the sum of the protection afforded by the individual layers. Although this annex discusses layering of protective clothing without testing of the entire system, consultation with the clothing manufacturer is necessary.

EXHIBIT M.1

An arc-rated PPE system of clothing. (Courtesy of Salisbury by Honeywell)

M.1 Layering of Protective Clothing.

M.1.1 Layering of arc-rated clothing is an effective approach to achieving the required arc rating. The use of all arc-rated clothing layers will result in achieving the required arc rating with the lowest number of layers and lowest clothing system weight. Garments that are not arc-rated should not be used to increase the arc rating of a garment or of a clothing system.

M.1.2 The total system of protective clothing can be selected to take credit for the protection provided by all the layers of clothing that are worn. For example, to achieve an arc rating of 40 cal/cm^2 (167.5 J/cm^2), an arc flash suit with an arc rating of 40 cal/cm^2 (167.5 J/cm^2) could be worn over a cotton shirt and cotton pants. Alternatively, an arc flash suit with a 25 cal/cm^2 (104.7 J/cm^2) arc rating could be worn over an arc-rated shirt and arc-rated pants with an arc rating of 8 cal/cm^2 (33.5 J/cm^2) to achieve a total system arc rating of 40 cal/cm^2 (167.5 J/cm^2). This latter approach provides the required arc rating at a lower weight and with fewer total layers of fabric and, consequently, would provide the required protection with a higher level of worker comfort.

The arc rating of a layered system of PPE is not simply a matter of adding together the ratings of the individual pieces; some manufacturers provide data on the arc ratings of individual parts. Exhibit M.2 is an example of how a manufacturer might supply such data.

EXHIBIT M.2

Curve showing the probability of injury based on arc rating materials in a layered PPE system. (Courtesy of ArcWear.com)

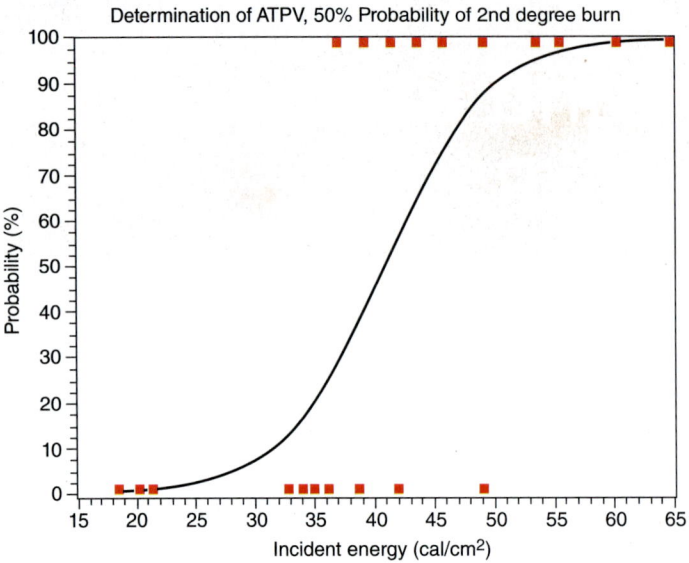

Fabric description:
Two layers, style 85917 - protera 1808.0 oz/yd² 271 g/m² 2 × 1 LH twill, 65% modacrylic 35% N317, navy 10057Q, AAD 8.0 oz/yd² 271 g/m² over style S961 indura ultra soft 11 oz/yd 373 g/m² duck, 88% cotton 12% nylon, brown, AAD 11.6 oz/yd² 393 g/m², ArcWear# 1102P86

M.2 Layering Using Arc-Rated Clothing over Natural Fiber Clothing Underlayers.

M.2.1 Under some exposure conditions, natural fiber underlayers can ignite even when they are worn under arc-rated clothing.

M.2.2 If the arc flash exposure is sufficient to break open all the arc-rated clothing outerlayer or underlayers, the natural fiber underlayer can ignite and cause more severe burn injuries to an expanded area of the body. This is due to the natural fiber underlayers burning onto areas of the worker's body that were not exposed by the arc flash event. This can occur when the natural fiber underlayer continues to burn underneath arc-rated clothing layers even in areas in which the arc-rated clothing layer or layers are not broken open due to a "chimney effect."

M.3 Total System Arc Rating.

M.3.1 The total system arc rating is the arc rating obtained when all clothing layers worn by a worker are tested as a multilayer test sample. An example of a clothing system is an arc-rated coverall worn over an arc-rated shirt and arc-rated pants in which all of the garments are constructed from the same arc-rated fabric. For this two-layer arc-rated clothing system, the arc rating would typically be more than three times higher than the arc ratings of the individual layers; that is, if the arc ratings of the arc-rated coverall, shirt, and pants were all in the range of 5 cal/cm² (20.9 J/cm²) to 6 cal/cm² (25.1 J/cm²), the total two-layer system arc rating would be over 20 cal/cm² (83.7 J/cm²).

M.3.2 It is important to understand that the total system arc rating cannot be determined by adding the arc ratings of the individual layers. In a few cases, it has been observed that the total system arc rating actually decreased when another arc-rated layer of a specific type was added to the system as the outermost layer. The only way to determine the total system arc rating is to conduct a multilayer arc test on the combination of all of the layers assembled as they would be worn.

> A total system arc rating is not simply a matter of adding together the ratings of the individual pieces; the layered system as a whole requires testing to obtain an arc rating.

Example Industrial Procedures and Policies for Working Near Overhead Electrical Lines and Equipment

INFORMATIVE ANNEX N

This informative annex is not a part of the requirements of this NFPA document but is included for informational purposes only.

> Informative Annex N illustrates electrical safety measures that might be appropriate for working near overhead lines. Although the content of this informative annex is not enforceable, the measures contained here are effective. See Supplement 3 for another safety procedure example, which illustrates the types of information that should comprise a typical safety procedure.

N.1 Introduction.

This informative annex is an example of an industrial procedure for working near overhead electrical systems. Areas covered include operations that could expose employees or equipment to contact with overhead electrical systems.

When working near electrical lines or equipment, avoid direct or indirect contact. Direct contact is contact with any part of the body. Indirect contact is when part of the body touches or is in dangerous proximity to any object in contact with energized electrical equipment. The following two assumptions should always be made:

(1) Lines are "live" (energized).
(2) Lines are operating at high voltage (over 1000 volts).

As the voltage increases, the minimum working clearances increase. Through arc-over, injuries or fatalities could occur, even if actual contact with high-voltage lines or equipment is not made. Potential for arc-over increases as the voltage increases.

N.2 Overhead Power Line Policy (OPP).

This informative annex applies to all overhead conductors, regardless of voltage, and requires the following:

(1) That employees not place themselves in close proximity to overhead power lines. "Close proximity" is within a distance of 3 m (10 ft) for systems up to 50 kV, and should be increased 100 mm (4 in.) for every 10 kV above 50 kV.
(2) That employees be informed of the hazards and precautions when working near overhead lines.
(3) That warning decals be posted on cranes and similar equipment regarding the minimum clearance of 3 m (10 ft).

(4) That a "spotter" be designated when equipment is working near overhead lines. This person's responsibility is to observe safe working clearances around all overhead lines and to direct the operator accordingly.

(5) That warning cones be used as visible indicators of the 3 m (10 ft) safety zone when working near overhead power lines.

Informational Note: "Working near," for the purpose of this informative annex, is defined as working within a distance from any overhead power line that is less than the combined height or length of the lifting device plus the associated load length and the required minimum clearance distance [as stated in N.2(1)]. Required clearance is expressed as follows:

Required clearance = lift equipment height or length + load length + at least 3 m (10 ft)

(6) That the local responsible person be notified at least 24 hours before any work begins to allow time to identify voltages and clearances or to place the line in an electrically safe work condition.

N.3 Policy.

All employees and contractors shall conform to the OPP. The first line of defense in preventing electrical contact accidents is to remain outside the limited approach boundary. Because most company and contractor employees are not qualified to determine the system voltage level, a qualified person shall be called to establish voltages and minimum clearances and take appropriate action to make the work zone safe.

N.4 Procedures.

N.4.1 General. Prior to the start of all operations where potential contact with overhead electrical systems is possible, the person in charge shall identify overhead lines or equipment, reference their location with respect to prominent physical features, or physically mark the area directly in front of the overhead lines with safety cones, survey tape, or other means. Electrical line location shall be discussed at a pre-work safety meeting of all employees on the job (through a job briefing). All company employees and contractors shall attend this meeting and require their employees to conform to electrical safety standards. New or transferred employees shall be informed of electrical hazards and proper procedures during orientations.

On construction projects, the contractor shall identify and reference all potential electrical hazards and document such actions with the on-site employers. The location of overhead electrical lines and equipment shall be conspicuously marked by the person in charge. New employees shall be informed of electrical hazards and of proper precautions and procedures.

Where there is potential for contact with overhead electrical systems, local area management shall be called to decide whether to place the line in an electrically safe work condition or to otherwise protect the line against unintentional contact. Where there is a suspicion of lines with low clearance [height under 6 m (20 ft)], the local on-site electrical supervisor shall be notified to verify and take appropriate action.

All electrical contact incidents, including "near misses," shall be reported to the local area health and safety specialist.

N.4.2 Look Up and Live Flags. In order to prevent unintentional contact with all aerial lifts, cranes, boom trucks, service rigs, and similar equipment shall use look up and live flags. The flags are visual indicators that the equipment is currently being used or has been returned to its "stowed or cradled" position. The flags shall be yellow with black lettering and shall state in bold lettering "LOOK UP AND LIVE."

Example Industrial Procedures

The procedure for the use of the flag follows.

(1) When the boom or lift is in its stowed or cradled position, the flag shall be located on the load hook or boom end.

(2) Prior to operation of the boom or lift, the operator of the equipment shall assess the work area to determine the location of all overhead lines and communicate this information to all crews on site. Once completed, the operator shall remove the flag from the load hook or boom and transfer the flag to the steering wheel of the vehicle. Once the flag is placed on the steering wheel, the operator can begin to operate the equipment.

(3) After successfully completing the work activity and returning the equipment to its stowed or cradled position, the operator shall return the flag to the load hook.

(4) The operator of the equipment is responsible for the placement of the look up and live flag.

N.4.3 High Risk Tasks.

N.4.3.1 Heavy Mobile Equipment. Prior to the start of each workday, a high-visibility marker (orange safety cones or other devices) shall be temporarily placed on the ground to mark the location of overhead wires. The supervisors shall discuss electrical safety with appropriate crew members at on-site tailgate safety talks. When working in the proximity of overhead lines, a spotter shall be positioned in a conspicuous location to direct movement and observe for contact with the overhead wires. The spotter, equipment operator, and all other employees working on the job location shall be alert for overhead wires and remain at least 3 m (10 ft) from the mobile equipment.

All mobile equipment shall display a warning decal regarding electrical contact. Independent truck drivers delivering materials to field locations shall be cautioned about overhead electrical lines before beginning work, and a properly trained on-site or contractor employee shall assist in the loading or off-loading operation. Trucks that have emptied their material shall not leave the work location until the boom, lift, or box is down and is safely secured.

N.4.3.2 Aerial Lifts, Cranes, and Boom Devices. Where there is potential for near operation or contact with overhead lines or equipment, work shall not begin until a safety meeting is conducted and appropriate steps are taken to identify, mark, and warn against unintentional contact. The supervisor will review operations daily to ensure compliance.

Where the operator's visibility is impaired, a spotter shall guide the operator. Hand signals shall be used and clearly understood between the operator and spotter. When visual contact is impaired, the spotter and operator shall be in radio contact. Aerial lifts, cranes, and boom devices shall have appropriate warning decals and shall use warning cones or similar devices to indicate the location of overhead lines and identify the 3 m (10 ft) minimum safe working boundary.

N.4.3.3 Tree Work. Wires shall be treated as live and operating at high voltage until verified as otherwise by the local area on-site employer. The local maintenance organization or an approved electrical contractor shall remove branches touching wires before work begins. Limbs and branches shall not be dropped onto overhead wires. If limbs or branches fall across electrical wires, all work shall stop immediately and the local area maintenance organization is to be called. When climbing or working in trees, pruners shall try to position themselves so that the trunk or limbs are between their bodies and electrical wires. If possible, pruners shall not work with their backs toward electrical wires. An insulated bucket truck is the preferred method of pruning when climbing poses a greater threat of electrical contact. Personal protective equipment (PPE) shall be used while working on or near lines.

N.4.4 Underground Electrical Lines and Equipment. Before excavation starts and where there exists reasonable possibility of contacting electrical or utility lines or equipment, the local area supervision (or USA DIG organization, when appropriate) shall be called and a request is to be made for identifying/marking the line location(s).

When USA DIG is called, their representatives will need the following:

(1) Minimum of two working days' notice prior to start of work, name of county, name of city, name and number of street or highway marker, and nearest intersection
(2) Type of work
(3) Date and time work is to begin
(4) Caller's name, contractor/department name and address
(5) Telephone number for contact
(6) Special instructions

Utilities that do not belong to USA DIG must be contacted separately. USA DIG might not have a complete list of utility owners. Utilities that are discovered shall be marked before work begins. Supervisors shall periodically refer their location to all workers, including new employees, subject to exposure.

N.4.5 Vehicles with Loads in Excess of 4.25 m (14 ft) in Height. This policy requires that all vehicles with loads in excess of 4.25 m (14 ft) in height use specific procedures to maintain safe working clearances when in transit below overhead lines.

The specific procedures for moving loads in excess of 4.25 m (14 ft) in height or via routes with lower clearance heights are as follows:

(1) Prior to movement of any load in excess of 4.25 m (14 ft) in height, the local health and safety department, along with the local person in charge, shall be notified of the equipment move.
(2) An on-site electrician, electrical construction representative, or qualified electrical contractor should check the intended route to the next location before relocation.
(3) The new site is to be checked for overhead lines and clearances.
(4) Power lines and communication lines shall be noted, and extreme care used when traveling beneath the lines.
(5) The company moving the load or equipment will provide a driver responsible for measuring each load and ensuring each load is secured and transported in a safe manner.
(6) An on-site electrician, electrical construction representative, or qualified electrical contractor shall escort the first load to the new location, ensuring safe clearances, and a service company representative shall be responsible for subsequent loads to follow the same safe route.

If proper working clearances cannot be maintained, the job must be shut down until a safe route can be established or the necessary repairs or relocations have been completed to ensure that a safe working clearance has been achieved.

All work requiring movement of loads in excess of 4.25 m (14 ft) in height are required to begin only after a general work permit has been completed detailing all pertinent information about the move.

N.4.6 Emergency Response. If an overhead line falls or is contacted, the following precautions should be taken:

(1) Keep everyone at least 3 m (10 ft) away.
(2) Use flagging to protect motorists, spectators, and other individuals from fallen or low wires.
(3) Call the local area electrical department or electric utility immediately.

Example Industrial Procedures

(4) Place barriers around the area.

(5) Do not attempt to move the wire(s).

(6) Do not touch anything that is touching the wire(s).

(7) Be alert to water or other conductors present.

(8) Crews shall have emergency numbers readily available. These numbers shall include local area electrical department, utility, police/fire, and medical assistance.

(9) If an individual becomes energized, DO NOT TOUCH the individual or anything in contact with the person. Call for emergency medical assistance and call the local utility immediately. If the individual is no longer in contact with the energized conductors, CPR, rescue breathing, or first aid should be administered immediately, but only by a trained person. It is safe to touch the victim once contact is broken or the source is known to be de-energized.

(10) Wires that contact vehicles or equipment will cause arcing, smoke, and possibly fire. Occupants should remain in the cab and wait for the local area electrical department or utility. If it becomes necessary to exit the vehicle, leap with both feet as far away from the vehicle as possible, without touching the equipment. Jumping free of the vehicle is the last resort.

(11) If operating the equipment and an overhead wire is contacted, stop the equipment immediately and, if safe to do so, jump free and clear of the equipment. Maintain your balance, keep your feet together and either shuffle or bunny hop away from the vehicle another 3 m (10 ft) or more. Do not return to the vehicle or allow anyone else for any reason to return to the vehicle until the local utility has removed the power line from the vehicle and has confirmed that the vehicle is no longer in contact with the overhead lines.

INFORMATIVE ANNEX O

Safety-Related Design Requirements

This informative annex is not a part of the requirements of this NFPA document but is included for informational purposes only.

> The design of a facility, equipment, or circuit could determine if a work task can be performed safely. In large measure, the facility and circuit design determines whether or how an employee is or might be exposed to an electrical hazard when performing tasks necessary to troubleshoot, repair, or maintain a facility.
>
> The circuit and equipment design determines the amount of incident energy that might be available at various points in the system and whether an electrically safe work condition can be created for sectors of the circuit. The location of components and isolating or insulating barriers determines whether or how an employee might be exposed to shock or electrocution.

O.1 Introduction.

This informative annex addresses the responsibilities of the facility owner or manager or the employer having responsibility for facility ownership or operations management to perform a risk assessment during the design of electrical systems and installations.

O.1.1 This informative annex covers employee safety-related design concepts for electrical equipment and installations in workplaces covered by the scope of this standard. This informative annex discusses design considerations that have impact on the application of the safety-related work practices only.

O.1.2 This informative annex does not discuss specific design requirements. The facility owner or manager or the employer should choose design options that eliminate hazards or reduce risk and enhance the effectiveness of safety-related work practices.

O.2 General Design Considerations.

O.2.1 Employers, facility owners, and managers who have responsibility for facilities and installations having electrical energy as a potential hazard to employees and other personnel should ensure that electrical hazard risk assessments are performed during the design of electrical systems and installations.

O.2.2 Design option decisions should facilitate the ability to eliminate hazards or reduce risk by doing the following:

(1) Reducing the likelihood of exposure
(2) Reducing the magnitude or severity of exposure
(3) Enabling achievement of an electrically safe work condition

△ **O.2.3 Incident Energy Reduction Methods.** The following methods have proved to be effective in reducing incident energy:

(1) Zone-selective interlocking. This is a method that allows two or more circuit breakers to communicate with each other so that a short circuit or ground fault will be cleared by the breaker closest to the fault with no intentional delay. Clearing the fault in the shortest time aids in reducing the incident energy.

(2) Differential relaying. The concept of this protection method is that current flowing into protected equipment must equal the current out of the equipment. If these two currents are not equal, a fault must exist within the equipment, and the relaying can be set to operate for a fast interruption. Differential relaying uses current transformers located on the line and load sides of the protected equipment and fast acting relay.

(3) Energy-reducing maintenance switching with a local status indicator. An energy-reducing maintenance switch allows a worker to set a circuit breaker trip unit to operate faster while the worker is working within an arc flash boundary, as defined in *NFPA 70E*, and then to set the circuit breaker back to a normal setting after the work is complete.

(4) Energy-reducing active arc flash mitigation system. This system can reduce the arcing duration by creating a low impedance current path, located within a controlled compartment, to cause the arcing fault to transfer to the new current path, while the upstream breaker clears the circuit. The system works without compromising existing selective coordination in the electrical distribution system.

(5) Arc flash relay. An arc flash relay typically uses light sensors to detect the light produced by an arc flash event. Once a certain level of light is detected, the relay will issue a trip signal to an upstream overcurrent device.

(6) High-resistance grounding. A great majority of electrical faults are of the phase-to-ground type. High-resistance grounding will insert an impedance in the ground return path and will typically limit the fault current to 10 amperes and below (at 5 kV nominal or below), leaving insufficient fault energy and thereby helping reduce the arc flash hazard level. High-resistance grounding will not affect arc flash energy for line-to-line or line-to-line-to-line arcs.

(7) Current-limiting devices. Current-limiting protective devices reduce incident energy by clearing the fault faster and by reducing the current seen at the arc source. The energy reduction becomes effective for current above the current-limiting threshold of the current-limiting fuse or current limiting circuit breaker.

(8) Shunt-trip. Adding a shunt-trip that is signaled to open from an open-fuse relay to switches 800 amperes and greater reduces incident energy by opening the switch immediately when the first fuse opens. The reduced clearing time reduces incident energy. This is especially helpful for arcing currents that are not within the current-limiting threshold of the three current-limiting fuses.

O.2.4 Additional Safety-by-Design Methods. The following methods have proven to be effective in reducing risk associated with an arc flash or shock hazard:

> The following is a list of commonly used engineering controls to either reduce available current, restrict access to energized conductors and circuit parts, or reduce the likelihood of initiating an arc flash hazard.

Safety-Related Design Requirements

O.2.4

(1) Installing finger-safe components, covers, and insulating barriers reduces exposure to energized parts.

Finger-safe components, often called IP-20 components, make it more difficult to accidentally contact an energized part, thereby reducing the likelihood of receiving an electric shock or creating an arcing fault.

(2) Installing disconnects within sight of each motor or driven machine increases the likelihood the chances that the equipment will be put into an electrically safe work condition before work has begun.

NFPA 70®, National Electrical Code® (*NEC®*), has allowances for a disconnecting means to not be within sight of a motor. However, installing a disconnecting means within sight of a motor increases the probability that an employee will utilize it to put the equipment into an electrically safe work condition.

(3) Installing current limiting cable limiters can help reduce incident energy. Additionally, cable limiters can be used to provide short-circuit protection (and therefore incident energy reduction) for feeder tap conductors that are protected at up to 10 times their ampacity, a situation where the tap conductor can easily vaporize.

(4) Installing inspection windows for noncontact inspection reduces the need to open doors or remove covers.

Infrared and viewing windows eliminate the high-risk task of opening energized electrical equipment when employees perform periodic diagnostic inspections to evaluate the condition of equipment. Eliminating this task reduces the likelihood of initiating an incident.

(5) Installing a single service fused disconnect switch or circuit breaker provides protection for buses that would be unprotected if six disconnect switches are used.

A main disconnecting means provides an easy method to de-energize all but the incoming terminals. The use of the six-disconnect rule permitted by the *NEC* can leave an unprotected, energized bus inside the enclosure. The presence of an unprotected, energized bus increases the likelihood of an employee accidentally contacting the bus or initiating an arc flash incident.

(6) Installing metering to provide remote monitoring of voltage and current levels reduces exposure to electrical hazards by placing the worker farther away from the hazard.

(7) Installing Type 2 "no damage" current limiting protection to motor controllers reduces incident energy whenever the arcing current is within the current limiting threshold of the current-limiting fuse or current-limiting circuit breaker.

In order to achieve Type 2 "no damage" protection of a motor controller, it is generally necessary to utilize overcurrent devices with the highest degree of current limitation. For example, most motor controllers cannot achieve Type 2 protection with Class RK5 fuses. A Class RK1, Class J, or Class CC fuse must be used. This very high degree of current limitation then is also able to reduce incident energy during an arc flash incident, if the fault current is high enough to be within the overcurrent protective device's current-limiting threshold.

(8) Installing adjustable instantaneous trip protective devices and lowering the trip settings can reduce the incident energy.

(9) Installing arc-resistant equipment, designed to divert hot gases, plasma, and other products of an arc-flash out of the enclosure so that a worker is not exposed when standing in front of the equipment with all doors and covers closed and latched, reduces the risk of arc flash exposure.

> When its doors and covers are closed and latched, arc-resistant switchgear provides protection for an employee who is energizing or de-energizing the equipment. Products of an arcing incident are diverted out of the enclosure and away from the employee. Arc-resistant equipment does not protect the worker when the doors and covers are not properly closed and latched.

(10) Installing provisions that provide remote racking of equipment, such as remote-controlled motorized remote racking of a circuit breaker or an MCC bucket, allows the worker to be located outside the arc-flash boundary. An extended length hand-operated racking tool also adds distance between the worker and the equipment, reducing the worker's exposure.

(11) Installing provisions that provide remote opening and closing of circuit breakers and switches could permit workers to operate the equipment from a safe distance, outside the arc flash boundary.

(12) Class C, D, and E special purpose ground fault circuit interrupters exist for circuits operating at voltages outside the range for Class A GFCI protection. See UL 943C for additional information.

> The reader should be aware of the following documents:
> - ANSI/IEEE C37.20.7-2007, *IEEE Guide for Testing Metal-Enclosed Switchgear Rated Up to 38 kV for Internal Arcing Faults*. This guide includes a procedure for testing and evaluating the performance of metal-enclosed switchgear for internal arcing faults. It also includes a method of identifying the capabilities of this equipment and discusses service conditions, installation, and application of equipment.
> - ANSI/IEEE C37.20.7-2007/Cor. 1-2010, *IEEE Guide for Testing Metal-Enclosed Switchgear Rated up to 38 kV for Internal Arcing Faults, Corrigendum 1*. This corrects technical errors found in IEEE C37.20.7-2007 concerning current values and arc initiation in low-voltage testing and supply frequency for equipment used in laboratories.

Aligning Implementation of This Standard with Occupational Health and Safety Management Standards

INFORMATIVE ANNEX P

This informative annex is not a part of the requirements of this NFPA document but is included for informational purposes only.

ANSI/AIHA Z10, *American National Standard for Occupational Health and Safety Management Systems*, defines the minimum basic requirements for an organization's overall occupational health and safety management system. The standard addresses management leadership, employee participation, planning, implementation, evaluation, corrective action, and management review. It covers basic activities such as incident investigation, inspections, and training.

The system in ANSI/AIHA Z10 allows for continual improvement of health and safety management. The standard includes required interrelated processes suitable for continual improvement that align with the Deming Cycle. The Deming Cycle, Plan – Do – Check – Act, or PDCA, is an iterative four-step management process also known as the Shewhart Cycle or PDSA (plan – do – study – act). The Deming Cycle is shown in Exhibit P.1.

PDCA is a successive cycle that starts off from a known base and tests small potential effects on the process, then gradually leads to larger and more targeted change based on a continuous process. The cycle is comprised of the following phases:

- Plan phase — The objectives and processes necessary to deliver results in accordance with the expected output or goal are established.
- Do phase — The new process is implemented on a small scale to test possible effects.
- Check phase — The new process is measured and the results of the Do phase are compared against the expected results to determine any differences.
- Act phase — The differences are analyzed to determine their cause. Under this phase, the changes to be made and where they apply to cause improvements are determined.

When a cycle through these four steps does not result in an improvement, the original base is returned to and the process is tried again until there is a plan that involves improvement.

A fundamental principle of PDCA is reiteration. Reiterating the PDCA cycle brings a company, organization, group, or production area closer to its goals. PDCA needs to be repeated in ever-tightening circles that represent increasing knowledge of the system, ultimately ending on or near the fundamental goals of that system. Small steps from a solid base provide feedback to justify hypotheses and increase understanding of the system being studied. If a small misstep is made, it is easy to repeat the previous iteration. The power of this concept lies in its simplicity. The simple cycle can be continually reapplied to the process in question for improvement.

EXHIBIT P.1

The Deming (PDCA) Cycle.

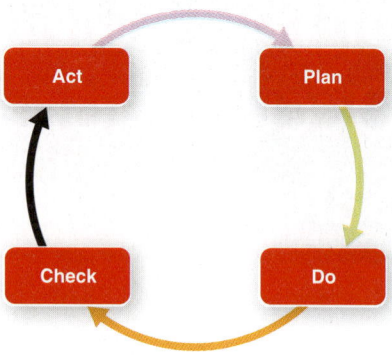

P.1 General.

Injuries from electrical energy are a significant cause of occupational fatalities in the workplace in the United States. This standard specifies requirements unique to the hazards of electrical energy. By itself, however, this standard does not constitute a comprehensive and effective electrical safety program. The most effective application of the requirements of this standard can be achieved within the framework of a recognized health and safety management system standard. ANSI/AIHA Z10, *American National Standard for Occupational Health and Safety Management Systems*, provides comprehensive guidance on the elements of an effective health and safety management system and is one recognized standard. ANSI/AIHA Z10 is harmonized with other internationally recognized standards, including CAN/CSA Z1000, *Occupational Health and Safety Management*; ANSI/ISO 14001, *Environmental Management Systems - Requirements with Guidance for Use*; and BS OSHAS 18001, *Occupational Health and Safety Management Systems*. Some companies and other organizations have proprietary health and safety management systems that are aligned with the key elements of ANSI/AIHA Z10.

The most effective design and implementation of an electrical safety program can be achieved through a joint effort involving electrical subject matter experts and safety professionals knowledgeable about safety management systems.

Such collaboration can help ensure that proven safety management principles and practices applicable to any hazard in the workplace are appropriately incorporated into the electrical safety program.

This informative annex provides guidance on implementing this standard within the framework of ANSI/AIHA Z10 and other recognized or proprietary comprehensive occupational health and safety management system standards.

> According to ANSI/AIHA Z10, a *hazard* is defined as "[a] condition, set of circumstances, or inherent property that can cause injury, illness, or death." *Incident* is defined as "[a]n event in which a work-related injury or illness (regardless of severity) or fatality occurred or could have occurred (commonly referred to as a 'close call' or 'near miss')." *Risk* is defined as "[a]n estimate of the combination of the likelihood of an occurrence of a hazardous event or exposure(s), and the severity of injury or illness that may be caused by the event or exposures."
>
> ANSI/AIHA Z10 outlines the use of a hierarchy of controls — health and safety controls. The hierarchy of health and safety controls offers a methodical approach to reducing the risk associated with a hazard. ANSI/AIHA Z10 lists the following methods of reducing risk, from most effective to least effective: elimination, substitution, engineering controls, warnings, administrative controls, and PPE. Exhibit P.2 provides a graphical representation of the hierarchy of health and safety controls. NFPA *70E* is specifically interested in electrical safety controls.

Aligning Implementation

EXHIBIT P.2

The AIHA hierarchy of health and safety controls.

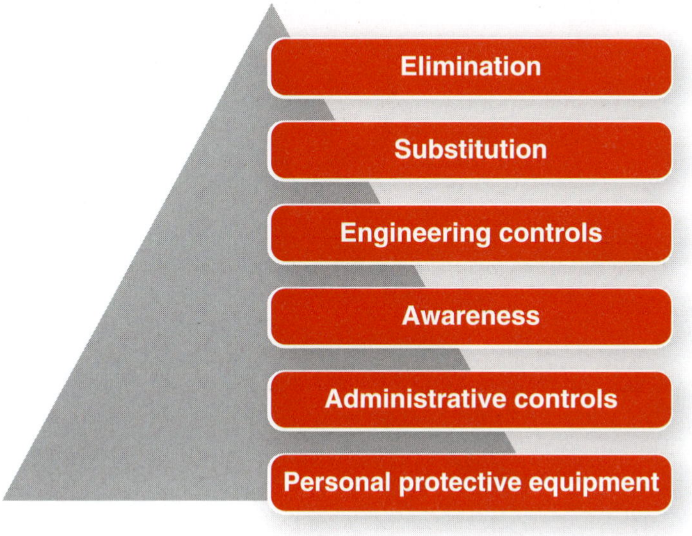

- Elimination
- Substitution
- Engineering controls
- Awareness
- Administrative controls
- Personal protective equipment

> The highest level of practical control should be used. In many cases, it may be found that a combination of controls is the most effective method. This is frequently the case where a higher order control, such as substitution, is not practical or does not reduce the risk to an acceptable level. In this case, a combination of the lower order controls, such as warnings and PPE, may be required when performing tasks such as testing equipment or creating an electrically safe work condition.
>
> The use of arc-resistant switchgear may be considered substitution or an engineering control. Administrative controls include items such as job planning, training, work procedures and practices, temporary barricades, and the like.

Human Performance and Workplace Electrical Safety

INFORMATIVE ANNEX Q

This informative annex is not a part of the requirements of this NFPA document but is included for informational purposes only.

> **Annex Q** introduces the concept of human performance (i.e., human error) and demonstrates how it can be applied to workplace electrical safety. The basic principle of human performance is that humans are fallible — even the best intentioned person errs. The objective of human performance is to identify and address human error and its negative consequences on people, programs, processes, work environment, equipment, or an organization. Risk assessment is a fundamental part of NFPA *70E*. For a risk assessment to be comprehensive it must include organizational, leader, and individual human performance factors that can either lead to or prevent errors and their consequences.

Q.1 Introduction.

This annex introduces the concept of human performance and how this concept can be applied to workplace electrical safety.

Human performance is an aspect of risk management that addresses organizational, leader, and individual performance as factors that either lead to or prevent errors and their events. The objective of human performance is to identify and address human error and its negative consequences on people, programs, processes, the work environment, an organization, or equipment.

Studies by high-risk industries indicate that human error is often a root cause of incidents. The premise of this annex is that human error is similarly a frequent root cause of electrical incidents. In occupational health and safety terms, an incident is an occurrence arising in the course of work that resulted in or could have resulted in an injury, illness, damage to health, or a fatality (see ANSI/AIHA Z10-2012, *Definition of Incident*).

The hierarchy of risk control methods identified in this and other standards is:

(1) Eliminating the hazard
(2) Substituting other materials, processes, or equipment
(3) Using engineering controls
(4) Establishing systems that increase awareness of potential hazards
(5) Setting administrative controls, e.g., training and procedures, instructions, and scheduling
(6) Using PPE, including measures to ensure its appropriate selection, use, and maintenance

The purpose of these controls is to either reduce the likelihood of an incident occurring or to prevent or mitigate the severity of consequence if an incident occurs. No control is infallible. All of the controls are subject to errors in human performance, whether at the design, implementation, or use phase.

Human performance addresses managing human error as a unique control that is complementary to the hierarchy of risk control methods.

N Q.2 Principles of Human Performance.

The following are basic principles of human performance:

(1) People are fallible, and even the best people make mistakes.
(2) Error-likely situations and conditions are predictable, manageable, and preventable.
(3) Individual performance is influenced by organizational processes and values.
(4) People achieve high levels of performance largely because of the encouragement and reinforcement received from leaders, peers, and subordinates.
(5) Incidents can be avoided through an understanding of the reasons mistakes occur and application of the lessons learned from past incidents.

N Q.3 Information Processing and Attention.

The brain processes information in a series of interactive stages:

(1) Attention — where and to what we intentionally or unintentionally direct our concentration.
(2) Sensing — sensory inputs (hearing, seeing, touching, smelling, etc.) receive and transfer information.
(3) Encoding, storage, thinking — incoming information is encoded and stored for later use in decision making (i.e., what to do with information). This stage of information processing involves interaction between the working memory and long-term memory (capabilities, knowledge, past experiences, opinions, and perspectives).
(4) Retrieval, acting — taking physical human action based on the synthesis of attention, sensation, encoded information, thinking, and decision-making. In a workplace environment this would include changing the state of a component using controls, tools, and computers, including verbal statements to inform or direct others.

According to Rasmussen's model used to classify human error, workers operate in one or more of three human performance modes: rule-based mode, skill-based mode, and knowledge-based mode.

Note: See Rasmussen, J. (1983); Skills, rules, and knowledge; signals, signs, and symbols, and other distinctions in human performance models. *IEEE Transactions on Systems, Man, and Cybernetics*, (3), 257-266.

Reason's Human Performance Generic Error Modeling System is an extension of Rasmussen's model. An individual consciously or subconsciously selects a human performance mode based on his or her perception of the situation. This perception is usually a function of the individual's familiarity with a specific task and the level of attention (information processing) applied to accomplish the activity.

Note: See Reason, J. *Human Error*. Cambridge, UK: Cambridge University Press, 1990.

Most cognitive psychologists agree that humans have a limited pool of attentional resources available to divide up among tasks. This pool of shared attentional resources enables the mind to process information while performing one or sometimes multiple tasks. Some tasks require more attentional resources than others. The amount of attentional resource required to perform a task satisfactorily defines the mental workload for an individual and is inversely proportional to the individual's familiarity with the task. An increase in knowledge, skill, and experience with a task decreases the level of attentional resources required to perform that task and therefore decreases the level of attentional resource allocated to that task.

Critical points in activities when risk is higher (increased likelihood of harm or increased severity of harm, or both) require an increased allocation of attentional resources. Allocation at these critical points can be improved by training, procedures, equipment design, and teamwork.

Each human performance mode has associated errors. Awareness of which human performance mode the individual might be in helps identify the kind of errors that could be made and which error prevention techniques would be the most effective.

N Q.4 Human Performance Modes and Associated Errors.

N Q.4.1 Rule-Based Human Performance Mode.

N Q.4.1.1 General. An individual operates in rule-based human performance mode when the work situation is likely to be one that he or she has encountered before or has been trained to deal with, or which is covered by a procedure. It is called the rule-based mode because the individual applies memorized or written rules. These rules might have been learned as a result of interaction at the workplace, through formal training, or by working with experienced workers.

The level of required attentional resources when in the rule-based mode fits between that of the knowledge- and skill-based modes. The time devoted to processing the information (reaction time) to select an appropriate response to the work situation is in the order of seconds.

The rule-based level follows an *IF* (symptom X), *THEN* (situation Y) logic. The individual operates by matching the signs and symptoms of the situation to some stored knowledge structure, and will usually react in a predicable manner.

In human performance theory, rule-based is the most desirable performance mode. The individual can use conscious thinking to challenge whether or not the proposed solution is appropriate. This can result in additional error prevention being integrated into the solution.

Not all activities guided by a procedure are necessarily executed in rule-based mode. An experienced worker might unconsciously default to the skill-based mode when executing a procedure that is normally done in the rule-based mode.

N Q.4.1.2 Rule-Based Human Performance Mode Errors. Since the rule-based human performance mode requires interpretation using an "if-then" logic, misinterpretation is the prevalent type error mode. Errors involve deviating from an approved procedure, applying the wrong response to a work situation, or applying the correct procedure to the wrong situation.

N Q.4.2 Knowledge-Based Human Performance Mode.

N Q.4.2.1 General. A worker operates in knowledge-based human performance mode when there is uncertainty about what to do; no skill or rule is readily identifiable. The individual relies on their understanding and knowledge of the situation and related scientific principles and fundamental theory to develop an appropriate response. Uncertainty creates a need for information. To gather information more effectively, the individual's attentional resources become more focused. Thinking takes more effort and energy, and the time devoted to processing the information to select an appropriate response to the situation can be in the order of minutes to hours.

Q.4.2.2 Knowledge-Based Human Performance Mode Errors. The prevalent error when operating in knowledge-based mode is that decisions are often based on an inaccurate mental picture of the work situation. Knowledge-based activities require decision making based on diagnosis and problem-solving. Humans do not usually perform optimally in high-stress, unfamiliar situations where they are required to "think on their feet" in the absence of rules, routines, and procedures to handle the situation. The tendency is to use only information that is readily available to evaluate the situation and to become enmeshed in one aspect of the problem to the exclusion of all other considerations. Decision-making is erroneous if problem-solving is based on incomplete or inaccurate information.

Q.4.3 Skill-Based Human Performance Mode.

Q.4.3.1 General. A person is in skill-based mode when executing a task that involves practiced actions in a very familiar and common situation. Human performance is governed by mental instructions developed by either practice or experience and is less dependent on external conditions. The time devoted to processing the information is in the order of milliseconds. Writing one's signature is an example of skill-based performance mode. A familiar workplace procedure is typically performed in skill-based performance mode, such as the operation of a low-voltage molded case circuit breaker.

Q.4.3.2 Skill-Based Human Performance Mode Errors. The relatively low demand on attentional resources required when an individual is in skill-based human performance mode can create the following errors:

(1) Inattention: Skill-based performance mode errors are primarily execution errors involving omissions triggered by human variability, or not recognizing changes in task requirements or work conditions related to the task.
(2) Perceived reduction in risk: As familiarity with a task increases, the individual's perception of the associated risk is less likely to match actual risk. A perceived reduction in risk can create "inattentional blindness" and insensitivity to the presence of hazards.

Q.5 Error Precursors. Error precursors are situations when the demands of the task and the environment it is performed in exceed the capabilities of the individual(s) or the limitations of human nature. Error precursors can also be unfavorable conditions that increase the probability for error during a specific action. Error precursors can be grouped into four broad categories.

(1) Task demands – when specific mental, physical, or team requirements to perform a task either exceed the capabilities or challenge the limitations of the individual assigned to the task.
(2) Work environment – when general influences of the workplace, organizational, and cultural conditions affect individual performance.
(3) Individual capabilities – when an individual's unique mental, physical, and emotional characteristics do not match the demands of the specific task.
(4) Human nature – when traits, dispositions, and limitations common to all persons incline an individual to err under unfavorable conditions.

Table Q.5 provides a list of specific examples for each category.
When error precursors are identified and addressed then the likelihood of human error is reduced.

N TABLE Q.5 Error Precursor Identification and Human Performance Tool Selection (see Q.5 and Q.6.1)

Error precursors	Optimal tool(s)	Human performance tools
Task Demands Time pressure (in a hurry) High workload (memory requirements) Simultaneous or multiple tasks Repetitive actions or monotony Critical steps or irreversible acts Interpretation requirements Unclear goals, roles, or responsibilities Lack of or unclear standards **Work Environment** Distractions/interruptions Changes/departures from routine Confusing displays or controls Workarounds/out of service instrumentation Obscure electrical supplies or configurations Unexpected equipment conditions Lack of alternative indication Personality conflicts **Individual Capabilities** Unfamiliar with, or first time performing task Lack of knowledge (faulty mental model) New technique not used before Imprecise communication habits Lack of proficiency or experience Indistinct problem-solving skills Unsafe attitudes for critical task Inappropriate values **Human Nature** Stress (limits attention) Habit patterns Assumptions Complacency/overconfidence Mind-set Inaccurate risk perception Mental shortcuts (biases) or limited short-term memory		**1 Pre-job briefing** Identify hazards, assess risk and select and implement risk controls from a hierarchy of methods **2 Job site review** Increased situational awareness **3 Post-job review** Identify ways to improve and best practices Peer check **4 Procedure use and adherence** Step-by-step procedure read, outcome understood Circle the task to be performed, check off each task as it is completed **5 Self-check with verbalization** Stop, Think, Act, Review (STAR) Verbalize intent before, during, and after each task **6 Three-way communication** Directives are repeated by receiver back to sender; receiver is acknowledged by sender Use of the phonetic alphabet for clarity **7 Stop when unsure** Stop and obtain further direction when unable to follow a procedure or process step or if something unexpected occurs Maintain a questioning attitude **8 Flagging and blocking** Identify (flag) equipment and controls that will be operated Prevent access (block) equipment and controls that should not be operated

Notes: This Table may be utilized when identifying workplace hazards. Identify the error precursors in the left-hand column. Select the optimal human performance tool or combination of tools from the right-hand column. List the selected tool(s) in the centre column beside the associated error. This Table does not include all possible human performance tools; however, all tools listed can be applied to each error precursor.

Q.6 Human Performance Tools.

Q.6.1 Application. Human performance tools reduce the likelihood of error when applied to error precursors. Consistent use of human performance tools by an organization will facilitate the incorporation of best practice work. The following are some human performance tools. See Table Q.5 for a list of these tools.

Q.6.2 Job Planning and Pre-job Briefing Tool *[see 110.1(H)]*. Creating a job plan and conducting pre-job briefing assists personnel to focus on the performance of the tasks and to understand their roles in the execution of the tasks.

The following is a graded approach that can be used when job planning to identify error precursors and select an appropriate human performance tool, or combination of tools, proportionate to the potential consequences of error:

(1) Summarize the critical steps of the job that, if performed improperly, will cause irreversible harm to persons or equipment, or will significantly impact operation of a process.
(2) Anticipate error precursors for each critical step.
(3) Foresee probable and worst-case consequences if an error occurs during each critical step.
(4) Evaluate controls or contingencies at each critical step to prevent, catch, and recover from errors and to reduce their consequences.
(5) Review previous experience and lessons learned relevant to the specific task and critical steps.

If one or more human performance tools are identified, then each tool should be discussed regarding its advantages, disadvantages, and when and how it should be applied.

Q.6.3 Job Site Review Tool. Incorporating a job site review into job planning facilitates the identification of hazards and potential barriers and delays. A job site review can be performed any time prior or during work.

Q.6.4 Post-Job Review Tool. A post-job review is a positive opportunity to capture feedback and lessons learned from the job that can be applied to future jobs. The use of or lack of use of human performance tools should be incorporated into the review.

The pre-job briefing and the post-job review are effective communication tools.

Q.6.5 Procedure Use and Adherence Tool. Adhering to a written step-by-step sequential procedure is a human performance tool. The worker should proactively read and understand the purpose, scope, and intent of all actions as written and in the sequence specified.

An accurate and current account of progress should be kept by marking each step in the procedure as it is completed. This ensures that if the procedure is interrupted before all the steps are completed, the job site or activity can be left in a safe state and the procedure can be resumed at the point it was interrupted.

If the procedure cannot be used as written, or if the expected result cannot be accurately predicted, then the activity should be stopped and the issues resolved before continuing.

An example of adhering to a written step-by-step sequential procedure is a switching sequence, wherein the sequential order of operation of electrical distribution equipment is identified and documented for the purposes of de-energizing and re-energizing.

Q.6.6 Self-Check with Verbalization Tool. The self-check with verbalization tool is also known by the acronym STAR – Stop, Think, Act, and Review. Before, during, and after performing a task that cannot be reversed, the worker should stop, think, and openly verbalize their actions. Verbalizing permits the individual's brain to slow down to their body speed. It has the effect of keeping the individual focused, thus enabling them to act and then review their actions.

Example: A worker has one more routine task to complete before the end of shift — to approach a group of motor control panels and close a circuit breaker in one of those panels. The error precursors are task demands (in a hurry) and human nature (complacency). If the worker verbalizes each step in the task and the expected outcome of each step, he or she is less likely to operate the wrong circuit breaker and will be prepared in the event that the outcome of an action does not match the expectation. For example, the worker self checks and verbalizes:

(1) I am at Panel 12 Bravo (12B).
(2) I am about to close Circuit Breaker 4 Bravo (4B).
(3) The pump motor heater indicator light will engage bright red on Panel 10 Bravo (10B).
(4) The pump motor should not start.
(5) If the pump motor starts then I will open Circuit Breaker 4 Bravo.
(6) I am now closing Circuit Breaker 4 Bravo.

N Q.6.7 Three-Way Communication Tool. The three-way communication tool facilitates a mutual understanding of the message between the sender and receiver. After a directive or statement is made by the sender, it is repeated by the receiver to confirm the accuracy of the message.

When the message includes the use of letters, then whenever possible the letters should be communicated using the phonetic alphabet.

Example: A sender issues a directive over a radio communication device: "Close circuit breaker 4 Bravo." The receiver repeats the message: "I understand, close circuit breaker 4 Bravo." The sender validates that the proper response was understood: "That is correct" or "Affirmative."

N Q.6.8 Stop When Unsure Tool. When a worker is unable to follow a procedure or process step, if something unexpected occurs or if the worker has a "gut feeling" that something is not right, then the worker should stop and obtain further direction. The "stop when unsure" tool requires that the worker maintain a questioning attitude at all times.

Phrases such as "I think" or "I'm pretty sure," whether verbalized or not, indicate that the worker is in knowledge-based mode and needs to transition to rule-based mode. This transition should be communicated to co-workers.

N Q.6.9 Flagging and Blocking Tools *[(see 130.7(E)]*. Flagging is a method to ensure the correct component is manipulated or worked on at the required time under the required conditions. A flag could be a marker, label, or device.

It should be used when an error-likely situation or condition is present, such as one of the following:

(1) Similar or "look-alike" equipment
(2) Work on multiple components
(3) Frequent operations performed in a short period of time
(4) Interruption of process critical equipment

Blocking is a method of physically preventing access to an area or equipment controls.

Hinged covers on control buttons or switches, barricades, fences or other physical barriers, whether temporary or permanent, are examples of blocking tools.

Blocking can be used in conjunction with flagging.

N Q.7 Human Performance Warning Flags.

N Q.7.1 General. There are common process, organizational, supervisory, and worker performance weaknesses that serve as human performance warning flags. These warning flags should be identified by the organization and action should be taken to address the root cause.

N Q.7.2 Program or Process. The following are program or process human performance warning flags:

(1) Risk management processes are over-relied on, instead of personal ownership and accountability for managing risk.
(2) Risk management processes are inefficient or cumbersome ("more" is often not better).

N Q.7.3 Organizational Performance. The following are organizational human performance warning flags:

(1) Personnel in the organization tend to engage in consensus or group thinking, without encouraging counterview points.
(2) Personnel overly defer to managers and perceived experts.
(3) Activities with high risk are not assigned clear owners.
(4) Past success without adverse outcomes becomes the basis for continuing current practices.
(5) The organization assumes that risk management is healthy because a program or process was established (i.e., complacency exists).

N Q.7.4 Supervisory Performance. The following are supervisory human performance warning flags:

(1) Delegation is lacking, with a few individuals relied on to make major decisions.
(2) Supervision is physically or mentally separated from the job site and is insufficiently aware of current conditions and attitudes.
(3) Personnel in the organization do not understand how risk is perceived and managed at the worker level.
(4) Past success without adverse outcomes becomes the basis for continuing current practices.
(5) Performance indicators are used to justify existing risk management strategies.

N Q.7.5 Worker Performance. The following are worker human performance warning flags:

(1) Individuals or groups exhibit self-imposed production pressure.
(2) Work activities are considered routine.
(3) Individuals are quick to make risky judgments without taking the time to fully understand the situation.
(4) Past success without adverse outcomes becomes the basis for continuing current practices.
(5) Personnel take pride in their ability to work through or with levels of risk that could have been mitigated or eliminated.
(6) Risk is not communicated effectively up the company. Individuals assume that the next level of supervision knows or understands the risk involved or that there are insufficient resources to manage the risk.
(7) Problem reporting is not transparent. Individuals are not willing to report high-risk conditions.

N Q.8 Workplace Culture.

N Q.8.1 General. The reduction or elimination of electrical incidents requires that all members at the workplace cultivate and consistently exhibit a culture that supports the use of human performance tools and principles. Workers, supervisors, and managers must all work together to implement strong human performance practices.

N Q.8.2 Workers. The safe performance of activities by workers is a product of mental processes influenced by factors related to the work environment, the task demands, and the capabilities of the worker. All need to take responsibility for their actions and strive to improve themselves, the task at hand, and the work environment. Five general practices that should be consistently demonstrated by workers include the following:

(1) Communication to support a consistent understanding
(2) Anticipation of error-likely situations and conditions
(3) Desire to improve personal capabilities
(4) Reports on all incidents (including "near-miss" incidents)
(5) A commitment to utilize human performance tools and principles

N Q.8.3 Supervisors and Managers. Through their actions, supervisors focus worker and team efforts in order to accomplish a task. To be effective, supervisors must understand what influences worker performance. Supervisors promote positive outcomes into the workplace environment to encourage desired performance and results. Supervisors must demonstrate a passion for identifying and preventing human performance errors. They influence both individual and company performance in order to achieve high levels of workplace electrical safety. Five general practices that should be consistently demonstrated by supervisors include the following:

(1) Promote open communication
(2) Encourage teamwork to eliminate error-likely situations and conditions
(3) Seek out and eliminate broader company weaknesses that may create opportunity for error
(4) Reinforce desired workplace culture
(5) Recognize the value in preventing errors, reporting of near-miss incidents, and the utilization of human performance tools and principles

N Q.8.4 The Organization. It is important that an organization's procedures, processes, and values recognize and accept that people make mistakes. The policies and goals of an organization influence worker and supervisor performance. Five general practices that should be consistently demonstrated by an organization include the following:

(1) Promote open communication
(2) Foster a culture that values error prevention and the use of human performance tools
(3) Identify and prevent the formation of error-likely situations and conditions
(4) Support continuous improvement and learning across the entire organization
(5) Establish a blame-free culture that supports incident reporting and proactively identifies and reacts appropriately to risk

PART 2

Supplements

The three supplements included in Part 2 of the *Handbook for Electrical Safety in the Workplace* provide additional information as well as supporting reference material to assist users of NFPA *70E*®, *Standard for Electrical Safety in the Workplace*®. These supplements are not part of the NFPA *70E* standard.

Supplement 1 *National Electrical Code*® Requirements Associated with Safety-Related Work Practices

Supplement 2 Electrical Preventive Maintenance Programs

Supplement 3 Typical Safety Procedure (Procedure for Selection, Inspection, and Care of Rubber Insulating Gloves and Leather Protectors)

SUPPLEMENT 1

National Electrical Code Requirements Associated with Safety-Related Work Practices

Editor's Note: *This supplement consists of a list of requirements from the 2017 edition of NFPA 70®, National Electrical Code® (NEC®), that directly impact the implementation of safety-related work practices from NFPA 70E®, Standard for Electrical Safety in the Workplace®. This list is not intended to be all-inclusive of applicable NEC requirements for any indicated equipment. Although the requirements are listed and categorized as applicable to an employee, employer, or electrical system designer, the employer and designer must be aware of each requirement.*

NEC Requirements for Employees

These requirements are those that should be identifiable to employees when they are put at risk of injury from the use of electricity.

Disconnecting Means and Where to Find Them

225.31	Feeders passing through the building or structure	426.50	Fixed outdoor deicing and snow-melting equipment
225.32	Location for outside feeders	427.55	Fixed electric pipeline or vessel heating equipment
225.33	Maximum number of outside feeder disconnects	430.75	Motor control circuits
225.34	Grouping of outside feeder disconnects	430.102	Motor controller
225.51	Isolating switches for outside feeders	430.111	Switch or circuit breaker as both controller and disconnecting means
225.52	Outside feeders over 1000 volts		
240.40	Fuses	430.112	Motors served by single disconnecting means
410.130	Electric-discharge lighting systems of 1000 volts or less	430.113	Motors with energy from more than one source
410.141	Luminaires or lamp installation	430.227	Motor controller over 1000 volts, nominal
422.30	Appliances	440.14	Air-conditioning or refrigerating equipment
422.31	Permanently connected appliances	440.63	Single-phase room air conditioner
424.19	Fixed electric space-heating equipment	450.14	Transformers
424.20	Thermostatically controlled switching devices	455.9	Phase converter connection of single-phase loads
424.65	Duct heater controller equipment		
425.19	Fixed industrial process heating equipment	455.20	Utilization equipment — phase converters
425.65	Duct heater controller equipment	480.7	Stationary battery system over 60 volts dc

Supplement 1

Disconnecting Means and Where to Find Them (Continued)

514.13	Provisions for maintenance and service of fuel dispensing equipment	669.8	Electroplating, anodizing, electropolishing, and electrostripping
525.21(A)	Rides, tents, and concessions	670.4(B)	Industrial machinery
547.9	Electrical supply to agricultural building(s) or structure(s)	680.13	Swimming, wading, therapeutic, and decorative pools; fountains; hot tubs; spas; and hydromassage bathtubs
555.17	Shore power connections		
590.4(E)	Temporary circuits disconnecting means	690.13	Building or other structure supplied by a photovoltaic system
600.6(A)	Signs and outline lighting systems		
610.32	Cranes and monorail hoists	690.15	Photovoltaic equipment
620.51	Elevator, dumbwaiter, escalator, moving walk, platform lift, or stairway chairlift	692.17	Fuel cell system
		694.22	Wind electric systems
620.52	Single-car and multicar elevator	694.24	Wind electric system equipment
620.53	Elevator car light, receptacle(s), and ventilation	694.26	Wind electric systems — fuses
		695.4(B)	Electric motor–driven fire pumps
620.54	Elevator heating and air-conditioning	705.21	Power production equipment
620.55	Elevator utilization equipment	705.20	Interconnected electric power production sources
625.43	Electric vehicle charging		
630.13	Arc welder	705.22	Interconnected electric power production sources
630.33	Resistance welder and control equipment		
660.5	X-ray equipment	706.7	Energy storage systems
660.24	Multi x-ray equipment independent control	712.34	Direct current microgrids
665.12	Dielectric heating, induction heating, induction melting, and induction welding equipment	712.35	Solidly grounded two- and three-wire direct current microgrid systems
668.13	Direct-current cell line		

Working Space Necessary to Conduct Tasks Safely

110.26	Access and working space for electrical equipment	480.10(C)	Stationary storage battery systems
110.30	Working space for electrical equipment over 1000 volts, nominal	530.62	Television and motion picture studio portable substations
		620.5	Elevators, dumbwaiters, escalators, moving walks, platform lifts, and stairway chairlifts
110.32	Access and work space for electrical equipment over 1000 volts, nominal		
		646.20	Modular data centers
110.34	Equipment likely to require examination, adjustment, servicing, or maintenance while energized	646.21	Modular data center battery systems
		646.22	Routine service and maintenance — modular data center
425.8(B)	Fixed resistance and electrode industrial process heating equipment	668.10	Electrolytic cell line working zone
		706.10	Energy storage system battery locations

Guarding Employees from Injury

110.4	Enclosure for electrical systems	230.62	Service equipment — enclosed or guarded
110.25	Locking requirements for disconnecting means	240.41	Guarded or isolated arcing or suddenly moving parts
110.27	Guarding of live parts operating at 50 to 1000 volts, nominal	408.20	Location of switchboards and switchgear
		410.5	Live parts of luminaires, portable luminaires, lampholders, and lamps
110.33	Entrance to enclosures and access to working space		
		422.4	Appliances — live parts
110.75	Access to manholes	426.12	Outdoor electric deicing and snow-melting equipment — thermal protection
110.76	Access to vaults and tunnels		

NEC Requirements for Employees

Guarding Employees from Injury (Continued)

427.12	Pipeline and vessel heating equipment — thermal protection
427.25	Pipeline and vessel heating equipment — personnel protection
427.36	Pipeline and vessel heating equipment induction coils — personnel protection
430.232	Guarding exposed live parts of motors and controllers
430.233	Motors — guards for attendants
445.14	Generator — protection of live parts
445.15	Generators — guards for attendants
450.8	Transformers — guarding
450.13	Transformers — accessibility
460.2	Capacitors — enclosing and guarding
470.18(B)	Resistors and reactors — isolated by enclosure or elevation
480.10(B)	Stationary storage battery locations
490.21(B)	Power fuses and fuse holders — equipment operating at more than 1000 volts, nominal
490.21(D)	Oil-filled cutout requirements
490.32	Guarding of high-voltage energized parts within a compartment
490.33	Guarding of energized parts operating at 1000 volts, nominal, or less within compartments
490.35	Accessibility of energized parts operating at more than 1000 volts, nominal
490.42	Interlocks — interrupter switches operating at more than 1000 volts, nominal
490.45	Circuit breaker interlocks operating at more than 1000 volts, nominal
490.46	Circuit breaker operating at more than 1000 volts, nominal — locking
490.53	Enclosures for equipment operating at more than 1000 volts, nominal
490.55	Power cable connections to mobile machines operating at more than 1000 volts, nominal
525.10(A)	Services for carnivals, circuses, fairs, and similar functions
590.7	Temporary wiring over 600 volts, nominal — guarding
620.4	Elevators, dumbwaiters, escalators, moving walks, platform lifts, and stairway chairlifts — live parts enclosed
620.71	Elevators, dumbwaiters, escalators, moving walks, platform lifts, and stairway chairlifts — guarding equipment
665.22	Induction and dielectric heating equipment — access to internal equipment
706.34(A)	Energy storage system battery locations — live parts

Identifying Hazards and Other Identification Requirements

110.15	Four-wire, delta-connected system high-leg marking
110.16	Arc flash hazard warning
110.22	Disconnecting means
200.6	Grounded conductors
210.5	Branch circuits
215.12	Feeders
225.30	Outside feeders — number of supplies
225.37	Services, feeders, or branch circuits supplying building or structure
408.3(F)	Switchboard, switchgear, or panelboard
408.4	Switchboard, switchgear, or panelboard circuit directory
409.110	Industrial control panel marking
424.86	Electrode-type boiler markings
425.86	Fixed industrial process electrode-type boilers markings
490.25	Backfeed of equipment operating at more than 1000 volts, nominal
665.23	Induction and dielectric heating equipment warning labels or signs
690.56	Solar photovoltaic (PV) systems — identification of power sources
692.56	Fuel cell system — stored energy
694.50	Interactive system point of interconnection
694.52	Wind electric systems employing energy storage
694.54	Wind electric systems — identification of power sources
700.7	On-site emergency power source signs
701.7	On-site legally required standby power source signs
702.7	On-site optional standby power source signs
705.10	Electric power production sources directory
705.12(B)	Electric power production sources — load side of service disconnect
706.11	Energy storage system directory

Supplement 1

NEC Requirements for Employers

These requirements are those that an employer must ensure are applied to reduce the risk of an electrical injury to an employee.

Responsibility for Installation

90.1	NEC purpose	400.12	Flexible cords and flexible cables uses not permitted
90.4	Enforcement of the NEC	400.13	Flexible cords and flexible cables splices
90.7	Examination of equipment for safety	400.17	Flexible cords and flexible cables protection from damage
110.2	Equipment approval	400.36	Flexible cords and flexible cables splices and terminations
110.3	Examination, identification, installation, and use of equipment	406.10(E)	Grounding-type attachment plugs
210.8	Ground-fault circuit-interrupter protection for personnel	410.82	Portable luminaire wiring
225.56	Inspections and tests for outside branch circuits and feeders	450.48	Storage in vaults
250.34	Portable and vehicle-mounted generator grounding electrodes	522.7	Permanent amusement attraction maintenance
250.188	Grounding of systems supplying portable or mobile equipment	590.3	Temporary electric power and lighting installation time constraints
400.10	Flexible cords and flexible cables uses permitted	590.6	Temporary wiring installation ground-fault protection for personnel

Disconnecting Means

230.70	Service	409.22	Industrial control panel short-circuit current rating
230.71	Maximum number of service disconnects	424.21	Switch and circuit breaker to be indicating type
230.72	Grouping of service disconnects	430.103	Open all ungrounded supply conductors
230.74	Simultaneous opening of poles of all ungrounded service conductors	430.128	Adjustable-speed drive systems
230.77	Indicating the open (off) or closed (on) position	460.8(C)	Capacitor bank
230.82	Equipment permitted to be connected to the supply side of service disconnect	460.24(B)	Isolation of capacitor, capacitor bank
230.91	Location of service overcurrent device	490.22	Isolating means for equipment over 1000 volts, nominal
230.92	Service overcurrent devices accessible to the occupant,	490.39	Gas discharge from interrupting devices
230.200	Services exceeding 1000 volts, nominal	490.40	Visual inspection windows for equipment over 1000 volts, nominal
230.204	Isolating switches for oil switches or air, oil, vacuum, or sulfur hexafluoride circuit breakers	490.45	Circuit breakers — interlocks for equipment over 1000 volts, nominal
230.205	Service disconnecting means	490.51(D)	Mobile and portable high-voltage equipment
240.24	Location for service disconnecting means exceeding 1000 volts, nominal	692.13	Fuel cell systems
404.6	Position and connection of single-throw knife switches	665.7	Induction and dielectric heating equipment remote control
404.7	General-use and motor-circuit switches, circuit breakers, and molded case switches indicating open (off) or closed (on) position	669.8	Electroplating
		694.20	Wind electric systems
		694.28	Installation and service of a wind turbine
		705.20	Electric power production source
404.8	Accessibility and grouping of switches and circuit breakers used as switches	705.23	Interactive system

NEC Requirements for Designers

Working Space

110.31	Enclosure for electrical installations over 1000 volts, nominal	425.8	Fixed industrial process heating equipment
110.70	Manholes and other electrical enclosures intended for personnel entry	610.57	Cranes and hoists
110.74	Conductors installed in manholes and other enclosures intended for personnel entry	680.9	Overhead conductor clearances for swimming pools, fountains, and similar installations

Equipment Marking

110.21	Equipment marking requirement	490.48	Substation design, documentation, and required diagram for equipment over 1000 volts, nominal
110.24	Service equipment available fault current		
230.56	Service conductor with the higher voltage to ground	692.54	Fuel cell systems fuel shut-off
		694.56	Instructions for disabling turbine

NEC Requirements for Designers

These requirements are those that an electrical system designer must apply to reduce the risk of an electrical injury to an employee.

110.9	Interrupting rating of equipment intended to interrupt current at fault levels	240.8	Fuses or circuit breakers in parallel
		240.12	Electrical system coordination
110.10	Overcurrent protective device circuit impedance, short-circuit current ratings, and other characteristics	240.82	Nontamperable circuit breaker
		240.86	Series ratings
110.72	Cabling work space	240.67	Arc energy reduction — fuses
110.73	Equipment work space	240.87	Arc energy reduction — circuit breakers
210.13	Branch circuit ground-fault protection of equipment	250.6	Grounding arrangement to prevent objectionable current
215.5	Diagram of feeders		
215.10	Feeder ground-fault protection of equipment	430.74	Electrical arrangement of control circuits
225.18	Outside branch circuit and feeder clearance for overhead conductors and cables	440.12	Hermetic refrigerant motor-compressor disconnecting means rating and interrupting capacity
225.19	Outside branch circuit and feeder clearances from buildings for conductors of not over 1000 volts, nominal	440.13	Cord-connected air-conditioning and refrigerating equipment
225.60	Outside branch circuit and feeder clearances over roadways, walkways, rail, water, and open land	460.6	Capacitors — discharge of stored energy
		460.28	Capacitor — means for discharge
225.61	Outside branch circuit and feeder clearances over buildings and other structures	490.21	Circuit-interrupting devices for equipment over 1000 volts, nominal
230.2	Number of services	490.48	Substation design, documentation, and required diagram
230.3	One building or other structure not to be supplied through another	517.17	Ground-fault protection for hospitals, and other buildings with Category 1 spaces or utilizing electrical life-support equipment
230.9	Service conductor clearances on buildings		
230.24	Service conductor clearances		
230.26	Service point of attachment	690.7	PV system dc circuits maximum voltage
230.75	Disconnection of service grounded conductor	700.31	Ground-fault protection of equipment for alternate source for emergency systems
230.76	Manually or power operable service disconnecting means	701.26	Ground-fault protection of equipment for alternate source legally required standby systems
230.95	Ground-fault protection of equipment		

SUPPLEMENT 2

Electrical Preventive Maintenance Programs

> **Editor's Note:** *This supplement contains extracts from Chapters 4, 5, and 6 of the 2016 edition of NFPA 70B, Recommended Practice for Electrical Equipment Maintenance. Entire sections of NFPA 70B are not included in all cases. Associated commentary explains the subject of the referenced sections. Refer to NFPA 70B for the full text of each section and chapter.*

NFPA 70B provides detailed information on the maintenance of electrical equipment. Chapter 4 explains the benefits of an electrical preventative maintenance program, and Chapters 5 and 6 provide specific information on how to set up a maintenance program. Scheduled maintenance tends to be systematic and orderly, while breakdown maintenance is often performed under stressful conditions that could tempt workers to take dangerous safety shortcuts.

Businesses can no longer tolerate equipment failures as a signal that maintenance of equipment is necessary. Just-in-time (JIT) manufacturing and Six Sigma programs dictate an effective preventive maintenance program that ensures continuity of operations and prevents equipment breakdowns. Breakdowns affect quality and production schedules, but they also disrupt customers' supply chains. JIT falls apart when suppliers cannot perform.

CHAPTER 4 Why an Effective Electrical Preventive Maintenance (EPM) Program Pays Dividends

4.1 Why EPM?

4.1.1 Electrical equipment deterioration is normal, and equipment failure is inevitable. However, equipment failure can be delayed through appropriate EPM. As soon as new equipment is installed, a process of normal deterioration begins. Unchecked, the deterioration process can cause malfunction or an electrical failure. Deterioration can be accelerated by factors such as a hostile environment, overload, or severe duty cycle. An effective EPM program identifies and recognizes these factors and provides measures for coping with them.

4.1.2 In addition to normal deterioration, other potential causes of equipment degradation can be detected and corrected through EPM. Among these are load changes or additions, circuit alterations, improperly set or improperly selected protective devices, and changing voltage conditions.

4.1.3 Without an EPM program, management assumes a greatly increased risk of a serious electrical failure and its consequences.

4.2 Value and Benefits of a Properly Administered EPM Program.

4.2.1 A well-administered EPM program reduces accidents, saves lives, and minimizes costly breakdowns and unplanned shutdowns of production equipment. Impending troubles can be identified — and solutions applied — before they become major problems requiring more expensive, time-consuming solutions.

4.2.2 Benefits of an effective EPM program fall into two general categories. Direct, measurable economic benefits are derived from reduced cost of repairs and reduced equipment downtime. Less measurable but very real benefits result from improved safety. To understand fully how personnel and equipment safety are served by an EPM program, the mechanics of the program — inspection, testing, and repair procedures — should be understood. Such an understanding explains other intangible benefits such as improved employee morale, better workmanship and increased productivity, reduced absenteeism, reduced interruption of production, and improved insurance considerations. Improved morale comes with employee awareness of a conscious management effort to promote safety by reducing the likelihood of electrical injuries or fatalities, electrical explosions, and fires. Reduced personnel injuries and property loss claims can help keep insurance premiums at favorable rates.

4.2.3 Some of the benefits that result from improved safety are difficult to measure. However, direct and measurable economic benefits can be documented by equipment repair cost and equipment downtime records after an EPM program has been implemented.

4.2.4 Dependability can be engineered and built into equipment, but effective maintenance is required to keep it dependable. Experience shows that equipment is reduced when it is covered by an EPM program. In many cases, the investment in EPM is small compared with the cost of accidents, equipment repair, and the production losses associated with unexpected outages.

4.2.5 Careful planning is the key to the economic success of an EPM program. With proper planning, maintenance costs can be held to a practical minimum, while production is maintained at a practical maximum.

4.2.6 An EPM program requires the support of top management, because top management provides the funds that are required to initiate and maintain the program. The maintenance of industrial electrical equipment is essentially a matter of business economics. Maintenance costs can be placed in either of two basic categories: preventive maintenance or breakdown repairs. The money spent for preventive maintenance will be reflected as less money required for breakdown repairs. An effective EPM program holds the sum of these two expenditures to a minimum.

4.2.7 An EPM program is a form of protection against accidents, lost production, and loss of profit. An EPM program enables management to place a monetary value on the cost of such protection. An effective EPM program satisfies an important part of management's responsibility for keeping costs down and production up.

CHAPTER 5   What Is an Effective Electrical Preventive Maintenance (EPM) Program?

5.1 Introduction. An effective electrical preventive maintenance (EPM) program should enhance safety and also reduce equipment failure to a minimum consistent with good economic judgment.

5.2 Essential Elements of an EPM Program. An EPM program should consist of the following essential elements:

Electrical Preventive Maintenance Programs

Supplement 2

(1) Responsible and qualified personnel
(2) Regularly scheduled inspection, testing, and servicing of equipment
(3) Survey and analysis of electrical equipment and systems to determine maintenance requirements and priorities
(4) Programmed routine inspections and suitable tests
(5) Accurate analysis of inspection and test reports so that proper corrective measures can be prescribed
(6) Performance of necessary work
(7) Concise but complete records

> NFPA 70B contains detailed information about each of these elements. A survey and analysis of essential equipment will evaluate its operating parameters and current condition to determine any necessary repair as well as the nature and frequency of required inspection and testing. Analysis of the inspection reports requires follow-through with necessary repairs, replacement, and adjustment for an effective electrical preventive maintenance (EPM) program. A facility might not have qualified personnel to perform the maintenance duties, and qualified contractors may be necessary to follow the EPM program. Programmed inspection and testing may require coordination between maintenance and production to schedule outages of production equipment under the maintenance program. Records should be kept not only of the condition and repair of equipment but also of the training and skills of the employee conducting the maintenance.

5.3 Planning an EPM Program. The following factors should be considered in the planning of an EPM program.

(1) *Personnel Safety*: Will an equipment failure endanger or threaten the safety of any personnel? What can be done to ensure personnel safety?
(2) *Equipment Loss*: Is installed equipment — both electrical and mechanical — complex or so unique that required repairs would be unusually expensive?
(3) *Production Economics*: Will breakdown repairs or replacement of failed equipment require extensive downtime? How many production dollars will be lost in the event of an equipment failure? Which equipment is most vital to production?

> A plan that prioritizes essential equipment will determine how, where, and when each piece fits into the maintenance program. An effective EPM program needs to consider not only equipment loss but the economics of lost production and the impact of an equipment failure on employee safety.
> Effective EPM programs begin with good design. A conscious effort to ensure optimum maintainability should be part of the design of new facilities. For example, auxiliary power sources can make it easier to schedule and perform maintenance work with minimal interruption of production.

CHAPTER 6 Planning and Developing an Electrical Preventive Maintenance (EPM) Program

6.1 Introduction.

6.1.1 The purpose of an EPM program is to reduce hazard to life and property resulting from the failure or malfunction of electrical systems and equipment. This chapter explains the planning and development considerations that can be used to establish such a program.

6.1.2 The following four basic steps should be taken in the planning and development of an EPM program:

(1) Compile a listing of all equipment and systems.
(2) Determine which equipment and systems are most critical.
(3) Develop a system for monitoring.
(4) Determine the internal and/or external personnel needed to implement and maintain the EPM program.

6.1.5 The work center of each maintenance work group should be conveniently located. This work center should contain the following:

(1) Copies of all the inspection and testing procedures for that zone
(2) Copies of previous reports
(3) Single-line diagrams
(4) Schematic diagrams
(5) Records of complete nameplate data
(6) Vendors' catalogs
(7) Facility stores' catalogs
(8) Supplies of report forms

6.2 Survey of Electrical Installation.

6.2.1 Data Collection.

6.2.1.1 The first step in organizing a survey should be to examine available resources. Will the available personnel permit the survey of an entire system, process, or building, or should it be divided into segments?

6.2.1.2 Where the project will be divided into segments, a priority should be assigned to each segment. Segments found to be related should be identified before the actual work commences.

6.2.1.3 The third step should be the assembling of all documentation. This might necessitate a search of desks, cabinets, computers, and such, and might also require that manufacturers be contacted, to replace lost documents. All of the documents should be centralized, controlled, and maintained. The documentation should include recommended practices and procedures for some or all of the following:

(1) Installation
(2) Disassembly/assembly (interconnections)
(3) Wiring diagrams, schematics, bills of materials
(4) Operation (set-up and adjustment)
(5) Maintenance (including parts list and recommended spares)
(6) Software program (if applicable)
(7) Troubleshooting

6.2.2 Diagrams and Data. The availability of up-to-date, accurate, and complete diagrams is the foundation of a successful EPM program. The diagrams discussed in 6.2.2.1 through 6.2.2.8.2 are some of those in common use.

Electrical Preventive Maintenance Programs

> Single line, circuit-routing, and schematic diagrams are just a few of the diagrams discussed in 6.2.2. These diagrams assist maintenance personnel by providing information such as equipment ratings, the physical location of conductors and equipment, and access points for raceways or pull boxes. The manufacturer's service manuals and instructions are also important for the diagrams and recommended practices and procedures. Another important aspect of the EPM program is that equipment installation changes be highlighted and noted or revised in an appropriate manner to keep the documentation current.

6.2.3 System Diagrams. System diagrams should be provided to complete the data being assembled. The importance of the system determines the extent of information shown. The information can be shown on the most appropriate type of diagram but should include the same basic information, source and type of power, conductor and raceway information, and switching and protective devices with their physical locations. It is vital to show where the system might interface with another system, such as with emergency power; hydraulic, pneumatic, or mechanical systems; security and fire-alarm systems; and monitoring and control systems. Some of the more common of these are described in 6.2.3.1 through 6.2.3.3.

> System diagrams for lighting; heating, ventilation, and air-conditioning; and control and monitoring are also important. Lighting diagrams may show lighting that is used for night security personnel or the location of emergency lighting. Diagrams for ventilation systems should show the interface with other systems, such as for smoke removal. Control and monitoring systems are often complicated, and the diagram should describe how these systems function. The referenced sections of NFPA 70B provide further information on these system diagrams.

6.2.5 Test and Maintenance Equipment.

6.2.5.1 All maintenance work requires the use of proper tools and equipment to properly perform the task to be done. In addition to their ordinary tools, maintenance personnel (such as carpenters, pipe fitters, and machinists) use special tools or equipment based on the nature of the work to be performed. The electrician is no exception, but for EPM, special-use tools should be readily available. The size of the facility, the nature of its operations, and the extent of its maintenance, repair, and test facilities are all factors that determine the use frequency of the equipment. Economics seldom justify purchasing an infrequently used, expensive tool when it can be rented. However, a corporation having a number of facilities in the area might well justify common ownership of the same device for joint use, making it quickly available at any time to any facility. Typical examples might be high-current test equipment, infrared thermography equipment, or a ground-fault locator.

6.2.5.2 Because a certain amount of mechanical maintenance is often a part of the EPM program being conducted on associated equipment, the electrical maintenance personnel should have ready access to such items as the following:

(1) Assorted lubrication tools and equipment
(2) Various types and sizes of wrenches
(3) Nonmetallic hammers and blocks to protect against injury to machined surfaces
(4) Feeler gauges to function as inside- and outside-diameter measuring gauges
(5) Instruments for measuring torque, tension, compression, vibration, and speed
(6) Standard and special mirrors with light sources for visual inspection
(7) Industrial-type portable blowers and vacuums having insulated nozzles for removal of dust and foreign matter

(8) Nontoxic, nonflammable cleaning solvents
(9) Clean, lint-free wiping cloths

6.2.5.3 The use of well-maintained safety equipment is essential and should be mandatory for work on energized electrical conductors or circuit parts. Prior to performing maintenance on energized electrical conductors or circuit parts, NFPA *70E* should be used to identify the degree of personal protective equipment (PPE) required. Some of the more important equipment that should be provided includes the following:

(1) Heavy leather gloves
(2) Insulating gloves, mats, blankets, baskets, boots, jackets, and coats
(3) Insulated hand tools such as screwdrivers and pliers
(4) Nonmetallic hard hats with suitable arc-rated face protection
(5) Poles with hooks and hot sticks to safely open isolating switches

> Paragraphs 6.2.5.4 through 6.2.5.9 of NFPA 70B further describe various test and maintenance equipment.

6.3 Identification of Critical Equipment.

6.3.1 Equipment (electric or otherwise) should be considered critical if its failure to operate normally and under complete control will cause a serious threat to people, property, or the product. Electric power, like process steam, water, and so forth, might be essential to the operation of a machine, but unless loss of one or more of these supplies causes the machine to become hazardous to people, property, or production, that machine might not be critical. The combined knowledge and experience of several people might be needed to make this determination. In a small facility, the facility engineer or master mechanic working with the operating superintendent should be able to make this determination.

> Section 6.3 describes some systems or segments of systems that may be critical to the operation of a facility. The equipment's relation to the entire operation and the effect of its loss on safety and production should be considered. An entire system may be critical but due to its size or complexity may be segmented.

6.4 Establishment of a Systematic Program. The purpose of any inspection and testing program is to establish the condition of equipment to determine what work should be done and to verify that it will continue to function until the next scheduled servicing occurs. Inspection and testing are best done in conjunction with routine maintenance. In this way, many minor items that require no special tools, training, or equipment can be corrected as they are found. The inspection and testing program is probably the most important function of a maintenance department in that it establishes what should be done to keep the system in service to perform the function for which it is required.

> Several aspects of an installation can have an impact on the frequency of inspection and testing. Section 6.4 points out that the atmosphere or environment, as well as the load the equipment is operating under, should be taken into consideration for the EPM program. For example, dust may impede a motor's ability to dissipate heat, or a motor designed for continuous operation but installed with an intermittent load could overheat the motor windings. Section 6.4 also expands on considerations for inspection frequencies, such as for equipment operating continuously or considered critical.

Electrical Preventive Maintenance Programs

6.5 Methods and Procedures.

6.5.1 General.

6.5.1.1 If a system is to operate without failure, not only should the discrete components of the system be maintained, but the connections between these components also should be covered by a thorough set of methods and procedures. Overlooking this important link in the system causes many facilities to suffer high losses every year.

6.5.1.2 Other areas where the maintenance department should develop its own procedures are shutdown safeguards, interlocks, and alarms. Although the individual pieces of equipment can have testing and calibrating procedures furnished by the manufacturer, the equipment application is probably unique, so the system should have an inspection and testing procedure developed.

> Section 6.5 breaks methods and procedures into five categories: forms and reports, planning, analysis of safety procedures, records, and emergency procedures. Forms can come in many varieties, and Section 6.5 lists items that should be included on a form. Some examples of forms for inspection, testing, and repair are provided in Annex H of NFPA 70B. The planning stage is where the scheduling of the inspections can be set to reduce production downtime. Many details involved in setting safety procedures are beyond the scope of NFPA 70B. Nonetheless, general considerations are covered in Section 6.5. Records are important to provide a method of evaluating the results of the EPM program, including the cost not only of the program but of the estimated cost of business interruption. Lastly, Section 6.5 recognizes the need for maintenance personnel to be prepared for emergencies.

6.8 Outsourcing of Electrical Equipment Maintenance.

6.8.1 General. This section describes the process for a facility to request the services of qualified contractors to perform maintenance on electrical equipment.

6.8.2 Contract Elements. Elements in a contract for outsourcing electrical maintenance service are to include, but are not limited to, the following:

(1) Define project scope of work, what is included and not included, along with equipment specifications on any new or replacement parts, and the time period(s) in which the activities are to be performed.
(2) Determine if it is a performance-based or detailed (step-by-step) specification.
(3) Determine which safety and maintenance codes and standards are to be followed, including appropriate permits.
(4) Determine methodology for pricing: lump sum or unit price.
(5) Determine the qualifications of potential contractors and develop and maintain a list of such.
(6) Obtain appropriate liability, insurance coverage, and warranty information.
(7) Assemble the appropriate up-to-date and accurate facility and equipment specific documents, such as, but not limited to, the following:
    (a) Facility one line diagrams
    (b) Facility layout drawings showing location of substations and major facility electrical equipment
    (c) Facility equipment list (if facility drawings show equipment, facility drawings may be used in lieu of specific equipment lists)

(d) Equipment manufacturers' requirements (these include equipment service manuals, equipment drawings, etc.)

(e) Risk assessment, short circuit analysis, and time-current coordination studies

(8) Conduct a pre-bid/negotiation walk through with the potential contractor.

(9) Conduct a post-work walk-through to verify proper completion of scope of work, and review written report from the contractor on findings and recommendations, as applicable.

> Often facilities do not have qualified personnel to conduct inspections, tests, or repairs of all or some of the equipment installed. NFPA *70E* provides guidance on host and contractor relationships from the worker safety aspect. NFPA 70B addresses items that should be included in a service contract for outsourced equipment maintenance.

SUPPLEMENT 3

Typical Safety Procedure (Procedure for Selection, Inspection, and Care of Rubber Insulating Gloves and Leather Protectors)

Editor's Note: *To help users to develop their own safety procedures, this supplement describes a typical safety procedure regarding a common subject in an electrical safety program — rubber insulating gloves and leather protectors. This procedure illustrates the type of information and format that can be used to develop an electrical safety procedure. Users must develop a method for identifying their procedures so that each electrical safety procedure is uniquely identified. This sample is provided for reference only, to illustrate the types of information that should comprise a typical safety procedure.*

Supplement 3

Title: Procedure for Selection, Inspection, and Care of Rubber Insulating Gloves and Leather Protectors	Doc. ID No.: ESP.100.000.003.01 Page: 001 of 010	
Eff. Date: 10/23/2017	Revision No.: 001 Revision Date: 10/06/2017	Supersedes: N/A
Reviewer: MK Rev. Date: 10/05/2017	Approved by: MDF Approval Date: 10/05/2017	Covers: All Personnel Within Restricted Approach Boundary

1.0 **Purpose:** The purpose of this procedure is to detail the selection, inspection, and care requirements for rubber insulating gloves and leather protectors.

2.0 **Scope:** This procedure covers all rubber insulating gloves regardless of Class and Type.

3.0 **Revision History:** This is the first revision and is a general upgrade.

4.0 **Background:** This procedure is required to meet Occupational Safety and Health Administration (OSHA) regulations and the requirements contained in NFPA *70E*®.

5.0 **Definitions:**

5.1 Class. A rubber insulating glove *class* defines the maximum ac rms and dc use values in volts and the ac rms and dc proof test voltage values to be used in volts. There are six voltage classes as follows:

  a. 00, 0, 1, 2, 3, and 4, with cuff labels colored beige, red, white, yellow, green, and orange, respectively.

5.2 Work Instruction. A work instruction tells the reader the necessary steps and the order in which the steps are to be taken to safely perform the required task, and is action oriented.

  a. Each step is stated simply in a clear and concise manner that is easy to read and understand.
  b. Work instructions can be prepared using an outline type format, a flow chart format, a playscript format, or a question and answer format.
  c. The format selected is to be the one that is best suited for the situation.

5.3 Type. A rubber insulating glove *type* defines whether the material is ozone (natural) resistant – Type I, or non-ozone (synthetic) resistant – Type II.

6.0 **Work Instructions:**

6.1 Cleaning:

  a. General:

    1) Cleaning should be done under good lighting conditions.
    2) Cleaning can uncover damage that may be hidden under soiled surfaces as contamination may mask color or hide defects.
    3) Cleaning removes contaminants (chemicals) that are less obvious or cannot be seen but that can degrade rubber such as fertilizers, herbicides, and pesticide residues.
    4) Contaminants may be conductive, especially when wet.
    5) Regular cleaning is good practice.

This sample is for illustrative purposes only. Users should develop their own safety procedures.

Typical Safety Procedure

Supplement 3

Title: Procedure for Selection, Inspection, and Care of Rubber Insulating Gloves and Leather Protectors		Doc. ID No.: ESP.100.000.003.01
		Page: 002 of 010
Eff. Date: 10/23/2017	Revision No. : 001	Supersedes: N/A
	Revision Date: 10/06/2017	
Reviewer: MK	Approved by: MDF	Covers: All Personnel Within Restricted Approach Boundary
Rev. Date: 10/05/2017	Approval Date: 10/05/2017	

    b. Hands Prior to Inspection, Handling, or Use:

       1) Prior to wearing or handling rubber insulating gloves or leather protectors, hands are to be cleaned using a non-petroleum based hand cleaner or towelettes made specifically for workers who wear rubber gloves.

       2) The cleaner is to be capable of dissolving and removing grease, oil, ink, tar, pipe dope, creosote, paint, etc., without harming natural or synthetic rubber.

       3) The cleaner is to be capable of cleaning hands with or without water.

       4) Workers should be aware that the cleaner may contain skin conditioners or perfume.

       5) Only approved hand cleaner is to be used.

       6) Approved hand cleaner for those using rubber insulating gloves or leather protectors is to be obtained from inventory control.

    c. Rubber Insulating Gloves:

       1) Prior to inspection or use, as necessary, rubber insulating gloves should be cleaned to ensure that only clean gloves are used.

       2) Rubber insulating gloves are generally to be cleaned by washing with a mild soap and water combination.

       3) The label area may be cleaned using soapy water or denatured alcohol.

       4) After washing, the gloves are to be thoroughly rinsed with water.

       5) Finally, the gloves are to be air-dried in an area away from direct sunlight and other sources (ozone) and where the temperature is less than 120°F (49°C).

       6) The cleaning is to be done, as necessary, prior to use to ensure that only clean gloves are used.

       7) The mild soap to be used is to be a concentrated detergent with a special grease release formula that removes oils, grease, and dirt from both natural and synthetic rubber.

       8) Only an approved cleaner for use on rubber insulating gloves obtained from inventory control is to be used.

6.2 Use of Sunscreen:

    a. Only approved sunscreen is to be used.

    b. If sunscreen is used by those handling or using rubber insulating gloves and leather protectors, it must be of a non-oily type that leaves no residue or slippery hands.

    c. It must be of a type made specifically for use with rubber protectors and rubber insulating gloves (e.g., it must be safe for use with leather protectors and rubber insulating gloves).

    d. Approved sunscreen for those using or handling rubber insulating gloves and leather protectors is to be obtained from inventory control.

6.3 Determine that the rubber insulating gloves have an adequate voltage rating (class) for the nominal system voltage.

    a. This is done by examining the glove label and the NFPA *70E* equipment label.

    b. Verify that the glove class is suitable for the maximum possible rms voltage in accordance with the ANSI C84.1 "B" range, based on nominal system voltage designated on the NFPA *70E* equipment label and the location of use within the system:

This sample is for illustrative purposes only. Users should develop their own safety procedures.

Title: Procedure for Selection, Inspection, and Care of Rubber Insulating Gloves and Leather Protectors		Doc. ID No.: ESP.100.000.003.01
		Page: 003 of 010
Eff. Date: 10/23/2017	Revision No. : 001	Supersedes: N/A
	Revision Date: 10/06/2017	
Reviewer: MK	Approved by: MDF	Covers: All Personnel Within Restricted Approach Boundary
Rev. Date: 10/05/2017	Approval Date: 10/05/2017	

      1) 508 V for a 480 V nominal system at the service location

   c) Refer to the Electrical Safety Procedure (ESP) on *Matching Rubber Insulating Goods to Nominal System Voltage at Point of Use* for further information.

6.4 Use only properly sized gloves:

   a. Glove size is measured by using a soft tape measure.
   b. Measure the dominant hand around the palm, not including the thumb, at its widest point in inches and the distance from the base of the palm to the tip of the index finger in inches of the dominant hand.
   c. The glove size is the longer of the above two measurement taken to the closest ½ inch above the measured value (e.g., 8" = 8, 8¼" = 8.5). Gloves come in sizes from 7 to 11 inches depending on the class, type, and length specified.
   d. If cotton glove liners are used, the glove size is to be increased one half-size (e.g., for 8.5, use 9).

6.5 Each rubber insulating glove is labeled in a color denoting the "class" and the maximum voltage the glove can be used for as indicated in the following table:

Class	Label Color[1]	Proof Test Voltage		Max. Use Voltage	
N/A	N/A	ac (rms)	dc	ac (rms)[2]	dc[2]
00	Beige	2,500	10,000	500	750
0	Red	5,000	20,000	1,000	1,500
1	White	10,000	40,000	7,500	11,250
2	Yellow	20,000	50,000	17,000	25,500
3	Green	30,000	60,000	26,500	39,750
4	Orange	40,000	70,000	36,000	54,000

Notes:

1. Rubber insulating gloves are to have a color-coded label that meets the requirements contained in ASTM D120.
2. Maximum use voltage when worn with leather protectors.

6.6 Verify that the rubber insulating gloves are the right type (category) for the use location (e.g., ozone resistant or non-ozone resistant):

   a. Type I – natural rubber – non-ozone resistant – indoor use
   b. Type II – synthetic – ozone resistant – outdoor or indoor use
   c. Where Type I gloves are used in outdoor locations, the amount of time they are exposed to sunlight (ozone) is to be minimized.

This sample is for illustrative purposes only. Users should develop their own safety procedures.

Typical Safety Procedure

Supplement 3

Title: Procedure for Selection, Inspection, and Care of Rubber Insulating Gloves and Leather Protectors		Doc. ID No.: ESP.100.000.003.01 Page: 004 of 010
Eff. Date: 10/23/2017	Revision No. : 001 Revision Date: 10/06/2017	Supersedes: N/A
Reviewer: MK Rev. Date: 10/05/2017	Approved by: MDF Approval Date: 10/05/2017	Covers: All Personnel Within Restricted Approach Boundary

6.7 The following table and notes indicate a breakdown of rubber insulating gloves that are generally available:

Breakdown of Generally Available Rubber Insulating Gloves[1]					
Class	Length in. (mm)[2]	Type[3]	Cuff Type[4]	Color[5,6]	Sizes[7,8]
00	11 (279), 14 (356)	I	SC	R, B	7, 8, 8H, 9, 9H, 10, 10H, 11, 12
00	11 (279), 14 (356)	II	SC	BL, BLO	7, 8, 8H, 9, 9H, 10, 10H, 11, 12
0	11 (279), 14 (356)	I	SC	R, B, Y, BY	7, 8, 8H, 9, 9H, 10, 10H, 11, 12
0	11 (279), 14 (356)	II	SC	BL, BLO	7, 8, 8H, 9, 9H, 10, 10H, 11, 12
1	14 (356), 16 (406), 18 (457)	I	SC, BC, CC	B, YB, RB	7, 8, 8H, 9, 9H, 10, 10H, 11, 12
2	14 (356), 16 (406), 18 (457)	I	SC, BC, CC	B, YB, RB	7, 8, 8H, 9, 9H, 10, 10H, 11, 12
3	14 (356), 16 (406), 18 (457)	I	SC, BC, CC	B, YB, RB	7, 8, 8H, 9, 9H, 10, 10H, 11, 12
4	14 (356), 16 (406), 18 (457)	I	SC, BC, CC	B, YB, RB	9, 9H, 10, 10H, 11, 12

Notes:

1. This chart is intended to provide guidance on the types of rubber insulating gloves that are generally available. The various manufacturers and suppliers of rubber insulated gloves and leather protectors should be consulted to determine the types and characteristics of gloves that are readily available.
2. Contour cuff (CC) gloves are available only on 18 in. (457 mm) gloves.
3. Type I equals natural rubber, which is non-ozone resistant; Type II equals synthetic rubber, which is ozone resistant.
4. Rubber insulating gloves come in one of three types of cuffs styles — straight cuff, contour cuff, or bell cuff:
   a. SC equals straight cuff, which is the default cuff style.
   b. CC equals a contour cuff, which is angled to prevent bunching or binding at the elbow when bent, and is only available on 18 in. gloves.
   c. BC equals a bell cuff, which accommodates heavier winter clothing and allows for greater air flow in warmer weather.

This sample is for illustrative purposes only. Users should develop their own safety procedures.

Title: Procedure for Selection, Inspection, and Care of Rubber Insulating Gloves and Leather Protectors		Doc. ID No.: ESP.100.000.003.01 Page: 005 of 010
Eff. Date: 10/23/2017	Revision No. : 001 Revision Date: 10/06/2017	Supersedes: N/A
Reviewer: MK Rev. Date: 10/05/2017	Approved by: MDF Approval Date: 10/05/2017	Covers: All Personnel Within Restricted Approach Boundary

Notes (continued):

5. Color code is as follows:
   a. R equals Red.
   b. B equals Black.
   c. Y equals Yellow.
   d. O equals Orange.
   e. RB equals Red on the inside and Black on the outside.
   f. YB equals Yellow on the inside and Black on the outside.
   e. BLO equals Blue inner color and Orange outer color.

6. The contrast between the outer color and the inner color makes inspection for cuts and tears easier when the glove is inflated or stretched.
7. Bell cuff (BC) gloves are not available in sizes 7, 8, or 8H.
8. The H in the size designation stands for a half (½) size.

6.8 Verify that the voltage insulation certification is still current:

   a. Check the marked test date and issue date or expiration date, as appropriate, to confirm that glove voltage insulation certification is still current.
   b. Rubber insulating gloves must be issued from inventory by inventory control within 1 year of the date they are voltage tested or they must be retested, and they must be retested no later than 6 months after issue.
   c. The gloves must be returned to inventory control to be sent for retesting at the time their replacement is obtained.

6.9 Ensure that hand jewelry, or other objects which could damage the gloves, are removed prior to inspection or use of the gloves.

6.10 Perform a visual inspection prior to each use, paying particular attention to the body of the glove, between the fingers, and each finger, inspecting both the inside surface and the outside surface for:

   a. Holes
   b. Rips
   c. Tears
   d. Cuts
   e. Cracks
   f. Punctures
   g. Snags
   h. Ozone cutting, checking, cracking, breaks, or pitting
   i. UV checking
   j. Embedded material, such as wire or metal shavings, that could cause punctures
   k. Textural changes, such as the following:

This sample is for illustrative purposes only. Users should develop their own safety procedures.

Title: Procedure for Selection, Inspection, and Care of Rubber Insulating Gloves and Leather Protectors		Doc. ID No.: ESP.100.000.003.01 Page: 006 of 010
Eff. Date: 10/23/2017	Revision No. : 001 Revision Date: 10/06/2017	Supersedes: N/A
Reviewer: MK Rev. Date: 10/05/2017	Approved by: MDF Approval Date: 10/05/2017	Covers: All Personnel Within Restricted Approach Boundary

      1) Swelling
      2) Softening
      3) Hardening
      4) Stickiness
      5) Inelasticity

  l. Oil contamination

  m. Other such defects that may damage the insulating properties

    Note: Surface irregularities may be present on all rubber goods because of imperfections on forms or molds or because of inherent difficulties in the manufacturing process. They may appear as indentations, protuberances or imbedded foreign materials that are acceptable under the following conditions:

      1) The indentation or protuberance blends into a smooth slope when the material is stretched.
      2) Foreign material remains in place when the insulating material is folded and stretches with the insulating material surrounding it.

    If defects are found that cannot be rectified, cut a finger off of each glove and turn into inventory control for proper disposal.

6.11 Perform an air leak test to test for punctures for each glove that may not be caught by the visual inspection by one of the following means or methods:

  a. Inflating gloves makes checking for cuts, tears, or ozone easier.
  b. The roll test:

      1) Hold the glove downward and grasp the cuff.
      2) Roll the glove cuff tightly, forcing air into the palm and finger area.
      3) Apply pressure to the various areas of the glove.
      4) Hold the glove close to the face and ear to listen for or feel leaking air from holes while the glove is inflated and pressure applied.

  c. Check for air leaks by means of a glove inflator:

      1) Inflate the glove following the instructions included with the glove inflator.
      2) Hold the glove close to the face and ear to listen for or feel leaking air from holes in the inflated glove.

  d. Do not over inflate:

      1) Type I – natural rubber – maximum of 1.5 times normal
      2) Type II – synthetic rubber – maximum of 1.25 times normal

This sample is for illustrative purposes only. Users should develop their own safety procedures.

Title: Procedure for Selection, Inspection, and Care of Rubber Insulating Gloves and Leather Protectors		Doc. ID No.: ESP.100.000.003.01 Page: 007 of 010
Eff. Date: 10/23/2017	Revision No. : 001 Revision Date: 10/06/2017	Supersedes: N/A
Reviewer: MK Rev. Date: 10/05/2017	Approved by: MDF Approval Date: 10/05/2017	Covers: All Personnel Within Restricted Approach Boundary

    6.12 Use leather protectors over rubber insulating gloves:

        a. Leather protectors must be sized for the rubber insulating gloves (e.g., size 10 for size 10).
        b. Perform a visual inspection of the leather protectors, checking for

            1) Cuts
            2) Tears
            3) Rips
            4) Abrasions
            5) Holes
            6) Contaminants, such as oil or petroleum products, or
            7) Other such damage
            8) If damaged discard by cutting off at least one glove finger on each glove and turn into in inventory control
            9) Leather protectors are not to be used as work gloves and work gloves are not to be used as leather protectors

    6.13 Verify that the distance between the end of the cuff of the rubber insulating glove and the cuff of the leather protector is not less than the distance required by ASTM F496, as shown in the following table:

Class	Distance (inches)
00	½
0	½
1	1
2	2
3	3
4	4

    6.14 Use of Glove Liners and Glove Dust:

        a. Only approved glove liners of an appropriate material, such as cotton, cotton with Lycra, or wool blends with substantial wool content, can be used for perspiration control or to provide additional warmth.
        b. Glove liners come only in one size (e.g., one size fits all).
        c. Glove liners can have a knit or straight cuff.
        d. Where glove liners are used, glove size is required to be increased one half (½) size.
        e. Only approved glove dust may be used to control perspiration.
        f. Do not use talc, baby powder, or similar products as they may contain acids and dyes that can cause the rubber insulating gloves to deteriorate.
        g. The glove dust is to be a type suggested or approved by the manufacturer of the gloves.
        h. Only approved glove liners are to be used, and they are to be obtained from inventory control.
        i. Only approved glove dust is to be used, and it may be obtained from inventory control.

This sample is for illustrative purposes only. Users should develop their own safety procedures.

Typical Safety Procedure

Supplement 3

Title: Procedure for Selection, Inspection, and Care of Rubber Insulating Gloves and Leather Protectors	Doc. ID No.: ESP.100.000.003.01 Page: 008 of 010
Eff. Date: 10/23/2017	Revision No.: 001 Revision Date: 10/06/2017	Supersedes: N/A
Reviewer: MK Rev. Date: 10/05/2017	Approved by: MDF Approval Date: 10/05/2017	Covers: All Personnel Within Restricted Approach Boundary

    j. The request to inventory control is to indicate whether the liners are to be used for perspiration control or warmth. The request may be made for more than one pair of glove liners.

    k. Damaged or soiled glove liners are not be used.

    l. Damaged glove liners must have a finger cut off and be returned to inventory control for replacement.

    m. The cleaner is to be diluted in accordance with the manufacturer's instructions prior to use and applied by means of a clean rag or sponge obtained from inventory control.

    n. Only cleaners tested for compatibility with the type of rubber compound employed in accordance with ASTM D471 and ASTM F496 are to be used.

6.15 Properly store:

    a. Store in a canvas storage bag with ventilation holes in bottom for proper ventilation.

    b. Do not store more than a single pair of rubber insulating gloves or leather protectors in a single bag that has a storage compartment for only one glove.

        1) Where the rubber insulating glove manufacturer permits, leather protectors may be stored over rubber insulating gloves inside a single glove bag storage compartment.

    c. Bags with multiple storage compartments designed to store more than one pair of gloves may be used to store both the rubber insulating gloves and the leather protectors.

    d. Store rubber insulating gloves with the cuffs down and the fingers up.

    e. Ensure that gloves lay flat in the bag.

    f. Store only in properly sized canvas storage bag(s).

    g. Do not store inside out, as storing inside out strains the rubber severely and promotes early ozone cutting.

    h. Do not allow gloves to be stored in a folded condition, as folds and creases strain rubber and cause it to crack from ozone prematurely.

    i. Do not store near sources of heat; store in cool, dry areas only.

6.16 Follow the manufacturer's instructions regarding inspection, storage, and use.

6.17 Training:

    a. Employees are to receive training on the proper use, care, storage, and replacement of rubber insulating gloves prior to issue of their first pair. This training is to include at least the following:

        1) How to determine proper size
        2) How to determine proper voltage class
        3) How to determine proper glove category
        4) How to determine the certification is current
        5) How to properly inspect prior to use
        6) How to clean properly
        7) How to store properly
        8) How to take damaged gloves out of service properly
        9) How to request a new or replacement pair of rubber insulating gloves

This sample is for illustrative purposes only. Users should develop their own safety procedures.

Title: Procedure for Selection, Inspection, and Care of Rubber Insulating Gloves and Leather Protectors		Doc. ID No.: ESP.100.000.003.01 Page: 009 of 010	
Eff. Date: 10/23/2017	Revision No.: 001 Revision Date: 10/06/2017		Supersedes: N/A
Reviewer: MK Rev. Date: 10/05/2017	Approved by: MDF Approval Date: 10/05/2017		Covers: All Personnel Within Restricted Approach Boundary

    b. After training, the employee must demonstrate to the satisfaction of the trainer that the employee is competent in the above procedures.

    c. The training, the content of the training, and demonstrated ability are to be documented for each employee.

    d. This training is to be done on at least a yearly basis or any time it is determined that an employee is failing to comply with this procedure.

6.18 Rubber insulating gloves, leather protectors, and glove liners must conform to company specifications.

7.0 **Responsibilities:**

    a. Supervisors are responsible for seeing that this procedure is followed and enforced.

    b. Trainers are responsible for seeing:

        1) That workers are properly trained
        2) That workers show demonstrated ability in the selection, use, and care of rubber insulating gloves and leather protectors
        3) That training is properly documented

8.0 **References:**

    a. Company specifications:

        1) Specifications for rubber insulating gloves
        2) Specifications for leather protectors
        3) Specifications for cotton glove liners
        4) Specifications for canvas carrying bags for rubber insulating gloves
        5) Specifications for cleaning products for rubber insulating goods

    b. Governmental standards:

        1) Occupational Safety and Health Administration (OSHA):

            a). 29 CFR 1910.137, *Occupational Safety and Health Standards, Personal Protective Equipment, Electrical Protective Devices*

    c. Industry standards:

        1) American Society of Testing and Materials (ASTM):

            a) ASTM D120, *Standard Specification for Rubber Insulating Gloves*
            b) ASTM F496, *Standard Specification for In-Service Care of Insulating Gloves and Sleeves*
            c) ASTM F696, *Standard Specification for Leather Protectors for Insulating Gloves and Mittens*
            d) ASTM F2675, *Test Method For Determining Arc Ratings of Hand Protective Products Developed and Used for Electrical Arc Flash Protection*

This sample is for illustrative purposes only. Users should develop their own safety procedures.

Typical Safety Procedure

Title: Procedure for Selection, Inspection, and Care of Rubber Insulating Gloves and Leather Protectors		Doc. ID No.: ESP.100.000.003.01 Page: 010 of 010
Eff. Date: 10/23/2017	Revision No. : 001 Revision Date: 10/06/2017	Supersedes: N/A
Reviewer: MK Rev. Date: 10/05/2017	Approved by: MDF Approval Date: 10/05/2017	Covers: All Personnel Within Restricted Approach Boundary

      2) National Fire Protection Association (NFPA):

          a) NFPA *70E, Standard for Electrical Safety in the Workplace*

   d. Company electrical safety procedures:

      1) ESP-100.000.001.01, *Matching Rubber Insulating Goods to Nominal System Voltage at Point of Use*
      2) ESP-100.000.002.01, *Purchasing Procedures for Rubber Insulating Gloves and Leather Protectors*
      3) ESP-100.000.004.01, *Limitations on Use of Rubber Insulating Gloves without Leather Protectors*
      4) ESP-100.000.005.01, *Issue and Replacement of Electrical Protective Equipment*
      5) ESP-100.000.006.01, *After Issue Storage of Rubber Insulating Goods*
      6) ESP-100.000.007.01, *Inventory Storage of Electrical Protective Equipment*
      7) ESP-100.000.008.01, *Cleaning of Rubber Insulating Goods*
      8) ESP-100.000.009.01, *Proper Disposal of Electrical Protective Equipment* c. Industry Standards:
      9) ESP-100.000.010.01, *Electrical Safety Training on the Issue, Inspection, Use, Cleaning, Replacement, and Proper Disposal of Rubber Insulating Gloves and Leather Protectors*
      10) ESP-100.000.011.01, *Procedure for Having Rubber Insulating Goods Retested*
      11) ESP-100.000.012.01, *Repair Procedure for Allowable Repairs to Rubber Insulating Gloves*

9.0 **Attachments:**

   a. 29 CFR 1910.137, *Occupational Safety and Health Standards, Personal Protective Equipment, Electrical Protective Devices*

This sample is for illustrative purposes only. Users should develop their own safety procedures.

Index

A

Accessible (as applied to equipment)
  Definition, Art. 100
Accessible (as applied to wiring methods), 120.4(B)(6), 330.4(A)
  Definition, Art. 100
Accessible, readily (readily accessible), 320.3(A)(3)
  Definition, Art. 100
Access plates, 230.2
Aerial lifts, 130.8(F)(1)
Alarms, battery operation, 320.3(A)(5)
Approach distances, *see also* Boundary
  Limits of, Annex C
  Preparation for, C.1
  Qualified persons, 130.4(E)(3), 130.4(F), C.1.1, C.1.2
  Unqualified persons, 130.4(E), 130.8(E), C.1.1
Approved (definition), Art. 100
Arc blast, K.4
Arc flash boundary, *see* Boundary, arc flash
Arc flash hazard, 130.2, K.3
  Battery room warning signs, 320.3(A)(6)
  Cell line working zone, 310.5(C)(4)
  Definition, Art. 100
  Protection from, *see* Arc flash protective equipment
Arc flash protective equipment, 130.5(F), 130.5(G), 130.5(H), 130.7
  Qualified persons, use by, C.1.2.1, C.1.2.3
  Unqualified persons, use by, C.1.1
Arc flash risk assessment, 130.2(B)(2), 130.3, 130.5
  Batteries, 320.3(A)(2)
  Electrolytic cell line working zones, 310.5(C)
Arc flash suit, 130.7(C)(10)(a), 130.7(C)(13), 130.7(C)(15)
  Definition, Art. 100
Arc rating
  Definition, Art. 100
  Total system arc rating, protective clothing, M.3
Arc-resistant switchgear, 130.7(C)(15)
Attachment plug (plug cap) (plug), 110.5(B), 110.5(C)
  Definition, Art. 100
  Maintenance, 245.1
Attendants, to warn and protect employees, 130.7(E)(3)
Auditing, 110.1(K)
Authority having jurisdiction (definition), Art. 100
Authorized person
  Battery rooms or areas restricted to, 320.3(A)(3)
  Definition, 320.2
Automatic (definition), Art. 100

B

Balaclava (sock hood), 130.5(G), 130.7(C)(10), 130.7(C)(15)
  Definition, Art. 100
Barricades, 130.7(E)(2)
  Definition, Art. 100
Barriers, *see also* Protective barriers
  Definition, Art. 100
  Electrolytic cells, safe work practices, 310.5(D)(3)
  Laser systems, 330.5(D)
  Maintenance of, 250.1
  Physical or mechanical, 130.6(F), 130.7(D)(1)
  Rotating equipment, 230.2
Batteries
  Abnormal battery conditions, alarms for, 320.3(A)(5)
  Cell flame arresters, 320.3(D)
  Definition, 320.2
  Direct-current ground-fault detection, 320.3(C)(1)
  Electrolyte hazards, 320.3(B)
  Maintenance requirements, safety-related, Art. 240, 320.3(C)
  Operation, 320.3(C)
  Personal protective equipment (PPE), use of, 320.3(A)(6)
  Safety requirements, Art. 320
  Testing, 320.3(C)
  Tools and equipment, use of, 320.3(C)(2)
  Valve-regulated lead acid cell (definition), 320.2
  Vented cell (definition), 320.2
  Ventilation, 240.1, 320.3(D)
  VRLA (valve-regulated lead acid cell) (definition), 320.2
Battery effect (definition), 310.2
Battery enclosures, 320.3(A)(3)
Battery rooms
  Definition, 320.2
  Requirements, 320.3(A)(3)
Blind reaching, electrical safety program, 130.6(B)
Body wash apparatus, 240.2
Bonded (bonding)
  Definition, Art. 100
  Maintenance of bonding, 205.6
Bonding conductor or jumper (definition), Art. 100
Boundary, *see also* Approach distances
  Approach boundaries to energized conductors or circuits, 130.2(B)(2), 130.4, C.1.1, C.1.2
  Arc flash, 130.2(B)(2), 130.5(E), C.1.1, C.1.2
    Calculations, Annex D
    Definition, Art. 100
    Protective equipment, use of, 130.7(C)(15), C.1.1, C.1.2.1, C.1.2.3

351

Index

Limited approach, 130.2, 130.4(B), 130.4(D), 130.4(E), 130.7(D)(1), 130.8, C.1.1, C.1.2.2; *see also* Approach distances
    Definition, Art. 100
Restricted approach, 130.2(B)(1), 130.2(B)(2), 130.2(B)(3), 130.4(D), 130.4(F), 130.7(C), 130.7(D)(1), C.1.1, C.1.2.3; *see also* Approach distances
    Definition, Art. 100
Shock protection, 130.2(B)(2), 130.4(B)(1), 130.4(D)
Branch circuit (definition), Art. 100
Building (definition), Art. 100

C

Cabinets (definition), Art. 100
Cable
    Flexible, *see* Flexible cords and cables
    Maintenance of, 205.13
Cable trays, maintenance, 215.3
Cell
    Definition, 320.2
    Electrolytic, *see* Electrolytic cell
Cell line, *see* Electrolytic cell line
Chemical hazard, 320.3(A)(2), 320.3(A)(6)
Circuit breakers
    Definition, Art. 100
    Low-voltage circuit breakers, calculations for incident energy and arc flash protection boundary for, D.4.7
    Molded-case, 225.2
    Reclosing circuits after operation, 130.6(M)
    Routine opening and closing of circuits, 130.6(L)
    Safety-related maintenance requirements, Art. 225
    Testing, 225.3
Circuits
    De-energized, *see* De-energized
    Energized, working on or near parts that are or might become; *see* Working on energized electrical conductors or circuit
    Identification, maintenance of, 205.12
    Impedance, 120.5(3)
    Interlocks, re-energizing by, 120.2(E)
    Reclosing after protective device operation, 130.6(M)
    Routine opening and closing of, 130.6(L)
Clear spaces, 130.6(H), 205.9
Combustible dust, 130.6(J)
Competent person, 350.4
    Definition, 350.2
Complex lockout/tagout procedure, 120.2(I), 120.4(A)(5), Annex G
Condition of maintenance, *see* Maintenance, condition of
Conductive (definition), Art. 100
Conductive work locations, 110.5(D)
Conductors
    Bare (definition), Art. 100
    Covered (definition), Art. 100
    De-energized, *see* De-energized
    Energized, *see* Working on energized electrical conductors or circuit
    Grounding conductors, equipment (EGC), 110.5(B)
        Definition, Art. 100
    Grounding electrode conductors (definition), Art. 100
    Identification, *see* Identified/identification
    Insulated
        Definition, Art. 100
        Integrity of insulation, maintenance of, 210.4
    Maintenance of, 205.13, 210.3
Contractors, relationship with, 110.3
Control devices, 120.2(F)
Controllers (definition), Art. 100
Cord- and plug-connected equipment, 110.5
    Connecting attachment plugs, 110.5(E)
    Grounding-type equipment, 110.5(B)
    Handling, 110.5(A)
    Safety-related maintenance requirements, Art. 245
    Visual inspection, 110.5(C)
Cords, flexible, *see* Flexible cords and cables
Covers, 215.1
Cranes, 310.5(D)(9)
Current-limiting overcurrent protective device (definition), Art. 100
Cutout
    Definition, Art. 100
    Portable cutout–type switches, 310.5(D)(8)
Cutting, 130.10

D

De-energized, *see also* Electrically safe work condition
    Conductors or circuit parts that have lockout/tagout devices applied, 120.4(A)(4), 120.4(B)(6)
    Definition, Art. 100
    Failure of equipment, 130.6(K)
    Process to de-energize equipment, 120.4(B)(1), 120.4(B)(3)
    Protective device operation, reclosing circuits after, 130.6(M)
    Testing of parts, 120.4(B)(6), 120.5
    Uninsulated overhead lines, 130.8(C)
Definitions, Art. 100
    Batteries and battery rooms, 320.2
    Electrolytic cells, 310.2
    Lasers, 330.2
    Power electronic equipment, 340.2
    Research and development laboratories, 350.2
Device (definition), Art. 100
Direct-current ground-fault detection, batteries, 320.3(C)(1)
Disconnecting means, 120.2(F), 120.5; *see also* Circuit breakers
    Definition, Art. 100
    Lockout/tagout devices, use of, 120.4(B)(3), 120.4(B)(11)
    Reclosing circuits after operation, 130.6(M)
    Routine opening and closing of circuits, 130.6(L)
Disconnecting (or isolating) switches (disconnector, isolator), *see also* Disconnecting means
    Definition, Art. 100
    Safety-related maintenance requirements, Art. 210
Documentation
    Arc flash risk assessment, 130.5(D)
    Electrical safety program, 105.3(A), 110.1(A), 110.1(K)(4), 110.3(C)
    Equipment labeling, 130.5(H)
    Laboratory, unlisted equipment for, 350.7(A)
    Of maintenance, 205.3
    Shock risk assessment, 130.4(C)
    Training, employees, 110.2(C)(4)
Doors, secured, 130.6(G)
Drilling, 130.10
Dust, combustible, 130.6(J)
Dwelling unit (definition), Art. 100

E

Electrical hazard, Art. 130; *see also* Arc flash hazard; Risk; Shock hazard
   Alerting techniques, 130.7(E)
   Categories of
      General, Annex K
      Personal protective equipment required for, *see* Personal protective equipment (PPE)
   Definition, Art. 100
   Identification procedure, 110.1(G)
   Lasers, 330.3, 330.5
   Risk assessment, F.4

Electrically safe work condition, Art. 120; *see also* Lockout/tagout
   Definition, Art. 100
   For lasers, 330.5(B)
   Process for establishing and verifying, 120.5
   Temporary protective grounding equipment, 120.5
   Verification of, 120.4(B)(5), 120.5
   Work involving electrical hazards, 130.2

Electrical safety (definition), Art. 100

Electrical safety program, 110.1, Annex E
   Auditing, 110.1(K)
   Awareness and self-discipline, 110.1(D)
   Contractors, relationship with, 110.3
   Controls, 110.1(F), E.2
   Definition, Art. 100
   Documentation of, 105.3(A), 110.1(A), 110.1(K)(4), 110.3(C)
   General, 110.1(A)
   Incident investigations, 110.1(J)
   Inspection, 110.1(B)
   Job briefing, 110.1(I)
   Maintenance, 110.1(C)
   Principles, 110.1(E), E.1
   Procedures, 110.1(G), E.3
   Risk assessment procedure, 110.1(H), Annex F

Electrolyte (definition), 320.2

Electrolyte hazards, storage battery, 320.3(B)(1)

Electrolytic cell, Art. 310
   Auxiliary nonelectric connections, 310.6(B)
   Employee training, 310.3, 310.4, 310.5(D)(6)

Electrolytic cell line working zone
   Attachments, 310.5(D)(10)
   Cranes and hoists, 310.5(D)(9)
   Employee training, 310.3, 310.4(A), 310(4)(B)(2), 310.5(D)(6)
   Portable equipment and tools, use of, 310.6
   Safeguards, employee, 310.5, Annex L

Elevated equipment, 130.8(F)(1)

Emergency response, training in, 110.2(C)

Employees
   Electrical safety program, 110.1
   Lockout/tagout procedure, 120.1, 120.2(B), 120.4
   Responsibilities, 105.3, 130.8(D)
      Lasers, 330.6
      Power electronic equipment, 340.5(B)
      Special equipment, 300.2
   Safeguarding, *see* Safeguarding
   Training, *see* Training, employees

Employers
   Electrical safety program, 110.1
   Responsibilities, 105.3, 120.4
      Host and contract employers, 110.3
      Lockout/tagout procedure, 120.1
      Power electronic equipment, 340.5(A)
      Safety related design requirements, Annex O
      Special equipment, 300.2
      Uninsulated overhead lines, work on or near, 130.8(D)

Enclosed (definition), Art. 100

Enclosures
   Definition, Art. 100
   Maintenance of, 205.6, 205.7, 210.1, 210.2

Energized
   Definition, Art. 100
   Electrical conductors or circuit, *see* Working on energized electrical conductors or circuit
   Electrolytic cells, *see* Electrolytic cell; Electrolytic cell line working zone
   Lasers, testing of, 330.5(B)

Energized electrical work permit, 130.2(B), Annex J

Equipment, *see also* specific equipment
   Batteries, for work on, 320.3(C)(2)
   Definition, Art. 100
   Grounding
      Portable equipment within energized cell line working zone, 310.6(A)
      Vehicle or mechanical equipment, 130.8(F)(3)
   Grounding-type, 110.5(B)
   Overhead, *see* Overhead lines and equipment
   Spaces about, maintenance of, 205.5, 205.9
   Special, *see* Special equipment
   Use of, 110.4

Equipment grounding conductors (EGC), 110.5(B)
   Definition, Art. 100

Explanatory material, 90.4

Exposed (as applied to energized electrical conductors or circuit parts), 105.1, 130.2, 130.3
   Definition, Art. 100
   Safe work practices, *see* Working on energized electrical conductors or circuit; Work practices, safety-related

Exposed (as applied to wiring methods) (definition), Art. 100

Extension cords, *see* Flexible cord sets

Eye wash apparatus, 240.2

F

Fault current, *see also* Short circuit current
   Available, 130.5(C), 130.7(C)(15), 210.3
      Definition, Art. 100
   Definition, Art. 100

Fiberglass-reinforced plastic rods, 130.7(D)(1)

Fiber or flyings, combustible, 130.6(J)

Field evaluated, 330.2, 330.5(E), 350.2, 350.6

Field work audit, 110.1(K)(2)

Fittings (definition), Art. 100

Flame arresters, battery cell, 320.3(D)

Flammable gases, 130.6(J)

Flammable liquids, 130.6(J)

Flexible cords and cables
   Grounding-type utilization equipment, 110.5(B)
   Handling, 110.5(A)
   Maintenance of, 205.14

Flexible cord sets, 110.5
   Connecting attachment plugs, 110.5(E)
   Visual inspection, 110.5(C)

Formal interpretation procedures, 90.5

Fuses, 130.6(L), 130.6(M)
   Current-limiting fuses, calculating arc-flash energies for use with, D.4.6

Index

Definition, Art. 100
Fuse or fuse-holding handling equipment, 130.7(D)(1)(b)
Safety-related maintenance requirements, 225.1

G
Gases, flammable, 130.6(J)
Ground (definition), Art. 100
Grounded (grounding), 120.4(B)(2)
    Definition, Art. 100
    Equipment
        Portable equipment within energized cell line working zone, 310.6(A)
        Vehicle or mechanical equipment, 130.8(F)(3)
    Lockout/tagout procedures, 120.4(B)(7)
    Maintenance of, 205.6
    Safety grounding equipment, maintenance of, 250.3
Grounded, solidly (definition), Art. 100
Grounded conductors (definition), Art. 100
Ground fault (definition), Art. 100
Ground-fault circuit-interrupters (GFCIs), 110.5(D), 110.6
    Definition, Art. 100
    Testing, 110.6(D)
Ground-fault protection, battery, 320.3(C)(1)
Grounding conductors, equipment (EGC), 110.5(B)
    Definition, Art. 100
Grounding electrode (definition), Art. 100
Grounding electrode conductors (definition), Art. 100
Grounding-type equipment, 110.5(B)
Guarded, 205.7; *see also* Barriers; Enclosures
    Definition, Art. 100
    Lasers, 330.5(A)
    Rotating equipment, 230.2
    Uninsulated overhead lines, 130.8(C), 130.8(D)

H
Handlines, 130.7(D)(1)
Hazard (definition), Art. 100; *see also* Electrical hazard
Hazardous (definition), Art. 100
Hazardous (classified) locations, maintenance requirements for, Art. 235
Hinged panels, secured, 130.6(G)
Hoists, 310.5(D)(9)
Human performance and workplace electrical safety, Annex Q

I
Identified/identification
    Equipment, field marking of, 130.5(H)
    Laboratory, unlisted equipment for, 350.7(A)
    Maintenance of, 205.10
    Temporary protective grounding equipment, 120.5(1)
Illumination
    Battery rooms, 320.3(A)(3)
    Working on energized electrical conductors or circuits, 130.6(C)
Implanted pacemakers and metallic medical devices, 310.5(D)(11)
Incident energy
    Calculation methods, Annex D
    Definition, Art. 100
    Equipment, labeling of, 130.5(H)
Incident energy analysis, 130.5(F), 130.5(G), 130.7(C)(15)
    Definition, Art. 100

Incident investigations, 110.1(J)
Informative publications, Annex A
Inspection
    Electrical safety program, 110.1(B), 110.4(D), 110.5(C)
    Visual
        Cord- and plug-connected equipment, 110.5(C)
        Electrical hazards, work involving, 130.2(B)(3), 130.7(B)
        Return to service after lockout/tagout, 120.4(B)(13)
        Safety and protective equipment, 130.7(B), 250.2(A)
        Safety grounding equipment, 250.3(A)
        Test instruments and equipment, 110.4(D)
Insulated (definition), Art. 100
Insulated conductors, maintenance of, 210.4
Insulated tools and equipment, 130.7(D)(1)
Insulating floor surface, L.1
Insulation, electrolytic cells, 310.5(D)(1)
Insulation rating, overhead lines, 130.8(B)
Interlocks
    Circuit, 120.2(E)
    Safety, 130.6(N), 205.8
Interrupter switch (definition), Art. 100
Interrupting rating (definition), Art. 100
Investigations, incident, 110.1(J)
Isolated (as applied to location)
    Definition, Art. 100
    Electrolytic cells, 310.5(D)(5)
Isolating switches
    Definition, Art. 100
    Safety-related maintenance requirements, Art. 210

J
Job briefing, 110.1(I), 130.2(B)(2), 350.5(A)
    Checklist, Annex I

L
Labeled (definition), Art. 100
Laboratory
    Custom built unlisted equipment
        Greater than 1000 volts, 350.8
        1000 volts or less, 350.7
    Definition, 350.2
    Safety-related work requirements, Art. 350
Laser
    Definition, 330.2
    Energy source (definition), 330.2
    Radiation (definition), 330.2
    System (definition), 330.2
    Work practices, safety-related, Art. 330
        Responsibility for, 330.6
        Safeguarding persons in operating area, 330.5
        Training, 330.4
Limited approach boundary, *see* Boundary, limited approach
Listed
    Definition, Art. 100
    Lasers, 330.5(E)
    Research and development laboratory equipment or systems, 350.6
Live parts
    Guarding of, *see* Guarded
    Safe work conditions, *see* Electrical safety program; Working on energized electrical conductors or circuit; Work practices, safety-related

Index

Lockout/tagout
   Accountability for personnel, 120.4(B)(10)
   Control, elements of, 120.4(B)
   Control devices, use of, 120.2(F)
   Control of energy, 120.2(D)
   Coordination, 120.4(B)(9)
   Equipment, 120.3
   Grounding, 120.4(B)(7)
   Hazardous electrical energy control, forms of, 120.2(I); *see also* Complex lockout/tagout procedure; Simple lockout/tagout procedure
   Identification of devices, 120.2(G)
   Maintenance of devices, 205.8
   Person in charge, 120.2(I), 120.4(A)(3), 120.4(A)(5)
   Plans for, 120.4(A)
   Principles, 120.2
   Procedures, 120.2(C), 120.4, 120.5, Annex G
     Coordination, 120.2(H)
   Programs, 120.1
     Audit, 110.1(K)(3)
   Release
     For return to service, 120.4(B)(13)
     Temporary, 120.4(B)(14)
   Removal of devices, 120.4(B)(12)
   Responsibility, 120.1, 120.4(A), 120.4(B)(4), 120.4(B)(8)
   Shift change, 120.4(B)(9)
   Testing, 120.4(B)(6)
   Working on/near conductors or circuit parts, 120.2(A)
Luminaires (definition), Art. 100

M
Maintenance, condition of, 110.1(C)
   Definition, Art. 100
Maintenance requirements, Chap. 2, 110.1(C)
   Batteries and battery rooms, Art. 240
   Controller equipment, Art. 220
   Fuses and circuit breakers, Art. 225
   General, Art. 205
   Hazardous (classified) locations, Art. 235
   Introduction, Art. 200
   Laboratory, unlisted equipment for, 350.7(B)
   Personal safety and protective equipment, Art. 250
   Portable electric tools and equipment, Art. 245
   Premises wiring, Art. 215
   Rotating equipment, Art. 230
   Substation, switchgear assemblies, switchboards, panelboards, motor control centers, and disconnect switches, Art. 210
Mandatory rules, 90.4
Marking, *see* Identified/identification
Mechanical equipment, working on or near uninsulated overhead lines, 130.8(F)
Motor control centers
   Definition, Art. 100
   Personal protective equipment required for tasks, 130.7(C)(15)
   Safety-related maintenance requirements, Art. 210
Multi-employer relationship, 120.4(A)(5)

N
Nominal voltage (definition), 320.2
Nonelectric equipment connections, electrolytic cell line, 310.6(B)

O
Occupational health and safety management standards, alignment with, Annex P
Open wiring protection, 215.2
Outdoors, GFCI protection, 110.6(C)
Outlets (definition), Art. 100
Overcurrent (definition), Art. 100
Overcurrent protection
   Maintenance of devices, 205.4, 210.5
   Modification, 110.7
Overhead lines and equipment, 120.3(D)(5)
   Clearances, maintenance of, 205.15
   Industrial procedure for working near overhead systems, example of, Annex N
   Insulation rating, 130.8(B)
   Working within limited approach boundary of uninsulated, 130.8
Overload (definition), Art. 100

P
Pacemakers, implanted, 310.5(D)(11)
Panelboards
   Definition, Art. 100
   Personal protective equipment required for tasks, 130.7(C)(15)
   Safety-related maintenance requirements, Art. 210
Permissive rules, 90.4
Personal protective equipment (PPE), 110.1(H)(3), 130.2(B)(2), 130.2(B)(3), 130.9, 130.10, L.1; *see also* Protective clothing
   Arc flash protection, 130.5(F), 130.5(G), 130.5(H), 130.7, C.1.1, C.1.2.1, C.1.2.3, Annex H
   Batteries and battery rooms, 320.3(A)(6), 320.3(B)
   Body protection, 130.7(C)(6)
   Care of, 130.7(B)
   Electrical equipment labeling for, 130.5(H)
   Eye protection, 130.7(C)(4)
   Flash protection, *see* Arc flash protective equipment
   Foot and leg protection, 130.7(C)(8)
   Hand and arm protection, 130.7(C)(7)
   Head, face, neck, and chin protection, 130.7(C)(3)
   Hearing protection, 130.7(C)(5)
   Maintenance, Art. 250
   Required for various tasks, 130.7(C)(15)
   Safeguarding of employees in electrolytic cell line working zone, 310.5(C)(1), 310.5(D)(2)
   Selection of, 130.7(C)(15), Annex H
   Shock protection, 130.4(A), 130.4(B), 130.7, C.1.1
   Standards for, 130.7(C)(14)
Pilot cell (definition), 320.2
Planning checklist, Annex I
Portable electric equipment, 110.5(A)
   Connecting attachment plugs, 110.5(E)
   Electrolytic cells, 310.6(A), L.2
   Grounding-type, 110.5(B)
   Handling, 110.5(A)
   Safety-related maintenance requirements, Art. 245
   Visual inspection, 110.5(C)
Power electronic equipment, safety-related work practices, Art. 340
   Definitions, 340.2
   Hazards associated with, 340.4
   Specific measures, 340.5
Power supply
   Cell line working area, L.2
   Portable electric equipment, circuits for, 310.6(A)

Index

Premises wiring (system)
    Definition, Art. 100
    Maintenance of, Art. 215
Prohibited approach boundary, *see* Boundary
Prospective fault current (definition), 320.2
Protective barriers, 130.6(F), 130.7(D)(1), 250.1, 330.5(D)
    Definition, 330.2
Protective clothing, 130.7(C), L.1
    Arc flash protection, 130.7(C)(9), 130.7(C)(10), 130.7(C)(13), 130.7(C)(15), C.1.1, Annex H
    Care and maintenance, 130.7(C)(13)
    Characteristics, 130.7(C)(11)
    Layering of, M.1, M.2
    Prohibited clothing, 130.7(C)(12)
    Selection of, 130.7(C)(9), Annex H
    Total system arc rating, M.3
Protective equipment, 130.7, 130.8(D), 130.8(F)(2)
    Alerting techniques, 130.7(E)
    Arc flash protection, *see* Arc flash protective equipment
    Barricades, 130.7(E)(2)
    Barriers, *see* Barriers
    Batteries, maintenance of, 320.3(A)(6)
    Care of equipment, 130.7(B)
    Insulated tools, 130.7(D)(1)
    Maintenance, Art. 250
    Nonconductive ladders, 130.7(D)(1)
    Personal, *see* Personal protective equipment (PPE)
    Rubber insulating equipment, 130.7(D)(1)
    Safety signs and tags, 130.7(E)(1)
    Shock protection, 130.4(B), 130.7, C.1.1
    Standards for, 130.7(G)
    Temporary protective grounding equipment, 120.5
    Voltage-rated plastic guard equipment, 130.7(D)(1)
Purpose of standard, 90.1

Q

Qualified persons, 130.2(B)(3), 130.3
    Approach distances, 130.4(E)(3), 130.4(F), C.1.1, C.1.2
    Definition, Art. 100
    Electrolytic cells, training for, 310.4(A)
    Lockout/tagout procedures, 120.2(I), 120.4(A)(4), 120.4(B)(14)
    Maintenance, performance of, 205.1
    Overhead lines, determining insulation rating of, 130.8(B)

R

Raceways
    Definition, Art. 100
    Maintenance, 215.3
Radiation worker (definition), 340.2
Readily accessible
    Battery enclosures, 320.3(A)(3)
    Definition, Art. 100
Receptacles
    Definition, Art. 100
    Electrolytic cell lines, L.2
    Maintenance, 245.1
    Portable electric equipment, 110.5(B), 110.5(C), 110.5(E)
Research and development
    Definition, 350.2
    Safety-related work requirements for laboratories, Art. 350
Restricted approach boundary, *see* Boundary, restricted approach

Risk
    Control, 110.1(H)(3), F.3
    Definition, Art. 100
Risk assessment
    Arc flash, 130.2(B)(2), 130.3, 320.3(A)(2)
    Definition, Art. 100
    Hazard-based, F.4
    Methods, F.6
    Procedure, 110.1(H), Annex F
    Shock, 130.2(B)(2), 130.3, 130.4, 320.3(A)(2)
    Task-based, F.5
Ropes, 130.7(D)(1)
Rules, mandatory and permissive, 90.4

S

Safeguarding
    In cell line working zone, 310.5, Annex L
    Definition, 310.2
    In laser operating area, 330.5
Safety grounding equipment, maintenance of, 250.3
Safety interlocks, 130.6(N), 205.8
    Maintenance of, 205.8
Safety-related design requirements, Annex O
Safety-related maintenance requirements, *see* Maintenance requirements
Safety-related work practices, *see* Work practices, safety-related
Scope of standard, 90.2
Service drop (definition), Art. 100
Service lateral (definition), Art. 100
Service point (definition), Art. 100
Shock hazard, K.2
    Battery room warning signs, 320.3(A)(6)
    Definition, Art. 100
    Protection from, 130.7, C.1.1
Shock hazard risk assessment, 320.3(A)(2)
Shock protection boundaries, 130.4(B)(1), 130.4(D)
Shock risk assessment, 130.2(B)(2), 130.3, 130.4
Short circuit, 320.3(C)(1), O.2.3(1)
Short circuit current
    Calculations, Annex D
    Prospective, 320.2, 320.3(A)(6)
    Rating (definition), Art. 100
    Unintended ground, caused by, 320.3(C)(1)
Signs, electrolytic cell areas, 310.5(B)
Simple lockout/tagout procedure, 120.2(I), 120.4(A)(4), Annex G
Single-line diagram
    Definition, Art. 100
    Maintenance of, 205.2
Special equipment, Chap. 3; *see also* Batteries; Electrolytic cell; Laser; Power electronic equipment
    Battery rooms
        Definition, 320.2
        Requirements, 320.3(A)(3)
    Organization, 300.3
    Responsibility, 300.2
Special permission (definition), Art. 100
Standard arrangement, 90.3
Step potential (definition), Art. 100
Stored energy, 120.4(B)(2), 120.5, 330.3(B)
Structure (definition), Art. 100
Substations, safety-related maintenance requirements, Art. 210
Supervisory performance, Q.7.4

Index

Switchboards
  Definition, Art. 100
  Safety-related maintenance requirements, Art. 210
Switches, *see also* Switching devices
  Disconnecting (or isolating) switches (disconnector, isolator); *see also* Disconnecting means
    Definition, Art. 100
    Safety-related maintenance requirements, Art. 210
  Load-rated, 130.6(L)
  Portable cutout type, 310.5(D)(8)
Switchgear
  Arc-resistant, 130.7(C)(15)
    Definition, Art. 100
  Metal-clad, 130.7(C)(15)
    Definition, Art. 100
  Metal-enclosed, 130.7(C)(15)
    Definition, Art. 100
  Personal protective equipment required for tasks, 130.7(C)(15)
  Safety-related maintenance requirements, Art. 210
Switching devices (definition), Art. 100; *see also* Circuit breakers; Disconnecting means; Switches

T
Tagout, *see* Lockout/tagout
Temporary protective grounding equipment, 120.5
Terminals, maintenance of, 230.1
Testing
  De-energized parts, 120.4(B)(6), 120.5
  Energized equipment, 130.2(B)(3)
  Equipment safeguards, 310.5(D)(12)
  Ground-fault circuit-interrupters, 110.6(D)
  Lockout/tagout procedure, 120.4(B)(6)
  Personal protective equipment, 310.5(D)(2)
  Safety and protective equipment, insulation of, 250.2(B)
  Safety grounding equipment, 250.3(B), 250.3(C)
Test instruments and equipment, 110.4
  Cell line working zone, 310.6(D)
  Maintenance of, 250.4
  Visual inspection, 110.4(D)
Thermal hazard, 320.3(A)(6)
Tools
  Batteries, for work on, 320.3(C)(2)
  Electrolytic cells, safe work practices, 310.5(D)(7), 310.6, L.2
Touch potential (definition), Art. 100
Training, employees, 105.3(A)
  Documentation, 110.2(C)(4)
  Emergency responses, 110.2(C)
  Lockout/tagout practices, 120.1, Annex G
  Work practices, safety-related, 105.3(A), 110.2, 110.3(B), 310.3, 310.4, 310.5(D)(6), 330.4

U
Underground electrical lines and equipment, 130.9
Ungrounded (definition), Art. 100
Uninsulated overhead lines, working within limited approach boundary of, 130.8(A)
Unqualified persons, 130.2(B)(2)
  Approach distances, 130.4(E), 130.8(E), C.1.1
  Definition, Art. 100
  Electrolytic cells, training for, 310.4(B)
Utilization equipment
  Definition, Art. 100
  Grounding-type, 110.5(B)

V
Valve-regulated lead acid cell (definition), 320.2
Vehicular equipment, working on or near uninsulated overhead lines, 130.8(F)
Ventilation, batteries, 240.1, 320.3(D)
Voltage
  (Of a circuit) (definition), Art. 100
  Electrolytic cells, voltage equalization, 310.5(D)(4)
  Lasers, 330.3(A)
  Nominal (definition), Art. 100
VRLA (valve-regulated lead acid cell) (definition), 320.2

W
Warning signs
  Battery rooms and enclosures, 320.3(A)(6)
  Lasers, 330.5(D)
  Maintenance of, 205.11
Welding machines, 310.6(C)
Wiring, premises
  Definition, Art. 100
  Maintenance of, Art. 215
Working distance, 130.2(B)(2), 130.5(G), 130.5(H), 130.7(C)(15), D.3.1, D.4.3, D.4.4
  Definition, Art. 100
Working on energized electrical conductors or circuit parts, Art. 130; *see also* Work practices, safety-related
  Alerting techniques, 130.7(E)
  Alertness of personnel, 130.6(A)
  Approach boundaries, *see* Boundary
  Blind reaching by employees, 130.6(B)
  Conductive articles being worn, 130.6(D)
  Conductive materials, tools, and equipment being handled, 130.6(E)
  Confined or enclosed work spaces, 130.6(F)
  Definition, Art. 100
  Electrically safe working conditions, 130.2
  Energized electrical work permit, 130.2(B)
  Failure, anticipation of, 130.6(K)
  Flash risk assessment, 130.5
  Housekeeping duties, 130.6(I)
  Illumination, 130.6(C)
  Insulated tools and equipment, 130.7(D)(1)
  Occasional use of flammable materials, 130.6(J)
  Opening and closing of circuits, routine, 130.6(L)
  Overhead lines, working within limited approach boundary of, 130.8
  Portable ladders, 130.7(D)(1)
  Protective shields, 130.6(F), 130.7(D)(1)
  Reclosing circuits after protective device operation, 130.6(M)
  Safe work conditions, 130.3
Working spaces
  Clear spaces, 130.6(H), 205.9
  Maintenance of, 205.5, 205.9
Work permit, energized electrical, 130.2(B), Annex J
Work practices, safety-related, Chap. 1; *see also* Electrically safe work condition; Working on energized electrical conductors or circuit
  Approach distances, *see* Approach distances
  Batteries and battery rooms, Art. 320
  Contractors, relationship with, 110.3
  De-energized equipment, *see* Electrically safe work condition
  Electrical conductors or circuit parts that are or might become energized, work on or near, 130.3
  Electrical safety program, 110.1

Index

Electrolytic cells, Art. 310, Annex L
Lasers, Art. 330
Power electronic equipment, Art. 340
Purpose, 105.2
Research and development laboratories, Art. 350

Responsibility for, 105.3
Scope, 105.1
Special equipment, *see* Special equipment
Training requirements, 105.3(A), 110.2, 110.3(B)
Use of equipment, 110.4

IMPORTANT NOTICES AND DISCLAIMERS CONCERNING NFPA® STANDARDS

NOTICE AND DISCLAIMER OF LIABILITY CONCERNING THE USE OF NFPA STANDARDS

NFPA® codes, standards, recommended practices, and guides ("NFPA Standards"), of which the document contained herein is one, are developed through a consensus standards development process approved by the American National Standards Institute. This process brings together volunteers representing varied viewpoints and interests to achieve consensus on fire and other safety issues. While the NFPA administers the process and establishes rules to promote fairness in the development of consensus, it does not independently test, evaluate, or verify the accuracy of any information or the soundness of any judgments contained in NFPA Standards.

The NFPA disclaims liability for any personal injury, property or other damages of any nature whatsoever, whether special, indirect, consequential or compensatory, directly or indirectly resulting from the publication, use of, or reliance on NFPA Standards. The NFPA also makes no guaranty or warranty as to the accuracy or completeness of any information published herein.

In issuing and making NFPA Standards available, the NFPA is not undertaking to render professional or other services for or on behalf of any person or entity. Nor is the NFPA undertaking to perform any duty owed by any person or entity to someone else. Anyone using this document should rely on his or her own independent judgment or, as appropriate, seek the advice of a competent professional in determining the exercise of reasonable care in any given circumstances.

The NFPA has no power, nor does it undertake, to police or enforce compliance with the contents of NFPA Standards. Nor does the NFPA list, certify, test, or inspect products, designs, or installations for compliance with this document. Any certification or other statement of compliance with the requirements of this document shall not be attributable to the NFPA and is solely the responsibility of the certifier or maker of the statement.

ADDITIONAL NOTICES AND DISCLAIMERS

Updating of NFPA Standards

Users of NFPA codes, standards, recommended practices, and guides ("NFPA Standards") should be aware that these documents may be superseded at any time by the issuance of new editions or may be amended from time to time through the issuance of Tentative Interim Amendments or corrected by Errata. An official NFPA Standard at any point in time consists of the current edition of the document together with any Tentative Interim Amendments and any Errata then in effect. In order to determine whether a given document is the current edition and whether it has been amended through the issuance of Tentative Interim Amendments or corrected through the issuance of Errata, consult appropriate NFPA publications such as the National Fire Codes® Subscription Service, visit the NFPA website at www.nfpa.org, or contact the NFPA at the address listed below.

Interpretations of NFPA Standards

A statement, written or oral, that is not processed in accordance with Section 6 of the Regulations Governing the Development of NFPA Standards shall not be considered the official position of NFPA or any of its Committees and shall not be considered to be, nor be relied upon as, a Formal Interpretation.

Patents

The NFPA does not take any position with respect to the validity of any patent rights referenced in, related to, or asserted in connection with an NFPA Standard. The users of NFPA Standards bear the sole responsibility for determining the validity of any such patent rights, as well as the risk of infringement of such rights, and the NFPA disclaims liability for the infringement of any patent resulting from the use of or reliance on NFPA Standards.

NFPA adheres to the policy of the American National Standards Institute (ANSI) regarding the inclusion of patents in American National Standards ("the ANSI Patent Policy"), and hereby gives the following notice pursuant to that policy:

> **NOTICE:** The user's attention is called to the possibility that compliance with an NFPA Standard may require use of an invention covered by patent rights. NFPA takes no position as to the validity of any such patent rights or as to whether such patent rights constitute or include essential patent claims under the ANSI Patent Policy. If, in connection with the ANSI Patent Policy, a patent holder has filed a statement of willingness to grant licenses under these rights on reasonable and nondiscriminatory terms and conditions to applicants desiring to obtain such a license, copies of such filed statements can be obtained, on request, from NFPA. For further information, contact the NFPA at the address listed below.

Law and Regulations

Users of NFPA Standards should consult applicable federal, state, and local laws and regulations. NFPA does not, by the publication of its codes, standards, recommended practices, and guides, intend to urge action that is not in compliance with applicable laws, and these documents may not be construed as doing so.

Copyrights

NFPA Standards are copyrighted. They are made available for a wide variety of both public and private uses. These include both use, by reference, in laws and regulations, and use in private self-regulation, standardization, and the promotion of safe practices and methods. By making these documents available for use and adoption by public authorities and private users, the NFPA does not waive any rights in copyright to these documents.

Use of NFPA Standards for regulatory purposes should be accomplished through adoption by reference. The term "adoption by reference" means the citing of title, edition, and publishing information only. Any deletions, additions, and changes desired by the adopting authority should be noted separately in the adopting instrument. In order to assist NFPA in following the uses made of its documents, adopting authorities are requested to notify the NFPA (Attention: Secretary, Standards Council) in writing of such use. For technical assistance and questions concerning adoption of NFPA Standards, contact NFPA at the address below.

For Further Information

All questions or other communications relating to NFPA Standards and all requests for information on NFPA procedures governing its codes and standards development process, including information on the procedures for requesting Formal Interpretations, for proposing Tentative Interim Amendments, and for proposing revisions to NFPA standards during regular revision cycles, should be sent to NFPA headquarters, addressed to the attention of the Secretary, Standards Council, NFPA, 1 Batterymarch Park, P.O. Box 9101, Quincy, MA 02269-9101; email: stds_admin@nfpa.org

For more information about NFPA, visit the NFPA website at www.nfpa.org. All NFPA codes and standards can be viewed at no cost at www.nfpa.org/docinfo.

Hierarchy of Risk Control Methods

There are six risk control methods required to be implemented by NFPA *70E*, Section 110.1(H)(3). The purpose of the hierarchy of risk control methods is to identify the most effective individual preventative or protective measure, or combination of measures, to reduce the risk associated with a hazard. Each risk control method is considered less effective than the one before it. The hierarchy of risk control methods includes:

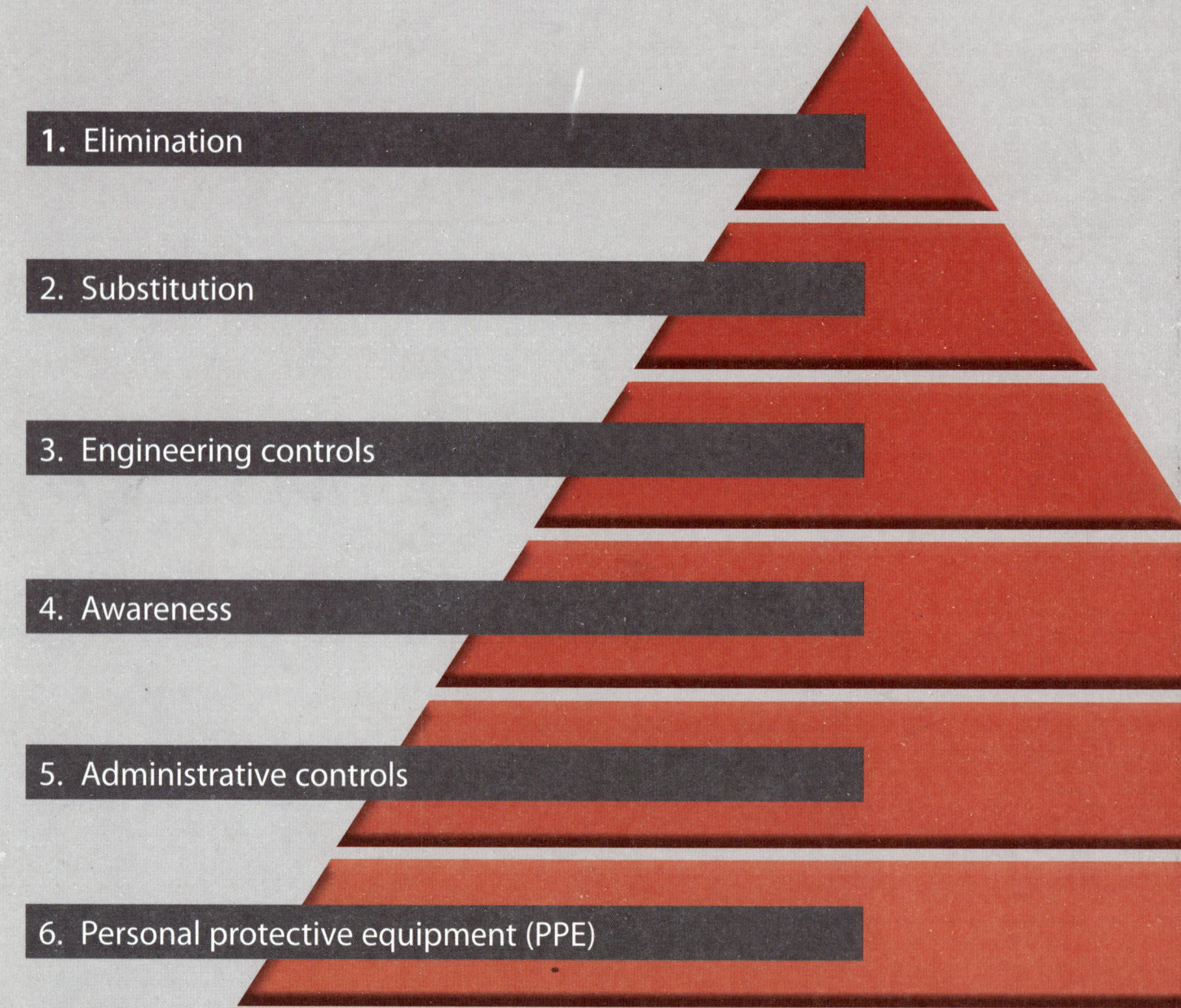

1. Elimination
2. Substitution
3. Engineering controls
4. Awareness
5. Administrative controls
6. Personal protective equipment (PPE)

Human factors are generally recognized as one of the leading causes of injuries. Elimination, substitution, and engineering controls are the most effective methods to reduce risk because they are usually applied at the source of possible injury and are less likely to be affected by human error. Awareness, administrative controls, and PPE are the least effective methods to reduce risk because they are not applied at the source and are more likely to be affected by human error. Informative Annex F provides guidance on risk assessment methods and the use of the hierarchy of risk control methods.